OpenGL

SuperBible

Sixth Edition

OpenGL®

SuperBible
Sixth Edition

*Comprehensive Tutorial
and Reference*

Graham Sellers
Richard S. Wright, Jr.
Nicholas Haemel

⚡Addison-Wesley

Upper Saddle River, NJ • Boston • Indianapolis • San Francisco
New York • Toronto • Montreal • London • Munich • Paris • Madrid
Capetown • Sydney • Tokyo • Singapore • Mexico City

The publisher offers excellent discounts on this book when ordered in quantity for bulk purchases or special sales, which may include electronic versions and/or custom covers and content particular to your business, training goals, marketing focus, and branding interests. For more information, please contact:

U.S. Corporate and Government Sales
(800) 382-3419
corpsales@pearsontechgroup.com

For sales outside the United States, please contact:

International Sales
international@pearsoned.com

Visit us on the Web: informit.com/aw

Library of Congress Cataloging-in-Publication Data

Wright, Richard S., Jr., 1965- author.
    OpenGL superBible : comprehensive tutorial and reference.—Sixth edition / Graham Sellers, Richard S. Wright, Jr., Nicholas Haemel.
        pages   cm
    Includes bibliographical references and index.
    ISBN-13: 978-0-321-90294-8 (pbk. : alk. paper)
    ISBN-10: 0-321-90294-7 (pbk. : alk. paper)
    1. Computer graphics. 2. OpenGL. I. Sellers, Graham, author. II. Haemel, Nicholas, author. III. Title.
    T385.W728 2013
    006.6'8—dc23
                                                    2013016852

ISBN-13: 978-0-321-90294-8
ISBN-10:   0-321-90294-7
Text printed in the United States on recycled paper at RR Donnelley in Crawfordsville, Indiana.
First printing, July 2013

Editor-in-Chief
Mark L. Taub

Executive Editor
Laura Lewin

Development Editor
Sheri Cain

Managing Editor
John Fuller

Full-Service Production Manager
Julie B. Nahil

Copy Editor
Teresa D. Wilson

Indexer
Larry Sweazey

Proofreader
Andrea Fox

Technical Reviewers
Piers Daniell
Daniel Koch
Daniel Rakos

Editorial Assistant
Olivia Basegio

Compositor
LaurelTech

For my family and my friends.
For those from whom I have learned.
For people who love to learn.
—Graham Sellers

For my wife LeeAnne,
for not killing me in my sleep
(when I deserved it).
To the memory of Richard S. Wright, Sr.
Thanks, Dad, for just letting me be a nerd.
—Richard S. Wright, Jr.

For my wife, Anna,
who has put up with all my engineering nonsense all these
years and provided undying love and support.
And to my parents for providing me with encouragement and
more LEGOs than I could get both arms around.
—Nicholas Haemel

Contents

Figures   xv

Tables   xxiii

Listings   xxv

Foreword   xxxiii

Preface   xxxv
    About This Book   xxxv
    The Architecture of the Book   xxxvi
    What's New in This Edition   xxxviii
    How to Build the Samples   xxxix
    Errata   xl

Acknowledgments   xli

About the Authors   xlv

I   Foundations   1

1   Introduction   3
    OpenGL and the Graphics Pipeline   4
    The Origins and Evolution of OpenGL   6
        Core Profile OpenGL   8
    Primitives, Pipelines, and Pixels   10
    Summary   11

2 Our First OpenGL Program   **13**
Creating a Simple Application   14
Using Shaders   16
Drawing Our First Triangle   24
Summary   25

3 Following the Pipeline   **27**
Passing Data to the Vertex Shader   28
    Vertex Attributes   28
Passing Data from Stage to Stage   29
    Interface Blocks   31
Tessellation   32
    Tessellation Control Shaders   33
    The Tessellation Engine   34
    Tessellation Evaluation Shaders   34
Geometry Shaders   36
Primitive Assembly, Clipping, and Rasterization   38
    Clipping   38
    Viewport Transformation   39
    Culling   40
    Rasterization   41
Fragment Shaders   42
Framebuffer Operations   45
    Pixel Operations   45
Compute Shaders   47
Summary   48

4 Math for 3D Graphics   **49**
Is This the Dreaded Math Chapter?   50
A Crash Course in 3D Graphics Math   51
    Vectors, or Which Way Is Which?   51
    Common Vector Operators   54
    Matrices   58
    Matrix Construction and Operators   60
Understanding Transformations   63
    Coordinate Spaces in OpenGL   63
    Coordinate Transformations   66
    Concatenating Transformations   73
    Quaternions   75
    The Model-View Transform   76
    Projection Transformations   79

Interpolation, Lines, Curves, and Splines 82
    Curves 83
    Splines 87
Summary 90

5   Data   91
Buffers 92
    Allocating Memory using Buffers 92
    Filling and Copying Data in Buffers 95
    Feeding Vertex Shaders from Buffers 97
Uniforms 103
    Default Block Uniforms 103
    Uniform Blocks 108
    Using Uniforms to Transform Geometry 121
Shader Storage Blocks 126
    Synchronizing Access to Memory 129
Atomic Counters 133
    Synchronizing Access to Atomic Counters 137
Textures 137
    Creating and Initializing Textures 138
    Texture Targets and Types 139
    Reading from Textures in Shaders 141
    Loading Textures from Files 144
    Controlling How Texture Data Is Read 148
    Array Textures 160
    Writing to Textures in Shaders 165
    Synchronizing Access to Images 176
    Texture Compression 177
    Texture Views 181
Summary 185

6   Shaders and Programs   187
Language Overview 188
    Data Types 188
    Built-In Functions 194
Compiling, Linking, and Examining Programs 201
    Getting Information from the Compiler 201
    Getting Information from the Linker 204
    Separate Programs 206
    Shader Subroutines 213
    Program Binaries 216
Summary 219

II In Depth   221

7   Vertex Processing and Drawing Commands   223
Vertex Processing 224
   Vertex Shader Inputs 224
   Vertex Shader Outputs 229
Drawing Commands 231
   Indexed Drawing Commands 231
   Instancing 237
   Indirect Draws 250
Storing Transformed Vertices 259
   Using Transform Feedback 260
   Starting, Pausing, and Stopping Transform Feedback 264
   Ending the Pipeline with Transform Feedback 266
   Transform Feedback Example — Physical Simulation 266
Clipping 276
   User-Defined Clipping 279
Summary 282

8   Primitive Processing   283
Tessellation 284
   Tessellation Primitive Modes 285
   Tessellation Subdivision Modes 294
   Passing Data between Tessellation Shaders 296
   Communication between Shader Invocations 299
   Tessellation Example — Terrain Rendering 300
   Tessellation Example — Cubic Bézier Patches 304
Geometry Shaders 310
   The Pass-Through Geometry Shader 311
   Using Geometry Shaders in an Application 313
   Discarding Geometry in the Geometry Shader 317
   Modifying Geometry in the Geometry Shader 320
   Generating Geometry in the Geometry Shader 322
   Changing the Primitive Type in the Geometry
      Shader 325
   Multiple Streams of Storage 328
   New Primitive Types Introduced by the Geometry
      Shader 329
   Multiple Viewport Transformations 336
Summary 340

9   Fragment Processing and the Framebuffer   341
    Fragment Shaders 342
        Interpolation and Storage Qualifiers 342
    Per-Fragment Tests 345
        Scissor Testing 345
        Stencil Testing 348
        Depth Testing 351
        Early Testing 355
    Color Output 357
        Blending 357
        Logical Operations 362
        Color Masking 363
    Off-Screen Rendering 364
        Multiple Framebuffer Attachments 368
        Layered Rendering 370
        Framebuffer Completeness 376
        Rendering in Stereo 379
    Antialiasing 384
        Antialiasing by Filtering 385
        Multi-sample Antialiasing 387
        Multi-sample Textures 389
        Sample Rate Shading 393
        Centroid Sampling 395
    Advanced Framebuffer Formats 399
        Rendering with No Attachments 399
        Floating-Point Framebuffers 401
        Integer Framebuffers 415
        The sRGB Color Space 416
    Point Sprites 419
        Texturing Points 420
        Rendering a Star Field 420
        Point Parameters 423
        Shaped Points 424
        Rotating Points 426
    Getting at Your Image 428
        Reading from a Framebuffer 429
        Copying Data between Framebuffers 431
        Reading Back Texture Data 434
    Summary 435

10 Compute Shaders   437
    Using Compute Shaders 438

Executing Compute Shaders 439
Compute Shader Communication 444
Examples 449
Compute Shader Parallel Prefix Sum 450
Compute Shader Flocking 462
Summary 471

11 Controlling and Monitoring the Pipeline   **473**
Queries 474
Occlusion Queries 475
Timer Queries 484
Transform Feedback Queries 487
Synchronization in OpenGL 493
Draining the Pipeline 493
Synchronization and Fences 494
Summary 498

III In Practice   **501**

12 Rendering Techniques   **503**
Lighting Models 504
The Phong Lighting Model 504
Blinn-Phong Lighting 513
Rim Lighting 515
Normal Mapping 518
Environment Mapping 522
Material Properties 532
Casting Shadows 534
Atmospheric Effects 540
Non-Photo-Realistic Rendering 544
Cell Shading — Texels as Light 545
Alternative Rendering Methods 548
Deferred Shading 548
Screen-Space Techniques 558
Rendering without Triangles 565
Summary 580

13 Debugging and Performance Optimization   **581**
Debugging Your Applications 582
Debug Contexts 582

Performance Optimization 589
   Performance Analysis Tools 589
   Tuning Your Application for Speed 597
Summary 616

14 Platform Specifics   617

Using Extensions in OpenGL 618
   Enhancing OpenGL with Extensions 619
OpenGL on Windows 623
   OpenGL Implementations on Windows 623
   Basic Window Setup 627
   The OpenGL Rendering Context 632
   Full-Screen Rendering 644
   Cleaning Up 646
OpenGL on Mac OS X 647
   The Faces of OpenGL on the Mac 648
   OpenGL with Cocoa 649
   Introducing GLKit 662
   Retina Displays 673
   Core OpenGL 674
   Full-Screen Rendering 675
   Sync Frame Rate 677
   Multi-threaded OpenGL 679
   GLUT 680
OpenGL on Linux 682
   The Basics 682
   Brief History 682
   What Is X? 683
   Getting Started 683
   Building OpenGL Apps 687
   Windows and Render Surfaces 693
   GLX Strings 695
   Context Management 695
   Using Contexts 699
   Putting It All Together 701
   Going Full Screen on X 704
OpenGL on Mobile Platforms 705
   OpenGL on a Diet 705
   OpenGL ES 3.0 709
   The OpenGL ES Environment 713
   EGL: A New Windowing Environment 718
   More EGL 727

Negotiating Embedded Environments 728
Android Development Environments 729
iOpenGL 734
Summary 744

A   **Further Reading**   **747**

B   **The SBM File Format**   **751**

C   **The SuperBible Tools**   **759**

Glossary   **765**
Index   **773**

Figures

Figure 1.1   Simplified graphics pipeline   6
Figure 1.2   Future Crew's 1992 demo *Unreal*   8

Figure 2.1   The output of our first OpenGL application   15
Figure 2.2   Rendering our first point   23
Figure 2.3   Making our first point bigger   23
Figure 2.4   Our very first OpenGL triangle   25

Figure 3.1   Our first tessellated triangle   36
Figure 3.2   Tessellated triangle after adding a geometry shader . .   38
Figure 3.3   Clockwise (left) and counterclockwise (right) winding
             order   41
Figure 3.4   Result of Listing 3.10   43
Figure 3.5   Result of Listing 3.12   45

Figure 4.1   A point in space is both a vertex and a vector   52
Figure 4.2   The dot product — cosine of the angle between two
             vectors   55
Figure 4.3   A cross product returns a vector perpendicular to its
             parameters   56
Figure 4.4   Reflection and refraction   58
Figure 4.5   A 4×4 matrix representing rotation and
             translation   62

Figure 4.6   Modeling transformations: rotation then translation,
              and translation then rotation   63
Figure 4.7   Two perspectives of view coordinates   65
Figure 4.8   The modeling transformations   67
Figure 4.9   A cube translated ten units in the positive y direction   69
Figure 4.10   A cube rotated about an arbitrary axis   71
Figure 4.11   A non-uniform scaling of a cube   74
Figure 4.12   A side-by-side example of an orthographic versus
              perspective projection   81
Figure 4.13   Finding a point on a line   83
Figure 4.14   A simple Bézier curve   84
Figure 4.15   A cubic Bézier curve   85
Figure 4.16   A cubic Bézier spline   88

Figure 5.1   Binding buffers and uniform blocks to binding
              points   118
Figure 5.2   A few frames from the spinning cube application . . .   124
Figure 5.3   Many cubes!   125
Figure 5.4   A simple textured triangle   142
Figure 5.5   A full-screen texture loaded from a .KTX file   146
Figure 5.6   An object wrapped in simple textures   148
Figure 5.7   Texture filtering — nearest (left) and linear (right) . .   153
Figure 5.8   A series of mipmapped images   155
Figure 5.9   A tunnel rendered with three textures and
              mipmapping   158
Figure 5.10   Example of texture coordinate wrapping modes   160
Figure 5.11   Output of the alien rain sample   165
Figure 5.12   Resolved per-fragment linked lists   177

Figure 6.1   Shape of a Hermite curve   198

Figure 7.1   Indices used in an indexed draw   232
Figure 7.2   Base vertex used in an indexed draw   235
Figure 7.3   Triangle strips with and without primitive restart . . .   237
Figure 7.4   First attempt at an instanced field of grass   241
Figure 7.5   Slightly perturbed blades of grass   242
Figure 7.6   Control over the length and orientation of our grass   243
Figure 7.7   The final field of grass   244
Figure 7.8   Result of instanced rendering   249
Figure 7.9   Result of asteroid rendering program   258
Figure 7.10   Relationship of transform feedback binding points . .   262
Figure 7.11   Connections of vertices in the spring-mass system . .   267

Figure 7.12   Simulation of points connected by springs 273
Figure 7.13   Visualizing springs in the spring-mass system 275
Figure 7.14   Clipping lines 276
Figure 7.15   Clipping triangles 277
Figure 7.16   Clipping triangles using a guard band 278
Figure 7.17   Rendering with user clip distances 282

Figure 8.1   Schematic of OpenGL tessellation 285
Figure 8.2   Tessellation factors for quad tessellation 286
Figure 8.3   Quad tessellation example 286
Figure 8.4   Tessellation factors for triangle tessellation 288
Figure 8.5   Triangle tessellation example 289
Figure 8.6   Tessellation factors for isoline tessellation 290
Figure 8.7   Isoline tessellation example 292
Figure 8.8   Tessellated isoline spirals example 293
Figure 8.9   Triangle tessellated using point mode 294
Figure 8.10   Tessellation using different subdivision modes 295
Figure 8.11   Displacement map used in terrain sample 300
Figure 8.12   Terrain rendered using tessellation 305
Figure 8.13   Tessellated terrain in wireframe 305
Figure 8.14   Final rendering of a cubic Bézier patch 309
Figure 8.15   A Bézier patch and its control cage 310
Figure 8.16   Geometry culled from different viewpoints 320
Figure 8.17   Exploding a model using the geometry shader 322
Figure 8.18   Basic tessellation using the geometry shader 325
Figure 8.19   Displaying the normals of a model using a geometry
              shader 328
Figure 8.20   Lines produced using lines with adjacency primitives 331
Figure 8.21   Triangles produced using
              GL_TRIANGLES_ADJACENCY 331
Figure 8.22   Triangles produced using
              GL_TRIANGLE_STRIP_ADJACENCY 332
Figure 8.23   Ordering of vertices for
              GL_TRIANGLE_STRIP_ADJACENCY 332
Figure 8.24   Rendering a quad using a pair of triangles 333
Figure 8.25   Parameterization of a quad 334
Figure 8.26   Quad rendered using a geometry shader 337
Figure 8.27   Result of rendering to multiple viewports 339

Figure 9.1   Contrasting perspective-correct and linear
              interpolation 345
Figure 9.2   Rendering with four different scissor rectangles 347

Figure 9.3   Effect of depth clamping at the near plane 354
Figure 9.4   A clipped object with and without depth clamping . . 355
Figure 9.5   All possible combinations of blending functions . . . 360
Figure 9.6   Result of rendering into a texture 369
Figure 9.7   Result of the layered rendering example 374
Figure 9.8   Result of stereo rendering to a stereo display 384
Figure 9.9   Antialiasing using line smoothing 385
Figure 9.10   Antialiasing using polygon smoothing 386
Figure 9.11   Antialiasing sample positions 387
Figure 9.12   No antialiasing (left) and 8-sample antialiasing
               (center and right) 388
Figure 9.13   Antialiasing of high-frequency shader output 394
Figure 9.14   Partially covered multi-sampled pixels 396
Figure 9.15   Different views of an HDR image 404
Figure 9.16   Histogram of levels for treelights.ktx 405
Figure 9.17   Naïve tone mapping by clamping 406
Figure 9.18   Transfer curve for adaptive tone mapping 407
Figure 9.19   Result of adaptive tone mapping program 409
Figure 9.20   The effect of light bloom on an image 409
Figure 9.21   Original and thresholded output for bloom example   412
Figure 9.22   Blurred thresholded bloom colors 413
Figure 9.23   Result of the bloom program 414
Figure 9.24   Gamma curves for sRGB and simple powers 418
Figure 9.25   A particle effect in the flurry screen saver 419
Figure 9.26   The star texture map 421
Figure 9.27   Flying through space with point sprites 423
Figure 9.28   Two potential orientations of textures on a point
               sprite 424
Figure 9.29   Analytically generated point sprite shapes 425

Figure 10.1   Global and local compute work group dimensions . . 443
Figure 10.2   Effect of race conditions in a compute shader 448
Figure 10.3   Effect of barrier() on race conditions 449
Figure 10.4   Sample input and output of a prefix sum operation . . 450
Figure 10.5   Breaking a prefix sum into smaller chunks 452
Figure 10.6   A 2D prefix sum 454
Figure 10.7   Computing the sum of a rectangle in a summed area
               table 456
Figure 10.8   Variable filtering applied to an image 457
Figure 10.9   Depth of field in a photograph 458
Figure 10.10   Applying depth of field to an image 461
Figure 10.11   Effects achievable with depth of field 461

Figure 10.12 Stages in the iterative flocking algorithm 463
Figure 10.13 Output of compute shader flocking program 471

Figure 12.1 Vectors used in Phong lighting 506
Figure 12.2 Per-vertex lighting (Gouraud shading) 509
Figure 12.3 Per-fragment lighting (Phong shading) 510
Figure 12.4 Varying specular parameters of a material 513
Figure 12.5 Phong lighting (left) vs. Blinn-Phong lighting (right) 515
Figure 12.6 Rim lighting vectors 516
Figure 12.7 Result of rim lighting example 517
Figure 12.8 Example normal map 518
Figure 12.9 Result of normal mapping example 522
Figure 12.10 A selection of spherical environment maps 523
Figure 12.11 Result of rendering with spherical environment
mapping 525
Figure 12.12 Example equirectangular environment map 526
Figure 12.13 Rendering result of equirectangular environment map 527
Figure 12.14 The layout of six cube faces in the Cubemap sample
program 528
Figure 12.15 Cube map environment rendering with a sky box . . 532
Figure 12.16 Pre-filtered environment maps and gloss map 533
Figure 12.17 Result of per-pixel gloss example 535
Figure 12.18 Depth as seen from a light 537
Figure 12.19 Results of rendering with shadow maps 540
Figure 12.20 Graphs of exponential decay 543
Figure 12.21 Applying fog to tessellated landscape 544
Figure 12.22 A one-dimensional color lookup table 545
Figure 12.23 A toon-shaded torus 547
Figure 12.24 Visualizing components of a G-buffer 553
Figure 12.25 Final rendering using deferred shading 554
Figure 12.26 Deferred shading with and without normal maps . . . 556
Figure 12.27 Bumpy surface occluding points 559
Figure 12.28 Selection of random vector in an oriented
hemisphere 561
Figure 12.29 Effect of increasing direction count on ambient
occlusion 562
Figure 12.30 Effect of introducing noise in ambient occlusion . . . 562
Figure 12.31 Ambient occlusion applied to a rendered scene 563
Figure 12.32 A few frames from the Julia set animation 568
Figure 12.33 Simplified 2D illustration of ray tracing 570
Figure 12.34 Our first ray-traced sphere 573
Figure 12.35 Our first lit ray-traced sphere 574

Figure 12.36 Implementing a stack using framebuffer objects 575
Figure 12.37 Ray-traced spheres with increasing ray bounces 576
Figure 12.38 Adding a ray-traced plane 578
Figure 12.39 Ray-traced spheres in a box 579

Figure 13.1 GPUView in action 591
Figure 13.2 VSync seen in GPUView 592
Figure 13.3 A packet dialog in GPUVIew 593
Figure 13.4 GPU PerfStudio 2 running the displacement mapping
example 594
Figure 13.5 GPU PerfStudio 2 frame debugger 595
Figure 13.6 GPU PerfStudio 2 HUD control window 596
Figure 13.7 GPU PerfStudio 2 overlaying information 596
Figure 13.8 GPU PerfStudio 2 showing AMD performance
counters 597
Figure 13.9 GPUView showing the effect of `glReadPixels()` into
system memory 599
Figure 13.10 GPUView showing the effect of `glReadPixels()` into
a buffer 600

Figure 14.1 Realtech VR's OpenGL Extensions Viewer 619
Figure 14.2 AMD and NVIDIA OpenGL drivers 625
Figure 14.3 The OpenGL Extensions Viewer is free on the Mac
App Store 650
Figure 14.4 The initial `CocoaGL` project 651
Figure 14.5 Interface Builder is ready to build your OpenGL app . 651
Figure 14.6 The OpenGL window ready to go... or is it? 652
Figure 14.7 Creating the basic NSView view class 653
Figure 14.8 Turn off the One Shot memory attribute 659
Figure 14.9 This chapter's demo rendering in a Cocoa view 664
Figure 14.10 The Cocoa sample with the supporting files 670
Figure 14.11 Tearing caused by an unsynced buffer swap 678
Figure 14.12 Here's looking at you! 703
Figure 14.13 OpenGL ES rendering on a cell phone 714
Figure 14.14 A typical embedded system diagram 719
Figure 14.15 StonehengeES rendered on an Android phone 731
Figure 14.16 The Xcode welcome screen 735
Figure 14.17 Selecting an OpenGL-ES-based game (application)
template 735
Figure 14.18 The starter OpenGL ES application 736
Figure 14.19 The "dancing cubes" default OpenGL ES code 736

Figure 14.20 The Xcode project with the Stonehenge model code
added 739
Figure 14.21 The completed Stonehenge model on an iOS device   743

Figure B.1   Dump of example SBM file 757

Tables

Table 1.1 OpenGL Versions and Publication Dates 7

Table 4.1 Common Coordinate Spaces Used in 3D Graphics . . . 64

Table 5.1 Buffer Object Usage Models 93
Table 5.2 Basic OpenGL Type Tokens and Their Corresponding
C Types 96
Table 5.3 Uniform Parameter Queries via
glGetActiveUniformsiv() 114
Table 5.4 Atomic Operations on Shader Storage Blocks 130
Table 5.5 Texture Targets and Description 139
Table 5.6 Basic Texture Targets and Sampler Types 142
Table 5.7 Texture Filters, Including Mipmapped Filters 156
Table 5.8 Image Types 166
Table 5.9 Image Data Format Classes 168
Table 5.10 Image Data Format Classes 169
Table 5.11 Atomic Operations on Images 172
Table 5.12 Native OpenGL Texture Compression Formats 178
Table 5.13 Texture View Target Compatibility 183
Table 5.14 Texture View Format Compatibility 184

Table 6.1 Scalar Types in GLSL 188
Table 6.2 Vector and Matrix Types in GLSL 190

Table 7.1   Vertex Attribute Types 226
Table 7.2   Draw Type Matrix 232
Table 7.3   Values for primitiveMode 265

Table 8.1   Allowed Draw Modes for Geometry Shader Input
             Modes   313
Table 8.2   Sizes of Input Arrays to Geometry Shaders   315

Table 9.1   Stencil Functions 349
Table 9.2   Stencil Operations 350
Table 9.3   Depth Comparison Functions 353
Table 9.4   Blend Functions 359
Table 9.5   Blend Equations 362
Table 9.6   Logic Operations 363
Table 9.7   Framebuffer Completeness Return Values 378
Table 9.8   Floating-Point Texture Formats 402

Table 11.1   Possible Return Values for **glClientWaitSync()** 496

Table 13.1   Map Buffer Access Types 601

Table 14.1   Pixel Format Attributes 636
Table 14.2   Buffer Swap Values for WGL_SWAP_METHOD_ARB 637
Table 14.3   OpenGL Technologies in OS X 648
Table 14.4   Cocoa Pixel Format Attributes 655
Table 14.5   Read-Only Properties of the GLKTextureInfo Class . . . 663
Table 14.6   GLX Config Attribute List 690
Table 14.7   Base OpenGL Versions for OpenGL ES 708
Table 14.8   EGL Config Attribute List 721
Table 14.9   EGL Config Attribute List 723
Table 14.10 Configuration Members and Flags for GLKView 738

Listings

Listing 2.1 Our first OpenGL application 14
Listing 2.2 Animating color over time 16
Listing 2.3 Our first vertex shader 18
Listing 2.4 Our first fragment shader 18
Listing 2.5 Compiling a simple shader 18
Listing 2.6 Creating the program member variable 21
Listing 2.7 Rendering a single point 22
Listing 2.8 Producing multiple vertices in a vertex shader 24
Listing 2.9 Rendering a single triangle 25

Listing 3.1 Declaration of a vertex attribute 28
Listing 3.2 Updating a vertex attribute 29
Listing 3.3 Vertex shader with an output 30
Listing 3.4 Fragment shader with an input 31
Listing 3.5 Vertex shader with an output interface block 31
Listing 3.6 Fragment shader with an input interface block 32
Listing 3.7 Our first tessellation control shader 34
Listing 3.8 Our first tessellation evaluation shader 35
Listing 3.9 Our first geometry shader 37
Listing 3.10 Deriving a fragment's color from its position 43
Listing 3.11 Vertex shader with an output 44
Listing 3.12 Deriving a fragment's color from its position 44
Listing 3.13 Simple do-nothing compute shader 47

Listing 5.1	Generating, binding, and initializing a buffer	94
Listing 5.2	Updating the content of a buffer with `glBufferSubData()`	94
Listing 5.3	Mapping a buffer's data store with `glMapBuffer()` . .	95
Listing 5.4	Setting up a vertex attribute	99
Listing 5.5	Using an attribute in a vertex shader	99
Listing 5.6	Declaring two inputs to a vertex shader	100
Listing 5.7	Multiple separate vertex attributes	101
Listing 5.8	Multiple interleaved vertex attributes	102
Listing 5.9	Example uniform block declaration	109
Listing 5.10	Declaring a uniform block with the `std140` layout . .	110
Listing 5.11	Example of a uniform block with offsets	111
Listing 5.12	Retrieving the indices of uniform block members . .	112
Listing 5.13	Retrieving the information about uniform block members	113
Listing 5.14	Setting a single float in a uniform block	114
Listing 5.15	Retrieving the indices of uniform block members . .	115
Listing 5.16	Specifying the data for an array in a uniform block	115
Listing 5.17	Setting up a matrix in a uniform block	116
Listing 5.18	Specifying bindings for uniform blocks	119
Listing 5.19	Uniform blocks binding layout qualifiers	119
Listing 5.20	Setting up cube geometry	121
Listing 5.21	Building the model-view matrix for a spinning cube	122
Listing 5.22	Updating the projection matrix for the spinning cube	123
Listing 5.23	Rendering loop for the spinning cube	123
Listing 5.24	Spinning cube vertex shader	123
Listing 5.25	Spinning cube fragment shader	124
Listing 5.26	Rendering loop for the spinning cube	125
Listing 5.27	Example shader storage block declaration	126
Listing 5.28	Using a shader storage block in place of vertex attributes	127
Listing 5.29	Setting up an atomic counter buffer	134
Listing 5.30	Setting up an atomic counter buffer	134
Listing 5.31	Counting area using an atomic counter	135
Listing 5.32	Using the result of an atomic counter in a uniform block	136
Listing 5.33	Generating, binding, and initializing a texture	138
Listing 5.34	Updating texture data with `glTexSubImage2D()`	138
Listing 5.35	Reading from a texture in GLSL	141
Listing 5.36	The header of a .KTX file	144
Listing 5.37	Loading a .KTX file	145

Listing 5.38   Vertex shader with single texture coordinate 147
Listing 5.39   Fragment shader with single texture coordinate . . . 147
Listing 5.40   Initializing an array texture 161
Listing 5.41   Vertex shader for the alien rain sample 162
Listing 5.42   Fragment shader for the alien rain sample 163
Listing 5.43   Rendering loop for the alien rain sample 164
Listing 5.44   Fragment shader performing image loads and
               stores 171
Listing 5.45   Filling a linked list in a fragment shader 174
Listing 5.46   Traversing a linked list in a fragment shader 175

Listing 6.1   Retrieving the compiler log from a shader 202
Listing 6.2   Fragment shader with external function
               declaration 206
Listing 6.3   Configuring a separable program pipeline 208
Listing 6.4   Printing interface information 212
Listing 6.5   Example subroutine uniform declaration 213
Listing 6.6   Setting values of subroutine uniforms 216
Listing 6.7   Retrieving a program binary 217

Listing 7.1   Declaration of a Multiple Vertex Attributes 225
Listing 7.2   Setting up indexed cube geometry 233
Listing 7.3   Drawing indexed cube geometry 234
Listing 7.4   Drawing the same geometry many times 238
Listing 7.5   Pseudo-code for **glDrawArraysInstanced()** 240
Listing 7.6   Pseudo-code for **glDrawElementsInstanced()** 240
Listing 7.7   Simple vertex shader with per-vertex color 246
Listing 7.8   Simple instanced vertex shader 247
Listing 7.9   Getting ready for instanced rendering 248
Listing 7.10   Example use of an indirect draw command 253
Listing 7.11   Setting up the indirect draw buffer for asteroids . . . 254
Listing 7.12   Vertex shader inputs for asteroids 255
Listing 7.13   Per-indirect draw attribute setup 255
Listing 7.14   Asteroid field vertex shader 255
Listing 7.15   Drawing asteroids 257
Listing 7.16   Spring-mass system vertex setup 268
Listing 7.17   Spring-mass system vertex shader 271
Listing 7.18   Spring-mass system iteration loop 274
Listing 7.19   Spring-mass system rendering loop 274
Listing 7.20   Clipping an object against a plane and a sphere . . . 281

Listing 8.1   Simple quad tessellation control shader example . . . 287
Listing 8.2   Simple quad tessellation evaluation shader
              example 287
Listing 8.3   Simple triangle tessellation control shader
              example 289
Listing 8.4   Simple triangle tessellation evaluation shader
              example 290
Listing 8.5   Simple isoline tessellation control shader
              example 291
Listing 8.6   Simple isoline tessellation evaluation shader
              example 291
Listing 8.7   Isoline spirals tessellation evaluation shader 292
Listing 8.8   Vertex shader for terrain rendering 301
Listing 8.9   Tessellation control shader for terrain rendering . . . 302
Listing 8.10 Tessellation evaluation shader for terrain
              rendering 303
Listing 8.11 Fragment shader for terrain rendering 304
Listing 8.12 Cubic Bézier patch vertex shader 306
Listing 8.13 Cubic Bézier patch tessellation control shader 307
Listing 8.14 Cubic Bézier patch tessellation evaluation shader . . 307
Listing 8.15 Cubic Bézier patch fragment shader 309
Listing 8.16 Source code for a simple geometry shader 311
Listing 8.17 Geometry shader layout qualifiers 311
Listing 8.18 Iterating over the elements of gl_in[] 312
Listing 8.19 The definition of gl_in[] 314
Listing 8.20 Configuring the custom culling geometry shader . . . 318
Listing 8.21 Finding a face normal in a geometry shader 318
Listing 8.22 Conditionally emitting geometry in a geometry
              shader 319
Listing 8.23 Setting up the "explode" geometry shader 321
Listing 8.24 Pushing a face out along its normal 321
Listing 8.25 Pass-through vertex shader 323
Listing 8.26 Setting up the "tessellator" geometry shader 323
Listing 8.27 Generating new vertices in a geometry shader 323
Listing 8.28 Emitting a single triangle from a geometry shader . . 324
Listing 8.29 Using a function to produce faces in a geometry
              shader 324
Listing 8.30 A pass-through vertex shader that includes
              normals 326
Listing 8.31 Setting up the "normal visualizer" geometry
              shader 326
Listing 8.32 Producing lines from normals in the geometry
              shader 327

Listing 8.33   Drawing a face normal in the geometry shader 327
Listing 8.34   Geometry shader for rendering quads 335
Listing 8.35   Fragment shader for rendering quads 336
Listing 8.36   Rendering to multiple viewports in a geometry
              shader 338

Listing 9.1   Setting up scissor rectangle arrays 346
Listing 9.2   Example stencil buffer usage, border decorations . . . 350
Listing 9.3   Rendering with all blending functions 359
Listing 9.4   Setting up a simple framebuffer object 367
Listing 9.5   Rendering to a texture 367
Listing 9.6   Setting up an FBO with multiple attachments 369
Listing 9.7   Declaring multiple outputs in a fragment shader . . . 370
Listing 9.8   Setting up a layered framebuffer 371
Listing 9.9   Layered rendering using a geometry shader 372
Listing 9.10   Displaying an array texture — vertex shader 373
Listing 9.11   Displaying an array texture — fragment shader 373
Listing 9.12   Attaching texture layers to a framebuffer 375
Listing 9.13   Checking completeness of a framebuffer object 378
Listing 9.14   Creating a stereo window 380
Listing 9.15   Drawing into a stereo window 381
Listing 9.16   Rendering to two layers with a geometry shader . . . 382
Listing 9.17   Copying from an array texture to a stereo back
              buffer 383
Listing 9.18   Turning on line smoothing 386
Listing 9.19   Choosing 8-sample antialiasing 388
Listing 9.20   Setting up a multi-sample framebuffer attachment . . 390
Listing 9.21   Simple multi-sample "maximum" resolve 391
Listing 9.22   Fragment shader producing high-frequency
              output 393
Listing 9.23   A 100-megapixel virtual framebuffer 401
Listing 9.24   Applying simple exposure coefficient to an HDR
              image 406
Listing 9.25   Adaptive HDR to LDR conversion fragment
              shader 407
Listing 9.26   Bloom fragment shader; output bright data to a
              separate buffer 410
Listing 9.27   Blur fragment shader 412
Listing 9.28   Adding bloom effect to scene 414
Listing 9.29   Creating integer framebuffer attachments 415
Listing 9.30   Texturing a point sprite in the fragment shader 420
Listing 9.31   Vertex shader for the star field effect 422

Listing 9.32 Fragment shader for the star field effect 423
Listing 9.33 Fragment shader for generating shaped points 425
Listing 9.34 Naïve rotated point sprite fragment shader 427
Listing 9.35 Rotated point sprite vertex shader 427
Listing 9.36 Rotated point sprite fragment shader 427
Listing 9.37 Taking a screenshot with `glReadPixels()` 430

Listing 10.1 Creating and compiling a compute shader 438
Listing 10.2 Compute shader image inversion 444
Listing 10.3 Dispatching the image copy compute shader 444
Listing 10.4 Compute shader with race conditions 447
Listing 10.5 Simple prefix sum implementation in C++ 450
Listing 10.6 Prefix sum implementation using a compute shader 453
Listing 10.7 Compute shader to generate a 2D prefix sum 455
Listing 10.8 Depth of field using summed area tables 459
Listing 10.9 Initializing shader storage buffers for flocking 464
Listing 10.10 The rendering loop for the flocking example 465
Listing 10.11 Compute shader for updates in flocking example . . . 466
Listing 10.12 The first rule of flocking 467
Listing 10.13 The second rule of flocking 467
Listing 10.14 Main body of the flocking update compute shader . . 468
Listing 10.15 Inputs to the flock rendering vertex shader 469
Listing 10.16 Flocking vertex shader body 470

Listing 11.1 Getting the result from a query object 478
Listing 11.2 Figuring out if occlusion query results are ready . . . 478
Listing 11.3 Simple, application-side conditional rendering 479
Listing 11.4 Rendering when query results aren't available 480
Listing 11.5 Basic conditional rendering example 481
Listing 11.6 A more complete conditional rendering example . . . 482
Listing 11.7 Timing operations using timer queries 484
Listing 11.8 Timing operations using `glQueryCounter()` 485
Listing 11.9 Drawing data written to a transform feedback
             buffer 491
Listing 11.10 Working while waiting for a sync object 495

Listing 12.1 The Gouraud shading vertex shader 507
Listing 12.2 The Gouraud shading fragment shader 508
Listing 12.3 The Phong shading vertex shader 510
Listing 12.4 The Phong shading fragment shader 511

Listing 12.5   Blinn-Phong fragment shader 514

Listing 12.6   Rim lighting shader function 516

Listing 12.7   Vertex shader for normal mapping 520

Listing 12.8   Fragment shader for normal mapping 521

Listing 12.9   Spherical environment mapping vertex shader 523

Listing 12.10 Spherical environment mapping fragment shader . . 524

Listing 12.11 Equirectangular environment mapping fragment
               shader 526

Listing 12.12 Loading a cube map texture 528

Listing 12.13 Vertex shader for sky box rendering 530

Listing 12.14 Fragment shader for sky box rendering 530

Listing 12.15 Vertex shader for cube map environment
               rendering 531

Listing 12.16 Fragment shader for cube map environment
               rendering 531

Listing 12.17 Fragment shader for per-fragment shininess 534

Listing 12.18 Getting ready for shadow mapping 536

Listing 12.19 Setting up matrices for shadow mapping 536

Listing 12.20 Setting up a shadow matrix 538

Listing 12.21 Simplified vertex shader for shadow mapping 538

Listing 12.22 Simplified fragment shader for shadow mapping . . . 539

Listing 12.23 Displacement map tessellation evaluation shader . . 541

Listing 12.24 Application of fog in a fragment shader 543

Listing 12.25 The toon vertex shader 546

Listing 12.26 The toon fragment shader 546

Listing 12.27 Initializing a G-buffer 550

Listing 12.28 Writing to a G-buffer 551

Listing 12.29 Unpacking data from a G-buffer 552

Listing 12.30 Lighting a fragment using data from a G-buffer 553

Listing 12.31 Deferred shading with normal mapping (fragment
               shader) 555

Listing 12.32 Ambient occlusion fragment shader 564

Listing 12.33 Setting up the Julia set renderer 567

Listing 12.34 Inner loop of the Julia renderer 567

Listing 12.35 Using a gradient texture to color the Julia set 568

Listing 12.36 Ray-sphere intersection test 571

Listing 12.37 Determining closest intersection point 572

Listing 12.38 Ray-plane intersection test 578

Listing 13.1   Creating a debug context with the sb6 framework . . 582

Listing 13.2   Setting the debug callback function 583

Listing 14.1   Registering a window class 628

Listing 14.2   Creating a simple window 629

Listing 14.3   Declaration of `PIXELFORMATDESCRIPTOR` 631

Listing 14.4   Choosing and setting a pixel format 632

Listing 14.5   Windows main message loop 633

Listing 14.6   Finding a pixel format with
`wglChoosePixelFormatARB()` 639

Listing 14.7   Enumerating pixel formats on Windows 640

Listing 14.8   Creating shared contexts on Windows 643

Listing 14.9   Setting up a full-screen window 645

Listing 14.10 Definition of the Objective-C
`GLCoreProfileView` class 653

Listing 14.11 Initialization of our core context OpenGL view 654

Listing 14.12 Outputting information about the OpenGL
context 660

Listing 14.13 Code called whenever the view changes size 660

Listing 14.14 Code called whenever the view changes size 661

Listing 14.15 Controlling movement smoothly with keyboard
bit flags and a timer 672

Listing 14.16 Creating and initializing the full-screen window . . . 676

Listing 14.17 GLUT main function to set up OpenGL 681

Listing 14.18 Extending `GLSurfaceView` 732

Listing 14.19 Setting up and rendering 733

Listing 14.20 Construction and initialization of the `GLKView` 738

Listing 14.21 Redirecting the current folder to point our
resources 742

Foreword

OpenGL® SuperBible has long been an essential reference for 3D graphics developers, and this new edition is more relevant than ever, particularly given the increasing importance of multi-platform deployment. In our line of work, we spend a lot of time at the interface between high-level rendering algorithms and fast-moving GPU and API targets. Even though, between us, we have more than thirty-five years of experience with real-time graphics programming, there is always more to learn. This is why we are so excited about this new edition of the *OpenGL® SuperBible*.

Many programmers of our generation used OpenGL back in the nineties before market forces dictated that we ship Windows games using Direct3D, which first shipped in 1995. While Direct3D initially followed in the footsteps of OpenGL, it eventually surpassed OpenGL in its rapid exposure of advanced GPU functionality, particularly in the transition to programmable graphics hardware.

During this transition, Microsoft consistently shipped new versions of Direct3D for a period of eight years, ending in 2002 with DirectX 9. With DirectX 10, however, Microsoft adopted a release strategy that tied new versions of DirectX to new versions of Windows, not only in terms of timing but in terms of legacy support. That is, not only did new versions of DirectX come out less frequently — only two major versions have come out in the last 11 years — but they were not supported on certain older versions of Windows. Naturally, this change in strategy by Microsoft curtailed the GPU vendors' ability to expose their innovations on Windows.

Fortunately, in this same timeframe, the OpenGL Architecture Review Board accelerated development, putting OpenGL back in a position of leadership. In fact, there has been so much progress in the past five years that OpenGL has reached a tipping point and is again viable for game development, particularly as more and more developers are adopting a multiplatform strategy that includes OS X and Linux.

OpenGL even has advantages to developers primarily targeting Windows, allowing them to access the very latest GPU features on all Windows versions, not just recent ones that have support for DirectX 10 or DirectX 11. In the growing Asian market, for example, Steam customers have the same caliber of PC hardware as their Western counterparts, but far more of them are running Windows XP, where DirectX 10 and DirectX 11 are not available. An application written using OpenGL, rather than Direct3D, can use the advanced features of customers' hardware and not have to maintain a reduced-quality rendering codepath for customers using Windows XP.

This edition of *OpenGL® SuperBible* is an outstanding resource for a wide variety of software developers, from students who may have some of the math and programming fundamentals but need a nudge in the right direction, to seasoned professional developers who need to quickly find out the nitty-gritty details of a particular API feature. In fact, we suspect that many professionals may be coming back to OpenGL after a number of years away, and this book is an excellent resource for doing just that.

Specifically, this edition of *OpenGL® SuperBible* introduces many of the new features of OpenGL 4.3, such as compute shaders, texture views, indirect multi-draw, enhanced API debugging, and more. As readers of previous editions have come to expect, the SuperBible continues to go well beyond the information provided in the API documentation and into the fundamentals of popular application techniques. Just having all of the essential platform-specific API initialization material for Linux, OS X, and Windows in one place is worth the price of admission, not to mention the detailed discussions of modern debugging techniques, shadow mapping, non-photo-realistic rendering, deferred rendering, and more.

We believe that, for newcomers, OpenGL is the right place to start writing 3D graphics code that will run on a wide array of platforms in order to reach the largest possible audience. Likewise, for professionals, there has never been a better time to come back to OpenGL.

Rich Geldreich and Jason Mitchell
Valve

Preface

About This Book

This book is designed both for people who are learning computer graphics through OpenGL and for people who may already know about graphics but want to learn about OpenGL. The intended audience is students of computer science, computer graphics, or game design; professional software engineers; or simply just hobbyists and people who are interested in learning something new. We begin by assuming that the reader knows nothing about either computer graphics or OpenGL. The reader should be familiar with computer programming in C++, however.

One of our goals with this book is to ensure that there are as few forward references as possible and to require little or no assumed knowledge. The book should be accessible and readable, and if you start from the beginning and read all the way through, you should come away with a good comprehension of how OpenGL works and how to use it effectively in your applications. After reading and understanding the content of this book, you will be well placed to read and learn from more advanced computer graphics research articles and be confident that you could take the principles that they cover and implement them in OpenGL.

It is *not* a goal of this book to cover every last feature of OpenGL, or to mention every function in the specification or every value that can be passed to a command. Rather, the goal is to provide a solid understanding of OpenGL, introduce its fundamentals, and explore some of its more advanced features. After reading this book, readers should be comfortable looking up finer details in the OpenGL specification, experimenting with

OpenGL on their own machines and using extensions (bonus features that add capabilities to OpenGL not required by the main specification).

The Architecture of the Book

This book breaks down roughly into three major parts. In the first part, we explain what OpenGL is, how it connects to the graphics pipeline, and give minimal working examples that are sufficient to demonstrate each section of it without requiring much, if any, knowledge of any other part of the whole system. We lay a foundation in the math behind 3D computer graphics, and describe how OpenGL manages the large amounts of data that are required to provide a compelling experience to the users of your applications. We also describe the programming model for *shaders*, which will form a core part of any OpenGL application.

In the second part of the book, we begin to introduce features of OpenGL that require some knowledge of multiple parts of the graphics pipeline and may refer to concepts already introduced. This allows us to introduce more complex topics without glossing over details or telling you to skip forward in the book to find out how something really works. By taking a second pass over the OpenGL system, we are able to delve into where data goes as it leaves each part of OpenGL, as you'll already have at least been briefly introduced to its destination.

In the final part of the book, we dive deeper into the graphics pipeline, cover some more advanced topics, and give a number of examples that use multiple features of OpenGL. We provide a number of worked examples that implement various rendering techniques, give a series of suggestions and advice on OpenGL best practices and performance considerations, and end up with a practical overview of OpenGL on several popular platforms, including mobile devices.

In Part I, we start gently and then blast through OpenGL to give you a taste of what's to come. Then, we lay the groundwork of knowledge that will be essential to you as you progress through the rest of the book. In this part, you will find

- Chapter 1, "Introduction," which provides a brief introduction to OpenGL, its origins, history, and current state.

- Chapter 2, "Our First OpenGL Program," which jumps right into OpenGL and shows you how to create a simple OpenGL application using the source code provided with this book.

- Chapter 3, "Following the Pipeline," takes a more careful look at OpenGL and its various components, introducing each in a little more detail and adding to the simple example presented in the previous chapter.

- Chapter 4, "Math for 3D Graphics," introduces the foundations of math that will be essential for effective use of OpenGL and the creation of interesting 3D graphics applications.

- Chapter 5, "Data," provides you with the tools necessary to manage data that will be consumed and produced by OpenGL.

- Chapter 6, "Shaders and Programs," takes a deeper look at *shaders*, which are fundamental to the operation of modern graphics applications.

In Part II, we take a more detailed look at several of the topics introduced in the first chapters. We dig deeper into each of the major parts of OpenGL, and our example applications will start to become a little more complex and interesting. In this part, you will find

- Chapter 7, "Vertex Processing and Drawing Commands," which covers the inputs to OpenGL and the mechanisms by which semantics are applied to the raw data you provide.

- Chapter 8, "Primitive Processing," covers some higher level concepts in OpenGL, including connectivity information, higher-order surfaces, and tessellation.

- Chapter 9, "Fragment Processing and the Framebuffer," looks at how high-level 3D graphics information is transformed by OpenGL into 2D images, and how your applications can determine the appearance of objects on the screen.

- Chapter 10, "Compute Shaders," illustrates how your applications can harness OpenGL for more than just graphics, and make use of the incredible computing power locked up in a modern graphics card.

- Chapter 11, "Controlling and Monitoring the Pipeline," shows you how you can get a glimpse of how OpenGL executes the commands you give it — how long they take to execute, and the amount of data that they produce.

In Part III, we build on the knowledge that you will have gained in reading the first two-thirds of the book and use it to construct example applications that touch on multiple aspects of OpenGL. We also get into the practicalities of building larger OpenGL applications and deploying them across multiple platforms. In this part, you will find

- Chapter 12, "Rendering Techniques," covers several applications of OpenGL for graphics rendering, from simulation of light to artistic methods and even some non-traditional techniques.

- Chapter 13, "Debugging and Performance Optimization," provides advice and tips on how to get your applications running without errors, and how to get them going fast.

- Chapter 14, "Platform Specifics," covers issues that may be particular to certain platforms, including Windows, Mac, Linux, and mobile devices.

Finally, several appendices are provided that describe the tools and file formats used in this book, and give pointers to more useful OpenGL resources.

What's New in This Edition

This edition of the book differs somewhat from previous editions. This is the sixth edition of the book. The first edition of the book was published in 1996, more than fifteen years ago. Over time, OpenGL has evolved and so has the book's audience. Even since the fifth edition, which was published in 2010, a lot has changed. In some ways, OpenGL has become more complex, with more bells and whistles, more features, and more that you have to do to make something — really anything — show up on the screen. This has raised the barrier to entry for students, and in the fifth edition, we tried to lower that barrier again by glossing over a lot of details or hiding them in utility classes, functions, wrappers, and libraries.

In this edition, we do not hide anything from the reader. What this means is that it might take a while to draw something really impressive, but the extra effort will give you a deeper understanding of what OpenGL is and how it interacts with the underlying graphics hardware. Only the most basic of application frameworks are provided, and our first few programs will be thoroughly underwhelming. However, we're working on the assumption that you'll read the whole book and that by the end of it, you'll have something to show your friends, colleagues, or potential employers that you can be proud of.

In this edition, the printed copy of the OpenGL reference pages, or "man" pages, is gone. The reference pages are available online at http://www.opengl.org/sdk/docs/man4/ and as a live document are kept up to date. A printed copy of those pages is somewhat redundant and leads to errors — several were found in the reference pages after the fifth edition went to print with no reasonable means of distributing an errata. Further, the reference pages consumed hundreds of printed pages of the book, adding to its cost and size. We'd rather fill a bunch of those pages with more content and save a few trees with the rest.

We've also changed the structure of the book somewhat and make several passes over OpenGL. Rather than having a whole chapter dedicated to a single topic, for example, we introduce as much as possible as early as possible using worked, minimal examples, and then bring in features that touch multiple aspects of OpenGL. This should greatly reduce the number of forward or circular references, and reduce the number of times we need to tell you *don't worry about this, we'll explain it later*.

We hope you enjoy it.

How to Build the Samples

Retrieve the sample code from the book's Web site, http://www.openglsuperbible.com, unpack the archive to a directory on your computer, and follow the instructions in the included HOWTOBUILD.TXT file for your platform of choice. The book's source code has been built and tested on Microsoft Windows (Windows XP or later is required), Linux (several major distributions), and Mac OS X. It is recommended that you install any available operating system updates and obtain the most recent graphics drivers from your graphics card manufacturer.

You may notice some minor discrepancies between the source code printed in this book and that in the source files. There are a number of reasons for this:

- This book is about OpenGL 4.3 — the most recent version at time of writing. The samples printed in the book are written assuming that OpenGL 4.3 is available on the target platform. However, we understand that in practice, operating systems, graphics drivers, and platforms may not have the *latest and greatest* available, and so, where possible, we've made minor modifications to the sample applications to allow them to run on earlier versions of OpenGL.

- There were several months between when this book's text was finalized for printing and when the sample applications were packaged and posted to the Web. In that time, we discovered opportunities for improvement, whether that was uncovering new bugs, platform dependencies, or optimizations. The latest version of the source code on the Web has those fixes and tweaks applied and therefore deviates from the necessarily static copy printed in the book.

- There is not necessarily a one-to-one mapping of listings in the book's text and sample applications in the Web package. Some sample applications demonstrate more than one concept, some aren't mentioned in the book at all, and some listings in the book don't have an equivalent sample application.

Errata

We made a bunch of mistakes — we're certain of it. It's incredibly frustrating as an author to spot an error that you made and know that it has been printed, in books that your readers paid for, thousands and thousands of times. We have to accept that this will happen, though, and do our best to correct issues as we are able. If you think you see something that doesn't quite gel, check the book's Web site for errata.

```
http://www.openglsuperbible.com
```

Acknowledgments

First and foremost, I would like to thank my wife, Chris, and my two wonderful kids, Jeremy and Emily. For the never-ending evenings, weekends, and holidays that I spent holed up in my office or curled up with a laptop instead of hanging out with you guys.... I appreciate your patience. I'd like to extend a huge thank you to our tech reviewers, Piers Daniell, Daniel Koch, and Daniel Rákos. You guys did a fantastic job, finding my mistakes and helping to make this book as good as it could be. Your feedback was particularly thorough, and the book grew by at least one hundred pages after I received your reviews. Thanks also to my co-authors Nick Haemel and Richard Wright, Jr. In particular to Richard, thanks for trusting me with taking the lead on this edition. I can only hope that this one turned out as well as the five that preceded it. Thanks to Laura Lewin, Olivia Basegio, Sheri Cain, and the rest of the staff at Addison-Wesley for putting up with me delivering whatever I felt, whenever I felt, and pretty much ignoring schedules and processes. Finally, thanks to you, our readers. Without you, there'd be no book.

Graham Sellers

Thanks to Nick and Graham, my very qualified co-authors. Especially thanks to Graham for taking over the role of lead author for the sixth edition of this book. I fear this revision simply would not have happened without him taking over both the management and the majority of the rewrite for this edition. Two editions ago, Addison-Wesley added this book to its "OpenGL Library" lineup, and I continue to be grateful for that move years later. For more than fifteen years, countless editors, reviewers, and publishers have made me look good and smarter than I am. There are too many to name, but I have to single out Debra Williams-Cauley for braving more than half this book's lifetime, and, yes, thank you Laura Lewin for taking over for Debra.... You are a brave soul!

Thanks to Full Sail University for letting me teach OpenGL for more than ten years now, while still continuing my "day job." Especially Rob Catto for looking the other way more than once, and running interference when things get in my way on a regular basis. My very good friends and associates in the graphics department there, particularly my department chair, Johnathan Burnside, who simply tolerates my schedule. To Wendy "Kitty" Jones, thanks for all the Thai food! Very special thanks also to my muse, Callisto, for your continuing inspiration and support, not to mention listening to me complain all the time. Special thanks to Software Bisque (Steve, Tom, Daniel, and Matt) for giving me something "real" to do with OpenGL every day, and providing me with possibly the coolest day (and night) job anybody could ever ask for. I also have to thank my family, LeeAnne, Sara, Stephen, and Alex. You've all put up with a lot of mood swings, rapidly changing priorities, and an unpredictable work schedule, and you've provided a good measure of motivation when I really needed it over the years.

Richard S. Wright, Jr.

Thanks to Richard and Graham for collaborating on one more project supporting OpenGL through creating great instructional content. Without your dedication and commitment, computer graphics students would not have the necessary tools to learn 3D graphics. It has been a pleasure working with you over the years to help support 3D graphics and OpenGL specifically. Thanks to Addison-Wesley and Laura Lewin for supporting our project.

I'd also like to thank NVIDIA for the great experiences that have expanded my 3D horizons. It has been great having opportunities to break new ground squeezing OpenGL into incredibly small products. I can't wait to ship all of the exciting things we have been working on! Thanks to Barthold Lichtenbelt for pulling me back into graphics and giving me an opportunity to work on some of the most exciting technology I've seen to date. Thanks to Piers Daniell for your vigilance and help in keeping us all on track and making sure we get all the details right. Special thanks to Xi Chen at NVIDIA for all your help on Android sample code.

And of course, I couldn't have completed yet another project without the support of my family and friends. To my wife, Anna: You have put up with all of my techno mumbo jumbo all these years while at the same time saving lives and making a significant difference in medicine in your own right. Thanks for your patience and support — I could never be successful without you.

Nicholas Haemel

About the Authors

Graham Sellers is a classic geek. His family got their first computer (a BBC Model B) right before his sixth birthday. After his mum and dad stayed up all night programming it to play "Happy Birthday," he was hooked and determined to figure out how it worked. Next came basic programming and then assembly language. His first real exposure to graphics was via "demos" in the early nineties, and then through Glide, and finally OpenGL in the late nineties. He holds a master's degree in engineering from the University of Southampton, England.

Currently, Graham is a senior manager and software architect on the OpenGL driver team at AMD. He represents AMD at the ARB and has contributed to many extensions and to the core OpenGL Specification. Prior to that, he was a team lead at Epson, implementing OpenGL ES and OpenVG drivers for embedded products. Graham holds several patents in the fields of computer graphics and image processing. When he's not working on OpenGL, he likes to disassemble and reverse engineer old video game consoles (just to see how they work and what he can make them do). Originally from England, Graham now lives in Orlando, Florida, with his wife and two children.

Richard S. Wright, Jr., has been using OpenGL for more than eighteen years, since version 1.1, and has taught OpenGL programming in the game design degree program at Full Sail University near Orlando, Florida, for more than a decade. Currently, Richard is a senior engineer at Software Bisque, where he is the technical lead and product manager for a 3D solar system simulator and their full-dome theater planetarium products, and works on their mobile products and scientific imaging applications.

Previously with Real 3D/Lockheed Martin, Richard was a regular OpenGL ARB attendee and contributed to the OpenGL 1.2 specification and conformance tests back when mammoths still walked the earth. Since then, Richard has worked in multi-dimensional database visualization, game development, medical diagnostic visualization, and astronomical space simulation on Windows, Linux, Mac OS X, and various handheld platforms.

Richard first learned to program in the eighth grade in 1978 on a paper terminal. At age 16, his parents let him buy a computer instead of a car with his grass-cutting money, and he sold his first computer program less than a year later (and it was a graphics program!). When he graduated from high school, his first job was teaching programming and computer literacy for a local consumer education company. He studied electrical engineering and computer science at the University of Louisville's Speed Scientific School and made it halfway through his senior year before his career got the best of him and took him to Florida. A native of Louisville, Kentucky, he now lives in Lake Mary, Florida. When not programming or dodging hurricanes, Richard is an avid amateur astronomer and photography buff. Richard is also, proudly, a Mac.

Nicholas Haemel has been involved with OpenGL for more than fifteen years, since soon after its wide acceptance. He graduated from the Milwaukee School of Engineering with a degree in computer engineering and a love for embedded systems, computer hardware, and making things work. Soon after graduation he put these skills to work for the 3D drivers group at ATI, developing graphics drivers and working on new GPUs.

Nick is now a senior manager of Tegra OpenGL Driver Development at NVIDIA. He leads a team of software developers working on NVIDIA mobile graphics drivers, represents NVIDIA at the Khronos Standards Body, has authored many OpenGL extensions, and contributed to all OpenGL specifications since version 3.0 and to the OpenGL ES 3.0 specification.

Nick's graphics career began at age nine when he first learned to program 2D graphics using Logo Writer. After convincing his parents to purchase a state-of-the-art 286 IBM-compatible PC, it immediately became the central control unit for robotic arms and other remotely programmable devices. Fast-forward twenty-five years and the devices being controlled are GPUs and SoCs smaller than the size of a fingernail but with more than eight billion transistors. Nick's interests also extend to business leadership and management, bolstered by an MBA from the University of Wisconsin–Madison. Nick currently resides in the Bay Area in California. When not working on accelerating the future of graphics, Nick enjoys the outdoors as a competitive sailor, mountaineer, ex-downhill ski racer, road biker, and photographer.

Part I

Foundations

Chapter 1

Introduction

WHAT YOU'LL LEARN IN THIS CHAPTER

- What the graphics pipeline is and how OpenGL relates to it

- The origins of OpenGL and how it came to be the way that it is today

- Some of the fundamental concepts that we'll be building on throughout the book

This book is about OpenGL. OpenGL is an interface that your application can use to access and control the graphics subsystem of the device upon which it runs. This could be anything from a high-end graphics workstation to a commodity desktop computer, a video game console, or even a mobile phone. Standardizing the interface to a subsystem increases portability and allows software developers to concentrate on creating quality products, on producing interesting content, and on the overall performance of their applications, rather than worrying about the specifics of the platforms they want them to run on. These standard interfaces are called Application Programming Interfaces (or APIs), of which OpenGL is one. This chapter introduces OpenGL, describes how it relates to the underlying graphics subsystem, and provides some history on the origin and evolution of OpenGL.

OpenGL and the Graphics Pipeline

Generating a product at high efficiency and volume generally requires two things: scalability and parallelism. In factories, this is achieved by using production lines. While one worker installs the engine in a car, another can be installing the doors and yet another can be installing the wheels. By overlapping the phases of production of the product, with each phase being executed by a skilled technician that concentrates their energy on that single task, each phase becomes more efficient and overall productivity goes up. Also, by making many cars at the same time, a factory can have multiple workers installing multiple engines or wheels or doors, and many cars can be on the production line at the same time, each at different stages of completion.

The same is true in computer graphics. The commands from your program are taken by OpenGL and sent to the underlying graphics hardware, which works on them in an efficient manner to produce the desired result as quickly and efficiently as possible. There could be many commands lined up to execute on the hardware (a term referred to as *in flight*), and some may even be partially completed. This allows their execution to be overlapped such that a later stage of one command might run concurrently with an earlier stage of another command. Furthermore, computer graphics generally consist of many repetitions of very similar tasks (such as figuring out what color a pixel should be), and these tasks are usually independent of one another — that is, the result of coloring one pixel doesn't depend on any other. Just as a car plant can build multiple cars simultaneously, so can OpenGL break up the work you give it and work on its fundamental elements *in parallel*. Through a combination of *pipelining* and *parallelism*, incredible performance of modern graphics processors is realized.

The goal of OpenGL is to provide an *abstraction layer* between your application and the underlying graphics subsystem, which is often a hardware accelerator made up of one or more custom, high performance processors with dedicated memory, display outputs, and so on. This abstraction layer allows your application to not need to know who made the graphics processor (or GPU — graphics processing unit), how it works, or how well it performs. Certainly it is possible to determine this information, but the point is that applications don't need to.

As a design principle, OpenGL must strike a balance between too high and too low an abstraction level. On the one hand, it must hide differences between various manufacturers' products (or between the various products of a single manufacturer) and system-specific traits such as screen resolution, processor architecture, installed operating system, and so on. On the other hand, the level of abstraction must be low enough that programmers can gain access to the underlying hardware and make best use of it. If OpenGL presented too high of an abstraction level, then it would be easy to create programs that fit the model, but very hard to use advanced features of the graphics hardware that weren't included. This is the type of model followed by software such as game engines — new features of the graphics hardware generally require pretty large changes in the engine in order for games built on top of it to gain access to them. If the abstraction level is too low, applications need to start worrying about architectural peculiarities of the system they're running on. Low levels of abstraction are common in video game consoles, for example, but don't fit well into a graphics library that spans in support from mobile phones through gaming PCs to high power professional graphics workstations.

As technology advances, more and more research is conducted into computer graphics, best practices are developed, and bottlenecks and requirements move, and so OpenGL must move to keep up.

The current state-of-the-art in graphics processing units, which most OpenGL implementations are based on, are capable of many teraflops of computing power, have gigabytes of memory that can be accessed at hundreds of gigabytes per second, and can drive multiple, multi-megapixel displays at high refresh rates. GPUs are also extremely flexible, and are able to work on tasks that might not be considered graphics at all such as physical simulations, artificial intelligence, and even audio processing.

Current GPUs consist of large number of small programmable processors called *shader cores* which run mini-programs called *shaders*. Each core has a relatively low throughput, processing a single instruction of the shader in one or more clock cycles and normally lacking advanced features such as out-of-order execution, branch prediction, super-scalar issue, and so on. However, each GPU might contain anywhere from a few tens to a few thousand of these cores, and together they can perform an immense amount of work. The graphics system is broken into a number *stages*, each represented either by a shader or by a fixed-function, possibly configurable processing block. Figure 1.1 shows a simplified schematic of the graphics pipeline.

In Figure 1.1, the boxes with rounded corners are considered *fixed-function* stages whereas the boxes with square corners are programmable, which means that they execute shaders that you supply. In practice, some or all of the fixed-function stages may really be implemented in shader code too — it's just that you don't supply that code, but rather the GPU

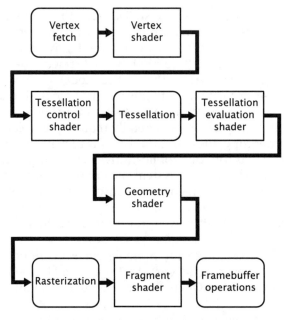

Figure 1.1: Simplified graphics pipeline

manufacturer would generally supply it as part of a driver, firmware, or other system software.

The Origins and Evolution of OpenGL

OpenGL has its origins at Silicon Graphics, Inc., (SGI) and their IRIS GL. GL stood for (and still stands for) "Graphics Library" and in much of the modern OpenGL documentation you will see the term "the GL," meaning "the graphics library," originating from this era. Silicon Graphics was[1] a manufacturer of high-end graphics workstations. These were extremely expensive, and using a proprietary API for graphics wasn't helping. Other manufacturers were producing much more inexpensive solutions running on competing APIs that were often compatible with each other. In the early nineties, SGI realized that portability was important and so decided to clean up IRIS GL, remove system-specific parts of the API and release it as an open standard that could be implemented, royalty free by anyone. The very first version of OpenGL was released in June of 1992 and was marked as OpenGL 1.0.

---

1. Silicon Graphics, or more accurately SGI, still exists today, but went bankrupt in 2009, with its assets and brands acquired by Rackable Systems, who assumed the moniker SGI, but do not operate in the high-end graphics market.

That year, SGI was also instrumental in establishing the OpenGL Architectural Review Board (ARB), the original members of which included companies such as Compaq, DEC, IBM, Intel, and Microsoft. Soon, other companies such as Hewlett Packard, Sun Microsystems, Evans & Sutherland, and Intergraph joined the group. The OpenGL ARB is the standards body that designs, governs, and produces the OpenGL specification and is now a part of Khronos Group, which is a larger consortium of companies that oversees the development of many open standards. Some of these original members either no longer exist (perhaps having gone out of business or having been acquired by or merged with other companies) or are no longer members of the ARB, having left the graphics business or otherwise gone their own ways. However, some still exist, either under new names or as the entity that was involved in the development of that very first version of OpenGL more than 20 years ago.

At time of writing, there have been 17 editions of the OpenGL specification. Their version numbers and dates of publication are shown in Table 1.1. This book covers version 4.3 of the OpenGL specification.

Table 1.1: OpenGL Versions and Publication Dates

Version	Publication Date
OpenGL 1.0	January 1992
OpenGL 1.1	January 1997
OpenGL 1.2	March 1998
OpenGL 1.2.1	October 1998
OpenGL 1.3	August 2001
OpenGL 1.4	July 2002
OpenGL 1.5	July 2003
OpenGL 2.0	September 2004
OpenGL 2.1	July 2006
OpenGL 3.0	August 2008
OpenGL 3.1	March 2009
OpenGL 3.2	August 2009
OpenGL 3.3	March 2010
OpenGL 4.0	March 2010[2]
OpenGL 4.1	July 2010
OpenGL 4.2	August 2011
OpenGL 4.3	August 2012

2. Yes, two versions at the same time!

Core Profile OpenGL

Twenty years is a long time in the development of cutting edge technology. In 1992, the top-of-the-line Intel CPU was the 80486, math co-processors were still optional, and the Pentium had not yet been invented (or at least released). Apple computers were still using Motorola 68K derived processors, and the PowerPC processors to which they would later switch would be made available during the second half of 1992. High-performance graphics acceleration was simply not something that was common in commodity home computers. If you didn't have access to a high-performance graphics workstation, you probably would have no hope of using OpenGL for anything. Software rendering ruled the world, and the Future Crew's *Unreal* demo won the Assembly '92 demo party. The best you could hope for in a home computer was some basic filled polygons or sprite rendering capabilities. The state of the art in 1992 home computer 3D graphics is shown in Figure 1.2.

Figure 1.2: Future Crew's 1992 demo *Unreal*

Over time, the price of graphics hardware came down, performance went up, and, partly due to low cost acceleration add-in boards for PCs and partly due to the increased performance of video game consoles, new features and capabilities showed up in affordable graphics processors and were added to OpenGL. Most of these features originated in *extensions* proposed by members of the OpenGL ARB. Some interacted well with each other and with existing features in OpenGL, and some did not. Also, as newer, better ways of squeezing performance out of graphics systems were invented, they were simply added to OpenGL, resulting in it having multiple ways of doing the same thing.

For many years, the ARB held a strong position on backwards compatibility, as it still does today. However, this backwards compatibility comes at a significant cost. Best practices have changed — what may have worked well or was not really a significant bottleneck on mid-1990s graphics hardware doesn't fit modern graphics processor architecture well. Specifying how new features interact with the older legacy features isn't easy and, in many cases, can make it almost impossible to cleanly introduce a new feature to OpenGL. As for implementing OpenGL, this has become such a difficult task that drivers tend to have more bugs than they really should, and graphics vendors need to spend considerable amounts of energy maintaining support for all kinds of legacy features that don't contribute to the advancement of or innovation in graphics.

For these reasons, in 2008, the ARB decided it would "fork" the OpenGL specification into two *profiles*. The first is the modern, *core* profile, which removes a number of legacy features leaving only those that are truly accelerated by current graphics hardware. This specification is several hundred pages shorter[3] than the other version of the specification, the *compatibility* profile. The compatibility profile maintains backwards compatibility with all revisions of OpenGL back to version 1.0. That means that software written in 1992 should compile and run on a modern graphics card with a thousand times higher performance today than when that program was first produced.

However, the compatibility profile really exists to allow software developers to maintain legacy applications and to add features to them without having to tear out years of work in order to shift to a new API. However, the core profile is strongly recommended by most OpenGL experts to be the profile that should be used for new application development. In particular, on some platforms, newer features are only available if you are using the core profile of OpenGL, and on others, an application written using the core profile of OpenGL will run *faster* than that same application unmodified, except to request the compatibility profile, even if it only uses features that are available in core profile OpenGL. Finally, if a feature's in the compatibility profile but has been removed from the core profile of OpenGL, there's probably a good reason for that, and it's a reasonable indication that you shouldn't be using it.

---

3. The core profile specification is still pretty hefty at well over 700 pages long.

This book covers only the core profile of OpenGL, and this is the last time we will mention the compatibility profile.

Primitives, Pipelines, and Pixels

As discussed, the model followed by OpenGL is that of a production line, or pipeline. Data flow within this model is generally one way, with data formed from commands called by your programs entering the front of the pipeline and flowing from stage to stage until it reaches the end of the pipeline. Along the way, shaders or other fixed-function blocks within the pipeline may pick up more data from *buffers* or *textures*, which are structures designed to store information that will be used during rendering. Some stages in the pipeline may even save data into these buffers or textures, allowing the application to read or save the data, or even for feedback to occur.

The fundamental unit of rendering in OpenGL is known as the *primitive*. OpenGL supports many types of primitives, but the three basic renderable primitive types are points, lines, and triangles. Everything you see rendered on the screen is a collection of (perhaps cleverly colored) points, lines, and triangles. Applications will normally break complex surfaces into a very large number of triangles and send them to OpenGL where they are rendered using a hardware accelerator called a *rasterizer*. Triangles are, relatively speaking, pretty easy to draw. As polygons, triangles are always *convex*, and therefore filling rules are easy to devise and follow. Concave polygons can always be broken down into two or more triangles, and so hardware natively supports rendering triangles directly and relies on other subsystems[4] to break complex geometry into triangles. The rasterizer is dedicated hardware that converts the three-dimensional representation of a triangle into a series of pixels that need to be drawn onto the screen.

Points, lines, and triangles are formed from collections of one, two, or three vertices, respectively. A *vertex* is simply a point within a coordinate space. In our case, we primarily consider a three-dimensional coordinate system. The graphics pipeline is broken down into two major parts. The first part, often known as the *front end*, processes vertices and primitives, eventually forming them into the points, lines, and triangles that will be handed off to the rasterizer. This is known as *primitive assembly*. After the rasterizer, the geometry has been converted from what

---

4. Sometimes, these subsystems are more hardware modules, and sometimes they are functions of drivers implemented in software.

is essentially a vector representation into a large number of independent pixels. These are handed off to the *back end*, which includes depth and stencil testing, fragment shading, blending, and updating the output image.

As you progress through this book, you will see how to tell OpenGL to start working for you. We'll go over how to create buffers and textures and hook them up to your programs. We'll also see how to write shaders to process your data and how to configure the fixed-function blocks of OpenGL to do what you want. OpenGL is really a large collection of fairly simple concepts, built upon each other. Having a good foundation and *big-picture* view of the system is essential, and over the next few chapters, we hope to provide that to you.

Summary

In this chapter you've been introduced to OpenGL and have read a little about its origins, history, status, and direction. You have seen the OpenGL pipeline and have been told how this book is going to progress. We have mentioned some of the terminology that we'll be using throughout the book. Over the next few chapters, you'll create our first OpenGL program, dig a little deeper into the various stages of the OpenGL pipeline, and then lay some foundations with some of the math that's useful in the world of computer graphics.

Chapter 2

Our First OpenGL Program

WHAT YOU'LL LEARN IN THIS CHAPTER

- How to create and compile shader code

- How to draw with OpenGL

- How to use the book's application framework to initialize your programs and clean up after yourself

In this chapter, we introduce the simple application framework that is used for almost all of the samples in this book. This shows you how to create the main window with the book's application framework and how to render simple graphics into it. You'll also see what a very simple GLSL shader looks like, how to compile it, and how to use it to render simple points. The chapter concludes with your very first OpenGL triangle.

Creating a Simple Application

To introduce the application framework that'll be used in the remainder of this book, we'll start with an extremely simple example application. The application framework is brought into your application by including sb6.h in your source code. This is a C++ header file that defines a namespace called sb6 that includes the declaration of an application class, sb6::application, from which we can derive our examples. The framework also includes a number of utility functions and a simple math library called vmath to help you with some of the number crunching involved in OpenGL.

To create an application, we simply include sb6.h, derive a class v sb6::application, and (in exactly one of our source files) include an instance of the DECLARE_MAIN macro. This defines the main entry point of our application, which creates an instance of our class (the type of which is passed as a parameter to the macro) and calls its run() method, which implements the application's main loop.

In turn, this performs some initialization by calling the startup() method and then calls the render() method in a loop. In the default implementation, both methods are virtual functions with empty bodies. We override the render() method in our derived class and write our drawing code inside it. The application framework takes care of creating a window, handling input, and displaying the rendered results to the user. The complete source code for our first example is given in Listing 2.1, and its output is shown in Figure 2.1.

```
// Include the "sb6.h" header file
#include "sb6.h"

// Derive my_application from sb6::application
class my_application : public sb6::application
{
public:
    // Our rendering function
    void render(double currentTime)
    {
        // Simply clear the window with red
        static const GLfloat red[] = { 1.0f, 0.0f, 0.0f, 1.0f };
        glClearBufferfv(GL_COLOR, 0, red);
    }
};

// Our one and only instance of DECLARE_MAIN
DECLARE_MAIN(my_application);
```

Listing 2.1: Our first OpenGL application

Figure 2.1: The output of our first OpenGL application

The example shown in Listing 2.1 simply clears the whole screen to red. This introduces our first OpenGL function, **glClearBufferfv()**. The prototype of **glClearBufferfv()** is

```
void glClearBufferfv(GLenum buffer,
                     GLint drawBuffer,
                     const GLfloat * value);
```

All OpenGL functions start with gl and follow a number of naming conventions such as encoding some of their parameter types as suffixes on the end of the function names. This allows a limited form of *overloading* even in languages that don't directly support this. In this case, the suffix fv means that the function consumes a vector (v) of floating-point (f) values, where arrays (generally referenced by pointers in languages like C) and vectors are used interchangeably by OpenGL.

The **glClearBufferfv()** function tells OpenGL to clear the buffer specified by the first parameter (in this case GL_COLOR) to the value specified in its third parameter. The second parameter, drawBuffer, is used when there are multiple output buffers that could be cleared. Because we're only using one here and drawBuffer is a zero-based index, we'll just set it to zero in this example. Here, that color is stored in the array red, which contains four floating-point values — one each for red, green, blue, and alpha, in that order. The red, green, and blue terms should be self-explanatory. Alpha is a fourth component that is associated with a color and is often used to encode the *opacity* of a fragment. When used this way, setting alpha to zero will make the fragment completely transparent, and setting it to one will make it completely opaque. The alpha value can also be stored in the output image and used in some parts of OpenGL's calculations, even though you can't see it. You can see that we set both the red and alpha values to one and the others to zero. This specifies an opaque red color. The result of running this application is shown in Figure 2.1.

This initial application isn't particularly interesting[1] as all it does is fill the window with a solid red color. You will notice that our render() function takes a single parameter — currentTime. This contains the number of seconds since the application was started, and we can use it to create a simple animation. In this case, we can use it to change the color that we use to clear the window. Our modified render() function[2] is shown in Listing 2.2.

```
// Our rendering function
void render(double currentTime)
{
    const GLfloat color[] = { (float)sin(currentTime) * 0.5f + 0.5f,
                              (float)cos(currentTime) * 0.5f + 0.5f,
                              0.0f, 1.0f };
    glClearBufferfv(GL_COLOR, 0, color);
}
```

Listing 2.2: Animating color over time

Now our window fades from red through yellow, orange, green, and back to red again. Still not that exciting, but at least it does *something*.

Using Shaders

As we mentioned in the introduction to the graphics pipeline in Chapter 1, "Introduction," OpenGL works by connecting a number of mini-programs called shaders together with fixed-function glue. When you draw, the graphics processor executes your shaders and pipes their

---

1. This sample is especially uninteresting if you are reading this book in black and white!

2. If you're copying this code into your own example, you'll need to include <math.h> in order to get the declarations of sin() and cos().

inputs and outputs along the pipeline until pixels[3] come out the end. In order to draw anything at all, you'll need to write at least a couple of shaders.

OpenGL shaders are written in a language called the OpenGL Shading Language, or GLSL. This is a language that has its origins in C, but has been modified over time to make it better suited to running on graphics processors. If you are familiar with C, then it shouldn't be hard to pick up GLSL. The compiler for this language is built into OpenGL. The source code for your shader is placed into a *shader object* and compiled, and then multiple shader objects can be linked together to form a *program object*. Each program object can contain shaders for one or more shader stages. The shader stages of OpenGL are vertex shaders, tessellation control and evaluation shaders, geometry shaders, fragment shaders, and compute shaders. The minimal useful pipeline configuration consists only of a vertex shader[4] (or just a compute shader), but if you wish to see any pixels on the screen, you will also need a fragment shader.

Our first couple of shaders are extremely simple. Listing 2.3 shows our first vertex shader. This is about as simple as it gets. In the first line, we have the #version 430 core declaration, which tells the shader compiler that we intend to use version 4.3 of the shading language. Notice that we include the keyword core to indicate that we only intend to use features from the core profile of OpenGL.

Next, we have the declaration of our main function, which is where the shader starts executing. This is exactly the same as in a normal C program, except that the main function of a GLSL shader has no parameters. Inside our main function, we assign a value to gl_Position, which is part of the plumbing that connects the shader to the rest of OpenGL. All variables that start with gl_ are part of OpenGL and connect shaders to each other or to the various parts of fixed functionality in OpenGL. In the vertex shader, gl_Position represents the output position of the vertex. The value we assign (vec4(0.0, 0.0, 0.5, 1.0)) places the vertex right in the middle of OpenGL's *clip space*, which is the coordinate system expected by the next stage of the OpenGL pipeline.

---

3. Actually, there are a number of use cases of OpenGL that create no pixels at all. We will cover those in a while. For now, let's just draw some pictures.

4. If you try to draw anything when your pipeline does not contain a vertex shader, the results will be undefined and almost certainly not what you were hoping for.

```
#version 430 core

void main(void)
{
    gl_Position = vec4(0.0, 0.0, 0.5, 1.0);
}
```

Listing 2.3: Our first vertex shader

Next, our fragment shader is given in Listing 2.4. Again, this is extremely simple. It too starts with a **#version** 430 core declaration. Next, it declares color as an output variable using the **out** keyword. In fragment shaders, the value of output variables will be sent to the window or screen. In the main function, it assigns a constant to this output. By default, that value goes directly onto the screen and is a vector of four floating-point values, one each for red, green, blue, and alpha, just like in the parameter to **glClearBufferfv()**. In this shader, the value we've used is **vec4(0.0, 0.8, 1.0, 1.0)**, which is a cyan color.

```
#version 430 core

out vec4 color;

void main(void)
{
    color = vec4(0.0, 0.8, 1.0, 1.0);
}
```

Listing 2.4: Our first fragment shader

Now that we have both a vertex and a fragment shader, it's time to compile them and link them together into a program that can be run by OpenGL. This is similar to the way that programs written in C++ or other similar languages are compiled and linked to produce executables. The code to link our shaders together into a program object is shown in Listing 2.5.

```
GLuint compile_shaders(void)
{
    GLuint vertex_shader;
    GLuint fragment_shader;
    GLuint program;

    // Source code for vertex shader
    static const GLchar * vertex_shader_source[] =
    {
        "#version 430 core                                \n"
        "                                                 \n"
        "void main(void)                                  \n"
        "{                                                \n"
        "    gl_Position = vec4(0.0, 0.0, 0.5, 1.0);      \n"
```

```
    "}                                                          \n"
};

// Source code for fragment shader
static const GLchar * fragment_shader_source[] =
{
    "#version 430 core                                          \n"
    "                                                           \n"
    "out vec4 color;                                            \n"
    "                                                           \n"
    "void main(void)                                            \n"
    "{                                                          \n"
    "    color = vec4(0.0, 0.8, 1.0, 1.0);                      \n"
    "}                                                          \n"
};

// Create and compile vertex shader
vertex_shader = glCreateShader(GL_VERTEX_SHADER);
glShaderSource(vertex_shader, 1, vertex_shader_source, NULL);
glCompileShader(vertex_shader);

// Create and compile fragment shader
fragment_shader = glCreateShader(GL_FRAGMENT_SHADER);
glShaderSource(fragment_shader, 1, fragment_shader_source, NULL);
glCompileShader(fragment_shader);

// Create program, attach shaders to it, and link it
program = glCreateProgram();
glAttachShader(program, vertex_shader);
glAttachShader(program, fragment_shader);
glLinkProgram(program);

// Delete the shaders as the program has them now
glDeleteShader(vertex_shader);
glDeleteShader(fragment_shader);

return program;
}
```

Listing 2.5: Compiling a simple shader

In Listing 2.5, we introduce a handful of new functions:

- **glCreateShader()** creates an empty shader object, ready to accept source code and be compiled.

- **glShaderSource()** hands shader source code to the shader object so that it can keep a copy of it.

- **glCompileShader()** compiles whatever source code is contained in the shader object.

- **glCreateProgram()** creates a program object to which you can attach shader objects.

- **glAttachShader()** attaches a shader object to a program object.

- **glLinkProgram()** links all of the shader objects attached to a program object together.

- **glDeleteShader()** deletes a shader object. Once a shader has been linked into a program object, the program contains the binary code and the shader is no longer needed.

The shader source code from Listing 2.3 and Listing 2.4 is included in our program as constant strings that are passed to the **glShaderSource()** function, which copies them into the shader objects that we created with **glCreateShader()**. The shader object stores a copy of our source code, and then when we call **glCompileShader()**, it compiles the GLSL shader source code into an intermediate binary representation, which is also stored in the shader object. The program object represents the linked executable that we will use for rendering. We attach our shaders to the program object using **glAttachShader()** and then call **glLinkProgram()**, which links the objects together into code that can be run on the graphics processor. Attaching a shader object to a program object creates a reference to the shader and so we can delete it, knowing that the program object will hold onto the shader's contents as long as it needs it. The compile_shaders function in Listing 2.5 returns the newly created program object.

When we call this function, we need to keep the returned program object somewhere so that we can use it to draw things. Also, we really don't want to recompile the whole program every time we want to use it. So, we need a function that is called once when the program starts up. The sb6 application framework provides just such a function: application::startup(), which we can override in our sample application and perform any one-time setup work.

One final thing that we need to do before we can draw anything is to create a *vertex array object* (VAO), which is an object that represents the vertex fetch stage of the OpenGL pipeline and is used to supply input to the vertex shader. As our vertex shader doesn't have any inputs right now, we don't need to do much with the VAO. Nevertheless, we still need to create the VAO so that OpenGL will let us draw. To create the VAO, we call the OpenGL function **glGenVertexArrays()**, and to attach it to our context, we call **glBindVertexArray()**. Their prototypes are

```
void glGenVertexArrays(GLsizei n,
                       GLuint * arrays);

void glBindVertexArray(GLuint array);
```

The vertex array object maintains all of the state related to the input to the OpenGL pipeline. We will add calls to **glGenVertexArrays()** and **glBindVertexArray()** to our startup() function.

In Listing 2.6, we have overridden the startup() member function of the sb6::application class and put our own initialization code in it. Again, as with render(), the startup() function is defined as an empty virtual function in sb6::application and is called automatically by the run() function. From startup(), we call compile_shaders and store the resulting program object in the rendering_program member variable in our class. When our application is done running, we should also clean up after ourselves, and so we have also overridden the shutdown() function and in it, we delete the program object that we created at start-up. Just as when we were done with our shader objects, we called **glDeleteShader()**, so when we are done with our program objects, we call **glDeleteProgram()**. In our shutdown() function, we also delete the vertex array object we created in our startup() function.

```
class my_application : public sb6::application
{
public:
    // <snip>

    void startup()
    {
        rendering_program = compile_shaders();
        glGenVertexArrays(1, &vertex_array_object);
        glBindVertexArray(vertex_array_object);
    }

    void shutdown()
    {
        glDeleteVertexArrays(1, &vertex_array_object);
        glDeleteProgram(rendering_program);
        glDeleteVertexArrays(1, &vertex_array_object);
    }

private:
    GLuint  rendering_program;
    GLuint  vertex_array_object;
};
```

Listing 2.6: Creating the program member variable

Now that we have a program, we need to execute the shaders in it and actually get to drawing something on the screen. We modify our render() function to call **glUseProgram()** to tell OpenGL to use our program object for rendering and then call our first drawing command, **glDrawArrays()**. The updated listing is shown in Listing 2.7.

```
// Our rendering function
void render(double currentTime)
{
    const GLfloat color[] = { (float)sin(currentTime) * 0.5f + 0.5f,
                              (float)cos(currentTime) * 0.5f + 0.5f,
                              0.0f, 1.0f };
    glClearBufferfv(GL_COLOR, 0, color);

    // Use the program object we created earlier for rendering
    glUseProgram(rendering_program);

    // Draw one point
    glDrawArrays(GL_POINTS, 0, 1);
}
```

Listing 2.7: Rendering a single point

The **glDrawArrays()** function sends vertices into the OpenGL pipeline. Its prototype is

```
void glDrawArrays(GLenum mode,
                  GLint first,
                  GLsizei count);
```

For each vertex, the vertex shader (the one in Listing 2.3) is executed. The first parameter to **glDrawArrays()** is the mode parameter and tells OpenGL what type of graphics primitive we want to render. In this case, we specified GL_POINTS because we want to draw a single point. The second parameter (first) is not relevant in this example, and so we've set it to zero. Finally, the last parameter is the number of vertices to render. Each point is represented by a single vertex, and so we tell OpenGL to render only one vertex, resulting in just one point being rendered. The result of running this program is shown in Figure 2.2.

As you can see, there is a tiny point in the middle of the window. For your viewing pleasure, we've zoomed in on the point and shown it in the inset at the bottom right of the image. Congratulations! You've made your very first OpenGL rendering. Although it's not terribly impressive yet, it lays the groundwork for more and more interesting drawing and proves that our application framework and our first, extremely simple shaders are working.

In order to make our point a little more visible, we can ask OpenGL to draw it a little larger than a single pixel. To do this, we'll call the **glPointSize()** function, whose prototype is

```
void glPointSize(GLfloat size);
```

This function sets the diameter of the point in pixels to the value you specify in size. The maximum value that you can use for points is

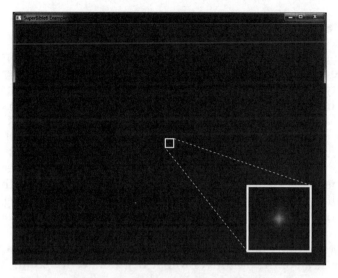

Figure 2.2: Rendering our first point

Figure 2.3: Making our first point bigger

implementation defined, but OpenGL guarantees that it's at least 64 pixels. By adding the following line

```
glPointSize(40.0f);
```

to our rendering function in Listing 2.7, we set the diameter of points to 40 pixels, and are presented with the image in Figure 2.3.

Drawing Our First Triangle

Drawing a single point is not really that impressive (even if it is really big!) — we already mentioned that OpenGL supports many different primitive types, and that the most important are points, lines, and triangles. In our toy example, we draw a single point by passing the token GL_POINTS to the **glDrawArrays()** function. What we really want to do is draw lines or triangles. As you may have guessed, we could also have passed GL_LINES or GL_TRIANGLES to **glDrawArrays()**, but there's one hitch: The vertex shader we showed you in Listing 2.3 places every vertex in the same place, right in the middle of clip space. For points, that's fine as OpenGL assigns area to points for you, but for lines and triangles, having two or more vertices in the exact same place produces a *degenerate primitive*, which is a line with zero length, or a triangle with zero area. If we try to draw anything but points with this shader, we won't get any output at all because all of the primitives will be degenerate. To fix this, we need to modify our vertex shader to assign a different position to each vertex.

Fortunately, GLSL includes a special input to the vertex shader called gl_VertexID, which is the index of the vertex that is being processed at the time. The gl_VertexID input starts counting from the value given by the first parameter of **glDrawArrays()** and counts upwards one vertex at a time for count vertices (the third parameter of **glDrawArrays()**). This input is one of the many *built-in variables* provided by GLSL that represent data that is generated by OpenGL or that you should generate in your shader and give to OpenGL (gl_Position, which we just covered, is another example of a built-in variable). We can use this index to assign a different position to each vertex (see Listing 2.8, which does exactly this).

```
#version 430 core

void main(void)
{
    // Declare a hard-coded array of positions
    const vec4 vertices[3] = vec4[3](vec4( 0.25, -0.25, 0.5, 1.0),
                                     vec4(-0.25, -0.25, 0.5, 1.0),
                                     vec4( 0.25,  0.25, 0.5, 1.0));

    // Index into our array using gl_VertexID
    gl_Position = vertices[gl_VertexID];
}
```

Listing 2.8: Producing multiple vertices in a vertex shader

By using the shader of Listing 2.8, we can assign a different position to each of the vertices based on their value of gl_VertexID. The points in the array `vertices` form a triangle, and if we modify our rendering function to pass GL_TRIANGLES to **glDrawArrays()** instead of GL_POINTS, as shown in Listing 2.9, then we obtain the image shown in Figure 2.4.

```
// Our rendering function
void render(double currentTime)
{
    const GLfloat color[] = { 0.0f, 0.2f, 0.0f, 1.0f };
    glClearBufferfv(GL_COLOR, 0, color);

    // Use the program object we created earlier for rendering
    glUseProgram(rendering_program);

    // Draw one triangle
    glDrawArrays(GL_TRIANGLES, 0, 3);
}
```

Listing 2.9: Rendering a single triangle

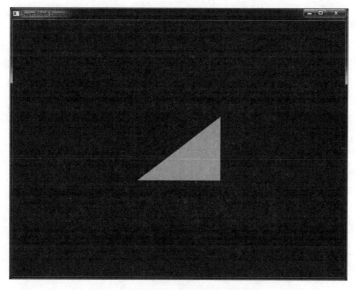

Figure 2.4: Our very first OpenGL triangle

Summary

This concludes the construction of our first OpenGL program. Shortly, we will cover how to get data into your shaders from your application, how to pass your own inputs to the vertex shader, how to pass data from shader stage to shader stage, and more.

In this chapter, you have been briefly introduced to the sb6 application framework, compiled a shader, cleared the window, and drawn points and triangles. You have seen how to change the size of points using the `glPointSize()` function and have seen your first drawing command — `glDrawArrays()`.

Chapter 3

Following the Pipeline

WHAT YOU'LL LEARN IN THIS CHAPTER

- What each of the stages in the OpenGL pipeline does

- How to connect your shaders to the fixed-function pipeline stages

- How to create a program that uses every stage of the graphics pipeline simultaneously

In this chapter, we will walk all the way along the OpenGL pipeline from start to finish, providing insight into each of the stages, which include fixed-function blocks and programmable shader blocks. You have already read a whirlwind introduction to the vertex and fragment shader stages. However, the application that you constructed simply drew a single triangle at a fixed position. If we want to render anything interesting with OpenGL, we're going to have to learn a lot more about the pipeline and all of the things you can do with it. This chapter introduces every part of the pipeline, hooks them up to each other, and provides an example shader for each stage.

Passing Data to the Vertex Shader

The vertex shader is the first *programmable* stage in the OpenGL pipeline and has the distinction of being the only mandatory stage in the pipeline. However, before the vertex shader runs, a fixed-function stage known as *vertex fetching*, or sometimes *vertex pulling*, is run. This automatically provides inputs to the vertex shader.

Vertex Attributes

In GLSL, the mechanism for getting data in and out of shaders is to declare global variables with the `in` and `out` storage qualifiers. You were briefly introduced to the `out` qualifier back in Chapter 2 when Listing 2.4 used it to output a color from the fragment shader. At the start of the OpenGL pipeline, we use the `in` keyword to bring inputs into the vertex shader. Between stages, `in` and `out` can be used to form conduits from shader to shader and pass data between them. We'll get to that shortly. For now, consider the input to the vertex shader and what happens if you declare a variable with an `in` storage qualifier. This marks the variable as an input to the vertex shader, which means that it is automatically filled in by the fixed-function vertex fetch stage. The variable becomes known as a *vertex attribute*.

Vertex attributes are how vertex data is introduced into the OpenGL pipeline. To declare a vertex attribute, declare a variable in the vertex shader using the `in` storage qualifier. An example of this is shown in Listing 3.1, where we declare the variable `offset` as an input attribute.

```
#version 430 core

// "offset" is an input vertex attribute
layout (location = 0) in vec4 offset;

void main(void)
{
    const vec4 vertices[3] = vec4[3](vec4( 0.25, -0.25, 0.5, 1.0),
                                     vec4(-0.25, -0.25, 0.5, 1.0),
                                     vec4( 0.25,  0.25, 0.5, 1.0));

    // Add "offset" to our hard-coded vertex position
    gl_Position = vertices[gl_VertexID] + offset;
}
```

Listing 3.1: Declaration of a vertex attribute

In Listing 3.1, we have added the variable `offset` as an input to the vertex shader. As it is an input to the first shader in the pipeline, it will be filled automatically by the vertex fetch stage. We can tell this stage what to fill the variable with by using one of the many variants of the vertex attribute functions, **glVertexAttrib*()**. The prototype for **glVertexAttrib4fv()**, which we use in this example, is

```
void glVertexAttrib4fv(GLuint index,
                       const GLfloat * v);
```

Here, the parameter index is used to reference the attribute and v is a pointer to the new data to put into the attribute. You may have noticed the layout (location = 0) code in the declaration of the offset attribute. This is a *layout qualifier,* and we have used it to set the *location* of the vertex attribute to zero. This location is the value we'll pass in index to refer to the attribute.

Each time we call **glVertexAttrib*()**, it will update the value of the vertex attribute that is passed to the vertex shader. We can use this to animate our one triangle. Listing 3.2 shows an updated version of our rendering function that updates the value of offset in each frame.

```
// Our rendering function
virtual void render(double currentTime)
{
    const GLfloat color[] = { (float)sin(currentTime) * 0.5f + 0.5f,
                              (float)cos(currentTime) * 0.5f + 0.5f,
                              0.0f, 1.0f };
    glClearBufferfv(GL_COLOR, 0, color);

    // Use the program object we created earlier for rendering
    glUseProgram(rendering_program);

    GLfloat attrib[] = { (float)sin(currentTime) * 0.5f,
                         (float)cos(currentTime) * 0.6f,
                         0.0f, 0.0f };

    // Update the value of input attribute 0
    glVertexAttrib4fv(0, attrib);

    // Draw one triangle
    glDrawArrays(GL_TRIANGLES, 0, 3);
}
```

Listing 3.2: Updating a vertex attribute

When we run the program with the rendering function of Listing 3.2, the triangle will move in a smooth oval shape around the window.

Passing Data from Stage to Stage

So far, you have seen how to pass data into a vertex shader by creating a vertex attribute using the in keyword, how to communicate with fixed-function blocks by reading and writing built-in variables such as gl_VertexID and gl_Position, and how to output data from the fragment shader using the out keyword. However, it's also possible to send your own data from shader stage to shader stage using the same in and out keywords. Just as you used the out keyword in the fragment shader to create the output variable that it writes its color values to, you can create an output variable in the vertex shader by using the out keyword as well. Anything you write to output variables in one shader get sent to similarly named variables declared with the in keyword in the subsequent stage. For example, if your vertex shader declares a variable called vs_color using the out keyword, it would match up with a variable named vs_color declared with the in keyword in the fragment shader stage (assuming no other stages were active in between).

If we modify our simple vertex shader as shown in Listing 3.3 to include vs_color as an output variable, and correspondingly modify our simple fragment shader to include vs_color as an input variable as shown in Listing 3.4, we can pass a value from the vertex shader to the fragment shader. Then, rather than outputting a hard-coded value, the fragment can simply output the color passed to it from the vertex shader.

```
#version 430 core

// "offset" and "color" are input vertex attributes
layout (location = 0) in vec4 offset;
layout (location = 1) in vec4 color;

// "vs_color" is an output that will be sent to the next shader stage
out vec4 vs_color;

void main(void)
{
    const vec4 vertices[3] = vec4[3](vec4( 0.25, -0.25, 0.5, 1.0),
                                     vec4(-0.25, -0.25, 0.5, 1.0),
                                     vec4( 0.25,  0.25, 0.5, 1.0));

    // Add "offset" to our hard-coded vertex position
    gl_Position = vertices[gl_VertexID] + offset;

    // Output a fixed value for vs_color
    vs_color = color;
}
```

Listing 3.3: Vertex shader with an output

As you can see in Listing 3.3, we declare a second input to our vertex shader, color (this time at location 1), and write its value to the vs_output output. This is picked up by the fragment shader of Listing 3.4 and written to the framebuffer. This allows us to pass a color all the way from a vertex attribute that we can set with **glVertexAttrib*()** through the vertex shader, into the fragment shader and out to the framebuffer, meaning that we can draw different colored triangles!

```
#version 430 core

// Input from the vertex shader
in vec4 vs_color;

// Output to the framebuffer
out vec4 color;

void main(void)
{
    // Simply assign the color we were given by the vertex shader
    // to our output
    color = vs_color;
}
```

Listing 3.4: Fragment shader with an input

Interface Blocks

Declaring interface variables one at a time is possibly the simplest way to
communicate data between shader stages. However, in most non-trivial
applications, you may wish to communicate a number of different pieces
of data between stages, and these may include arrays, structures, and other
complex arrangements of variables. To achieve this, we can group together
a number of variables into an *interface block*. The declaration of an
interface block looks a lot like a structure declaration, except that it is
declared using the in or out keyword depending on whether it is an input
to or output from the shader. An example interface block definition is
shown in Listing 3.5.

```
#version 430 core

// "offset" is an input vertex attribute
layout (location = 0) in vec4 offset;
layout (location = 1) in vec4 color;

// Declare VS_OUT as an output interface block
out VS_OUT
{
    vec4 color;     // Send color to the next stage
} vs_out;

void main(void)
{
    const vec4 vertices[3] = vec4[3](vec4( 0.25, -0.25, 0.5, 1.0),
                                     vec4(-0.25, -0.25, 0.5, 1.0),
                                     vec4( 0.25,  0.25, 0.5, 1.0));

    // Add "offset" to our hard-coded vertex position
    gl_Position = vertices[gl_VertexID] + offset;

    // Output a fixed value for vs_color
    vs_out.color = color;
}
```

Listing 3.5: Vertex shader with an output interface block

Note that the interface block in Listing 3.5 has both a block name (VS_OUT, upper case) and an instance name (vs_out, lower case). Interface blocks are matched between stages using the block name (VS_OUT in this case), but are referenced in shaders using the instance name. Thus, modifying our fragment shader to use an interface block gives the code shown in Listing 3.6.

```
#version 430 core

// Declare VS_OUT as an input interface block
in VS_OUT
{
    vec4 color;      // Send color to the next stage
} fs_in;

// Output to the framebuffer
out vec4 color;

void main(void)
{
    // Simply assign the color we were given by the vertex shader
    // to our output
    color = fs_in.color;
}
```

Listing 3.6: Fragment shader with an input interface block

Matching interface blocks by block name but allowing block instances to have different names in each shader stage serves two important purposes: First, it allows the name by which you refer to the block to be different in each stage, avoiding confusing things such as having to use vs_out in a fragment shader, and second, it allows interfaces to go from being single items to arrays when crossing between certain shader stages, such as the vertex and tessellation or geometry shader stages as we will see in a short while. Note that interface blocks are only for moving data from shader stage to shader stage — you can't use them to group together inputs to the vertex shader or outputs from the fragment shader.

Tessellation

Tessellation is the process of breaking a high-order primitive (which is known as a *patch* in OpenGL) into many smaller, simpler primitives such as triangles for rendering. OpenGL includes a fixed-function, configurable tessellation engine that is able to break up quadrilaterals, triangles, and lines into a potentially large number of smaller points, lines, or triangles that can be directly consumed by the normal rasterization hardware further down the pipeline. Logically, the tessellation phase sits directly after the vertex shading stage in the OpenGL pipeline and is made up of three parts: the tessellation control shader, the fixed-function tessellation engine, and the tessellation evaluation shader.

Tessellation Control Shaders

The first of the three tessellation phases is the tessellation control shader (sometimes known as simply the control shader, or abbreviated to TCS). This shader takes its input from the vertex shader and is primarily responsible for two things: the first being the determination of the level of tessellation that will be sent to the tessellation engine, and the second being the generation of data that will be sent to the tessellation evaluation shader that is run after tessellation has occurred.

Tessellation in OpenGL works by breaking down high-order surfaces known as *patches* into points, lines, or triangles. Each patch is formed from a number of *control points*. The number of control points per patch is configurable and set by calling **glPatchParameteri()** with pname set to GL_PATCH_VERTICES and value set to the number of control points that will be used to construct each patch. The prototype of **glPatchParameteri()** is

```
void glPatchParameteri(GLenum pname,
                       GLint value);
```

By default, the number of control points per patch is three, and so if this is what you want (as in our example application), you don't need to call it at all. When tessellation is active, the vertex shader runs once per control point whilst the tessellation control shader runs in batches on groups of control points where the size of each batch is the same as the number of vertices per patch. That is, vertices are used as control points, and the result of the vertex shader is passed in batches to the tessellation control shader as its input. The number of control points per patch can be changed such that the number of control points that is output by the tessellation control shader can be different from the number of control points that it consumes. The number of control points produced by the control shader is set using an output layout qualifier in the control shader's source code. Such a layout qualifier looks like:

```
layout (vertices = N) out;
```

Here, N is the number of control points per patch. The control shader is responsible for calculating the values of the output control points and for setting the tessellation factors for the resulting patch that will be sent to the fixed-function tessellation engine. The output tessellation factors are written to the gl_TessLevelInner and gl_TessLevelOuter built-in output variables, whereas any other data that is passed down the pipeline is written to user-defined output variables (those declared using the **out** keyword, or the special built-in gl_out array) as normal.

Listing 3.7 shows a simple tessellation control shader. It sets the number of output control points to three (the same as the default number of input control points) using the `layout` (vertices = 3) `out`; layout qualifier, copies its input to its output (using the built-in variables gl_in and gl_out), and sets the inner and outer tessellation level to 5. The built-in input variable gl_InvocationID is used to index into the gl_in and gl_out arrays. This variable contains the zero-based index of the control point within the patch being processed by the current invocation of the tessellation control shader.

```
#version 430 core

layout (vertices = 3) out;

void main(void)
{
    if (gl_InvocationID == 0)
    {
        gl_TessLevelInner[0] = 5.0;
        gl_TessLevelOuter[0] = 5.0;
        gl_TessLevelOuter[1] = 5.0;
        gl_TessLevelOuter[2] = 5.0;
    }
    gl_out[gl_InvocationID].gl_Position = gl_in[gl_InvocationID].gl_Position;
}
```

Listing 3.7: Our first tessellation control shader

The Tessellation Engine

The tessellation engine is a fixed-function part of the OpenGL pipeline that takes high-order surfaces represented as patches and breaks them down into simpler primitives such as points, lines, or triangles. Before the tessellation engine receives a patch, the tessellation control shader processes the incoming control points and sets tessellation factors that are used to break down the patch. After the tessellation engine produces the output primitives, the vertices representing them are picked up by the tessellation evaluation shader. The tessellation engine is responsible for producing the parameters that are fed to the invocations of the tessellation evaluation shader, which it then uses to transform the resulting primitives and get them ready for rasterization.

Tessellation Evaluation Shaders

Once the fixed-function tessellation engine has run, it produces a number of output vertices representing the primitives it has generated. These are passed to the tessellation evaluation shader. The tessellation evaluation shader (evaluation shader, or TES for short) runs an invocation for each vertex produced by the tessellator. When the tessellation levels are high, this means that the tessellation evaluation shader could run an extremely large number of times, and so you should be careful with complex evaluation shaders and high tessellation levels.

Listing 3.8 shows a tessellation evaluation shader that accepts input vertices produced by the tessellator as a result of running the control shader shown in Listing 3.7. At the start of the shader is a layout qualifier that sets the tessellation mode. In this case, we selected that the mode should be triangles. Other qualifiers, equal_spacing and cw, select that new vertices should be generated equally spaced along the tessellated polygon edges and that a clockwise vertex winding order should be used for the generated triangles. We will cover the other possible choices in the section "Tessellation" in Chapter 8.

In the remainder of the shader, you will see that it assigns a value to gl_Position just like a vertex shader does. It calculates this using the contents of two more built-in variables. The first is gl_TessCoord, which is the *barycentric coordinate* of the vertex generated by the tessellator. The second is the gl_Position member of the gl_in[] array of structures. This matches the gl_out structure written to in the tessellation control shader earlier in Listing 3.7. This shader essentially implements pass-through tessellation. That is, the tessellated output patch is the exact same shape as the original, incoming triangular patch.

```
#version 430 core

layout (triangles, equal_spacing, cw) in;

void main(void)
{
    gl_Position = (gl_TessCoord.x * gl_in[0].gl_Position +
                   gl_TessCoord.y * gl_in[1].gl_Position +
                   gl_TessCoord.z * gl_in[2].gl_Position);
}
```

Listing 3.8: Our first tessellation evaluation shader

In order to see the results of the tessellator, we need to tell OpenGL to draw only the outlines of the resulting triangles. To do this, we call **glPolygonMode()**, whose prototype is

```
void glPolygonMode(GLenum face,
                   GLenum mode);
```

The face parameter specifies what type of polygons we want to affect and as we want to affect everything, we set it to GL_FRONT_AND_BACK. The other modes will be explained shortly. mode says how we want our polygons to be rendered. As we want to render in wireframe mode (i.e., lines), we set this to GL_LINE. The result of rendering our one triangle example with tessellation enabled and the two shaders of Listing 3.7 and Listing 3.8 is shown in Figure 3.1.

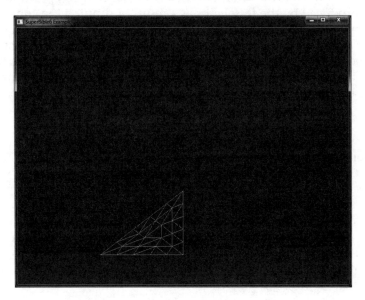

Figure 3.1: Our first tessellated triangle

Geometry Shaders

The geometry shader is logically the last shader stage in the front end, sitting after vertex and tessellation stages and before the rasterizer. The geometry shader runs once per primitive and has access to all of the input vertex data for all of the vertices that make up the primitive being processed. The geometry shader is also unique amongst the shader stages in that it is able to increase or reduce the amount of data flowing in through the pipeline in a programmatic way. Tessellation shaders can also increase or decrease the amount of work in the pipeline, but only implicitly by setting the tessellation level for the patch. Geometry shaders, on the other hand, include two functions — EmitVertex() and EndPrimitive() — that explicitly produce vertices that are sent to primitive assembly and rasterization.

Another unique feature of geometry shaders is that they can change the primitive mode mid-pipeline. For example, they can take triangles as input and produce a bunch of points or lines as output, or even create triangles from independent points. An example geometry shader is shown in Listing 3.9.

```
#version 430 core

layout (triangles) in;
layout (points, max_vertices = 3) out;

void main(void)
{
    int i;

    for (i = 0; i < gl_in.length(); i++)
    {
        gl_Position = gl_in[i].gl_Position;
        EmitVertex();
    }
}
```

Listing 3.9: Our first geometry shader

The shader shown in Listing 3.9 acts as another simple pass-through shader that converts triangles into points so that we can see their vertices. The first layout qualifier indicates that the geometry shader is expecting to see triangles as its input. The second layout qualifier tells OpenGL that the geometry shader will produce points and that the maximum number of points that each shader will produce will be three. In the main function, we have a loop that runs through all of the members of the gl_in array, which is determined by calling its .length() function.

We actually know that the length of the array will be three because we are processing triangles and every triangle has three vertices. The outputs of the geometry shader are again similar to those of a vertex shader. In particular, we write to gl_Position to set the position of the resulting vertex. Next, we call EmitVertex(), which produces a vertex at the output of the geometry shader. Geometry shaders automatically call EndPrimitive() for you at the end of your shader, and so calling it explicitly is not necessary in this example. As a result of running this shader, three vertices will be produced and they will be rendered as points.

By inserting this geometry shader into our simple one tessellated triangle example, we obtain the output shown in Figure 3.2. To create this image, we set the point size to 5.0 by calling **glPointSize()**. This makes the points large and highly visible.

Figure 3.2: Tessellated triangle after adding a geometry shader

Primitive Assembly, Clipping, and Rasterization

After the front end of the pipeline has run (which includes vertex shading, tessellation, and geometry shading) comes a fixed-function part of the pipeline that performs a series of tasks that take the vertex representation of our scene and convert it into a series of pixels that in turn need to be colored and written to the screen. The first step in this process is *primitive assembly*, which is the grouping of vertices into lines and triangles. Primitive assembly still occurs for points, but it is trivial in that case. Once primitives have been constructed from their individual vertices, they are *clipped* against the displayable region, which usually means the window or screen, but can be a smaller area known as the *viewport*. Finally, the parts of the primitive that are determined to be potentially visible are sent to a fixed-function subsystem called the *rasterizer*. This block determines which pixels are covered by the primitive (point, line, or triangle) and sends the list of pixels on to the next stage, which is fragment shading.

Clipping

As vertices exit the vertex shader, their position is said to be in *clip space*. This is one of the many coordinate systems that can be used to represent positions. You may have noticed that the gl_Position variable that we have written to in our vertex, tessellation, and geometry shaders has a **vec4** type and that the positions that we have produced by writing to it are all four-component vectors. This is what is known as a *homogeneous coordinate*. The homogeneous coordinate system is used in projective geometry as much of the math ends up simpler in homogeneous coordinate space than it does in a regular Cartesian space. Homogeneous coordinates have one more component than their equivalent Cartesian coordinate, which is why our three-dimensional position vector is represented as a four-component variable.

Although the output of the front end is a four-component homogeneous coordinate, clipping occurs in Cartesian space, and so to convert from homogeneous coordinates to Cartesian coordinates, OpenGL performs a *perspective division*, which is the process of dividing all four components of the position by the last component, w. This has the effect of projecting the vertex from the homogeneous space to the Cartesian space, leaving w as 1.0. In all of the examples so far, we have set the w component of gl_Position as 1.0, and so this division has no effect. When we explore projective geometry in a short while, we will discuss the effect of setting w to values other than one.

After the projective division, the resulting position is now in *normalized device space*. In OpenGL, the visible region of normalized device space is the volume that extends from −1.0 to 1.0 in the x and y dimensions and from 0.0 to 1.0 in the z dimension. Any geometry that is contained in this region may become visible to the user, and anything outside of it should be discarded. The six sides of this volume are formed by planes in three-dimensional space. As a plane divides a coordinate space in two, the volumes on each side of the plane are called *half-spaces*.

Before passing primitives on to the next stage, OpenGL performs clipping by determining which side of each of these planes the vertices of each primitive lie on. Each plane effectively has an "outside" and an "inside." If a primitive's vertices all lie on the "outside" of any one plane, then the whole thing is thrown away. If all of primitive's vertices are on the "inside" of all the planes (and therefore inside the view volume), then it is passed through unaltered. Primitives that are partially visible (which means that they cross one of the planes) must be handled specially. More details about how this works is given in the section "Clipping" in Chapter 7.

Viewport Transformation

After clipping, all of the vertices of your geometry have coordinates that lie between −1.0 and 1.0 in the x and y dimensions. Along with a z coordinate that lies between 0.0 and 1.0, these are known as *normalized device coordinates.* However, the window that you're drawing to has coordinates that start from $(0, 0)$ at the bottom left and range to $(w - 1, h - 1)$, where w and h are the width and height of the window in pixels, respectively. In order to place your geometry into the window, OpenGL applies the *viewport transform*, which applies a scale and offset to the vertices' normalized device coordinates to move them into *window coordinates*. The scale and bias to apply are determined by the viewport bounds, which you can set by calling `glViewport()` and `glDepthRange()`.

This transform takes the form

$$
\begin{pmatrix} x_w \\ y_w \\ z_w \end{pmatrix} = \begin{pmatrix} \frac{p_x}{2} x_d + o_x \\ \frac{p_y}{2} y_d + o_y \\ \frac{f-n}{2} z_d + \frac{n+f}{2} \end{pmatrix}
$$

Here, x_w, y_w, and z_w are the resulting coordinates of the vertex in window space, and x_d, y_d, and z_d are the incoming coordinates of the vertex in normalized device space. p_x and p_y are the width and height of the viewport, in pixels, and n and f are the near and far plane distances in the z coordinate, respectively. Finally, o_x, o_y, and o_z are the origins of the viewport.

Culling

Before a triangle is processed further, it may be optionally passed through a stage called *culling*, which determines whether the triangle faces towards or away from the viewer and can decide whether to actually go ahead and draw it based on the result of this computation. If the triangle faces towards the viewer, then it is considered to be *front-facing*; otherwise, it is said to be *back-facing*. It is very common to discard triangles that are back-facing because when an object is closed, any back-facing triangle will be hidden by another front-facing triangle.

To determine whether a triangle is front- or back-facing, OpenGL will determine its *signed* area in window space. One way to determine the area of a triangle is to take the cross product of two of its edges. The equation for this is

$$
a = \frac{1}{2} \sum_{i=0}^{n-1} x_w^i y_w^{i \oplus 1} - x_w^{i \oplus 1} y_w^i
$$

Here, x_w^i and y_w^i are the coordinates of the ith vertex of the triangle in window space, and $i \oplus 1$ is $(i + 1)$ mod 3. If the area is positive, then the triangle is considered to be front-facing, and if it is negative, then it is considered to be back-facing. The sense of this computation can be reversed by calling **glFrontFace()** with either dir set to either GL_CW or GL_CCW (where CW and CCW stand for clockwise and counter clockwise, respectively). This is known as the *winding order* of the triangle, and the clockwise or counterclockwise terms refer to the order in which the vertices appear in window space. By default, this state is set to GL_CCW, indicating that triangles whose vertices are in counterclockwise order are considered to be front-facing and those whose vertices are in clockwise order are considered to be back-facing. If the state is GL_CW, then a is simply negated before being used in the culling process. Figure 3.3 shows this pictorially for the purpose of illustration.

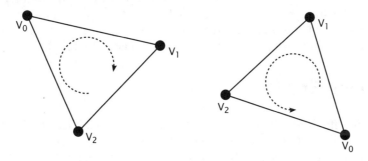

Figure 3.3: Clockwise (left) and counterclockwise (right) winding order

Once the direction that the triangle is facing has been determined, OpenGL is capable of discarding either front-facing, back-facing, or even both types of triangles. By default, OpenGL will render all triangles, regardless of which way they face. To turn on culling, call **glEnable()** with cap set to GL_CULL_FACE. When you enable culling, OpenGL will cull back-facing triangles by default. To change which types of triangles are culled, call **glCullFace()** with face set to GL_FRONT, GL_BACK, or GL_FRONT_AND_BACK.

As points and lines don't have any geometric[1] area, this facing calculation doesn't apply to them and they can't be culled at this stage.

Rasterization

Rasterization is the process of determining which fragments might be covered by a primitive such as a line or a triangle. There are a myriad of algorithms

---

1. Obviously, once they are rendered to the screen, points and lines have area; otherwise, we wouldn't be able to see them. However, this area is artificial and can't be calculated directly from their vertices.

for doing this, but most OpenGL systems will settle on a half-space-based method for triangles as it lends itself well to parallel implementation. Essentially, OpenGL will determine a bounding box for the triangle in window coordinates and test every fragment inside it to determine whether it is inside or outside the triangle. To do this, it treats each of the triangle's three edges as a half-space that divides the window in two.

Fragments that lie on the interior of all three edges are considered to be inside the triangle, and fragments that lie on the exterior of any of the three edges are considered to be outside the triangle. Because the algorithm to determine which side of a line a point lies on is relatively simple and is independent of anything besides the position of the line's endpoints and of the point being tested, many tests can be performed concurrently, providing the opportunity for massive parallelism.

Fragment Shaders

The fragment[2] shader is the last programmable stage in OpenGL's graphics pipeline. This stage is responsible for determining the color of each fragment before it is sent to the framebuffer for possible composition into the window. After the rasterizer processes a primitive, it produces a list of fragments that need to be colored and passes it to the fragment shader. Here, an explosion in the amount of work in the pipeline occurs as each triangle could produce hundreds, thousands, or even millions of fragments.

Listing 2.4 back in Chapter 2 contains the source code of our first fragment shader. It's an extremely simple shader that declares a single output and then assigns a fixed value to it. In a real-world application, the fragment shader would normally be substantially more complex and be responsible for performing calculations related to lighting, applying materials, and even determining the depth of the fragment. Available as input to the fragment shader are several built-in variables such as gl_FragCoord, which contains the position of the fragment within the window. It is possible to use these variables to produce a unique color for each fragment.

Listing 3.10 provides a shader that derives its output color from gl_FragCoord, and Figure 3.4, shows the output of running our original single-triangle program with this shader installed.

---

2. The term *fragment* is used to describe an element that may ultimately contribute to the final color of a pixel. The pixel may not end up being the color produced by any particular invocation of the fragment shader due to a number of other effects such as depth or stencil tests, blending, or multi-sampling, all of which will be covered later in the book.

```
#version 430 core

out vec4 color;

void main(void)
{
    color = vec4(sin(gl_FragCoord.x * 0.25) * 0.5 + 0.5,
                 cos(gl_FragCoord.y * 0.25) * 0.5 + 0.5,
                 sin(gl_FragCoord.x * 0.15) * cos(gl_FragCoord.y * 0.15),
                 1.0);
}
```

Listing 3.10: Deriving a fragment's color from its position

As you can see, the color of each pixel in Figure 3.4 is now a function of its position, and a simple screen-aligned pattern has been produced. It is the shader of Listing 3.10 that created the checkered patterns in the output.

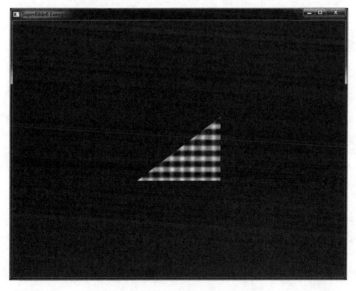

Figure 3.4: Result of Listing 3.10

The gl_FragCoord variable is one of the built-in variables available to the fragment shader. However, just as with other shader stages, we can define our own inputs to the fragment shader, which will be filled in based on the outputs of whichever stage is last before rasterization. For example, if we have a simple program with only a vertex shader and fragment shader in it, we can pass data from the fragment shader to the vertex shader.

The inputs to the fragment shader are somewhat unlike inputs to other shader stages in that OpenGL *interpolates* their values across the primitive that's being rendered. To demonstrate, we take the vertex shader of Listing 3.3 and modify it to assign a different, fixed color for each vertex, as shown in Listing 3.11.

```
#version 430 core

// "vs_color" is an output that will be sent to the next shader stage
out vec4 vs_color;

void main(void)
{
    const vec4 vertices[3] = vec4[3](vec4( 0.25, -0.25, 0.5, 1.0),
                                     vec4(-0.25, -0.25, 0.5, 1.0),
                                     vec4( 0.25,  0.25, 0.5, 1.0));
    const vec4 colors[] = vec4[3](vec4( 1.0, 0.0, 0.0, 1.0),
                                  vec4( 0.0, 1.0, 0.0, 1.0),
                                  vec4( 0.0, 0.0, 1.0, 1.0));

    // Add "offset" to our hard-coded vertex position
    gl_Position = vertices[gl_VertexID] + offset;

    // Output a fixed value for vs_color
    vs_color = color[gl_VertexID];
}
```

Listing 3.11: Vertex shader with an output

As you can see, in Listing 3.11, we added a second constant array that contains colors and index into it using `gl_VertexID`, writing its content to the `vs_color` output. Now, we modify our simple fragment shader to include the corresponding input and write its value to the output, as shown in Listing 3.12.

```
#version 430 core

// "vs_color" is the color produced by the vertex shader
in vec4 vs_color;

out vec4 color;

void main(void)
{
    color = vs_color;
}
```

Listing 3.12: Deriving a fragment's color from its position

The result of using this new pair of shaders is shown in Figure 3.5. As you can see, the color changes smoothly across the triangle.

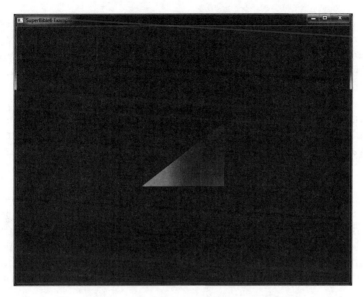

Figure 3.5: Result of Listing 3.12

Framebuffer Operations

The framebuffer represents the last stage of the OpenGL graphics pipeline. It can represent the visible content of the screen and a number of additional regions of memory that are used to store per-pixel values other than color. On most platforms, this means the window you see on your desktop (or possibly the whole screen if your application covers it) and it is owned by the operating system (or windowing system to be more precise). The framebuffer provided by the windowing system is known as the default framebuffer, but it is possible to provide your own if you wish to do things like render into off-screen areas. The state held by the framebuffer includes states such as where the data produced by your fragment shader should be written, what the format of that data should be, and so on. This state is stored in an object, called a *framebuffer object*. Also considered part of the framebuffer, but not stored per framebuffer object, is the pixel operation state.

Pixel Operations

After the fragment shader has produced an output, several things may happen to the fragment before it is written to the window, such as whether it even belongs in the window. Each of these things may be turned on or off by your application. The first thing that could happen is the *scissor test*, which tests your fragment against a rectangle that you can define. If it's inside the rectangle, then it'll get processed further, and if it's outside, it'll get thrown away.

Next comes the *stencil test*. This compares a reference value provided by your application with the contents of the stencil buffer, which stores a single[3] value per-pixel. The content of the stencil buffer has no particular semantic meaning and can be used for any purpose.

After the stencil test has been performed, a second test called the *depth test* is performed. The depth test is an operation that compares the fragment's z coordinate against the contents of the *depth buffer*. The depth buffer is a region of memory that, like the stencil buffer, is another part of the framebuffer with enough space for a single value for each pixel, and it contains the depth (which is related to distance from the viewer) of each pixel.

Normally, the values in the depth buffer range from zero to one, with zero being the closest possible point in the depth buffer and one being the furthest possible point in the depth buffer. To determine whether a fragment is closer than other fragments that have already been rendered in the same place, OpenGL can compare the z component of the fragment's window-space coordinate against the value already in the depth buffer, and if it is less than what's already there, then the fragment is visible. The sense of this test can also be changed. For example, you can ask OpenGL to let fragments through that have a z coordinate that is greater than, equal to, or not equal to the content of the depth buffer. The result of the depth test also affects what OpenGL does to the stencil buffer.

Next, the fragment's color is sent either to the blending or logical operation stage, depending on whether the framebuffer is considered to store floating-point, normalized, or integer values. If the content of the framebuffer is either floating-point or normalized integer values, then blending is applied. Blending is a highly configurable stage in OpenGL and will be covered in detail in its own section. In short, OpenGL is capable of using a wide range of functions that take components of the output of your fragment shader and of the current content of the

---

3. It's actually possible for a framebuffer to store multiple depth, stencil, or color values per-pixel when a technique called *multi-sampling* is employed. We'll dig into this later in the book.

framebuffer and calculate new values that are written back to the framebuffer. If the framebuffer contains unnormalized integer values, then logical operations such as logical AND, OR, and XOR can be applied to the output of your shader and the value currently in the framebuffer to produce a new value that will be written back into the framebuffer.

Compute Shaders

The first sections of this chapter describe the *graphics pipeline* in OpenGL. However, OpenGL also includes the *compute shader* stage, which can almost be thought of as a separate pipeline that runs independently of the other graphics-oriented stages.

Compute shaders are a way of getting at the computational power possessed by the graphics processor in the system. Unlike the graphics-centric vertex, tessellation, geometry, and fragment shaders, compute shaders could be considered as a special, single-stage pipeline all on their own. Each invocation of the compute shader operates on a single unit of work known as a *work item*, several of which are formed together into small groups called *local workgroups*. Collections of these workgroups can be sent into OpenGL's compute pipeline to be processed. The compute shader doesn't have any fixed inputs or outputs besides a handful of built-in variables to tell the shader which item it's working on. All processing performed by a compute shader is explicitly written to memory by the shader itself rather than being consumed by a subsequent pipeline stage. A very basic compute shader is shown in Listing 3.13.

```
#version 430 core

layout (local_size_x = 32, local_size_y = 32) in;

void main(void)
{
    // Do nothing
}
```

Listing 3.13: Simple do-nothing compute shader

Compute shaders are otherwise just like any other shader stage in OpenGL. To compile one, you create a shader object with the type GL_COMPUTE_SHADER, attach your GLSL source code to it with **glShaderSource()**, compile it with **glCompileShader()**, and then link it into a program with **glAttachShader()** and **glLinkProgram()**. The result is a program object with a compiled compute shader in it that can be launched to do work for you.

The shader in Listing 3.13 tells OpenGL that the size of the local workgroup is going to be 32 by 32 work items, but then proceeds to do nothing. In order to make a compute shader that actually does something useful, you're going to need to know a bit more about OpenGL, and so we'll revisit this later in the book.

Summary

In this chapter, you have taken a whirlwind trip down OpenGL's graphics pipeline. You have been (very) briefly introduced to each major stage and have created a program that uses each of them, if only to do nothing impressive. We've glossed over or even neglected to mention several useful features of OpenGL with the intention of getting you from zero to rendering in as few pages as possible. Over the next few chapters, you'll learn more fundamentals of computer graphics and of OpenGL, and then we'll take a second trip down the pipeline, dig deeper into the topics from this chapter, and get into some of the things we skipped in this preview of what OpenGL can do.

Chapter 4

Math for 3D Graphics

WHAT YOU'LL LEARN IN THIS CHAPTER

- What a vector is, and why you should care

- What a matrix is, and why you should care more

- How we use matrices and vectors to move geometry around

- The OpenGL conventions and coordinate spaces

So far, you have learned to draw points, lines, and triangles and have written simple shaders that pass your hard-coded vertex data through unmodified. We haven't really been rendering in 3D—which is odd for a book on 3D graphics! Well, to turn a collection of shapes into a coherent scene, you must arrange them in relation to one another and to the viewer. In this chapter, you start moving shapes and objects around in your coordinate system. The ability to place and orient your objects in a scene is a crucial tool for any 3D graphics programmer. As you will see, it is actually convenient to describe your objects' dimensions around the origin and then transform the objects into the desired positions.

Is This the Dreaded Math Chapter?

In most books on 3D graphics programming, yes, this would be the dreaded math chapter. However, you can relax; we take a more moderate approach to these principles than some texts.

One of the fundamental mathematical operations that will be performed by your shaders is the coordinate transform, which boils down to multiplying matrices with vectors and with each other. The keys to object and coordinate transformations are two matrix conventions used by OpenGL programmers. To familiarize you with these matrices, this chapter strikes a compromise between two extremes in computer graphics philosophy. On the one hand, we could warn you, "Please review a textbook on linear algebra before reading this chapter." On the other hand, we could perpetuate the deceptive reassurance that you can "learn to do 3D graphics without all those complex mathematical formulas." But we don't agree with either camp.

In reality, you can get along just fine without understanding the finer mathematics of 3D graphics, just as you can drive your car every day without having to know anything at all about automotive mechanics and the internal combustion engine. But you had better know enough about your car to realize that you need an oil change every so often, that you have to fill the tank with gas regularly, and that you must change the tires when they get bald. This knowledge makes you a responsible (and safe!) automobile owner. If you want to be a responsible and capable OpenGL programmer, the same standards apply. You need to understand at least the basics so you know what can be done and what tools best suit the job. If you are a beginner, you will find that, with some practice, matrix math and vectors will gradually make more and more sense, and you will develop a more intuitive (and powerful) ability to make full use of the concepts we introduce in this chapter.

So even if you don't already have the ability to multiply two matrices in your head, you need to know what matrices are and that they are the means to OpenGL's 3D magic. But before you go dusting off that old linear algebra textbook (doesn't everyone have one?), have no fear: The sb6 library has a component called vmath that contains a number of useful classes and functions that can be used to represent and manipulate vectors and matrices. They can be used directly with OpenGL and are very similar in syntax and appearance to GLSL — the language you'll be writing your shaders in. So, although you don't have to do all your matrix and vector manipulation yourself, it's still a good idea to know what they are and how to apply them. See — you can eat your cake and have it too!

A Crash Course in 3D Graphics Math

There are a good many books on the math behind 3D graphics, and a few of the better ones that we have found are listed in Appendix A, "Further Reading." We do not pretend here that we are going to cover everything that is important for you to know. We are not even going to try and cover everything you should know. In this chapter, we are just going to cover what you really need to know. If you're already a math whiz, you should skip immediately to the section ahead on the standard 3D transformations. Not only do you already know what we are about to cover, but most math fans will be somewhat offended that we did not give sufficient space to their favorite feature of homogeneous coordinate spaces. Imagine one of those reality TV shows where you must escape a virtual swamp filled with crocodiles. How much 3D math do you really need to know to survive? That's what the next two sections are going to be about, 3D math survival skills. The crocodiles do not care if you really know what a homogeneous coordinate space is or not.

Vectors, or Which Way Is Which?

The main input to OpenGL is the vertex, which has a number of attributes that normally include a position. Basically, this is a position in xyz coordinate space, and a given position in space is defined by exactly one and only one unique xyz triplet. An xyz triplet, however, can be represented as a vector (in fact, for the mathematically pure in heart, a position is actually a vector too... there, we threw you a bone). A vector is perhaps the single most important foundational concept to understand when it comes to manipulating 3D geometry. Those three values (x, y, and z) combined represent two important values: a direction and a magnitude.

Figure 4.1 shows a point in space (picked arbitrarily) and an arrow drawn from the origin of the coordinate system to that point in space. The point can be thought of as a vertex when you are stitching together triangles, but the arrow can be thought of as a vector. A vector is first, simply a direction from the origin toward the point in space. We use vectors all the time in OpenGL to represent directional quantities. For example, the x axis is the vector (1, 0, 0). This says to go positive one unit in the x direction, and zero in the y and z directions. A vector is also how we point where we are going, for example, which way is the camera pointing, or in which direction do we want to move to get away from that crocodile! The vector is so fundamental to the operation of OpenGL that vectors of various sizes are first-class types in GLSL and are given names such as `vec3` and `vec4` (representing 3- and 4-element vectors, respectively).

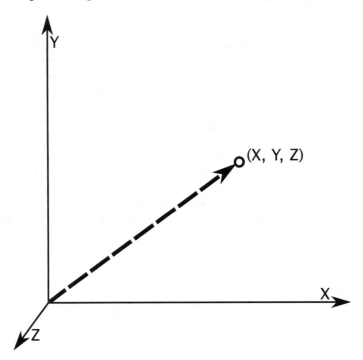

Figure 4.1: A point in space is both a vertex and a vector.

The second quantity a vector can represent is the magnitude. The magnitude of a vector is the length of the vector. For our x axis vector (1, 0, 0), the length of the vector is one. A vector with a length of one we call a *unit vector*. If a vector is not a unit vector and we want to scale it to make it one, we call that *normalization*. Normalizing a vector scales it such that its length becomes one and the vector is then said to be *normalized*. Unit vectors are important when we only want to represent a direction and not a magnitude. Also, if vector lengths appear in the equations we'll be using, they get a whole lot simpler when those lengths are 1! A magnitude can be important as well; for example, it can tell us how far we need to move in a given direction — how far away I need to get from that crocodile.

Vectors (and matrices) are such important concepts in 3D graphics that they are first class citizens in GLSL — the language in which you write your shaders. However, this is not so in languages like C++. To allow you to use them in your C++ programs, the vmath library that is provided with this book's source code contains classes that can represent vectors and matrices that are named similarly to their GLSL counterparts: For instance, vmath::vec3 can represent a three-component floating-point vector (x, y, z), and vmath::vec4 can represent a four-component floating-point vector (x, y, z, w) and so on. The w coordinate is added to make the vector *homogeneous* but is typically set to 1.0. The x, y, and z values might later be divided by w, which when it is 1.0, essentially leaves the xyz values alone. The classes in vmath are actually templated classes with type definitions to represent common types such as single- and double-precision floating-point values, and signed- and unsigned-integer variables. vmath::vec3 and vmath::vec4 are defined simply as follows:

```
typedef Tvec3<float> vec3;
typedef Tvec4<float> vec4;
```

Declaring a three-component vector is as simple as

```
sb6::vmath::vec3 vVector;
```

If you include "`using namespace vmath`" in your source code, you can even write

```
vec3 vVector;
```

However, in these examples, we'll always qualify our use of the vmath library by explicitly using the vmath:: namespace. All of the vmath classes define a number of constructors and copy operators, which means you can declare and initialize a vectors as follows:

```
vec3 vVertex1(0.0f, 0.0f, 1.0f);
vec4 vVertex2 = vec4(1.0f, 0.0f, 1.0f, 1.0f);
vec4 vVertex3(vVertex1, 1.0f);
```

Now, an array of three-component vertices, such as for a triangle can be declared as

```
vec3 vVerts[] = { vec3(-0.5f, 0.0f, 0.0f),
                  vec3( 0.5f, 0.0f, 0.0f),
                  vec3( 0.0f, 0.5f, 0.0f) } ;
```

This should look similar to the code that we introduced you to in the section "Drawing Our First Triangle" back in Chapter 2. The vmath library also includes lots and lots of math-related functions and overrides most operators on its class to allow vectors and matrices to be added, subtracted, multiplied, transposed, and so on.

We need to be careful here not to gloss over that fourth W component too much. Most of the time when you specify geometry with vertex positions, a three-component vertex is all you want to store and send to OpenGL. For many directional vectors, such as a surface normal (a vector pointing perpendicular to a surface that is used for lighting calculations), again, a three-component vector suffices. However, we soon delve into the world of matrices, and to transform a 3D vertex, you must multiply it by a 4×4 transformation matrix. The rules are you must multiply a four-component vector by a 4×4 matrix; if you try and use a three-component vector with a 4×4 matrix... the crocodiles will eat you! More on what all this means soon. Essentially, if you are going to do your own matrix operations on vectors, then you will probably want four-component vectors in many cases.

Common Vector Operators

Vectors behave as you would expect for operations such as addition, subtraction, unary negation, and so on. These operators perform a per-component calculation and result in a vector of the same size as their inputs. The vmath vector classes override the addition, subtraction, and unary negation operators, along with several others, to provide such functionality. This allows you to use code such as

```
vmath::vec3 a(1.0f, 2.0f, 3.0f);
vmath::vec3 b(4.0f, 5.0f, 6.0f);
vmath::vec3 c;

c = a + b;
c = a - b;
c += b;
c = -c;
```

However, there are many more operations on vectors that are explained from a mathematical perspective in the following subsections. They also have implementations in the vmath library, which will be outlined here.

Dot Product

Vectors can be added, subtracted, and scaled by simply adding, subtracting, or scaling their individual XYZ components. An interesting and useful operation, however, that can be applied only to two vectors is called the *dot product*, which is also sometimes known as the *inner product*. The dot product between two (three-component) vectors returns a scalar (just one value) that is the cosine of the angle between the two vectors scaled by the product of their lengths. If the two vectors are of unit length, the value returned falls between −1.0 and 1.0 and is equal to the cosine of the angle between them. Of course, to get the actual angle between the vectors, you'd need to take the inverse cosine (or arc-cosine) of this value. The dot product is used extensively during lighting calculations and is taken between a surface normal vector and a vector pointing toward a light source in diffuse lighting calculations. We will delve deeper into this type of shader code in the section "Lighting Models" in Chapter 12. Figure 4.2 shows two vectors, $v1$ and $v2$, and how the angle between them is represented by θ

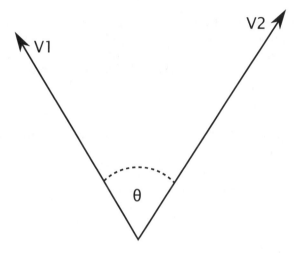

Figure 4.2: The dot product — cosine of the angle between two vectors

Mathematically, the dot product of two vectors $v1$ and $v2$ is calculated as

$$v1 \times v2 = v1.x \times v2.x + v1.y \times v2.y + v1.z \times v2.z$$

The vmath library has some useful functions that use the dot product operation. For starters, you can actually get the dot product itself between two vectors with the function vmath::dot, or with the dot member function of the vector classes.

```
vmath::vec3 a(...);
vmath::vec3 b(...);

float c = a.dot(b);
float d = dot(a, b);
```

As we mentioned, the dot product between a pair of unit vectors is a value between −1.0 and +1.0) that represents the cosine of the angle between them. A slightly higher level function, vmath::angle, actually returns this angle in radians.

```
float angle(const vmath::vec3& u, const vmath::vec3& v);
```

Cross Product

Another useful mathematical operation between two vectors is the *cross product*, which is also sometimes known as the *vector product*. The cross product between two vectors is a third vector that is perpendicular to the plane in which the first two vectors lie. The cross product of two vectors $v1$ and $v2$ is defined as

$$v1 \times v2 = \|v1\| \, \|v2\| \, sin(\theta)\vec{n}$$

where $\vec{n}$ is the unit vector that is perpendicular to both $v1$ and $v2$. This means that if you normalize the result of a cross product, you get the normal to the plane. If $v1$ and $v2$ are both unit length, and are known to be perpendicular to one another, then you don't even need to normalize the result as it will also be unit length. Figure 4.3 shows two vectors, $v1$ and $v2$, and their cross product $v3$.

The cross product of two three-dimensional vectors $v1$ and $v2$ can be calculated as

$$\begin{bmatrix} v3.x \\ v3.y \\ v3.z \end{bmatrix} = \begin{bmatrix} v1.y \cdot v2.z - v1.z \cdot v2.y \\ v1.z \cdot v2.x - v1.x \cdot v2.z \\ v1.x \cdot v2.y - v1.y \cdot v2.x \end{bmatrix}$$

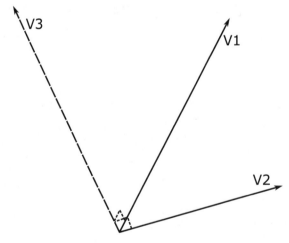

Figure 4.3: A cross product returns a vector perpendicular to its parameters

Again, the vmath library has functions that take the cross product of two vectors and return the resulting vector: one member function of the three-component vector classes and one global function.

```
vec3 a(...);
vec3 b(...);

vec3 c = a.cross(b);
vec3 d = cross(a, b);
```

Unlike the dot product, the order of the vectors is important. In
Figure 4.3, $v3$ is the result of $v2$ cross $v1$. If you were to reverse the order of
$v1$ and $v2$, the resulting vector $v3$ would point in the opposite direction.
Applications of the cross product are numerous, from finding surface
normals of triangles to constructing transformation matrices.

Length of a Vector

As we have already discussed, vectors have a direction and a magnitude.
The magnitude of a vector is also known as its length. The magnitude of a
three-dimensional vector can be found by using the following equation:

$$length(v) = \sqrt{v.x^2 + v.y^2 + v.z^2}$$

This can be generalized as the square root of the sum of the squares of the
components of the vector.[1] In only two dimensions, this is simply
Pythagoras's theorem — the square of the hypotenuse is equal to the sum
of the squares of the other two sides. This extends to any number of
dimensions, and the vmath library includes functions to calculate this for
you.

```
template <typename T, int len>
static inline T length(const vecN<T,len>& v) { ... }
```

Reflection and Refraction

Common operations in computer graphics are calculating reflection and
refraction vectors. Given an incoming vector R_{in} and a normal to a
surface N, we wish to know the direction in which R_{in} will be reflected
($R_{reflect}$), and given a particular index of refraction η, what direction R_{in}
will be refracted. We show this in Figure 4.4, with the refracted vectors for
various values of η shown as $R_{refract,\eta1}$ through $R_{refract,\eta4}$.

---

1. The sum of the squares of the components of a vector is also the dot product of a vector
with itself.

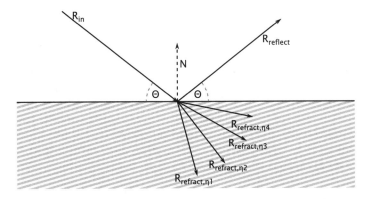

Figure 4.4: Reflection and refraction

Although Figure 4.4 shows the system in only two dimensions, we are interested in computing this in three dimensions (this is a 3D graphics book, after all). The math for calculating $R_{reflect}$ is

$$R_{reflect} = R_{in} - (2N \cdot R_{in})N$$

and the math for calculating $R_{refract}$ for a given value of η is

$$k = 1 - \eta^2(1 - (N \cdot R)^2)$$

$$R_{refract} = \begin{cases} 0.0 & \text{if } k < 0.0 \\ \eta R - (\eta(N \cdot R) + \sqrt{k})N & \text{if } k \geq 0.0 \end{cases}$$

To get the desired result, both R and N must be unit-length vectors (i.e., they should be normalized before use). The two vmath functions, reflect() and refract(), implement these equations.

Matrices

The matrix is not just a Hollywood movie trilogy, but an exceptionally powerful mathematical tool that greatly simplifies the process of solving one or more equations with variables that have complex relationships to each other. One common example of this, near and dear to the hearts of graphics programmers, is coordinate transformations. For example, if you have a point in space represented by x, y, and z coordinates, and you need to know where that point is if you rotate it some number of degrees around some arbitrary point and orientation, you would use a matrix. Why? Because the new x coordinate depends not only on the old x coordinate and the other rotation parameters, but also on what the y and *z* coordinates were as well. This kind of dependency between the variables and solution is just the sort of problem that matrices excel at. For fans of *Matrix* movies who have a mathematical inclination, the term matrix is indeed an appropriate title.

Mathematically, a matrix is nothing more than a set of numbers arranged in uniform rows and columns — in programming terms, a two-dimensional array. A matrix doesn't have to be square, but all of the rows must have the same number of elements and all of the columns must have the same number of elements. The following are a selection of matrices. They don't represent anything in particular but serve only to demonstrate matrix structure. Note that it is also valid for a matrix to have a single column or row. A single row or column of numbers would more simply be called a vector, as discussed previously. In fact, as you will soon see, we can think of some matrices as a table of column vectors.

$$\begin{bmatrix} 1 & 4 & 7 \\ 2 & 5 & 8 \\ 3 & 6 & 9 \end{bmatrix} \begin{bmatrix} 0 & 42 \\ 1.5 & 0.877 \\ 2 & 14 \end{bmatrix} \begin{bmatrix} 1 \\ 2 \\ 3 \\ 4 \end{bmatrix}$$

Matrix and vector are two important terms that you see often in 3D graphics programming literature. When dealing with these quantities, you also see the term scalar. A *scalar* is just an ordinary single number used to represent magnitude or a specific quantity (you know — a regular old, plain, simple number... like before you cared or had all this jargon added to your vocabulary). Matrices can be multiplied and added together, but they can also be multiplied by vectors and scalar values. Multiplying a point (represented by a vector) by a matrix (representing a transformation) yields a new transformed point (another vector). Matrix transformations are actually not too difficult to understand but can be intimidating at first. Because an understanding of matrix transformations is fundamental to many 3D tasks, you should still make an attempt to become familiar with them. Fortunately, only a little understanding is enough to get you going and doing some pretty incredible things with OpenGL. Over time, and with a little more practice and study, you will master this mathematical tool yourself.

In the meantime, as previously for vectors, you will find a number of useful matrix functions and features available in the vmath library. The source code to this library is also available in the file vmath.h in the book's source code folder. This 3D math library greatly simplifies many tasks in this chapter and the ones to come. One *useful* feature of this library is that it lacks incredibly clever and highly optimized code! This makes the library highly portable and easy to understand. You'll also find it has a very GLSL-like syntax.

In your 3D programming tasks with OpenGL, you will use three sizes of matrix extensively; 2×2, 3×3, and 4×4. The vmath library has matrix data types that match those defined by GLSL, such as

```
vmath::mat2 m1;
vmath::mat3 m2;
vmath::mat4 m3;
```

As in GLSL, the matrix classes in vmath define common operators such as addition, subtraction, unary negation, multiplication, and division, along with constructors and relational operators. Again, the matrix classes in vmath are built using templates and include type definitions for single- and double-precision floating-point and signed and unsigned integer matrix types.

Matrix Construction and Operators

OpenGL represents a 4×4 matrix not as a two-dimensional array of floating values but as a single array of 16 floating-point values. By default, OpenGL uses a *column major* or *column primary* layout for matrices. That means that, for a 4×4 matrix, the first four elements represent the first column of the matrix, the next four elements represent the second column, and so on. This approach is different from many math libraries, which do take the two-dimensional array approach. For example, OpenGL prefers the first of these two examples:

```
GLfloat matrix[16];    // Nice OpenGL-friendly matrix
```

```
GLfloat matrix[4][4]; // Not as convenient for OpenGL programmers
```

OpenGL can use the second variation, but the first is a more efficient representation. The reason for this becomes clear in a moment. These 16 elements represent the 4×4 matrix, as shown below. When the array elements traverse down the matrix columns one by one, we call this column-major matrix ordering. In memory, the 4×4 approach of the two-dimensional array (the second option in the preceding code) is laid out in a row-major order. In math terms, the two orientations are the transpose of one another.

$$\begin{bmatrix} A_{00} & A_{10} & A_{20} & A_{30} \\ A_{01} & A_{11} & A_{21} & A_{31} \\ A_{02} & A_{12} & A_{22} & A_{32} \\ A_{03} & A_{13} & A_{23} & A_{33} \end{bmatrix}$$

Representing the above matrix in column-major order in memory produces an array as follows:

```
static const float A[] =
{
    A00, A01, A02, A03, A10, A11, A12, A13,
    A20, A21, A22, A23, A30, A31, A32, A33
};
```

Whereas representing it in row-major order would require a layout such as

```
static const float A[] =
{
    A00, A10, A20, A30, A01, A11, A21, A31,
    A20, A21, A22, A23, A30, A31, A32, A33,
};
```

The real magic lies in the fact that these 16 values can represent a particular position in space and an orientation of the three axes with respect to the viewer. Interpreting these numbers is not hard at all. The four columns each represent a four-element vector.[2] To keep things simple for this book, we focus our attention on just the first three elements of the vectors in the first three columns. The fourth column vector contains the x, y, and z values of the transformed coordinate system's origin.

The first three elements of the first three columns are just directional vectors that represent the orientation (vectors here are used to represent a direction) of the x, y, and z axes in space. For most purposes, these three vectors are always at 90° angles from each other and are usually each of unit length (unless you are also applying a scale or shear). The mathematical term for this (in case you want to impress your friends) is orthonormal when the vectors are unit length, and orthogonal when they are not. Figure 4.5 shows the 4×4 transformation matrix with its components highlighted. Notice that the last row of the matrix is all 0s with the exception of the very last element, which is 1.

The upper left 3×3 submatrix of the matrix shown in Figure 4.5 represents a rotation or orientation. The last column of the matrix represents a translation or position.

The most amazing thing is that if you have a 4×4 matrix that contains the position and orientation of a coordinate system, and you multiply a vertex expressed in the identity coordinate system (written as a column matrix or vector) by this matrix, the result is a new vertex that has been

---

2. In fact, the vmath library internally represents matrices as arrays of its own vector classes, with each vector holding a column of the matrix.

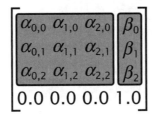

$$\begin{bmatrix} \alpha_{0,0} & \alpha_{1,0} & \alpha_{2,0} & \beta_0 \\ \alpha_{0,1} & \alpha_{1,1} & \alpha_{2,1} & \beta_1 \\ \alpha_{0,2} & \alpha_{1,2} & \alpha_{2,2} & \beta_2 \\ 0.0 & 0.0 & 0.0 & 1.0 \end{bmatrix}$$

Figure 4.5: A 4 × 4 matrix representing rotation and translation

transformed to the new coordinate system. This means that any position in space and any desired orientation can be uniquely defined by a 4 × 4 matrix, and if you multiply all of an object's vertices by this matrix, you transform the entire object to the given location and orientation in space!

Not only this, but if you transform an object's vertices from one space to another using one matrix, you can then transform *those* vertices by yet another matrix, transforming them again into another coordinate space. Given matrices A and B and vector v, we know that

$$A \cdot (B \cdot v)$$

is equivalent to

$$(A \cdot B) \cdot v$$

This is because matrix multiplication is *associative*. Herein lies the magic — it is possible to stack a whole bunch of transforms together by multiplying the matrices that represent those transforms and using the resulting matrix as a single term in the final product.

The final appearance of your scene or object can depend greatly on the order in which the modeling transformations are applied. This is particularly true of translation and rotation. We can see this as a consequence of the associativity and commutativity rules for matrix multiplication — we can group together sequences of transformations in any way we like as matrix multiplication is associative, but the order that the matrices appear in the multiplication matters because matrix multiplication is *not* commutative.

Figure 4.6 illustrates a progression of a square rotated first about the z axis and then translated down the newly transformed x axis on the top, and first translating the same square along the x axis and then rotating it around the z axis on the bottom. The difference in the final dispositions of the square occurs because each transformation is performed with respect to the last transformation performed. On the top of Figure 4.6, the square is rotated with respect to the origin first. On the bottom of Figure 4.6, after the square is translated, the rotation is performed around the newly translated origin.

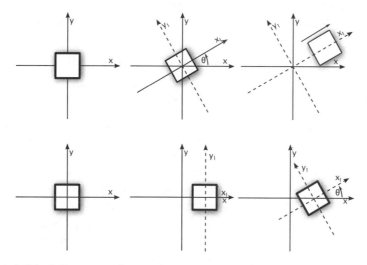

Figure 4.6: Modeling transformations: rotation then translation, and translation then rotation

Understanding Transformations

If you think about it, most 3D graphics aren't really 3D. We use 3D concepts and terminology to describe what something looks like; then this 3D data is "squished" onto a 2D computer screen. We call the process of squishing 3D data down into 2D data *projection*. We refer to the projection whenever we want to describe the type of transformation (orthographic or perspective) that occurs during vertex processing, but projection is only one of the types of transformations that occur in OpenGL. Transformations also allow you to rotate objects around; move them about; and even stretch, shrink, and warp them.

Coordinate Spaces in OpenGL

A series of one or more transforms can be represented as a matrix, and multiplication by that matrix effectively moves a vector from one coordinate space to another. There are several coordinate spaces that are commonly used in OpenGL programming. Any number of geometric transformations can occur between the time you specify your vertices and the time they appear on the screen, but the most common are modeling, viewing, and projection. In this section, we examine each of the coordinate spaces commonly used in 3D computer graphics (and summarized in Table 4.1) and the transforms used to move vectors between them.

Table 4.1: Common Coordinate Spaces Used in 3D Graphics

Coordinate Space	What It Represents
Model Space	Positions relative to a local origin. This is also sometimes known as *object space*.
World Space	Positions relative to a global origin (i.e., their location within the world).
View Space	Positions relative to the viewer. This is also sometimes called *camera* or *eye space*.
Clip Space	Positions of vertices after projection into a non-linear homogeneous coordinate.
Normalized Device Coordinate (NDC) Space	Vertex coordinates are said to be in NDC after their clip-space coordinates have been divided by their own w component.
Window Space	Positions of vertices in pixels, relative to the origin of the window.

A matrix that moves coordinates from one space to another is normally named for those spaces. For example, a matrix that transforms an object's vertices from model space into view space is commonly referred to as a model-view matrix.

Object Coordinates

Most of your vertex data will typically begin life in *object space*, which is also commonly known as *model space*. In object space, positions of vertices are interpreted as relative to a local origin. Consider a spaceship model. The origin of the model is probably going to be somewhere logical such as the tip of the craft's nose, at its center of gravity, or where the pilot might sit. In a 3D modeling program, returning to the origin and zooming out sufficiently should show you the whole spaceship. The origin of a model is often the point about which you might rotate it to place it into a new orientation. It wouldn't make sense to place the origin far outside the model as rotating the object about that point would apply significant translation as well as rotation.

World Coordinates

The next common coordinate space is *world space*. This is where coordinates are stored relative to a fixed, global origin. To continue the spaceship analogy, this could be the center of a play-field or other fixed body such as a nearby planet. Once in world space, all objects exist in a common frame. Often, this is the space in which lighting and physics calculations are performed.

View Coordinates

An important concept throughout this chapter is that of view coordinates. These are often referred to as *camera* or *eye* coordinates. View coordinates are relative to the position of the observer (hence the terms camera and eye), regardless of any transformations that may occur; you can think of them as "absolute" coordinates. Thus, eye coordinates represent a virtual fixed coordinate system that is used as a common frame of reference.

Figure 4.7 shows the view coordinate system from two viewpoints. On the left, the view coordinates are represented as seen by the observer of the scene (that is, perpendicular to the monitor). On the right, the view coordinate system is translated slightly so you can better see the relation of the z axis. Positive x and y are pointed right and up, respectively, from the viewer's perspective. Positive z travels away from the origin toward the user, and negative z values travel farther away from the viewpoint into the screen. The screen lies at the z coordinate 0.

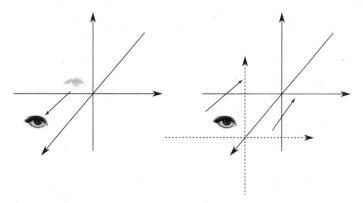

Figure 4.7: Two perspectives of view coordinates

When you draw in 3D with OpenGL, you use the Cartesian coordinate system. In the absence of any transformations, the system in use is identical to the eye coordinate system just described.

Clip and Normalized Device Space

Clip space is the coordinate space in which OpenGL performs clipping. When your vertex shader writes to gl_Position, this coordinate is considered to be in clip space. This is always a four-dimensional homogenous coordinate. Upon exiting clip space, all four of the vertex's components are divided through by its w component. Obviously, after this, w becomes equal to 1.0. If w is not 1.0 before this division, the x, y, and z components are effectively scaled by the inverse of w. This allows for effects such as perspective foreshortening and projection. The result of the division is considered to be in *normalized device coordinate space* (NDC space). Clearly, if the resulting w component of a clip-space coordinate is 1.0, then clip space and NDC space become identical.

Coordinate Transformations

As noted, coordinates may be moved from space to space by multiplying their vector representations by *transformation matrices*. Transformations are used to manipulate your model and the particular objects within it. These transformations move objects into place, rotate them, and scale them. Figure 4.8 illustrates three of the most common modeling transformations that you will apply to your objects. Figure 4.8 (a) shows translation, in which an object is moved along a given axis. Figure 4.8 (b) shows a rotation, in which an object is rotated about one of the axes. Finally, Figure 4.8 (c) shows the effects of scaling, where the dimensions of the object are increased or decreased by a specified amount. Scaling can occur non-uniformly (the various dimensions can be scaled by different amounts), so you can use scaling to stretch and shrink objects.

Each of these standard transforms can be represented as a matrix by which you can multiply your vertex coordinates to calculate their position after the transformation. The following subsections discuss the construction of those matrices, both mathematically and using the functions provided in the vmath library.

The Identity Matrix

There are a number of important types of transformation matrices you need to be familiar with before we start trying to use them. The first is the

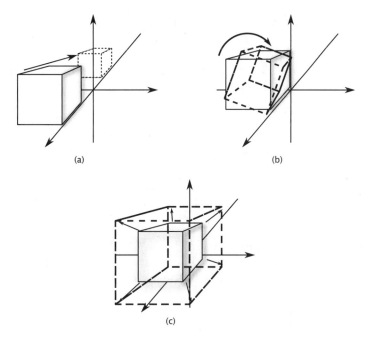

(a)

(b)

(c)

Figure 4.8: The modeling transformations

identity matrix. As shown below, the identity matrix contains all zeros except a series of ones that traverse the matrix diagonally. The 4×4 identity matrix looks like this:

$$\begin{bmatrix} 1.0 & 0.0 & 0.0 & 0.0 \\ 0.0 & 1.0 & 0.0 & 0.0 \\ 0.0 & 0.0 & 1.0 & 0.0 \\ 0.0 & 0.0 & 0.0 & 1.0 \end{bmatrix}$$

Multiplying a vertex by the identity matrix is equivalent to multiplying it by one; it does nothing to it.

$$\begin{bmatrix} 1.0 & 0.0 & 0.0 & 0.0 \\ 0.0 & 1.0 & 0.0 & 0.0 \\ 0.0 & 0.0 & 1.0 & 0.0 \\ 0.0 & 0.0 & 0.0 & 1.0 \end{bmatrix} \begin{bmatrix} v.x \\ v.y \\ v.z \\ v.w \end{bmatrix} = \begin{bmatrix} 1 \cdot v.x + 0 \cdot v.y + 0 \cdot v.z + 0 \cdot v.w \\ 0 \cdot v.x + 1 \cdot v.y + 0 \cdot v.z + 0 \cdot v.w \\ 0 \cdot v.x + 0 \cdot v.y + 1 \cdot v.z + 0 \cdot v.w \\ 0 \cdot v.x + 0 \cdot v.y + 0 \cdot v.z + 1 \cdot v.w \end{bmatrix} = \begin{bmatrix} v.x \\ v.y \\ v.z \\ v.w \end{bmatrix}$$

Objects drawn using the identity matrix are untransformed; they are at the origin (last column), and the x, y, and z axes are defined to be the same as those in eye coordinates.

Obviously, identity matrices for 2×2 matrices, 3×3 matrices, and matrices of other dimensions exist and simply have ones in their diagonal as you can see above. All identity matrices are square. There are no non-square identity matrices. Any identity matrix is its own transpose. You can make an identity matrix for OpenGL in C++ code like this:

```
// Using a raw array:
GLfloat m1[] = { 1.0f, 0.0f, 0.0f, 0.0f,    // X Column
                 0.0f, 1.0f, 0.0f, 0.0f,    // Y Column
                 0.0f, 0.0f, 1.0f, 0.0f,    // Z Column
                 0.0f, 0.0f, 0.0f, 1.0f };  // W Column

// Or using the vmath::mat4 constructor:
vmath::mat4 m2( vmath::vec4(1.0f, 0.0f, 0.0f, 0.0f),    // X Column
                vmath::vec4(0.0f, 1.0f, 0.0f, 0.0f),    // Y Column
                vmath::vec4(0.0f, 0.0f, 1.0f, 0.0f),    // Z Column
                vmath::vec4(0.0f, 0.0f, 0.0f, 1.0f) };  // W Column
```

There are also a shortcut functions in the vmath library which construct identity matrices for you; each matrix class has a static member function which produces an identity matrix of the appropriate dimensions:

```
vmath::mat2 m2 = vmath::mat2::identity();
vmath::mat3 m3 = vmath::mat3::identity();
vmath::mat4 m4 = vmath::mat4::identity();
```

If you recall, the very first vertex shader we used in the book back in Chapter 2 was a pass-through shader. It did not transform your vertices at all, but simply passed its hard-coded data on untouched, in the default coordinate system with no matrix applied to the vertices at all. We could have multiplied them all by the identity matrix, but that would have been a wasteful and pointless operation.

Translation Matrices

A *translation matrix* simply moves your vertices along one or more of the three axes. Figure 4.9 shows, for example, translating a cube up the y axis ten units.

The formulation of a 4×4 translation matrix is as follows:

$$\begin{bmatrix} 1.0 & 0.0 & 0.0 & t_x \\ 0.0 & 1.0 & 0.0 & t_y \\ 0.0 & 0.0 & 1.0 & t_z \\ 0.0 & 0.0 & 0.0 & 1.0 \end{bmatrix}$$

Here, t_x, t_y, and t_z represent the translation in the x, y, and z axes, respectively. Examining the structure of the translation matrix reveals one

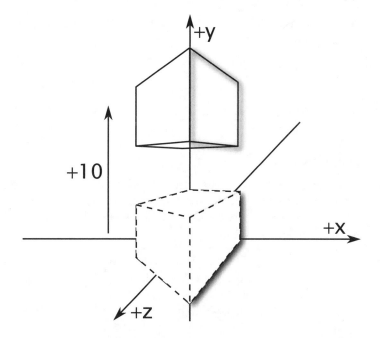

Figure 4.9: A cube translated ten units in the positive *y* direction

of the reasons why we need to use four-dimensional homogeneous coordinates to represent positions in 3D graphics. Consider the position vector v, whose w component is 1.0. Multiplying by a translation matrix of the form above yields

$$\begin{bmatrix} 1.0 & 0.0 & 0.0 & t_x \\ 0.0 & 1.0 & 0.0 & t_y \\ 0.0 & 0.0 & 1.0 & t_z \\ 0.0 & 0.0 & 0.0 & 1.0 \end{bmatrix} \begin{bmatrix} v_x \\ v_y \\ v_z \\ 1.0 \end{bmatrix} \begin{bmatrix} v_x + t_x \\ v_y + t_y \\ v_z + t_z \\ 1.0 \end{bmatrix}$$

As you can see, t_x, t_y, and t_z have been added to the components of v, producing translation. Had the w component of v not been 1.0, then using this matrix for translation would have resulted in t_x, t_y, and t_z being scaled by that value, affecting the output of the transform. In practice, position vectors are almost always encoded using four components with w (the last) being 1.0, whereas direction vectors are either encoded simply using three components or as four components with w being zero. Thus, multiplying a four-component direction vector by a translation matrix doesn't change it at all. The vmath library contains two functions that will construct a 4×4 translation matrix for you from either three separate components or from a 3D vector:

```
template <typename T>
static inline Tmat4<T> translate(T x, T y, T z) { ... }

template <typename T>
static inline Tmat4<T> translate(const vecN<T,3>& v) { ... }
```

Rotation Matrices

To rotate an object about one of the three coordinate axes, or indeed any arbitrary vector, you have to devise a *rotation matrix*. The form of a rotation matrix depends on the axis about which we wish to rotate. To rotate about the x axis, we use

$$R_x(\theta) = \begin{bmatrix} 1.0 & 0.0 & 0.0 & 0.0 \\ 0.0 & \cos\theta & \sin\theta & 0.0 \\ 0.0 & -\sin\theta & \cos\theta & 0.0 \\ 0.0 & 0.0 & 0.0 & 1.0 \end{bmatrix}$$

Here, $R_x(\theta)$ represents a rotation around the x axis by an angle of θ. Likewise, to rotate around the y or z axes, we can use

$$R_y(\theta) = \begin{bmatrix} \cos\theta & 0.0 & -\sin\theta & 0.0 \\ 0.0 & 1.0 & 0.0 & 0.0 \\ \sin\theta & 0.0 & \cos\theta & 0.0 \\ 0.0 & 0.0 & 0.0 & 1.0 \end{bmatrix} \quad R_z(\theta) = \begin{bmatrix} \cos\theta & -\sin\theta & 0.0 & 0.0 \\ \sin\theta & \cos\theta & 0.0 & 0.0 \\ 0.0 & 0.0 & 1.0 & 0.0 \\ 0.0 & 0.0 & 0.0 & 1.0 \end{bmatrix}$$

It is possible to multiply these three matrices together in order to produce a composite transform to rotate by a given amount around each of the three axes in a single matrix-vector multiplication operation. The matrix to do this is

$$R_z(\psi)\,R_y(\theta)\,R_x(\phi) = \begin{bmatrix} c_\theta c_\psi & c_\phi s_\psi + s_\phi s_\theta c_\psi & s_\phi s_\psi - c_\phi s_\theta c_\psi & 0.0 \\ -c_\theta s_\psi & c_\phi c_\psi - s_\phi s_\theta s_\psi & s_\phi c_\psi + c_\phi s_\theta s_\psi & 0.0 \\ s_\theta & -s_\phi c_\theta & c_\phi c_\theta & 0.0 \\ 0.0 & 0.0 & 0.0 & 1.0 \end{bmatrix}$$

Here, s_ψ, s_θ, and s_ϕ indicate the sine of ψ, θ, and ϕ, respectively, and c_ψ, c_θ, and c_ϕ indicate the cosine of ψ, θ, and ϕ. If this seems like a huge chunk of math, don't worry — again, a couple of vmath functions come to the rescue:

```
template <typename T>
static inline Tmat4<T> rotate(T angle_x, T angle_y, T_angle_z);
```

You can also perform a rotation around an arbitrary axis by specifying x, y, and z values for that vector. To see the axis of rotation, you can just draw a line from the origin to the point represented by (x,y,z). The vmath library also includes code to produce this matrix from an angle-axis representation:

```
template <typename T>
static inline Tmat4<T> rotate(T angle, T x, T y, T z);

template <typename T>
static inline Tmat4<T> rotate(T angle, const vecN<T,3>& axis);
```

These two overloads of the vmath::rotate function produce a rotation matrix representing a rotation of angle degrees round the axis specified by x, y, and z for the first variant, or by the vector v for the second. Here, we perform a rotation around the vector specified by the x, y, and z arguments. The angle of rotation is in the counterclockwise direction measured in degrees and specified by the argument angle. In the simplest of cases, the rotation is around only one of the coordinate systems' cardinal axes (x, y, or z).

The following code, for example, creates a rotation matrix that rotates vertices 45° around an arbitrary axis specified by (1,1,1), as illustrated in Figure 4.10.

```
vmath::mat4 rotation_matrix = vmath::rotate(45.0, 1.0, 1.0, 1.0);
```

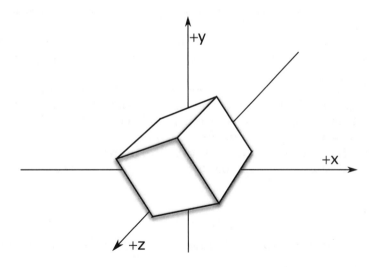

Figure 4.10: A cube rotated about an arbitrary axis

Notice in this example the use of degrees. This function internally converts degrees to radians because unlike computers, many programmers prefer to think in terms of degrees.

Euler Angles

Euler angles are a set of three angles[3] that represent orientation in space. Each angle represents a rotation around one of three orthogonal vectors that define our frame (for example, the x, y and z axes). As you have read, the order that matrix transformations are performed is important as performing some transformations (such as rotations) in different orders will produce different results. This is due to the non-commutative nature of matrix multiplication. Thus, given a set of Euler angles, should you rotate first around the x axis, then around y and then z, or should you perform the rotations in the opposite order, or even do y first? Well, so long as you're consistent, it doesn't really matter.

Representation of orientations as a set of three angles has some advantages. For example, this type of representation is fairly intuitive, which is important if you plan to hook the angles up to a user interface. Another benefit is that it's pretty straightforward to interpolate angles, construct a rotation matrix at each point, and see smooth, consistent motion in your final animation. However, Euler angles also come with a serious pitfall — *gimbal lock*.

Gimbal lock occurs when a rotation by one angle reorients one of the axes to be aligned with another of the axes. Any further rotation around either of the two now colinear axes will result in the same transformation of the model, removing a degree of freedom from the system. Thus, Euler angles are not suitable for concatenating transforms or accumulating rotations.

To avoid this, you will notice that our `vmath::rotate` functions are able to take an angle by which to rotate and an axis about which to rotate. Of course, stacking three rotations together, one in each of the x, y, and z axes, allows you to use Euler angles if you must, but it is much preferable to use angle-axis representation for rotations, or to use *quaternions* to represent transformations and convert them to matrices as needed.

Scaling Matrices

Our final "standard" transformation matrix is a *scaling matrix*. A scaling transform changes the size of your object by expanding or contracting all

---

3. In a three-dimensional frame.

the vertices along the three axes by the factors specified. A scaling matrix has the form

$$\begin{bmatrix} s_x & 0.0 & 0.0 & 0.0 \\ 0.0 & s_y & 0.0 & 0.0 \\ 0.0 & 0.0 & s_z & 0.0 \\ 0.0 & 0.0 & 0.0 & 1.0 \end{bmatrix}$$

Here, s_x, s_y, and s_z represent the scaling factors in the x, y, and z dimensions, respectively. Creating a scaling matrix with the vmath library is similar to the method for creating a translation or rotation matrix. Three functions exist to construct this matrix for you:

```
template <typename T>
static inline Tmat4<T> scale(T x, T y, T z) { ... }

template <typename T>
static inline Tmat4<T> scale(const Tvec3<T>& v) { ... }

template <typename T>
static inline Tmat4<T> scale(T x) { ... }
```

The first of these scales independently in the x, y, and z axes by the values given in the x, y, and z parameters. The second performs the same function but uses a three-component vector rather than three separate parameters to represent the scale factors. The final function scales by the same amount, x, in all three dimensions. Scaling does not have to be uniform, and you can use it to both stretch and squeeze objects along different directions. For example, a 10 x 10 x 10 cube could be scaled by two in the x and z directions as shown in Figure 4.11.

Concatenating Transformations

As you have learned, coordinate transforms can be represented by matrices, and transformation of a vector from one space to another comprises a simple matrix-vector multiplication operation. Multiplying by a sequence of matrices can apply a sequence of transformations. It is not necessary to store the intermediate vectors after each matrix-vector multiplication. Rather, it is possible and generally preferable to first multiply together all of the matrices comprising a single set of related transformations to produce a single matrix representing the entire transformation sequence. This matrix can then be used to transform vectors directly from the source to the destination coordinate spaces.

Remember, order is important. When writing code with vmath or in GLSL, you should always multiply a matrix by a vector and read the sequence of

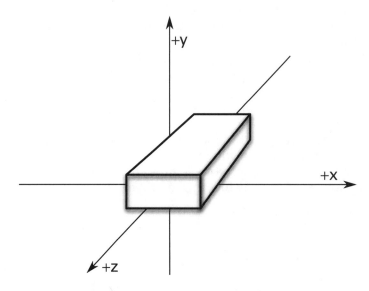

Figure 4.11: A non-uniform scaling of a cube

transformations in reverse order. For example, consider the following code sequence:

```
vmath::mat4 translation_matrix = vmath::translate(4.0f, 10.0f, -20.0f);
vmath::mat4 rotation_matrix = vmath::rotate(45.0f,
                                            vmath::vec3(0.0f, 1.0f, 0.0f));
vmath::vec4 input_vertex = vmath::vec4(...);

vmath::vec4 transformed_vertex = translation_matrix *
                                 rotation_matrix *
                                 input_vertex;
```

This code first rotates a model 45° around the y axis (due to rotation_matrix) and then translates it 4 units in the x axis, 10 units in the y axis and negative 20 units in the z axis (due to translation_matrix). This places the model in a particular orientation and then moves it into position. Reading the sequence of transformations backwards gives the order of operations (rotation then translation). We could rewrite this code as follows:

```
vmath::mat4 translation_matrix = vmath::translate(4.0f, 10.0f, -20.0f);
vmath::mat4 rotation_matrix = vmath::rotate(45.0f,
                                            vmath::vec3(0.0f, 1.0f, 0.0f));
vmath::mat4 composite_matrix = translation_matrix * rotation_matrix;
vmath::vec4 input_vertex = vmath::vec4(...);

vmath::vec4 transformed_vertex = composite_matrix *
                                 input_vertex;
```

Here, `composite_matrix` is formed by multiplying the translation matrix by the rotation matrix, forming a composite that represents the rotation followed by the translation. This matrix can then be used to transform any number of vertices or other vectors. If you have a lot of vertices to transform, this can greatly speed up your calculation. Each vertex now takes only one matrix-vector multiply rather than two.

Care must be taken here. It's too easy to read (or write) the sequence of transformations left-to-right as you would code. If we were to multiply our translation and rotation matrices together in that order, then in the first transform we would move the origin of the model and the rotation operation would then take place around that new origin, potentially sending our model flying off into space!

Quaternions

A *quaternion* is a four-dimensional quantity that is similar in some ways to a complex number. It has a real part and *three* imaginary parts (as compared to a complex number's one imaginary part). Just as a complex number has an imaginary part i, a quaternion has three imaginary parts, i, j, and k. Mathematically, a quaternion q is represented as

$$q = (x + yi + zj + wk)$$

The imaginary parts of the quaternion have properties similar to the imaginary part of a complex number. In particular,

$$i^2 = j^2 = k^2 = ikj = -1$$

Also, the product of any two of i, j, and k gives whichever one was not part of that product. Thus,

$$i = jk$$
$$j = ik$$
$$k = jk$$

Given this, we can see that it is possible to multiply two quaternions together as follows:

$$q_1 = (x_1 + y_1 i + z_1 j + w_1 k)$$
$$q_2 = (x_2 + y_2 i + z_2 j + w_2 k)$$
$$q_1 q_2 = x_1 x_2 - y_1 y_2 - z_1 z_2 - w_1 w_2$$
$$+ (x_1 y_2 + y_1 x_2 + z_1 w_2 - w_1 z_2)i$$
$$+ (x_1 z_2 - y_1 w_2 + z_1 x_2 + w_1 y_2)j$$
$$+ (x_1 w_2 + y_1 z_2 - z_1 y_2 + w_1 x_2)k$$

As with complex numbers, multiplication of quaternions is non-commutative. Addition and subtraction for quaternions is defined as simple vector addition and subtraction, with the terms being added or subtracted on a component-by-component basis. Other functions such as unary negation and magnitude also behave as expected for a four-component vector. Although a quaternion is a four-component entity, it is common to represent a quaternion as a real scalar part and a three-component imaginary vector part. Such representation is often written

$$q = (r, \vec{v})$$

Okay, great — but this isn't the dreaded math chapter, right? This is about computer graphics, OpenGL, and all that fun stuff. Well, here's where quaternions get really useful. Remember that our rotation functions take an angle and an axis to rotate around? Well, we can represent those two quantities as a quaternion by stuffing the angle in the real part and the axis in the vector part, yielding a quaternion that represents a rotation around any axis.

A sequence of rotations can be represented by a series of quaternions multiplied together, producing a single resulting quaternion that encodes the whole lot in one go. While it's possible to make a bunch of matrices that represent rotation around the various Cartesian axes and then multiply them all together, that method is susceptible to *gimbal lock*. If you do the same thing with a sequence of quaternions, gimbal lock cannot occur. For your coding pleasure, vmath includes the vmath::quaterion class that implements most of the functionality described here.

The Model-View Transform

In a simple OpenGL application, one of the most common transformations is to take a model from model space to view space in order to render it. In effect, we move the model first into world space (i.e., place it relative to the world's origin) and then from there into view space (placing it relative to the viewer). This process establishes the vantage point of the scene. By default, the point of observation in a perspective projection is at the origin (0,0,0) looking down the negative z axis (*into* the monitor or screen). This point of observation is moved relative to the eye coordinate system to provide a specific vantage point. When the point of observation is located at the origin, as in a perspective projection, objects drawn with positive z values are behind the observer. In an orthographic projection, however, the viewer is assumed to be infinitely far away on the positive z axis and can see everything within the viewing volume.

Because this transform takes vertices from model space (which is also sometimes known as object space) directly into view space and effectively bypasses world space, it is often referred to as the *model-view transform* and the matrix that encodes this transformation is known as the *model-view matrix*.

The model transform essentially places objects into world space. Each object is likely to have its own model transform, which will generally consist of a sequence of scale, rotation, and translation operations. The result of multiplying the positions of vertices in model space by the model transform is a set of positions in world space. This transformation is sometimes called the model-world transform.

The view transformation allows you to place the point of observation anywhere you want and look in any direction. Determining the viewing transformation is like placing and pointing a camera at the scene. In the grand scheme of things, you must apply the viewing transformation before any other modeling transformations. The reason is that it appears to move the current working coordinate system with respect to the eye coordinate system. All subsequent transformations then occur based on the newly modified coordinate system. The transform that moves coordinates from world space to view space is sometimes called the world-view transform.

Concatenating the model-world and world-view transform matrices by multiplying them together yields the model-view matrix (i.e., the matrix that takes coordinates from model to view space). There are some advantages to doing this. First, there are likely to be many models in your scene and many vertices in each model. Using a single composite transform to move the model into view space is more efficient than moving it into world space and then into view space as explained earlier. The second advantage has more to do with the numerical accuracy of single-precision floating-point numbers — the world could be huge, and computation performed in world space will have different precision depending on how far the vertices are from the world origin. However, if you perform the same calculations in view space, then precision is dependent on how far vertices are *from the viewer*, which is probably what you want — a great deal of precision is applied to objects that are close to the viewer at the expense of precision very far from the viewer.

The Lookat Matrix

If you have a vantage point at a known location and a thing you want to look at, you would wish to place your virtual camera at that location and then point it in the right direction. In order to orient the camera correctly, you also need to know which way is up. Otherwise, the camera could spin around its forward axis, and even though it would still be technically be pointing in the right direction, this is almost certainly not what you want. So, given an origin, a point of interest, and a direction that we consider to be up, we would like to construct a sequence of transforms, ideally baked together into a single matrix, that will represent a rotation that will point a camera in the correct direction and a translation that will move the origin to the center of the camera. This matrix is known as a *lookat matrix* and can be constructed using only the math covered in this chapter so far.

First, we know that subtracting two positions gives us a vector that would move a point from the first position to the second and that normalizing that vector result gives us its directional. So, if we take the coordinates of a point of interest, subtract from that the position of our camera, and then normalize the resulting vector, we have a new vector that represents the direction of view from the camera to the point of interest. We call this the *forward* vector.

Next, we know that if we take the cross product of two vectors, we will receive a third vector that is orthogonal (which means, at a right angle) to both input vectors. Well, we have two vectors — the forward vector we just calculated and the *up* vector that represents the direction we consider to be upwards. Taking the cross product of those two vectors results in a third vector that is orthogonal to each of them and points sideways with respect to our camera. We call this the *sideways* vector. However, the up and forward vectors are not necessarily orthogonal to each other, and we need a third orthogonal vector to construct a rotation matrix. To obtain this vector, we can simply apply the same process again — taking the cross product of the forward vector and our sideways vector to produce a third that is orthogonal to both and represents *up* with respect to the camera.

These three vectors are of unit length and are all orthogonal to one another, and so they form a set of orthonormal basis vectors and represent our view frame. Given these three vectors, we can construct a rotation matrix that will take a point in the standard Cartesian basis and move it into the basis of our camera. In the following math, e is the eye (or camera) position, p is the point of interest, and u is the up vector. Here we go...

First, construct our forward vector, f:

$$f = \frac{p - e}{\|p - e\|}$$

Next, take the cross of f and u to construct a side vector s:

$$s = f \times u$$

Now, construct a new up vector, u' in our camera's reference:

$$u' = s \times f$$

Finally, we construct a rotation matrix representing a reorientation into our newly constructed orthonormal basis:

$$R = \begin{bmatrix} s.x & u'.x & f.x & 0.0 \\ s.y & u'.y & f.y & 0.0 \\ s.z & u'.z & f.z & 0.0 \\ 0.0 & 0.0 & 0.0 & 1.0 \end{bmatrix}$$

Right, we're not quite finished. In order to transform objects into the camera's frame, not only do we need to orient everything correctly, but we also need to move the origin to the position of the camera. We do this by simply translating the resulting vectors by the negative of the camera's position. Remember how a translation matrix is simply constructed by placing the offset into that rightmost column of the matrix? Well, we can do that here too:

$$T = \begin{bmatrix} s.x & u'.x & f.x & -e.x \\ s.y & u'.y & f.y & -e.y \\ s.z & u'.z & y.z & -e.z \\ 0.0 & 0.0 & 0.0 & 1.0 \end{bmatrix}$$

Finally, we have our lookat matrix, T. If this seems like a lot of steps to you, you're in luck. There's a function in the vmath library that will construct the matrix for you:

```
template <typename T>
static inline Tmat4<T> lookat(const vecN<T,3>& eye,
                              const vecN<T,3>& center,
                              const vecN<T,3>& up) { ... }
```

The matrix produced by the vmath::lookat function can be used as the basis for your camera matrix — the matrix that represents the position and orientation of your camera. In other words, this can be your view matrix.

Projection Transformations

The projection transformation is applied to your vertices after the model-view transformation. This projection actually defines the viewing volume and establishes clipping planes. The clipping planes are plane equations in 3D space that OpenGL uses to determine whether geometry can be seen by the viewer. More specifically, the projection transformation specifies how a finished scene (after all the modeling is done) is projected to the final image on the screen. You will learn more about two types of projections — orthographic and perspective.

In an orthographic, or parallel, projection, all the polygons are drawn on-screen with exactly the relative dimensions specified. Lines and polygons are mapped directly to the 2D screen using parallel lines, which means no matter how far away something is, it is still drawn the same size, just flattened against the screen. This type of projection is typically used for rendering two-dimensional images such as the front, top, and side elevations in blueprints or two-dimensional graphics such as text or on-screen menus.

A perspective projection shows scenes more as they appear in real life instead of as a blueprint. The hallmark of perspective projections is foreshortening, which makes distant objects appear smaller than nearby objects of the same size. Lines in 3D space that might be parallel do not always appear parallel to the viewer. With a railroad track, for instance, the rails are parallel, but using perspective projection, they appear to converge at some distant point. The benefit of perspective projection is that you don't have to figure out where lines converge or how much smaller distant objects are. All you need to do is specify the scene using the model-view transformations and then apply the perspective projection matrix. Linear algebra works all the magic for you.

Figure 4.12 compares orthographic and perspective projections on two different scenes. As you can see, in the orthographic projection shown on the left, the cubes do not appear to change in size as they move further from the viewer. However, in the perspective projection shown on the right, the cubes get smaller and smaller as they get further from the viewer.

Orthographic projections are used most often for 2D drawing purposes where you want an exact correspondence between pixels and drawing units. You might use them for a schematic layout, text, or perhaps a 2D graphing application. You also can use an orthographic projection for 3D renderings when the depth of the rendering has a very small depth in comparison to the distance from the viewpoint. Perspective projections are used for rendering scenes that contain wide-open spaces or objects that need to have foreshortening applied. For the most part, perspective projections are typical for 3D graphics. In fact, looking at a 3D object with an orthographic projection can be somewhat unsettling.

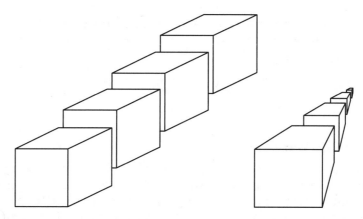

Figure 4.12: A side-by-side example of an orthographic versus perspective projection

Perspective Matrices

Once your vertices are in view space, we need to get them into clip space, which we do by applying our projection matrix, which may represent a perspective or orthographic projection (or some other projection all together). A commonly used perspective matrix is called a *frustum matrix*. A frustum matrix is a projection matrix that produces a perspective projection such that clip space takes the shape of a rectangular frustum, which is a truncated rectangular pyramid. Its parameters are the distance to the near and far planes and the world space coordinate of the left, right, top, and bottom clipping planes. It takes the following form:

$$\begin{bmatrix} \frac{2 \cdot near}{right-left} & 0.0 & \frac{right+left}{right-left} & 0.0 \\ 0.0 & \frac{2 \cdot near}{top-bottom} & \frac{top+bottom}{top-bottom} & 0.0 \\ 0.0 & 0.0 & \frac{near+far}{near-far} & \frac{2 \cdot near \cdot far}{near-far} \\ 0.0 & 0.0 & -1.0 & 0.0 \end{bmatrix}$$

The `vmath` function to do this is `vmath::frustum`:

```
static inline mat4 frustum(float left,
                           float right,
                           float bottom,
                           float top,
                           float n,
                           float f) { ... }
```

Another common method for construction of a perspective matrix is to directly specify a field of view as an angle (in degrees, perhaps), an aspect ratio (generally derived by dividing the window's width by its height), and the view-space positions of the near and far planes. This is somewhat simpler to specify, and only produces symmetric frustra. However, this is almost always what you'll want. The `vmath` function to do this is `vmath::perspective`:

```
static inline mat4 perspective(float fovy /* in degrees */,
                               float aspect,
                               float n,
                               float f) { ... }
```

Orthographic Matrices

If you wish to use an orthographic projection for your scene, then you can construct a (somewhat simpler) orthographic projection matrix. An orthographic projection matrix is simply a scaling matrix that linearly maps view-space coordinates into clip-space coordinates. The parameters to construct the orthographic projection matrix are the left, right, top, and bottom coordinates in view space of the bounds of the scene, and the position of the near and far planes. The form of the matrix is

$$
\begin{bmatrix}
\frac{2}{right-left} & 0.0 & 0.0 & \frac{left+right}{left-right} \\
0.0 & \frac{2}{top-bottom} & 0.0 & \frac{bottom+top}{bottom-top} \\
0.0 & 0.0 & \frac{2}{near-far} & \frac{near+far}{far-near} \\
0.0 & 0.0 & 0.0 & 1.0
\end{bmatrix}
$$

Again, there's a `vmath` function to construct this matrix for you, `vmath::ortho`:

```
static inline mat4 ortho(float left,
                         float right,
                         float bottom,
                         float top,
                         float near,
                         float far) { ... }
```

Interpolation, Lines, Curves, and Splines

Interpolation is a term used to describe the process of finding values that lie between a set of known points. Consider the equation of the line passing through points A and B:

$$P = A + t\vec{D}$$

where P is any point on the line and the $\vec{D}$ is the vector from A to B:

$$\vec{D} = (B - A)$$

We can therefore write this equation as

$$P = A + t(B - A) \quad \text{or}$$
$$P = (1 - t)A + tB$$

It is easy to see that when t is zero, P is equal to A, and when t is one, P is equal to $A + B - A$, which is simply B. Such a line is shown in Figure 4.13.

Figure 4.13: Finding a point on a line

If t lies between 0.0 and 1.0, then P is going to end up somewhere between A and B. Values of t outside this range will push P off the ends of the line. You should be able to see that by smoothly varying t, we can move point P from A to B and back. This is known as *linear interpolation*. The values of A and B (and therefore P) can be have any number of dimensions. For example, they could be scalar values; two-dimensional values such as points on a graph; three-dimensional values such as coordinates in 3D space, colors, and so on; or even higher dimension quantities such as matrices, arrays, or even whole images. In many cases, linear interpolation doesn't make much sense (for example, linearly interpolating between two matrices generally doesn't produce a meaningful result), but angles, positions, and other coordinates can normally be interpolated safely.

Linear interpolation is such a common operation in graphics that GLSL includes a built-in function specifically for this purpose, `mix`:

```
vec4 mix(vec4 A, vec4 B, float t);
```

The `mix` function comes in several versions taking various different dimensionalities of vectors or scalars as the A and B inputs and taking scalars or matching vectors for t.

Curves

If moving everything along a straight line between two points is all we wanted to do, then this would be enough. However, in the real world, objects move in smooth curves and accelerate and decelerate smoothly. A curve can be represented by three or more *control points*. For most curves, there are more than three control points, two of which form the end-points and the others define the shape of the curve. Consider the simple curve shown in Figure 4.14.

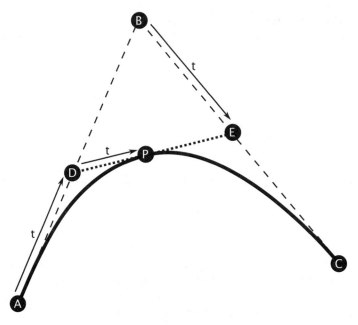

Figure 4.14: A simple Bézier curve

The curve shown in Figure 4.14 has three control points, A, B, and C. A and C are the end points of the curve and B defines the shape of the curve. If we join points A and B with one line and points B and C together with another line, then we can interpolate along the two lines using a simple linear interpolation to find a new pair of points, D and E. Now, given these two points, we can again join them with yet another line and interpolate along it to find a new point, P. As we vary our interpolation parameter, t, point P will move in a smooth curved path from A to D. Expressed mathematically, this is

$$D = A + t(B - A)$$
$$E = B + t(C - B)$$
$$P = D + t(E - D)$$

Substituting for D and E and doing a little crunching, we come up with the following:

$$P = A + t(B - A) + t((B + (t(C - B))) - (A + t(B - A))))$$
$$P = A + t(B - A) + tB + t^2(C - B) - tA - t^2(B - A)$$
$$P = A + t(B - A + B - A) + t^2(C - B - B + A)$$
$$P = A + 2t(B - A) + t^2(C - 2B + A)$$

You should recognize this as a *quadratic* equation in t. The curve that it describes is known as a *quadratic Bézier curve*. We can actually implement this very easily in GLSL using the `mix` function as all we're doing is linearly interpolating (mixing) the results of two previous interpolations.

```
vec4 quadratic_bezier(vec4 A, vec4 B, vec4 C, float t)
{
    vec4 D = mix(A, B, t);      // D = A + t(B - A)
    vec4 E = mix(B, C, t);      // E = B + t(C - B)

    vec4 P = mix(D, E, t);      // P = D + t(E - D)

    return P;
}
```

By adding a fourth control point as shown in Figure 4.15, we can increase the order by one and produce a *cubic* Bézier curve.

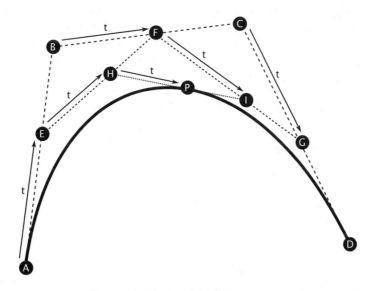

Figure 4.15: A cubic Bézier curve

We now have four control points, A, B, C, and D. The process for constructing the curve is similar to the quadratic Bézier curve. We form a first line from A to B, a second from B to C, and a third from C to D. Interpolating along each of the three lines gives rise to three new points, E, F, and G. Using these three points, we form two more lines, one from E to F and another from F to G, interpolating along which gives rise to points H and I, between which we can interpolate to find our final point, P. Therefore, we have the equations shown below.

$$E = A + t(B - A)$$
$$F = B + t(C - B)$$
$$G = C + t(D - C)$$

$$H = E + t(F - E)$$
$$I = F + t(G - F)$$

$$P = H + t(I - H)$$

If you think the equations above look familiar, you'd be right — our points E, F, and G form a quadratic Bézier curve that we use to interpolate to our final point P. If we were to substitute the equations for E, F, and G into the equations for H and I, substitute *those* into the equation for P, and crunch through the expansions, we would be left with a cubic equation with terms in t^3 — hence the name *cubic Bézier curve*. Again, we can implement this simply and efficiently in terms of linear interpolations in GLSL using the mix function:

```
vec4 cubic_bezier(vec4 A, vec4 B, vec4 C, vec4 D, float t)
{
    vec4 E = mix(A, B, t);      // E = A + t(B - A)
    vec4 F = mix(B, C, t);      // F = B + t(C - B)
    vec4 G = mix(C, D, t);      // G = C + t(D - C)

    vec4 H = mix(E, F, t);      // H = E + t(F - E)
    vec4 I = mix(F, G, t);      // I = F + t(G - F)

    vec4 P = mix(H, I, t);      // P = H + t(I - H)

    return P;
}
```

Just as the structure of the equations for a cubic Bézier curve "includes" the equations for a quadratic curve, so too does the code to implement them. In fact, we can layer these curves on top of each other, using the code for one to build the next:

```
vec4 cubic_bezier(vec4 A, vec4 B, vec4 C, vec4 D, float t)
{
    vec4 E = mix(A, B, t);      // E = A + t(B - A)
    vec4 F = mix(B, C, t);      // F = B + t(C - B)
    vec4 G = mix(C, D, t);      // G = C + t(D - C)

    return quadratic_bezier(E, F, G, t);
}
```

Now that we see this pattern, we can take it further and produce even higher order curves. For example, a *quintic* Bézier curve (one with five control points) can be implemented as

```
vec4 quintic_bezier(vec4 A, vec4 B, vec4 C, vec4 D, vec4 E, float t)
{
    vec4 F = mix(A, B, t);      // F = A + t(B - A)
    vec4 G = mix(B, C, t);      // G = B + t(C - B)
    vec4 H = mix(C, D, t);      // H = C + t(D - C)
    vec4 I = mix(D, E, t);      // I = D + t(E - D)

    return cubic_bezier(F, G, H, I, t);
}
```

This layering could theoretically be applied over and over for any number of control points. However, in practice, curves with more than four control points are not commonly used. Rather, we use *splines*.

Splines

A spline is effectively a long curve made up of several smaller curves (such as Béziers) that locally define their shape. At least the control points representing the ends of the curves are shared between segments,[4] and often one or more of the interior control points are either shared or linked in some way between adjacent segments. Any number of curves can be joined together in this way allowing arbitrarily long paths to be formed. Take a look at the curve shown in Figure 4.16.

In Figure 4.16, the curve is defined by ten control points, A through J, which form three cubic Bézier curves. The first is defined by A, B, C, and D; the second shares D and further uses E, F, and G; with the third sharing G and adding H, I, and J. This type of spline is known as a *cubic Bézier spline* because it is constructed from a sequence of cubic Bézier curves. This is also known as a *cubic B-spline* — a term that may be familiar to anyone who has read much about graphics in the past.

To interpolate point P along the spline, we simply divide it into three regions, allowing t to range from 0.0 to 3.0. Between 0.0 and 1.0, we interpolate along the first curve, moving from A to D. Between 1.0 and 2.0, we interpolate along the second curve, moving from D to G, and when t is between 2.0 and 3.0, we interpolate along the final curve between G and J.

---

4. This is what sticks the curves together to form a spline. These control points are known as *welds*, and the control points in between are sometimes referred to as *knots*.

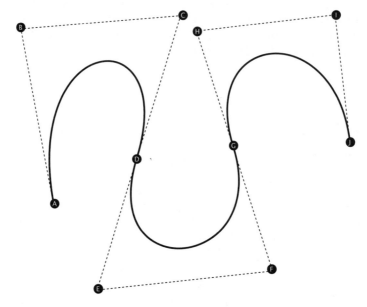

Figure 4.16: A cubic Bézier spline

Thus, the integer part of t determines the curve segment along which we are interpolating, and the fractional part of t is used to interpolate along that segment. Of course, we can scale t as we wish. For example, if we take a value between 0.0 and 1.0 and multiply it by the number of segments in the curve, we can continue to use our original range of values for t regardless of the number of control points in a curve.

The following code will interpolate a vector along a cubic Bézier spline with ten control points (and thus three segments):

```
vec4 cubic_bspline_10(vec4 CP[10], float t)
{
    float f = t * 3.0;
    int i = int(floor(f));
    float s = fract(t);

    if (t <= 0.0)
        return CP[0];

    if (t >= 1.0)
        return CP[9];

    vec4 A = CP[i * 3];
    vec4 B = CP[i * 3 + 1];
    vec4 C = CP[i * 3 + 2];
    vec4 D = CP[i * 3 + 3];

    return cubic_bezier(A, B, C, D, s);
}
```

If we use a spline to determine the position or orientation of an object, we will find that we must be very careful about our choice of control point locations in order to keep motion smooth and fluid. The rate of change in the value of our interpolated point P (i.e., its velocity) is the differential of the equation of the curve with respect to t. If this function is discontinuous, then P will suddenly change direction and our objects will appear to jump around. Furthermore, the rate of change of P's velocity (its acceleration) is the second-order derivative of the spline equation with respect to t. If the acceleration is not smooth, then P will appear to suddenly speed up or slow down.

A function that has a continuous first derivative is known as C^1 continuous, and likewise a curve that has a continuous second derivative is known as C^2 continuous. Bézier curve segments are both C^1 and C^2 continuous, but to ensure that we maintain continuity over the welds of a spline, we need to ensure that each segment starts off where the previous ended in position, direction of movement, and rate of change. Well, a rate of travel in a particular direction is simply a velocity. So, rather than assigning arbitrary control points to our spline, we can assign a velocity at each weld. If the same velocity of the curve at each weld is used in the computation of the curve segments on either side of that weld, then we will have a spline function that is both C^1 and C^2 continuous.

This should make sense if you take another look at Figure 4.16 — there are no kinks, and the curve is nice and smooth through the welds (points D and G). Now look at the control points on either side of the welds. For example, take points C and E, which surround D. C and E form a straight line, and D lies right in the middle of it. In fact, we can call the line segment from D to E the velocity at D, or $\vec{V_D}$. Given the position of point D (the weld) and velocity of the curve $\vec{V_D}$ at D, then C and E can be calculated as

$$C = D - \vec{V_D}$$
$$E = D + \vec{V_D}$$

Likewise, if $\vec{V_A}$ represents the velocity at A, B can be calculated as

$$B = A + \vec{V_A}$$

Thus, you should be able to see that given the positions and velocities at the welds of a cubic B-spline, we can dispense with all of the other control points and compute them on the fly as we evaluate each of the control points. A cubic B-spline that is represented this way (as a set of weld positions and velocities) is known as a *cubic Hermite spline*, or sometimes simply a *cspline*. The *cspline* is an extremely useful tool for producing smooth and natural animations.

Summary

In this chapter, you learned some mathematical concepts crucial to using OpenGL for the creation of 3D scenes. Even if you can't juggle matrices in your head, you now know what matrices are and how they are used to perform the various transformations. You also learned how to construct and manipulate the matrices that represent the viewer and viewport properties. You should now understand how to place your objects in the scene and determine how they are viewed on-screen. This chapter also introduced the powerful concept of a frame of reference, and you saw how easy it is to manipulate frames and convert them into transformations.

Finally, we introduced the use of the vmath library that accompanies this book. This library is written entirely in portable C++ and provides you with a handy toolkit of miscellaneous math and helper routines that can be used along with OpenGL.

Surprisingly, we did not cover a single new OpenGL function call in this entire chapter. Yes, this was the math chapter, and you might not have even noticed if you think math is just about formulas and calculations. Vectors, matrices, and the application thereof are absolutely crucial to being able to use OpenGL to render 3D objects and worlds. However, it's important to note that OpenGL doesn't impose any particular math convention upon you and does not itself provide any math functionality. Even if you use a different 3D math library, or even roll your own, you will still find yourself following the patterns laid out in this chapter for manipulating your geometry and 3D worlds. Now, go ahead and start making some!

Chapter 5

Data

WHAT YOU'LL LEARN IN THIS CHAPTER

- How to create buffers and textures that you can use to store data that your program can access

- How to get OpenGL to supply the values of your vertex attributes automatically

- How to access textures from your shaders for both reading and writing

In the examples you've seen so far, we have either used hard-coded data directly in our shaders, or we have passed values to shaders one at a time. While sufficient to demonstrate the configuration of the OpenGL pipeline, this is hardly representative of modern graphics programming. Recent graphics processors are designed as streaming processors that consume and produce huge amounts of data. Passing a few values to OpenGL at a time is extremely inefficient. To allow data to be stored and accessed by OpenGL, we include two main forms of data storage — buffers and textures. In this chapter, we first introduce buffers, which are linear blocks of un-typed data and can be seen as generic memory allocations. Next, we introduce textures, which are normally used to store multi-dimensional data, such as images or other data types.

Buffers

In OpenGL, buffers are linear allocations of memory that can be used for a number of purposes. They are represented by *names,* which are essentially opaque handles that OpenGL uses to identify them. Before you can start using buffers, you have to ask OpenGL to reserve some names for you and then use them to allocate memory and put data into that memory. The memory allocated for a buffer object is called its *data store.* Once you have the name of a buffer, you can attach it to the OpenGL context by *binding* it to a buffer binding point. Binding points are sometimes referred to as *targets,*[1] and the terms may be used interchangeably. There are a large number of buffer binding points in OpenGL, and each has a different use. For example, you can use the contents of a buffer to automatically supply the inputs of a vertex shader, to store the values of variables that will be used by your shaders, or as a place for shaders to store the data they produce.

Allocating Memory using Buffers

The function that is used to allocate memory using a buffer object is **glBufferData()**, whose prototype is

```
void glBufferData(GLenum target,
                  GLsizeiptr size,
                  const GLvoid * data,
                  GLenum usage);
```

The `target` parameter tells OpenGL which target the buffer you want to allocate storage for is bound to. For example, the binding point that is used when you want to use a buffer to store data that OpenGL can put into your vertex attributes is called the GL_ARRAY_BUFFER binding point. Although you may hear the term *vertex buffer* or *uniform buffer,* unlike some graphics libraries, OpenGL doesn't really assign *types* to buffers — a buffer is just a buffer and can be used for any purpose at any time (and even multiple purposes at the same time, if you like). The `size` parameter tells OpenGL how big the buffer should be, and `data` is a pointer to some initial data for the buffer (it can be NULL if you don't have data to put in the buffer right away). Finally, `usage` tells OpenGL how you plan to use the buffer. There are a number of possible values for `usage`, which are listed in Table 5.1.

---

1. It's not technically correct to conflate *target* and *binding point* as a single target may have multiple binding points. However, for most use cases, it is well understood what is meant.

Table 5.1: Buffer Object Usage Models

Buffer Usage	Description
GL_STREAM_DRAW	Buffer contents will be set once by the application and used infrequently for drawing.
GL_STREAM_READ	Buffer contents will be set once as output from an OpenGL command and used infrequently for drawing.
GL_STREAM_COPY	Buffer contents will be set once as output from an OpenGL command and used infrequently for drawing or copying to other images.
GL_STATIC_DRAW	Buffer contents will be set once by the application and used frequently for drawing or copying to other images.
GL_STATIC_READ	Buffer contents will be set once as output from an OpenGL command and queried many times by the application.
GL_STATIC_COPY	Buffer contents will be set once as output from an OpenGL command and used frequently for drawing or copying to other images.
GL_DYNAMIC_DRAW	Buffer contents will be updated frequently by the application and used frequently for drawing or copying to other images.
GL_DYNAMIC_READ	Buffer contents will be updated frequently as output from OpenGL commands and queried many times by the application.
GL_DYNAMIC_COPY	Buffer contents will be updated frequently as output from OpenGL commands and used frequently for drawing or copying to other images.

Listing 5.1 shows how a name for a buffer is reserved by calling **glGenBuffers()**, how it is bound to the context using **glBindBuffer()**, and how storage for it is allocated by calling **glBufferData()**.

```
// The type used for names in OpenGL is GLuint
GLuint buffer;

// Generate a name for the buffer
glGenBuffers(1, &buffer);

// Now bind it to the context using the GL_ARRAY_BUFFER binding point
glBindBuffer(GL_ARRAY_BUFFER, buffer);

// Specify the amount of storage we want to use for the buffer
glBufferData(GL_ARRAY_BUFFER, 1024 * 1024, NULL, GL_STATIC_DRAW);
```

Listing 5.1: Generating, binding, and initializing a buffer

After the code in Listing 5.1 has executed, buffer contains the name of a
buffer object that has been initialized to represent one megabyte of storage
for whatever data we choose. Using the GL_ARRAY_BUFFER target to refer to
the buffer object suggests to OpenGL that we're planning to use this buffer
to store vertex data, but we'll still be able to take that buffer and bind it to
some other target later. There are a handful of ways to get data into the
buffer object. You may have noticed the NULL pointer that we pass as the
third argument to **glBufferData()** in Listing 5.1. Had we instead supplied
a pointer to some data, that data would have been used to initialize the
buffer object. Another way to get data into a buffer is to give it to OpenGL
and tell it to copy data there. To do this, we call **glBufferSubData()**,
passing the size of the data we want to put into the buffer, the offset in the
buffer where we want it to go, and a pointer to the data in memory that
should be put into the buffer. **glBufferSubData()** is declared as

```
void glBufferSubData(GLenum target,
                     GLintptr offset,
                     GLsizeiptr size,
                     const GLvoid * data);
```

Listing 5.2 shows how we can put the data originally used in Listing 3.1
into a buffer object, which is the first step in automatically feeding a
vertex shader with data.

```
// This is the data that we will place into the buffer object
static const float data[] =
{
     0.25, -0.25, 0.5, 1.0,
    -0.25, -0.25, 0.5, 1.0,
     0.25,  0.25, 0.5, 1.0
};

// Put the data into the buffer at offset zero
glBufferSubData(GL_ARRAY_BUFFER, 0, sizeof(data), data);
```

Listing 5.2: Updating the content of a buffer with **glBufferSubData()**

Another method for getting data into a buffer object is to ask OpenGL for a pointer to the memory that the buffer object represents and then copy the data there yourself. Listing 5.3 shows how to do this using the `glMapBuffer()` function.

```
// This is the data that we will place into the buffer object
static const float data[] =
{
     0.25, -0.25, 0.5, 1.0,
    -0.25, -0.25, 0.5, 1.0,
     0.25,  0.25, 0.5, 1.0
};

// Get a pointer to the buffer's data store
void * ptr = glMapBuffer(GL_ARRAY_BUFFER, GL_WRITE_ONLY);

// Copy our data into it...
memcpy(ptr, data, sizeof(data));

// Tell OpenGL that we're done with the pointer
glUnmapBuffer(GL_ARRAY_BUFFER);
```

Listing 5.3: Mapping a buffer's data store with `glMapBuffer()`

The `glMapBuffer()` function is useful if you don't have all the data handy when you call the function. For example, you might be about to generate the data, or to read it from a file. If you wanted to use `glBufferSubData()` (or the initial pointer passed to `glBufferData()`), you'd have to generate or read the data into a temporary memory and then get OpenGL to make another copy of it into the buffer object. If you map a buffer, you can simply read the contents of the file directly into the mapped buffer. When you unmap it, if OpenGL can avoid making a copy of the data, it will. Regardless of whether we used `glBufferSubData()` or `glMapBuffer()` and an explicit copy to get data into our buffer object, it now contains a copy of data[] and we can use it as a source of data to feed our vertex shader.

Filling and Copying Data in Buffers

After allocating storage space for your buffer object using `glBufferData()`, one possible next step is to fill the buffer with known data. Whether you use the initial data parameter of `glBufferData()`, use `glBufferSubData()` to put the initial data in the buffer, or use `glMapBuffer()` to obtain a pointer to the buffer's data store and fill it with your application, you will need to overwrite the entire buffer. If the data you want to put into a buffer is a constant value, it is probably much more efficient to call `glClearBufferSubData()`, whose prototype is

```
void glClearBufferSubData(GLenum target,
                          GLenum internalformat,
                          GLintptr offset,
                          GLsizeiptr size,
                          GLenum format,
                          GLenum type,
                          const void * data);
```

The **glClearBufferSubData()** function takes a pointer to a variable
containing the values that you want to clear the buffer object to and, after
converting it to the format specified in internalformat, replicates it
across the range of the buffer's data store specified by offset and size,
both of which are measured in bytes. format and type tell OpenGL about
the data pointed to by data. Format can be one of GL_RED, GL_RG, GL_RGB,
or GL_RGBA to specify 1-, 2-, 3-, or 4-channel data, for example.
Meanwhile, type should represent the data type of the components. For
instance, it could be GL_UNSIGNED_BYTE or GL_FLOAT to specify unsigned
bytes or floating-point data. The most common types supported by
OpenGL and their corresponding C data types are listed in Table 5.2.

Table 5.2: Basic OpenGL Type Tokens and Their Corresponding C Types

Type Token	C Type
GL_BYTE	GLchar
GL_UNSIGNED_BYTE	GLuchar
GL_SHORT	GLshort
GL_UNSIGNED_SHORT	GLushort
GL_INT	GLint
GL_UNSIGNED_INT	GLuint
GL_FLOAT	GLfloat
GL_DOUBLE	GLdouble

Once your data has been sent to the GPU, it's entirely possible you may
want to share that data between buffers or copy the results from one
buffer into another. OpenGL provides an easy-to-use way of doing that.
glCopyBufferSubData() lets you specify which buffers are involved as well
as the size and offsets to use.

```
void glCopyBufferSubData(GLenum readtarget,
                         GLenum writetarget,
                         GLintptr readoffset,
                         GLintptr writeoffset,
                         GLsizeiptr size);
```

The readtarget and writetarget are the targets where the two buffers you want to copy data between are bound. These can be buffers bound to any of the available buffer binding points. However, since buffer binding points can only have one buffer bound at a time, you couldn't copy between two buffers both bound to the GL_ARRAY_BUFFER target, for example. This means that when you perform the copy, you need to pick two targets to bind the buffers to, which will disturb OpenGL state.

To resolve this, OpenGL provides the GL_COPY_READ_BUFFER and GL_COPY_WRITE_BUFFER targets. These targets were added specifically to allow you to copy data from one buffer to another without any unintended side effects. They are not used for anything else in OpenGL, and so you can bind your read and write buffers to these binding points without affecting any other buffer target. The readoffset and writeoffset parameters tell OpenGL where in the source and destination buffers to read or write the data, and the size parameter tells it how big the copy should be. Be sure that the ranges you are reading from and writing to remain within the bounds of the buffers; otherwise, your copy will fail.

You may notice the types of readoffset, writeoffset, and size, which are GLintptr and GLsizeiptr. These types are special definitions of integer types that are at least wide enough to hold a pointer variable.

Feeding Vertex Shaders from Buffers

Back in Chapter 2, you were briefly introduced to the vertex array object (VAO) where we explained how it represented the inputs to the vertex shader — even though at the time, we didn't use any real inputs to our vertex shaders and opted instead for hard-coded arrays of data. Then, in Chapter 3 we introduced the concept of *vertex attributes*, but we only discussed how to change their static values. Although the vertex array object stores these static attribute values for you, it can do a whole lot more. Before we can proceed, we need to create a vertex array object to store our vertex array state:

```
GLuint vao;
glGenVertexArrays(1, &vao);
glBindVertexArray(vao);
```

Now that we have our VAO created and bound, we can start filling in its state. Rather than using hard-coded data in the vertex shader, we can instead rely entirely on the value of a vertex attribute and ask OpenGL to fill it automatically using the data stored in a buffer object that we supply. To tell OpenGL where in the buffer object our data is, we use the **glVertexAttribPointer()** function[2] to describe the data, and then enable automatic filling of the attribute by calling **glEnableVertexAttribArray()**. The prototypes of **glVertexAttribPointer()** and **glEnableVertexAttribArray()** are

```
void glVertexAttribPointer(GLuint index,
                           GLint size,
                           GLenum type,
                           GLboolean normalized,
                           GLsizei stride,
                           const GLvoid * pointer);

void glEnableVertexAttribArray(GLuint index);
```

For **glVertexAttribPointer()**, the first parameter, index, is the index of the vertex attribute. You can define a large number of attributes as input to a vertex shader and then refer to them by their index as explained in "Vertex Attributes" in Chapter 3. size is the number of components that are stored in the buffer for each vertex, and type is the type of the data, which would normally be one of the types in Table 5.2.

The normalized parameter tells OpenGL whether the data in the buffer should be normalized (scaled between 0.0 and 1.0) before being passed to the vertex shader or if it should be left alone and passed as is. This is ignored for floating-point data, but for integer data types such as GL_UNSIGNED_BYTE or GL_INT, it is important. For example, if GL_UNSIGNED_BYTE data is normalized, it is divided by 255 (the maximum value representable by an unsigned byte) before being passed to a floating-point input to the vertex shader. The shader will therefore see values of the input attribute between 0.0 and 1.0. However, if the data is not normalized, it is simply casted to floating point and the shader will receive numbers between 0.0 and 255.0, even though the input to the vertex shader is floating-point.

The stride parameter tells OpenGL how many bytes are between the start of one vertex's data and the start of the next, but you can set this to zero to let OpenGL calculate it for you based on the values of size and type.

---

2. **glVertexAttribPointer()** is so named for historical reasons. Way back in times of yore, OpenGL didn't have buffer objects and all of the data it read was from your application's memory. When you called **glVertexAttribPointer()**, you really did give it a pointer to real data. On modern architectures, that's horribly inefficient, especially if the data will be read more than once, and so now OpenGL only supports reading data from buffer objects. Although the name of the function remains to this day, the pointer parameter is really interpreted as an offset into a buffer object.

Finally, `pointer` is, despite its name, the offset into the buffer that is currently bound to GL_ARRAY_BUFFER where the vertex attribute's data starts.

An example showing how to use **glVertexAttribPointer()** to configure a vertex attribute is shown in Listing 5.4. Notice that we also call **glEnableVertexAttribArray()** after setting up the pointer. This tells OpenGL to use the data in the buffer to fill the vertex attribute rather than using data we give it using one of the **glVertexAttrib*()** functions.

```
// First, bind our buffer object to the GL_ARRAY_BUFFER binding
// The subsequent call to glVertexAttribPointer will reference this buffer
glBindBuffer(GL_ARRAY_BUFFER, buffer);

// Now, describe the data to OpenGL, tell it where it is, and turn on
// automatic vertex fetching for the specified attribute
glVertexAttribPointer(0,              // Attribute 0
                      4,              // Four components
                      GL_FLOAT,       // Floating-point data
                      GL_FALSE,       // Not normalized
                                      // (floating-point data never is)
                      0,              // Tightly packed
                      NULL);          // Offset zero (NULL pointer)
glEnableVertexAttribArray(0);
```

Listing 5.4: Setting up a vertex attribute

After Listing 5.4 has been executed, OpenGL will automatically fill the first attribute in the vertex shader with data it has read from the buffer that was bound when **glVertexAttribPointer()** was called. We can modify our vertex shader to use only its input vertex attribute rather than a hard-coded array. This updated shader is shown in Listing 5.5.

```
#version 430 core

layout (location = 0) in vec4 position;

void main(void)
{
    gl_Position = position;
}
```

Listing 5.5: Using an attribute in a vertex shader

As you can see, the shader of Listing 5.5 is greatly simplified over the original shader shown in Chapter 2. Gone is the hard-coded array of data, and as an added bonus, this shader can be used with an arbitrary number of vertices. You can literally put millions of vertices worth of data into your buffer object and draw them all with a single command such as a call to **glDrawArrays()**.

If you are done using data from a buffer object to fill a vertex attribute, you can disable that attribute again with a call to **glDisableVertexAttribArray()**, whose prototype is

```
void glDisableAttribArray(GLuint index);
```

Once you have disabled the vertex attribute, it goes back to being static and passing the value you specify with **glVertexAttrib*()** to the shader.

Using Multiple Vertex Shader Inputs

As you have learned, you can get OpenGL to feed data into your vertex shaders for you and using data you've placed in buffer objects. You can also declare multiple inputs to your vertex shaders and assign each one a unique location that can be used to refer to it. Combining these things together means that you can get OpenGL to provide data to multiple vertex shader inputs simultaneously. Consider the input declarations to a vertex shader shown in Listing 5.6

```
layout (location = 0) in vec3 position;
layout (location = 1) in vec3 color;
```

Listing 5.6: Declaring two inputs to a vertex shader

If you have a linked program object whose vertex shader has multiple inputs, you can determine the locations of those inputs by calling

```
GLint glGetAttribLocation(GLuint program,
                          const GLchar * name);
```

Here, program is the name of the program object containing the vertex shader, and name is the name of the vertex attribute. In our example declarations of Listing 5.6, passing "position" to **glGetAttribLocation()** will cause it to return 0, and passing "color" will cause it to return 1. Passing something that is not the name of a vertex shader input will cause **glGetAttribLocation()** to return -1. Of course, if you always specify locations for your vertex attributes in your shader code, then **glGetAttribLocation()** should return whatever you specified. If you don't specify locations in shader code, OpenGL will assign locations for you, and those locations will be returned by **glGetAttribLocation()**.

There are two ways to connect vertex shader inputs to your application's data, and they are referred to as *separate attributes* and *interleaved attributes*.

When attributes are separate, that means that they are either located in different buffers, or at least at different locations in the same buffer. For example, if you want to feed data into two vertex attributes, you could create two buffer objects, bind the first to the GL_ARRAY_BUFFER target and call **glVertexAttribPointer()**, then bind the second buffer to the GL_ARRAY_BUFFER target and call **glVertexAttribPointer()** again for the second attribute. Alternatively, you can place the data at different offsets within the same buffer, bind it to the GL_ARRAY_BUFFER target, then call **glVertexAttribPointer()** twice — once with the offset to the first chunk of data and then again with the offset of the second chunk of data. Code demonstrating this is shown in Listing 5.7

```
GLuint buffer[2];

static const GLfloat positions[] = { ... };
static const GLfloat colors[] = { ... };

// Get names for two buffers
glGenBuffers(2, &buffers);

// Bind the first and initialize it
glBindBuffer(GL_ARRAY_BUFFER, buffer[0]);
glBufferData(GL_ARRAY_BUFFER, sizeof(positions), positions, GL_STATIC_DRAW);
glVertexAttribPointer(0, 3, GL_FLOAT, GL_FALSE, 0, NULL);
glEnableVertexAttribArray(0);

// Bind the second and initialize it
glBindBuffer(GL_ARRAY_BUFFER, buffer[1]);
glBufferData(GL_ARRAY_BUFFER, sizeof(colors), colors, GL_STATIC_DRAW);
glVertexAttribPointer(1, 3, GL_FLOAT, GL_FALSE, 0, NULL);
glEnableVertexAttribArray(1);
```

Listing 5.7: Multiple separate vertex attributes

In both cases of separate attributes, we have used *tightly packed* arrays of data to feed both attributes. This is effectively structure-of-arrays (SoA) data. We have a set of tightly packed, independent arrays of data. However, it's also possible to use an array-of-structures form of data. Consider how the following structure might represent a single vertex:

```
struct vertex
{
    // Position
    float x;
    float y;
    float z;

    // Color
    float r;
    float g;
    float b;
};
```

Now we have two inputs to our vertex shader (position and color) interleaved together in a single structure. Clearly, if we make an array of these structures, we have an array-of-structures (AoS) layout for our data. To represent this with calls to **glVertexAttribPointer()**, we have to use its `stride` parameter. The `stride` parameter tells OpenGL how far apart *in bytes* the start each vertex's data is. If we leave it as zero, it's a signal to OpenGL that the data is tightly packed and that it can work it out for itself given the `type` and `stride` parameters. However, to use the `vertex` structure declared above, we can simply use `sizeof`(vertex) for the `stride` parameter and everything will work out. Listing 5.8 shows the code to do this.

```
GLuint buffer;

static const vertex vertices[] = { ... };

// Allocate and initialize a buffer object
glGenBuffers(1, &buffer);
glBindBuffer(GL_ARRAY_BUFFER, buffer);
glBufferData(GL_ARRAY_BUFFER, sizeof(vertices), vertices, GL_STATIC_DRAW);

// Set up two vertex attributes - first positions
glVertexAttribPointer(0, 3, GL_FLOAT, GL_FALSE,
                      sizeof(vertex), (void *)offsetof(vertex, x));
glEnableVertexAttribArray(0);

// Now colors
glVertexAttribPointer(1, 3, GL_FLOAT, GL_FALSE,
                      sizeof(vertex), (void *)offsetof(vertex, r));
glEnableVertexAttribArray(1);
```

Listing 5.8: Multiple interleaved vertex attributes

Loading Objects from Files

As you can see, you could potentially use a large number of vertex attributes in a single vertex shader, and as we progress through various techniques, you will see that we'll regularly use four or five, possibly more. Filling buffers with data to feed all of these attributes and then setting up the vertex array object and all of the vertex attribute pointers can be a chore. Further, encoding all of your geometry data directly in your application just simply isn't practical for anything but the simplest models. Therefore, it makes sense to store model data in files and load it into your application. There are plenty of model file formats out there, and most modeling programs support several of the more common formats.

For the purpose of this book, we have devised a simple object file definition called an .SBM file that stores the information we need without being either too simple or too over-engineered. Complete documentation for the format is contained in Appendix B. The sb6 framework also includes a loader for this model format, called `sb6::object`. To load an object file, create an instance of `sb6::object`, and call its load function as follows:

```
sb6::object my_object;

my_object.load("filename.sbm");
```

If successful, the model will be loaded into the instance of `sb6::object`, and you will be able to render it. During loading, the class will create and set up the object's vertex array object and then configure all of the vertex attributes contained in the model file. The class also includes a render function that binds the object's vertex array object and calls the appropriate drawing command. For example, calling

```
my_object.render();
```

will render a single copy of the object with the current shaders. In many of the examples in the remainder of this book, we'll simply use our object loader to load object files (several of which are included with the book's source code) and render them.

Uniforms

Although not really a form of storage, uniforms are an important way to get data into shaders and to hook them up to your application. You have already seen how to pass data to a vertex shader using vertex attributes, and you have seen how to pass data from stage to stage using interface blocks. Uniforms allow you to pass data directly from your application into any shader stage. There are two flavors of uniforms that depend on how they are declared. The first are uniforms declared in the default block, and the second are uniform blocks, whose values are stored in buffer objects. We will discuss both now.

Default Block Uniforms

While attributes are needed for per-vertex positions, surface normals, texture coordinates, and so on, a uniform is how we pass data into a shader that stays the same — is uniform — for an entire primitive batch or longer. Probably the single most common uniform for a vertex shader is the transformation matrix. We use transformation matrices in our vertex shaders to manipulate vertex positions and other vectors. Any shader variable can be specified as a uniform, and uniforms can be in any of the shader stages (even though we only talk about vertex and fragment shaders in this chapter). Making a uniform is as simple as placing the keyword `uniform` at the beginning of the variable declaration:

```
uniform float fTime;
uniform int iIndex;
uniform vec4 vColorValue;
uniform mat4 mvpMatrix;
```

Uniforms are always considered to be constant, and they cannot be assigned to by your shader code. However, you can initialize their default values at declaration time in a manner such as

```
uniform answer = 42;
```

If you declare the same uniform in multiple shader stages, each of those stages will "see" the same value of that uniform.

Arranging Your Uniforms

After a shader has been compiled and linked into a program object, you can use one of many functions defined by OpenGL to set their values (assuming you don't want the defaults defined by the shader). Just as with vertex attributes, these functions refer to uniforms by their *location* within their program object. It is possible to specify the locations of uniforms in your shader code by using a location *layout qualifier*. When you do this, OpenGL will try to assign the locations that you specify to the uniforms in your shaders. The location layout qualifier looks like

```
layout (location = 17) uniform vec4 myUniform;
```

You'll notice the similarity between the location layout qualifier for uniforms and the one we've used for vertex shader inputs. In this case, myUniform will be allocated to location 17. If you don't specify a location for your uniforms in your shader code, OpenGL will automatically assign locations to them for you. You can figure out what locations were assigned by calling the **glGetUniformLocation()** function, whose prototype is

```
GLint glGetUniformLocation(GLuint program,
                           const GLchar* name);
```

This function returns a signed integer that represents the location of the variable named by name in the program specified by program. For example, to get the location of a uniform variable named vColorValue, we would do something like this:

```
GLint iLocation = glGetUniformLocation(myProgram, "vColorValue");
```

In the previous example, passing "myUniform" to **glGetUniformLocation()** would result in the value 17 being returned. If you know a priori where your uniforms are because you assigned locations to them in your shaders, then you don't need to find them and you can avoid the calls to **glGetUniformLocation()**. This is the recommended way of doing things.

If the return value of **glGetUniformLocation()** is -1, it means the uniform name could not be located in the program. You should bear in mind that even if a shader compiles correctly, a uniform name may still "disappear" from the program if it is not used directly in at least one of the attached shaders — even if you assign it a location explicitly in your shader source code. You do not need to worry about uniform variables being optimized away, but if you declare a uniform and then do not use it, the compiler will toss it out. Also, know that shader variable names are case sensitive, so you must get the case right when you query their locations.

Setting Scalars and Vector Uniforms

OpenGL supports a large number of data types both in the shading language and in the API, and in order to allow you to pass all this data around, it includes a huge number of functions just for setting the value of uniforms. A single scalar or vector data type can be set with any of the following variations on the **glUniform*()** function:

```
void glUniform1f(GLint location, GLfloat v0);
void glUniform2f(GLint location, Glfloat v0, GLfloat v1);
void glUniform3f(GLint location, GLfloat v0, GLfloat v1,
                 GLfloat v2);
void glUniform4f(GLint location, GLfloat v0, GLfloat v1,
                 GLfloat v2, GLfloat v3);
void glUniform1i(GLint location, GLint v0);
void glUniform2i(GLint location, GLint v0, GLint v1);
void glUniform3i(GLint location, GLint v0, GLint v1,
                 GLint v2);
void glUniform4i(GLint location, GLint v0, GLint v1,
                 GLint v2, GLint v3);
void glUniform1ui(GLint location, GLuint v0);
void glUniform2ui(GLint location, GLuint v0, GLuint v1);
void glUniform3ui(GLint location, GLuint v0, GLuint v1,
                  GLuint v2);
void glUniform4ui(GLint location, GLuint v0, GLuint v1,
                  GLuint v2, GLint v3);
```

For example, consider the following four variables declared in a shader:

```
uniform float fTime;
uniform int iIndex;
uniform vec4 vColorValue;
uniform bool bSomeFlag;
```

To find and set these values in the shader, your C/C++ code might look something like this:

```
GLint locTime, locIndex, locColor, locFlag;
locTime  = glGetUniformLocation(myShader, "fTime");
locIndex = glGetUniformLocation(myShader, "iIndex");
locColor = glGetUniformLocation(myShader, "vColorValue");
locFlag  = glGetUniformLocation(myShader, "bSomeFlag");
...
...
glUseProgram(myShader);
glUniform1f(locTime, 45.2f);
glUniform1i(locIndex, 42);
glUniform4f(locColor, 1.0f, 0.0f, 0.0f, 1.0f);
glUniform1i(locFlag, GL_FALSE);
```

Note that we used an integer version of `glUniform*()` to pass in a `bool` value. Booleans can also be passed in as floats, with 0.0 representing `false`, and any non-zero value representing `true`.

Setting Uniform Arrays

The `glUniform*()` function also comes in flavors that take a pointer, potentially to an array of values.

```
void glUniform1fv(GLint location, GLuint count, const GLfloat* value);
void glUniform2fv(GLint location, GLuint count, const Glfloat* value);
void glUniform3fv(GLint location, GLuint count, const GLfloat* value);
void glUniform4fv(GLint location, GLuint count, const GLfloat* value);

void glUniform1iv(GLint location, GLuint count, const GLint* value);
void glUniform2iv(GLint location, GLuint count, const GLint* value);
void glUniform3iv(GLint location, GLuint count, const GLint* value);
void glUniform4iv(GLint location, GLuint count, const GLint* value);

void glUniform1uiv(GLint location, GLuint count, constGLuint* value);
void glUniform2uiv(GLint location, GLuint count, constGLuint* value);
void glUniform3uiv(GLint location, GLuint count, constGLuint* value);
void glUniform4uiv(GLint location, GLuint count, constGLuint* value);
```

Here, the count value represents how many elements are in each array of x number of components, where x is the number at the end of the function name. For example, if you had a uniform with four components, such as one shown here:

```
uniform vec4 vColor;
```

then in C/C++, you could represent this as an array of floats:

```
GLfloat vColor[4] = {  1.0f, 1.0f, 1.0f, 1.0f };
```

But this is a single array of four values, so passing it into the shader would look like this:

```
glUniform4fv(iColorLocation, 1, vColor);
```

On the other hand, if you had an array of color values in your shader,

```
uniform vec4 vColors[2];
```

then in C++, you could represent the data and pass it in like this:

```
GLfloat vColors[4][2] = { {  1.0f, 1.0f, 1.0f, 1.0f } ,
                          {  1.0f, 0.0f, 0.0f, 1.0f } };
...
glUniform4fv(iColorLocation, 2, vColors);
```

At its simplest, you can set a single floating-point uniform like this:

```
GLfloat fValue = 45.2f;
glUniform1fv(iLocation, 1, &fValue);
```

Setting Uniform Matrices

Finally, we see how to set a matrix uniform. Shader matrix data types only come in the single and double-precision floating-point variety, and thus we have far less variation. The following functions set the values of 2×2, 3×3, and 4×4 single-precision floating-point matrix uniforms, respectively:

```
glUniformMatrix2fv(GLint location, GLuint count,
                   GLboolean transpose, const GLfloat *m);
glUniformMatrix3fv(GLint location, GLuint count,
                   GLboolean transpose, const GLfloat *m);
glUniformMatrix4fv(GLint location, GLuint count,
                   GLboolean transpose, const GLfloat *m);
```

Similarly, the following functions set the values of 2×2, 3×3, and 4×4 double-precision floating-point matrix uniforms:

```
glUniformMatrix2dv(GLint location, GLuint count,
                   GLboolean transpose, const GLdouble *m);
glUniformMatrix3dv(GLint location, GLuint count,
                   GLboolean transpose, const GLdouble *m);
glUniformMatrix4dv(GLint location, GLuint count,
                   GLboolean transpose, const GLdouble *m);
```

In all of these functions, the variable count represents the number of matrices stored at the pointer parameter m (yes, you can have arrays of matrices!). The Boolean flag transpose is set to GL_FALSE if the matrix is already stored in column-major ordering (the way OpenGL prefers). Setting this value to GL_TRUE causes the matrix to be transposed when it is copied into the shader. This might be useful if you are using a matrix library that uses a row-major matrix layout instead (for example, some other graphics APIs use row-major ordering and you may wish to use a library designed for one of them).

Uniform Blocks

Eventually, the shaders you'll be writing will become very complex. Some of them will require a lot of constant data, and passing all this to the shader using uniforms can become quite inefficient. If you have a lot of shaders in an application, you'll need to set up the uniforms for every one of those shaders, which means a lot of calls to the various `glUniform*()` functions. You'll also need to keep track of which uniforms change. Some change for every object, some change once per frame, while others may only require initializing once for the whole application. This means that you either need to update different sets of uniforms in different places in your application (making it more complex to maintain) or update all the uniforms all the time (costing performance).

To alleviate the cost of all the `glUniform*()` calls, to make updating a large set of uniforms simpler, and to be able to easily share a set of uniforms between different programs, OpenGL allows you to combine a group of uniforms into a *uniform block* and store the whole block in a buffer object. The buffer object is just like any other that has been described earlier. You can quickly set the whole group of uniforms by either changing your buffer binding or overwriting the content of a bound buffer. You can also leave the buffer bound while you change programs, and the new program will see the current set of uniform values. This functionality is called the uniform buffer object, or UBO. In fact, the uniforms you've used up until now live in the default block. Any uniform declared at the global scope in a shader ends up in the default uniform block. You can't keep the default block in a uniform buffer object; you need to create one or more named uniform blocks.

To declare a set of uniforms to be stored in a buffer object, you need to use a named uniform block in your shader. This looks a lot like the interface blocks described in the section "Interface Blocks" back in Chapter 3, but it uses the `uniform` keyword instead of `in` or `out`. Listing 5.9 shows what the code looks like in a shader.

```
uniform TransformBlock
{
    float scale;              // Global scale to apply to everything
    vec3  translation;        // Translation in X, Y, and Z
    float rotation[3];        // Rotation around X, Y, and Z axes
    mat4 projection_matrix;   // A generalized projection matrix to apply
                              // after scale and rotate
}  transform;
```

Listing 5.9: Example uniform block declaration

This code declares a uniform block whose name is TransformBlock. It also declares a single instance of the block called transform. Inside the shader, you can refer to the members of the block using its instance name, transform (e.g., transform.scale or transform.projection_matrix). However, to set up the data in the buffer object that you'll use to back the block, you need to know the location of a member of the block, and for that, you need the block name, TransformBlock. If you wanted to have multiple instances of the block, each with its own buffer, you could make transform an array. The members of the block will have the same locations within each block, but there will now be several instances of the block that you can refer to in the shader. Querying the location of members within a block is important when you want to fill the block with data, which is explained in the following section.

Building Uniform Blocks

Data accessed in the shader via named uniform blocks can be stored in buffer objects. In general, it is the application's job to fill the buffer objects with data using functions like **glBufferData()** or **glMapBuffer()**. The question is, then, what is the data in the buffer supposed to look like? There are actually two possibilities here, and whichever one you choose is a trade-off.

The first method is to use a standard, agreed upon layout for the data. This means that your application can just copy data into the buffers and assume specific locations for members within the block — you can even store the data on disk ahead of time and simply read it straight into a buffer that's been mapped using **glMapBuffer()**. The standard layout may leave some empty space between the various members of the block, making the buffer larger than it needs to be, and you might even trade some performance for this convenience, but even so, using the standard layout is probably safe in almost all situations.

Another alternative is to let OpenGL decide where it would like the data. This can produce the most efficient shaders, but it means that your application needs to figure out where to put the data so that OpenGL can read it. Under this scheme, the data stored in uniform buffers is arranged in a *shared* layout. This is the default layout and is what you get if you don't explicitly ask OpenGL for something else. With the shared layout, the data in the buffer is laid out however OpenGL decides is best for runtime performance and access from the shader. This can sometimes allow for greater performance to be achieved by the shaders, but requires more work from the application. The reason this is called the shared layout is that while OpenGL has arranged the data within the buffer, that arrangement will be the same between multiple programs and shaders sharing the same declaration of the uniform block. This allows you to use the same buffer object with any program. To use the shared layout, the application must determine the locations within the buffer object of the members of the uniform block.

First, we'll describe the *standard* layout, which is what we would recommend that you use for your shaders (even though it's not the default). To tell OpenGL that you want to use the standard layout, you need to declare the uniform block with a layout qualifier. A declaration of our `TransformBlock` uniform block, with the standard layout qualifier, `std140`, is shown in Listing 5.10.

```
layout(std140) uniform TransformBlock
{
    float scale;            // Global scale to apply to everything
    vec3  translation;      // Translation in X, Y, and Z
    float rotation[3];      // Rotation around X, Y, and Z axes
    mat4 projection_matrix; // A generalized projection matrix to
                            // apply after scale and rotate
} transform;
```

Listing 5.10: Declaring a uniform block with the `std140` layout

Once a uniform block has been declared to use the standard, or `std140`, layout, each member of the block consumes a predefined amount of space in the buffer and begins at an offset that is predictable by following a set of rules. A summary of the rules is as follows:

Any type consuming N bytes in a buffer begins on an N-byte boundary within that buffer. That means that standard GLSL types such as `int`, `float`, and `bool` (which are all defined to be 32-bit or four-byte quantities) begin on multiples of four bytes. A vector of these types of length two always begins on a $2N$-byte boundary. For example, that means a `vec2`, which is eight bytes long in memory, always starts on an eight-byte boundary. Three- and four-element vectors always start on a $4N$-byte boundary; so `vec3` and `vec4` types start on 16-byte boundaries, for instance. Each member of an array of scalar or vector types (`int`s or `vec3`s, for example) always start boundaries defined by these same rules, but rounded up to the alignment of a `vec4`. In particular, this means that arrays of anything but `vec4` (and $N \times 4$ matrices) won't be tightly packed, but instead there will be a gap between each of the elements. Matrices are essentially treated like short arrays of vectors, and arrays of matrices are treated like very long arrays of vectors. Finally, structures and arrays of structures have additional packing requirements; the whole structure starts on the boundary required by its largest member, rounded up to the size of a `vec4`.

Particular attention must be paid to the difference between the `std140` layout and the packing rules that are often followed by your C++ (or other application language) compiler of choice. In particular, an array in a uniform block is not necessarily tightly packed. This means that you can't create, for example, an array of `float` in a uniform block and simply copy data from a C array into it because the data from the C array will be packed, and the data in the uniform block won't be.

This all sounds complex, but it is logical and well defined, and allows a large range of graphics hardware to implement uniform buffer objects efficiently. Returning to our `TransformBlock` example, we can figure out the offsets of the members of the block within the buffer using these rules. Listing 5.11 shows an example of a uniform block declaration along with the offsets of its members.

```
layout(std140) uniform TransformBlock
{
//  Member                      base alignment  offset    aligned offset
    float scale;             // 4               0         0
    vec3  translation;       // 16              4         16
    float rotation[3];       // 16              28        32 (rotation[0])
                             //                           48 (rotation[1])
                             //                           64 (rotation[2])
    mat4 projection_matrix;  // 16              80        80 (column 0)
                             //                           96 (column 1)
                             //                           112 (column 2)
                             //                           128 (column 3)
} transform;
```

Listing 5.11: Example of a uniform block with offsets

There is a complete example of the alignments of various types in the original `ARB_uniform_buffer_object` extension specification.

If you really want to use the shared layout, you can determine the offsets that OpenGL assigned to your block members. Each member of a uniform block has an index that is used to refer to it to find its size and location within the block. To get the index of a member of a uniform block, call

```
void glGetUniformIndices(GLuint program,
                         GLsizei uniformCount,
                         const GLchar ** uniformNames,
                         GLuint * uniformIndices);
```

This function allows you to get the indices of a large set of uniforms — perhaps even all of the uniforms in a program with a single call to OpenGL, even if they're members of different blocks. It takes a count of the number of uniforms you'd like the indices for (`uniformCount`) and an array of uniform names (`uniformNames`) and puts their indices in an array for you (`uniformIndices`). Listing 5.12 contains an example of how you would retrieve the indices of the members of `TransformBlock`, which we declared earlier.

```
static const GLchar * uniformNames[4] =
{
    "TransformBlock.scale",
    "TransformBlock.translation",
    "TransformBlock.rotation",
    "TransformBlock.projection_matrix"
};
GLuint uniformIndices[4];

glGetUniformIndices(program, 4, uniformNames, uniformIndices);
```

Listing 5.12: Retrieving the indices of uniform block members

After this code has run, you have the indices of the four members of the uniform block in the `uniformIndices` array. Now that you have the indices, you can use them to find the locations of the block members within the buffer. To do this, call

```
void glGetActiveUniformsiv(GLuint program,
                           GLsizei uniformCount,
                           const GLuint * uniformIndices,
                           GLenum pname,
                           GLint * params);
```

This function can give you a lot of information about specific uniform block members. The information that we're interested in is the offset of the member within the buffer, the array stride (for `TransformBlock.rotation`), and the matrix stride (for `TransformBlock.projection_matrix`). These values tell us where to put data within the buffer so that it can be seen in the shader. We can retrieve these from OpenGL by setting pname to `GL_UNIFORM_OFFSET`,

GL_UNIFORM_ARRAY_STRIDE, and GL_UNIFORM_MATRIX_STRIDE, respectively.
Listing 5.13 shows what the code looks like.

```
GLint uniformOffsets[4];
GLint arrayStrides[4];
GLint matrixStrides[4];
glGetActiveUniformsiv(program, 4, uniformIndices,
                      GL_UNIFORM_OFFSET, uniformOffsets);
glGetActiveUniformsiv(program, 4, uniformIndices,
                      GL_UNIFORM_ARRAY_STRIDE, arrayStrides);
glGetActiveUniformsiv(program, 4, uniformIndices,
                      GL_UNIFORM_MATRIX_STRIDE, matrixStrides);
```

Listing 5.13: Retrieving the information about uniform block members

Once the code in Listing 5.13 has run, uniformOffsets contains the offsets
of the members of the TransformBlock block, arrayStrides contains the
strides of the array members (only rotation, for now), and matrixStrides
contains the strides of the matrix members (only projection_matrix).

The other information that you can find out about uniform block
members includes the data type of the uniform, the size in bytes that it
consumes in memory, and layout information related to arrays and
matrices within the block. You need some of that information to initialize
a buffer object with more complex types, although the size and types of
the members should be known to you already if you wrote the shaders.
The other accepted values for pname and what you get back are listed in
Table 5.3.

If the type of the uniform you're interested in is a simple type such as int,
float, bool, or even vectors of these types (vec4 and so on), all you need
is its offset. Once you know the location of the uniform within the buffer,
you can either pass the offset to **glBufferSubData()** to load the data at the
appropriate location, or you can use the offset directly in your code to
assemble the buffer in memory. We demonstrate the latter option here
because it reinforces the idea that the uniforms are stored in memory, just
like vertex information can be stored in buffers. It also means fewer calls
to OpenGL, which can sometimes lead to higher performance. For these
examples, we assemble the data in the application's memory and then
load it into a buffer using **glBufferData()**. You could alternatively use
glMapBuffer() to get a pointer to the buffer's memory and assemble the
data directly into that.

Let's start by setting the simplest uniform in the TransformBlock block,
scale. This uniform is a single float whose location is stored in the first

element of our `uniformIndices` array. Listing 5.14 shows how to set the value of the single float.

Table 5.3: Uniform Parameter Queries via **`glGetActiveUniformsiv()`**

Value of pname	What You Get Back
GL_UNIFORM_TYPE	The data type of the uniform as a GLenum.
GL_UNIFORM_SIZE	The size of arrays, in units of whatever GL_UNIFORM_TYPE gives you. If the uniform is not an array, this will always be one.
GL_UNIFORM_NAME_LENGTH	The length, in characters of the names of the uniforms.
GL_UNIFORM_BLOCK_INDEX	The index of the block that the uniform is a member of.
GL_UNIFORM_OFFSET	The offset of the uniform within the block.
GL_UNIFORM_ARRAY_STRIDE	The number of bytes between consecutive elements of an array. If the uniform is not an array, this will be zero.
GL_UNIFORM_MATRIX_STRIDE	The number of bytes between the first element of each column of a column-major matrix or row of a row-major matrix. If the uniform is not a matrix, this will be zero.
GL_UNIFORM_IS_ROW_MAJOR	Each element of the output array will either be one if the uniform is a row-major matrix, or zero if it is a column-major matrix or not a matrix at all.

```
// Allocate some memory for our buffer (don't forget to free it later)
unsigned char * buffer = (unsigned char *)malloc(4096);

// We know that TransformBlock.scale is at uniformOffsets[0] bytes
// into the block, so we can offset our buffer pointer by that value and
// store the scale there.
*((float *)(buffer + uniformOffsets[0])) = 3.0f;
```

Listing 5.14: Setting a single float in a uniform block

Next, we can initialize data for `TransformBlock.translation`. This is a `vec3`, which means it consists of three floating-point values packed tightly together in memory. To update this, all we need to do is find the location of the first element of the vector and store three consecutive floats in memory starting there. This is shown in Listing 5.15.

```
// Put three consecutive GLfloat values in memory to update a vec3
((float *)(buffer + uniformOffsets[1]))[0] = 1.0f;
((float *)(buffer + uniformOffsets[1]))[1] = 2.0f;
((float *)(buffer + uniformOffsets[1]))[2] = 3.0f;
```

Listing 5.15: Retrieving the indices of uniform block members

Now, we tackle the array `rotation`. We could have also used a `vec3` here, but for the purposes of this example, we use a three-element array to demonstrate the use of the `GL_UNIFORM_ARRAY_STRIDE` parameter. When the **shared** layout is used, arrays are defined as a sequence of elements separated by an implementation-defined stride in bytes. This means that we have to place the data at locations in the buffer defined both by `GL_UNIFORM_OFFSET` and `GL_UNIFORM_ARRAY_STRIDE`, as in the code snippet of Listing 5.16.

```
// TransformBlock.rotations[0] is at uniformOffsets[2] bytes into
// the buffer. Each element of the array is at a multiple of
// arrayStrides[2] bytes past that
const GLfloat rotations[] = {  30.0f, 40.0f, 60.0f };
unsigned int offset = uniformOffsets[2];

for (int n = 0; n < 3; n++)
{
    *((float *)(buffer + offset)) = rotations[n];
    offset += arrayStrides[2];
}
```

Listing 5.16: Specifying the data for an array in a uniform block

Finally, we set up the data for `TransformBlock.projection_matrix`. Matrices in uniform blocks behave much like arrays of vectors. For column-major matrices (which is the default), each column of the matrix is treated like a vector, the length of which is the height of the matrix. Likewise, row-major matrices are treated like an array of vectors where each row is an element in that array. Just like normal arrays, the starting offset for each column (or row) in the matrix is determined by an implementation defined quantity. This can be queried by passing the `GL_UNIFORM_MATRIX_STRIDE` parameter to **glGetActiveUniformsiv()**. Each column of the matrix can be initialized using similar code to that which was used to initialize the `vec3` `TransformBlock.translation`. This setup code is given in Listing 5.17.

```
// The first column of TransformBlock.projection_matrix is at
// uniformOffsets[3] bytes into the buffer. The columns are
// spaced matrixStride[3] bytes apart and are essentially vec4s.
// This is the source matrix - remember, it's column major so
const GLfloat matrix[] =
{
    1.0f, 2.0f, 3.0f, 4.0f,
    9.0f, 8.0f, 7.0f, 6.0f,
    2.0f, 4.0f, 6.0f, 8.0f,
    1.0f, 3.0f, 5.0f, 7.0f
};

for (int i = 0; i < 4; i++)
{
    GLuint offset = uniformOffsets[3] + matrixStride[3] * i;
    for (j = 0; j < 4; j++)
    {
        *((float *)(buffer + offset)) = matrix[i * 4 + j];
        offset += sizeof(GLfloat);
    }
}
```

Listing 5.17: Setting up a matrix in a uniform block

This method of querying offsets and strides works for any of the layouts. With the shared layout, it is the only option. However, it's somewhat inconvenient, and as you can see, you need quite a lot of code to lay out your data in the buffer in the correct way. This is why we recommend that you use the *standard* layout. This allows you to determine where in the buffer data should be placed based on a set of rules that specify the size and alignments for the various data types supported by OpenGL. These rules are common across all OpenGL implementations, and so you don't need to query anything to use it (although, should you query offsets and strides, the results will be correct). There is some chance that you'll trade a small amount of shader performance for its use, but the savings in code complexity and application performance are well worth it.

Regardless of which packing mode you choose, you can bind your buffer full of data to a uniform block in your program. Before you can do this, you need to retrieve the index of the uniform block. Each uniform block in a program has an index that is compiler assigned. There is fixed maximum number of uniform blocks that can be used by a single program, and a maximum number that can be used in any given shader stage. You can find these limits by calling `glGetIntegerv()` with the GL_MAX_UNIFORM_BUFFERS parameter (for the total per program) and either GL_MAX_VERTEX_UNIFORM_BUFFERS, GL_MAX_GEOMETRY_UNIFORM_BUFFERS,

GL_MAX_TESS_CONTROL_UNIFORM_BUFFERS,
GL_MAX_TESS_EVALUATION_UNIFORM_BUFFERS, or
GL_MAX_FRAGMENT_UNIFORM_BUFFERS for the vertex, tessellation control
and evaluation, geometry, and fragment shader limits, respectively. To
find the index of a uniform block in a program, call

```
GLuint glGetUniformBlockIndex(GLuint program,
                         const GLchar * uniformBlockName);
```

This returns the index of the named uniform block. In our example
uniform block declaration here, uniformBlockName would be
"TransformBlock". There is a set of buffer binding points to which you
can bind a buffer to provide data for the uniform blocks. It is essentially a
two-step process to bind a buffer to a uniform block. Uniform blocks are
assigned binding points, and then buffers can be bound to those binding
points, matching buffers with uniform blocks. This way, different
programs can be switched in and out without changing buffer bindings,
and the fixed set of uniforms will automatically be seen by the new
program. Contrast this to the values of the uniforms in the default block,
which are per-program state. Even if two programs contain uniforms with
the same names, their values must be set for each program and will
change when the active program is changed.

To assign a binding point to a uniform block, call

```
void glUniformBlockBinding(GLuint program,
                       GLuint uniformBlockIndex,
                       GLuint uniformBlockBinding);
```

where program is the program where the uniform block you're changing
lives. uniformBlockIndex is the index of the uniform block you're
assigning a binding point to. You just retrieved that by calling
glGetUniformBlockIndex(). uniformBlockBinding is the index of the
uniform block binding point. An implementation of OpenGL
supports a fixed maximum number of binding points, and you can
find out what that limit is by calling **glGetIntegerv()** with the
GL_MAX_UNIFORM_BUFFER_BINDINGS parameter.

Alternatively, you can specify the binding index of your uniform blocks
right in your shader code. To do this, we again use the layout qualifier,
this time with the binding keyword. For example, to assign our
TransformBlock block to binding 2, we could declare it as

```
layout(std140, binding = 2) uniform TransformBlock
{
    ...
} transform;
```

Notice that the `binding` layout qualifier can be specified at the same time as the `std140` (or any other) qualifier. Assigning bindings in your shader source code avoids the need to call **glUniformBlockBinding()**, or even to determine the block's index from your application, and so is usually the best method of assigning block location. Once you've assigned binding points to the uniform blocks in your program, whether through the **glUniformBlockBinding()** function or through a layout qualifier, you can bind buffers to those same binding points to make the data in the buffers appear in the uniform blocks. To do this, call

```
glBindBufferBase(GL_UNIFORM_BUFFER, index, buffer);
```

Here, GL_UNIFORM_BUFFER tells OpenGL that we're binding a buffer to one of the uniform buffer binding points. index is the index of the binding point and should match what you specified either in your shader or in uniformBlockBinding in your call to **glUniformBlockBinding()**. buffer is the name of the buffer object that you want to attach. It's important to note that index is not the index of the uniform block (uniformBlockIndex in **glUniformBlockBinding()**), but the index of the uniform buffer binding point. This is a common mistake to make and is easy to miss.

This mixing and matching of binding points with uniform block indices is illustrated in Figure 5.1.

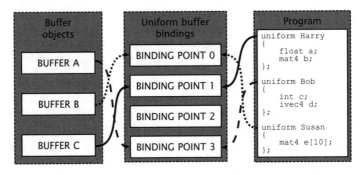

Figure 5.1: Binding buffers and uniform blocks to binding points

In Figure 5.1, there is a program with three uniform blocks (Harry, Bob, and Susan) and three buffer objects (A, B, and C). Harry is assigned to binding point 1, and buffer C is bound to binding point 1, so Harry's data comes from buffer C. Likewise, Bob is assigned to binding point 3, to which buffer A is bound, and so Bob's data comes from buffer A. Finally, Susan is assigned to binding point 0, and buffer B is bound to binding point 0, so Susan's data comes from buffer B. Notice that binding point 2 is not used.

That doesn't matter. There could be a buffer bound there, but the program doesn't use it.

The code to set this up is simple and is given in Listing 5.18.

```
// Get the indices of the uniform blocks using glGetUniformBlockIndex
GLuint harry_index = glGetUniformBlockIndex(program, "Harry");
GLuint bob_index   = glGetUniformBlockIndex(program, "Bob");
GLuint susan_index = glGetUniformBlockIndex(program, "Susan");

// Assign buffer bindings to uniform blocks, using their indices
glUniformBlockBinding(program, harry_index, 1);
glUniformBlockBinding(program, bob_index, 3);
glUniformBlockBinding(program, susan_index, 0);

// Bind buffers to the binding points
// Binding 0, buffer B, Susan's data
glBindBufferBase(GL_UNIFORM_BUFFER, 0, buffer_b);
// Binding 1, buffer C, Harry's data
glBindBufferBase(GL_UNIFORM_BUFFER, 1, buffer_c);
// Note that we skipped binding 2
// Binding 3, buffer A, Bob's data
glBindBufferBase(GL_UNIFORM_BUFFER, 3, buffer_a);
```

Listing 5.18: Specifying bindings for uniform blocks

Again, if we had set the bindings for our uniform blocks in our shader code by using the `binding` layout qualifier, we could avoid the calls to **glUniformBlockBinding()** in Listing 5.18. This example is shown in Listing 5.19.

```
layout (binding = 1) uniform Harry
{
    // ...
};

layout (binding = 3) uniform Bob
{
    // ...
};

layout (binding = 0) uniform Susan
{
    // ...
};
```

Listing 5.19: Uniform blocks binding layout qualifiers

After a shader containing the declarations shown in Listing 5.19 is compiled and linked into a program object, the bindings for the Harry, Bob, and Susan uniform blocks will be set to the same things as they would be after executing Listing 5.18. Setting the uniform block binding in the shader can be useful for a number of reasons. First is that it reduces the number of calls to OpenGL that your application must make. Second, it allows the shader to associate a uniform block with a particular binding point without the application needing to know its name. This can be helpful if you have some data in a buffer with a standard layout, but want to refer to it with different names in different shaders.

A common use for uniform blocks is to separate steady state from transient state. By setting up the bindings for all your programs using a standard convention, you can leave buffers bound when you change the program. For example, if you have some relatively fixed state — say the projection matrix, the size of the viewport, and a few other things that change once a frame or less often — you can leave that information in a buffer bound to binding point zero. Then, if you set the binding for the fixed state to zero for all programs, whenever you switch program objects using **glUseProgram()**, the uniforms will be sitting there in the buffer, ready to use.

Now let's say that you have a fragment shader that simulates some material (e.g., cloth or metal); you could put the parameters for the material into another buffer. In your program that shades that material, bind the uniform block containing the material parameters to binding point 1. Each object would maintain a buffer object containing the parameters of its surface. As you render each object, it uses the common material shader and simply binds its parameter buffer to buffer binding point 1.

A final significant advantage of uniform blocks is that they can be quite large. The maximum size of a uniform block can be determined by calling **glGetIntegerv()** and passing the GL_MAX_UNIFORM_BLOCK_SIZE parameter. Also, the number of uniform blocks that you can access from a single program can be retrieved by calling **glGetIntegerv()** and passing the GL_MAX_UNIFORM_BLOCK_BINDINGS. OpenGL guarantees that at least 64KB in size, and you can have at least 14 of them referenced by a single program. Taking the example of the previous paragraph a little further, you could pack all of the properties for all of the materials used by your application into a single, large uniform block containing a big array of structures. As you render the objects in your scene, you only need to communicate the index within that array of the material you wish to use. You can achieve that with a static vertex attribute or traditional uniform, for example. This could be substantially faster than replacing the contents of a buffer object or changing uniform buffer bindings between each object. If you're really clever, you can even render objects made up from multiple surfaces with different materials using a single drawing command.

Using Uniforms to Transform Geometry

Back in Chapter 4, "Math for 3D Graphics," you learned how to construct matrices that represent several common transformations including scale, translation, and rotation, and how to use the sb6::vmath library to do the heavy lifting for you. You also saw how to multiply matrices to produce a composite matrix that represents the whole transformation sequence. Given a point of interest and the camera's location and orientation, you can build a matrix that will transform objects into the coordinate space of the viewer. Also, you can build matrices that represent perspective and orthographic projections onto the screen.

Furthermore, in this chapter you have seen how to feed a vertex shader with data from buffer objects, and how to pass data into your shaders through uniforms (whether in the default uniform block, or in a uniform buffer). Now it's time to put all this together and build a program that does a little more than pass vertices through un-transformed.

Our example program will be the classic spinning cube. We'll create geometry representing a unit cube located at the origin and store it in buffer objects. Then, we will use a vertex shader to apply a sequence of transforms to it to move it into world space. We will construct a basic view matrix, multiply our model and view matrices together to produce a model-view matrix, and create a perspective transformation matrix representing some of the properties of our camera. Finally, we will pass these into a simple vertex shader using uniforms and draw the cube on the screen.

First, let's set up the cube geometry using a vertex array object. The code to do this is shown in Listing 5.20.

```
// First, create and bind a vertex array object
glGenVertexArrays(1, &vao);
glBindVertexArray(vao);

static const GLfloat vertex_positions[] =
{
    -0.25f,  0.25f, -0.25f,
    -0.25f, -0.25f, -0.25f,
     0.25f, -0.25f, -0.25f,
```

```
    0.25f, -0.25f, -0.25f,
    0.25f,  0.25f, -0.25f,
   -0.25f,  0.25f, -0.25f,

    /* MORE DATA HERE */

   -0.25f,  0.25f, -0.25f,
    0.25f,  0.25f, -0.25f,
    0.25f,  0.25f,  0.25f,

    0.25f,  0.25f,  0.25f,
   -0.25f,  0.25f,  0.25f,
   -0.25f,  0.25f, -0.25f
};

// Now generate some data and put it in a buffer object
glGenBuffers(1, &buffer);
glBindBuffer(GL_ARRAY_BUFFER, buffer);
glBufferData(GL_ARRAY_BUFFER,
             sizeof(vertex_positions),
             vertex_positions,
             GL_STATIC_DRAW);
// Set up our vertex attribute
glVertexAttribPointer(0, 3, GL_FLOAT, GL_FALSE, 0, NULL);
glEnableVertexAttribArray(0);
```

Listing 5.20: Setting up cube geometry

Next, on each frame, we need to calculate the position and orientation of
our cube and calculate the matrix that represents them. We also build the
camera matrix by simply translating in the z direction. Once we have built
these matrices, we can multiply them together and pass them as uniforms
into our vertex shader. The code to do this is shown in Listing 5.21.

```
float f = (float)currentTime * (float)M_PI * 0.1f;
vmath::mat4 mv_matrix =
    vmath::translate(0.0f, 0.0f, -4.0f) *
    vmath::translate(sinf(2.1f * f) * 0.5f,
                     cosf(1.7f * f) * 0.5f,
                     sinf(1.3f * f) * cosf(1.5f * f) * 2.0f) *
    vmath::rotate((float)currentTime * 45.0f, 0.0f, 1.0f, 0.0f) *
    vmath::rotate((float)currentTime * 81.0f, 1.0f, 0.0f, 0.0f);
```

Listing 5.21: Building the model-view matrix for a spinning cube

The projection matrix can be rebuilt whenever the window size changes.
The sb6::application framework provides a function called onResize
that handles resize events. If we override this function, then when the
window size changes it will be called and we can projection matrix. We
can load that into a uniform as well in our rendering loop. If the window
size changes, we'll also need to update our viewport with a call to
glViewport(). Once we have put all our matrices into our uniforms, we
can draw the cube geometry with the **glDrawArrays()** function. The code

to update the projection matrix is shown in Listing 5.22 and the remainder of the rendering loop is shown in Listing 5.23.

```
void onResize(int w, int h)
{
    sb6::application::onResize(w, h);
    aspect = (float)info.windowWidth / (float)info.windowHeight;
    proj_matrix = vmath::perspective(50.0f,
                                     aspect,
                                     0.1f,
                                     1000.0f);
}
```

Listing 5.22: Updating the projection matrix for the spinning cube

```
// Clear the framebuffer with dark green
static const GLfloat green[] = { 0.0f, 0.25f, 0.0f, 1.0f };
glClearBufferfv(GL_COLOR, 0, green);

// Activate our program
glUseProgram(program);

// Set the model-view and projection matrices
glUniformMatrix4fv(mv_location, 1, GL_FALSE, mv_matrix);
glUniformMatrix4fv(proj_location, 1, GL_FALSE, proj_matrix);

// Draw 6 faces of 2 triangles of 3 vertices each = 36 vertices
glDrawArrays(GL_TRIANGLES, 0, 36);
```

Listing 5.23: Rendering loop for the spinning cube

Before we can actually render anything, we'll need to write a simple vertex shader to transform the vertex positions using the matrices we've been given and to pass along the color information so that the cube isn't just a flat blob. The vertex shader is shown in Listing 5.24 and the fragment shader is shown in Listing 5.25.

```
#version 430 core

in vec4 position;

out VS_OUT
{
    vec4 color;
} vs_out;

uniform mat4 mv_matrix;
uniform mat4 proj_matrix;

void main(void)
{
    gl_Position = proj_matrix * mv_matrix * position;
    vs_out.color = position * 2.0 + vec4(0.5, 0.5, 0.5, 0.0);
}
```

Listing 5.24: Spinning cube vertex shader

```
#version 430 core

out vec4 color;

in VS_OUT
{
    vec4 color;
} fs_in;

void main(void)
{
    color = fs_in.color;
}
```

Listing 5.25: Spinning cube fragment shader

A few frames of the resulting application are shown in Figure 5.2.

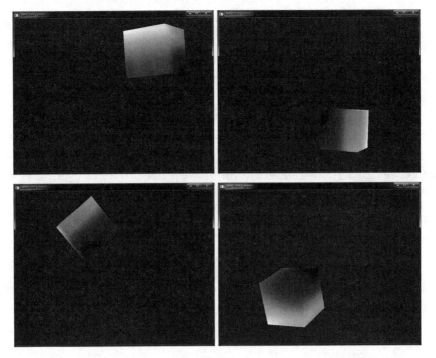

Figure 5.2: A few frames from the spinning cube application

Of course, now that we have our cube geometry in a buffer object and a model-view matrix in a uniform, there's nothing to stop us from updating the uniform and drawing many copies of the cube in a single frame. In Listing 5.26 we've modified the rendering function to calculate a new model-view matrix many times and repeatedly draw our cube. Also, because we're going to render many cubes in this example, we'll need to clear the depth buffer before rendering the frame. Although not shown here, we also modified our `startup` function to enable depth testing and set the depth test function to `GL_LEQUAL`. The result of rendering with our modified program is shown in Figure 5.3.

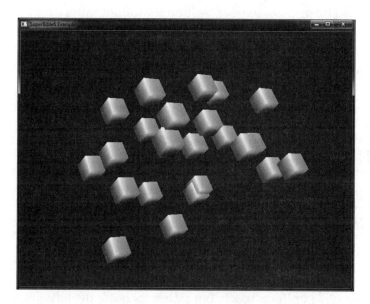

Figure 5.3: Many cubes!

```
// Clear the framebuffer with dark green and clear
// the depth buffer to 1.0
static const GLfloat green[] = { 0.0f, 0.25f, 0.0f, 1.0f };
static const GLfloat one = 1.0f;
glClearBufferfv(GL_COLOR, 0, green);
glClearBufferfv(GL_DEPTH, 0, &one);

// Activate our program
glUseProgram(program);

// Set the model-view and projection matrices
glUniformMatrix4fv(proj_location, 1, GL_FALSE, proj_matrix);

// Draw 24 cubes...
for (i = 0; i < 24; i++)
{
    // Calculate a new model-view matrix for each one
    float f = (float)i + (float)currentTime * 0.3f;
    vmath::mat4 mv_matrix =
        vmath::translate(0.0f, 0.0f, -20.0f) *
        vmath::rotate((float)currentTime * 45.0f, 0.0f, 1.0f, 0.0f) *
        vmath::rotate((float)currentTime * 21.0f, 1.0f, 0.0f, 0.0f) *
        vmath::translate(sinf(2.1f * f) * 2.0f,
                         cosf(1.7f * f) * 2.0f,
```

```
                    sinf(1.3f * f) * cosf(1.5f * f) * 2.0f);
    // Update the uniform
    glUniformMatrix4fv(mv_location, 1, GL_FALSE, mv_matrix);

    // Draw - notice that we haven't updated the projection matrix
    glDrawArrays(GL_TRIANGLES, 0, 36);
}
```

Listing 5.26: Rendering loop for the spinning cube

Shader Storage Blocks

In addition to the read-only access to buffer objects that is provided by
uniform blocks, buffer objects can also be used for general storage from
shaders using *shader storage blocks*. These are declared in a similar manner
to uniform blocks and backed in the same way by binding a range of
buffer objects to one of the indexed GL_SHADER_STORAGE_BUFFER targets.
However, the biggest difference between a uniform block and a shader
storage block is that your shader can *write* into the shader storage block
and, furthermore, it can even perform *atomic operations* on members of a
shader storage block. Shader storage blocks also have a much higher upper
size limit.

To declare a shader storage block, simply declare a block in the shader just
like you would a uniform block, but rather than use the `uniform` keyword,
use the `buffer` qualifier. Like uniform blocks, shader storage blocks
support the `std140` packing layout qualifier, but also support the `std430`[3]
packing layout qualifier, which allows arrays of integers and floating-point
variables (and structures containing them) to be tightly packed
(something that is sorely lacking from `std140`). This allows better
efficiency of memory use and tighter cohesion with structure layouts
generated by compilers for languages such as C++. An example shader
storage block declaration is shown in Listing 5.27.

```
#version 430 core

struct my_structure
{
    int         pea;
    int         carrot;
    vec4        potato;
};
```

---

3. The `std140` and `std430` packing layouts are named for the version of the shading language
with which they were introduced — `std140` with GLSL 1.40 (which was part of OpenGL 3.1),
and `std430` with GLSL 4.30, which was the version released with OpenGL 4.3.

```
layout (binding = 0, std430) buffer my_storage_block
{
    vec4            foo;
    vec3            bar;
    int             baz[24];
    my_structure    veggies;
};
```

Listing 5.27: Example shader storage block declaration

The members of a shader storage block can be referred to just as any other variable. To read from them, you could, for example use them as a parameter to a function, and to write into them you simply assign to them. When the variable is used in an expression, the source of data will be the buffer object, and when the variable is assigned to, the data will be written into the buffer object. You can place data into the buffer using functions like **glBufferData()** just as you would with a uniform block. Because the buffer is writable by the shader, if you call **glMapBuffer()** with GL_READ_ONLY (or GL_READ_WRITE) as the access mode, you will be able read the data produced by your shader.

Shader storage blocks and their backing buffer objects provide additional advantages over uniform blocks. For example, their size is not really limited. Of course, if you go overboard, OpenGL may fail to allocate memory for you, but there really isn't a hard-wired practical upper limit to the size of a shader storage block. Also, the newer packing rules for std430 allow an application's data to be more efficiently packed and directly accessed than would a uniform block. It is worth noting, though, that due to the stricter alignment requirements of uniform blocks and smaller minimum size, some hardware may handle uniform blocks differently than shader storage blocks and execute more efficiently when reading from them. Listing 5.28 shows how you might use a shader storage block in place of regular inputs in a vertex shader.

```
#version 430 core

struct vertex
{
    vec4            position;
    vec3            color;
};

layout (binding = 0, std430) buffer my_vertices
{
    vertex          vertices[];
};

uniform mat4 transform_matrix;
```

```
out VS_OUT
{
    vec3        color;
} vs_out;

void main(void)
{
    gl_Position = transform_matrix * vertices[gl_VertexID].position;
    vs_out.color = vertices[gl_VertexID].color;
}
```

Listing 5.28: Using a shader storage block in place of vertex attributes

Although it may seem that shader storage blocks offer so many advantages
that they almost make uniform blocks and vertex attributes redundant,
you should be aware that all of this additional flexibility makes it difficult
for OpenGL to make access to storage blocks truly optimal. For example,
some OpenGL implementations may be able to provide faster access to
uniform blocks given the knowledge that their content will always be
constant. Also, reading the input data for vertex attributes may happen
long before your vertex shader runs, letting OpenGL's memory subsystem
keep up. Reading vertex data right in the middle of your shader might
well slow it down quite a bit.

Atomic Memory Operations

In addition to simply reading and writing of memory, shader storage
blocks allow you to perform *atomic operations* on memory. An atomic
operation is a sequence of a read from memory potentially followed by a
write to memory that must be uninterrupted for the result to be correct.
Consider a case where two shader invocations perform the operation
m = m + 1; using the same memory location represented by m. Each
invocation will load the current value stored in the memory location
represented by m, add one to it, and then write it back to memory at the
same location.

If each invocation operates in lockstep, then we will end up with the
wrong value in memory unless the operation can be made atomic. This is
because the first invocation will load the value from memory, and then
the second invocation will read the *same* value from memory. Both
invocations will increment their copy of the value. The first invocation
will write its incremented value back to memory, and then finally, the
second invocation will overwrite that value with the same, incremented
value that it calculated. This problem only gets worse when there are
many more than two invocations running at a time.

To get around this problem, atomic operations cause the complete read-modify-write cycle to complete for one invocation before any other invocation gets a chance to even read from memory. In theory, if multiple shader invocations perform atomic operations on different memory locations, then everything should run nice and fast and work just as if you had written the naïve m = m + 1; code in your shader. If two invocations access the same memory locations (this is known as *contention*), then they will be *serialized* and only one will get to go at one time. To execute an atomic operation on a member of a shader storage block, you call one of the atomic memory functions listed in Table 5.4.

In Table 5.4, all of the functions have an integer (`int`) and unsigned integer (`uint`) version. For the integer versions, mem is declared as `inout int` mem, data and comp (for `atomicCompSwap`) are declared as `int` data, and `int` comp and the return value of all functions is `int`. Likewise, for the unsigned integer versions, all parameters are declared using `uint` and the return type of the function is `uint`. Notice that there are no atomic operations on floating-point variables, vectors, or matrices or integer values that are not 32 bits wide. All of the atomic memory access functions shown in Table 5.4 return the value that was in memory *prior* to the atomic operation taking place. When an atomic operation is attempted by multiple invocations of your shader to the same location at the same time, they are *serialized*, which means that they take turns. This means that you're not guaranteed to receive any particular return value of an atomic memory operation.

Synchronizing Access to Memory

When you are only reading from a buffer, data is *almost* always going to be available when you think it should be and you don't need to worry about the order in which your shaders read from it. However, when your shader starts writing data into buffer objects, either through writes to variables in shader storage blocks or through explicit calls to the atomic operation functions that might write to memory, there are cases where you need to avoid *hazards*.

Memory hazards fall roughly into three categories:

- A Read-After-Write (RAW) hazard can occur when your program attempts to read from a memory location right after it's written to it. Depending on the system architecture, the read and write may be re-ordered such that the read actually ends up being executed *before* the write is complete, resulting in the old data being returned to the application.

Table 5.4: Atomic Operations on Shader Storage Blocks

Atomic Function	Behavior
`atomicAdd(mem, data)`	Reads from mem, adds it to data, writes the result back to mem, and then returns the value originally stored in mem.
`atomicAnd(mem, data)`	Reads from mem, logically ANDs it with data, writes the result back to mem, and then returns the value originally stored in mem.
`atomicOr(mem, data)`	Reads from mem, logically ORs it with data, writes the result back to mem, and then returns the value originally stored in mem.
`atomicXor(mem, data)`	Reads from mem, logically exclusive ORs it with data, writes the result back to mem, and then returns the value originally stored in mem.
`atomicMin(mem, data)`	Reads from mem, determines the minimum of the retrieved value and data, writes the result back to mem, and then returns the value originally stored in mem.
`atomicMax(mem, data)`	Reads from mem, determines the maximum of the retrieved value and data, writes the result back to mem, and then returns the value originally stored in mem.
`atomicExchange(mem, data)`	Reads from mem, writes the value of data into mem, and then returns the value originally stored in mem.
`atomicCompSwap(mem, comp, data)`	Reads from mem, compares the retrieved value with comp, and if they are equal, writes the data into mem, but always returns the value originally stored in mem.

- A Write-After-Write (WAW) hazard can occur when a program performs a write to the same memory location twice in a row. You might expect that whatever data was written last would overwrite the data written first and be the values that end up staying in memory. Again, on some architectures this is not guaranteed, and in some circumstances the *first* data written by the program might actually be the data that ends up in memory.

- Finally, a Write-After-Read (WAR) hazard normally only occurs in parallel processing systems (such as graphics processors) and may happen when one thread of execution (such as a shader invocation) performs a write to memory after another thread believes that it has written to memory. If these operations are re-ordered, the thread that performed the read may end up getting the data that was written by the second thread without expecting it.

Because of the deeply pipelined and highly parallel nature of the systems that OpenGL is expected to be running on, it includes a number of mechanisms to alleviate and control memory hazards. Without these features, OpenGL implementations would need to be far more conservative about reordering your shaders and running them in parallel. The main apparatus for dealing with memory hazards is the *memory barrier*.

A memory barrier essentially acts as a marker that tells OpenGL, "Hey, if you're going to start reordering things, that's fine — just don't let anything I say after this point actually happen before anything I say before it." You can insert barriers both in your application code with calls to OpenGL, and in your shaders.

Using Barriers in Your Application

The function to insert a barrier is **glMemoryBarrier()** and its prototype is

```
void glMemoryBarrier(GLbitfield barriers);
```

The **glMemoryBarrier()** function takes a GLbitfield parameter, barriers, which allows you to specify which of OpenGL's memory subsystems should obey the barrier and which ones are free to ignore it and continue as they would have. The barrier affects ordering of memory operations in the categories specified in barriers. If you want to bash OpenGL with a big hammer and just synchronize everything, you can set barriers to GL_ALL_BARRIER_BITS. However, there are quite a number of bits defined that you can add together to be more precise about what you want to synchronize. A few examples are listed below:

- Including GL_SHADER_STORAGE_BARRIER_BIT tells OpenGL that you want it to let any accesses (writes in particular) performed by shaders that are run before the barrier complete before letting any shaders access the data after the barrier. This means that if you write into a shader storage buffer from a shader and then call **glMemoryBarrier()** with GL_SHADER_STORAGE_BARRIER_BIT included in barriers, shaders you run after the barrier will "see" that data. Without such a barrier, this is not guaranteed.

- Including GL_UNIFORM_BARRIER_BIT in barriers tells OpenGL that you might have written into memory that might be used as a uniform buffer after the barrier, and it should wait to make sure that shaders that write into the buffer have completed before letting shaders that use it as a uniform buffer run. You would set this, for example, if you wrote into a buffer using a shader storage block in a shader and then wanted to use that buffer as a uniform buffer later.

- Including GL_VERTEX_ATTRIB_ARRAY_BARRIER_BIT ensures that OpenGL will wait for shaders that write to buffers have completed before using any of those buffers as the source of vertex data through a vertex attribute. For example, you would set this if you write into a buffer through a shader storage block and then want to use that buffer as part of a vertex array to feed data into the vertex shader of a subsequent drawing command.

There are plenty more of these bits that control the ordering of shaders with respect to OpenGL's other subsystems, and we will introduce them as we talk more in depth about those subsystems. The key to remember about **glMemoryBarrier()** is that the items included in barriers are the *destination* subsystems and that the mechanism by which you updated the data isn't relevant.

Using Barriers in Your Shaders

Just as you can insert memory barriers in your application's code to control the ordering of memory accesses performed by your shaders relative to your application, you can also insert barriers into your shaders to stop OpenGL from reading or writing memory in some order other than what your shader code says. The basic memory barrier function in GLSL is

```
void memoryBarrier();
```

If you call `memoryBarrier()` from your shader code, any memory reads or writes that you might have performed will complete before the function returns. This means that it's safe to go read data back that you might have just written. Without a barrier, it's even possible that when you read from a memory location that you just wrote to that OpenGL will return *old* data to you instead of the new!

To provide finer control over what types of memory accesses are ordered, there are some more specialized versions of the `memoryBarrier()`. For example, `memoryBarrierBuffer()` orders only transactions on reads and writes to buffers, but to nothing else. We'll introduce the other barrier functions as we talk about the types of data that they protect.

Atomic Counters

Atomic counters are a special type of variable that represents storage that is shared across multiple shader invocations. This storage is backed by a buffer object, and functions are provided in GLSL to increment and decrement the values stored in the buffer. What is special about these operations is that they are *atomic*, and just as with the equivalent functions for members of shader storage blocks (shown in Table 5.4), they return the original value of the counter before it was modified. Just like the other atomic operations, if two shader invocations increment the same counter at the same time, OpenGL will make them take turns. One shader invocation will receive the original value of the counter, the other will receive the original value plus one, and the final value of the counter will be that of the original value plus two. Also, just as with shader storage block atomics, it should be noted that there is no guarantee of the order that these operations will occur, and so you can't rely on receiving any specific value.

To declare an atomic counter in a shader, do this:

```
layout (binding = 0) uniform atomic_uint my_variable;
```

OpenGL provides a number of binding points to which you can bind the buffers where it will store the values of atomic counters. Additionally, each atomic counter is stored at a specific offset within the buffer object. The buffer binding index and the offset within the buffer bound to that binding can be specified using the **binding** and **offset** layout qualifiers that can be applied to an atomic counter uniform declaration. For example, if we wish to place `my_variable` at offset 8 within the buffer bound to the buffer bound to atomic counter binding point 3, then we could write

```
layout (binding = 3, offset = 8) uniform atomic_uint my_variable;
```

In order to provide storage for the atomic counter, we can now bind a buffer object to the GL_ATOMIC_COUNTER_BUFFER indexed binding point. Listing 5.29 shows how to do this.

```
// Generate a buffer name
GLuint buf;
glGenBuffers(1, &buf);
// Bind it to the generic GL_ATOMIC_COUNTER_BUFFER target and
// initialize its storage
glBindBuffer(GL_ATOMIC_COUNTER_BUFFER, buf);
glBufferData(GL_ATOMIC_COUNTER_BUFFER, 16 * sizeof(GLuint),
             NULL, GL_DYNAMIC_COPY);
// Now bind it to the fourth indexed atomic counter buffer target
glBindBufferBase(GL_ATOMIC_COUNTER_BUFFER, 3, buf);
```

Listing 5.29: Setting up an atomic counter buffer

Before using the atomic counter in your shader, it's a good idea to reset it first. To do this, you can either call **glBufferSubData()** and pass the address of a variable holding the value you want to reset the counter(s) to, map the buffer using **glMapBufferRange()**, and write the values directly into it, or use **glClearBufferSubData()**. Listing 5.30 shows an example of all three methods.

```
// Bind our buffer to the generic atomic counter buffer
// binding point
glBindBuffer(GL_ATOMIC_COUNTER_BUFFER, buf);

// Method 1 - use glBufferSubData to reset an atomic counter.
const GLuint zero = 0;
glBufferSubData(GL_ATOMIC_COUNTER_BUFFER, 2 * sizeof(GLuint),
                sizeof(GLuint), &zero);

// Method 2 - Map the buffer and write the value directly into it
GLuint * data =
    (GLuint *)glMapBufferRange(GL_ATOMIC_COUNTER_BUFFER,
                               0, 16 * sizeof(GLuint),
                               GL_MAP_WRITE_BIT |
                               GL_MAP_INVALIDATE_RANGE_BIT);
data[2] = 0;
glUnmapBuffer(GL_ATOMIC_COUNTER_BUFFER);

// Method 3 - use glClearBufferSubData
glClearBufferSubData(GL_ATOMIC_COUNTER_BUFFER,
                     GL_R32UI,
                     2 * sizeof(GLuint),
                     sizeof(GLuint),
                     GL_RED_INTEGER, GL_UNSIGNED_INT,
                     &zero);
```

Listing 5.30: Setting up an atomic counter buffer

Now that you have created a buffer and bound it to an atomic counter buffer target, and you declared an atomic counter uniform in your shader, you are ready to start counting things. First, to increment an atomic counter, call

```
uint atomicCounterIncrement(atomic_uint c);
```

This function reads the current value of the atomic counter, adds one to it, writes the new value back to the atomic counter, and returns the original value it read, and it does it all atomically. Because the order of execution between different invocations of your shader is not defined, calling atomicCounterIncrement twice in a row won't necessarily give you two consecutive values. To decrement an atomic counter, call

```
uint atomicCounterDecrement(atomic_uint c);
```

This function reads the current value of the atomic counter, subtracts one from it, writes the value back into the atomic counter and returns the *new* value of the counter to you. Notice that this is the opposite of atomicCounterIncrement. If only one invocation of a shader is executing, and it calls atomicCounterIncrement followed by atomicCounterDecrement, it should receive the same value from both functions. However, in most cases, many invocations of the shader will be executing in parallel, and in practice, it is unlikely that you will receive the same value from a pair of calls to these functions. If you simply want to know the value of an atomic counter, you can call

```
uint atomicCounter(atomic_uint c);
```

This function simply returns the current value stored in the atomic counter c. As an example of using atomic counters, Listing 5.31 shows a simple fragment shader that increments an atomic counter each time it executes. This has the effect of producing the screen space area of the objects rendered with this shader in the atomic counter.

```
#version 430 core

layout (binding = 0, offset = 0) uniform atomic_uint area;

void main(void)
{
    atomicCounterIncrement(area);
}
```

Listing 5.31: Counting area using an atomic counter

One thing you might notice about the shader in Listing 5.31 is that it doesn't have any regular outputs (variables declared with the **out** storage qualifier) and won't write any data into the framebuffer. In fact, we'll disable writing to the framebuffer while we run this shader. To turn off writing to the framebuffer, we can call

```
glColorMask(GL_FALSE, GL_FALSE, GL_FALSE, GL_FALSE);
```

To turn framebuffer writes back on again, we can call

```
glColorMask(GL_TRUE, GL_TRUE, GL_TRUE, GL_TRUE);
```

Because atomic counters are stored in buffers, it's possible now to bind our atomic counter to another buffer target, such as one of the GL_UNIFORM_BUFFER targets, and retrieve its value in a shader. This allows us to use the value of an atomic counter to control the execution of shaders that your program runs later. Listing 5.32 shows an example shader that reads the result of our atomic counter through a uniform block and uses it as part of the calculation of its output color.

```
#version 430 core

layout (binding = 0) uniform area_block
{
    uint    counter_value;
};

out vec4 color;

uniform float max_area;

void main(void)
{
    float brightness = clamp(float(counter_value) / max_area,
                             0.0, 1.0);

    color = vec4(brightness, brightness, brightness, 1.0);
}
```

Listing 5.32: Using the result of an atomic counter in a uniform block

When we execute the shader in Listing 5.31, it simply counts the area of the geometry that's being rendered. That area then shows up in Listing 5.32 as the first and only member of the area_block uniform buffer block. We divide it by the maximum expected area and then use that as the brightness of further geometry. Consider what happens when we render with these two shaders. If an object is close to the viewer, it will appear larger and cover more screen area — the ultimate value of the atomic counter will be greater. When the object is far from the viewer, it will be smaller and the atomic counter won't reach such a high value. The value of the atomic counter will be reflected in the uniform block in the second shader, affecting the brightness of the geometry it renders.

Synchronizing Access to Atomic Counters

Atomic counters represent locations in buffer objects. While shaders are executing, their values may well reside in special memory inside the graphics processor (which is what makes them faster than simple atomic memory operations on members of shader storage blocks, for example). However, when your shader is done executing, the values of the atomic counters will be written back into memory. As such, incrementing and decrementing atomic counters is considered a form of memory operation and so can be susceptible to the *hazards* described earlier in this chapter. In fact, the **glMemoryBarrier()** function supports a bit specifically for synchronizing access to atomic counters with other parts of the OpenGL pipeline. Calling

```
glMemoryBarrier(GL_ATOMIC_COUNTER_BARRIER_BIT);
```

will ensure that any access to an atomic counter in a buffer object will reflect updates to that buffer by a shader. You should call **glMemoryBarrier()** with the GL_ATOMIC_COUNTER_BARRIER_BIT set when something has *written* to a buffer that you want to see reflected in the values of your atomic counters. If you update the values in a buffer using an atomic counter and then use that buffer for something else, the bit you include in the barriers parameter to **glMemoryBarrier()** should correspond to what you want that buffer to be used for, which will not necessarily include GL_ATOMIC_COUNTER_BARRIER_BIT.

Similarly, there is a version of the GLSL memoryBarrier() function, memoryBarrierAtomicCounter(), that ensures that operations on atomic counters are completed before it returns.

Textures

Textures are a structured form of storage that can be made accessible to shaders both for reading and writing. They are most often used to store image data and come in many forms. Perhaps the most common texture layout is two dimensional, but textures can also be created in one-dimensional or three-dimensional layouts, array forms (with multiple textures stacked together to form one logical object), cubes, and so on. Textures are represented as objects that can be generated, bound to *texture units*, and manipulated. To create a texture, first we need to ask OpenGL to reserve a name for us by calling **glGenTextures()**. At this point, the name we get back represents a yet-to-be-created texture object, and it only begins its life as a texture once it's been bound to a *texture target*. This is similar to binding a buffer object to one of the buffer binding points. However, once you bind a texture name to a texture target, it takes the *type* of that target until it is destroyed.

Creating and Initializing Textures

The full creation of a texture involves generating a name and binding it to one of the texture targets, and then telling OpenGL what size image you want to store in it. Listing 5.33 shows how to generate a name for a texture object using **glGenTextures()**, use **glBindTexture()** to bind it to the GL_TEXTURE_2D target (which is one of several available texture targets), and then use the **glTexStorage2D()** function to allocate storage for the texture.

```
// The type used for names in OpenGL is GLuint
GLuint texture;

// Generate a name for the texture
glGenTextures(1, &texture);

// Now bind it to the context using the GL_TEXTURE_2D binding point
glBindTexture(GL_TEXTURE_2D, texture);

// Specify the amount of storage we want to use for the texture
glTexStorage2D(GL_TEXTURE_2D,    // 2D texture
               1,                // 1 mipmap level
               GL_RGBA32F,       // 32-bit floating-point RGBA data
               256, 256);        // 256 x 256 texels
```

Listing 5.33: Generating, binding, and initializing a texture

Compare Listing 5.33 and Listing 5.1 and note how similar they are. In both cases, you reserve a name for an object, bind it to a target, and then define the storage for the data they contain. For textures, the function we've used to do this is **glTexStorage2D()**. It takes as parameters the target for the operation, which is the one we used to bind the texture; the number of *levels* that are used in *mipmapping*, which we are not using here (but will explain shortly); the *internal format* of the texture (we chose GL_RGBA32F here, which is a four-channel floating-point format); and the width and height of the texture. When we call this function, OpenGL will allocate enough memory to store a texture with those dimensions for us. Next, we need to specify some data for the texture. To do this, we use **glTexSubImage2D()** as shown in Listing 5.34.

```
// Define some data to upload into the texture
float * data = new float[256 * 256 * 4];

// generate_texture() is a function that fills memory with image data
```

```
generate_texture(data, 256, 256);

// Assume the texture is already bound to the GL_TEXTURE_2D target
glTexSubImage2D(GL_TEXTURE_2D,    // 2D texture
                0,                // Level 0
                0, 0,             // Offset 0, 0
                256, 256,         // 256 x 256 texels, replace entire image
                GL_RGBA,          // Four channel data
                GL_FLOAT,         // Floating-point data
                data);            // Pointer to data

// Free the memory we allocated before - OpenGL now has our data
delete [] data;
```

Listing 5.34: Updating texture data with **glTexSubImage2D()**

Texture Targets and Types

The example in Listing 5.34 demonstrates how to create a 2D texture by binding a new name to the 2D texture target specified with GL_TEXTURE_2D. This is just one of several targets that are available to bind textures to, and a new texture object takes on the type determined by the target to which it is first bound. Thus, texture targets and types are often used interchangeably. Table 5.5 lists the available targets and describes the type of texture that will be created when a new name is bound to that target.

Table 5.5: Texture Targets and Description

Texture Target (GL_TEXTURE_*)	Description
1D	One-dimensional texture
2D	Two-dimensional texture
3D	Three-dimensional texture
RECTANGLE	Rectangle texture
1D_ARRAY	One-dimensional array texture
2D_ARRAY	Two-dimensional array texture
CUBE_MAP	Cube map texture
CUBE_MAP_ARRAY	Cube map array texture
BUFFER	Buffer texture
2D_MULTISAMPLE	Two-dimensional multi-sample texture
2D_MULTISAMPLE_ARRAY	Two-dimensional array multi-sample texture

The GL_TEXTURE_2D texture target is probably the one you will deal with the most. This is our standard, two-dimensional image that you imagine could be wrapped around objects. The GL_TEXTURE_1D and GL_TEXTURE_3D types allow you to create one-dimensional and three-dimensional textures, respectively. A 1D texture behaves just like a 2D texture with a height of 1, for the most part. A 3D texture, on the other hand, can be used to represent a *volume* and actually has a three-dimensional texture coordinate. The rectangle texture[4] is a special case of 2D textures that have subtle differences in how they are read in shaders and which parameters they support.

The GL_TEXTURE_1D_ARRAY and GL_TEXTURE_2D_ARRAY types represent arrays of texture images aggregated into single object. They are covered in more detail later in this chapter. Likewise, cube map textures (created by binding a texture name to the GL_TEXTURE_CUBE_MAP target) represent a collection of six square images that form a cube, which can be used to simulate lighting environments, for example. Just as the GL_TEXTURE_1D_ARRAY and GL_TEXTURE_2D_ARRAY represent 1D and 2D textures that are arrays of 1D or 2D images, the GL_TEXTURE_CUBE_MAP_ARRAY target represents a texture that is an array of cube maps.

Buffer textures, represented by the GL_TEXTURE_BUFFER target, are a special type of texture that are much like a 1D texture, except that their storage is actually represented by a buffer object. Besides this, they differ from a 1D texture in that their maximum size can be much larger than a 1D texture. The minimum requirement from the OpenGL specification is 65536 texels, but in practice most implementations will allow you to create much larger buffers — usually in the range of several hundred megabytes. Buffer textures also lack a few of the features supported by the 1D texture type such as filtering and mipmaps.

Finally, the multi-sample texture types GL_TEXTURE_2D_MULTISAMPLE and GL_TEXTURE_2D_MULTISAMPLE_ARRAY are used for *multi-sample antialiasing*, which is a technique for improving image quality, especially at the edges of lines and polygons.

---

4. Rectangle textures were introduced into OpenGL when not all hardware could support textures whose dimensions were not integer powers of two. Modern graphics hardware supports this almost universally, and so rectangle textures have essentially become a subset of the 2D texture and there isn't much need to use one in preference to a 2D texture.

Reading from Textures in Shaders

Once you've created a texture object and placed some data in it, you can read that data in your shaders and use it to color fragments, for example. Textures are represented in shaders as *sampler variables* and are hooked up to the outside world by declaring uniforms with sampler types. Just as there can be textures with various dimensionalities and that can be created and used through the various texture targets, there are corresponding sampler variable types that can be used in GLSL to represent them. The sampler type that represents two-dimensional textures is `sampler2D`. To access our texture in a shader, we can create a uniform variable with the `sampler2D` type, and then use the `texelFetch` built-in function with that uniform and a set of texture coordinates at which to read from the texture. Listing 5.35 shows an example of how to read from a texture in GLSL.

```
#version 430 core

uniform sampler2D s;

out vec4 color;

void main(void)
{
    color = texelFetch(s, ivec2(gl_FragCoord.xy), 0);
}
```

Listing 5.35: Reading from a texture in GLSL

The shader of Listing 5.35 simply reads from the uniform sampler s using a texture coordinate derived from the built-in variable `gl_FragCoord`. This variable is an input to the fragment shader that holds the floating-point coordinate of the fragment being processed in window coordinates. However, the `texelFetch` function accepts integer-point coordinates that range from $(0, 0)$ to the width and height of the texture. Therefore, we construct a two-component integer vector (**ivec2**) from the x and y components of `gl_FragCoord`. The third parameter to `texelFetch` is the mipmap level of the texture. Because the texture in this example has only one level, we set this to zero. The result of using this shader with our single-triangle example is shown in Figure 5.4.

Sampler Types

Each dimensionality of texture has a target to which texture objects are bound, which were introduced in the previous section, and each target has a corresponding sampler type that is used in your shader to access

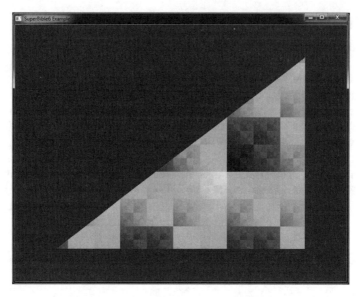

Figure 5.4: A simple textured triangle

them. Table 5.6 lists the basic texture types and the sampler that should be used in shaders to access them.

Table 5.6: Basic Texture Targets and Sampler Types

Texture Target	Sampler Type
GL_TEXTURE_1D	sampler1D
GL_TEXTURE_2D	sampler2D
GL_TEXTURE_3D	sampler3D
GL_TEXTURE_RECTANGLE	sampler2DRect
GL_TEXTURE_1D_ARRAY	sampler1DArray
GL_TEXTURE_2D_ARRAY	sampler2DArray
GL_TEXTURE_CUBE_MAP	samplerCube
GL_TEXTURE_CUBE_MAP_ARRAY	samplerCubeArray
GL_TEXTURE_BUFFER	samplerBuffer
GL_TEXTURE_2D_MULTISAMPLE	sampler2DMS
GL_TEXTURE_2D_MULTISAMPLE_ARRAY	sampler2DMSArray

You should be able to see from the table that to create a 1D texture and then use it in your shader, you would bind a new texture name to the

GL_TEXTURE_1D target and then use a `sampler1D` variable in your shader to read from it. Likewise, for 2D textures, you'd use GL_TEXTURE_2D and `sampler2D`, and for 3D textures, you'd use GL_TEXTURE_3D and `sampler3D`, and so on.

The GLSL sampler types `sampler1D`, `sampler2D`, and so on represent floating-point data. It is also possible to store signed and unsigned integer data in textures and retrieve that in your shader. To represent a texture containing signed integer data, we prefix the equivalent floating-point sampler type with i. Similarly, to represent a texture containing unsigned integer data, we prefix the equivalent floating-point sampler type with u. For example, a 2D texture containing signed integer data would be represented by a variable of type `isampler2D`, and a 2D texture containing unsigned integer data would be represented by a variable of type `usampler2D`.

As shown in our introductory example of Listing 5.35, we read from textures in shaders using the `texelFetch` built-in function. There are actually many variations of this function as it is *overloaded*. This means that there are several versions of the function that each have a different set of function parameters. Each function takes a sampler variable as the first parameter, with the main differentiator between the functions being the type of that sampler. The remaining parameters to the function depend on the type of sampler being used. In particular, the number of components in the texture coordinate depend on the dimensionality of the sampler, and the return type of the function depends on the type of the sampler (floating point, signed integer, or unsigned integer). For example, the following are all declarations of the `texelFetch` function:

```
vec4 texelFetch(sampler1D s, int P, int lod);
vec4 texelFetch(sampler2D s, ivec2 P, int lod);
ivec4 texelFetch(isampler2D s, ivec2 P, int lod);
uvec4 texelFetch(usampler3D s, ivec3 P, int lod);
```

Notice how the version of `texelFetch` that takes a `sampler1D` sampler type expects a one-dimensional texture coordinate, `int` P, but the version that takes a `sampler2D` expects a two-dimensional coordinate, `ivec2` P. You can also see that the return type of the `texelFetch` function is influenced by the type of sampler that it takes. The version of `texelFetch` that takes a `sampler2D` produces a floating-point vector, whereas the version that takes a `isampler2D` sampler returns an integer vector. This type of overloading is similar to that supported by languages such as C++. That is, functions can be overloaded by parameter types, but not by return type, unless that return type is determined by one of the parameters.

All of the texture functions return a four-component vector, regardless of whether that vector is floating point or integer, and independently from the format of the texture object bound to the texture unit referenced by the sampler variable. If you read from a texture that contains fewer than four channels, the default value of zero will be filled in for the green and blue channels and one for the alpha channel. If one or more channels of the returned data never gets used by your shader, that's fine, and it is likely that the shader compiler will optimize away any code that becomes redundant as a result.

Loading Textures from Files

In our simple example, we generated the texture data directly in our application. However, this clearly isn't practical in a real-world application where you most likely have images stored on disk or on the other end of a network connection. Your options are either to convert your textures into hard-coded arrays (yes, there are utilities that will do this for you) or to load them from files within your application.

There are lots of image file formats that store pictures with or without compression, some of which are more suited to photographs and some more suited to line drawings or text. However, very few image formats exist that can properly store all of the formats supported by OpenGL or represent advanced features such as mipmaps, cubemaps, and so on. One such format is the .KTX format, or the *Khronos TeXture format*, which was specifically designed for the storage of pretty much anything that can be represented as an OpenGL texture. In fact, the .KTX file format includes most of the parameters you need to pass to texturing functions such as **glTexStorage2D()** and **glTexSubImage2D()** in order to load the texture directly in the file.

The structure of a .KTX file header is shown in Listing 5.36.

```
struct header
{
    unsigned char      identifier[12];
    unsigned int       endianness;
    unsigned int       gltype;
    unsigned int       gltypesize;
    unsigned int       glformat;
    unsigned int       glinternalformat;
    unsigned int       glbaseinternalformat;
    unsigned int       pixelwidth;
    unsigned int       pixelheight;
    unsigned int       pixeldepth;
```

```
            unsigned int        arrayelements;
            unsigned int        faces;
            unsigned int        miplevels;
            unsigned int        keypairbytes;
        };
```

Listing 5.36: The header of a .KTX file

In this header, identifier contains a series of bytes that allow the
application to verify that this is a legal .KTX file and endianness
contains a known value that will be different depending on whether a
little-endian or big-endian machine created the file. The gltype,
glformat, glinternalformat, and glbaseinternalformat fields are
actually the raw values of the GLenum types that will be used to load the
texture. The gltypesize field stores the size, in bytes, of one element of
data in the gltype type, and is used in case the endianness of the file does
not match the native endianness of the machine loading the file, in which
case, each element of the texture must be byte-swapped as it is loaded. The
remaining fields, pixelwidth, pixelheight, pixeldepth, arrayelements,
faces, and miplevels, store information about the dimensions of the
texture. Finally, the keypairbytes field is used to allow applications to
store additional information after the header and before the texture data.
After this information, the raw texture data begins.

Because the .KTX file format was designed specifically for use in
OpenGL-based applications, writing the code to load .KTX file is actually
pretty straightforward. Even so, a basic loader for .KTX files is included in
this book's source code. To use the loader, you can simply reserve a new
name for a texture using **glGenTextures()**, and then pass it, along with the
filename of the .KTX file, to the loader. If you wish, you can even omit the
OpenGL name for the texture (or pass zero) and the loader will call
glGenTextures() for you. If the .KTX file is recognized, the loader will bind
the texture to the appropriate target and load it with the data from the
.KTX file. An example is shown in Listing 5.37.

```
// Generate a name for the texture
glGenTextures(1, &texture);

// Load texture from file
sb6::ktx::file::load("media/textures/icemoon.ktx", texture);
```

Listing 5.37: Loading a .KTX file

If you think that Listing 5.37 looks simple... you'd be right. The .KTX
loader takes care of almost all the details for you. If the loader was
successful in loading and allocating the texture, it will return the name

of the texture you passed in (or the one it generated for you), and if it fails for some reason, it will return zero. After the loader returns, it leaves the texture bound to the texture unit that was active when it was called. That means that you can call **glActiveTexture()**, then call sb6::ktx::file::load, and the texture will be left bound to your selected texture unit. Don't forget to delete the texture when you're done with it by calling **glDeleteTextures()** on the name returned by the .KTX loader. Applying the texture loaded in the example above to the whole viewport produces the image shown in Figure 5.5.

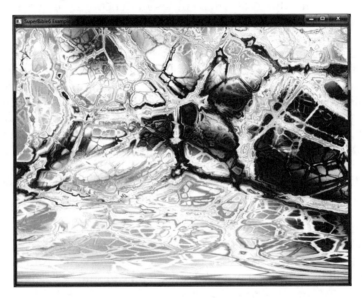

Figure 5.5: A full-screen texture loaded from a .KTX file

Texture Coordinates

In the simple example shown earlier in this chapter, we simply used the current fragment's window-space coordinate as the position at which to read from the texture. However, you can use any value you want, but in a fragment shader, they will usually be derived from one of the inputs that are smoothly interpolated from across each primitive by OpenGL. It is then the vertex (or geometry or tessellation evaluation) shader's responsibility to produce the values of these coordinates. The vertex shader will generally pull the texture coordinates from a per-vertex input and pass them through unmodified. When you use multiple textures in your fragment shader, there is nothing to stop you from using a unique set of texture coordinates for each texture, but for most applications, a single set of texture coordinates would be used for every texture.

A simple vertex shader that accepts a single texture coordinate and passes it through to the fragment shader is shown in Listing 5.38 with the corresponding fragment shader shown in Listing 5.39.

```
#version 430 core

uniform mat4 mv_matrix;
uniform mat4 proj_matrix;

layout (location = 0) in vec4 position;
layout (location = 4) in vec2 tc;

out VS_OUT
{
    vec2 tc;
} vs_out;

void main(void)
{
    // Calculate the position of each vertex
    vec4 pos_vs = mv_matrix * position;

    // Pass the texture coordinate through unmodified
    vs_out.tc = tc;

    gl_Position = proj_matrix * pos_vs;
}
```

Listing 5.38: Vertex shader with single texture coordinate

The shader shown in Listing 5.39 not only takes as input the texture coordinate produced by the vertex shader, but also scales it non-uniformly. The textures wrapping modes are set to GL_REPEAT, which means that the texture will be repeated several times across the object.

```
#version 430 core

layout (binding = 0) uniform sampler2D tex_object;

// Input from vertex shader
in VS_OUT
{
    vec2 tc;
} fs_in;

// Output to framebuffer
out vec4 color;

void main(void)
{
    // Simply read from the texture at the (scaled) coordinates, and
    // assign the result to the shader's output.
    color = texture(tex_object, fs_in.tc * vec2(3.0, 1.0));
}
```

Listing 5.39: Fragment shader with single texture coordinate

By passing a texture coordinate with each vertex, we can *wrap* a texture around an object. Texture coordinates can then be generated offline procedurally or assigned by hand by an artist using a modeling program and stored in an object file. If we load a simple checkerboard pattern into a texture and apply it to an object, we can see how the texture is wrapped around it. Such an example is shown in Figure 5.6. On the left is the object with a checkerboard pattern wrapped around it. On the right is the same object using a texture loaded from a file.

Figure 5.6: An object wrapped in simple textures

Controlling How Texture Data Is Read

OpenGL provides a lot of flexibility in how it reads data from textures and returns it to your shader. Usually, texture coordinates are normalized — that is, they range between 0.0 and 1.0. OpenGL lets you control what happens when the texture coordinates you supply fall outside this range. This is called the *wrapping mode* of the sampler. Also, you get to decide how values *between* the real samples are calculated. This is called the *filtering mode* of a sampler. The parameters controlling the wrapping and filtering mode of a sampler are stored in a *sampler object*.

To create one or more sampler objects, call

```
void glGenSamplers(GLsizei n, GLuint * samplers);
```

Here, n is the number of sampler objects you want to create, and `samplers` is the address of at least n unsigned integer variables that will be used to store the names of the newly created sampler objects.

Sampler objects are manipulated slightly differently than other objects in OpenGL. The two main functions you will use to set the parameters of a sampler object are

```
void glSamplerParameteri(GLuint sampler,
                         GLenum pname,
                         GLint param);
```

and

```
void glSamplerParameterf(GLuint sampler,
                         GLenum pname,
                         GLfloat param);
```

Notice that **glSamplerParameteri()** and **glSamplerParameterf()** both take the sampler object name as the first parameter. This means that you can directly modify a sampler object without binding it to a target first. You will need to bind a sampler object to use it, but in this case, you bind it to a texture unit just as you would a texture. The function used to bind a sampler object to one of the texture units is **glBindSampler()**, whose prototype is

```
void glBindSampler(GLuint unit, GLuint sampler);
```

For **glBindSampler()**, rather than taking a texture target, it takes the index of the texture unit to which to bind the sampler object. Together, the sampler object and texture object bound to a given texture unit form a complete set of data and parameters required for constructing texels as demanded by your shaders. By separating the parameters of the texture sampler from the texture data, this provides three important behaviors:

- It allows you to use the same set of sampling parameters for a large number of textures without needing to specify those parameters for each of the textures.

- It allows you to change the texture bound to a texture unit without updating the sampler parameters.

- It allows you to read from the same texture with multiple sets of sampler parameters at the same time.

Although non-trivial applications will likely opt to use their own sampler objects, each texture effectively contains an embedded sampler object that contains the sampling parameters to be used for that texture when no sampler object is bound to the corresponding texture unit. You can think of this as the default sampling parameters for a texture. To access the sampler object stored inside a texture object, you need to bind it to its target and then call

```
void glTexParameterf(GLenum target,
                     GLenum pname,
                     GLfloat param);
```

or

```
void glTexParameteri(GLenum target,
                     GLenum pname,
                     GLint param);
```

In these cases, the `target` parameter specifies the target to which the texture you want to access is bound, and pname and param have the same meanings as for **glSamplerParameteri()** and **glSamplerParameterf()**.

Using Multiple Textures

If you want to use multiple textures in a single shader, you will need to create multiple sampler uniforms and set them up to reference different texture units. You'll also need to bind multiple textures to your context at the same time. To allow this, OpenGL supports multiple texture units. The number of units supported can be queried by calling **glGetIntegerv()** with the GL_MAX_COMBINED_TEXTURE_IMAGE_UNITS parameter, as in

```
GLint units;
glGetIntegerv(GL_MAX_COMBINED_TEXTURE_IMAGE_UNITS, &units);
```

This will tell you the maximum number of texture units that might be accessible to all shader stages at any one time. To bind a texture to a specific texture unit, you first need to change the active texture unit *selector*, by calling **glActiveTexture()** with a texture unit identifier. This identifier is the value of the token GL_TEXTURE0 plus the index of the texture unit you want to select. For example, to select texture unit 5, call

```
glActiveTexture(GL_TEXTURE0 + 5);
```

For your convenience, the standard OpenGL header files define the tokens GL_TEXTURE1 through GL_TEXTURE31 as the values of GL_TEXTURE0 plus the values 1 through 31. Given this, to bind three textures to your context, you could use code such as

```
GLuint textures[3];

glGenTextures(3, &textures);

glActiveTexture(GL_TEXTURE0);
glBindTexture(GL_TEXTURE_2D, textures[0]);

glActiveTexture(GL_TEXTURE1);
glBindTexture(GL_TEXTURE_2D, textures[1]);

glActiveTexture(GL_TEXTURE2);
glBindTexture(GL_TEXTURE_2D, textures[2]);
```

Once you have bound multiple textures to your context, you need to make the sampler uniforms in your shaders refer to the different units. There are two ways to do this; the first is to use the `glUniform1i()` function to set the value of the sampler uniform directly from your application's code. Because samplers are declared as uniforms in your shader code, you can call `glGetUniformLocation()` to find their location and then modify their value. Sampler variables don't have a value that can actually be read as an integer in shaders, but for the purposes of setting the texture unit to which it refers, it is treated as an integer uniform and hence the use of the `glUniform1i()` function. The second way to set the texture unit referred to by a sampler uniform is to initialize its value at shader compilation time by using the `binding` layout qualifier in your shader code. To create three sampler uniforms referring to texture units 0, 1, and 2, we can write

```
layout (binding = 0) uniform sampler2D foo;
layout (binding = 1) uniform sampler2D bar;
layout (binding = 2) uniform sampler2D baz;
```

After compiling this code and linking it into a program object, the sampler `foo` will reference texture unit 0, `bar` will reference unit 1, and `baz` will reference unit 2. The unit to which the sampler uniform refers can still be changed after the program has been linked by calling the `glUniform1i()` function. However, setting the unit directly in the shader code is far more convenient and does not require changes to the application's source code. This is the method we will use in the majority of the samples in the remainder of the book.

Texture Filtering

There is almost never a one-to-one correspondence between texels in the texture map and pixels on the screen. A careful programmer could achieve this result, but only by texturing geometry that was carefully planned to appear on-screen such that the texels and pixels lined up. (This is actually often done when OpenGL is used for image processing applications.) Consequently, texture images are always either stretched or shrunk as they are applied to geometric surfaces. Due to the orientation of the geometry, a given texture could even be stretched and shrunk at the same time across the surface of some object.

In the samples presented so far, we have been using the `texelFetch()` function, which fetches a single texel from the selected texture at specific integer texture coordinates. Clearly, to achieve a fragment-to-texel ratio that is not an integer, this function isn't going to cut it. Here, we need a more flexible function, and that function is simply called `texture()`. Like `texelFetch()`, it has several overloaded prototypes:

```
vec4  texture(sampler1D s, float P);
vec4  texture(sampler2D s, vec2 P);
ivec4 texture(isampler2D s, vec2 P);
uvec4 texture(usampler3D s, vec3 P);
```

As you might have noticed, unlike the `texelFetch()` function, the `texture()` function accepts *floating-point* texture coordinates. The range 0.0 to 1.0 in each dimension maps exactly once onto the texture. However, the texture coordinates can have any value in between, and can even stray far outside the range 0.0 to 1.0. The next few sections describe how OpenGL takes these floating-point numbers and uses them to produce texel values for your shaders.

The process of calculating color fragments from a stretched or shrunken texture map is called *texture filtering*. Stretching a texture is also known as *magnification*, and shrinking a texture is also known as *minification*. Using the sampler parameter functions, OpenGL allows you to set both magnification and minification filters. The parameter names for these two filters are `GL_TEXTURE_MAG_FILTER` and `GL_TEXTURE_MIN_FILTER`. For now, you can select from two basic texture filters for them, `GL_NEAREST` and `GL_LINEAR`, which correspond to nearest neighbor and linear filtering. Make sure you always choose one of these two filters for the `GL_TEXTURE_MIN_FILTER` — the default filter setting does not work without mipmaps (see the next section "Mipmaps").

Nearest neighbor filtering is the simplest and fastest filtering method you can choose. Texture coordinates are evaluated and plotted against a texture's texels, and whichever texel the coordinate falls in, that color is used for the fragment texture color. Nearest neighbor filtering is characterized by large blocky pixels when the texture is stretched especially large. An example is shown on the left of Figure 5.7. You can set the texture filter for both the minification and the magnification filter by using these two function calls:

```
glSamplerParameteri(sampler, GL_TEXTURE_MIN_FILTER, GL_NEAREST);
glSamplerParameteri(sampler, GL_TEXTURE_MAG_FILTER, GL_NEAREST);
```

Linear filtering requires more work than nearest neighbor but often is worth the extra overhead. On today's commodity hardware, the extra cost of linear filtering is usually zero. Linear filtering works by not taking the nearest texel to the texture coordinate, but by applying the weighted average of the texels surrounding the texture coordinate (a linear interpolation). For this interpolated fragment to match the texel color exactly, the texture coordinate needs to fall directly in the center of the texel. Linear filtering is characterized by "fuzzy" graphics when a texture is stretched. This fuzziness, however, often lends a more realistic and less artificial look than the jagged blocks of the nearest neighbor filtering mode. A contrasting example is shown on the right of Figure 5.7. You can set linear filtering simply enough by using the following lines:

```
glSamplerParameteri(sampler, GL_TEXTURE_MIN_FILTER, GL_LINEAR);
glSamplerParameteri(sampler, GL_TEXTURE_MAG_FILTER, GL_LINEAR);
```

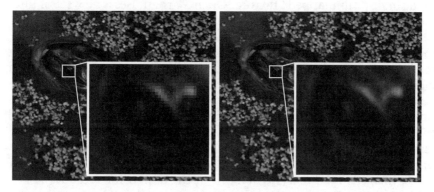

Figure 5.7: Texture filtering — nearest (left) and linear (right)

Mipmaps

Mipmapping is a powerful texturing technique that can improve both the rendering performance and the visual quality of a scene. It does this by addressing two common problems with standard texture mapping. The first is an effect called scintillation (aliasing artifacts) that appears on the surface of objects rendered very small on-screen compared to the relative size of the texture applied. Scintillation can be seen as a sort of sparkling that occurs as the sampling area on a texture map moves disproportionately to its size on the screen. The negative effects of scintillation are most noticeable when the camera or the objects are in motion.

The second issue is more performance related but is due to the same scenario that leads to scintillation. That is, a large amount of texture memory is used to store the texture, but it is accessed very sparsely as adjacent fragments on the screen access texels that are disconnected in texture space. This causes texturing performance to suffer greatly as the size of the texture increases and the sparsity of access becomes greater.

The solution to both of these problems is to simply use a smaller texture map. However, this solution then creates a new problem: When near the same object, it must be rendered larger, and a small texture map will then be stretched to the point of creating a hopelessly blurry or blocky textured object. The solution to both of these issues is *mipmapping*. Mipmapping gets its name from the Latin phrase *multum in parvo*, which means "many things in a small place." In essence, you load not only a single image into the texture object, but a whole series of images from largest to smallest into a single "mipmapped" texture. OpenGL then uses a new set of filter modes to choose the best-fitting texture or textures for the given geometry. At the cost of some extra memory (and possibly considerably more processing work), you can eliminate scintillation and the texture memory processing overhead for distant objects simultaneously, while maintaining higher resolution versions of the texture available when needed.

A mipmapped texture consists of a series of texture images, each one-half the size on each axis or one-fourth the total number of pixels of the previous image. This scenario is shown in Figure 5.8. Mipmap levels do not have to be square, but the halving of the dimensions continues until the last image is 1×1 texel. When one of the dimensions reaches 1, further divisions occur on the other dimension only. For 2D textures, using a square set of mipmaps requires about one-third more memory than not using mipmaps at all.

Mipmap levels are loaded with **glTexSubImage2D()** (for 2D textures). Now the level parameter comes into play because it specifies which mip level the image data is for. The first level is 0, then 1, 2, and so on. If mipmapping is not being used, you would usually use only level 0. When you allocate your texture with **glTexStorage2D()** (or the appropriate function for the type of texture you're allocating), you can set the number of levels to include in the texture in the levels parameter. Then, you can use mipmapping with the levels present in the texture. You can further constrain the number of mipmap levels that will be used during rendering by setting the base and maximum levels to be used with the GL_TEXTURE_BASE_LEVEL and GL_TEXTURE_MAX_LEVEL texture parameters. For example, if you want to specify that only mip levels 0 through 4 should be accessed, you call glTexParameteri twice, as shown here:

```
glTexParameteri(GL_TEXTURE_2D, GL_TEXTURE_BASE_LEVEL, 0);
glTexParameteri(GL_TEXTURE_2D, GL_TEXTURE_MAX_LEVEL, 4);
```

Figure 5.8: A series of mipmapped images

Mipmap Filtering

Mipmapping adds a new twist to the two basic texture filtering modes
GL_NEAREST and GL_LINEAR by giving four permutations for mipmapped
filtering modes. They are listed in Table 5.7.

Table 5.7: Texture Filters, Including Mipmapped Filters

Constant	Description
GL_NEAREST	Perform nearest neighbor filtering on the base mip level.
GL_LINEAR	Perform linear filtering on the base mip level.
GL_NEAREST_MIPMAP_NEAREST	Select the nearest mip level, and perform nearest neighbor filtering.
GL_NEAREST_MIPMAP_LINEAR	Perform a linear interpolation between mip levels, and perform nearest neighbor filtering.
GL_LINEAR_MIPMAP_NEAREST	Select the nearest mip level, and perform linear filtering.
GL_LINEAR_MIPMAP_LINEAR	Perform a linear interpolation between mip levels, and perform linear filtering; also called trilinear filtering.

Just loading the mip levels with **glTexStorage2D()** does not by itself enable mipmapping. If the texture filter is set to GL_LINEAR or GL_NEAREST, only the base texture level is used, and any mip levels loaded are ignored. You must specify one of the mipmapped filters listed for the loaded mip levels to be used. The constants have the form GL_<FILTER>_MIPMAP_<SELECTOR>, where <FILTER> specifies the texture filter to be used on the mip level selected. The <SELECTOR> specifies how the mip level is selected; for example, NEAREST selects the nearest matching mip level. Using LINEAR for the selector creates a linear interpolation between the two nearest mip levels, which is again filtered by the chosen texture filter.

Which filter you select varies depending on the application and the performance requirements at hand. GL_NEAREST_MIPMAP_NEAREST, for example, gives very good performance and low aliasing (scintillation) artifacts, but nearest neighbor filtering is often not visually pleasing. GL_LINEAR_MIPMAP_NEAREST is often used to speed up games because a higher quality linear filter is used, but a fast selection (nearest) is made between the different-sized mip levels available. Note that you can only use the GL_<*>_MIPMAP_<*> filter modes for the GL_TEXTURE_MIN_FILTER setting — the GL_TEXTURE_MAG_FILTER setting must always be one of GL_NEAREST or GL_NEAREST.

Using nearest as the mipmap selector (as in both examples in the preceding paragraph), however, can also leave an undesirable visual artifact. For oblique views, you can often see the transition from one mip level to another across a surface. It can be seen as a distortion line or a sharp transition from one level of detail to another. The GL_LINEAR_MIPMAP_LINEAR and GL_NEAREST_MIPMAP_LINEAR filters perform an additional interpolation between mip levels to eliminate this transition zone, but at the extra cost of substantially more processing overhead. The GL_LINEAR_MIPMAP_LINEAR filter is often referred to as trilinear mipmapping and, although there are more advanced techniques for image filtering, produces very good results.

Generating Mip Levels

As mentioned previously, mipmapping for 2D textures requires approximately one-third more texture memory than just loading the base texture image. It also requires that all the smaller versions of the base texture image be available for loading. Sometimes this can be inconvenient because the lower resolution images may not necessarily be available to either the programmer or the end user of your software. While having precomputed mip levels for your textures yields the very best results, it is convenient and somewhat common to have OpenGL generate the textures for you. You can generate all the mip levels for a texture once you loaded level zero with the function **glGenerateMipmap()**:

```
void glGenerateMipmap(GLenum target);
```

The target parameter can be GL_TEXTURE_1D, GL_TEXTURE_2D, GL_TEXTURE_3D, GL_TEXTURE_CUBE_MAP, GL_TEXTURE_1D_ARRAY, or GL_TEXTURE_2D_ARRAY (more on these last three later). The quality of the filter used to create the smaller textures may vary widely from implementation to implementation. In addition, generating mipmaps on the fly may not be any faster than actually loading prebuilt mipmaps. This is something to think about in performance-critical applications. For the very best visual quality (as well as for consistency), you should load your own pregenerated mipmaps.

Mipmaps in Action

The example program tunnel shows off mipmapping as described in this chapter and demonstrates visually the different filtering and mipmap modes. This sample program loads three textures at startup and then switches between them to render a tunnel. The pre-filtered images that make up the textures are stored in the .KTX files containing the texture data. The tunnel has a brick wall pattern with different materials on the floor and ceiling. The output from tunnel is shown in Figure 5.9 with the texture minification mode set to GL_LINEAR_MIPMAP_LINEAR. As you can see, the texture becomes blurrier as you get further down the tunnel.

Figure 5.9: A tunnel rendered with three textures and mipmapping

Texture Wrap

Normally, you specify texture coordinates between 0.0 and 1.0 to map out the texels in a texture map. If texture coordinates fall outside this range, OpenGL handles them according to the current texture wrapping mode specified in the sampler object. You can set the wrap mode for each component of the texture coordinate individually by calling **glSamplerParameteri()** with GL_TEXTURE_WRAP_S, GL_TEXTURE_WRAP_T, or GL_TEXTURE_WRAP_R as the parameter name. The wrap mode can then be set to one of the following values: GL_REPEAT, GL_MIRRORED_REPEAT, GL_CLAMP_TO_EDGE, or GL_CLAMP_TO_BORDER. The value of GL_TEXTURE_WRAP_S affects 1D, 2D, and 3D textures; GL_TEXTURE_WRAP_T affects only 2D and 3D textures; and GL_TEXTURE_WRAP_R affects only 3D textures.

The GL_REPEAT wrap mode simply causes the texture to repeat in the direction in which the texture coordinate has exceeded 1.0. The texture repeats again for every integer texture coordinate. This mode is useful for applying a small tiled texture to large geometric surfaces. Well-done seamless textures can lend the appearance of a seemingly much larger texture, but at the cost of a much smaller texture image. The GL_MIRRORED_REPEAT mode is similar, but as each component of the texture passes 1.0, it starts moving back towards the origin of the texture until it reaches 2.0, at which point the pattern repeats. it is The other modes do not repeat, but are "clamped" — thus their name.

If the only implication of the wrap mode is whether the texture repeats, you would need only two wrap modes: repeat and clamp. However, the texture wrap mode also has a great deal of influence on how texture filtering is done at the edges of the texture maps. For GL_NEAREST filtering, there are no consequences to the wrap mode because the texture coordinates are always snapped to some particular texel within the texture map. However, the GL_LINEAR filter takes an average of the pixels surrounding the evaluated texture coordinate, and this creates a problem for texels that lie along the edges of the texture map. This problem is resolved quite neatly when the wrap mode is GL_REPEAT. The texel samples are simply taken from the next row or column, which in repeat mode wraps back around to the other side of the texture. This mode works perfectly for textures that wrap around an object and meet on the other side (such as spheres).

The clamped texture wrap mode offers a couple of options for the way texture edges are handled. For GL_CLAMP_TO_BORDER, the needed texels are taken from the texture border color (which can be set by passing GL_TEXTURE_BORDER_COLOR to **glSamplerParameterfv()**). The GL_CLAMP_TO_EDGE wrap mode forces texture coordinates out of range to be sampled along the last row or column of valid texels.

Figure 5.10 shows a simple example of the various texture wrapping modes. The same mode is used for both the S and T components of the texture coordinates. The four squares in the image have the same texture applied to them, but with different texture wrapping modes applied. The texture is a simple square with nine arrows pointing up and to the left, with a bright band around the top and right edges. For the top left square, the GL_CLAMP_TO_BORDER mode is used. The border color has been set to a dark color and it is clear that when OpenGL ran out of texture data, it used the dark color instead. However, in the bottom left square, the

GL_CLAMP_TO_EDGE mode is used. In this case, the bright band is continued to the top and right of the texture data.

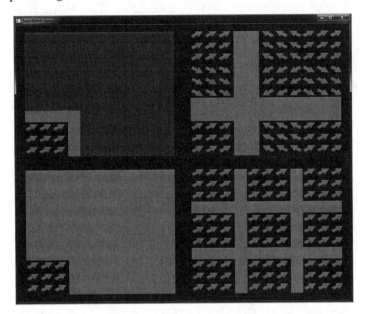

Figure 5.10: Example of texture coordinate wrapping modes

The bottom right square is drawn using the GL_REPEAT mode, which wraps the texture over and over. As you can see, there are several copies of our arrow texture, and all the arrows are pointing in the same direction. Compare this to the square on the top right of Figure 5.10. It is using the GL_MIRRORED_REPEAT mode and as you can see, the texture has been repeated across the square. However, the first copy of the image is the right way around, then the next copy is flipped, the next copy is the right way around again, and so on.

Array Textures

Previously we discussed the idea that multiple textures could be accessed at once via different texture units. This is extremely powerful and useful as your shader can gain access to several texture objects at the same time by declaring multiple sampler uniforms. We can actually take this a bit further by using a feature called *array textures*. With an array texture, you can load up several 1D, 2D, or cube map images into a single texture object. The concept of having more than one image in a single texture is not new. This happens with mipmapping, as each mip level is a distinct image, and with cube mapping, where each face of the cube map has its own image and even its own set of mip levels. With texture arrays, however, you can have a whole array of texture images bound to a single texture object and then index through them in the shader, thus greatly increasing the amount of texture data available to your application at any one time.

Most texture types have an array equivalent. You can create 1D and 2D array textures, and even cube map array textures. However, you can't create a 3D array texture as this is not supported by OpenGL. As with cube maps, array textures can have mip maps. Another interesting thing to note is that if you were to create an array of sampler uniforms in your shader, the value you use to index into that array must be uniform. However, with a texture array, each lookup into the texture map can come from a different element of the array. In part to distinguish between elements of an array of textures and a single element of an array texture, the elements are usually referred to as *layers*.

You may be wondering what the difference between a 2D array texture and a 3D texture is (or a 1D array texture and a 2D texture, for that matter). The biggest difference is probably that no filtering is applied between the layers of an array texture. Also, the maximum number of array texture layers supported by an implementation may be greater than the maximum 3D texture size, for example.

Loading a 2D Array Texture

To create a 2D array, simply create a new texture object bound to the GL_TEXTURE_2D_ARRAY target, allocate storage for it using **glTexStorage3D()**, and then load the images into it using one or more calls to **glTexSubImage3D()**. Notice the use of the 3D versions of the texture storage and data functions. These are required because the depth and z coordinates passed to them are interpreted as the array element, or *layer*. Simple code to load a 2D array texture is shown in Listing 5.40.

```
GLuint tex;

glGenTextures(1, &tex);
glBindTexture(GL_TEXTURE_2D_ARRAY, tex);

glTexStorage3D(GL_TEXTURE_2D_ARRAY,
               8,
               GL_RGBA8,
               256,
               256,
               100);
```

```
for (int i = 0; i < 100; i++)
{
    glTexSubImage3D(GL_TEXTURE_2D_ARRAY,
                    0,
                    0, 0,
                    i,
                    256, 256,
                    1,
                    GL_RGBA,
                    GL_UNSIGNED_BYTE,
                    image_data[i]);
}
```

Listing 5.40: Initializing an array texture

Conveniently, the .KTX file format supports array textures, and so the book's loader code can load them directly from disk. Simply use sb6::ktx::file::load to load an array texture from a file.

To demonstrate texture arrays, we create a program that renders a large number of cartoon aliens raining on the screen. The sample uses an array texture where each slice of the texture holds one of 64 separate images of an alien. The array texture is packed into a single .KTX file called alienarray.ktx, which we load into a single texture object. To render the alien rain, we draw hundreds of instances of a four-vertex triangle strip that makes a screen-aligned quad. Using the instance number as the index into the texture array gives each quad a different texture, even though they are all drawn with the same command. Additionally, we use a uniform buffer to store a per-instance orientation, x offset, and y offset, which are set up by the application.

In this case, our vertex shader uses no vertex attributes and is shown in its entirety in Listing 5.41.

```
#version 430 core

layout (location = 0) in int alien_index;

out VS_OUT
{
    flat int alien;
    vec2 tc;
} vs_out;

struct droplet_t
{
    float x_offset;
    float y_offset;
    float orientation;
    float unused;
};
```

```
layout (std140) uniform droplets
{
    droplet_t droplet[256];
};

void main(void)
{
    const vec2[4] position = vec2[4](vec2(-0.5, -0.5),
                                     vec2( 0.5, -0.5),
                                     vec2(-0.5,  0.5),
                                     vec2( 0.5,  0.5));
    vs_out.tc = position[gl_VertexID].xy + vec2(0.5);
    float co = cos(droplet[alien_index].orientation);
    float so = sin(droplet[alien_index].orientation);
    mat2 rot = mat2(vec2(co, so),
                    vec2(-so, co));
    vec2 pos = 0.25 * rot * position[gl_VertexID];
    gl_Position = vec4(pos.x + droplet[alien_index].x_offset,
                       pos.y + droplet[alien_index].y_offset,
                       0.5, 1.0);
}
```

Listing 5.41: Vertex shader for the alien rain sample

In our vertex shader, the position of the vertex and its texture coordinate
are taken from a hard-coded array. We calculate a per-instance rotation
matrix, rot, allowing our aliens to spin. Along with the texture
coordinate, vs_out.tc, we pass the value of gl_InstanceID (modulo 64)
to the fragment shader via vs_out.alien. In the fragment shader, we
simply use the incoming values to sample from the texture and write to
our output. The fragment shader is shown in Listing 5.42.

```
#version 430 core

layout (location = 0) out vec4 color;

in VS_OUT
{
    flat int alien;
    vec2 tc;
} fs_in;

layout (binding = 0) uniform sampler2DArray tex_aliens;

void main(void)
{
    color = texture(tex_aliens, vec3(fs_in.tc, float(fs_in.alien)));
}
```

Listing 5.42: Fragment shader for the alien rain sample

Accessing Texture Arrays

In the fragment shader (shown in Listing 5.42) we declare our sampler for
the 2D array texture, sampler2DArray. To sample this texture we use the

texture function as normal, but pass in a three-component texture coordinate. The first two components of this texture coordinate, the s and t components, are used as typical two-dimensional texture coordinates. The third component, the p element, is actually an integer index into the texture array. Recall we set this in the vertex shader, and it is going to vary from 0 to 63, with a different value for each alien.

The complete rendering loop for the alien rain sample is shown in Listing 5.43.

```
void render(double currentTime)
{
    static const GLfloat black[] = { 0.0f, 0.0f, 0.0f, 0.0f };
    float t = (float)currentTime;

    glViewport(0, 0, info.windowWidth, info.windowHeight);
    glClearBufferfv(GL_COLOR, 0, black);

    glUseProgram(render_prog);

    glBindBufferBase(GL_UNIFORM_BUFFER, 0, rain_buffer);
    vmath::vec4 * droplet =
        (vmath::vec4 *)glMapBufferRange(
                        GL_UNIFORM_BUFFER,
                        0,
                        256 * sizeof(vmath::vec4),
                        GL_MAP_WRITE_BIT |
                        GL_MAP_INVALIDATE_BUFFER_BIT);

    for (int i = 0; i < 256; i++)
    {
        droplet[i][0] = droplet_x_offset[i];
        droplet[i][1] = 2.0f - fmodf((t + float(i)) *
                                droplet_fall_speed[i], 4.31f);
        droplet[i][2] = t * droplet_rot_speed[i];
        droplet[i][3] = 0.0f;
    }
    glUnmapBuffer(GL_UNIFORM_BUFFER);

    int alien_index;
    for (alien_index = 0; alien_index < 256; alien_index++)
    {
        glVertexAttribI1i(0, alien_index);
        glDrawArrays(GL_TRIANGLE_STRIP, 0, 4);
    }
}
```

Listing 5.43: Rendering loop for the alien rain sample

As you can see, there is only a simple loop around one drawing command in our rendering function. On each frame, we update the values of the data in the rain_buffer buffer object, which we use to store our per-droplet values. Then, we execute a loop of 256 calls to **glDrawArrays()**, which will draw 256 individual aliens. On each iteration of the loop, we update the alien_index input to the vertex shader. Note that we use the

glVertexAttribI*() 1i variant of **glVertexAttrib*()** as we are using an integer input to our vertex shader. The final output of the alien rain sample program is shown in Figure 5.11.

Figure 5.11: Output of the alien rain sample

Writing to Textures in Shaders

A texture object is a collection of images that, when the mipmap chain is included, support filtering, texture coordinate wrapping, and so on. Not only does OpenGL allow you to read from textures with all of those features, but it also allows you to read from *and write to* textures directly in your shaders. Just as you use a sampler variable in shaders to represent an entire texture and the associated sampler parameters (whether from a sampler object or from the texture object itself), you can use an *image* variable to represent a single image from a texture.

Image variables are declared just like sampler uniforms. There are several types of image variables that represent different data types and image dimensionalities. Table 5.8 shows the image types available to OpenGL.

First, you need to declare an image variable as a uniform so that you can associate it with an *image unit*. Such a declaration generally looks like

```
uniform image2D my_image;
```

Table 5.8: Image Types

Image Type	Description
image1D	1D image
image2D	2D image
image3D	3D image
imageCube	Cube map image
imageCubeArray	Cube map array image
imageRect	Rectangle image
image1DArray	1D array image
image2DArray	2D array image
imageBuffer	Buffer image
image2DMS	2D multi-sample image
image2DMSArray	2D multi-sample array image

Once you have an image variable, you can read from it using the imageLoad function and write into it using the imageStore function. Both of these functions are *overloaded*, which means that there are multiple versions of each of them for various parameter types. The versions for the image2D type are

```
vec4 imageLoad(readonly image2D image, ivec2 P);
void imageStore(image2D image, ivec2 P, vec4 data);
```

The imageLoad() function will read the data from image at the coordinates specified in P and return it to your shader. Similarly, the imageStore() function will take the values you provide in data and store them into image at P. Notice that the type of P is an *integer* type (an integer vector for the case of 2D iamges). This is just like the texelFetch() function — no filtering is performed for loads and filtering really doesn't make sense for stores. The dimension of P and the return type of the function depend on the type of the image parameter.

Just as with sampler types, image variables can represent floating-point data stored in images. However, it's also possible to store signed and unsigned integer data in images, in which case the image type is prefixed with a i or u (as in iimage2D and uimage2D), respectively. When an integer image variable is used, the return type of the imageLoad function and the data type of the data parameter to imageStore change appropriately. For example, we have

```
ivec4 imageLoad(readonly iimage2D image, ivec2 P);
void  imageStore(iimage2D image, ivec2 P, ivec4 data);
uvec4 imageLoad(readonly uimage2D image, ivec2 P);
void  imageStore(uimage2D image, ivec2 P, uvec4 data);
```

To bind a texture for load and store operations, you need to bind it to an
image unit using the **glBindImageTexture()** function, whose prototype is

```
void glBindImageTexture(GLuint unit,
                        GLuint texture,
                        GLint level,
                        GLboolean layered,
                        GLint layer,
                        GLenum access,
                        GLenum format);
```

The function looks like it has a lot of parameters, but they're all fairly
self-explanatory. First, the unit parameter is a zero-based index of the
image unit[5] to which you want to bind the image. Next, the texture
parameter is the name of a texture object that you've created using
glGenTextures() and allocated storage for with **glTexStorage2D()** (or the
appropriate function for the type of texture you're using). level specifies
which mipmap level you want to access in your shader, starting with zero
for the base level and progressing to the number of mipmap levels in the
image.

The layered parameter should be set to GL_FALSE if you want to bind a
single layer of an array texture as a regular 1D or 2D image, in which case
the layer parameter specifies the index of that layer. Otherwise, layered
should be set to GL_TRUE, and a whole level of an array texture will be
bound to the image unit (with layer being ignored).

Finally, the access and format parameters describe how you will use the
data in the image. access should be one of GL_READ_ONLY, GL_WRITE_ONLY,
or GL_READ_WRITE to say that you plan to only read, only write, or to do
both to the image, respectively. The format parameter specifies what
format the data in the image should be interpreted as. There is a lot of
flexibility here, with the only real requirement being that the image's
internal format (the one you specified in **glTexStorage2D()**) is in the same
class as the one specified in the format parameter. Table 5.9 lists the
acceptable image formats and their classes.

---

5. Note that there is no glActiveImageUnit function and there is no selector for image units.
You can just bind an image to a unit directly.

Table 5.9: Image Data Format Classes

Format	Class
GL_RGBA32F	4x32
GL_RGBA32I	4x32
GL_RGBA32UI	4x32
GL_RGBA16F	4x16
GL_RGBA16UI	4x16
GL_RGBA16I	4x16
GL_RGBA16_SNORM	4x16
GL_RGBA16	4x16
GL_RGBA8UI	4x8
GL_RGBA8I	4x8
GL_RGBA8_SNORM	4x8
GL_RGBA8	4x8
GL_R11F_G11F_B10F	(a)
GL_RGB10_A2UI	(b)
GL_RGB10_A2	(b)
GL_RG32F	2x32
GL_RG32UI	2x32
GL_RG32I	2x32
GL_RG16F	2x16
GL_RG16UI	2x16
GL_RG16I	2x16
GL_RG16_SNORM	2x16
GL_RG16	2x16
GL_RG8UI	2x8
GL_RG8I	2x8
GL_RG8	2x8
GL_RG8_SNORM	2x8
GL_R32F	1x32
GL_R32UI	1x32
GL_R32I	1x32
GL_R16F	1x16
GL_R16UI	1x16
GL_R16I	1x16
GL_R16_SNORM	1x16

continued

Table 5.9: *Continued*

Format	Class
GL_R16	1x16
GL_R8UI	1x8
GL_R8I	1x8
GL_R8	1x8
GL_R8_SNORM	1x8

Referring to Table 5.9, you can see that the GL_RGBA32F, GL_RGBA32I, and GL_RGBA32UI formats are in the same format class (4x32), which means that you can take a texture that has a GL_RGBA32F internal format and bind one of its levels to an image unit using the GL_RGBA32I or GL_RGBA32UI image formats. When you store into an image, the appropriate number of bits from your source data are chopped off and written to the image as is. However, if you want to read from an image, you must also supply a matching image format using a *format layout qualifier* in your shader code.

The GL_R11F_G11F_B10F format, which has the marker (a) for its format class, and GL_RGB10_A2UI and GL_RGB10_A2, which have the marker (b) for their format class, have their own special classes. GL_R11F_G11F_B10F is not compatible with anything else, and GL_RGB10_A2UI and GL_RGB10_A2 are only compatible with each other.

The appropriate format layout qualifiers for each of the various image formats are shown in Table 5.10.

Table 5.10: Image Data Format Classes

Format	Format Qualifier
GL_RGBA32F	rgba32f
GL_RGBA32I	rgba32i
GL_RGBA32UI	rgba32ui
GL_RGBA16F	rgba16f
GL_RGBA16UI	rgba16ui
GL_RGBA16I	rgba16i
GL_RGBA16_SNORM	rgba16_snorm

continued

Table 5.10: *Continued*

Format	Format Qualifier
GL_RGBA16	rgba16
GL_RGB10_A2UI	rgb10_a2ui
GL_RGB10_A2	rgb10_a2
GL_RGBA8UI	rgba8ui
GL_RGBA8I	rgba8i
GL_RGBA8_SNORM	rgba8_snorm
GL_RGBA8	rgba8
GL_R11F_G11F_B10F	r11f_g11f_b10f
GL_RG32F	rg32f
GL_RG32UI	rg32ui
GL_RG32I	rg32i
GL_RG16F	rg16f
GL_RG16UI	rg16ui
GL_RG16I	rg16i
GL_RG16_SNORM	rg16_snorm
GL_RG16	rg16
GL_RG8UI	rg8ui
GL_RG8I	rg8i
GL_RG8_SNORM	rg8_snorm
GL_RG8	rg8
GL_R32F	r32f
GL_R32UI	r32ui
GL_R32I	r32i
GL_R16F	r16f
GL_R16UI	r16ui
GL_R16I	r16i
GL_R16_SNORM	r16_snorm
GL_R16	r16
GL_R8UI	r8ui
GL_R8I	r8i
GL_R8_SNORM	r8_snorm
GL_R8	r8

Listing 5.44 shows an example fragment shader that copies data from one image to another using image loads and stores, logically inverting that data along the way.

```
#version 430 core

// Uniform image variables:
// Input image - note use of format qualifier because of loads
layout (binding = 0, rgba32ui) readonly uniform uimage2D image_in;
// Output image
layout (binding = 1) uniform writeonly uimage2D image_out;

void main(void)
{
    // Use fragment coordinate as image coordinate
    ivec2 P = ivec2(gl_FragCoord.xy);

    // Read from input image
    uvec4 data = imageLoad(image_in, P);

    // Write inverted data to output image
    imageStore(image_out, P, ~data);
}
```

Listing 5.44: Fragment shader performing image loads and stores

Obviously, the shader shown in Listing 5.44 is quite trivial. However, the power of image loads and stores is that you can include any number of them in a single shader and their coordinates can be anything. This means that a fragment shader is not limited to writing out to a fixed location in the framebuffer, but can write anywhere in an image, and write to multiple images by using multiple image uniforms. Furthermore, it allows any shader stage to write data into images, not just fragment shaders. Be aware, though that with this power comes a lot of responsibility. It's perfectly easy for your shader to trash its own data — if multiple shader invocations write to the same location in an image, it's not well defined what will happen unless you use *atomics*, which are described in the context of images in the next section.

Atomic Operations on Images

Just as with shader storage blocks described in the section "Atomic Memory Operations," you can perform *atomic operations* on data stored in images. Again, an atomic operation is a sequence of a read, a modification, and a write that must be indivisible in order to achieve the desired result. Also, like atomic operations on members of a shader storage block, atomic operations on images are performed using a number of built-in functions in GLSL. These functions are listed in Table 5.11.

For all of the functions listed in Table 5.11 except for imageAtomicCompSwap, the parameters are an image variable, a coordinate, and a piece of data. The dimension of the coordinate depends on the type

Table 5.11: Atomic Operations on Images

Atomic Function	Behavior
imageAtomicAdd	Reads from image at P, adds it to data, writes the result back to image at P, and then returns the value originally stored in image at P.
imageAtomicAnd	Reads from image at P, logically ANDs it with data, writes the result back to image at P, and then returns the value originally stored in image at P.
imageAtomicOr	Reads from image at P, logically ORs it with data, writes the result back to image at P, and then returns the value originally stored in image at P.
imageAtomicXor	Reads from image at P, logically exclusive ORs it with data, writes the result back to image at P, and then returns the value originally stored in image at P.
imageAtomicMin	Reads from image at P, determines the minimum of the retrieved value and data, writes the result back to image at P, and returns the value originally stored in image at P.
imageAtomicMax	Reads from image at P, determines the maximum of the retrieved value and data, writes the result back to image at P, and returns the value originally stored in image at P.
imageAtomicExchange	Reads from image at P, writes the value of data into mem, and then returns the value originally stored in image at P.
imageAtomicCompSwap	Reads from image at P, compares the retrieved value with comp, and if they are equal, writes data into image at P, and returns the value originally stored in image at P.

of image variable. 1D images use a single integer coordinate, 2D images and 1D array images take a 2D integer vector (i.e., ivec2), and 3D images and 2D array images take a 3D integer vector (i.e., ivec3).

For example, we have

```
uint imageAtomicAdd(uimage1D image, int P, uint data);
uint imageAtomicAdd(uimage2D image, ivec2 P, uint data);
uint imageAtomicAdd(uimage3D image, ivec3 P, uint data);
```

and so on. The imageAtomicCompSwap is unique in that it takes an additional parameter, comp, which it compares with the existing content in memory. If the value of comp is equal to the value already in memory, then it is replaced with the value of data. The prototypes of imageAtomicCompSwap include

```
uint imageAtomicCompSwap(uimage1D image, int P, uint comp, uint data);
uint imageAtomicCompSwap(uimage2D image, ivec2 P, uint comp, uint data);
uint imageAtomicCompSwap(uimage3D image, ivec3 P, uint comp, uint data);
```

All of the atomic functions return the data that was originally in memory before the operation was performed. This is useful if you wish to append data to a list, for example. To do this, you would simply determine how many items you want to append to the list, call imageAtomicAdd with the number of elements and then start writing your new data into memory at the location that it returns. Note that while you can't add an arbitrary number to an atomic counter (and the number of atomic counters supported in a single shader is usually not great), you can do similar things with shader storage buffers.

The memory you write to could be a shader storage buffer or another image variable. If the image containing the "filled count" variables is pre-initialized to zero, then the first shader invocation to attempt to append to the list will receive zero and write there, the next invocation will receive whatever the first added, the next will receive whatever the third added, and so on.

Another application for atomics is constructing data structures such as linked lists in memory. To build a linked list from a shader, you need three pieces of storage — the first is somewhere to store the list items, the second is somewhere to store the item count, and the third is the "head pointer," which is the index of the last item on in the list. Again, you can use a shader storage buffer to store items for the linked list, an atomic counter to store the current item count, and an image to store the head pointer for the list(s). To append an item to the list, you would follow three steps:

1. Increment the atomic counter, and retrieve its previous value, which is returned by atomicCounterIncrement.

2. Use `imageAtomicExchange` to exchange the updated counter value with the current head pointer.

3. Store your data into your data store. The structure for each element includes a *next* index, which you fill with the previous value of the head pointer retrieved in step 2.

If the "head pointer" image is a 2D image the size of the framebuffer, then you can use this method to create a per-pixel list of fragments. You can later walk this list and perform whatever operations you like. The shader shown in Listing 5.45 demonstrates how to append fragments to a linked list stored in a shader storage buffer using a 2D image to store the head pointers and an atomic counter to keep the fill count.

```
#version 430 core

// Atomic counter for filled size
layout (binding = 0, offset = 0) uniform atomic_uint fill_counter;

// 2D image to store head pointers
layout (binding = 0) uniform uimage2D head_pointer;

// Shader storage buffer containing appended fragments
struct list_item
{
    vec4        color;
    float       depth;
    int         facing;
    uint        next;
};

layout (binding = 0, std430) buffer list_item_block
{
    list_item   item[];
};

// Input from vertex shader
in VS_OUT
{
    vec4 in;
} fs_in;

void main(void)
{
    ivec2 P = ivec2(gl_FragCoord.xy);

    uint index = atomicCounterIncrement(fill_counter);

    uint old_head = imageAtomicExchange(head_pointer, P, index);

    item[index].color = fs_in.color;
    item[index].depth = gl_FragCoord.z;
    item[index].facing = gl_FrontFacing ? 1 : 0;
    item[index].next = old_head;
}
```

Listing 5.45: Filling a linked list in a fragment shader

You might notice the use of the `gl_FrontFacing` built-in variable. This is a Boolean input to the fragment shader whose value is generated by the back-face culling stage that is described in "Primitive Assembly, Clipping, and Rasterization" back in Chapter 3, "Following the Pipeline." Even if back-face culling is disabled, this variable will still contain `true` if the polygon is considered front facing and `false` otherwise.

Before executing this shader, the head pointer image is cleared to a known value that can't possibly be the index of an item in the list (such as the maximum value of an unsigned integer), and the atomic counter is reset to zero. The first item appended will be item zero, that value will be written to the head pointer, and its *next* index will contain the reset value of the head pointer image. The next value appended to the list will be at index 1, which is written to the head pointer, the old value of which (0) is written to the *next* index, and so on. The result is that the head pointer image contains the index of the last item appended to the list, and each item contains the index of the previous one appended. Eventually, the *next* index of an item will be the value originally used to clear the head image, which indicates that the end of the list.

To traverse the list, we load the index of the first item in it from the head pointer image and read it from the shader storage buffer. For each item, we simply follow the *next* index until we reach the end of the list, or until the maximum number of fragments have been traversed (which protects us from accidentally running off the end of the list). The shader shown in Listing 5.46 shows an example of this. The shader walks the linked list, keeping a running total of the depth of the fragments stored for each pixel. The depth value of front-facing primitives is added to the running total, and the depth value of back-facing primitives is subtracted from the total. The result is the total filled depth of the interior of convex objects, which can be used to render volumes and other filled spaces.

```
#version 430 core

// 2D image to store head pointers
layout (binding = 0, r32ui) coherent uniform uimage2D head_pointer;

// Shader storage buffer containing appended fragments
struct list_item
{
    vec4        color;
    float       depth;
    int         facing;
    uint        next;
};

layout (binding = 0, std430) buffer list_item_block
```

```
{
    list_item    item[];
};

layout (location = 0) out vec4 color;

const uint max_fragments = 10;

void main(void)
{
    uint frag_count = 0;
    float depth_accum = 0.0;
    ivec2 P = ivec2(gl_FragCoord.xy);

    uint index = imageLoad(head_pointer, P).x;

    while (index != 0xFFFFFFFF && frag_count < max_fragments)
    {
        list_item this_item = item[index];

        if (this_item.facing != 0)
        {
            depth_accum -= this_item.depth;
        }
        else
        {
            depth_accum += this_item.depth;
        }

        index = this_item.next;
        frag_count++;
    }

    depth_accum *= 3000.0;

    color = vec4(depth_accum, depth_accum, depth_accum, 1.0);
}
```

Listing 5.46: Traversing a linked list in a fragment shader

The result of rendering with the shaders of Listings 5.45 and 5.46 is shown in Figure 5.12.

Synchronizing Access to Images

As images represent large regions of memory and we have just explained how to write directly into images from your shaders, you may have guessed that we'll now explain the memory barrier types that you can use to synchronize access to that memory. Just as with buffers and atomic counters, you can call

```
glMemoryBarrier(GL_SHADER_IMAGE_ACCESS_BIT);
```

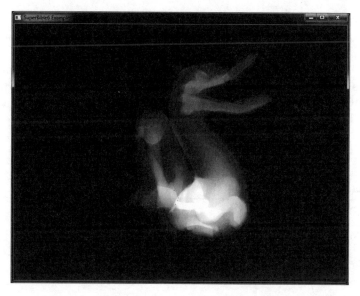

Figure 5.12: Resolved per-fragment linked lists

You should call **glMemoryBarrier()** with the GL_SHADER_IMAGE_ACCESS_BIT set when something has *written* to an image that you want read from images later — including other shaders.

Similarly, there is a version of the GLSL memoryBarrier() function, memoryBarrierImage(), that ensures that operations on images from inside your shader are completed before it returns.

Texture Compression

Textures can take up an incredible amount of space! Some modern games can easily use 1GB of texture data in a given level. That's a lot of data! Where do you put it all? Textures are an important part to making rich, realistic, and impressive scenes, but if you can't load all of the data onto the GPU, your rendering will be slow if not impossible. One way to deal with storing and using a large amount of texture data is to compress the data. Compressed textures have two major benefits. First, they reduce the amount of storage space required for image data. Although the texture formats supported by OpenGL are not generally not compressed as aggressively as in formats such as JPEG, they do provide substantial space benefits. The second (and possibly more important) benefit is that because the graphics processor needs to read less data when fetching from a compressed texture, less *memory bandwidth* is required when compressed textures are used.

There are a number of compressed texture formats supported by OpenGL. All OpenGL implementations support at least the compression schemes listed in Table 5.12.

Table 5.12: Native OpenGL Texture Compression Formats

Formats (GL_COMPRESSED_*)	Type
RED	Generic
RG	Generic
RGB	Generic
RGBA	Generic
SRGB	Generic
SRGB_ALPHA	Generic
RED_RGTC1	RGTC
SIGNED_RED_RGTC1	RGTC
RG_RGTC2	RGTC
SIGNED_RG_RGTC2	RGTC
RGBA_BPTC_UNORM	BPTC
SRGB_ALPHA_BPTC_UNORM	BPTC
RGB_BPTC_SIGNED_FLOAT	BPTC
RGB_BPTC_UNSIGNED_FLOAT	BPTC
RGB8_ETC2	ETC2
SRGB8_ETC2	ETC2
RGB8_PUNCHTHROUGH_ALPHA1_ETC2	ETC2
SRGB8_PUNCHTHROUGH_ALPHA1_ETC2	ETC2
RGBA8_ETC2_EAC	ETC2
SRGB8_ALPHA8_ETC2_EAC	ETC2
R11_EAC	EAC
SIGNED_R11_EAC	EAC
RG11_EAC	EAC
SIGNED_RG11_EAC	EAC

The first six formats listed in Table 5.12 are generic and allow the OpenGL driver to decide what compression mechanism to use. This means your driver can use the format that best meets current conditions. The catch is that it is implementation specific, and although your code will work on many platforms, the result of rendering with them might not be the same.

The RGTC (Red-Green Texture Compression) format breaks a texture image into 4×4 texel blocks, compressing the individual channels within that block using a series of codes. This compression mode works only for one- and two-channel signed and unsigned textures, and only for certain texel formats. You don't need to worry about the exact compression scheme unless you are planning on writing a compressor. Just note that space savings from using RGTC is 50%.

The BPTC (Block Partitioned Texture Compression) format also breaks textures up into blocks of 4×4 texels, each represented as 128 bits (16 bytes) of data in memory. The blocks are encoded using a rather complex scheme that essentially comprises a pair of endpoints and a representation of the position on a line between those two endpoints. It allows the endpoints to be manipulated to generate a variety of values as output for each texel. The BPTC formats are capable of compressing 8-bit per-channel normalized data and 32-bit per-channel floating-point data. The compression ratio for BPTC formats ranges from 25% for RGBA floating-point data to 33% for RGB 8-bit data.

The other formats listed, Ericsson Texture Compression (ETC2) and Ericsson Alpha[6] Compression (EAC) are low-bandwidth formats that are also[7] available in OpenGL ES 3.0. They are designed for extremely low bit-per-pixel applications such as those found in mobile devices that have substantially less memory bandwidth than the high-performance GPUs found in desktop and workstation computers.

Your implementation may also support other compressed formats such as S3TC[8] and ETC1. You should check for the availability of formats not required by OpenGL before attempting to use them. The best way to do this is to check for support of the related extension. For example, if your implementation of OpenGL supports the S3TC, it will advertise the GL_EXT_texture_compression_s3tc extension string.

---

6. Although this is the official acronym, it's a bit of a misnomer as EAC can be used for more than just alpha.

7. The EAC and ETC2 formats were added to OpenGL 4.3 in an effort to drive convergence between desktop and mobile versions of the API, and at time of writing, few if any desktop GPUs actually support them natively, with most OpenGL implementations decompressing the data you give them. Use them with caution.

8. S3TC is also known as the earlier versions of the DXT format.

Using Compression

You can ask OpenGL to compress a texture in some formats when you load it, although it's strongly recommended to compress textures yourself and store the compressed texture in a file. If OpenGL does support compression for your selected format, all you have to do is request that the internal format be one of the compressed formats and OpenGL will take your uncompressed data and compress it as the texture image is loaded. There is no real difference in how you use compressed textures and uncompressed textures. The GPU handles the conversion when it samples from the texture. Many imaging tools used for creating textures and other images allow you to save your data directly in a compressed format.

The .KTX file format allows compressed data to be stored in it, and the book's texture loader will load compressed images transparently to your application. You can check whether a texture is compressed by calling **glGetTexLevelParameteriv()** with one of two parameters. As one option, you can check the GL_TEXTURE_INTERNAL_FORMAT parameter of the texture and explicitly test whether it's one of the compressed formats. To do this, either keep a lookup table of recognized formats in your application or call **glGetInternalFormativ()** with the parameter GL_TEXTURE_COMPRESSED. Alternatively, simply pass the GL_TEXTURE_COMPRESSED parameter directly to **glGetTexLevelParameteriv()**, which will return GL_TRUE if the texture has compressed data in it and GL_FALSE otherwise.

Once you have loaded a texture using a non-generic compressed internal format, you can get the compressed image back by calling **glGetCompressedTexImage()**. Just pick the texture target and mipmap level you are interested in. Because you may not know how the image is compressed or what format is used, you should check the image size to make sure you have enough room for the whole surface. You can do this by calling **glGetTexParameteriv()** and passing the GL_TEXTURE_COMPRESSED_IMAGE_SIZE token.

```
Glint imageSize = 0;
glGetTexParameteriv(GL_TEXTURE_2D,
                    GL_TEXTURE_COMPRESSED_IMAGE_SIZE,
                    &imageSize);
void *data = malloc(imageSize);
glGetCompressedTexImage(GL_TEXTURE_2D, 0, data);
```

If you wish to load compressed texture images yourself rather than using the book's .KTX loader, you can call **glTexStorage2D()** or **glTexStorage3D()** with the desired compressed internal format to allocate storage for the texture, and then call **glCompressedTexSubImage2D()** or `glCompressedTexSubImage3D()` to upload data into it. When you do this, you need to ensure that the `xoffset`, `yoffset`, and other parameters obey texture format specific rules. In particular, most texture compression formats compress blocks of texels. These blocks are usually sizes such as 4 × 4 texels. The regions that you update with `glCompressedTexSubImage2D()` need to line up on block boundaries for these formats to work.

Shared Exponents

Although shared exponent textures are not technically a compressed format in the truest sense, they do allow you to use floating-point texture data while saving storage space. Instead of storing an exponent for each of the R, G, and B values, shared exponent formats use the same exponent value for the whole texel. The fractional and exponential parts of each value are stored as integers and then assembled when the texture is sampled. For the format GL_RGB9_E5, 9 bits are used to store each color and 5 bits are the common exponent for all channels. This format packs three floating-point values into 32 bits; that's a savings of 67%! To make use of shared exponents, you can get the texture data directly in this format from a content creation tool or write a converter that compresses your float RGB values into a shared exponent format.

Texture Views

Usually, when you're using textures, you'll know ahead of time what format your textures are, what you're going to use them for and your shaders will match the data they're fetching. For instance, a shader that's expecting to read from a 2D array texture might declare a sampler uniform as a `sampler2DArray`. Likewise, a shader that's expecting to read from an integer format texture might declare a corresponding sampler as `isampler2D`. However, there may be times when the textures you create and load might not match what your shaders expect. In this case, you can use *texture views* to re-use the texture data in one texture object with another. This has two main use cases (although there are certainly many more):

- A texture view can be used to "pretend" that a texture of one type is actually a texture of a different type. For example, you can take a 2D texture and create a view of it that treats it as a 2D array texture with only one layer.

- A texture view can be used to pretend that the data in the texture object is actually a different format than what is really stored in memory. For example, you might take a texture with an internal format of GL_RGBA32F (i.e., four 32-bit floating-point components per texel) and create a view of it that sees them as GL_RGBA32UI (four 32-bit unsigned integers per texel) so that you can get at the individual bits of the texels.

Of course, you can do both of these things at the same time — that is, take a texture and create a view of it with both a different format and different type.

Creating Texture Views

To create a view of a texture, we use the **glTextureView()** function, whose prototype is

```
void glTextureView(GLuint texture,
                   GLenum target,
                   GLuint origtexture,
                   GLenum internalformat,
                   GLuint minlevel,
                   GLuint numlevels,
                   GLuint minlayer,
                   GLuint numlayers);
```

The first parameter, texture, is the name of the texture object you'd like to make into a view. You should get this name from a call to **glGenTextures()**. Next, target specifies what *type* of texture you'd like to create. This can be pretty much any of the texture targets (GL_TEXTURE_1D, GL_TEXTURE_CUBE_MAP, or GL_TEXTURE_2D_ARRAY, for example), but it must be *compatible* with the type of the original texture, whose name is given in origtexture. The compatibility between various targets is given in Table 5.13.

As you can see, for most texture targets you can at least create a view of the texture with the same target. The exception is buffer textures as these are essentially already views of a buffer object — you can simply attach the same buffer object to another buffer texture to get another view of its data.

The internalformat parameter specifies the internal format for the new texture view. This must be compatible with the internal format of the original texture. This can be tricky to understand, so we'll explain it in a moment.

The last four parameters allow you to make a view of a *subset* of the original texture's data. The minlevel and numlevels parameter specify the first mipmap level and number of mipmap levels to include in the view. This allows you to create a texture view that represents part of an entire mipmap pyramid of another texture. For example, to create a texture that represented just the base level (level 0) of another texture, you can set minlevel to 0 and numlevels to 1. To create a view that represented the 4 lowest resolution mipmaps of a 10-level texture, you would set minlevel to 6 and numlevels to 4.

Table 5.13: Texture View Target Compatibility

If origtexture is... (GL_TEXTURE_*)	You can create a view of it as... (GL_TEXTURE_*)
1D	1D or 1D_ARRAY
2D	2D or 2D_ARRAY
3D	3D
CUBE_MAP	CUBE_MAP, 2D, 2D_ARRAY, or CUBE_MAP_ARRAY
RECTANGLE	RECTANGLE
BUFFER	none
1D_ARRAY	1D or 1D_ARRAY
2D_ARRAY	2D or 2D_ARRAY
CUBE_MAP_ARRAY	CUBE_MAP, 2D, 2D_ARRAY, or CUBE_MAP_ARRAY
2D_MULTISAMPLE	2D_MULTISAMPLE or 2D_MULTISAMPLE_ARRAY
2D_MULTISAMPLE_ARRAY	2D_MULTISAMPLE or 2D_MULTISAMPLE_ARRAY

Similarly, minlayer and numlayers are used to create a view of a subset of the layers of an array texture. For instance, if you want to create an array texture view that represents the middle 4 layers of a 20-layer array texture, you can set minlayer to 8 and numlayers to 4. Whatever you choose for the minlevel, numlevels, minlayer, and numlayers parameters, they must be consistent with the source and destination textures. For example, if you want to create a non-array texture view representing a single layer of an array texture, you must set minlayer to a layer that actually exists in the source texture and numlayers to 1 because the destination doesn't have any layers (rather, it effectively has 1 layer).

We mentioned that the internal format of the source texture and the new texture view (specified in the internalformat parameter) must be compatible with one another. To be compatible, two formats must be in the same *class*. There are several format classes, and they are listed, along with the internal formats that are members of that class, in Table 5.14.

Table 5.14: Texture View Format Compatibility

Format Class	Members of the Class
128-bit	GL_RGBA32F, GL_RGBA32UI, GL_RGBA32I
96-bit	GL_RGB32F, GL_RGB32UI, GL_RGB32I
64-bit	GL_RGBA16F, GL_RG32F, GL_RGBA16UI, GL_RG32UI, GL_RGBA16I, GL_RG32I, GL_RGBA16, GL_RGBA16_SNORM
48-bit	GL_RGB16, GL_RGB16_SNORM, GL_RGB16F, GL_RGB16UI, GL_RGB16I
32-bit	GL_RG16F, GL_R11F_G11F_B10F, GL_R32F, GL_RGB10_A2UI, GL_RGBA8UI, GL_RG16UI, GL_R32UI, GL_RGBA8I, GL_RG16I, GL_R32I, GL_RGB10_A2, GL_RGBA8, GL_RG16, GL_RGBA8_SNORM, GL_RG16_SNORM, GL_SRGB8_ALPHA8, GL_RGB9_E5
24-bit	GL_RGB8, GL_RGB8_SNORM, GL_SRGB8, GL_RGB8UI, GL_RGB8I
16-bit	GL_R16F, GL_RG8UI, GL_R16UI, GL_RG8I, GL_R16I, GL_RG8, GL_R16, GL_RG8_SNORM, GL_R16_SNORM
8-bit	GL_R8UI, GL_R8I, GL_R8, GL_R8_SNORM
RGTC1_RED	GL_COMPRESSED_RED_RGTC1, GL_COMPRESSED_SIGNED_RED_RGTC1
RGTC2_RG	GL_COMPRESSED_RG_RGTC2, GL_COMPRESSED_SIGNED_RG_RGTC2
BPTC_UNORM	GL_COMPRESSED_RGBA_BPTC_UNORM, GL_COMPRESSED_SRGB_ALPHA_BPTC_UNORM
BPTC_FLOAT	GL_COMPRESSED_RGB_BPTC_SIGNED_FLOAT, GL_COMPRESSED_RGB_BPTC_UNSIGNED_FLOAT

In addition to formats that match each other's classes, you can always create a view of a texture with the same format as the original — even for formats that are not listed in Table 5.14.

Once you have created a view of a texture, you can use it like any other texture of the new type. For instance, if you have a 2D array texture, and you create a 2D non-array texture view of one of its layers, you can call **glTexSubImage2D()** to put data into the view, and the same data will end up in the corresponding layer of the array texture. As another example, you can create a 2D non-array texture view of a single layer of a 2D array texture and access it from a `sampler2D` uniform in a shader. Likewise, you could create a single-layer 2D array texture view of a 2D non-array texture and access that from a `sampler2DArray` uniform in a shader.

Summary

In this chapter, you have learned about how OpenGL deals with the vast amounts of data required for graphics rendering. At the start of the pipeline, you saw how to automatically feed your vertex shaders with data using buffer objects. We also discussed methods of getting constant values, known as uniforms, into your shaders — first using buffers and then using the *default uniform block*. This block is where the uniforms that represent textures, images, and storage buffers live too, and we used them to show you how to directly read and write images to and from textures and buffers using your shader code. You saw how to take a texture and pretend that part of it's actually a different type of texture, possibly with a different data format. You also learned about atomic operations, which touched on the massively parallel nature of modern graphics processors.

Chapter 6

Shaders and Programs

WHAT YOU'LL LEARN IN THIS CHAPTER

- The fundamentals of the OpenGL shading language

- How to find out if your shaders compiled, and what went wrong if they didn't

- How to retrieve and cache binaries of your compiled shaders and use them later for rendering

By this point in the book, you have read about the OpenGL pipeline, written some simple OpenGL programs, and seen some rendering. We have covered basic computer graphics fundamentals, some 3D math, and more. Modern graphics applications spend most of their time executing shaders, and graphics programmers spend a lot of their time writing shaders. Before you can write really compelling programs, you'll need to understand shaders, the OpenGL programming model, and the types of operations that a graphics processor does well (and those that it does poorly). In this chapter, we'll take a deeper dive into The OpenGL Shading Language, also known as GLSL. We'll discuss a number of its features and subtleties and provide you with a strong foundation with which you can put your ideas into practice.

Language Overview

GLSL is in the class of languages that can be considered "C-like." That is, its syntax and model are much like that of C with a number of differences that make it more suitable for graphics and parallel execution in general. One of the major differences between C and GLSL is that matrix and vector types are first class citizens. That means that they are built into the language. Another major difference between GLSL and C is that GLSL is designed to be run on massively parallel implementations — most graphics processors will run thousands of copies (or *invocations*) of your shaders at the same time. GLSL also has several limitations to make allowances for these types of implementations. For example, recursion is not allowed in GLSL, and precision requirements for floating-point numbers are not as strict as the IEEE standards that govern most C implementations.

Data Types

GLSL supports both scalar and vector data types, arrays and structures, and a number of opaque data types that represent textures and other data structures.

Scalar Types

The scalar data types supported in GLSL are 32- and 64-bit floating point, 32-bit signed and unsigned integers, and Boolean values. No support is provided for other commonly used types available in C such as `short`, `char`, or strings. Also, GLSL doesn't support pointers or integer types larger than 32 bits. The scalar types supported are shown in Table 6.1.

Table 6.1: Scalar Types in GLSL

Type	Definition
`bool`	A Boolean value that can either be `true` or `false`
`float`	IEEE-754 formatted 32-bit floating-point quantity
`double`	IEEE-754 formatted 64-bit floating-point quantity
`int`	32-bit two's-complement signed integer
`unsigned int`	32-bit unsigned integer

Signed and unsigned integers behave as would be expected in a C program. That is, signed integers are stored as two's complement and have a range from -2,147,483,648 to 2,147,483,647, and unsigned integers have a range from 0 to 4,294,967,295. If you add numbers together such that they overflow their ranges, they will wrap around.

Floating-point numbers are effectively defined as they are in the IEEE-754 standard. That is, 32-bit floating-point numbers have a sign bit, 8 exponent bits, and 23 mantissa bits. The sign bit is set if the number is negative and clear if it is positive. The 8 exponent bits represent a number between -127 and +127, which is biased into the range 0 to 254 by adding 127 to its value. The mantissa represents the significant digits of the number, and there are 23 of them, plus an implied binary 1 digit in the 24th position. Given the sign bit, s, exponent, e, and manitissa, m, the actual value of a 32-bit floating-point number is given by

$$n = (-1)^s (1 + \sum_{i=1}^{23} b_{-i} 2^{-i}) \times 2^{(e-127)}$$

Similarly, double-precision numbers also follow the IEEE-754 standard with a sign bit, 11 exponent bits, and 52 mantissa bits. The sign bit is defined as in 32-bit floating point, the exponent represents a value between -1022 and 1023, and the 52-bit mantissa represents the significant digits of the number, with an additional implied 1 in the 53rd position. The actual value of the 64-bit double-precision floating-point number is

$$n = (-1)^s (1 + \sum_{i=1}^{52} b_{-i} 2^{-i}) \times 2^{(e-1023)}$$

GLSL is not required to adhere strictly to the IEEE-754 standard for everything. For most operations the precision will be good enough and behavior is well defined. However, for some operations such as propagation of NaNs (Not a Number) and behavior of infinities and denormals, some deviation is allowed for. In general, though, writing code that relies on exact behavior of NaNs and infinities is not a good idea as many processors perform poorly on these types of values. For built-in functions such as trigonometric functions, even more leeway is given by GLSL. Finally, GLSL has no support for exceptions. That means that if you do something unreasonable such as dividing a number by zero, you won't know until you see unexpected results come out of your shader.

Vectors and Matrices

Vectors of all supported scalar types and matrices of single- and double-precision floating-point types are supported by GLSL. Vector and matrix type names are decorated with their underlying scalar type's name, except for floating-point vectors and matrices, which have no decoration. Table 6.2 shows all of the vector and matrix types in GLSL.

Table 6.2: Vector and Matrix Types in GLSL

Dimension	Scalar Type				
Scalar	bool	float	double	int	unsigned int
2-Element Vector	bvec2	vec2	dvec2	ivec2	uvec2
3-Element Vector	bvec3	vec3	dvec3	ivec3	uvec3
4-Element Vector	bvec4	vec4	dvec4	ivec4	uvec4
2 × 2 Matrix	—	mat2	dmat2	—	—
2 × 3 Matrix	—	mat2x3	dmat2x3	—	—
2 × 4 Matrix	—	mat2x4	dmat2x4	—	—
3 × 2 Matrix	—	mat3x2	dmat3x2	—	—
3 × 3 Matrix	—	mat3	dmat3	—	—
3 × 4 Matrix	—	mat3x4	dmat3x4	—	—
4 × 2 Matrix	—	mat4x2	dmat4x2	—	—
4 × 3 Matrix	—	mat4x3	dmat4x3	—	—
4 × 4 Matrix	—	mat4	dmat4	—	—

Vectors may be constructed from other vectors, a single scalar, from sequences of scalars, or from any combination of scalars and vectors of the appropriate type, so long as there are enough fields in total to fill the destination. Thus, the following are all legal constructors:

```
vec3 foo = vec3(1.0);
vec3 bar = vec3(foo);
vec4 baz = vec4(1.0, 2.0, 3.0, 4.0);
vec4 bat = vec4(1.0, foo);
```

The components of a vector may be accessed as if it were an array. That is, the four components of

```
vec4 foo;
```

may be accessed as

```
float x = foo[0];
float y = foo[1];
float z = foo[2];
float w = foo[3];
```

In addition to accesses as an array, vectors may be accessed as if they were structures with fields representing their components. The first component can be accessed through the .x, .s, or .r field. The second component is accessed through the .y, .t, or .g field. The third is accessed through the .z, .p, or .b field, and finally, the fourth component can be accessed through the .w, .q, or .a field. This seems confusing, but x, y, z, and w are often used to denote positions or directions, r, g, b, and a are often used to represent colors, and s, t, p,[1] and q[2] are used to denote texture coordinates. If you were to write the vector's structure in C, it would look something like this:

```
typedef union vec4_t
{
  struct
  {
    float x;
    float y;
    float z;
    float w;
  };
  struct
  {
    float s;
    float t;
    float p;
    float q;
  };
  struct
  {
    float r;
    float g;
    float b;
    float a;
  };
} vec4;
```

However, this isn't the end of the story — vectors also support what is called *swizzling*. This is the stacking of fields into vectors of their own. For example, the first three components of foo (which is a **vec4**) could be extracted by writing foo.xyz (or foo.rgb or foo.stp). The powerful thing is that you can also specify these fields in any order you wish, and you can repeat them. So, foo.zyx would produce a three-element vector with the x and z fields of foo swapped, and foo.rrrr would produce a four-element vector with the r component of foo in every field. Note that you can't mix and match the conceptually separate x, y, z, and w fields with the s, t, p, and q or r, g, b, and a fields. That is, you can't write foo.xyba, for example.

Matrices also first-class types in GLSL and may be treated like arrays. In GLSL, matrices appear as if they are arrays of vectors, and each element of

---

1. p is used as the third component of a texture coordinate because r is already taken for color.

2. q is used for the fourth component of a texture coordinate because it comes after p.

that array (which is therefore a vector) represents a column of the matrix. Because each of those vectors can also be treated like an array, a column of a matrix behaves as an array, effectively allowing matrices to be treated like two-dimensional arrays. For example, if we declare bar as a `mat4` type, then bar[0] is a `vec4` representing its first column, and bar[0][0] is the first component of that vector (as is bar[0].x), bar[0][1] is the second component of the vector (which is equivalent to bar[0].y), and so on. Continuing, bar[1] is the second column, bar[2] is the third, and so on. Again, if you were to write this in C, it would look something like

```
typedef vec4 mat4[4];
```

Standard operators, such as + and -, are defined for vectors and matrices. The multiplication operator (∗) is defined between two vectors to be component-wise, and between two matrices or a matrix and a vector as a matrix-matrix or matrix-vector multiplication operation. Division of vectors and matrices by scalars behaves as expected, and division of vectors and matrices by other vectors and matrices is executed component-wise, therefore requiring the two operands to be of the same dimension.

Arrays and Structures

You can build aggregate types both as arrays and structures, including arrays of structures and structures of arrays. Structure types are declared much as they would be in C++, and in particular, there is no **typedef** keyword in GLSL but rather structure definitions in GLSL implicitly declare a new type as they do in C++. Structure types may be forward declared by simply writing **struct** my_structure;, where my_structure is the name of the new structure type being declared.

There are two ways to declare an array in GLSL. The first is similar to that of C or C++, where the array size is appended to the variable name The following are examples of this type of declaration:

```
float foo[5];
ivec2 bar[13];
dmat3 baz[29];
```

The second syntax is to implicitly declare the type of the whole array by appending the size to the *element type* rather than the variable name. The above declaration could equivalently be written

```
float[5] foo;
ivec2[13] bar;
dmat3[29] baz;
```

To a C programmer, this may seem odd. However, it's actually a very powerful feature as it allows types to be implicitly defined without the typedef keyword, which GLSL lacks. One example use of this is to declare a function that returns an array:

```
vec4[4] functionThatReturnsArray()
{
    vec4[4] foo = ...

    return foo;
}
```

Declaring array types in this form also implicitly defines the constructor for the array. This means that you can write

```
float[6] var = float[6](1.0, 2.0, 3.0, 4.0, 5.0, 6.0);
```

However, in this case, recent versions[3] of GLSL also allow the traditional, C-style array initializer syntax to be used, as in

```
float var[6] = { 1.0, 2.0, 3.0, 4.0, 5.0, 6.0 };
```

Arrays may be included in structures, and you can build arrays of structure types (which may themselves include structures). So, for example, the following structure and array definitions are legal in GLSL:

```
struct foo
{
    int a;
    vec2 b;
    mat4 c;
};

struct bar
{
    vec3 a;
    foo[7] b;
};

bar[29] baz;
```

In this listing, baz is an array of 29 instances of bar, which contains one vec3 and 7 instances of foo, which contains an int, a vec2, and a mat4.

Arrays also include a special *method*[4] called .length(), which returns the number of elements in the array. This allows, for example, loops to be constructed that iterate over all the elements in array. It's also interesting

---

3. Curly brace {...} style initializer lists were introduced in GLSL 4.20 along with OpenGL 4.2. If you are writing shaders that might need to run in an earlier version of GLSL, you may want to stick to the implicit array type initialization by construction.

4. GLSL doesn't support member functions in the traditional C++ sense, but an exception is made in this case.

to note that because there is a duality between vectors and arrays in GLSL, the `.length()` function works on vectors (giving their size, naturally) and that because matrices are essentially arrays of vectors, `.length()` when applied to a matrix gives you the number of columns it has. The following are a few examples of applications of the `.length()` function:

```
float a[10];                // Declare an array of 10 elements
float b[a.length()];        // Declare an array of the same size
mat4 c;
float d = float(c.length()); // d is now 4
int e = c[0].length();      // e is the height of c (4)

int i;

// This loop iterates 10 times
for (i = 0; i < a.length(); i++)
{
  b[i] = a[i];
}
```

Although GLSL doesn't officially support multi-dimensional arrays, it does support arrays of arrays. This means that you can put array types into arrays — when you index into the first array, you get back an array, into which you can index, and so on. So, consider the following:

```
float a[10];        // "a" is an array of 10 floats
float b[10][2];     // "b" is an array of 2 arrays of 10 floats
float c[10][2][5];  // "c" is an array of 5 arrays of 2 arrays of 10 floats
```

Here, a is a regular, one-dimensional array. b may look like a two-dimensional array, but it's actually a one-dimensional array of arrays, each of which has ten elements. There is a subtle difference here. In particular, if you were to write b[1].length(), you would get 10. Following on then, c is a one-dimensional array of five one-dimensional arrays of two elements, each of which is a one-dimensional array of ten elements. c[3].length() produces 2, and c[3][1].length() produces 10.

Built-In Functions

There are literally hundreds of built-in functions in GLSL. Many of them are used to work with textures and memory and will be covered in detail in those contexts. In this subsection, we're going to look at functions that deal strictly with data — basic math, matrix, vector, and data packing and unpacking functions will be covered here.

Terminology

Given the very large number of types in GLSL, the language includes support for function *overloading*, which means that functions can have multiple definitions, each with a different set of parameters. Rather than enumerate all of the types supported for each of the functions, some standard terminology is used in the GLSL Specification to group classes of data types together such that families of functions can be referred to more concisely. We will sometimes use those terms here to refer to groups of types also. The following are terms that are used both in the GLSL Specification and in this book:

- genType means any single-precision floating-point scalar or vector, or one of `float`, `vec2`, `vec3`, or `vec4`.

- genUType means any unsigned integer scalar or vector, or one of `uint`, `uvec2`, `uvec3`, or `uvec4`.

- genIType means any signed integer scalar or vector, or one of `int`, `ivec2`, `ivec3`, or `ivec4`.

- genDType means any double-precision floating-point scalar or vector, or one of `double`, `dvec2`, `dvec3`, or `dvec4`.

- mat means any single-precision floating-point matrix. For example, `mat2`, `mat3`, `mat4`, or any of the non-square matrix forms.

- dmat means any double-precision floating-point matrix. For example, `dmat2`, `dmat3`, `dmat4`, or any of the non-square matrix forms.

Built–In Matrix and Vector Functions

As has been discussed in some detail, vectors and matrices are first-class citizens in GLSL, and where it makes sense, built-in operators such as +, -, *, and / work directly on vector and matrix types. However, a number of functions are provided to deal specifically with vectors and matrices.

The `matrixCompMult()` function performs a component-wise multiplication of two matrices. Remember, the * operator for two matrices is defined to perform a traditional matrix multiplication in GLSL. Clearly, the two matrix parameters to `matrixCompMult()` must be the same size.

Matrices may be transposed using the built-in `transpose()` function. If you transpose a non-square matrix, its dimensions are simply swapped.

To find the inverse of a matrix, GLSL provides the `inverse()` built-in function for the `mat2`, `mat3`, and `mat4` types as well as their double-precision equivalents, `dmat2`, `dmat3`, and `dmat4`. Be aware though, that finding the inverse of a matrix is fairly expensive, and so if the matrix is likely to be constant, calculate the inverse in your application and load it into your shader as a uniform. Non-square matrices do not have inverses and so are not supported by the inverse() function. Similarly, the determinant() function calculates the determinant of any square matrix. For ill-conditioned matrices, the determinant and inverse do not exist, and so calling inverse() or determinant() on such a matrix will produce an undefined result.

The outerProduct() function performs an outer product of two vectors. Effectively, this takes two vectors as input, treats the first as a $1 \times N$ matrix and the second as an $N \times 1$ matrix, and then multiplies them together. The resulting $N \times N$ matrix is returned.

If you need to compare two vectors to one another, a number of built-in functions will do this for you in a component-by-component manner. These are lessThan(), lessThanEqual(), greaterThan(), greaterThanEqual(), equal(), and notEqual(). Each of these functions takes two vectors of the same type and size, applies the operation that their name suggests, and returns a Boolean vector of the same size of the function's parameters (that is, a **bvec2**, **bvec3**, or **bvec4**). Each component of this Boolean vector contains the result of the comparison for the corresponding components in the source parameters.

Given a Boolean vector, you can test it to see if any of its components are **true** using the any() function, or to see if *all* of its components are **true** with the all() function. You can also invert the value of a Boolean vector using the not() function.

A large number of built-in functions for dealing with vectors are provided by GLSL. These include length(), which returns the length of a vector, and distance(), which returns the distance between two points (which is the same as the length of the vector produced by subtracting one point from the other). The normalize() function divides a vector by its own length, producing a vector that has a length of one, but points in the same direction as the source. The dot() and cross() functions can be used to find the dot and cross products of two vectors, respectively.

The reflect() and refract() functions take an input vector, a normal to a plane, and calculate the reflected or refracted vector that results. refract() takes the index of refraction, *eta*, as a parameter in addition to the incoming and normal vectors. The math behind this is explained in "Reflection and Refraction" in Chapter 4, "Math for 3D Graphics."

Likewise, the `faceforward()` function takes an input vector and two surface normals — if the dot product of the input vector and the second normal vector is negative, then it returns the first normal vector; otherwise, it returns the negative of the first normal vector. As you might have guessed from its name, this can be used to determine whether a plane is front- or back-facing with respect to a particular view direction. Facingness was covered in Chapter 3, "Following the Pipeline."

Built-In Math Functions

GLSL supports many built-in functions to perform mathematical operations and to manipulate data in variables. The common math functions include `abs()`, `sign()`, `ceil()`, `floor()`, `trunc()`, `round()`, `roundEven()`, `fract()`, `mod()`, `modf()`, `min()`, and `max()`. For the most part, these functions operate on vectors as well as scalars, but otherwise behave as their counterparts in the C standard libraries. The `roundEven()` function doesn't have a direct equivalent in C — this function rounds its argument to the nearest integer, but breaks ties when there is a fractional part of 0.5 by rounding to the nearest *even* number. That is, 7.5 and 8.5 will both round to 8, 42.5 will round to 42 and 43.5 will round to 44.

Two implicit declarations of the `clamp()` function are

```
vec4 clamp(vec4 x, float minVal, float maxVal);
vec4 clamp(vec4 x, vec4 minVal, vec4 maxVal);
```

This function clamps the incoming vector x to the range specified by minVal and maxVal (which may be scalars or vectors). For example, specifying minVal to be 0.0 and maxVal to be 1.0 constrains x to be in the range 0.0 to 1.0. This is such a common range to which to clamp numbers that graphics hardware often has a special case for this range, and some shading languages even include a built-in function specifically to clamp inputs to this range.

A few more special functions are `mix()`, `step()`, and `smoothstep()`. `mix()` performs a linear interpolation between two of its inputs using the third as a weighting factor. It can effectively be implemented as

```
vec4 mix(vec4 x, vec4 y, float a)
{
    return x + a * (y - x);
}
```

Again, this is such a common operation in graphics that it is a built-in function in the shading language, and graphics hardware may have special functionality to implement this directly.

The step() function generates a step function (a function that has a value of either 0.0 or 1.0) based on its two inputs. It is defined as

```
vec4 step(vec4 edge, vec4 x);
```

and it returns 0.0 if x < edge and 1.0 if x >= edge. The smoothstep() function is not as aggressive and produces a smooth fade between two of its inputs based on where the value of its third lies between the first two. It is defined as

```
vec4 smoothstep(vec4 edge0, vec4 edge1, vec4 x);
```

smoothstep() can effectively be implemented as

```
vec4 smoothstep(vec4 edge0, vec4 edge1, vec4 x)
{
  vec4 t = clamp((x - edge0) / (edge1 - edge0), 0.0, 1.0);

  return t * t * (vec4(3.0) - 2.0 * t);
}
```

The shape produced by smoothstep() is known as a Hermite curve, and the operation it performs is *Hermite interpolation*. The general shape of the curve is shown in Figure 6.1.

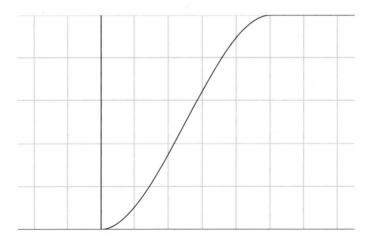

Figure 6.1: Shape of a Hermite curve

The fma() function performs a fused multiply-add operation. That is, it multiplies the first two of its parameters together and then adds the third. The intermediate result of the operation is generally kept at a higher precision than the source operands, producing a more accurate result than if you were to write those two operations directly in your code. In some graphics processors, the fused multiply-add function may be more efficient than a sequence of a multiplication followed by a separate addition operation.

Most of the math functions in GLSL presume that you are using floating-point numbers in the majority of your shader code. However, there are a few cases where you might be using integers, and GLSL includes a handful of functions that are designed to help you perform arithmetic on very large integer (or fixed-point) numbers. In particular, uaddCarry() and usubBorrow() allow you to perform add with carry and subtract with borrow operations, and imulExtended() and umulExtended() allow you to multiply a pair of 32-bit signed- or unsigned-integer values together, respectively, producing a 64-bit result as a further pair of 32-bit values.

In addition to all this low-level arithmetic functionality, GLSL also includes support for all of the expected trigonometry functions, such as sin(), cos(), and tan(); their inverses, asin(), acos() and atan(); and the hyperbolic forms of those functions, sinh(), cosh(), tanh(), asinh(), acosh(), and atanh(). Exponential functions are also included. These are pow(), exp(), log(), exp2(), log2(), sqrt(), and inversesqrt(). Because most of the GLSL functions dealing with angles work in *radians*, even though sometimes it might be convenient to work in degrees, GLSL also includes the radians() function (which takes an angle in degrees and converts it to radians) and the degrees() function (which takes an angle in radians and converts it into degrees).

Built-In Data Manipulation Functions

In addition to all of the functions that do real processing work, GLSL includes a lot of built-in functions that allow you to get at the innards of your data. For example, the frexp() allows you to break apart a floating-point number into its mantissa and exponent parts, and ldexp() allows you to build a new floating-point number from a mantissa and exponent that you supply. This allows some direct manipulation of the values of floating-point numbers.

If you need even more control over floating-point numbers, intBitsToFloat() and uintBitsToFloat() allow you to take a signed- or unsigned-integer number, respectively, and reinterpret its raw bits as a 32-bit floating-point number. To go the opposite way, floatBitsToInt() and floatBitsToUint() take a floating-point number and hand it back to you as either a signed- or unsigned-integer value, respectively. These four functions let you literally tear a floating-point number apart, mess with its bits, and put it back together again. You need to be careful when doing this, however, as not all bit combinations form valid floating-point numbers, and it's quite possible to generate NaNs (Not-a-Number), denormals or infinities. To test whether a floating-point number represents a NaN or an infinity, you can call `isnan()` or `isinf()`.

In addition to being able to tear apart floating-point numbers and then put them back together again, GLSL includes a number of functions to take floating-point vectors, scale them to various bit depths (such as 8- or 16-bit values), and pack them together into a single 32-bit quantity. For example, the `packUnorm4x8()` and `packSnorm4x8()` functions pack a `vec4` value into four unsigned- or signed- 8-bit integer values, respectively, and then pack those four 8-bit values together into a single `uint`. The `unpackUnorm4x8()` and `unpackSnorm4x8()` go the other way. The `packUnorm2x16()`, `packSnorm2x16()`, `unpackUnormx16()`, and `unpackSnorm16()` functions are the equivalents that handle `vec2` variables, packing and unpacking them as 16-bit quantities into a `uint`.

The term `norm` in these functions refers to *normalized*. In this context, normalization essentially means scaling a value to map it onto a new range. Here, floating-point values are either in the range 0.0 to 1.0 for unsigned normalized data, or -1.0 to 1.0 for signed normalized data. The ends of the input range are mapped to the lower and upper bounds of the output range. This means that for unsigned normalized 8-bit data, for example, an unsigned byte with a value of 0 corresponds to 0.0 in floating point, and an unsigned byte with a value of 255 (the maximum value representable by an unsigned 8-bit number) maps to 1.0.

The `packDouble2x32()` and `unpackDouble2x32()` functions perform similar operations on `double` variables, and the `packHalf2x16()` functions perform these operations on 16-bit floating-point quantities. It should be noted that GLSL does not include direct support for 16-bit floating-point variables, although data can be stored in memory in that format, and so GLSL includes functionality to unpack it into usable data types in the shading language.

If you just want to get at a subsection of the bits in a signed or unsigned integer, you can use the `bitfieldExtract()` function to pull a specified chunk of bits out of an unsigned integer (or vector of unsigned integers). If the input value to the function is a signed integer, then the result is sign extended, otherwise it is zero extended. Once you have manipulated the bits, you can put them back into the integer using the `bitfieldInsert()` function.

Other bitfield operations supported by GLSL include `bitfieldReverse()`, `bitCount()`, `findLSB()`, and `findMSB()` functions, which reverse the order of a subset of bits in an integer, count the number of set bits in an integer, and find the index of the least significant or most significant bit that is set in an integer, respectively.

Compiling, Linking, and Examining Programs

Each OpenGL implementation has a compiler and linker built in that will take your shader code, compile it to an internal binary form, and link it together so that it can be run on a graphics processor. This process may fail for various reasons, and so it is important to be able to figure out why. The compilation or link stage may have failed, and even if they succeed, it may be that some other factor has changed the way that your program behaves.

Getting Information from the Compiler

To this point in the book, all of the shaders we've presented have been perfect, tested and bug free. We've done very little, if any error checking and have just blasted ahead assuming that everything will work fine. However, in the real world, at least during development, your shaders will have bugs, typos, or errors in them, and the shader compiler can help you find problems and squash them. The first step is to determine whether a shader compiled or not. Once you have set the shader's source code and called **glCompileShader()**, you can get the compilation status back from OpenGL by calling **glGetShaderiv()**. Its prototype is

```
void glGetShaderiv(GLuint shader,
                   GLenum  pname,
                   GLint * params);
```

Here, `shader` is the name of the shader object you'd like to know about, `pname` is the parameter you want to get from the shader object, and `params` is the address of a variable where OpenGL should put the result. To find out if a shader compiled successfully, you can set `pname` to `GL_COMPILE_STATUS`. The variable pointed to by `params` will be set to zero if the shader failed to compile and to one if it compiled successfully. Incidentally, one and zero are the numerical values of `GL_TRUE` and `GL_FALSE`, so you can test against those defines if you wish.

Other values for pname that can be passed to **glGetShaderiv()** are

- GL_SHADER_TYPE, which returns the type of shader that the object is (GL_VERTEX_SHADER, GL_FRAGMENT_SHADER, etc.),

- GL_DELETE_STATUS, which will return GL_TRUE or GL_FALSE to indicate whether **glDeleteShader()** has been called on the shader object,

- GL_SHADER_SOURCE_LENGTH, which returns the total length of the source code associated with the shader object, and

- GL_INFO_LOG_LENGTH, which returns the length of the information log contained in the shader object.

This last token, GL_INFO_LOG_LENGTH, tells you the length of the information log that the shader object contains. This log is generated when the shader is compiled. Initially, it's empty, but as the shader compiler parses and compiles the shader, it generates a log that contains output similar to what you might be familiar with in the regular compiler world. You can then go ahead and retrieve the log from the shader object by calling **glGetShaderInfoLog()**, whose prototype is

```
void glGetShaderInfoLog(GLuint shader,
                        GLsizei bufSize,
                        GLsizei * length,
                        GLchar * infoLog);
```

Again, shader is the name of the shader object whose log you want to get at. infoLog should be pointed at a buffer that will have the log written into it by OpenGL. The buffer should be big enough to hold the entire log — the size of which you can get through the **glGetShaderiv()** function that we just introduced. If you only care about the first few lines of the log, you can use a fixed size buffer for infoLog, but regardless, the size of the buffer you're using should be in bufSize. The actual amount of data written into infoLog will be written into the variable pointed to by length by OpenGL. Listing 6.1 shows an example of how to retrieve the log from a shader object.

```
// Create, attach source to, and compile a shader...
GLuint fs = glCreateShader(GL_FRAGMENT_SHADER);
glShaderSource(fs, 1, &source, NULL);
glCompileShader(fs);

// Now, get the info log length...
GLint log_length;
glGetShaderiv(fs, GL_INFO_LOG_LENGTH, &log_length);
```

```
// Allocate a string for it...
std::string str;

str.reserve(log_length);

// Get the log...
glGetShaderInfoLog(fs, log_length, NULL, str.c_str());
```

Listing 6.1: Retrieving the compiler log from a shader

If your shader contains errors or suspect code that might generate compiler warnings, then OpenGL's shader compiler will tell you about it in the log. Consider the following shader, which contains deliberate errors:

```
#version 430 core

layout (location = 0) out vec4 color;

uniform scale;
uniform vec3 bias;

void main(void)
{
    color = vec4(1.0, 0.5, 0.2, 1.0) * scale + bias;
}
```

Compiling this shader produces the following log on this author's machine. You will likely see something similar on your own.

```
ERROR: 0:5: error(#12) Unexpected qualifier
ERROR: 0:10: error(#143) Undeclared identifier: scale
WARNING: 0:10: warning(#402) Implicit truncation of vector from
size: 4 to size: 3
ERROR: 0:10: error(#162) Wrong operand types: no operation "+" exists
that takes a left-hand operand of type "4-component vector of vec4" and
a right operand of type "uniform 3-component vector of vec3" (or there
is no acceptable conversion)
ERROR: error(#273) 3 compilation errors.  No code generated
```

As you can see, several errors and a warning have been generated and recorded in the shader's information log. For this particular compiler, the format of the error messages is ERROR or WARNING followed by the string index (remember, **glShaderSource()** allows you to attach multiple source strings to a single shader object), followed by the line number. Let's look at the errors one by one:

```
ERROR: 0:5: error(#12) Unexpected qualifier
```

Line 5 of our shader is this:

```
uniform scale;
```

It seems that we have forgotten the type of the `scale` uniform. We can fix that by giving `scale` a type (it's supposed to be `vec4`). The next three issues are on the same line:

```
ERROR: 0:10: error(#143) Undeclared identifier: scale
WARNING: 0:10: warning(#402) Implicit truncation of vector from
size: 4 to size: 3
ERROR: 0:10: error(#162) Wrong operand types: no operation "+" exists
that takes a left-hand operand of type "4-component vector of vec4" and
a right operand of type "uniform 3-component vector of vec3" (or there
is no acceptable conversion)
```

The first one says that `scale` is an undefined identifier — that is, the compiler doesn't know what `scale` is. This is because of that first error on line 5, and that because of that, we haven't actually defined `scale` yet. Next is a warning that we are attempting to truncate a vector from a four-component type to a three-component type. This might not be a serious issue, given that the compiler might be confused as a result of another error on the very same line. This one is saying that there is no version of the + operator that can add a `vec3` and a `vec4`. This is because, even once we've given `scale` its `vec4` type, bias has been declared as a `vec3` and therefore can't be added to a `vec4` variable. A potential fix is to change the type of bias to a `vec4`. If we apply our now known fixes to the shader (shown in Listing 6.1), we have

```
#version 430 core

layout (location = 0) out vec4 color;

uniform vec4 scale;
uniform vec4 bias;

void main(void)
{
    color = vec4(1.0, 0.5, 0.2, 1.0) * scale + bias;
}
```

Once we compile this updated shader, we should have success, calling **glGetShaderiv()** with pname set to GL_COMPILE_STATUS should return GL_TRUE, and the new info log should either be empty or simply indicate success.

Getting Information from the Linker

Just as compilation may fail, linking of programs may also fail or not go exactly the way you planned. Just as the compiler will produce an info log when you call **glCompileShader()**, when you call **glLinkProgram()**, the linker can also produce a log that you can query to figure out what went on. Also, a program object has several properties, including its link status, resource usage, and so on that you can retrieve. In fact, a linked program has quite a bit more status than a compiled shader, and you can retrieve it all by using **glGetProgramiv()**, whose prototype is

```
void glGetProgramiv(GLuint program,
                    GLenum  pname,
                    GLint * params);
```

You'll notice that **glGetProgramiv()** is very similar to **glGetShaderiv()**. The first parameter, program, is the name of the program object whose information you want to retrieve, and the last parameter, params, is the address of a variable where you would like OpenGL to write that information. Just like **glGetShaderiv()**, **glGetProgramiv()** takes a parameter called pname, which indicates what you would like to know about the program object. There are actually many more valid values for pname for program objects, and these are a few that we can look at now:

- GL_DELETE_STATUS, as with the same property of shaders, indicates whether **glDeleteProgram()** has been called for the program object.

- GL_LINK_STATUS, similarly to the GL_COMPILE_STATUS property of a shader, indicates the success of linking the program.

- GL_INFO_LOG_LENGTH returns the info log length for the program.

- GL_ATTACHED_SHADERS returns the number of shaders that are attached to the program.

- GL_ACTIVE_ATTRIBUTES returns the number of attributes that the vertex shader in the program actually[5] uses.

- GL_ACTIVE_UNIFORMS returns the number of uniforms used by the program.

- GL_ACTIVE_UNIFORM_BLOCKS returns the number of uniform blocks used by the program.

You can tell whether a program has been successfully linked by calling **glGetProgramiv()** with pname set to GL_LINK_STATUS, and if it returns GL_TRUE in params, then linking worked. You can also get the information log from a program just like you can from a shader. To do this, you can call **glGetProgramInfoLog()**, whose prototype is

```
void glGetProgramInfoLog(GLuint program,
                         GLsizei bufSize,
                         GLsizei * length,
                         GLchar * infoLog);
```

---

5. More precisely, that the compiler thinks the vertex shader uses.

The parameters to **glGetProgramInfoLog()** work just the same as they do for **glGetShaderInfoLog()**, except that in place of shader, we have program, which is the name of the program object whose log you want to read. Now, consider the shader shown in Listing 6.2.

```
#version 430 core

layout (location = 0) out vec4 color;

vec3 myFunction();

void main(void)
{
    color = vec4(myFunction(), 1.0);
}
```

Listing 6.2: Fragment shader with external function declaration

Listing 6.2 includes a declaration of an external function. This works similarly to C programs where the actual definition of the function is contained in a separate source file. OpenGL expects that the function body for myFunction is defined in one of the fragment shaders attached to the program object (remember, you can attach multiple shaders of the same type to the same program object and have them link together). When you call **glLinkProgram()**, OpenGL will go looking in all the fragment shaders for a function called myFunction, and if it's not there, will generate a link error. The result of trying to link just this fragment shader into a program object is

```
Vertex shader(s) failed to link, fragment shader(s) failed to link.
ERROR: error(#401) Function: myFunction() is not implemented
```

To resolve this error, we can either include the body of myFunction in the shader of Listing 6.2, or we can attach a second fragment shader to the same program object that includes the function body.

Separate Programs

So far, all of the programs you have used have been considered *monolithic* program objects. That is, they contain a shader for each stage that is active. You have attached a vertex shader, a fragment shader, and possibly tessellation or geometry shaders to a single program object and then have called glLinkProgram() to link the program object into a single representation of the entire pipeline. This type of linking might allow a compiler to perform inter-stage optimizations such as eliminating code in a vertex shader that contributes to an output that is never used by the subsequent fragment shader, for example. However, this scheme comes at a potential cost of flexibility and possibly performance to the application. For every combination of vertex, fragment, and possibly other shaders, you need to have a unique program object, and linking all those programs doesn't come cheap.

For example, consider the case where you want to change only a fragment shader. With a monolithic program, you would need to link the same vertex shader to two or more different fragment shaders, creating a new program object for each combination. If you have multiple fragment shaders and multiple vertex shaders, you now need a program object for each combination of shaders. This problem gets worse as you add more and more shaders and shader stages to the mix. You end up with a combinatorial explosion of shader combinations that can quickly balloon into thousands of permutations, or more.

To alleviate this, OpenGL supports linking program objects in *separable* mode. A program linked this way can contain shaders for only a single stage in the pipeline or for just a few of the stages. Multiple program objects, each representing a section of the OpenGL pipeline can then be attached to a *program pipeline object* and matched together at run-time rather than at link time. Shaders attached to a single program object can still benefit from inter-stage optimizations, but the program objects attached to a program pipeline object can be switched around at will with relatively little cost in performance.

To use a program object in separable mode, you need to tell OpenGL what you plan to do *before* you link it by calling **glProgramParameteri()** with pname set to GL_PROGRAM_SEPARABLE and value set to GL_TRUE. This tells OpenGL not to eliminate any outputs from a shader that it thinks aren't being used. It will also arrange any internal data layout such that the last shader in the program object can communicate with the first shader in another program object with the same input layout. Next, you should create a program pipeline object with **glGenProgramPipelines()**, and then attach programs to it representing the sections of the pipeline you wish to use. To do this, call **glUseProgramStages()**, passing the name of the program pipeline object, a bitfield indicating which stages to use, and the name of a program object that contains those stages.

An example of how to set up a program pipeline object with two programs, one containing only a vertex shader and one containing only a fragment shader, is shown in Listing 6.3.

```
// Create a vertex shader
GLuint vs = glCreateShader(GL_VERTEX_SHADER);

// Attach source and compile
glShaderSource(vs, 1, vs_source, NULL);
glCompileShader(vs);

// Create a program for our vertex stage and attach the vertex shader to it
GLuint vs_program = glCreateProgram();
glAttachShader(vs_program, vs);

// Important part - set the GL_PROGRAM_SEPARABLE flag to GL_TRUE *then* link
glProgramParameteri(vs_program, GL_PROGRAM_SEPARABLE, GL_TRUE);
glLinkProgram(vs_program);

// Now do the same with a fragment shader
GLuint fs = glCreateShader(GL_FRAGMENT_SHADER);
glShaderSource(fs, 1, fs_source, NULL);
glCompileShader(fs);
GLuint fs_program = glCreateProgram();
glAttachShader(fs_program, vs);
glProgramParameteri(fs_program, GL_PROGRAM_SEPARABLE, GL_TRUE);
glLinkProgram(fs_program);

// The program pipeline represents the collection of programs in use:
// Generate the name for it here.
GLuint program_pipeline;
glGenProgramPipelines(1, &program_pipeline);

// Now, use the vertex shader from the first program and the fragment shader
// from the second program.
glUseProgramStages(program_pipeline, GL_VERTEX_SHADER_BIT, vs_program);
glUseProgramStages(program_pipeline, GL_FRAGMENT_SHADER_BIT, fs_program);
```

Listing 6.3: Configuring a separable program pipeline

Although this simple example only includes two program objects, each with only a single shader in it, it's possible to have more complex arrangements where more than two program objects are used, or where one or more of the program objects contain more than one shader. For example, tessellation control and tessellation evaluation shaders are often tightly coupled, and one does not make much sense without the other. Also, very often when tessellation is used, it is possible to use a pass-through vertex shader and do all of the real vertex shader work either in the tessellation control shader or in the tessellation evaluation shader. In those cases, it may make sense to couple a vertex shader and both tessellation shaders in one program object, and still use separable programs to be able to switch the fragment shader on the fly.

If you really do want to create a simple program object with exactly one shader object in it, you can take a shortcut and call

```
GLuint glCreateShaderProgramv(GLenum type,
                              GLsizei count,
                              const char ** strings);
```

The **glCreateShaderProgramv()** function takes the type of shader you want to compile (GL_VERTEX_SHADER, GL_FRAGMENT_SHDAER, etc.), the number of source strings, and a pointer to an array of strings (just like **glShaderSource()**), and compiles those strings into a new shader object. Then, it internally attaches that shader object to a new program object, sets its separable hint to true, links it, deletes the shader object, and returns the program object to you. You can then go ahead and use this program object in your program pipeline objects.

Once you have a program pipeline object with a bunch of shader stages compiled into program objects and attached to it, you can make it the current pipeline by calling **glBindProgramPipeline()**:

```
void glBindProgramPipeline(GLuint pipeline);
```

Here, `pipeline` is the name of the program pipeline object that you wish to use. Once the program pipeline object is bound, its programs will be used for rendering or compute operations.

Interface Matching

GLSL provides a specific set of rules for how the outputs from one shader stage are matched up with the corresponding inputs in the next stage. When you link a set of shaders together into a single program object, OpenGL's linker will tell you if you didn't match things up correctly. However, when you use separate program objects for each stage, the matching occurs when you switch program objects, and not lining things up correctly can cause effects from subtle failures of your program to things not working at all. It is therefore very important to follow these rules to avoid these kind of issues, especially when you are using separate program objects.

In general, the output variables of one shader stage end up connected to the inputs of the subsequent stage if they match exactly in name and type. The variables must also match in qualification. For interface blocks, the two blocks on either side of the interface must have the same members, with the same names, declared in the same order. The same applies for structures (either used as inputs and outputs, or as members of interface blocks). If the interface variable is an array, both sides of the interface should declare the same number of elements in that array. The only exception is for the inputs and outputs for tessellation and geometry shaders that change from single elements to arrays along the way.

If you link shaders for multiple stages together in a single program object, OpenGL may realize that an interface member isn't required and that it can eliminate it from the shader(s). As an example, if the vertex shader only writes a constant to a particular output and the fragment shader then consumes that data as an input, OpenGL might remove the code to produce that constant from the vertex shader and instead use the constant directly in the fragment shader. When separate programs are used, OpenGL can't do this and must consider every part of the interface to be active and used.

It can be a pain to remember to name all of your input and output variables the same way in every shader in your application, especially as the number of shaders grows or as more developers start contributing shaders. However, it is possible to use a `layout` qualifier to assign a location to each input and output in a set of shaders. Where possible, OpenGL will use the locations of each input and output to match them together. In that case, the names of the variables don't matter, and they only need match in type and qualification.

It is possible to query the input and output interfaces of a program object by calling `glGetProgramInterfaceiv()` and `glGetProgramResourceiv()`, whose prototypes are

```
void glGetProgramInterfaceiv(GLuint program,
                             GLenum programInterface,
                             GLenum pname,
                             GLint * params);
```

and

```
void glGetProgramResourceiv(GLuint program,
                            GLenum programInterface,
                            GLuint index,
                            GLsizei propCount,
                            const Glenum * props,
                            GLsizei bufSize,
                            GLsizei * length,
                            GLint * params);
```

Here, `program` is the name of the program object you want to discover the interface properties of, and `programInterface` should be GL_PROGRAM_INPUT or GL_PROGRAM_OUTPUT to specify that you want to know about the inputs or outputs of the program, respectively.

For `glGetProgramInterfaceiv()`, pname should be GL_ACTIVE_RESOURCES, and the number of separate inputs or outputs of program will be written into the variable pointed to by params. You can then read from this list of inputs or outputs by passing the index of the resource in the index parameter of **glGetProgramResourceiv()**. **glGetProgramResourceiv()** returns multiple properties in a single function call, and the number of properties to return is given in propCount. props is an array of tokens specifying which properties you'd like to retrieve. Those properties will be written to the array whose address is given in params and the size of which (in elements) is given in bufSize. If length is not NULL, then the actual number of properties will be written into the variable that it points at.

The values in the props array can be any of the following:

- GL_TYPE returns the type of the interface member in the corresponding element of params.

- GL_ARRAY_SIZE returns the length of the interface array if it is an array, or zero if it is not.

- GL_REFERENCED_BY_VERTEX_SHADER,
  GL_REFERENCED_BY_TESS_CONTROL_SHADER,
  GL_REFERENCED_BY_TESS_EVALUATION_SHADER,
  GL_REFERENCED_BY_GEOMETRY_SHADER,
  GL_REFERENCED_BY_FRAGMENT_SHADER, and
  GL_REFERENCED_BY_COMPUTE_SHADER return zero or non-zero depending on whether the input or output is referenced by the vertex, tessellation control or evaluation, geometry, fragment, or compute shader stages, respectively.

- GL_LOCATION returns the shader-specified or OpenGL-generated location for the input or output in the corresponding element of params.

- GL_LOCATION_INDEX can be used only when programInterface specifies GL_PROGRAM_OUTPUT, and it returns the index of the output of a fragment shader.

- GL_IS_PER_PATCH lets you know if an output of a tessellation control shader or an input to a tessellation evaluation shader is declared as a per-patch interface.

You can determine the name of an input or output by calling **glGetProgramResourceName()**:

```
void glGetProgramResourceName(GLuint program,
                              GLenum programInterface,
                              GLuint index,
                              GLsizei bufSize,
                              GLsizei * length,
                              char * name);
```

Again, program, programInterface, and index have the same meaning as they do for **glGetProgramResourceiv()**. bufSize is the size of the buffer pointed to by name, and, if it is not NULL, length points to a variable that will have the actual length of the name written into it. As an example, Listing 6.4 shows a simple program that will print information about the active outputs of the program object.

```
// Get the number of outputs
GLint outputs;
glGetProgramInterfaceiv(program, GL_PROGRAM_OUTPUT,
                        GL_ACTIVE_RESOURCES, &outputs);

// A list of tokens describing the properties we wish to query
static const GLenum props[] = { GL_TYPE, GL_LOCATION };

// Various local variables
GLint i;
GLint params[2];
GLchar name[64];
const char * type_name;

for (i = 0; i < outputs; i++)
{
    // Get the name of the output
    glGetProgramResourceName(program, GL_PROGRAM_OUTPUT, i,
                             sizeof(name), NULL, name);

    // Get other properties of the output
    glGetProgramResourceiv(program, GL_PROGRAM_OUTPUT, i,
                           2, props, 2, NULL, params);

    // type_to_name() is a function that returns the GLSL name of
    // type given its enumerant value
    type_name = type_to_name(params[0]);

    // Print the result
    printf("Index %d: %s %s @ location %d.\n",
           i, type_name, name, params[1]);
}
```

Listing 6.4: Printing interface information

Look at the output declarations in the following snippet of a fragment shader:

```
out vec4 color;
layout (location = 2) out ivec2 data;
out float extra;
```

Given these declarations, the code shown in Listing 6.4 prints the following:

```
Index 0: vec4 color @ location 0.
Index 1: ivec2 data @ location 2.
Index 2: float extra @ location 1.
```

Notice that the listing of the active outputs appears in the order that they were declared in. However, since we explicitly specified output location 2 for data, the GLSL compiler went back and used location 1 for extra. We are also able to correctly tell the types of the outputs using this code. Although in your applications, you will likely know the types and names of all of your outputs, this kind of functionality is very useful for development tools and debuggers that may not know the origin of the shaders that they are working with.

Shader Subroutines

Even when your programs are linked in separable mode, switching between program objects can still be fairly expensive from a performance perspective. As an alternative, it may be possible to use *subroutine uniforms*. These are a special type of uniform that behaves something akin to a function pointer in C. To use a subroutine uniform, we declare a subroutine type, declare one or more compatible subroutines (which are essentially just functions with a special declaration format), and then "point" our subroutine uniforms at these functions. A simple example is shown in Listing 6.5.

```
#version 430 core

// First, declare the subroutine type
subroutine vec4 sub_mySubroutine(vec4 param1);

// Next declare a couple of functions that can be used as subroutine...
subroutine (sub_mySubroutine)
vec4 myFunction1(vec4 param1)
{
    return param1 * vec4(1.0, 0.25, 0.25, 1.0);
}

subroutine (sub_mySubroutine)
vec4 myFunction2(vec4 param1)
{
    return param1 * vec4(0.25, 0.25, 1.0, 1.0);
}

// Finally, declare a subroutine uniform that can be "pointed"
// at subroutine functions matching its signature
subroutine uniform sub_mySubroutine mySubroutineUniform;

// Output color
out vec4 color;

void main(void)
{
    // Call subroutine through uniform
    color = mySubroutineUniform(vec4(1.0));
}
```

Listing 6.5: Example subroutine uniform declaration

When you link a program that includes subroutines, each subroutine in each stage is assigned an index. If you are using version 430 of GLSL or newer (this is the version shipped with OpenGL 4.3), you can assign the indices yourself in shader code using the index layout qualifier. So, we could declare the subroutines from Listing 6.5 as follows:

```
layout (index = 2)
subroutine (sub_mySubroutine)
vec4 myFunction1(vec4 param1)
{
    return param1 * vec4(1.0, 0.25, 0.25, 1.0);
}

layout (index = 1);
subroutine (sub_mySubroutine)
vec4 myFunction2(vec4 param1)
{
    return param1 * vec4(0.25, 0.25, 1.0, 1.0);
}
```

If you are using a version of GLSL earlier than 430, then OpenGL will assign indices for you and you have no say in the matter. Either way, you can find out what those indices are by calling

```
GLuint glGetProgramResourceIndex(GLuint program,
                                 GLenum programInterface,
                                 const char * name);
```

Here, program is the name of the linked program containing the subroutine; programInterface is one of GL_VERTEX_SUBROUTINE, GL_TESS_CONTROL_SUBROUTINE, GL_TESS_EVALUATION_SUBROUTINE, GL_GEOMETRY_SUBROUTINE, GL_FRAGMENT_SUBROUTINE, or GL_COMPUTE_SUBROUTINE to indicate which shader stage that you're asking about; and name is the name of the subroutine. If a subroutine with the name name is not found in the appropriate stage of the program, then this function returns GL_INVALID_VALUE. Going the other way, given the indices of subroutines in a program, you can get their names by calling

```
void glGetProgramResourceName(GLuint program,
                              GLenum programInterface,
                              GLuint index,
                              GLsizei bufSize,
                              GLsizei * length,
                              char *  name);
```

Here, program is the name of the program object containing the subroutines, programInterface is one of the same tokens accepted by **glGetProgramResourceIndex()**, index is the index of the subroutine within the program, bufsize is the size of the buffer whose address is in name, and length is the address of a variable that will be filled with the actual number of characters written into name. The number of active subroutines

in a particular stage of a program can be determined by calling
glGetProgramStageiv():

```
void glGetProgramStageiv(GLuint program,
                         GLenum shadertype,
                         GLenum pname,
                         GLint *values);
```

Again, program is the name of the program object containing the shader, and shadertype indicates which stage of the program you're asking about. To get the number of active subroutines in the relevant stage of the program, pname should be set to GL_ACTIVE_SUBROUTINES. The result is written into the variable whose address you place in values. When you call **glGetActiveSubroutineName()**, index should be between zero and one less than this value. Once you know the names of the subroutines in a program object (either because you wrote the shader or because you queried the names), you can set their values by calling

```
void glUniformSubroutinesuiv(GLenum shadertype,
                             GLsizei count,
                             const GLunit *indices);
```

This function sets count subroutine uniforms in the shader stage given by shadertype in the active program to point at the subroutines whose indices are given in the first count elements of the array pointed to by indices. Subroutines uniforms are a little different from other uniforms in several ways:

- The state for subroutine uniforms is stored in the current OpenGL context rather than in the program object. This allows subroutine uniforms to have different values within the same program object when it's used in different contexts.

- The values of subroutine uniforms are lost when the current program object is changed using **glUseProgram()**, when you call **glUseProgramStages()** or **glBindProgramPipeline()**, or if you re-link the current program object. This means that you need to reset them every time you use a new program or new program stages.

- It is not possible to change the value of a subset of the subroutine uniforms in a stage of a program object. **glUniformSubroutinesuiv()** sets the value of count uniforms, starting from zero. Any uniforms beyond count will be left with their previous value. Remember, though, that the default value of subroutine uniforms is not defined, and so not setting them at all and then calling them could cause bad things to happen.

In our simple example, after linking our program object, we can run the following code to determine the indices of our subroutine functions as we haven't assigned explicit locations to them in our shader code:

```
subroutines[0] = glGetProgramResourceIndex(render_program,
                                           GL_FRAGMENT_SHADER_SUBROUTINE,
                                           "myFunction1");
subroutines[1] = glGetProgramResourceIndex(render_program,
                                           GL_FRAGMENT_SHADER_SUBROUTINE,
                                           "myFunction2");
```

Now, our rendering loop is shown in Listing 6.6.

```
void subroutines_app::render(double currentTime)
{
    int i = (int)currentTime;

    glUseProgram(render_program);

    glUniformSubroutinesuiv(GL_FRAGMENT_SHADER, 1, &subroutines[i & 1]);

    glDrawArrays(GL_TRIANGLE_STRIP, 0, 4);
}
```

Listing 6.6: Setting values of subroutine uniforms

This function draws a quad using a simple vertex shader that was also linked into our program object. After setting the current program with a call to **glUseProgram()**, it resets the values of the only subroutine uniform in the program. Remember, the values of all of the subroutine uniforms "go away" when you change the current program. The subroutine at which we point the uniform changes every second. Using the fragment shader shown in Listing 6.5, the window will be rendered red for one second, then blue for a second, then red again, and so on.

In general, you can expect that setting the value of a single subroutine uniform to take less time than changing a program object. Therefore, if you have several similar shaders, it may be worthwhile combining them into one and using a subroutine uniform to choose between which path to take. You can even declare multiple versions of your main() function (with different names), create a subroutine uniform that can point at any of them, and then call it from your real main() function.

Program Binaries

Once you have compiled and linked a program, it is possible to ask OpenGL to give you a binary object that represents its internal version of the program. At some point in the future, your application can hand that binary back to OpenGL and bypass the compiler and linker. If you wish to use this feature, you should call **glProgramParameteri()** with pname set to GL_PROGRAM_BINARY_RETRIEVABLE_HINT set to GL_TRUE before calling **glLinkProgram()**. This tells OpenGL that you plan to get the binary data back from it and that it should hang on to that binary and have it ready to pass to you.

Before you can retrieve the binary for a program object, you need to figure out how long it's going to be and allocate memory to store it. To do this, you can call **glGetProgramiv()** and set pname to GL_PROGRAM_BINARY_LENGTH. The resulting value written into params is the number of bytes you will need to set aside for the program binary.

Next, you can call **glGetProgramBinary()** to actually retrieve the binary representation of the program object. The prototype of **glGetProgramBinary()** is

```
void glGetProgramBinary(GLuint program,
                        GLsizei bufsize,
                        GLsizei * length,
                        GLenum * binaryFormat,
                        void * binary);
```

Given the name of a program object in program, it will write the binary representation of the program into the memory pointed to by binary, and write a token representing the format of that program binary into binaryFormat. The size of this region of memory is passed in bufsize and must be large enough to store the entire program binary, which is why it is necessary to query the binary size with **glGetProgramiv()** first. The actual number of bytes written is stored in the variable whose address is passed in length. The format of the binary is likely to be proprietary and specific to the vendor that made your OpenGL drivers. However, it's important to keep hold of the value written to binaryFormat because you'll need to pass this back to OpenGL later along with the contents of the binary to load it back up again. Listing 6.7 shows a simple example of how to retrieve a program binary from OpenGL.

```
// Create a simple program containing only a vertex shader
static const GLchar source[] = { ... };

// First create and compile the shader
GLuint shader;
shader = glCreateShader(GL_VERTEX_SHADER);
glShaderSource(shader, 1, suorce, NULL);
glCompileShader(shader);

// Create the program and attach the shader to it
```

```
GLuint program;
program = glCreateProgram();
glAttachShader(program, shader);

// Set the binary retrievable hint and link the program
glProgramParameteri(program, GL_PROGRAM_BINARY_RETRIEVABLE_HINT, GL_TRUE);
glLinkProgram(program);

// Get the expected size of the program binary
GLint binary_size = 0;
glGetProgramiv(program, GL_PROGRAM_BINARY_SIZE, &binary_size);

// Allocate some memory to store the program binary
unsigned char * program_binary = new unsigned char [binary_size];

// Now retrieve the binary from the program object
GLenum binary_format = GL_NONE;
glGetProgramBinary(program, binary_size, NULL, &binary_format,
  program_binary);
```

Listing 6.7: Retrieving a program binary

Once you have the program binary, you can save it to disk (possibly compressed) and use it next time your program starts. This can save you the time taken to compile shaders and link programs before you can start rendering. It should be noted that the program binary format is probably[6] going to be specific to your graphics card vendor and is not portable from machine to machine, or even from driver to driver on the same machine. This feature is not currently designed as a distribution mechanism, but as more of a caching mechanism.

This may seem like a fairly large limitation and as if program binaries are not of much use — and with relatively simple applications like those outlined in this book. However, consider a very large application such as a video game. It may include hundreds or thousands of shaders, and may compile multiple variants of those shaders. The startup time on many video games is very long, and using program binaries to cache compiled shaders from run-to-run of a game can save a lot of time. However, another issue that plagues complex application is run-time recompilation of shaders.

Most features of OpenGL are supported directly by modern graphics processors. However, some of them require some level of work in a shader. When your application compiles shaders, the OpenGL implementation will assume the most common case for most states and compile the shader

---

6. It is conceivable that one or more OpenGL vendors could get together and define a standard binary format in an extension that is understood by multiple parties. At time of writing, that has not happened.

assuming that is the way it will be used. If it is used in a way that is not handled by this default compilation of the shaders, the OpenGL implementation may need to at least partially recompile parts of the shader to deal with the changes. That can cause a noticeable stutter in the execution of the application.

For this reason, it's strongly recommended that you compile your shaders and then link your program with the GL_PROGRAM_BINARY_RETRIEVABLE_HINT set to GL_TRUE, but wait until you've used them a few times for real rendering before retrieving the binaries. This will give the OpenGL implementation a chance to recompile any shaders that need it and store a number of versions of each program in a single binary. Next time you load the binary and the OpenGL implementation realizes that it needs a particular variant of the program, it will find it already compiled in the binary blob you just handed it.

Once you're ready to give the program binary back to OpenGL, call **glProgramBinary()** on a fresh program object, and with binaryFormat and length set to the values you got back from **glGetProgramBinary()** and with the data loaded into the buffer that you pass in binary. This will reload the program object with the data it contained when you queried the binary on the last run of your application. If the OpenGL driver doesn't recognize the binary you give it or can't load it for some reason, the **glProgramBinary()** call will fail. In this case, you'll need to supply the original GLSL source for the shaders and recompile them.

Summary

This chapter discussed shaders, how they work, the GLSL programming language, how OpenGL uses them, and where they fit within the graphics pipeline. You should have a good understanding of the basic concepts involved in writing the shaders you'll need for your programs. You also learned how to retrieve binary shaders from OpenGL so that your applications can cache them and store them away for later. When your shaders don't work (which is inevitable during the development of any application), you should be able to get information from OpenGL that will help you figure out why. With a little practice, and with the topics covered earlier in this book, you should be in good stead to write some interesting OpenGL programs.

Part II

In Depth

Chapter 7

Vertex Processing and Drawing Commands

WHAT YOU'LL LEARN IN THIS CHAPTER

- How to get data from your application into the front of the graphics pipeline

- What the various OpenGL drawing commands are and what their parameters do

- How your transformed geometry gets into your application's window

In Chapter 3, we followed the OpenGL pipeline from start to finish, producing a simple application that exercised every shader stage with a minimal example that was just enough to make it do something. We even showed you a simple compute shader that did nothing at all! However, the result of all this was a single tessellated triangle broken into points. Since then, you have learned some of the math involved in 3D computer graphics, have seen how to set up the pipeline to do more than draw a single triangle, and have a deeper introduction to GLSL, the OpenGL Shading Language. In this chapter, we dig deeper into the first couple of stages of the OpenGL pipeline — that is, vertex assembly and vertex shading. We'll see how drawing commands are structured and how they can be used to send work into the OpenGL pipeline, and how that ends up in primitives being produced ready for rasterization.

Vertex Processing

The first programmable stage in the OpenGL pipeline (i.e., one that you can write a shader for) is the vertex shader. Before the shader runs, OpenGL will fetch the inputs to the vertex shader in the *vertex fetch* stage, which we will describe first. Your vertex shader's responsibility is to set the position[1] of the vertex that will be fed to the next stage in the pipeline. It can also set a number of other user-defined and built-in outputs that further describe the vertex to OpenGL.

Vertex Shader Inputs

The first step in any OpenGL graphics pipeline is the the vertex fetch stage, unless the configuration does not require any vertex attributes, as was the case in some of our earliest examples. This stage runs before your vertex shader and is responsible for forming its inputs. You have been introduced to the **glVertexAttribPointer()** function, and we have explained how it hooks data in buffers up to vertex shader inputs. Now, we'll take a closer look at vertex attributes.

In the example programs presented thus far, we've only used a single vertex attribute and have filled it with four-component floating-point data, which matches the data types we have used for our uniforms, uniform blocks, and hard-coded constants. However, OpenGL supports a large number of vertex attributes, and each can have its own format, data type, number of components, and so on. Also, OpenGL can read the data for each attribute from a different buffer object. **glVertexAttribPointer()** is a handy way to set up virtually everything about a vertex attribute. However, it can actually be considered more of a helper function that sits on top of a few lower level functions: **glVertexAttribFormat()**, **glVertexAttribBinding()**, and **glBindVertexBuffer()**. Their prototypes are

```
void glVertexAttribFormat(GLuint attribindex, GLint size,
                          GLenum type, GLboolean normalized,
                          GLuint relativeoffset);

void glVertexAttribBinding(GLuint attribindex,
                           GLuint bindingindex);

void glBindVertexBuffer(GLuint bindingindex,
                        GLuint buffer,
                        GLintptr offset,
                        GLintptr stride);
```

---

1. Under certain circumstances, you may even omit this.

In order to understand how these functions work, first, let's consider a simple vertex shader fragment that declares a number of inputs. In Listing 7.1, notice the use of the location layout qualifier to set the locations of the inputs explicitly in the shader code.

```
#version 430 core

// Declare a number of vertex attributes
layout (location = 0) in vec4 position;
layout (location = 1) in vec3 normal;
layout (location = 2) in vec2 tex_coord;
// Note that we intentionally skip location 3 here
layout (location = 4) in vec4 color;
layout (location = 5) in int material_id;
```

Listing 7.1: Declaration of a Multiple Vertex Attributes

The shader fragment in Listing 7.1 declares five inputs, position, normal, tex_coord, color, and material_id. Now, consider that we are using a data structure to represent our vertices that is defined in C as

```
typedef struct VERTEX_t
{
    vmath::vec4     position;
    vmath::vec3     normal;
    vmath::vec2     tex_coord;
    GLubyte         color[3];
    int             material_id;
} VERTEX;
```

Notice that our vertex structure in C mixes use of vmath types and plain old data (for color).

The first attribute is pretty standard and should be familiar to you — it's the position of the vertex, specified as a four-component floating-point vector. To describe this input using the **glVertexAttribFormat()** function, we would set size to 4 and type to GL_FLOAT. The second, the normal of the geometry at the vertex, is in normal and would be passed to **glVertexAttribFormat()** with size set to 3 and, again, type set to GL_FLOAT. Likewise, tex_coord can be used as a two-dimensional texture coordinate and might be specified by setting size to 2 and type to GL_FLOAT.

Now, the color input to the vertex shader is declared as a vec4, but the color member of our VERTEX structure is actually an array of 3 bytes. Both the size (number of elements) and the data type are different. OpenGL can convert the data for you as it reads it into the vertex shader. To hook our 3-byte color member up to our four-component vertex shader input, we call **glVertexAttribFormat()** with size set to 3 and type set to

GL_UNSIGNED_BYTE. This is where the `normalized` parameter comes in. As you probably know, the range of values representable by an unsigned byte is 0 to 255. However, that's not what we want in our vertex shader. There, we want to represent colors as values between 0.0 and 1.0. If you set `normalized` to `GL_TRUE`, then OpenGL will automatically divide through each component of the input by the maximum possible representable positive value, *normalizing* it.

Because two's-complement numbers are able to represent a greater magnitude negative number than a positive number, this can place one value below the -1.0 (-128 for `GLbyte`, -32,768 for `GLshort`, and -2,147,483,648 for `GLint`). Those most negative numbers are treated specially and are clamped to the floating-point value -1.0 during normalization. If `normalized` is `GL_FALSE`, then the value will be converted directly to floating point and presented to the vertex shader. In the case of unsigned byte data (like `color`), this means that the values will be between 0.0 and 255.0.

Table 7.1 shows the tokens that can be used for the `type` parameter, their corresponding OpenGL type, and the range of values that they can represent.

Table 7.1: Vertex Attribute Types

Type	OpenGL Type	Range
GL_BYTE	GLbyte	-128 to 127
GL_SHORT	Glshort	-32,768 to 32767
GL_INT	GLint	-2,147,483,648 to 2,147,483,647
GL_FIXED	GLfixed	-32,768 to 32767
GL_UNSIGNED_BYTE	GLubyte	0 to 255
GL_UNSIGNED_SHORT	GLushort	0 to 65535
GL_UNSIGNED_INT	GLuint	4,294,967,295
GL_HALF_FLOAT	GLhalf	—
GL_FLOAT	GLfloat	—
GL_DOUBLE	GLdouble	—

In Table 7.1, the floating-point types (`GLhalf`, `GLfloat`, and `GLdouble`) don't have ranges because they can't be normalized. The `GLfixed` type is a special case. It represents *fixed-point* data that is made up of 32 bits with the binary point at position 16 (halfway through the number), and as such, it is treated as one of the floating-point types and cannot be normalized.

In addition to the scalar types shown in Table 7.1, **glVertexAttribFormat()** also supports several *packed* data formats that use a single integer to store multiple components. The two packed data formats supported by OpenGL are GL_UNSIGNED_INT_2_10_10_10_REV and GL_INT_2_10_10_10_REV, which both represent four components packed into a single 32-bit word.

The GL_UNSIGNED_INT_2_10_10_10_REV format provides 10 bits for each of the x, y, and z components of the vector and only 2 bits for the w component, which are all treated as unsigned quantities. This gives a range of 0 to 1023 for each of x, y, and z and 0 to 3 for w. Likewise, the GL_INT_2_10_10_10_REV format provides 10 bits for x, y, and z and 2 bits for w, but in this case, each component is treated as a signed quantity. That means that while x, y, and z have a range of -512 to 511, w may range from -2 to 1. While this may not seem terribly useful, there are a number of use cases for three-component vectors with more than 8 bits of precision (24 bits in total), but that do not require 16 bits of precision (48 bits in total), and even though those last two bits might be wasted, 10 bits of precision per component provides what is needed.

When one of the packed data types (GL_UNSIGNED_INT_2_10_10_10_REV or GL_INT_2_10_10_10_REV) is specified, then size must be set either to 4 or to the special value GL_BGRA. This applies an automatic swizzle to the incoming data to reverse the order of the r, g, and b (which are equivalent to the x, y, and z) components of the incoming vectors. This provides compatibility with data stored in that order[2] without needing to modify your shaders.

Finally, returning to our example vertex declaration, we have the material_id field, which is an integer. In this case, because we want to pass an integer value as is to the vertex shader, we'll use a variation on the **glVertexAttribFormat()**, **glVertexAttribIFormat()**, whose prototype is

```
void glVertexAttribIFormat(GLuint attribindex,
                           GLint size,
                           GLenum type,
                           GLuint relativeoffset);
```

Again, the attribindex, size, type, and relativeoffset parameters specify the attribute index, number of components, type of those components, and the offset from the start of the vertex of the attribute that's being set up. However, you'll notice that the normalized parameter is missing. That's because this version of **glVertexAttribFormat()** is *only*

---

2. The BGRA ordering is quite common in some image formats and is the default ordering used by some graphics APIs.

for integer types — type must be one of the integer types (GL_BYTE, GL_SHORT, GL_INT, one of their unsigned counterparts, or one of the packed data formats), and integer inputs to a vertex shader are never normalized. Thus, the complete code to describe our vertex format is

```
// position
glVertexAttribFormat(0, 4, GL_FLOAT, GL_FALSE, offsetof(VERTEX, position));

// normal
glVertexAttribFormat(1, 3, GL_FLOAT, GL_FALSE, offsetof(VERTEX, normal));

// tex_coord
glVertexAttribFormat(2, 2, GL_FLOAT, GL_FALSE, offsetof(VERTEX, texcoord));

// color[3]
glVertexAttribFormat(4, 3, GL_UNSIGNED_BYTE, GL_TRUE, offsetof(VERTEX, color));

// material_id
glVertexAttribIFormat(5, 1, GL_INT, offsetof(VERTEX, material_id));
```

Now that you've set up the vertex attribute format, you need to tell OpenGL which buffers to read the data from. If you recall our discussion of uniform blocks and how they map to buffers, you can apply similar logic to vertex attributes. Each vertex shader can have any number of input attributes (up to an implementation-defined limit), and OpenGL can provide data for them by reading from any number of buffers (again, up to a limit). Some vertex attributes can share space in a buffer; others may reside in different buffer objects. Rather than individually specifying which buffer objects are used for each vertex shader input, we can instead group inputs together and associate groups of them with a set of buffer binding points. Then, when you change the buffer bound to one of these binding points, it will change the buffer used to supply data for all of the attributes that are mapped to that binding point.

To establish the mapping between vertex shader inputs and buffer binding points, you can call **glVertexAttribBinding()**. The first parameter to **glVertexAttribBinding()**, attribindex, is the index of the vertex attribute, and the second parameter, bindingindex, is the buffer binding point index. In our example, we're going to store all of the vertex attributes in a single buffer. To set this up, we'd simply call **glVertexAttribBinding()** once for each attribute and specify zero for the bindingindex parameter each time:

```
void glVertexAttribBinding(0, 0);   // position
void glVertexAttribBinding(1, 0);   // normal
void glVertexAttribBinding(2, 0);   // tex_coord
void glVertexAttribBinding(4, 0);   // color
void glVertexAttribBinding(5, 0);   // material_id
```

However, we could establish a more complex binding scheme. Let's say, for example, that we wanted to store `position`, `normal`, and `tex_coord` in one buffer, `color` in a second, and `material_id` in a third. We could set this up as follows:

```
void glVertexAttribBinding(0, 0);   // position
void glVertexAttribBinding(1, 0);   // normal
void glVertexAttribBinding(2, 0);   // tex_coord
void glVertexAttribBinding(4, 1);   // color
void glVertexAttribBinding(5, 2);   // material_id
```

Finally, we need to bind a buffer object to each of the binding points that is used by our mapping. To do this, we call **glBindVertexBuffer()**. This function takes four parameters, `bindingindex`, `buffer`, `offset`, and `stride`. The first is the index of the buffer binding point that you want to bind the buffer, and the second is the name of the buffer object that you're going to bind. `offset` is an offset into the buffer object where the vertex data starts, and `stride` is the distance, in bytes, between the start of each vertex's data in the buffer. If your data is tightly packed (i.e., there are no gaps between the vertices), you can just set this to the total size of your vertex data (which would be `sizeof(VERTEX)` in our example); otherwise, you'll need to add the size of the gaps to the size of the vertex data.

Vertex Shader Outputs

After your vertex shader has decided what to do with the vertex data, it must send it to its outputs. We have already discussed the `gl_Position` built-in output variable, and have shown you how you can create your own outputs from shaders that can be used to pass data into the following stages. Along with `gl_Position`, OpenGL also defines a couple more output variables, `gl_PointSize` and `gl_ClipDistance[]`, and wraps them up into an interface block called `gl_PerVertex`. Its declaration is

```
out gl_PerVertex
{
    vec4  gl_Position;
    float gl_PointSize;
    float gl_ClipDistance[];
};
```

Again, you should be familiar with `gl_Position`. `gl_ClipDistance[]` is used for clipping, which will be described in some detail later in this chapter. The other output, `gl_PointSize`, is used for controlling the size of points that might be rendered.

Variable Point Sizes

By default, OpenGL will draw points with a size of a single fragment. However, as you saw way back in Chapter 2, you can change the size of points that OpenGL draws by calling **glPointSize()**. The maximum size that OpenGL will draw your points is implementation defined, but it will be least 64 pixels. You find out what the actual upper limit is by calling **glGetIntegerv()** to find the value of GL_POINT_SIZE_RANGE. This will actually write *two* integers to the output variable, so make sure you point it at an array of two integers. The first element of the array will be filled with the minimum point size (which will be at most 1), and the second element will be filled with the maximum point size.

Now, setting all of your points to be big blobs isn't going to produce particularly appealing images. You can actually set the point size programmatically in the vertex shader (or whatever stage is last in the front end). To do this, write the desired value of the point diameter to the built-in variable gl_PointSize. Once you have a shader that does this, you need to tell OpenGL that you wish to use the size written to the point size variable. To do this, call

```
glEnable(GL_PROGRAM_POINT_SIZE);
```

A common use for this is to determine the size of a point based on its distance from the viewer. When you use the **glPointSize()** function to set the size of points, every point will have the same size no matter what their position is. By choosing a value for gl_PointSize, you can implement any function you wish, and each point produced by a single draw command can have a different size. This includes points generated in the geometry shader or by the tessellation engine when the tessellation evaluation shader specifies point_mode.

The following formula is often used to implement distance-based point size attenuation, where d is the distance of the point from the eye and a, b, and c are configurable parameters of a quadratic equation. You can store those in uniforms and update them with your application, or if you have a particular set of parameters in mind, you might want to make them constants in your vertex shader. For example, if you want a constant size, set a to a non-zero value and b and c to zero. If a and c are zero and b is non-zero, then point size will fall off linearly with distance. Likewise, if a and b are zero but c is non-zero, then point size will fall off quadratically with distance.

$$\text{size} = \text{clamp}\left(\sqrt{\frac{1.0}{a + b \times d + c \times d^2}}\right)$$

Drawing Commands

Until now, we have written every example using only a single drawing command — **glDrawArrays()**. OpenGL includes many drawing commands, however, and while some could be considered supersets of others, they can be generally categorized as either indexed or non-indexed and direct or indirect. Each of these will be covered in the next few sections.

Indexed Drawing Commands

The **glDrawArrays()** command is a non-indexed drawing command. That is, the vertices are issued in order, and any vertex data stored in buffers and associated with vertex attributes is simply fed to the vertex shader in the order that it appears in the buffer. An indexed draw, on the other hand, includes an indirection step that treats the data in each of those buffers as an array, and rather than index into that array sequentially, it reads from another array of indices, and after having read the index, OpenGL uses that to index into the array. To make an indexed drawing command work, you need to bind a buffer to the GL_ELEMENT_ARRAY_BUFFER target. This buffer will contain the indices of the vertices that you want to draw. Next, you call one of the indexed drawing commands, which all have the word Elements in their names. For example, **glDrawElements()** is the simplest of these functions and its prototype is

```
void glDrawElements(GLenum mode,
                    GLsizei count,
                    GLenum type,
                    const GLvoid * indices);
```

When you call **glDrawElements()**, mode and type have the same meaning as they do for **glDrawArrays()**. type specifies the type of data used to store each index and may be one of GL_UNSIGNED_BYTE to indicate one byte per index, GL_UNSIGNED_SHORT to indicate 16 bits per index, and GL_UNSIGNED_INT to indicate 32 bits per index. Although indices is defined as a pointer, it is actually interpreted as the offset into the buffer currently bound to the GL_ELEMENT_ARRAY_BUFFER binding where the first index is stored. Figure 7.1 shows how the indices specified by a call to **glDrawElements()** are used by OpenGL.

The **glDrawArrays()** and **glDrawElements()** commands are actually subsets of the complete functionality supported by the direct drawing commands

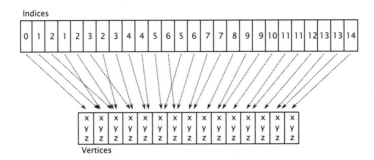

Figure 7.1: Indices used in an indexed draw

of OpenGL. The set of the most generalized OpenGL drawing commands is given in Table 7.2 — all other OpenGL drawing commands can be expressed in terms of these functions.

Table 7.2: Draw Type Matrix

Draw Type	Command
Direct, Non-Indexed	`glDrawArraysInstancedBaseInstance()`
Direct, Indexed	`glDrawElementsInstancedBaseVertexBaseInstance()`
Indirect, Non-Indexed	`glMultiDrawArraysIndirect()`
Indirect, Indexed	`glMultiDrawElementsIndirect()`

Remember back to the spinning cube example in Chapter 5 and in particular to the geometry setup performed in Listing 5.20. To draw a cube, we drew 12 triangles (two for each face of the cube), and each one consumed 36 vertices. However, a cube really only has 8 corners, and so should only need 8 vertices of information, right? Well, we can use an indexed draw to greatly cut down the amount of vertex data, especially for geometry that has a lot of vertices. We can re-write the setup code of Listing 5.20 to only define the 8 corners of the cube, but to also define a

set of 36 indices that tell OpenGL which corner to use for each vertex of
each triangle. The new setup code looks like this:

```
static const GLfloat vertex_positions[] =
{
    -0.25f, -0.25f, -0.25f,
    -0.25f,  0.25f, -0.25f,
     0.25f, -0.25f, -0.25f,
     0.25f,  0.25f, -0.25f,
     0.25f, -0.25f,  0.25f,
     0.25f,  0.25f,  0.25f,
    -0.25f, -0.25f,  0.25f,
    -0.25f,  0.25f,  0.25f,
};

static const GLushort vertex_indices[] =
{
    0, 1, 2,
    2, 1, 3,
    2, 3, 4,
    4, 3, 5,
    4, 5, 6,
    6, 5, 7,
    6, 7, 0,
    0, 7, 1,
    6, 0, 2,
    2, 4, 6,
    7, 5, 3,
    7, 3, 1
};

glGenBuffers(1, &position_buffer);
glBindBuffer(GL_ARRAY_BUFFER, position_buffer);
glBufferData(GL_ARRAY_BUFFER,
             sizeof(vertex_positions),
             vertex_positions,
             GL_STATIC_DRAW);
glVertexAttribPointer(0, 3, GL_FLOAT, GL_FALSE, 0, NULL);
glEnableVertexAttribArray(0);

glGenBuffers(1, &index_buffer);
glBindBuffer(GL_ELEMENT_ARRAY_BUFFER, index_buffer);
glBufferData(GL_ELEMENT_ARRAY_BUFFER,
             sizeof(vertex_indices),
             vertex_indices,
             GL_STATIC_DRAW);
```

Listing 7.2: Setting up indexed cube geometry

As you can see from Listing 7.2, the total amount of data required to
represent our cube is greatly reduced — it went from 108 floating-point
values (36 triangles times 3 components each, which is 432 bytes) down to
24 floating-point values (just the 8 corners at 3 components each, which is
72 bytes) and 36 16-bit integers (another 72 bytes), for a total of 144 bytes,
representing a reduction of two-thirds. To use the index data in

vertex_indices, we need to bind a buffer to the GL_ELEMENT_ARRAY_BUFFER and put the indices in it just as we did with the vertex data. In Listing 7.2, we do that right after we set up the buffer containing vertex positions.

Once you have a set of vertices and their indices in memory, you'll need to change your rendering code to use **glDrawElements()** (or one of the more advanced versions of it) instead of **glDrawArrays()**. Our new rendering loop for the spinning cube example is shown in Listing 7.3.

```
// Clear the framebuffer with dark green
static const GLfloat green[] = { 0.0f, 0.25f, 0.0f, 1.0f };
glClearBufferfv(GL_COLOR, 0, green);

// Activate our program
glUseProgram(program);

// Set the model-view and projection matrices
glUniformMatrix4fv(mv_location, 1, GL_FALSE, mv_matrix);
glUniformMatrix4fv(proj_location, 1, GL_FALSE, proj_matrix);

// Draw 6 faces of 2 triangles of 3 vertices each = 36 vertices
glDrawElements(GL_TRIANGLES, 36, GL_UNSIGNED_SHORT, 0);
```

Listing 7.3: Drawing indexed cube geometry

Notice that we're still drawing 36 vertices, but now 36 *indices* will be used to index into an array of only 8 unique vertices. The result of rendering with the vertex index and position data in our two buffers and a call to **glDrawElements()** is identical to that shown in Figure 5.2.

The Base Vertex

The first advanced version of **glDrawElements()** that takes an extra parameter is **glDrawElementsBaseVertex()**, whose prototype is

```
void glDrawElementsBaseVertex(GLenum mode,
                              GLsizei count,
                              GLenum type,
                              GLvoid * indices,
                              GLint  basevertex);
```

When you call **glDrawElementsBaseVertex()**, OpenGL will fetch the vertex index from the buffer bound to the GL_ELEMENT_ARRAY_BUFFER and then add basevertex to it before it is used to index into the array of vertices. This allows you to store a number of different pieces of geometry in the same buffer and then offset into it using basevertex. Figure 7.2 shows how basevertex is added to vertices in an indexed drawing command.

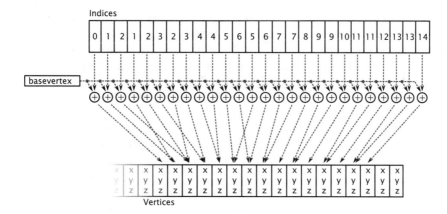

Figure 7.2: Base vertex used in an indexed draw

As you can see from Figure 7.2, vertex indices are essentially fed into an addition operation, which adds the base vertex to it before OpenGL uses it to fetch the underlying vertex data. Clearly, if basevertex is zero, then **glDrawElementsBaseVertex()** is equivalent to **glDrawElements()**. In fact, we consider calling **glDrawElements()** as equivalent to calling **glDrawElementsBaseVertex()** with basevertex set to zero.

Combining Geometry using Primitive Restart

There are many tools out there that "stripify" geometry. The idea of these tools is that by taking "triangle soup," which means a large collection of unconnected triangles, and attempting to merge it into a set of triangle strips, performance can be improved. This works because individual triangles are each represented by three vertices, but a triangle strip reduces this to a single vertex per triangle (not counting the first triangle in the strip). By converting the geometry from triangle soup to triangle strips, there is less geometry data to process, and the system should run faster. If the tool does a good job and produces a small number of long strips containing many triangles each, this generally works well. There has been a lot of research into this type of algorithm, and a new method's success is measured by passing some well-known models through the new "stripifier" and comparing the number and average length of the strips generated by the new tool to those produced by current state-of-the-art stripifiers.

Despite all of this research, the reality is that a soup can be rendered with a single call to **glDrawArrays()** or **glDrawElements()**, but unless the functionality that is about to be introduced is used, a set of strips needs to be rendered with separate calls to OpenGL. This means that there is likely to be a lot more function calls in a program that uses stripified geometry, and if the stripping application hasn't done a decent job or if the model just doesn't lend well to stripification, this can eat any performance gains seen by using strips in the first place.

A feature that can help here is *primitive restart*. Primitive restart applies to the GL_TRIANGLE_STRIP, GL_TRIANGLE_FAN, GL_LINE_STRIP, and GL_LINE_LOOP geometry types. It is a method of informing OpenGL when one strip (or fan or loop) has ended and that another should be started. To indicate the position in the geometry where one strip ends and the next starts, a special marker is placed as a reserved value in the element array. As OpenGL fetches vertex indices from the element array, it checks for this special index value, and whenever it comes across it, it ends the current strip and starts a new one with the next vertex. This mode is disabled by default but can be enabled by calling

```
glEnable(GL_PRIMITIVE_RESTART);
```

and disabled again by calling

```
glDisable(GL_PRIMITIVE_RESTART);
```

When primitive restart mode is enabled, OpenGL watches for the special index value as it fetches them from the element array buffer and when it comes across it, stops the current strip and starts a new one. To set the index that OpenGL should watch for, call

```
glPrimitiveRestartIndex(index);
```

OpenGL watches for the value specified by index and uses that as the primitive restart marker. Because the marker is a vertex index, primitive restart is best used with indexed drawing functions such as **glDrawElements()**. If you draw with a non-indexed drawing command such as **glDrawArrays()**, the primitive restart index is simply ignored.

The default value of the primitive restart index is zero. Because that's almost certainly the index of a real vertex that will be contained in the model, it's a good idea to set the restart index to a new value whenever you're using primitive restart mode. A good value to use is the maximum value representable by the index type you're using (0xFFFFFFFF for

GL_UNSIGNED_INT, 0xFFFF for GL_UNSIGNED_SHORT, and 0xFF for GL_UNSIGNED_BYTE) because you can be almost certain that it will not be used as a valid index of a vertex. Many stripping tools have an option to either create separate strips or to create a single strip with the restart index in it. The stripping tool may use a predefined index or output the index it used when creating the stripped version of the model (for example, one greater than the number of vertices in the model). You need to know this and set it using the **glPrimitiveRestartIndex()** function to use the output of the tool in your application. The primitive restart feature is illustrated in Figure 7.3.

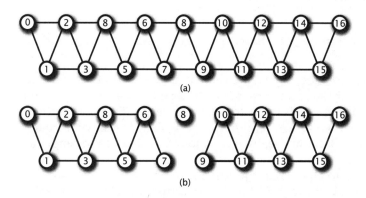

Figure 7.3: Triangle strips with and without primitive restart

In Figure 7.3, a triangle strip is pictured with the vertices marked with their indices. In (a), the strip is made up of 17 vertices, which produces a total of 15 triangles in a single, connected strip. By enabling primitive restart mode and setting the primitive restart index to 8, the 8th index (whose value is also 8) is recognized by OpenGL as the special restart marker, and the triangle strip is terminated at vertex 7. This is shown in (b). The actual position of vertex 8 is ignored because this is not seen by OpenGL as the index of a real vertex. The next vertex processed (vertex 9) becomes the start of a new triangle strip. So while 17 vertices are still sent to OpenGL, the result is that two separate triangle strips of 8 vertices and 6 triangles each are drawn.

Instancing

There will probably be times when you want to draw the same object many times. Imagine a fleet of starships, or a field of grass. There could be thousands of copies of what are essentially identical sets of geometry, modified only slightly from instance to instance. A simple application might just loop over all of the individual blades of grass in a field and render them separately, calling **glDrawArrays()** once for each blade and perhaps updating a set of shader uniforms on each iteration. Supposing each blade of grass were made up of a strip of four triangles, the code might look something like Listing 7.4.

```
glBindVertexArray(grass_vao);
for (int n = 0; n < number_of_blades_of_grass; n++)
{
    SetupGrassBladeParameters();
    glDrawArrays(GL_TRIANGLE_STRIP, 0, 6);
}
```

Listing 7.4: Drawing the same geometry many times

How many blades of grass are there in a field? What is the value of number_of_blades_of_grass? It could be thousands, maybe millions. Each blade of grass is likely to take up a very small area on the screen, and the number of vertices representing the blade is also very small. Your graphics card doesn't really have a lot of work to do to render a single blade of grass, and the system is likely to spend most of its time sending commands to OpenGL rather than actually drawing anything. OpenGL addresses this through instanced rendering, which is a way to ask it to draw many copies of the same geometry.

Instanced rendering is a method provided by OpenGL to specify that you want to draw many copies of the same geometry with a single function call. This functionality is accessed through instanced rendering functions, such as

```
void glDrawArraysInstanced(GLenum mode,
                           GLint first,
                           GLsizei count,
                           GLsizei instancecount);
```

and

```
void glDrawElementsInstanced(GLenum mode,
                             GLsizei count,
                             GLenum type,
                             const void * indices,
                             GLsizei instancecount);
```

These two functions behave much like **glDrawArrays()** and **glDrawElements()**, except that they tell OpenGL to render instancecount copies of the geometry. The first parameters of each (mode, first, and count for **glDrawArraysInstanced()**, and mode, count, type, and indices for **glDrawElementsInstanced()**) take the same meaning as in the regular, non-instanced versions of the functions. When you call one of these functions, OpenGL makes any preparations it needs to draw your geometry (such as copying vertex data to the graphics card's memory, for example) only once and then renders the same vertices many times.

If you set instancecount to one, then **glDrawArraysInstanced()** and **glDrawElementsInstanced()** will draw a single instance of your geometry. Obviously, this is equivalent to calling **glDrawArrays()** or **glDrawElements()**, but we normally state this equivalency the other way around — that is, we say that calling **glDrawArrays()** is equivalent to calling **glDrawArraysInstanced()** with instancecount set to one, and that, likewise, calling **glDrawElements()** is equivalent to calling **glDrawElementsInstanced()** with instancecount set to one. As we discussed earlier, though, calling **glDrawElements()** is also equivalent to calling **glDrawElementsBaseVertex()** with basevertex set to zero. In fact, there is another drawing command that combines both basevertex and instancecount together. This is **glDrawElementsInstancedBaseVertex()**, whose prototype is

```
void glDrawElementsInstancedBaseVertex(GLenum mode,
                                       GLsizei count,
                                       GLenum type,
                                       GLvoid * indices,
                                       GLsizei instancecount,
                                       GLint   basevertex);
```

So, in fact, calling **glDrawElements()** is equivalent to calling **glDrawElementsInstancedBaseVertex()** with instancecount set to one and basevertex set to zero, and likewise, calling **glDrawElementsInstanced()** is equivalent to calling **glDrawElementsInstancedBaseVertex()** with basevertex set to zero.

Finally, just as we can pass basevertex to **glDrawElementsBaseVertex()** and **glDrawElementsInstancedBaseVertex()**, we can pass a baseinstance parameter to versions of the instanced drawing commands. These functions are **glDrawArraysInstancedBaseInstance()**, **glDrawElementsInstancedBaseInstance()**, and the exceedingly long **glDrawElementsInstancedBaseVertexBaseInstance()**, which takes both a basevertex and baseinstance parameter. Now we have introduced all of the direct drawing commands, it should be clear that they are all subsets of **glDrawArraysInstancedBaseInstance()** and **glDrawElementsInstancedBaseVertexBaseInstance()**, and that where they are missing, basevertex and baseinstance are assumed to be zero, and instancecount is assumed to be one.

If all that these functions did were send many copies of the same vertices to OpenGL as if `glDrawArrays()` or `glDrawElements()` had been called in a tight loop, they wouldn't be very useful. One of the things that makes instanced rendering usable and very powerful is a special, built-in variable in GLSL named gl_InstanceID. The gl_InstanceID variable appears in the vertex as if it were a static integer vertex attribute. When the first copy of the vertices is sent to OpenGL, gl_InstanceID will be zero. It will then be incremented once for each copy of the geometry and will eventually reach instancecount - 1.

The **glDrawArraysInstanced()** function essentially operates as if the code in Listing 7.5 were executed.

```
// Loop over all of the instances (i.e., instancecount)
for (int n = 0; n < instancecount; n++)
{
    // Set the gl_InstanceID attribute - here gl_InstanceID is a C variable
    // holding the location of the "virtual" gl_InstanceID input.
    glVertexAttrib1i(gl_InstanceID, n);

    // Now, when we call glDrawArrays, the gl_InstanceID variable in the
    // shader will contain the index of the instance that's being rendered.
    glDrawArrays(mode, first, count);
}
```

Listing 7.5: Pseudo-code for **glDrawArraysInstanced()**

Likewise, the **glDrawElementsInstanced()** function operates similarly to the code in Listing 7.6.

```
for (int n = 0; n < instancecount; n++)
{
    // Set the value of gl_InstanceID
    glVertexAttrib1i(gl_InstanceID, n);

    // Make a normal call to glDrawElements
    glDrawElements(mode, count, type, indices);
}
```

Listing 7.6: Pseudo-code for **glDrawElementsInstanced()**

Of course, gl_InstanceID is not a real vertex attribute, and you can't get a location for it by calling **glGetAttribLocation()**. The value of gl_InstanceID is managed by OpenGL and is very likely generated in hardware, meaning that it's essentially free to use in terms of performance. The power of instanced rendering comes from imaginative use of this variable, along with instanced arrays, which are explained in a moment.

The value of gl_InstanceID can be used directly as a parameter to a shader function or to index into data such as textures or uniform arrays. To return to our example of the field of grass, let's figure out what we're going to do with gl_InstanceID to make our field not just be thousands of identical blades of grass growing out of a single point. Each of our grass blades is made out of a little triangle strip with four triangles in it, a total of just six vertices. It could be tricky to get them to all look different. However, with some shader magic, we can make each blade of grass look sufficiently different so as to produce an interesting output. We won't go over the shader code here, but we will walk through a few ideas of how you can use gl_InstanceID to add variation to your scenes.

First, we need each blade of grass to have a different position; otherwise, they'll all be drawn on top of each other. Let's arrange the blades of grass more or less evenly. If the number of blades of grass we're going to render is a power of 2, we can use half of the bits of gl_InstanceID to represent the x coordinate of the blade, and the other half to represent the z coordinate (our ground lies in the xz plane, with y being altitude). For this example, we render 2^{20}, or a little over a million, blades of grass (actually 1,048,576 blades, but who's counting?). By using the ten least significant bits (bits 9 through 0) as the x coordinate and the ten most significant bits (19 through 10) as the z coordinate, we have a uniform grid of grass blades. Let's take a look at Figure 7.4 to see what we have so far.

Figure 7.4: First attempt at an instanced field of grass

Our uniform grid of grass probably looks a little plain, as if a particularly attentive groundskeeper hand-planted each blade. What we really need to do is displace each blade of grass by some random amount within its grid square. That'll make the field look a little less uniform. A simple way of generating random numbers is to multiply a seed value by a large number and take a subset of the bits of the resulting product and use it as the input to a function. We're not aiming for a perfect distribution here, so this simple generator should do. Usually, with this type of algorithm, you'd reuse the seed value as input to the next iteration of the random number generator. In this case, though, we can just use `gl_InstanceID` directly as we're really generating the next few numbers after `gl_InstanceID` in a pseudo-random sequence. By iterating over our pseudo-random function only a couple of times, we can get a reasonably random distribution. Because we need to displace in both x and z, we generate two successive random numbers from `gl_InstanceID` and use them to displace the blade of grass within the plane. Look at Figure 7.5 to see what we get now.

Figure 7.5: Slightly perturbed blades of grass

At this point, our field of grass is distributed evenly with random perturbations in position for each blade of grass. All the grass blades look the same, though. (Actually, we used the same random number generator to assign a slightly different color to each blade of grass just so that they'd show up in the figures.) We can apply some variation over the field to make each blade look slightly different. This is something that we'd probably want to have control over, so we use a texture to hold information about blades of grass.

You have an x and a z coordinate for each blade of grass that was calculated by generating a grid coordinate directly from `gl_InstanceID` and then generating a random number and displacing the blade within the xz plane. That coordinate pair can be used as a coordinate to look up a texel within a 2D texture, and you can put whatever you want in it. Let's control the length of the grass using the texture. We can put a length parameter in the texture (let's use the red channel) and multiply the y coordinate of each vertex of the grass geometry by that to make longer or shorter grass. A value of zero in the texture would produce very short (or nonexistent) grass, and a value of one would produce grass of some maximum length. Now you can design a texture where each texel represents the length of the grass in a region of your field. Why not draw a few crop circles?

Now, the grass is evenly distributed over the field, and you have control of the length of the grass in different areas. However, the grass blades are still just scaled copies of each other. Perhaps we can introduce some more variation. Next, we rotate each blade of grass around its axis according to another parameter from the texture. We use the green channel of the texture to store the angle through which the grass blade should be rotated around the y axis, with zero representing no rotation and one representing a full 360 degrees. We've still only done one texture fetch in our vertex shader, and still the only input to the shader is `gl_InstanceID`. Things are starting to come together. Take a look at Figure 7.6.

Figure 7.6: Control over the length and orientation of our grass

Our field is still looking a little bland. The grass just sticks straight up and doesn't move. Real grass sways in the wind and gets flattened when things roll over it. We need the grass to bend, and we'd like to have control over that. Why not use another channel from the parameter texture (the blue channel) to control a bend factor? We can use that as another angle and rotate the grass around the x axis before we apply the rotation in the green channel. This allows us to make the grass bend over based on the parameter in the texture. Use zero to represent no bending (the grass stands straight up) and one to represent fully flattened grass. Normally, the grass will sway gently, and so the parameter will have a low value. When the grass gets flattened, the value can be much higher.

Finally, we can control the color of the grass. It seems logical to just store the color of the grass in a large texture. This might be a good idea if you want to draw a sports field with lines, markings, or advertising on it for example, but it's fairly wasteful if the grass is all varying shades of green. Instead, let's make a palette for our grass in a 1D texture and use the final channel within our parameter texture (the alpha channel) to store the index into that palette. The palette can start with an anemic looking dead-grass yellow at one end and a lush, deep green at the other end. Now we read the alpha channel from the parameter texture along with all the other parameters and use it to index into the 1D texture— a dependent texture fetch. Our final field is shown in Figure 7.7.

Figure 7.7: The final field of grass

Now, our final field has a million blades of grass, evenly distributed, with application control over length, "flatness," direction of bend, or sway and color. Remember, the only input to the shader that differentiates one blade of grass from another is gl_InstanceID, the total amount of geometry sent to OpenGL is six vertices, and the total amount of code required to draw all the grass in the field is a single call to **glDrawArraysInstanced()**.

The parameter texture can be read using linear texturing to provide smooth transitions between regions of grass and can be a fairly low resolution. If you want to make your grass wave in the wind or get trampled as hoards of armies march across it, you can animate the texture by updating it every frame or two and uploading a new version of it before you render the grass. Also, because the gl_InstanceID is used to generate random numbers, adding an offset to it before passing it to the random number generator allows a different but predetermined chunk of "random" grass to be generated with the same shader.

Getting Your Data Automatically

When you call one of the instanced drawing commands such as **glDrawArraysInstanced()** or **glDrawElementsInstanced()**, the built-in variable gl_InstanceID will be available in your shaders to tell you which instance you're working on, and it will increment by one for each new instance of the geometry that you're rendering. It's actually available even when you're not using one of the instanced drawing functions—it'll just be zero in those cases. This means that you can use the same shaders for instanced and non-instanced rendering.

You can use gl_InstanceID to index into arrays that are the same length as the number of instances that you're rendering. For example, you can use it to look up texels in a texture or to index into a uniform array. Really, what you'd be doing though is treating the array as if it were an "instanced attribute." That is, a new value of the attribute is read for each instance you're rendering. OpenGL can feed this data to your shader automatically using a feature called instanced arrays. To use instanced arrays, declare an input to your shader as normal. The input attribute will have an index that you would use in calls to functions like **glVertexAttribPointer()**. Normally, the vertex attributes would be read per vertex and a new value would be fed to the shader. However, to make OpenGL read attributes from the arrays once per instance, you can call

```
void glVertexAttribDivisor(GLuint index,
                           GLuint divisor);
```

Pass the index of the attribute to the function in `index` and set `divisor` to the number of instances you'd like to pass between each new value being read from the array. If `divisor` is zero, then the array becomes a regular vertex attribute array with a new value read per vertex. If `divisor` is non-zero, however, then new data is read from the array once every `divisor` instances. For example, if you set `divisor` to one, you'll get a new value from the array for each instance. If you set `divisor` to two, you'll get a new value for every second instance, and so on. You can mix and match the divisors, setting different values for each attribute. An example of using this functionality would be when you want to draw a set of objects with different colors. Consider the simple vertex shader in Listing 7.7.

```
#version 430 core

in vec4 position;
in vec4 color;

out Fragment
{
    vec4 color;
} fragment;

uniform mat4 mvp;

void main(void)
{
    gl_Position = mvp * position;
    fragment.color = color;
}
```

Listing 7.7: Simple vertex shader with per-vertex color

Normally, the attribute color would be read once per vertex, and so every vertex would end up having a different color. The application would have to supply an array of colors with as many elements as there were vertices in the model. Also, it wouldn't be possible for every instance of the object to have a different color because the shader doesn't know anything about instancing. We can make color an instanced array if we call

```
glVertexAttribDivisor(index_of_color, 1);
```

where `index_of_color` is the index of the slot to which the color attribute has been bound. Now, a new value of color will be fetched from the vertex array once per instance. Every vertex within any particular instance will receive the same value for color, and the result will be that each instance of the object will be rendered in a different color. The size of the vertex array holding the data for color only needs to be as long as the number of indices we want to render. If we increase the value of the divisor, new data will be read from the array with less and less frequency. If the divisor is two, a new value of color will be presented every second instance; if the divisor is three, color will be updated every third instance; and so on. If we render geometry using this simple shader, each instance will be drawn on top of the others. We need to modify the position of each instance so that we can see each one. We can use another instanced array for this. Listing 7.8 shows a simple modification to the vertex shader in Listing 7.7.

```
#version 430 core

in vec4 position;
in vec4 instance_color;
in vec4 instance_position;

out Fragment
{
    vec4 color;
} fragment;

uniform mat4 mvp;

void main(void)
{
    gl_Position = mvp * (position + instance_position);
    fragment.color = instance_color;
}
```

Listing 7.8: Simple instanced vertex shader

Now, we have a per-instance position as well as a per-vertex position. We can add these together in the vertex shader before multiplying with the model-view-projection matrix. We can set the `instance_position` input attribute to an instanced array by calling

```
glVertexAttribDivisor(index_of_instance_position, 1);
```

Again, `index_of_instance_position` is the index of the location to which the `instance_position` attribute has been bound. Any type of input attribute can be made instanced using glVertexAttribDivisor. This example is simple and only uses a translation (the value held in `instance_position`). A more advanced application could use matrix vertex attributes or pack some transformation matrices into uniforms and pass matrix weights in instanced arrays. The application can use this to render an army of soldiers, each with a different pose, or a fleet of spaceships all flying in different directions.

Now let's hook this simple shader up to a real program. First, we load our shaders as normal before linking the program. The vertex shader is shown in Listing 7.8, the fragment shader simply passes the `color` input to its output, and the application code to hook all this up is shown in Listing 7.9. In the code, we declare some data and load it into a buffer and attach it to a vertex array object. Some of the data is used as per-vertex positions, but the rest is used as per-instance colors and positions.

```
static const GLfloat square_vertices[] =
{
    -1.0f, -1.0f, 0.0f, 1.0f,
     1.0f, -1.0f, 0.0f, 1.0f,
     1.0f,  1.0f, 0.0f, 1.0f,
    -1.0f,  1.0f, 0.0f, 1.0f
};

static const GLfloat instance_colors[] =
{
    1.0f, 0.0f, 0.0f, 1.0f,
    0.0f, 1.0f, 0.0f, 1.0f,
    0.0f, 0.0f, 1.0f, 1.0f,
    1.0f, 1.0f, 0.0f, 1.0f
};

static const GLfloat instance_positions[] =
{
    -2.0f, -2.0f, 0.0f, 0.0f,
     2.0f, -2.0f, 0.0f, 0.0f,
     2.0f,  2.0f, 0.0f, 0.0f,
    -2.0f,  2.0f, 0.0f, 0.0f
};

GLuint offset = 0;

glGenVertexArrays(1, &square_vao);
glGenBuffers(1, &square_vbo);
glBindVertexArray(square_vao);
glBindBuffer(GL_ARRAY_BUFFER, square_vbo);
glBufferData(GL_ARRAY_BUFFER,
             sizeof(square_vertices) +
             sizeof(instance_colors) +
             sizeof(instance_positions), NULL, GL_STATIC_DRAW);
glBufferSubData(GL_ARRAY_BUFFER, offset,
                sizeof(square_vertices),
                square_vertices);
offset += sizeof(square_vertices);
glBufferSubData(GL_ARRAY_BUFFER, offset,
                sizeof(instance_colors), instance_colors);
offset += sizeof(instance_colors);
glBufferSubData(GL_ARRAY_BUFFER, offset,
                sizeof(instance_positions), instance_positions);
offset += sizeof(instance_positions);

glVertexAttribPointer(0, 4, GL_FLOAT, GL_FALSE, 0, 0);
glVertexAttribPointer(1, 4, GL_FLOAT, GL_FALSE, 0,
                      (GLvoid *)sizeof(square_vertices));
glVertexAttribPointer(2, 4, GL_FLOAT, GL_FALSE, 0,
                      (GLvoid *)(sizeof(square_vertices) +
                                 sizeof(instance_colors)));

glEnableVertexAttribArray(0);
glEnableVertexAttribArray(1);
glEnableVertexAttribArray(2);
```

Listing 7.9: Getting ready for instanced rendering

Now all that remains is to set the vertex attrib divisors for the
`instance_color` and `instance_position` attribute arrays:

```
glVertexAttribDivisor(1, 1);
glVertexAttribDivisor(2, 1);
```

Now we draw four instances of the geometry that we previously put into
our buffer. Each instance consists of four vertices, each with its own
position, which means that the same vertex in each instance has the same
position. However, all of the vertices in a single instance see the same
value of `instance_color` and `instance_position`, and a new value of
each is presented to each instance. Our rendering loop looks like this:

```
static const GLfloat black[] = { 0.0f, 0.0f, 0.0f, 0.0f };
glClearBufferfv(GL_COLOR, 0, black);

glUseProgram(instancingProg);
glBindVertexArray(square_vao);
glDrawArraysInstanced(GL_TRIANGLE_FAN, 0, 4, 4);
```

What we get is shown in Figure 7.8. In the figure, you can see that four
rectangles have been rendered. Each is at a different position, and each
has a different color. This can be extended to thousands or even millions
of instances, and modern graphics hardware should be able to handle this
without any issue.

Figure 7.8: Result of instanced rendering

When you have instanced vertex attributes, you can use the baseInstance parameter to drawing commands such as glDrawArraysInstancedBaseInstance() to *offset* where in their respective buffers the data is read from. If you set this to zero (or call one of the functions that lacks this parameter), the data for the first instance comes from the start of the array. However, if you set it to a non-zero value, the index within the instanced array from which the data comes is offset by that value. This is very similar to the baseVertex parameter described earlier.

The actual formula for calculating the index from which attributes are fetched is

$$\left\lfloor \frac{instance}{divisor} \right\rfloor + baseInstance$$

We will use the baseInstance parameter in some of the following examples to provide offsets into instanced vertex arrays.

Indirect Draws

So far, we have covered only direct drawing commands. In these commands, we pass the parameters of the draw such as the number of vertices or instances directly to the function. However, there is a family of drawing commands that allow the parameters of each draw to be stored in a buffer object. This means that at the time that your application calls the drawing command, it doesn't actually need to know those parameters, only the location in the buffer where the parameters are stored. This opens a few interesting possibilities. For instance,

- Your application can generate the parameters for a drawing command ahead of time, possibly even offline, load them into a buffer, and then send them to OpenGL when it's ready to draw.

- You can generate the parameters using OpenGL at runtime and store them in a buffer object from a shader, using them to render later parts of the scene.

There are four indirect drawing commands in OpenGL. The first two have direct equivalents; glDrawArraysIndirect() is the indirect equivalent to glDrawArraysInstancedBaseInstance(), and glDrawElementsIndirect() is equivalent to glDrawElementsInstancedBaseVertexBaseInstance(). The prototypes of these indirect functions are

```
void glDrawArraysIndirect(GLenum mode,
                          const void * indirect);
```

and

```
void glDrawElementsIndirect(GLenum mode,
                            GLenum type,
                            const void * indirect);
```

For both functions, mode is one of the primitive modes such as
GL_TRIANGLES or GL_PATCHES. For **glDrawElementsIndirect()**, type is the
type of the indices to be used (just like the type parameter to
glDrawElements()) and should be set to GL_UNSIGNED_BYTE,
GL_UNSIGNED_SHORT, or GL_UNSIGNED_INT. Again, for both functions,
indirect is interpreted as an offset into the buffer object bound to the
GL_DRAW_INDIRECT_BUFFER target, but the contents of the buffer at
this address are different, depending on which function is being used.
When expressed as a C-style structure definition, for
glDrawArraysIndirect(), the form of the data in the buffer is

```
typedef struct {
    GLuint vertexCount;
    GLuint instanceCount;
    GLuint firstVertex;
    GLuint baseInstance;
} DrawArraysIndirectCommand;
```

For **glDrawElementsIndirect()**, the form of the data in the buffer is

```
typedef  struct {
    GLuint vertexCount;
    GLuint instanceCount;
    GLuint firstIndex;
    GLint  baseVertex;
    GLuint baseInstance;
} DrawElementsIndirectCommand;
```

Calling **glDrawArraysIndirect()** will cause OpenGL to behave as if you
had called **glDrawArraysInstancedBaseInstance()** with the mode you
passed to **glDrawArraysIndirect()** but with the count, first,
instancecount, and baseinstance parameters taken from the
vertexCount, firstVertex, instanceCount, and baseInstance fields of
the DrawArraysIndirectCommand structure stored in the buffer object at
the offset given in the indirect parameter.

Likewise, calling **glDrawElementsIndirect()** will cause OpenGL to behave
as if you had called **glDrawElementsInstancedBaseVertexBaseInstance()**
with the mode and type parameters passed directly through, and with the
count, instancecount, basevertex, and baseinstance parameters taken
from the vertexCount, instanceCount, baseVertex, and baseInstance
fields of the DrawElementsIndirectCommand structure in the buffer.

However, the one difference here is that the `firstIndex` parameter is in units of indices rather than bytes, and so is multiplied by the size of the index type to form the offset that would have been passed in the `indices` parameter to **glDrawElements()**.

As handy as it may seem to be able to do this, what makes this feature particularly powerful is the *multi* versions of these two functions. These are

```
void glMultiDrawArraysIndirect(GLenum mode,
                               const void * indirect,
                               GLsizei drawcount,
                               GLsizei stride);
```

and

```
void glMultiDrawElementsIndirect(GLenum mode,
                                 GLenum type,
                                 const void * indirect,
                                 GLsizei  drawcount,
                                 GLsizei  stride);
```

These two functions behave very similarly to **glDrawArraysIndirect()** and **glDrawElementsIndirect()**. However, you have probably noticed two additional parameters to each of the functions. Both functions essentially perform the same operation as their non-multi variants in a loop on an array of `DrawArraysIndirectCommand` or `DrawElementsIndirectCommand`. structures. `drawcount` specifies the number of structures in the array, and `stride` specifies the number of bytes between the start of each of the structures in the buffer object. If `stride` is zero, then the arrays are considered to be tightly packed. Otherwise, it allows you to have structures with additional data in-between, and OpenGL will skip over that data as it traverses the array.

The practical upper limit on the number of drawing commands you can batch together using these functions really only depends on the amount of memory available to store them. The `drawcount` parameter can literally range to the billions, but with each command taking 16 or 20 bytes, a billion draw commands would consume 20 gigabytes of memory and probably take several seconds or even minutes to execute. However, it's perfectly reasonable to batch together tens of thousands of draw commands into a single buffer. Given this, you can either preload a buffer object with the parameters for many draw commands, or generate a very large number of commands on the GPU. When you generate the parameters for your drawing commands using the GPU directly into the buffer object, you don't need to wait for them to be ready before calling the indirect draw command that will consume them, and the parameters never make a round trip from the GPU to your application and back.

Listing 7.10 shows a simple example of how **glMultiDrawArraysIndirect()** might be used.

```
typedef struct {
    GLuint vertexCount;
    GLuint instanceCount;
    GLuint firstVertex;
    GLuint baseInstance;
} DrawArraysIndirectCommand;

DrawArraysIndirectCommand draws[] =
{
    {
        42,        // Vertex count
        1,         // Instance count
        0,         // First vertex
        0          // Base instance
    },
    {
        192,
        1,
        327,
        0,
    },
    {
        99,
        1,
        901,
        0
    }
};

// Put "draws[]" into a buffer object
GLuint buffer;

glGenBuffers(1, &buffer);
glBindBuffer(GL_DRAW_INDIRECT_BUFFER, buffer);
glBufferData(GL_DRAW_INDIRECT_BUFFER, sizeof(draws),
             draws, GL_STATIC_DRAW);

// This will produce 3 draws (the number of elements in draws[]), each
// drawing disjoint pieces of the bound vertex arrays
glMultiDrawArraysIndirect(GL_TRIANGLES,
                          NULL,
                          sizeof(draws) / sizeof(draws[0]),
                          0);
```

Listing 7.10: Example use of an indirect draw command

Simply batching together three drawing commands isn't really that interesting, though. To show the real power of the indirect draw command, we'll draw an asteroid field. This field will consist of 30,000 individual asteroids. First, we will take advantage of the sb6::object class's ability to store multiple meshes within a single file. When such a file is loaded from disk, all of the vertex data is loaded into a single buffer object and associated with a single vertex array object. Each of the sub-objects has a starting vertex and a count of the number of vertices used to describe it. We can retrieve these from the object loader by calling `sb6::object::get_sub_object_info()`. The total number of sub-objects in the `.sbm` file is made available through the `sb6::object::get_sub_object_count()` function. Therefore, we can construct an indirect draw buffer for our asteroid field using the code shown in Listing 7.11.

```
object.load("media/objects/asteroids.sbm");

glGenBuffers(1, &indirect_draw_buffer);
glBindBuffer(GL_DRAW_INDIRECT_BUFFER, indirect_draw_buffer);
glBufferData(GL_DRAW_INDIRECT_BUFFER,
             NUM_DRAWS * sizeof(DrawArraysIndirectCommand),
             NULL,
             GL_STATIC_DRAW);

DrawArraysIndirectCommand * cmd = (DrawArraysIndirectCommand *)
    glMapBufferRange(GL_DRAW_INDIRECT_BUFFER,
                     0,
                     NUM_DRAWS * sizeof(DrawArraysIndirectCommand),
                     GL_MAP_WRITE_BIT | GL_MAP_INVALIDATE_BUFFER_BIT);

for (i = 0; i < NUM_DRAWS; i++)
{
    object.get_sub_object_info(i % object.get_sub_object_count(),
                               cmd[i].first,
                               cmd[i].count);
    cmd[i].primCount = 1;
    cmd[i].baseInstance = i;
}

glUnmapBuffer(GL_DRAW_INDIRECT_BUFFER);
```

Listing 7.11: Setting up the indirect draw buffer for asteroids

Next, we need a way to communicate which asteroid we're drawing to the vertex shader. There is no direct way to get this information from the indirect draw command into the shader. However, we can take advantage of the fact that all drawing commands are actually instanced drawing commands — commands that only draw a single copy of the object can be considered to draw a single instance. Therefore, we can set up an instanced vertex attribute, set the `baseInstance` field of the indirect drawing command structure to the index within that attribute's array of the data that we wish to pass to the vertex shader, and then use that data for whatever we wish. You'll notice that in Listing 7.11, we set the `baseInstance` field of each structure to the loop counter.

Next, we need to set up a corresponding input to our vertex shader. The input declaration for our asteroid field renderer is shown in Listing 7.12.

```
#version 430 core

layout (location = 0) in vec4 position;
layout (location = 1) in vec3 normal;

layout (location = 10) in uint draw_id;
```

Listing 7.12: Vertex shader inputs for asteroids

As usual, we have a position and normal input. However, we've also used
an attribute at location 10, draw_id, to store our draw index. This
attribute is going to be instanced and associated with a buffer that simply
contains an identity mapping. We're going to use the sb6::object
loader's functions to access and modify its vertex array object to inject our
extra vertex attribute. The code to do this is shown in Listing 7.13.

```
glBindVertexArray(object.get_vao());

glGenBuffers(1, &draw_index_buffer);
glBindBuffer(GL_ARRAY_BUFFER, draw_index_buffer);
glBufferData(GL_ARRAY_BUFFER,
             NUM_DRAWS * sizeof(GLuint),
             NULL,
             GL_STATIC_DRAW);

GLuint * draw_index =
    (GLuint *)glMapBufferRange(GL_ARRAY_BUFFER,
                               0,
                               NUM_DRAWS * sizeof(GLuint),
                               GL_MAP_WRITE_BIT |
                               GL_MAP_INVALIDATE_BUFFER_BIT);

for (i = 0; i < NUM_DRAWS; i++)
{
    draw_index[i] = i;
}

glUnmapBuffer(GL_ARRAY_BUFFER);

glVertexAttribIPointer(10, 1, GL_UNSIGNED_INT, 0, NULL);
glVertexAttribDivisor(10, 1);
glEnableVertexAttribArray(10);
```

Listing 7.13: Per-indirect draw attribute setup

Once we've set up our draw_id vertex shader input, we can use it to make
each mesh unique. Without this, each asteroid would be a simple rock
placed at the origin. In this example, we will directly create an orientation
and translation matrix in the vertex shader from draw_id. The complete
vertex shader is shown in Listing 7.14.

```
#version 430 core

layout (location = 0) in vec4 position;
layout (location = 1) in vec3 normal;
```

```
layout (location = 10) in uint draw_id;

out VS_OUT
{
    vec3 normal;
    vec4 color;
} vs_out;

uniform float time = 0.0;

uniform mat4 view_matrix;
uniform mat4 proj_matrix;
uniform mat4 viewproj_matrix;

const vec4 color0 = vec4(0.29, 0.21, 0.18, 1.0);
const vec4 color1 = vec4(0.58, 0.55, 0.51, 1.0);

void main(void)
{
    mat4 m1;
    mat4 m2;
    mat4 m;
    float t = time * 0.1;
    float f = float(draw_id) / 30.0;

    float st = sin(t * 0.5 + f * 5.0);
    float ct = cos(t * 0.5 + f * 5.0);

    float j = fract(f);
    float d = cos(j * 3.14159);

    // Rotate around Y
    m[0] = vec4(ct, 0.0, st, 0.0);
    m[1] = vec4(0.0, 1.0, 0.0, 0.0);
    m[2] = vec4(-st, 0.0, ct, 0.0);
    m[3] = vec4(0.0, 0.0, 0.0, 1.0);

    // Translate in the XZ plane
    m1[0] = vec4(1.0, 0.0, 0.0, 0.0);
    m1[1] = vec4(0.0, 1.0, 0.0, 0.0);
    m1[2] = vec4(0.0, 0.0, 1.0, 0.0);
    m1[3] = vec4(260.0 + 30.0 * d, 5.0 * sin(f * 123.123), 0.0, 1.0);

    m = m * m1;

    // Rotate around X
    st = sin(t * 2.1 * (600.0 + f) * 0.01);
    ct = cos(t * 2.1 * (600.0 + f) * 0.01);

    m1[0] = vec4(ct, st, 0.0, 0.0);
    m1[1] = vec4(-st, ct, 0.0, 0.0);
    m1[2] = vec4(0.0, 0.0, 1.0, 0.0);
    m1[3] = vec4(0.0, 0.0, 0.0, 1.0);

    m = m * m1;

    // Rotate around Z
    st = sin(t * 1.7 * (700.0 + f) * 0.01);
    ct = cos(t * 1.7 * (700.0 + f) * 0.01);

    m1[0] = vec4(1.0, 0.0, 0.0, 0.0);
    m1[1] = vec4(0.0, ct, st, 0.0);
    m1[2] = vec4(0.0, -st, ct, 0.0);
    m1[3] = vec4(0.0, 0.0, 0.0, 1.0);
```

```
    m = m * m1;

    // Non-uniform scale
    float f1 = 0.65 + cos(f * 1.1) * 0.2;
    float f2 = 0.65 + cos(f * 1.1) * 0.2;
    float f3 = 0.65 + cos(f * 1.3) * 0.2;

    m1[0] = vec4(f1, 0.0, 0.0, 0.0);
    m1[1] = vec4(0.0, f2, 0.0, 0.0);
    m1[2] = vec4(0.0, 0.0, f3, 0.0);
    m1[3] = vec4(0.0, 0.0, 0.0, 1.0);

    m = m * m1;

    gl_Position = viewproj_matrix * m * position;
    vs_out.normal = mat3(view_matrix * m) * normal;
    vs_out.color = mix(color0, color1, fract(j * 313.431));
}
```

Listing 7.14: Asteroid field vertex shader

In the vertex shader shown in Listing 7.14, we calculate the orientation,
position, and color of the asteroid directly from draw_id. First, we convert
draw_id to floating point and scale it. Next, we calculate a number of
translation, scaling, and rotation matrices based on its value and the value
of the time uniform. These matrices are concatenated to form a model
matrix, m. The position is first transformed by the model matrix and then
the view-projection matrix. The vertex's normal is also transformed by the
model and view matrices. Finally, an output color is computed for the
vertex by interpolating between two colors (one is a chocolate brown, the
other a sandy gray) to give the asteroid its final color. A simple lighting
scheme is used in the fragment shader to give the asteroids a sense of
depth.

The rendering loop for this application is extremely simple. First, we set
up our view and projection matrices and then we render all of the models
with a single call to **glMultiDrawArraysIndirect()**. The drawing code is
shown in Listing 7.15.

```
glBindVertexArray(object.get_vao());

if (mode == MODE_MULTIDRAW)
{
    glMultiDrawArraysIndirect(GL_TRIANGLES, NULL, NUM_DRAWS, 0);
}
else if (mode == MODE_SEPARATE_DRAWS)
{
    for (j = 0; j < NUM_DRAWS; j++)
    {
        GLuint first, count;
        object.get_sub_object_info(j % object.get_sub_object_count(),
                                   first, count);
        glDrawArraysInstancedBaseInstance(GL_TRIANGLES,
```

```
                                        first,
                                        count,
                                        1, j);
            }
    }
```

Listing 7.15: Drawing asteroids

As you can see from Listing 7.15, we first bind the object's vertex array object by calling `object.get_vao()` and passing the result to **`glBindVertexArray()`**. When mode is `MODE_MULTIDRAW`, the entire scene is drawn with a single call to **`glMultiDrawArraysIndirect()`**. However, if mode is `MODE_SEPARATE_DRAWS`, we loop over all of the loaded sub-objects and draw each separately by passing the same parameters that are loaded into the indirect draw buffer directly to a call to **`glDrawArraysInstancedBaseInstance()`**. Depending on your OpenGL implementation, the separate draw mode could be substantially slower. The resulting output is shown in Figure 7.9.

Figure 7.9: Result of asteroid rendering program

In our example, using a typical consumer graphics card, we can achieve 60 frames per second with 30,000 unique[3] models, which is equivalent to 1.8 million drawing commands every second. Each mesh has approximately

---

3. The asteroids in this example are not truly unique — they are selected from a large batch of unique rock models, and then a different scale and color are applied to each one. The chances

500 vertices, which means that we're rendering almost a billion vertices per second, and our bottleneck is almost certainly not the rate at which we are submitting drawing commands.

With clever use of the `draw_id` input (or other instanced vertex attributes), more interesting geometry with more complex variation could be rendered. For example, we could use texture mapping to apply surface detail, storing a number of different surfaces in an array texture and selecting a layer using `draw_id`. There's also no reason why the content of the indirect draw buffer need be static. In fact, we can generate its content directly on the graphics process using various techniques that will be explained shortly to achieve truly dynamic rendering without application intervention.

Storing Transformed Vertices

In OpenGL, it is possible to save the results of the vertex, tessellation evaluation, or geometry shader into one or more buffer objects. This is a feature known as *transform feedback*, and is effectively the last stage in the front end. It is a non-programmable, fixed-function stage in the OpenGL pipeline that is nonetheless highly configurable. When transform feedback is used, a specified set of attributes output from the last stage in the current shader pipeline (whether that be a vertex, tessellation evaluation, or geometry shader) are written into a set of buffers.

When no geometry shader is present, vertices processed by the vertex shader and perhaps tessellation evaluation shader are recorded. When a geometry shader is present, the vertices generated by the `EmitVertex()` function are stored, allowing a variable amount of data to be recorded depending on what the shader does. The buffers used for capturing the output of vertex and geometry shaders are known as transform feedback buffers. Once data has been placed into a buffer using transform feedback, it can be read back using a function like **glGetBufferSubData()** or by mapping it into the application's address space using **glMapBuffer()** and reading from it directly. It can also be used as the source of data for subsequent drawing commands. For the remainder of this section, we will refer to the last stage in the front end as the vertex shader. However, be aware that if a geometry or tessellation evaluation shader is present, the last stage is the one whose outputs are saved by transform feedback.

---

of finding two rocks the same shape, at the same scale, and with the same color is vanishingly small.

Using Transform Feedback

To set up transform feedback, we must tell OpenGL which of the outputs from the front end we want to record. The outputs from the last stage of the front end are sometimes referred to as *varyings*. The function to tell OpenGL which ones to record is **glTransformFeedbackVaryings()**, and its prototype is

```
void glTransformFeedbackVaryings(GLuint program,
                                 GLsizei count,
                                 const GLchar * const * varying,
                                 GLenum bufferMode);
```

The first parameter to **glTransformFeedbackVaryings()** is the name of a program object. The transform feedback varying state is actually maintained as part of a program object. This means that different programs can record different sets of vertex attributes, even if the same vertex or geometry shaders are used in them. The second parameter is the number of outputs (or varyings) to record and is also the length of the array whose address is given in the third parameter, varying. This third parameter is simply an array of C-style strings giving the names of the varyings to record. These are the names of the out variables in the vertex shader. Finally, the last parameter (bufferMode) specifies the mode in which the varyings are to be recorded. This must be either GL_SEPARATE_ATTRIBS or GL_INTERLEAVED_ATTRIBS. If bufferMode is GL_INTERLEAVED_ATTRIBS, the varyings are recorded into a single buffer, one after another. If bufferMode is GL_SEPARATE_ATTRIBS, each of the varyings is recorded into its own buffer. Consider the following piece of vertex shader code, which declares the output varyings:

```
out vec4 vs_position_out;
out vec4 vs_color_out;
out vec3 vs_normal_out;
out vec3 vs_binormal_out;
out vec3 vs_tangent_out;
```

To specify that the varyings vs_position_out, vs_color_out, and so on should be written into a single interleaved transform feedback buffer, the following C code could be used in your application:

```
static const char * varying_names[] =
{
    "vs_position_out",
    "vs_color_out",
    "vs_normal_out",
    "vs_binormal_out",
    "vs_tangent_out"
};

const int num_varyings = sizeof(varying_names) /
                             sizeof(varying_names[0]);
```

```
glTransformFeedbackVaryings(program,
                            num_varyings,
                            varying_names,
                            GL_INTERLEAVED_ATTRIBS);
```

Not all of the outputs from your vertex (or geometry) shader need to be stored into the transform feedback buffer. It is possible to save a subset of the vertex shader outputs to the transform feedback buffer and send more to the fragment shader for interpolation. Likewise, it is also possible to save some outputs from the vertex shader into a transform feedback buffer that are not used by the fragment shader. Because of this, outputs from the vertex shader that may have been considered inactive (because they're not used by the fragment shader) may become active due to their being stored in a transform feedback buffer. Therefore, after specifying a new set of transform feedback varyings by calling **glTransformFeedbackVaryings()**, it is necessary to link the program object using

```
glLinkProgram(program);
```

If you change the set of varyings captured by transform feedback, you need to link the program object again otherwise your changes won't have any effect. Once the transform feedback varyings have been specified and the program has been linked, it may be used as normal. Before actually capturing anything, you need to create a buffer and bind it to an indexed transform feedback buffer binding point. Of course, before any data can be written to a buffer, space must be allocated in the buffer for it. To allocate space without specifying data, call

```
GLuint buffer;
glGenBuffers(1, &buffer);
glBindBuffer(GL_TARNSFORM_FEEDBACK_BUFFER, buffer);
glBufferData(GL_TRANSFORM_FEEDBACK_BUFFER, size, NULL, GL_DYNAMIC_COPY);
```

When you allocate storage for a buffer, there are many possible values for the usage parameter, but GL_DYNAMIC_COPY is probably a good choice for a transform feedback buffer. The DYNAMIC part tells OpenGL that the data is likely to change often but will likely be used a few times between each update. The COPY part says that you plan to update the data in the buffer through OpenGL functionality (such as transform feedback) and then hand that data back to OpenGL for use in another operation (such as drawing).

When you have specified the transform feedback mode as GL_INTERLEAVED_ATTRIBS, all of the stored vertex attributes are written one after another into a single buffer. To specify which buffer the transform feedback data will be written to, you need to bind a buffer to one of the indexed transform feedback binding points. There are actually multiple GL_TRANSFORM_FEEDBACK_BUFFER binding points for this purpose, which are conceptually separate but related to the general binding GL_TRANSFORM_FEEDBACK_BUFFER binding point. A schematic of this is shown in Figure 7.10.

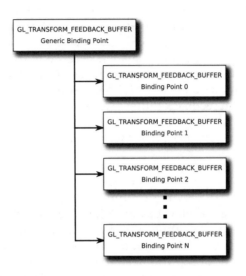

Figure 7.10: Relationship of transform feedback binding points

To bind a buffer to any of the indexed binding points, call

```
glBindBufferBase(GL_TRANSFORM_FEEDBACK_BUFFER, index, buffer);
```

As before, GL_TRANSFORM_FEEDBACK_BUFFER tells OpenGL that we're binding a buffer object to store the results of transform feedback, and the last parameter, buffer, is the name of the buffer object we want to bind. The extra parameter, index, is the index of the GL_TRANSFORM_FEEDBACK_BUFFER binding point. An important thing to note is that there is no way to directly address any of the extra binding points provided by **glBindBufferBase()** through functions like **glBufferData()** or **glCopyBufferSubData()**. However, when you call **glBindBufferBase()**, it actually binds the buffer to the indexed binding point and to the generic binding point. Therefore, you can use the extra binding points to allocate space in the buffer if you access the general binding point right after calling **glBindBufferBase()**.

A slightly more advanced version of **glBindBufferBase()** is **glBindBufferRange()**, whose prototype is

```
void glBindBufferRange(GLenum target,
                       GLuint index,
                       GLuint buffer,
                       GLintptr offset,
                       GLsizeiptr size);
```

The **glBindBufferRange()** function allows you to bind a section of a buffer to an indexed binding point, whereas **glBindBuffer()** and **glBindBufferBase()** can only bind the whole buffer at once. The first three parameters (target, index, and buffer) have the same meanings as in **glBindBufferBase()**. The offset and size parameters are used to specify the start and length of the section of the buffer that you'd like to bind, respectively. You can even bind different sections of the same buffer to several different indexed binding points simultaneously. This enables you to use transform feedback in GL_SEPARATE_ATTRIBS mode to write each attribute of the output vertices into separate sections of a single buffer. If your application packs all attributes into a single vertex buffer and uses **glVertexAttribPointer()** to specify non-zero offsets into the buffer, this allows you to make the output of transform feedback match the input of your vertex shader.

If you specified that all of the attributes should be recorded into a single transform feedback buffer by using the GL_INTERLEAVED_ATTRIBS parameter to **glTransformFeedbackVaryings()**, the data will be tightly packed and written into the buffer bound to the first GL_TRANSFORM_FEEDBACK_BUFFER binding point (that with index zero). However, if you specified that the mode for transform feedback is GL_SEPARATE_ATTRIBS, each output from the vertex shader will be recorded into its own separate buffer (or section of a buffer, if you used **glBindBufferRange()**). In this case, you need to bind multiple buffers or buffer sections as transform feedback buffers. The index parameter must be between zero and one less than the maximum number of varyings that can be recorded into separate buffers using transform feedback mode. This limit depends on your graphics hardware and drivers and can be found by calling **glGetIntegerv()** with the GL_MAX_TRANSFORM_FEEDBACK_SEPARATE_ATTRIBS parameter. This limit is also applied to the count parameter to **glTransformFeedbackVaryings()**.

There is no fixed limit on the number of separate varyings that can be written to transform feedback buffers in GL_INTERLEAVED_ATTRIBS mode, but there is a maximum number of components that can be written into a buffer. For example, it is possible to write more **vec3** varyings than **vec4** varyings into a buffer using transform feedback. Again, this limit depends on your graphics hardware and can be found using **glGetIntegerv()** with the GL_MAX_TRANSFORM_FEEDBACK_INTERLEAVED_COMPONENTS parameter.

If you need to, you can leave gaps in the output structures stored in the transform feedback buffer. When you do this, OpenGL will write a few elements, then skip some space in the output buffer, then write a few more components, and so on, leaving the unused space in the buffer unmodified. To do this you can include one of the "virtual" varying names, gl_SkipComponents1, gl_SkipComponents2, gl_SkipComponents3, or gl_SkipComponents4 to skip one, two, three, or four components' worth of storage space in the output buffer.

Finally, it also possible to write one set of output varyings interleaved into one buffer while writing another set of attributes into another buffer. To do this, we use another special "virtual" varying name, gl_NextBuffer, which tells **glTransformFeedbackVaryings()** to move on to the next buffer binding index. When you use gl_NextBuffer, the bufferMode parameter must be GL_INTERLEAVED_ATTRIBS. As an example, consider the code

```
static const char * varying_names[] =
{
    "carrots",
    "peas",
    "gl_NextBuffer",
    "beans",
    "potatoes"
};

const int num_varyings = sizeof(varying_names) / sizeof(varying_names[0]);

glTransformFeedbackVaryings(program,
                            num_varyings,
                            varying_names,
                            GL_INTERLEAVED_ATTRIBS);
```

After running this code and then calling **glLinkProgram()**, the transform feedback stage will be configured to write carrots and peas into the first of the transform feedback buffers and beans and potatoes to the second. You could even skip the first buffer binding altogether by setting the first varying name to gl_NextBuffer.

Starting, Pausing, and Stopping Transform Feedback

Once the buffers that are to receive the results of the transform feedback have been bound, transform feedback mode is activated by calling

```
void glBeginTransformFeedback(GLenum primitiveMode);
```

Now whenever vertices pass through OpenGL's front end, output varyings from the last shader will be written to the transform feedback buffers. The parameter to the function, primitiveMode, tells OpenGL what types of geometry to expect. The acceptable parameters are GL_POINTS, GL_LINES, and GL_TRIANGLES. When you call **glDrawArrays()** or another OpenGL drawing function, the basic geometric type must match what you have specified as the transform feedback primitive mode, or you must have a geometry shader that outputs the appropriate primitive type. For example, if primitiveMode is GL_TRIANGLES, then the last stage of the front end must produce triangles. This means that if you have a geometry shader, it must output triangle_strip primitives, if you have a tessellation evaluation shader (and no geometry shader), its output mode must be triangles, and if you have neither, you must call **glDrawArrays()** with GL_TRIANGLES, GL_TRIANGLE_STRIP or GL_TRIANGLE_FAN. The mapping of transform feedback primitive mode to draw types is shown in Table 7.3.

Table 7.3: Values for primitiveMode

Value of primitiveMode	Allowed Draw Types
GL_POINTS	GL_POINTS
GL_LINES	GL_LINES, GL_LINE_STRIP, GL_LINE_LOOP
GL_TRIANGLES	GL_TRIANGLES, GL_TRIANGLE_STRIP, GL_TRIANGLE_FAN

In addition to the modes listed in Table 7.3, GL_PATCHES can be used for the drawing command's mode parameter, so long as either the tessellation evaluation shader or geometry shader (if present) is configured to output the right type of primitives. Once transform feedback mode is activated, OpenGL will record your selected outputs from the front end into transform feedback buffers. You can temporarily suspend this recording by calling

```
void glPauseTransformFeedback();
```

When transform feedback mode is paused, it can be restarted again by calling

```
void glResumeTransformFeedback();
```

At this point, OpenGL will continue to record the output of the front end from wherever it left off in the transform feedback buffers. So long as transform feedback is not paused, vertices are recorded into the transform feedback buffers until transform feedback mode is exited or until the space allocated for the transform feedback buffers is exhausted. To exit transform feedback mode, call

```
glEndTransformFeedback();
```

All rendering that occurs between a call to **glBeginTransformFeedback()** and **glEndTransformFeedback()** results in data being written into the

currently bound transform feedback buffers. Each time
`glBeginTransformFeedback()` is called, OpenGL starts writing data at the
beginning of the buffers bound for transform feedback, overwriting what
might be there already. Some care should be taken while transform
feedback is active as changing transform feedback state between calls to
`glBeginTransformFeedback()` and `glEndTransformFeedback()` is not
allowed. For example, it's not possible to change the transform feedback
buffer bindings or to resize or reallocate any of the transform feedback
buffers while transform feedback mode is active. This includes cases where
transform feedback is paused, even though it's not recording during those
times.

Ending the Pipeline with Transform Feedback

In many applications of transform feedback, it may well be that you
simply want to store the vertices that the transform feedback stage
produces, but you don't actually want to *draw anything*. As transform
feedback logically sits right before rasterization in the OpenGL pipeline,
we can ask OpenGL to turn off rasterization (and therefore anything after
it) by calling

```
glEnable(GL_RASTERIZER_DISCARD);
```

This stops OpenGL from processing primitives any further after transform
feedback has been executed. The result is that our vertices are recorded
into the output transform feedback buffers, but nothing is actually
rasterized. To turn rasterization back on, we call

```
glDisable(GL_RASTERIZER_DISCARD);
```

This disables rasterizer discard, enabling rasterization.

Transform Feedback Example — Physical Simulation

In the `springmass` example, we build a physical simulation of a mesh of
springs and masses. Each vertex represents a weight, connected to up to
four neighbors by elastic tethers. The example iterates over the vertices,
processing each one with a vertex shader. A number of advanced features
are used in this example. We use a texture buffer object (TBO) to hold
vertex position data in addition to a regular attribute array. The same
buffer is bound to both the TBO and the vertex attribute associated with
the position input to the vertex shader. This allows us to arbitrarily access
the current position of other vertices in the system. We also use an integer
vertex attribute to hold indices of neighboring vertices. Furthermore, we

use transform feedback to store the positions and velocities of each of the masses between each iteration of the algorithm.

For each vertex, we need a position, velocity, and mass. We can pack the positions and masses into one vertex array and pack the velocities into another. Each element of the position array is actually a **vec4**, with the x, y, and z components containing the three-dimensional coordinate of the vertex, and the w component containing the weight of the vertex. The velocity array can simply be an array of **vec3**. Additionally, we use an array of **ivec4** to store information about the springs connecting the weights together. There is one **ivec4** for each vertex, and each of the four components of the vector contains the index of the vertex that is connected to the other end of the spring. We call this the connection vector. This means that we can connect each mass to up to four other masses. To record that there is no connection, we store a -1 in the corresponding component of the connection vector (see Figure 7.11).

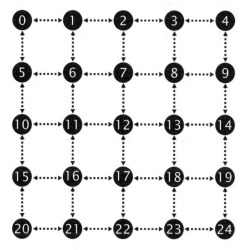

Figure 7.11: Connections of vertices in the spring-mass system

Consider vertex 12. It has associated with it an **ivec4** connection vector containing <7, 13, 17, 11> — the indices of the vertices to which it is connected. Likewise, the connection vector for vertex 13 contains <8, 14, 18, 12>. There is a bidirectional connection between vertices 12 and 13. The vertices at the edges of the mesh don't have all of their springs attached. So vertex 14 has a connection vector containing <9, -1, 19, 13>. Notice that the y component of the vector contains -1, indicating that there is no spring there.

Because for each of the connection vectors we either store the index of the vertex to which we are connected or -1 to indicate that no connection is present, we know that by storing a -1 in each of the connection vector components, we can fix that vertex in place. No matter what forces are acting on it, its position won't be updated. This allows us to fix the position of some of the vertices and hold the structure in place. If all components of the connection vector are -1, then the calculations for updating the position and velocity of the vertex will be skipped by simply setting the force associated with that vertex to zero. The code to set up the initial positions and velocities of each node and the connection vectors for our spring-mass system is shown in Listing 7.16.

```
vmath::vec4 * initial_positions = new vmath::vec4 [POINTS_TOTAL];
vmath::vec3 * initial_velocities = new vmath::vec3 [POINTS_TOTAL];
vmath::ivec4 * connection_vectors = new vmath::ivec4 [POINTS_TOTAL];

int n = 0;

for (j = 0; j < POINTS_Y; j++)
{
    float fj = (float)j / (float)POINTS_Y;
    for (i = 0; i < POINTS_X; i++)
    {
        float fi = (float)i / (float)POINTS_X;

        initial_positions[n] = vmath::vec4((fi - 0.5f) * (float)POINTS_X,
                                           (fj - 0.5f) * (float)POINTS_Y,
                                           0.6f * sinf(fi) * cosf(fj),
                                           1.0f);
        initial_velocities[n] = vmath::vec3(0.0f);

        connection_vectors[n] = vmath::ivec4(-1);

        if (j != (POINTS_Y - 1))
        {
            if (i != 0)
                connection_vectors[n][0] = n - 1;

            if (j != 0)
                connection_vectors[n][1] = n - POINTS_X;

            if (i != (POINTS_X - 1))
                connection_vectors[n][2] = n + 1;

            if (j != (POINTS_Y - 1))
                connection_vectors[n][3] = n + POINTS_X;
        }
        n++;
    }
}

glGenVertexArrays(2, m_vao);
glGenBuffers(5, m_vbo);

for (i = 0; i < 2; i++)
{
```

```
        glBindVertexArray(m_vao[i]);

        glBindBuffer(GL_ARRAY_BUFFER, m_vbo[POSITION_A + i]);
        glBufferData(GL_ARRAY_BUFFER,
                     POINTS_TOTAL * sizeof(vmath::vec4),
                     initial_positions, GL_DYNAMIC_COPY);
        glVertexAttribPointer(0, 4, GL_FLOAT, GL_FALSE, 0, NULL);
        glEnableVertexAttribArray(0);

        glBindBuffer(GL_ARRAY_BUFFER, m_vbo[VELOCITY_A + i]);
        glBufferData(GL_ARRAY_BUFFER,
                     POINTS_TOTAL * sizeof(vmath::vec3),
                     initial_velocities, GL_DYNAMIC_COPY);
        glVertexAttribPointer(1, 3, GL_FLOAT, GL_FALSE, 0, NULL);
        glEnableVertexAttribArray(1);

        glBindBuffer(GL_ARRAY_BUFFER, m_vbo[CONNECTION]);
        glBufferData(GL_ARRAY_BUFFER,
                     POINTS_TOTAL * sizeof(vmath::ivec4),
                     connection_vectors, GL_STATIC_DRAW);
        glVertexAttribIPointer(2, 4, GL_INT, 0, NULL);
        glEnableVertexAttribArray(2);
    }

    delete [] connection_vectors;
    delete [] initial_velocities;
    delete [] initial_positions;

    // Attach the buffers to a pair of TBOs.
    glGenTextures(2, m_pos_tbo);
    glBindTexture(GL_TEXTURE_BUFFER, m_pos_tbo[0]);
    glTexBuffer(GL_TEXTURE_BUFFER, GL_RGBA32F, m_vbo[POSITION_A]);
    glBindTexture(GL_TEXTURE_BUFFER, m_pos_tbo[1]);
    glTexBuffer(GL_TEXTURE_BUFFER, GL_RGBA32F, m_vbo[POSITION_B]);
```

Listing 7.16: Spring-mass system vertex setup

To update the system, we run a vertex shader that obtains its own position and connection vector using regular vertex attributes. It then looks up the current positions of the vertices it's connected to by indexing into the TBO using the elements of the connection vector (which is also a regular vertex attribute). The code for initializing the TBOs is also shown at the end of Listing 7.16.

For each connected vertex, the shader can calculate the distance to it and thus the extension of the virtual spring between them. From this, it can calculate the force exerted upon it by the spring, calculate the acceleration this produces given the mass of the vertex, and produce a new position and velocity vector to use in the next iteration. It sounds complex, but it's not—it's just Newtonian physics and Hooke's law.

Hooke's law is

$$F = -kx$$

where F is the force exerted by the spring, k is the spring constant (how stiff the spring is), and x is the extension of the spring. The spring's extension is relative to its resting length. For our system, we keep the rest length of the springs the same and store it in a uniform. Any stretching of the spring produces a positive value of x, and any compression of the spring produces a negative value of x. The instantaneous length of the spring is simply the length of the vector from one of its ends to the other—exactly what we'll calculate in the vertex shader. We give the force a direction by multiplying the linear force F by the direction along the spring. We introduce the variable $\vec{d}$, which is simply the normalized direction along the spring:

$$\vec{F} = \vec{d}F$$

This gives us the force applied to the mass due to the extension or compression of the spring. If we were to simply apply this force to the mass, the system would oscillate and, due to numerical imprecision, would eventually become unstable. All real spring systems have some loss due to friction, and this can be modeled by including damping into the force equation. The force due to damping is determined by the equation

$$\vec{F_d} = -c\vec{v}$$

where c represents the damping coefficient. Ideally, we would calculate the damping force for each spring, but for this simple system, a single force based on the mass's velocity will do. Also, we use the initial velocity at each time-step to approximate the continuous differential that would be required by this equation. In our shader, we initialize F by calculating the damping force and then accumulate the force exerted by each spring on the mass. Finally, we can apply gravity to the system by treating it as simply one more force acting on each mass. Gravity is a constant force that generally acts in a downward direction. We can just add that to the initial force acting on the mass:

$$F_{total} = G - \vec{d}kx - c\vec{v}$$

Once we have the total force, we can simply apply Newton's laws. First, Newton's second law allows us to calculate the acceleration of the mass:

$$F = m\vec{a}$$

$$\vec{a} = \frac{\vec{F}}{m}$$

Here, F is the force we just calculated using gravity, the damping coefficient, and Hooke's law; m is the mass of the vertex (stored in the w component of the position attribute); and a is the resulting acceleration. Given the initial velocity (which we get from our other attribute array), we can plug it into the following equations of motion to find out what our final velocity will be and how far we moved in a fixed time:

$$\vec{v} = \vec{u} + \vec{a}t$$

$$\vec{s} = \vec{u} + \frac{\vec{a}t^2}{2}$$

where u is the initial velocity (read from our velocity attribute array), v is the final velocity, t is our time-step (supplied by the application), and s is the distance we've travelled. Don't forget, a, u, v, and s are all vectors. All that's left to do is write the shaders and hook them up to an application. Listing 7.17 shows what the vertex shader looks like.

```
#version 430 core

// This input vector contains the vertex position in xyz, and the
// mass of the vertex in w
layout (location = 0) in vec4 position_mass;
// This is the current velocity of the vertex
layout (location = 1) in vec3 velocity;
// This is our connection vector
layout (location = 2) in ivec4 connection;

// This is a TBO that will be bound to the same buffer as the
// position_mass input attribute
layout (binding = 0) uniform samplerBuffer tex_position;

// The outputs of the vertex shader are the same as the inputs
out vec4 tf_position_mass;
out vec3 tf_velocity;

// A uniform to hold the time-step. The application can update this.
uniform float t = 0.07;

// The global spring constant
uniform float k = 7.1;

// Gravity
const vec3 gravity = vec3(0.0, -0.08, 0.0);

// Global damping constant
uniform float c = 2.8;

// Spring resting length
uniform float rest_length = 0.88;

void main(void)
{
    vec3 p = position_mass.xyz;    // p can be our position
    float m = position_mass.w;     // m is the mass of our vertex
    vec3 u = velocity;             // u is the initial velocity
```

```
vec3 F = gravity * m - c * u;   // F is the force on the mass
bool fixed_node = true;          // Becomes false when force is applied

for (int i = 0; i < 4; i++)
{
    if (connection[i] != -1)
    {
        // q is the position of the other vertex
        vec3 q = texelFetch(tex_position, connection[i]).xyz;
        vec3 d = q - p;
        float x = length(d);
        F += -k * (rest_length - x) * normalize(d);
        fixed_node = false;
    }
}

// If this is a fixed node, reset force to zero
if (fixed_node)
{
    F = vec3(0.0);
}

// Acceleration due to force
vec3 a = F / m;

// Displacement
vec3 s = u * t + 0.5 * a * t * t;

// Final velocity
vec3 v = u + a * t;

// Constrain the absolute value of the displacement per step
s = clamp(s, vec3(-25.0), vec3(25.0));

// Write the outputs
tf_position_mass = vec4(p + s, m);
tf_velocity = v;
}
```

Listing 7.17: Spring-mass system vertex shader

That wasn't so hard, was it? To execute the shader, we iterate over our set
of vertices that we placed in buffers earlier. We need to double-buffer the
position and velocity information, which means that we read from one set
of buffers and write to the other on one pass, and then swap the buffers
around so that the data moves back and forth from one buffer to the
other. The connection information remains the same on each pass, so it's
going to be constant. To do this, we use the two VAOs that we set up
earlier. The first VAO has one set of position and velocity attributes
attached to it, along with the common connection information. The other
VAO has the other set of position and velocity attributes attached and the
same, common connection information.

In addition to the VBOs, we need two TBOs. We use each buffer as a
position VBO and as a TBO, simultaneously. This seems strange, but is
perfectly legal in OpenGL— after all, we're just reading from the same

buffer via two different methods. To set this up, we generate two textures, bind them to the GL_TEXTURE_BUFFER binding point, and attach the buffers to them using **glTexBuffer()**, as explained earlier in this book. When we bind VAO A, we also bind texture A. When we bind VAO B, we bind texture B. That way, the same data appears in both the position vertex attribute and in the tex_position samplerBuffer buffer texture.

The code to set this up isn't particularly complex but is repetitive. A complete implementation can be found on this book's Web site. The example application includes the code to create and initialize the buffers, perform double buffering, and visualize the results. The application fixes a couple of the vertices in place so that the whole system doesn't just fall off the bottom of the screen. Once we have all of the buffers hooked up, we can simulate a time-step in the system with a single call to **glDrawArrays()**. Each node in the system is represented by a single GL_POINTS primitive. If we initialize the system and let it run, we see a result that looks like Figure 7.12.

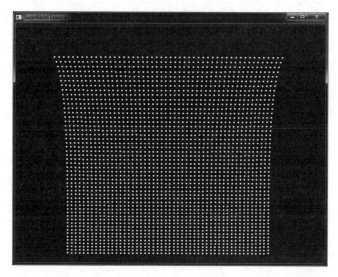

Figure 7.12: Simulation of points connected by springs

On each frame, we run the physical simulation several times, and on each iteration we swap the VAOs and TBOs. This iterative loop is shown in Listing 7.18. Each iteration of the loop updates the positions and velocities of all the nodes once. Iterating the simulation several times rather than just using a larger time-step in the simulation leads to greater stability and less oscillation of nodes, which leads to a better visual result.

```
int i;
glUseProgram(m_update_program);

glEnable(GL_RASTERIZER_DISCARD);

for (i = iterations_per_frame; i != 0; --i)
{
    glBindVertexArray(m_vao[m_iteration_index & 1]);
    glBindTexture(GL_TEXTURE_BUFFER, m_pos_tbo[m_iteration_index & 1]);
    m_iteration_index++;
    glBindBufferBase(GL_TRANSFORM_FEEDBACK_BUFFER, 0,
                    m_vbo[POSITION_A + (m_iteration_index & 1)]);
    glBindBufferBase(GL_TRANSFORM_FEEDBACK_BUFFER, 1,
                    m_vbo[VELOCITY_A + (m_iteration_index & 1)]);
    glBeginTransformFeedback(GL_POINTS);
    glDrawArrays(GL_POINTS, 0, POINTS_TOTAL);
    glEndTransformFeedback();
}

glDisable(GL_RASTERIZER_DISCARD);
```

Listing 7.18: Spring-mass system iteration loop

During iteration, we enable *rasterizer discard*, which stops data passing further down the pipeline beyond the transform feedback stage. We then disable rasterizer discard once we are done iterating so that we can render the resulting system to the screen. After enough iterations have been performed, we can render the points in the system in whatever way we wish. Using a simple program for rendering, we draw the nodes of the system as points and the connections between them as lines. Code to do this is shown in Listing 7.19, and the resulting image is shown in Figure 7.12.

```
static const GLfloat black[] = { 0.0f, 0.0f, 0.0f, 0.0f };

glViewport(0, 0, info.windowWidth, info.windowHeight);
glClearBufferfv(GL_COLOR, 0, black);

glUseProgram(m_render_program);

if (draw_points)
{
    glPointSize(4.0f);
    glDrawArrays(GL_POINTS, 0, POINTS_TOTAL);
}

if (draw_lines)
{
    glBindBuffer(GL_ELEMENT_ARRAY_BUFFER, m_index_buffer);
    glDrawElements(GL_LINES, CONNECTIONS_TOTAL * 2,
                GL_UNSIGNED_INT, NULL);
}
```

Listing 7.19: Spring-mass system rendering loop

The image in Figure 7.12 is not particularly interesting, but it does demonstrate that our simulation is running correctly. To make the visual result more appealing, we can set the point size to a larger value, and we can also issue a second, indexed draw using `glDrawElements()` and `GL_LINES` primitives to visualize the connections between nodes. Note that the same vertex positions can be used as input to this second pass, but we need to construct another buffer to use with the `GL_ELEMENT_ARRAY` binding that contains the indices of the vertices at the end of each spring. This additional step is also performed by the example program. Figure 7.13 shows the final result.

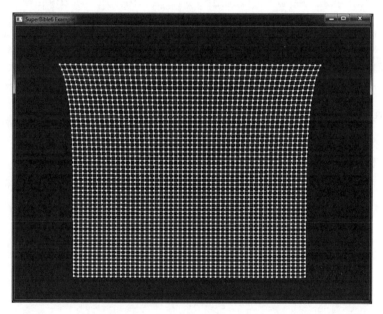

Figure 7.13: Visualizing springs in the spring-mass system

Of course, the physical simulation (and the vertex data produced by it) can be used for anything. This particular system would provide a reasonable approximation to cloth, although it is elementary. It does not, for instance, handle self-interaction, which would be important for a realistic cloth simulation. However, many systems in which particles interact in a deterministic way can be modeled and simulated using only a vertex shader and transform feedback.

Clipping

As explained in Chapter 3, "Following the Pipeline," clipping is the process of determining which primitives may be fully or partially visible and constructing a set of primitives from them that will lie entirely inside the viewport.

For points, clipping is trivial — if the coordinate of the point is inside the region, then it should be processed further, whereas if it is outside the region it should be discarded. Clipping lines is a little more complex. If both ends of the line lie on the outside of the same plane of the clipping volume (for example, if the x component of both ends of the line is less than -1.0), then the line is trivially discarded. If both ends of the line lie inside the clipping volume, then it is trivially accepted. If one end of the line is inside the clipping volume or if the endpoints of the line lie such that it may cut through the clipping volume, then the line must be clipped against the volume to create a shorter line that lies within it. Figure 7.14 demonstrates trivially accepted, trivially discarded, and non-trivially clipped lines shown in two dimensions for clarity.

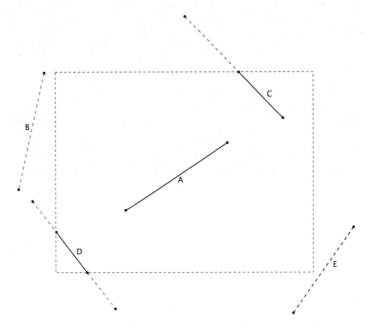

Figure 7.14: Clipping lines

In Figure 7.14 the line marked A is trivially accepted as both of its endpoints are entirely within the viewport (represented as a dotted rectangle). The line marked B is trivially rejected because both of its endpoints are outside the left edge of the viewport. Line C is clipped against the top edge of the viewport and line D is clipped against the left *and* bottom edges of the viewport. This is non-trivial clipping and results in vertices being moved along the line to make it fit into the viewport. Line E is a special case—the first endpoint is on the outside of the right edge of the viewport but the second is inside the right edge. However, the second endpoint of E is outside the bottom edge of the viewport whereas the first is inside that edge. OpenGL will still discard this line, but internally it may temporarily clip the line against one or other of the viewport edges before determining that there is nothing to be drawn.

The clipping of triangles poses a problem that appears to be more complex but is actually solved in a similar manner. As with lines, triangles may be trivially discarded if all three of their vertices lie on the outside of the same clipping plane and may be trivially accepted if all of their vertices lie inside the clipping volume. If the triangle lies partially inside and partially outside the clipping volume, then it must be clipped by cutting it into a number of smaller triangles that fit within the volume. Figure 7.15 demonstrates the process in two dimensions, although of course this really happens in three dimensions in OpenGL.

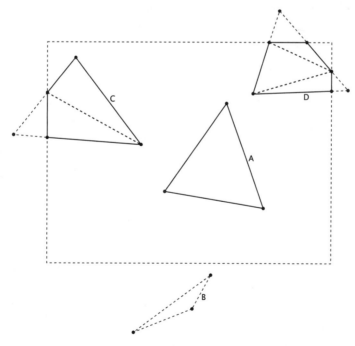

Figure 7.15: Clipping triangles

As you can see, the triangle marked A in Figure 7.15 is trivially accepted because all three of its vertices lie inside the viewport. Triangle B is trivially discarded because all three of its vertices lie outside of the same edge of the viewport. Triangle C crosses the left edge of the viewport and must be clipped. An additional vertex is generated by OpenGL, and the original triangle is split into two parts. Triangle D clips against the right and top edges of the viewport. An additional vertex is produced for each clipped edge, and new triangles are created to fill the polygonal shape that is produced. In fact, this is generally true — for each edge that a triangle clips, one extra vertex and one extra triangle are produced.

The Guard Band

As you can see in Figure 7.15, triangles that are partially visible but clip against one or more of the viewport edges can, depending on the implementation, be broken into multiple smaller triangles. This can cause a performance problem for GPUs that can process triangles at a fixed rate. In some cases, it may be faster to allow such triangles to pass through the clipping phase unmodified and instead have the rasterizer throw away parts that are not going to be visible. To implement this, some GPUs include a *guard band*, which is a region outside clip space in which triangles will be allowed to pass through even though they will not be visible. The guard band is illustrated in Figure 7.16.

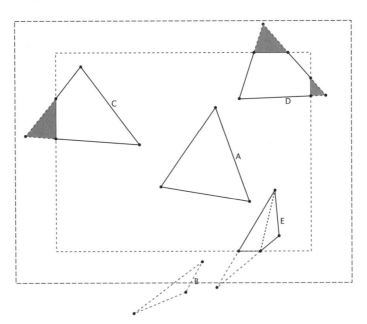

Figure 7.16: Clipping triangles using a guard band

The presence of a guard band does not affect trivially accepted or trivially rejected triangles — those are either passed through or thrown away as they were before. However, triangles that clip against one or more edge of the viewport but otherwise fall inside the guard band are also considered to be trivially accepted and not are broken up. Only triangles that clip against one or more edges of the guard band *and* protrude into the viewport are broken into multiple triangles. Referring to Figure 7.16, we see that triangle A is trivially accepted as before and triangle B is trivially rejected as before. However, triangles C and D are no longer broken up. Rather, they are passed through the clipper unmodified and the shaded areas later discarded during rasterization. Only the newly introduced triangle E is broken into sub-triangles for rasterization. This is because it clips against both the viewport (the inner dotted rectangle) and the guard band (the outer dotted rectangle).

In practice, the width of the guard band (the gap between the inner and outer dotted rectangles) is quite large — usually at least as big as the viewport itself, and you'd have to draw some pretty huge triangles to hit both. While none of this will have any visible effect on the output of your program, it may affect its performance, and so is useful information.

User-Defined Clipping

One way to determine which side of a plane a point lies on is to calculate the signed distance from that point to the plane. When you know the signed distance from a point to a plane, its absolute value determines how far the point is to the plane, and its sign determines which side of the plane the point is on. Therefore, you can use the sign of this distance to determine whether you are inside or outside a plane. OpenGL may or may not use that method to perform view volume clipping, but you can use it to implement your own clipping algorithms.

In addition to the six distances to the six standard clip planes making up the view frustum, a set of additional distances is available to the application that can be written inside the vertex or geometry shader. The clip distances are available for writing in the vertex shader through the built-in variable gl_ClipDistance[], which is an array of floating-point values. As you learned earlier in this chapter, gl_ClipDistance[] is a member of the gl_PerVertex block and can be written from the vertex shader, tessellation evaluation, or geometry shader — whichever comes last. The number of clip distances supported depends on your implementation of OpenGL. These distances are interpreted exactly as the built-in clip distances. If a shader writer wants to use user-defined clip distances, they should be enabled by the application by calling

```
glEnable(GL_CLIP_DISTANCE0 + n);
```

Here, n is the index of the clip distance to enable. The tokens GL_CLIP_DISTANCE1, GL_CLIP_DISTANCE2, and so on up to GL_CLIP_DISTANCE5 are usually defined in standard OpenGL header files. However, the maximum value of n is implementation defined and can be found by calling **glGetIntegerv()** with the token GL_MAX_CLIP_DISTANCES. You can disable the user-defined clip distance by calling **glDisable()** with the same token. If the user-defined clip distance at a particular index is not enabled, the value written to gl_ClipDistance[] at that index is ignored.

As with the built-in clipping planes, the sign of the distance written into the gl_ClipDistance[] array is used to determine whether a vertex is inside or outside the user-defined clipping volume. If the signs of all the distances for every vertex of a single triangle are negative, the triangle is clipped. If it is determined that the triangle may be partially visible, then the clip distances are linearly interpolated across the triangle and the visibility determination is made at each pixel. Thus, the rendered result will be a linear approximation to the per-vertex distance function evaluated by the vertex shader. This allows a vertex shader to clip geometry against an arbitrary set of planes (the distance of a point to a plane can be found with a simple dot product).

The gl_ClipDistance[] array is also available as an input to the fragment shader. Fragments that would have a negative value in any element of gl_ClipDistance[] are clipped away and never reach the fragment shader. However, any fragment that only has positive values in gl_ClipDistance[] passes through the fragment shader, and this value can then be read and used by the shader for any purpose. One example use of this functionality is to fade the fragment by reducing its alpha value based as its clip distance approaches zero. This allows a large primitive clipped against a plane by the vertex shader to fade smoothly or be antialiased by the fragment shader, rather than generating a hard clipped edge.

Note that if all of the vertices making up a single primitive (point, line, or triangle) are clipped against the same plane, then the whole primitive is eliminated. This seems to make sense and behaves as expected for regular polygon meshes. However, when using points and lines, you need to be careful. With points, you can render a point with a single vertex that covers multiple pixels by setting the gl_PointSize parameter to a value greater than 1.0. When gl_PointSize is large, a big point is rendered around the vertex. This means that if you have a large point that is moving slowly toward and eventually off the edge of the screen, it will suddenly disappear when the center of the point exits the view volume and the vertex representing that point is clipped. Likewise, OpenGL can render wide lines. If a line is drawn whose vertices are both outside one of the clipping planes but would otherwise be visible, nothing will be drawn. This can produce strange popping artifacts if you're not careful.

Listing 7.20 illustrates how a vertex shader might write to two clip distances. For the first clip distance, we determine the distance of the object-space vertex to a plane defined by the four-component vector, clip_plane. For the second distance, we consider the distance from each vertex to a sphere. To do this, we take the length of the vector from the view space vertex to the center of the sphere and subtract the sphere's radius (which is stored in the w component of the clip_sphere).

```
#version 430 core

// More uniforms here

// Clip plane
uniform vec4 clip_plane = vec4(1.0, 1.0, 0.0, 0.85);
uniform vec4 clip_sphere = vec4(0.0, 0.0, 0.0, 4.0);

void main(void)
{
    // Lighting code goes here

    // Write clip distances
    gl_ClipDistance[0] = dot(position, clip_plane);
    gl_ClipDistance[1] = length(position.xyz / position.w -
                                clip_sphere.xyz) - clip_sphere.w;

    // Calculate the clip-space position of each vertex
    gl_Position = proj_matrix * P;
}
```

Listing 7.20: Clipping an object against a plane and a sphere

The result of rendering with the shader shown in Listing 7.20 is shown in Figure 7.17.

As you can see in Figure 7.17, the dragon has not only been clipped against the flat plane, but also around the curved surface of the sphere. Be aware, though, that if the clip distance is linearly interpolated against a curved surface such as a sphere, the resulting clipped geometry will be a linear approximation to that curve. For good results, then, the original geometry must be reasonably detailed.

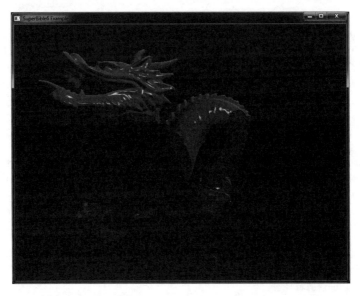

Figure 7.17: Rendering with user clip distances

Summary

This chapter covered in some detail the mechanisms by which OpenGL reads vertex data from the buffers that you provide and how you map the inputs to your vertex shader to those inputs. We've also discussed the responsibilities of the vertex shader and the built-in output variables that it can write. You have seen how the vertex shader can not only set the resulting position of the vertices that it produces, but also the size for any points that might be rendered, and even how it can control the clipping process to allow you to clip objects against arbitrary shapes.

You have been introduced to transform feedback — a powerful stage in OpenGL that allows the vertex shader to store arbitrary data into buffers. We have looked at how OpenGL clips the primitives it generates against the visible region of the window and how primitives are moved from clip space into not just a single viewport, but into many viewports. In the next chapter, we'll take another look at the front-end stages of tessellation and geometry shaders, which operate somewhat similarly to vertex shaders and will leverage the knowledge you've gained in this chapter.

Chapter 8

Primitive Processing

WHAT YOU'LL LEARN IN THIS CHAPTER

- How to use tessellation to add geometric detail to your scenes

- How to use geometry shaders to process whole primitives and create geometry on the fly

In the previous chapters, you've read about the OpenGL pipeline and have been at least briefly introduced to the functions of each of its stages. We've covered the vertex shader stage in some detail, including how its inputs are formed and where its outputs go. A vertex shader runs once on each of the vertices you send OpenGL and produces one set of outputs for each. The next few stages of the pipeline seem similar to vertex shaders at first, but can actually be considered *primitive processing* stages. First, the two tessellation shader stages and the fixed-function tessellator that they flank together process *patches*. Next, the geometry shader processes entire primitives (points, lines, and triangles) and runs once for each. In this chapter, we'll cover both tessellation and geometry shading, and investigate some of the OpenGL features that they unlock.

Tessellation

As introduced in the section "Tessellation" in Chapter 3, tessellation is the process of breaking a large primitive referred to as a *patch* into many smaller primitives before rendering them. There are many uses for tessellation, but the most common application is to add geometric detail to otherwise lower fidelity meshes. In OpenGL, tessellation is produced using three distinct stages of the pipeline — the tessellation control shader (TCS), the fixed-function tessellation engine, and the tessellation evaluation shader (TES). Logically, these three stages fit between the vertex shader and the geometry shader stage. When tessellation is active, incoming vertex data is first processed as normal by the vertex shader and then passed, in groups, to the tessellation control shader.

The tessellation control shader operates on groups of up to 32 vertices[1] at a time, collectively known as a patch. In the context of tessellation, the input vertices are often referred to as *control points*. The tessellation control shader is responsible for generating three things:

- The per-patch inner and outer tessellation factors
- The position and other attributes for each output control point
- Per-patch user-defined varyings

The tessellation factors are sent on to the fixed-function tessellation engine, which uses them to determine the way that it will break up the patch into smaller primitives. Besides the tessellation factors, the output of a tessellation control shader is a new patch (i.e., a new collection of vertices) that is passed to the tessellation evaluation shader after the patch has been tessellated by the tessellation engine. If some of the data is common to all output vertices (such as the color of the patch), then that data may be marked as *per patch*. When the fixed-function tessellator runs, it generates a new set of vertices spaced across the patch as determined by the tessellation factors and the tessellation mode, which is determined using a layout declaration in the tessellation evaluation shader. The only input to the tessellation evaluation shader generated by OpenGL is a set of coordinates indicating where in the patch the vertex lies. When the tessellator is generating triangles, those coordinates are *barycentric*

---

1. The minimum number of vertices per patch required to be supported by the OpenGL specification is 32. However, the upper limit is not fixed and may be determined by retrieving the value of GL_MAX_PATCH_VERTICES.

coordinates. When the tessellation engine is generating lines or triangles, those coordinates are simply a pair of normalized values indicating the relative position of the vertex. This is stored in the gl_TessCoord input variable. This setup is shown in the schematic of Figure 8.1.

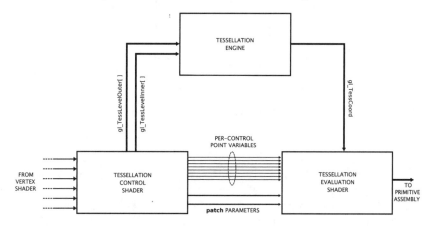

Figure 8.1: Schematic of OpenGL tessellation

Tessellation Primitive Modes

The tessellation mode is used to determine how OpenGL breaks up patches into primitives before passing them on to rasterization. This mode is set using an input layout qualifier in the tessellation evaluation shader and may be one of quads, triangles, or isolines. This primitive mode not only controls the form of the primitives produced by the tessellator, but also the interpretation of the gl_TessCoord input variable in the tessellation evaluation shader.

Tessellation Using Quads

When the chosen tessellation mode is set to quads, the tessellation engine will generate a quadrilateral (or quad) and break it up into a set of triangles. The two elements of the gl_TessLevelInner[] array should be written by the tessellation control shader and control the level of tessellation applied to the innermost region within the quad. The first element sets the tessellation in the horizontal (u) direction, and the second element sets the tessellation level applied in the vertical (v) direction. Also, all four elements of the gl_TessLevelOuter[] array should be written by the tessellation control shader and are used to determine the level of tessellation applied to the outer edges of the quad. This is shown in Figure 8.2.

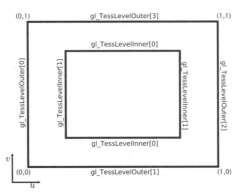

Figure 8.2: Tessellation factors for quad tessellation

When the quad is tessellated, the tessellation engine generates vertices across a two-dimensional domain normalized within the quad. The value stored in the gl_TessCoord input variable sent to the tessellation evaluation shader is then a two-dimensional vector (that is, only the x and y components of gl_TessCoord are valid) containing the normalized coordinate of the vertex within the quad. The tessellation evaluation shader can use these coordinates to generate its outputs from the inputs passed by the tessellation control shader. An example of quad tessellation produced by the tessmodes sample application is shown in Figure 8.3.

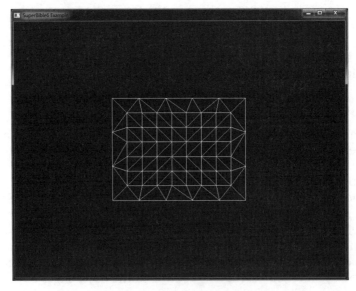

Figure 8.3: Quad tessellation example

In Figure 8.3, the inner tessellation factors in the u and v directions were set to 9.0 and 7.0, respectively. The outer tessellation factors were set to 3.0 and 5.0 in the u and v directions. This was accomplished using the very simple tessellation control shader shown in Listing 8.1.

```
#version 430 core

layout (vertices = 4) out;

void main(void)
{
    if (gl_InvocationID == 0)
    {
        gl_TessLevelInner[0] = 9.0;
        gl_TessLevelInner[1] = 7.0;
        gl_TessLevelOuter[0] = 3.0;
        gl_TessLevelOuter[1] = 5.0;
        gl_TessLevelOuter[2] = 3.0;
        gl_TessLevelOuter[3] = 5.0;
    }

    gl_out[gl_InvocationID].gl_Position =
        gl_in[gl_InvocationID].gl_Position;
}
```

Listing 8.1: Simple quad tessellation control shader example

The result of setting the tessellation factors in this way is visible in Figure 8.3. If you look closely, you will see that along the horizontal outer edges there are five divisions and along the vertical ones there are three divisions. On the interior, you can see that there are 9 divisions along the horizontal axis and 7 along the vertical.

The tessellation evaluation shader that generated Figure 8.3 is shown in Listing 8.2. Notice that the tessellation mode is set using the **quads** input layout qualifier near the front of the tessellation evaluation shader. The shader then uses the x and y components of gl_TessCoordinate to perform its own interpolation of the vertex position. In this case, the gl_in[] array is four elements long (as specified in the control shader shown in Listing 8.1).

```
#version 430 core

layout (quads) in;

void main(void)
{
    // Interpolate along bottom edge using x component of the
    // tessellation coordinate
    vec4 p1 = mix(gl_in[0].gl_Position,
                  gl_in[1].gl_Position,
                  gl_TessCoord.x);
    // Interpolate along top edge using x component of the
    // tessellation coordinate
    vec4 p2 = mix(gl_in[2].gl_Position,
```

```
                    gl_in[3].gl_Position,
                    gl_TessCoord.x);
        // Now interpolate those two results using the y component
        // of tessellation coordinate
        gl_Position = mix(p1, p2, gl_TessCoord.y);
    }
```

Listing 8.2: Simple quad tessellation evaluation shader example

Tessellation Using Triangles

When the tessellation mode is set to triangles (again, using an input layout qualifier in the tessellation control shader), the tessellation engine produces a triangle that is then broken into many smaller triangles. Only the first element of the gl_TessLevelInner[] array is used, and this level is applied to the entirety of the inner area of the tessellated triangle. The first three elements of the gl_TessLevelOuter[] array are used to set the tessellation factors for the three edges of the triangle. This is shown in Figure 8.4.

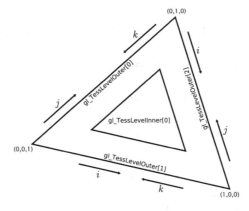

Figure 8.4: Tessellation factors for triangle tessellation

As the tessellation engine generates the vertices corresponding to the tessellated triangles, each vertex is assigned a three-dimensional coordinate called a *barycentric coordinate*. The three components of a barycentric coordinate can be used to form a weighted sum of three inputs representing the corners of a triangle and arrive at a value that is linearly interpolated across that triangle. An example of triangle tessellation is shown in Figure 8.5.

The tessellation control shader used to generate Figure 8.5 is shown in Listing 8.3. Notice how similar it is to Listing 8.1 in that all it does is write

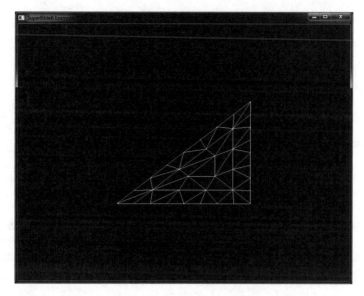

Figure 8.5: Triangle tessellation example

constants into the inner and outer tessellation levels and pass through the control point positions unmodified.

```
#version 430 core

layout (vertices = 3) out;

void main(void)
{
    if (gl_InvocationID == 0)
    {
        gl_TessLevelInner[0] = 5.0;
        gl_TessLevelOuter[0] = 8.0;
        gl_TessLevelOuter[1] = 8.0;
        gl_TessLevelOuter[2] = 8.0;
    }

    gl_out[gl_InvocationID].gl_Position =
        gl_in[gl_InvocationID].gl_Position;
}
```

Listing 8.3: Simple triangle tessellation control shader example

Listing 8.3 sets the inner tessellation level to 5.0 and all three outer tessellation levels to 8.0. Again, looking closely at Figure 8.5, you can see that each of the outer edges of the tessellated triangle has 8 divisions and the inner edges have 5 divisions. The tessellation evaluation shader that produced Figure 8.5 is shown in Listing 8.4.

```
#version 430 core

layout (triangles) in;

void main(void)
{
    gl_Position = (gl_TessCoord.x * gl_in[0].gl_Position) +
                  (gl_TessCoord.y * gl_in[1].gl_Position) +
                  (gl_TessCoord.z * gl_in[2].gl_Position);
}
```

Listing 8.4: Simple triangle tessellation evaluation shader example

Again, to produce a position for each vertex generated by the tessellation engine, we simply calculate a weighted sum of the input vertices. This time, all three components of gl_TessCoord are used and represent the relative weights of the three vertices making up the outermost tessellated triangle. Of course, we're free to do anything we wish with the barycentric coordinates, the inputs from the tessellation control shader, and any other data we have access to in the evaluation shader.

Tessellation Using Isolines

Isoline tessellation is a mode of the tessellation engine where, rather than producing triangles, it produces real line primitives running along lines of equal v coordinate in the tessellation domain. Each line is broken up into segments along the u direction. The two outer tessellation factors stored in the first two components of gl_TessLevelOuter[] are used to specify the number of lines and the number of segments per line, respectively, and the inner tessellation factors (gl_TessLevelInner[]) are not used at all. This is shown in Figure 8.6.

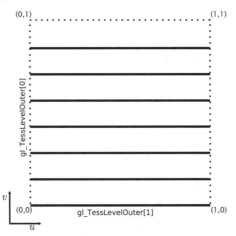

Figure 8.6: Tessellation factors for isoline tessellation

The tessellation control shader shown in Listing 8.5 simply set both the outer tessellation levels to 5.0 and doesn't write to the inner tessellation levels. The corresponding tessellation evaluation shader is shown in Listing 8.6.

```
#version 430 core

layout (vertices = 4) out;

void main(void)
{
    if (gl_InvocationID == 0)
    {
        gl_TessLevelOuter[0] = 5.0;
        gl_TessLevelOuter[1] = 5.0;
    }

    gl_out[gl_InvocationID].gl_Position =
        gl_in[gl_InvocationID].gl_Position;
}
```

Listing 8.5: Simple isoline tessellation control shader example

Notice that Listing 8.6 is virtually identical to Listing 8.2 except that the input primitive mode is set to isolines.

```
#version 430 core

layout (isolines) in;

void main(void)
{
    // Interpolate along bottom edge using x component of the
    // tessellation coordinate
    vec4 p1 = mix(gl_in[0].gl_Position,
                  gl_in[1].gl_Position,
                  gl_TessCoord.x);
    // Interpolate along top edge using x component of the
    // tessellation coordinate
    vec4 p2 = mix(gl_in[2].gl_Position,
                  gl_in[3].gl_Position,
                  gl_TessCoord.x);
    // Now interpolate those two results using the y component
    // of tessellation coordinate
    gl_Position = mix(p1, p2, gl_TessCoord.y);
}
```

Listing 8.6: Simple isoline tessellation evaluation shader example

The result of our extremely simple isoline tessellation example is shown in Figure 8.7.

Figure 8.7 doesn't really seem all that interesting. It's also difficult to see that each of the horizontal lines is actually made up of several segments.

Figure 8.7: Isoline tessellation example

If, however, we change the tessellation evaluation shader to that shown in Listing 8.7, we can generate the image shown in Figure 8.8.

```
#version 430 core

layout (isolines) in;

void main(void)
{
    float r = (gl_TessCoord.y + gl_TessCoord.x / gl_TessLevelOuter[0]);
    float t = gl_TessCoord.x * 2.0 * 3.14159;
    gl_Position = vec4(sin(t) * r, cos(t) * r, 0.5, 1.0);
}
```

Listing 8.7: Isoline spirals tessellation evaluation shader

The shader in Listing 8.7 converts the incoming tessellation coordinates into polar form, with the radius r calculated as smoothly extending from zero to one, and with the angle t as a scaled version of the x component of the tessellation coordinate to produce a single revolution on each isoline. This produces the spiral pattern shown in Figure 8.8, where the segments of the lines are clearly visible.

Tessellation Point Mode

In addition to being able to render tessellated patches using triangles or lines, it's also possible to render the generated vertices as individual

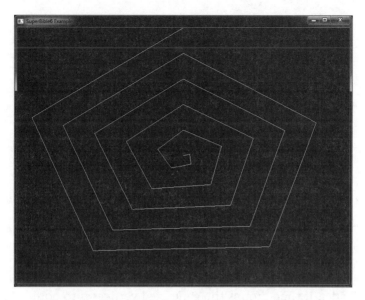

Figure 8.8: Tessellated isoline spirals example

points. This is known as *point mode* and is enabled using the `point_mode` input layout qualifier in the tessellation evaluation shader just like any other tessellation mode. When you specify that point mode should be used, the resulting primitives are points. However, this is somewhat orthogonal to the use of the `quads`, `triangles`, or `isolines` layout qualifiers. That is, you should specify `point_mode` *in addition* to one of the other layout qualifiers. The `quads`, `triangles`, and `isolines` still control the generation of `gl_TessCoord` and the interpretation of the inner and outer tessellation levels. For example, if the tessellation mode is `quads`, then `gl_TessCoord` is a two-dimensional vector, whereas if the tessellation mode is `triangles`, then it is a three-dimensional barycentric coordinate. Likewise, if the tessellation mode is `isolines`, only the outer tessellation levels are used, whereas if it is `triangles` or `quads`, the inner tessellation levels are used as well.

Figure 8.9 shows a version of Figure 8.5 rendered using point mode next to the original image. To produce the figure on the right, we simply change the input layout qualifier of Listing 8.4 to read:

```
layout (triangles, point_mode) in;
```

As you can see, the layout of the vertices is identical in both sides of Figure 8.9, but on the right, each vertex has been rendered as a single point.

Figure 8.9: Triangle tessellated using point mode

Tessellation Subdivision Modes

The tessellation engine works by generating a triangle or quad primitive and then subdividing its edges into a number of segments determined by the inner and outer tessellation factors produced by the tessellation control shader. It then groups the generated vertices into points, lines, or triangles and sends them on for further processing. In addition to the type of primitives generated by the tessellation engine, you have quite a bit of control about how it subdivides the edges of the generated primitives.

By default, the tessellation engine will subdivide each edge into a number of equal-sized parts where the number of parts is set by the corresponding tessellation factor. This is known as equal_spacing mode, and although it is the default, it can be made explicit by including the following layout qualifier in your tessellation evaluation shader:

```
layout (equal_spacing) in;
```

Equal spacing mode is perhaps the easiest mode to comprehend — simply set the tessellation factor to the number segments you wish to subdivide your patch primitive into along each edge, and the tessellation engine takes care of the rest. Although simple, the equal_spacing mode comes with a significant disadvantage — as you alter the tessellation factor, it is always rounded up to the next nearest integer and will produce a visible jump from one level to the next as the tessellation factor changes. The two other modes alleviate this problem by allowing the segments to be non-equal in length. These modes are fractional_even_spacing and fractional_odd_spacing, and again, you can set these modes by using input layout qualifiers as follows:

```
layout (fractional_even_spacing) in;
// or
layout (fractional_odd_spacing) in;
```

With fractional even spacing, the tessellation factor is rounded to the next lower even integer and the edge subdivided as if that were the tessellation factor. With fractional odd spacing, the tessellation factor is rounded down to the next lower odd number and the edge subdivided as if that were the tessellation factor. Of course, with either scheme, there is a small remaining segment that doesn't have the same length as the other segments. That last segment is then cut in half, each half having the same length as the other and is therefore a *fractional* segment.

Figure 8.10 shows the same triangle tessellated with equal_spacing mode on the left, fractional_even_spacing mode in the center, and fractional_odd_spacing mode on the right.

Figure 8.10: Tessellation using different subdivision modes

In all three images shown in Figure 8.10, the inner and outer tessellation factors have been set to 5.3. In the leftmost image showing equal_spacing mode, you should be able to see that the number of segments along each of the outer edges of the triangle is 6 — the next integer after 5.3. In the center image, which shows fractional_even_spacing spacing, there are 4 equal-sized segments (as 4 is the next lower even integer to 5.3) and then two additional smaller segments. Finally, in the rightmost image, which demonstrates fractional_odd_spacing, you can see that there are 5 equal-sized segments (5 being the next lower odd integer to 5.3) and there are two very skinny segments that make up the rest.

If the tessellation level is animated, either by being explicitly turned up and down using a uniform, or calculated in the tessellation control shader, the length of the equal-sized segments and the two filler segments will change smoothly and dynamically. Whether you choose fractional_even_spacing or fractional_odd_spacing really depends on which looks better in your application — there is generally no real advantage to either. However, unless you need a guarantee that tessellated edges have equal-sized segments and you can live with popping if the tessellation level changes, fractional_even_spacing or fractional_odd_spacing will generally look better in any dynamic application than equal_spacing.

Controlling the Winding Order

In Chapter 3, "Following the Pipeline," we introduced culling and explained how the *winding order* of a primitive affects how OpenGL decides whether to render it. Normally, the winding order of a primitive is determined by the order in which your application presents vertices to OpenGL. However, when tessellation is active, OpenGL generates all the vertices and connectivity information for you. In order to allow you to control the winding order of the resulting primitives, you can specify whether you want the vertices to be generated in clockwise or counterclockwise order. Again, this is specified using an input layout qualifier in the tessellation evaluation shader. To indicate that you want clockwise winding order, use the following layout qualifier:

```
layout (cw) in;
```

To specify that the winding order of the primitives generated by the tessellation engine be counterclockwise, include

```
layout (ccw) in;
```

The cw and ccw layout qualifiers can be combined with the other input layout qualifiers specified in the tessellation control shader. By default, the winding order is counterclockwise, and so you can omit this layout qualifier if that is what you need. Also, it should be self-evident that winding order only applies to triangles, and so if your application generates isolines or points, then the winding order is ignored — your shader can still include the winding order layout qualifier, but it won't be used.

Passing Data between Tessellation Shaders

In this section, we have looked at how to set the inner and outer tessellation levels for the quad, triangle, and point primitive modes. However, the resulting images in Figures 8.3 through 8.8 aren't particularly exciting, in part because we haven't done anything but compute the positions of the resulting vertices and then just shaded the resulting primitives solid white. In fact, we have rendered all of these images using lines by setting the polygon mode to GL_LINE with the **glPolygonMode()** function. To produce something a little more interesting, we're going to need to pass more data along the pipeline.

Before a tessellation control shader is run, each vertex represents a control point, and the vertex shader runs once for each input control point and produces its output as normal. The vertices (or control points) are then grouped together and passed together to the tessellation control shader.

The tessellation control shader processes this group of control points and produces a new group of control points that may or may not have the same number of elements in it as the original group. The tessellation control shader actually runs once for each control point in the *output* group, but each invocation of the tessellation control shader has access to all of the input control points. For this reason, both the inputs to and outputs from a tessellation control shader are represented as arrays. The input arrays are sized by the number of control points in each patch, which is set by calling

```
glPatchParameteri(GL_PATCH_VERTICES, n);
```

Here, n is the number of vertices per patch. By default, the number of vertices per patch is 3. The size of the input arrays in the tessellation control shader is set by this parameter, and their contents come from the vertex shader. The built-in variable gl_in[] is always available and is declared as an array of the gl_PerVertex structure. This structure is where the built-in outputs go after you write to them in your vertex shader. All other outputs from the vertex shader become arrays in the tessellation control shader as well. In particular, if you use an output block in your vertex shader, the instance of that block becomes an array of instances in the tessellation control shader. So, for example

```
out VS_OUT
{
    vec4        foo;
    vec3        bar;
    int         baz
} vs_out;
```

becomes

```
in VS_OUT
{
    vec4        foo;
    vec3        bar;
    int         baz;
} tcs_in[];
```

in the tessellation evaluation shader.

The output of the tessellation control shader is also an array, but its size is set by the vertices output layout qualifier at the front of the shader. It is quite common to set the input and output vertex count to the same value (as was the case in the samples earlier in this section) and then pass the input directly to the output from the tessellation control shader. However, there's no requirement for this, and the size of the output arrays in the tessellation control shader is limited by the value of the GL_MAX_PATCH_VERTICES constant.

As the outputs of the tessellation control shader are arrays, so the inputs to the tessellation evaluation shader are also similarly sized arrays. The tessellation evaluation shader runs once per generated vertex and, like the tessellation control shader, has access to all of the data for all of the vertices in the patch.

In addition to the per-vertex data passed from tessellation control shader to the tessellation evaluation shader in arrays, it's also possible to pass data directly between the stages that is constant across an entire patch. To do this, simply declare the output variable in the tessellation control shader and the corresponding input in the tessellation evaluation shader using the `patch` keyword. In this case the variable does not have to be declared as an array (although you are welcome to use arrays as `patch` qualified variables) as there is only one instance per patch.

Rendering without a Tessellation Control Shader

The purpose of the tessellation control shader is to perform tasks such as computing the value of per-patch inputs to the tessellation evaluation shader and to calculate the values of the inner and outer tessellation levels that will be used by the fixed-function tessellator. However, in some simple applications, there are no per-patch inputs to the tessellation evaluation shader, and the tessellation control shader only writes constants to the tessellation levels. In this case, it's actually possible to set up a program with a tessellation evaluation shader, but without a tessellation control shader.

When no tessellation control shader is present, the default values of all inner and outer tessellation levels is 1.0. You can change this by calling **glPatchParameterfv()**, whose prototype is

```
void glPatchParameterfv(GLenum pname,
                        const GLfloat * values);
```

If pname is GL_PATCH_DEFAULT_INNER_LEVEL, then values should point to an array of two floating-point values that will be used as the new default inner tessellation levels in the absence of a tessellation control shader. Likewise, if pname is GL_PATCH_DEFAULT_OUTER_LEVEL, then values should point to an array of four floating-point values that will be used as the new default outer tessellation levels.

If no tessellation control shader is part of the current pipeline, then the number of control points that is presented to the tessellation evaluation shader is the same as the number of control points per patch set by the **glPatchParameteri()** when the pname parameter is set to

GL_PATCH_VERTICES. In this case, the input to the tessellation evaluation shader comes directly from the vertex shader. That is, the input to the tessellation evaluation shader is an array formed from the outputs of the vertex shader invocations that generated the patch.

Communication between Shader Invocations

Although the purpose of output variables in tessellation control shaders is primarily to pass data to the tessellation evaluation shader, they also have a secondary purpose. That is, to communicate data between control shader invocations. As you have read, the tessellation control shader runs a single invocation for each *output* control point in a patch. Each output variable in the tessellation control shader is therefore an array, the length of which is the number of control points in the output patch. Normally, each tessellation control shader invocation will take responsibility for writing to one element of this array.

What might not be obvious is that tessellation control shaders can actually *read* from their output variables — including those that might be written by other invocations! Now, the tessellation control shader is designed in such a way that the invocations can run in parallel. However, there is no ordering guarantee over how those shaders actually execute your code. That means that you have no idea if, when you read from another invocation's output variable, that that invocation has actually written data there.

To deal with this, GLSL includes the barrier() function. This is known as a flow-control barrier, as it enforces relative order to the execution of multiple shader invocations. The barrier() function really shines when used in compute shaders — we'll get to that later. However, it's available in a limited form in tessellation control shaders, too, with a number of restrictions. In particular, in a tessellation control shader, barrier() may only be called directly from within your main() function, and can't be inside any control flow structures (such as if, else, while, or switch).

When you call barrier(), the tessellation control shader invocation will stop and wait for all the other invocations in the same patch to catch up. It won't continue execution until all the other invocations have reached the same point. This means that if you write to an output variable in a tessellation control shader and then call barrier(), you can be sure that all the other invocations have done the same thing by the time barrier() returns, and therefore it's safe to go ahead and read from the other invocations' output variables.

Tessellation Example — Terrain Rendering

To demonstrate a potential use for tessellation, we will cover a simple terrain rendering system based on quadrilateral patches and *displacement mapping*. The code for this example is part of the dispmap sample. A displacement map is a texture that contains the displacement from a surface at each location. Each patch represents a small region of a landscape that is tessellated depending on its likely screen-space area. Each tessellated vertex is moved along the tangent to the surface by the value stored in the displacement map. This adds geometric detail to the surface without needing to explicitly store the positions of each tessellated vertex. Rather, only the displacements from an otherwise flat landscape are stored in the displacement map and are applied at runtime in the tessellation evaluation shader. The displacement map (which is also known as a height map) used in the example is shown in Figure 8.11.

Figure 8.11: Displacement map used in terrain sample

Our first step is to set up a simple vertex shader. As each patch is effectively a simple quad, we can use constants in the shader to represent the four vertices rather than setting up vertex arrays for it. The complete shader is shown in Listing 8.8. The shader uses the instance number (stored in gl_InstanceID) to calculate an offset for the patch, which is a one-unit square in the xz plane, centered on the origin. In this application, we will render a grid of 64×64 patches, and so the x and y offsets for the patch are calculated by taking gl_InstanceID modulo 64 and gl_InstanceID divided by 64. The vertex shader also calculates the texture coordinates for the patch, which are passed to the tessellation control shader in vs_out.tc.

```
#version 430 core

out VS_OUT
{
    vec2 tc;
} vs_out;

void main(void)
{
    const vec4 vertices[] = vec4[](vec4(-0.5, 0.0, -0.5, 1.0),
                                   vec4( 0.5, 0.0, -0.5, 1.0),
                                   vec4(-0.5, 0.0,  0.5, 1.0),
                                   vec4( 0.5, 0.0,  0.5, 1.0));

    int x = gl_InstanceID & 63;
    int y = gl_InstanceID >> 6;
    vec2 offs = vec2(x, y);

    vs_out.tc = (vertices[gl_VertexID].xz + offs + vec2(0.5)) / 64.0;
    gl_Position = vertices[gl_VertexID] + vec4(float(x - 32), 0.0,
                                               float(y - 32), 0.0);
}
```

Listing 8.8: Vertex shader for terrain rendering

Next, we come to the tessellation control shader. Again, the complete shader is shown in Listing 8.9. In this example, the bulk of the rendering algorithm is implemented in the tessellation control shader, and the majority of the code is only executed by the first invocation. Once we have determined that we are the first invocation by checking that gl_InvocationID is zero, we calculate the tessellation levels for the whole patch. First, we project the corners of the patch into normalized device coordinates by multiplying the incoming coordinates by the model-view-projection matrix and then dividing each of the four points by their own homogeneous .w component.

Next, we calculate the length of each of the four edges of the patch in normalized device space after projecting them onto the xy plane by ignoring their z components. Then, the shader calculates the tessellation levels of each edge of the patch as a function of its length using a simple scale and bias. Finally, the inner tessellation factors are simply set to the minimum of the outer tessellation factors calculated from the edge lengths in the horizontal or vertical directions.

You may also have noticed a piece of code in Listing 8.9 that checks whether all of the z coordinates of the projected control points are less than zero and then sets the outer tessellation levels to zero if this happens. This is an optimization that culls entire patches that are behind[2] the viewer.

```
#version 430 core

layout (vertices = 4) out;

in VS_OUT
{
    vec2 tc;
} tcs_in[];

out TCS_OUT
{
    vec2 tc;
} tcs_out[];

uniform mat4 mvp;

void main(void)
{
    if (gl_InvocationID == 0)
    {
        vec4 p0 = mvp * gl_in[0].gl_Position;
        vec4 p1 = mvp * gl_in[1].gl_Position;
        vec4 p2 = mvp * gl_in[2].gl_Position;
        vec4 p3 = mvp * gl_in[3].gl_Position;
        p0 /= p0.w;
        p1 /= p1.w;
        p2 /= p2.w;
        p3 /= p3.w;
        if (p0.z <= 0.0 ||
            p1.z <= 0.0 ||
            p2.z <= 0.0 ||
            p3.z <= 0.0)
        {
            gl_TessLevelOuter[0] = 0.0;
            gl_TessLevelOuter[1] = 0.0;
            gl_TessLevelOuter[2] = 0.0;
            gl_TessLevelOuter[3] = 0.0;
        }
        else
        {
            float l0 = length(p2.xy - p0.xy) * 16.0 + 1.0;
            float l1 = length(p3.xy - p2.xy) * 16.0 + 1.0;
            float l2 = length(p3.xy - p1.xy) * 16.0 + 1.0;
            float l3 = length(p1.xy - p0.xy) * 16.0 + 1.0;
            gl_TessLevelOuter[0] = l0;
```

---

2. This optimization is actually not foolproof. If the viewer were at the bottom of a very steep cliff and looking directly upwards, all four corners of the base patch may be behind the viewer, whereas the cliff cutting through the patch will extend into the viewer's field of view.

```
            gl_TessLevelOuter[1] = l1;
            gl_TessLevelOuter[2] = l2;
            gl_TessLevelOuter[3] = l3;
            gl_TessLevelInner[0] = min(l1, l3);
            gl_TessLevelInner[1] = min(l0, l2);
        }
    }

    gl_out[gl_InvocationID].gl_Position = gl_in[gl_InvocationID].gl_Position;
    tcs_out[gl_InvocationID].tc = tcs_in[gl_InvocationID].tc;
}
```

Listing 8.9: Tessellation control shader for terrain rendering

Once the tessellation control shader has calculated the tessellation levels
for the patch, it simply copies its input to its output. It does this per
instance and passes the resulting data to the tessellation evaluation shader,
which is shown in Listing 8.10.

```
#version 430 core

layout (quads, fractional_odd_spacing) in;

uniform sampler2D tex_displacement;

uniform mat4 mvp;
uniform float dmap_depth;

in TCS_OUT
{
    vec2 tc;
} tes_in[];

out TES_OUT
{
    vec2 tc;
} tes_out;

void main(void)
{
    vec2 tc1 = mix(tes_in[0].tc, tes_in[1].tc, gl_TessCoord.x);
    vec2 tc2 = mix(tes_in[2].tc, tes_in[3].tc, gl_TessCoord.x);
    vec2 tc = mix(tc2, tc1, gl_TessCoord.y);

    vec4 p1 = mix(gl_in[0].gl_Position,
                  gl_in[1].gl_Position,
                  gl_TessCoord.x);
    vec4 p2 = mix(gl_in[2].gl_Position,
                  gl_in[3].gl_Position,
                  gl_TessCoord.x);
    vec4 p = mix(p2, p1, gl_TessCoord.y);

    p.y += texture(tex_displacement, tc).r * dmap_depth;

    gl_Position = mvp * p;
    tes_out.tc = tc;
}
```

Listing 8.10: Tessellation evaluation shader for terrain rendering

The tessellation evaluation shader shown in Listing 8.10 first calculates the texture coordinate of the generated vertex by linearly interpolating the texture coordinates passed from the tessellation control shader of Listing 8.9 (which were in turn generated by the vertex shader of Listing 8.8). It then applies a similar interpolation to the incoming control point positions to produce the position of the outgoing vertex. However, once it's done that, it uses the texture coordinate that it calculated to offset the vertex in the y direction before multiplying that result by the model-view-projection matrix (the same one that was used in the tessellation control shader). It also passes the computed texture coordinate on to the fragment shader in `tes_out.tc`. That fragment shader is shown in Listing 8.11.

```
#version 430 core

out vec4 color;

layout (binding = 1) uniform sampler2D tex_color;

in TES_OUT
{
    vec2 tc;
} fs_in;

void main(void)
{
    color = texture(tex_color, fs_in.tc);
}
```

Listing 8.11: Fragment shader for terrain rendering

The fragment shader shown in Listing 8.11 is really pretty simple. All it does is use the texture coordinate that the tessellation evaluation shader gave it to look up a color for the fragment. The result of rendering with this set of shaders is shown in Figure 8.12.

Of course, if we've done our job correctly, you shouldn't be able to tell that the underlying geometry is tessellated. However, if you look at the wireframe version of the image shown in Figure 8.13, you can clearly see the underlying triangular mesh of the landscape. The goals of the program are that all of the triangles rendered on the screen have roughly similar screen-space area and that sharp transitions in the level of tessellation are not visible in the rendered image.

Tessellation Example — Cubic Bézier Patches

In the displacement mapping example, all we did was use a (very large) texture to drive displacement from a flat surface and then use tessellation

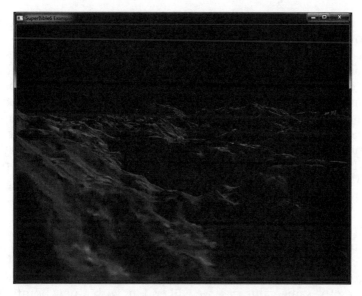

Figure 8.12: Terrain rendered using tessellation

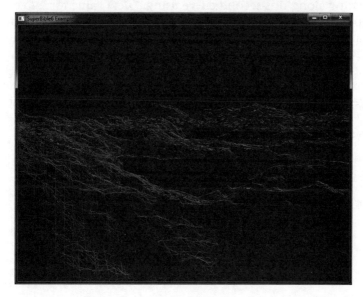

Figure 8.13: Tessellated terrain in wireframe

to increase the number of polygons in the scene. This is a type of brute force, data driven approach to geometric complexity. In the `cubicbezier` example described here, we will use math to drive geometry — we're going to render a *cubic Bézier patch*. If you look back to Chapter 4, you'll see that we've covered all the number crunching we'll need here.

A cubic Bézier patch is a type of *higher order surface* and is defined by a number of *control points*[3] that provide input to a number of interpolation functions that define the surface's shape. A Bézier patch has 16 control points, laid out in a 4×4 grid. Very often (including in this example), they are equally spaced in two dimensions varying only in distance from a shared plane. However, they don't have to be. Free-form Bézier patches are extremely powerful modeling tools, being used natively by many pieces of modeling and design software. With OpenGL tessellation, it's possible to render them directly.

The simplest method of rendering a Bézier patch is to treat the four control points in each row of the patch as the control points for a single cubic Bézier curve, just as was described in Chapter 4. Given our 4×4 grid of control points, we have 4 curves, and if we interpolate along each of them using the same value of t, we will end up with 4 new points. We use these 4 points as the control points for a second cubic Bézier curve. Interpolating along this second curve using a new value for t gives us a second point that lies on the patch. The two values of t (let's call them t_0 and t_1) are the *domain* of the patch and are what is handed to us in the tessellation evaluation shader in gl_TessCoord.xy.

In this example, we'll perform tessellation in view space. That means that in our vertex shader, we'll transform our patch's control points into view space by multiplying their coordinates by the model-view matrix — that is all. This simple vertex shader is shown in Listing 8.12.

```
#version 430 core

in vec4 position;

uniform mat4 mv_matrix;

void main(void)
{
    gl_Position = mv_matrix * position;
}
```

Listing 8.12: Cubic Bézier patch vertex shader

---

3. It should now be evident why the tessellation control shader is so named.

Once our control points are in view space, they are passed to our tessellation control shader. In a more advanced[4] algorithm, we could project the control points into screen space, determine the length of the curve, and set the tessellation factors appropriately. However, in this example, we'll settle with a simple fixed tessellation factor. As in previous examples, we set the tessellation factors only when gl_InvocationID is zero, but pass all of the other data through once per invocation. The tessellation control shader is shown in Listing 8.13.

```
#version 430 core

layout (vertices = 16) out;

void main(void)
{
    if (gl_InvocationID == 0)
    {
        gl_TessLevelInner[0] = 16.0;
        gl_TessLevelInner[1] = 16.0;
        gl_TessLevelOuter[0] = 16.0;
        gl_TessLevelOuter[1] = 16.0;
        gl_TessLevelOuter[2] = 16.0;
        gl_TessLevelOuter[3] = 16.0;
    }

    gl_out[gl_InvocationID].gl_Position =
        gl_in[gl_InvocationID].gl_Position;
}
```

Listing 8.13: Cubic Bézier patch tessellation control shader

Next, we come to the tessellation evaluation shader. This is where the meat of the algorithm lies. The shader in its entirety is shown in Listing 8.14. You should recognize the cubic_bezier and quadratic_bezier functions from Chapter 4. The evaluate_patch function is responsible for evaluating[5] the vertex's coordinate given the input patch coordinates and the vertex's position within the patch.

```
#version 430 core

layout (quads, equal_spacing, cw) in;

uniform mat4 mv_matrix;
uniform mat4 proj_matrix;
```

---

4. To do this right, we'd need to evaluate the length of the Bézier curve, which involves calculating an integral over a non-closed form... which is hard.

5. You should also now see why the tessellation evaluation shader is so named.

```
out TES_OUT
{
    vec3 N;
} tes_out;

vec4 quadratic_bezier(vec4 A, vec4 B, vec4 C, float t)
{
    vec4 D = mix(A, B, t);
    vec4 E = mix(B, C, t);

    return mix(D, E, t);
}

vec4 cubic_bezier(vec4 A, vec4 B, vec4 C, vec4 D, float t)
{
    vec4 E = mix(A, B, t);
    vec4 F = mix(B, C, t);
    vec4 G = mix(C, D, t);

    return quadratic_bezier(E, F, G, t);
}

vec4 evaluate_patch(vec2 at)
{
    vec4 P[4];
    int i;

    for (i = 0; i < 4; i++)
    {
        P[i] = cubic_bezier(gl_in[i + 0].gl_Position,
                            gl_in[i + 4].gl_Position,
                            gl_in[i + 8].gl_Position,
                            gl_in[i + 12].gl_Position,
                            at.y);
    }

    return cubic_bezier(P[0], P[1], P[2], P[3], at.x);
}

const float epsilon = 0.001;

void main(void)
{
    vec4 p1 = evaluate_patch(gl_TessCoord.xy);
    vec4 p2 = evaluate_patch(gl_TessCoord.xy + vec2(0.0, epsilon));
    vec4 p3 = evaluate_patch(gl_TessCoord.xy + vec2(epsilon, 0.0));

    vec3 v1 = normalize(p2.xyz - p1.xyz);
    vec3 v2 = normalize(p3.xyz - p1.xyz);

    tes_out.N = cross(v1, v2);

    gl_Position = proj_matrix * p1;
}
```

Listing 8.14: Cubic Bézier patch tessellation evaluation shader

In our tessellation evaluation shader, we calculate the surface normal to the patch by evaluating the patch position at two points very close to the point under consideration, using the additional points to calculate two vectors that lie on the patch and then taking their cross product. This is passed to the fragment shader shown in Listing 8.15.

```
#version 430 core

out vec4 color;

in TES_OUT
{
    vec3 N;
} fs_in;

void main(void)
{
    vec3 N = normalize(fs_in.N);

    vec4 c = vec4(1.0, -1.0, 0.0, 0.0) * N.z +
             vec4(0.0, 0.0, 0.0, 1.0);

    color = clamp(c, vec4(0.0), vec4(1.0));
}
```

Listing 8.15: Cubic Bézier patch fragment shader

This fragment shader performs a very simple lighting calculation using the z component of the surface normal. The result of rendering with this shader is shown in Figure 8.14.

Figure 8.14: Final rendering of a cubic Bézier patch

Because the rendered patch shown in Figure 8.14 is smooth, it is hard to see the tessellation that has been applied to the shape. The left of Figure 8.15 shows a wireframe representation of the tessellated patch, and the right side of Figure 8.15 shows the patch's control points and the control cage, which is formed by creating a grid of lines between the control points.

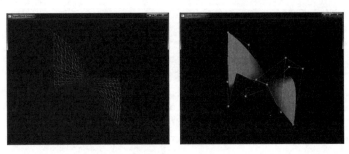

Figure 8.15: A Bézier patch and its control cage

Geometry Shaders

The geometry shader is unique in contrast to the other shader types in that it processes a whole primitive (triangle, line, or point) at once and can actually change the amount of data in the OpenGL pipeline programmatically. A vertex shader processes one vertex at a time; it cannot access any other vertex's information and is strictly one-in, one-out. That is, it cannot generate new vertices, and it cannot stop the vertex from being processed further by OpenGL. The tessellation shaders operate on patches and can set tessellation factors, but have little further control over how patches are tessellated, and cannot produce disjoint primitives. Likewise, the fragment shader processes a single fragment at a time, cannot access any data owned by another fragment, cannot create new fragments, and can only destroy fragments by discarding them. On the other hand, a geometry shader has access to all of the vertices in a primitive (up to six with the primitive modes GL_TRIANGLES_ADJACENCY and GL_TRIANGLE_STRIP_ADJACENCY), can change the type of a primitive, and can even create and destroy primitives.

Geometry shaders are an optional part of the OpenGL pipeline. When no geometry shader is present, the outputs from the vertex or tessellation evaluation shader are interpolated across the primitive being rendered and are fed directly to the fragment shader. When a geometry shader is present, however, the outputs of the vertex or tessellation evaluation shader become the inputs to the geometry shader, and the outputs of the geometry shader are what are interpolated and fed to the fragment shader. The geometry shader can further process the output of the vertex or tessellation evaluation shader, and if it is generating new primitives (this is called amplification), it can apply different transformations to each primitive as it creates them.

The Pass-Through Geometry Shader

As explained back in Chapter 3, "Following the Pipeline," the simplest geometry shader that allows you to render anything is the *pass-through* shader, which is shown in Listing 8.16.

```
#version 430 core

layout (triangles) in;
layout (triangle_strip) out;
layout (max_vertices = 3) out;

void main(void)
{
    int i;

    for (i = 0; i < gl_in.length(); i++)
    {
        gl_Position = gl_in[i].gl_Position;
        EmitVertex();
    }
    EndPrimitive();
}
```

Listing 8.16: Source code for a simple geometry shader

This is a very simple pass-through geometry shader, which sends its input to its output without modifying it. It looks similar to a vertex shader, but there are a few extra differences to cover. Going over the shader a few lines at a time makes everything clear. The first few lines simply set up the version number (430) of the shader just like in any other shader. The next couple of lines are the first geometry shader-specific parts. They are shown again in Listing 8.17.

```
#version 430 core

layout (triangles) in;
layout (triangle_strip) out;
layout (max_vertices = 3) out;
```

Listing 8.17: Geometry shader layout qualifiers

These set the input and output primitive modes using a layout qualifier. In this particular shader we're using `triangles` for the input and `triangle_strip` for the output. Other primitive types, along with the layout qualifier, are covered later. For the geometry shader's output, not only do we specify the primitive type, but the maximum number of vertices expected to be generated by the shader (through the `max_vertices` qualifier). This shader produces individual triangles (generated as very short triangle strips), so we specified 3 here.

Next is our `main()` function, which is again similar to what might be seen in a vertex or fragment shader. The shader contains a loop, and the loop runs a number of times determined by the length of the built-in array, `gl_in`. This is another geometry shader-specific variable. Because the geometry shader has access to all of the vertices of the input primitive, the input has to be declared as an array. All of the built-in variables that are written by the vertex shader (such as `gl_Position`) are placed into a structure, and an array of these structures is presented to the geometry shader in a variable called `gl_in`.

The length of the `gl_in[]` array is determined by the input primitive mode, and because in this particular shader, triangles are the input primitive mode, the size of `gl_in[]` is three. The inner loop is given again in Listing 8.18.

```
for (i = 0; i < gl_in.length(); i++)
{
    gl_Position = gl_in[i].gl_Position;
    EmitVertex();
}
```

Listing 8.18: Iterating over the elements of `gl_in[]`

Inside our loop, we're generating vertices by simply copying the elements of `gl_in[]` to the geometry shader's output. A geometry shader's outputs are similar to the vertex shader's outputs. Here, we're writing to `gl_Position`, just as we would in a vertex shader. When we're done setting up all of the new vertex's attributes, we call EmitVertex(). This is a built-in function, specific to geometry shaders that tells the shader that we're done with our work for this vertex and that it should store all that information away and prepare to start setting up the next vertex.

Finally, after the loop has finished executing, there's a call to another special, geometry shader-only function, EndPrimitive(). EndPrimitive() tells the shader that we're done producing vertices for the current primitive and to move on to the next one. We specified `triangle_strip` as the output for our shader, and so if we continue to call EmitVertex() more than three times, OpenGL continues adding triangles to the triangle strip. If we need our geometry shader to generate separate, individual triangles or multiple, unconnected triangle strips (remember, geometry shaders can create new or amplify geometry), we could call EndPrimitive() between each one to mark their boundaries. If you don't call EndPrimitive() somewhere in your shader, the primitive is automatically ended when the shader ends.

Using Geometry Shaders in an Application

Geometry shaders, like the other shader types, are created by calling the **glCreateShader()** function and using GL_GEOMETRY_SHADER as the shader type, as follows:

```
glCreateShader(GL_GEOMETRY_SHADER);
```

Once the shader has been created, it is used like any other shader object. You give OpenGL your shader source code by calling **glShaderSource()**, compile the shader using the **glCompileShader()** function, and attach it to a program object by calling the **glAttachShader()** function. Then the program is linked as normal using the **glLinkProgram()** function. Now that you have a program object with a geometry shader linked into it, when you draw geometry using a function like **glDrawArrays()**, the vertex shader will run once per vertex, the geometry shader will run once per primitive (point, line, or triangle), and the fragment will run once per fragment. The primitives received by a geometry shader must match what it is expecting based in its own input primitive mode. When tessellation is not active, the primitive mode you use in your drawing commands must match the input primitive mode of the geometry shader. For example, if the geometry shader's input primitive mode is points, then you may only use GL_POINTS when you call **glDrawArrays()**. If the geometry shader's input primitive mode is triangles, then you may use GL_TRIANGLES, GL_TRIANGLE_STRIP, or GL_TRIANGLE_FAN in your **glDrawArrays()** call. A complete list of the geometry shader input primitive modes and the allowed geometry types is given in Table 8.1.

Table 8.1: Allowed Draw Modes for Geometry Shader Input Modes

Geometry Shader Input Mode	Allowed Draw Modes
points	GL_POINTS
lines	GL_LINES, GL_LINE_LOOP, GL_LINE_STRIP
triangles	GL_TRIANGLES, GL_TRIANGLE_FAN, GL_TRIANGLE_STRIP
lines_adjacency	GL_LINES_ADJACENCY
triangles_adjacency	GL_TRIANGLES_ADJACENCY

When tessellation is active, the mode you use in your drawing commands should always be GL_PATCHES, and OpenGL will convert the patches into points, lines, or triangles during the tessellation process. In this case, the input primitive mode of the geometry shader should match the tessellation primitive mode. The input primitive type is specified in the body of the geometry shader using a layout qualifier. The general form of the input layout qualifier is

```
layout (primitive_type) in;
```

This specifies that primitive_type is the input primitive type that the geometry shader is expected to handle, and primitive_type must be one of the supported primitive modes: points, lines, triangles, lines_adjacency, or triangles_adjacency. The geometry shader runs once per primitive. This means that it'll run once per point for GL_POINTS; once per line for GL_LINES, GL_LINE_STRIP, and GL_LINE_LOOP; and once per triangle for GL_TRIANGLES, GL_TRIANGLE_STRIP, and GL_TRIANGLE_FAN. The inputs to the geometry shader are presented in arrays containing all of the vertices making up the input primitive. The predefined inputs are stored in a built-in array called gl_in[], which is an array of structures defined in Listing 8.19.

```
in gl_PerVertex
{
    vec4  gl_Position;
    float gl_PointSize;
    float gl_ClipDistance[];
} gl_in[];
```

Listing 8.19: The definition of gl_in[]

The members of this structure are the built-in variables that are written in the vertex shader: gl_Position, gl_PointSize, and gl_ClipDistance[]. You should recognize this structure from its declaration as an output block in the vertex shader described earlier in this chapter. These variables appear as global variables in the vertex shader because the block doesn't have an instance name there, but their values end up in the gl_in[] array of block instances when they appear in the geometry shader. Other variables written by the vertex shader also become arrays in the geometry shader. In the case of individual varyings, outputs in the vertex shader are declared as normal, and the inputs to the geometry shader have a similar declaration, except that they are arrays. Consider a vertex shader that defines outputs as

```
out vec4 color;
out vec3 normal;
```

The corresponding input to the geometry shader would be

```
in vec4 color[];
in vec3 normal[];
```

Notice that both the `color` and `normal` varyings have become arrays in the geometry shader. If you have a large amount of data to pass from the vertex to the geometry shader, it can be convenient to wrap per-vertex information passed from the vertex shader to the geometry shader into an interface block. In this case, your vertex shader will have a definition like this:

```
out VertexData
{
    vec4 color;
    vec3 normal;
} vertex;
```

And the corresponding input to the geometry shader would look like this:

```
in VertexData
{
    vec4 color;
    vec3 normal;
    // More per-vertex attributes can be inserted here
} vertex[];
```

With this declaration, you'll be able to access the per-vertex data in the geometry shader using `vertex[n].color` and so on. The length of the input arrays in the geometry shader depends on the type of primitives that it will process. For example, points are formed from a single vertex, and so the arrays will only contain a single element, whereas triangles are formed from three vertices, and so the arrays will be three elements long. If you're writing a geometry shader that's designed specifically to process a particular primitive type, you can explicitly size your input arrays, which provides a small amount of additional compile-time error checking. Otherwise, you can let your arrays be automatically sized by the input primitive type layout qualifier. A complete mapping of the input primitive modes and the resulting size of the input arrays is shown in Table 8.2.

Table 8.2: Sizes of Input Arrays to Geometry Shaders

Input Primitive Type	Size of Input Arrays
`points`	1
`lines`	2
`triangles`	3
`lines_adjacency`	4
`triangles_adjacency`	6

You also need to specify the primitive type that will be generated by the geometry shader. Again, this is determined using a layout qualifier, like so:

```
layout (primitive_type) out;
```

This is similar to the input primitive type layout qualifier, the only difference being that you are declaring the output of the shader using the out keyword. The allowable output primitive types from the geometry shader are `points`, `line_strip`, and `triangle_strip`. Notice that geometry shaders only support outputting the strip primitive types (not counting points—obviously, there is no such thing as a point strip).

There is one final layout qualifier that must be used to configure the geometry shader. Because a geometry shader is capable of producing a variable amount of data per vertex, OpenGL must be told how much space to allocate for all that data by specifying the maximum number of vertices that the geometry shader is expected to produce. To do this, use the following layout qualifier:

```
layout (max_vertices = n) out;
```

This sets the maximum number of vertices that the geometry shader may produce to n. Because OpenGL may allocate buffer space to store intermediate results for each vertex, this should be the smallest number possible that still allows your application to run correctly. For example, if you are planning to take points and produce one line at a time, then you can safely set this to two. This gives the shader hardware the best opportunity to run fast. If you are going to heavily tessellate the incoming geometry, you might want to set this to a much higher number, although this may cost you some performance. The upper limit on the number of vertices that a geometry shader can produce depends on your OpenGL implementation. It is guaranteed to be at least 256, but the absolute maximum can be found by calling **glGetIntegerv()** with the GL_MAX_GEOMETRY_OUTPUT_VERTICES parameter.

You can also declare more than one layout qualifier with a single statement by separating them with a comma, like so:

```
layout (triangle_strip, max_vertices = n) out;
```

With these layout qualifiers, a boilerplate **#version** declaration, and an empty main() function, you should be able to produce a geometry shader that compiles and links but does absolutely nothing. In fact, it will discard any geometry you send it, and nothing will be drawn by your application. We need to introduce two important functions: EmitVertex() and EndPrimitive(). If you don't call these, nothing will be drawn.

EmitVertex() tells the geometry shader that you've finished filling in all of the information for this vertex. Setting up the vertex works much like the vertex shader. You need to write into the built-in variable gl_Position. This sets the clip-space coordinates of the vertex that is produced by the geometry shader, just like in a vertex shader. Any other attributes that you want to pass from the geometry shader to the fragment shader can be declared in an interface block or as global variables in the geometry shader. Whenever you call EmitVertex, the geometry shader stores the values currently in all of its output variables and uses them to generate a new vertex. You can call EmitVertex() as many times as you like in a geometry shader, until you reach the limit you specified in your max_vertices layout qualifier. Each time, you put new values into your output variables to generate a new vertex.

An important thing to note about EmitVertex() is that it makes the values of any of your output variables (such as gl_Position) undefined. So, for example, if you want to emit a triangle with a single color, you need to write that color with every one of your vertices; otherwise, you will end up with undefined results.

EmitPrimitive() indicates that you have finished appending vertices to the end of the primitive. Don't forget, geometry shaders only support the strip primitive types (line_strip and triangle_strip). If your output primitive type is triangle_strip and you call EmitVertex() more than three times, the geometry shader will produce multiple triangles in a strip. Likewise, if your output primitive type is line_strip and you call EmitVertex() more than twice, you'll get multiple lines. In the geometry shader, EndPrimitive() refers to the strip. This means that if you want to draw individual lines or triangles, you have to call EndPrimitive() after every two or three vertices. You can also draw multiple strips by calling EmitVertex() many times between multiple calls to EndPrimitive().

One final thing to note about calling EmitVertex() and EndPrimitive() in the geometry shader is that if you haven't produced enough vertices to produce a single primitive (e.g., you're generating triangle_strip outputs and you call EndPrimitive() after two vertices), nothing is produced for that primitive, and the vertices you've already produced are simply thrown away.

Discarding Geometry in the Geometry Shader

The geometry shader in your program runs once per primitive. What you do with that primitive is entirely up to you. The two functions

EmitVertex() and EndPrimitive() allow you to programmatically append new vertices to your triangle or line strip and to start new strips. You can call them as many times as you want (until you reach the maximum defined by your implementation). You're also allowed to not call them at all. This allows you to clip geometry away and discard primitives. If your geometry shader runs and you never call EmitVertex() for that particular primitive, nothing will be drawn. To illustrate this, we can implement a custom backface culling routine that culls geometry as if it were viewed from an arbitrary point in space. This is implemented in the gsculling example.

First, we set up our shader version and declare our geometry shader to accept triangles and to produce triangle strips. Backface culling doesn't really make a lot of sense for lines or points. We also define a uniform that will hold our custom viewpoint in world space. This is shown in Listing 8.20.

```
#version 330

// Input is triangles, output is triangle strip. Because we're going
// to do a 1 in 1 out shader producing a single triangle output for
// each one input, max_vertices can be 3 here.
layout (triangles) in;
layout (triangle_strip, max_vertices=3) out;

// Uniform variables that will hold our custom viewpoint and
// model-view matrix
uniform vec3 viewpoint;
uniform mav4 mv_matrix;
```

Listing 8.20: Configuring the custom culling geometry shader

Now inside our main() function, we need to find the face normal for the triangle. This is simply the cross products of any two vectors in the plane of the triangle—we can use the triangle edges for this. Listing 8.21 shows how this is done.

```
// Calculate two vectors in the plane of the input triangle
vec3 ab = gl_in[1].gl_Position.xyz - gl_in[0].gl_Position.xyz;
vec3 ac = gl_in[2].gl_Position.xyz - gl_in[0].gl_Position.xyz;
vec3 normal = normalize(cross(ab, ac));
```

Listing 8.21: Finding a face normal in a geometry shader

Now that we have the normal, we can determine whether it faces toward or away from our user-defined viewpoint. To do this, we need to transform the normal into the same coordinate space as the viewpoint, which is world space. Assuming we have the model-view matrix in a uniform, simply multiply the normal by this matrix. To be more accurate, we should multiply the vector by the inverse of the transpose of the upper-left 3×3 submatrix of the model-view matrix. This is known as the normal matrix, and you're free to implement this and put it in its own uniform if you like. However, if your model-view matrix only contains translation, uniform scale (no shear), and rotation, you can use it directly. Don't forget, the normal is a three-element vector, and the model-view matrix is a 4×4 matrix. We need to extend the normal to a four-element vector before we can multiply the two. We can then take the dot product of the resulting vector with the vector from the viewpoint to any point on the triangle.

If the sign of the dot product is negative, that means that the normal is facing away from the viewer and the triangle should be culled. If it is positive, the triangle's normal is pointing toward the viewer, and we should pass the triangle on. The code to transform the face normal, perform the dot product, and test the sign of the result is shown in Listing 8.22.

```
// Calculate the transformed face normal and the view direction vector
vec3 transformed_normal = (vec4(normal, 0.0) * mv_matrix).xyz;
vec3 vt = normalize(gl_in[0].gl_Position.xyz - viewpoint);

// Take the dot product of the normal with the view direction
float d = dot(vt, normal);

// Emit a primitive only if the sign of the dot product is positive
if (d > 0.0)
{
    for (int i = 0; i < 3; i++)
    {
        gl_Position = gl_in[i].gl_Position;
        EmitVertex();
    }
    EndPrimitive();
}
```

Listing 8.22: Conditionally emitting geometry in a geometry shader

In Listing 8.22, if the dot product is positive, we copy the input vertices to the output of the geometry shader and call EmitVertex() for each one. If the dot product is negative, we simply don't do anything at all. This results in the incoming triangle being discarded altogether and nothing being drawn.

In this particular example, we are generating at most one triangle output for each triangle input to the geometry shader. Although the output of the geometry shader is a triangle strip, our strips only contain a single triangle. Therefore, there doesn't strictly need to be a call to EndPrimitive(). We just leave it there for completeness.

Figure 8.16 shows a the result of this shader.

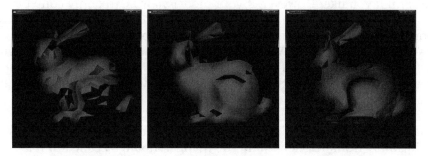

Figure 8.16: Geometry culled from different viewpoints

In Figure 8.16, the virtual viewer has been moved to different positions. As you can see, different parts of the model have been culled away by the geometry shader. It's not expected that this example is particularly useful, but it does demonstrate the ability for a geometry shader to perform geometry culling based on application-defined criteria.

Modifying Geometry in the Geometry Shader

The previous example either discarded geometry or passed it through unmodified. It is also possible to modify vertices as they pass through the geometry shader to create new, derived shapes. Even though your geometry shader is passing vertices on one-to-one (i.e., no amplification or culling is taking place), this still allows you to do things that would otherwise not be possible with a vertex shader alone. If the input geometry is in the form of triangle strips or fans, for example, the resulting geometry will have shared vertices and shared edges. Using the vertex shader to move shared vertices will move all of the triangles that share that vertex. It is not possible, then, to separate two triangles that share an edge in the original geometry using the vertex shader alone. However, this is trivial using the geometry shader.

Consider a geometry shader that accepts triangles and produces triangle_strip as output. The input to a geometry shader that accepts triangles is individual triangles, regardless of whether they originated from a **glDrawArrays()** or a **glDrawElements()** function call, or whether the primitive type was GL_TRIANGLES, GL_TRIANGLE_STRIP, or GL_TRIANGLE_FAN. Unless the geometry shader outputs more than three vertices, the result is independent, unconnected triangles.

In this next example, we "explode" a model by pushing all of the triangles out along their face normals. It doesn't matter whether the original model is drawn with individual triangles or with triangle strips or fans. As with the previous example, the input is triangles, the output is **triangle_strip**, and the maximum number of vertices produced by the geometry shader is three because we're not amplifying or decimating geometry. The setup code for this is shown in Listing 8.23.

```
#version 330

// Input is triangles, output is triangle strip. Because we're going to do a
// 1 in 1 out shader producing a single triangle output for each one input,
// max_vertices can be 3 here.
layout (triangles) in;
layout (triangle_strip, max_vertices=3) out;
```

Listing 8.23: Setting up the "explode" geometry shader

To project the triangle outward, we need to calculate the face normal of each triangle. Again, to do this we can take the cross product of two vectors in the plane of the triangle—two edges of the triangle. For this, we can reuse the code from Listing 8.21. Now that we have the triangle's face normal, we can project vertices along that normal by an application-controlled amount. That amount can be stored in a uniform (we call it explode_factor) and updated by the application. This simple code is shown in Listing 8.24.

```
for (int i = 0; i < 3; i++)
{
    gl_Position = gl_in[i].gl_Position +
                  vec4(explode_factor * normal, 0.0);
}
```

Listing 8.24: Pushing a face out along its normal

The result of running this geometry shader on a model is shown in Figure 8.17. The model has been deconstructed, and the individual triangles have become visible.

Figure 8.17: Exploding a model using the geometry shader

Generating Geometry in the Geometry Shader

Just as you are not required to call EmitVertex() or EndPrimitive() at all if you don't want to produce any output from the geometry shader, it is also possible to call EmitVertex() and EndPrimitive() as many times as you need to produce new geometry. That is, until you reach the maximum number of output vertices that you declared at the start of your geometry shader. This functionality can be used for things like making multiple copies of the input or breaking the input into smaller pieces. This is the subject of the next example, which is the gstessellate sample in the book's accompanying source code. The input to our shader is a tetrahedron centered around the origin. Each face of the tetrahedron is made from a single triangle. We tessellate incoming triangles by producing new vertices halfway along each edge and then moving all of the resulting vertices so that they are variable distances from the origin. This transforms our tetrahedron into a spiked shape.

Because the geometry shader operates in object space (remember, the tetrahedron's vertices are centered around the origin), we need to do no coordinate transforms in the vertex shader and, instead, do the transforms in the geometry shader after we've generated the new vertices. To do this, we need a simple, pass-through vertex shader. Listing 8.25 shows a simple pass-through vertex shader.

```
#version 330

in vec4 position;

void main(void)
{
    gl_Position = position;
}
```

Listing 8.25: Pass-through vertex shader

This shader only passes the vertex position to the geometry shader. If you have other attributes associated with the vertices such as texture coordinates or normals, you need to pass them through the vertex shader to the geometry shader as well.

As in the previous example, we accept triangles as input to the geometry shader and produce a triangle strip. We break the strip after every triangle so that we can produce separate, independent triangles. In this example, we produce four output triangles for every input triangle. We need to declare our maximum output vertex count as 12—four triangles times three vertices. We also need to declare a uniform matrix to store the model-view transformation matrix in the geometry shader because we do that transform after generating vertices. Listing 8.26 shows this code.

```
#version 430 core

layout (triangles) in;
layout (triangle_strip, max_vertices = 12) out;

// A uniform to store the model-view-projection matrix
uniform mat4 mvp;
```

Listing 8.26: Setting up the "tessellator" geometry shader

First, let's copy the incoming vertex coordinates into a local variable. Then, given the original, incoming vertices, we find the midpoint of each edge by taking their average. In this case, however, rather than simply dividing by two, we multiply by a scale factor, which will allow us to alter the *spikiness* of the resulting object. Code to do this is shown in Listing 8.27.

```
// Copy the incoming vertex positions into some local variables
vec3 a = gl_in[0].gl_Position.xyz;
vec3 b = gl_in[1].gl_Position.xyz;
vec3 c = gl_in[2].gl_Position.xyz;
```

```
// Find a scaled version of their midpoints
vec3 d = (a + b) * stretch;
vec3 e = (b + c) * stretch;
vec3 f = (c + a) * stretch;

// Now, scale the original vertices by an inverse of the midpoint
// scale
a *= (2.0 - stretch);
b *= (2.0 - stretch);
c *= (2.0 - stretch);
```

Listing 8.27: Generating new vertices in a geometry shader

Because we are going to generate several triangles using almost identical code, we can put that code into a function (shown in Listing 8.28) and call it from our main tessellation function.

```
void make_face(vec3 a, vec3 b, vec3 c)
{
    vec3 face_normal = normalize(cross(c - a, c - b));
    vec4 face_color = vec4(1.0, 0.2, 0.4, 1.0) * (mat3(mvMatrix) * face_normal
    gl_Position = mvpMatrix * vec4(a, 1.0);
    color = face_color;
    EmitVertex();

    gl_Position = mvpMatrix * vec4(b, 1.0);
    color = face_color;
    EmitVertex();

    gl_Position = mvpMatrix * vec4(c, 1.0);
    color = face_color;
    EmitVertex();

    EndPrimitive();
}
```

Listing 8.28: Emitting a single triangle from a geometry shader

Notice that the make_face function calculates a face color based on the face's normal in addition to emitting the positions of its vertices. Now, we simply call make_face four times from our main function, which is shown in Listing 8.29.

```
make_face(a, d, f);
make_face(d, b, e);
make_face(e, c, f);
make_face(d, e, f);
```

Listing 8.29: Using a function to produce faces in a geometry shader

Figure 8.18 shows the result of our simple geometry shader-based tessellation program.

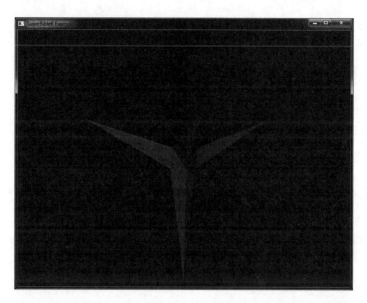

Figure 8.18: Basic tessellation using the geometry shader

Note that using the geometry shader for heavy tessellation may not produce the most optimal performance. If something more complex than that shown in this example is desired, it's best to use the hardware tessellation functions of OpenGL. However, if simple amplification of between two and four output primitives for each input primitive is desired, the geometry shader is probably the way to go.

Changing the Primitive Type in the Geometry Shader

So far, all of the geometry shader examples we've gone through have taken triangles as input and produced triangle strips as output. This doesn't change the geometry type. However, geometry shaders can input and output different types of geometry. For example, you can transform points into triangles or triangles into points. In the normalviewer example, which we'll describe next, we're going to change the geometry type from triangles to lines. For each vertex input to the shader, we take the vertex normal and represent it as a line. We also take the face normal and represent that as another line. This allows us to visualize the model's normals—both at each vertex and for each face. Note, though, that if you want to draw the normals on top of the original model, you need to draw everything twice—once with the geometry shader to visualize the normals and once without the geometry shader to show the model. You can't output a mix of two different primitives from a single geometry shader.

For our geometry shader, in addition to the members of the `gl_in` structure, we need the per-vertex normal, and that will have to be passed through the vertex shader. An updated version of the pass-through vertex shader from Listing 8.25 is given in Listing 8.30.

```
#version 330

in vec4 position;
in vec3 normal;

out Vertex
{
    vec3 normal;
} vertex;

void main(void)
{
    gl_Position = position;
    vertex.normal = normal;
}
```

Listing 8.30: A pass-through vertex shader that includes normals

This passes the position attribute straight through to the `gl_Position` built-in variable and places the normal into an output block.

The setup code for the geometry shader is shown in Listing 8.31. In this example, we accept triangles and produce line strips, each of a single line. Because we output a separate line for each normal we visualize, we produce two vertices for each vertex consumed, plus two more for the face normal. Therefore, the maximum number of vertices that we output per input triangle is eight. To match the Vertex output block that we declared in the vertex shader, we also need to declare a corresponding input interface block in the geometry shader. As we're going to do the object-space-to-world-space transformation in the geometry shader, we declare a mat4 uniform called mvp to represent the model-view-projection matrix. This is necessary so that we can keep the vertex's position in the same coordinate system as its normal until we produce the new vertices representing the line.

```
#version 330

layout (triangles) in;
layout (line_strip) out;
layout (max_vertices = 8) out;

in Vertex
{
    vec3 normal;
} vertex[];
```

```
// Uniform to hold the model-view-projection matrix
uniform mat4 mvp;

// Uniform to store the length of the visualized normals
uniform float normal_length;
```

Listing 8.31: Setting up the "normal visualizer" geometry shader

Each input vertex is transformed into its final position and emitted from the geometry shader, and then a second vertex is produced by displacing the input vertex along its normal and transforming that into its final position as well. This makes the length of all of our normals one but allows any scaling encoded in our model-view-projection matrix to be applied to them along with the model. We multiply the normals by the application-supplied uniform normal_length, allowing them to be scaled to match the model. Our inner loop is shown in Listing 8.32.

```
gl_Position = mvp * gl_in[0].gl_Position;
gs_out.normal = gs_in[0].normal;
gs_out.color = gs_in[0].color;
EmitVertex();

gl_Position = mvp * (gl_in[0].gl_Position +
                     vec4(gs_in[0].normal * normal_length, 0.0));
gs_out.normal = gs_in[0].normal;
gs_out.color = gs_in[0].color;
EmitVertex();
EndPrimitive();
```

Listing 8.32: Producing lines from normals in the geometry shader

This generates a short line segment at each vertex pointing in the direction of the normal. Now, we need to produce the face normal. To do this, we need to pick a suitable place from which to draw the normal, and we need to calculate the face normal itself in the geometry shader along which to draw the line.

As in the earlier example given in Listing 8.33, we use a cross product of two of the triangle's edges to find the face normal. To pick a starting point for the line, we choose the centroid of the triangle, which is simply the average of the coordinates of the input vertices. Listing 8.33 shows the shader code.

```
vec3 ab = gl_in[1].gl_Position.xyz - gl_in[0].gl_Position.xyz;
vec3 ac = gl_in[2].gl_Position.xyz - gl_in[0].gl_Position.xyz;
vec3 face_normal = normalize(cross(ab, ac));

vec4 tri_centroid = (gl_in[0].gl_Position +
                     gl_in[1].gl_Position +
                     gl_in[2].gl_Position) / 3.0;
```

```
gl_Position = mvp * tri_centroid;
gs_out.normal = gs_in[0].normal;
gs_out.color = gs_in[0].color;
EmitVertex();

gl_Position = mvp * (tri_centroid +
                     vec4(face_normal * normal_length, 0.0));
gs_out.normal = gs_in[0].normal;
gs_out.color = gs_in[0].color;
EmitVertex();
EndPrimitive();
```

Listing 8.33: Drawing a face normal in the geometry shader

Now when we render a model, we get the image shown in Figure 8.19.

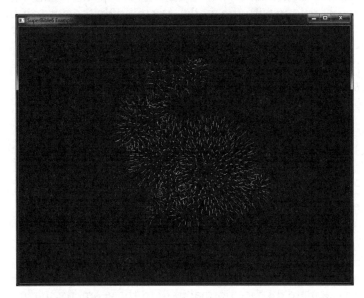

Figure 8.19: Displaying the normals of a model using a geometry shader

Multiple Streams of Storage

When only a vertex shader is present, there is a simple one-in, one-out
relationship between the vertices coming into the shader and the vertices
stored in the transform feedback buffer. When a geometry shader is
present, each shader invocation may store zero, one, or more vertices into
the bound transform feedback buffers. Not only this, but it's actually
possible to configure up to four output *streams* and use the geometry
shader to send its output to whichever one it chooses. This can be used,
for example, to sort geometry or to render some primitives while storing
other geometry in transform feedback buffers. There are a couple of pretty

major limitations when multiple output streams are used in a geometry shader; first, the output primitive mode from the geometry shader for all streams must be set to `points`. Second, although it's possible to simultaneously render geometry and to store data into transform feedback buffers, only the first stream may be rendered — the others are for storage only. If your application fits with these constraints, then this can be a very powerful feature.

To set up multiple output streams from your geometry shader, use the `stream` layout qualifier to select one of four streams. As with most other output layout qualifiers, the `stream` qualifier may be applied directly to a single output or to an output block. It can also be applied directly to the `out` keyword without declaring an output variable, in which case it will affect all further output declarations until another `stream` layout qualifier is encountered. For example, consider the following output declarations in a geometry shader:

```
out vec4                foo; // "foo" is in stream 0 (the default).
layout (stream=2) out vec4  bar; // "bar" is part of stream 2.
out vec4                baz; // "baz" is back in stream 0.
layout (stream=1) out;      // Everything from here on is in stream 1.
out int                 apple;  // "apple" and "orange" are part
out int                 orange; // of stream 1.
layout (stream=3) out MY_BLOCK  // Everything in "MY_BLOCK" is in
stream 3.
{
    vec3                purple;
    vec3                green;
};
```

In the geometry shader, when you call `EmitVertex()`, the vertex will be recorded into the first output stream (stream 0). Likewise, when you call `EndPrimitive()`, it will end the primitive being recorded to stream 0. However, you can call `EmitStreamVertex()` and `EndStreamPrimitive()`, both of which take an integer argument specifying the stream to send the output to:

```
void EmitStreamVertex(int stream);

void EndStreamPrimitive(int stream);
```

The `stream` argument must be a compile time constant. If rasterization is enabled, then any primitives sent to stream 0 will be rasterized.

New Primitive Types Introduced by the Geometry Shader

Four new primitive types were introduced with geometry shaders: `GL_LINES_ADJACENCY`, `GL_LINE_STRIP_ADJACENCY`,

GL_TRIANGLES_ADJACENCY, and GL_TRIANGLE_STRIP_ADJACENCY. These primitive types are really only useful when rendering with a geometry shader active. When the new adjacency primitive types are used, for each line or triangle passed into the geometry shader, it not only has access to the vertices defining that primitive, but it also has access to the vertices of the primitive that is next to the one it's processing.

When you render using GL_LINES_ADJACENCY, each line segment consumes four vertices from the enabled attribute arrays. The two center vertices make up the line; the first and last vertices are considered the adjacent vertices. The inputs to the geometry shader are therefore four-element arrays. In fact, because the input and output types of the geometry shader do not have to be related, GL_LINES_ADJACENCY can be seen as a way of sending generalized four-vertex primitives to the geometry shader. The geometry shader is free to transform them into whatever it pleases. For example, your geometry shader could convert each set of four vertices into a triangle strip made up of two triangles. This allows you to render quads using the GL_LINES_ADJACENCY primitive. It should be noted, though, that if you draw using GL_LINES_ADJACENCY when no geometry shader is active, regular lines will be drawn using the two innermost vertices of each set of four vertices. The two outermost vertices will be discarded, and the vertex shader will not run on them at all.

Using GL_LINE_STRIP_ADJACENCY produces a similar effect. The difference is that the entire strip is considered to be a primitive, with one additional vertex on each end. If you send eight vertices to OpenGL using GL_LINES_ADJACENCY, the geometry shader will run twice, whereas if you send the same vertices using GL_LINE_STRIP_ADJACENCY, the geometry shader will run five times. Figure 8.20 should make things clear. The eight vertices in the top row are sent to OpenGL with the GL_LINES_ADJACENCY primitive mode. The geometry shader runs twice on four vertices each time—ABCD and EFGH. In the second row, the same eight vertices are sent to OpenGL using the GL_LINE_STRIP_ADJACENCY primitive mode. This time, the geometry shader runs five times—ABCD, BCDE, and so on until EFGH. In each case, the solid arrows are the lines that would be rendered if no geometry shader were present.

The GL_TRIANGLES_ADJACENCY primitive mode works similarly to the GL_LINES_ADJACENCY mode. A triangle is sent to the geometry shader for each set of six vertices in the enabled attribute arrays. The first, third, and fifth vertices are considered to make up the real triangle, and the second, fourth, and sixth vertices are considered to be in between the triangle's

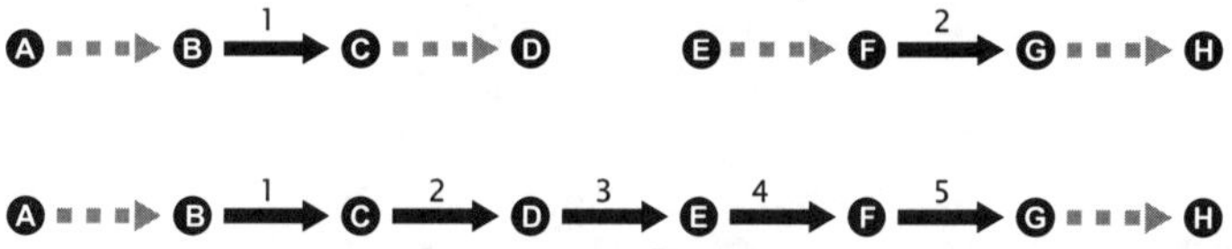

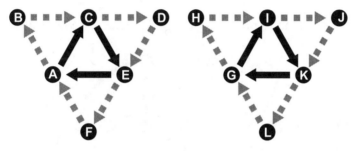

Figure 8.20: Lines produced using lines with adjacency primitives

vertices. This means that the inputs to the geometry shader are six-element arrays. As before, you can do anything you want to the vertices using the geometry shader; GL_TRIANGLES_ADJACENCY is a good way to get arbitrary six-vertex primitives into the geometry shader. Figure 8.21 shows this.

Figure 8.21: Triangles produced using GL_TRIANGLES_ADJACENCY

The final, and perhaps most complex (or alternatively the most difficult to understand), of these primitive types is GL_TRIANGLE_STRIP_ADJACENCY. This primitive represents a triangle strip with every other vertex (the first, third, fifth, seventh, ninth, and so on) forming the strip. The vertices in between are the adjacent vertices. Figure 8.22 demonstrates the principle. In the figure, the vertices A through P represent 16 vertices sent to OpenGL. A triangle strip is generated from every other vertex (A, C, E, G, I, and so on), and the vertices that come between them (B, D, F, H, J, and so on) are the adjacent vertices.

There are special cases for the triangles that come at the start and end of the strip, but once the strip is started, the vertices fall into a regular pattern that is more clearly seen in Figure 8.23.

The rules for the ordering of GL_TRIANGLE_STRIP_ADJACENCY are spelled out clearly in the OpenGL Specification—in particular, the special cases are noted there. You are encouraged to read that section of the specification if you want to work with this primitive type.

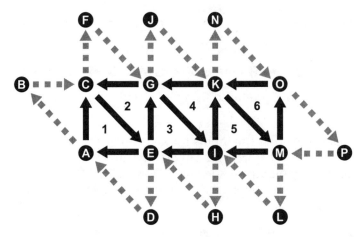

Figure 8.22: Triangles produced using GL_TRIANGLE_STRIP_ADJACENCY

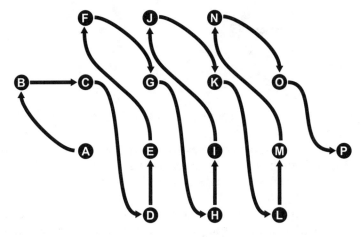

Figure 8.23: Ordering of vertices for GL_TRIANGLE_STRIP_ADJACENCY

Rendering Quads Using a Geometry Shader

In computer graphics, the word *quad* is used to describe a quadrilateral – a shape with four sides. Modern graphics APIs do not support rendering quads directly, primarily because modern graphics hardware does not support quads. When a modeling program produces an object made from quads, it will often include the option to export the geometry data by converting each quad into a pair of triangles. These are then rendered by the graphics hardware directly. In some graphics hardware, quads are supported, but internally the hardware will do this conversion from quads to pairs of triangles for you.

In many cases, breaking a quad into a pair of triangles works out just fine and the visual image isn't much different than what would have been rendered had native support for quads been present. However, there are a large class of cases where breaking a quad into a pair of triangles *doesn't* produce the correct result. Take a look at Figure 8.24.

Figure 8.24: Rendering a quad using a pair of triangles

In Figure 8.24, we have rendered a quad as a pair of triangles. In both images, the vertices are wound in the same order. There are three black vertices and one white vertex. In the left image, the split between the triangles runs vertically through the quad. The topmost and two side vertices are black and the bottommost vertex is white. The seam between the two triangles is clearly visible as a bright line. In the right image, the quad has been split horizontally. This has produced the topmost triangle, which contains only black vertices and is therefore entirely black, and the bottommost triangle, which contains one white vertex and two black ones, therefore displaying a black to white gradient.

The reason for this is that during rasterization and interpolation of the per-vertex colors presented to the fragment shader, we're only rendering a triangle. There are only three vertices' worth of information available to us at any given time, and therefore, we can't take into consideration the "other" vertex in the quad.

Clearly, neither image is correct, but neither is obviously better than the other. Also, the two images are radically different. If we rely on our export tools, or worse a runtime library, to split quads for us, we do not have any control over which of these two images we'll get. What can we do about that? Well, the geometry shader is able to accept primitives with the GL_LINES_ADJACENCY type, and each of these has four vertices — exactly enough to represent a quad. This means that by using lines with adjacency, we can get four vertices' worth of information at least as far as the geometry shader.

Next, we need to deal with the rasterizer. Recall, the output of the geometry shader can only be points, lines, or triangles, and so the best we can do is to break each quad (represented by a `lines_adjacency` primitive) into a pair of triangles. You might think this leaves us in the same spot as we were before. However, we now have the advantage that we can pass whatever information we like on to the fragment shader.

To correctly render a quad, we must consider the parameterization of the domain over which we want to interpolate our colors (or any other attribute). For triangles, we use barycentric coordinates, which are three-dimensional coordinates used to weight the three corners of the triangle. However, for a quad, we can use a two-dimensional parameterization. Consider the quad shown in Figure 8.25.

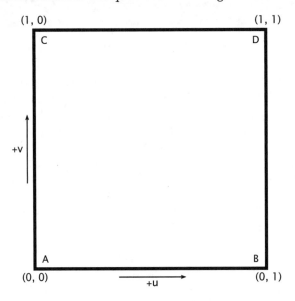

Figure 8.25: Parameterization of a quad

Domain parameterization of a quad is two-dimensional and can be represented as a two-dimensional vector. This can be smoothly interpolated over the quad to find the value of the vector at any point within it. For each of the quad's four vertices A, B, C, and D, the values of the vector will be $(0,0)$, $(0,1)$, $(1,0)$, and $(1,1)$, respectively. We can generate these values per vertex in our geometry shader and pass them to the fragment shader.

To use this vector to retrieve the interpolated values of our other per-fragment attributes, we make the following observation: The value of any interpolant will move smoothly between vertex A and B and between C and D with the x component of the vector. Likewise, a value along the edge AB will move smoothly to the corresponding value on edge CD. Thus, given the values of the attributes at the vertices A through D, we can use the domain parameter to interpolate a value of each attribute at any point inside the quad.

Thus, our geometry shader simply passes all four of the per-vertex attributes, unmodified, as `flat` outputs to the fragment shader, along with a smoothly varying domain parameter per vertex. The fragment shader then uses the domain parameter and *all four* per-vertex attributes to perform the interpolation directly.

The geometry shader is shown in Listing 8.34, and the fragment shader is shown in Listing 8.35 — both are taken from the gsquads example. Finally, the result of rendering the same geometry as shown in Figure 8.24 is shown in Figure 8.26.

```
#version 430 core

layout (lines_adjacency) in;
layout (triangle_strip, max_vertices = 6) out;

in VS_OUT
{
    vec4 color;
} gs_in[4];

out GS_OUT
{
    flat vec4 color[4];
    vec2 uv;
} gs_out;

void main(void)
{
    gl_Position = gl_in[0].gl_Position;
    gs_out.uv = vec2(0.0, 0.0);
    EmitVertex();

    gl_Position = gl_in[1].gl_Position;
    gs_out.uv = vec2(1.0, 0.0);
    EmitVertex();

    gl_Position = gl_in[2].gl_Position;
    gs_out.uv = vec2(1.0, 1.0);

    // We're only writing the output color for the last
    // vertex here because they're flat attributes,
    // and the last vertex is the provoking vertex by default
    gs_out.color[0] = gs_in[1].color;
    gs_out.color[1] = gs_in[0].color;
    gs_out.color[2] = gs_in[2].color;
    gs_out.color[3] = gs_in[3].color;
    EmitVertex();
```

```
    EndPrimitive();

    gl_Position = gl_in[0].gl_Position;
    gs_out.uv = vec2(0.0, 0.0);
    EmitVertex();

    gl_Position = gl_in[2].gl_Position;
    gs_out.uv = vec2(1.0, 1.0);
    EmitVertex();

    gl_Position = gl_in[3].gl_Position;
    gs_out.uv = vec2(0.0, 1.0);

    // Again, only write the output color for the last vertex
    gs_out.color[0] = gs_in[1].color;
    gs_out.color[1] = gs_in[0].color;
    gs_out.color[2] = gs_in[2].color;
    gs_out.color[3] = gs_in[3].color;
    EmitVertex();

    EndPrimitive();
}
```

Listing 8.34: Geometry shader for rendering quads

```
#version 430 core

in GS_OUT
{
    flat vec4 color[4];
    vec2 uv;
} fs_in;

out vec4 color;

void main(void)
{
    vec4 c1 = mix(fs_in.color[0], fs_in.color[1], fs_in.uv.x);
    vec4 c2 = mix(fs_in.color[2], fs_in.color[3], fs_in.uv.x);

    color = mix(c1, c2, fs_in.uv.y);
}
```

Listing 8.35: Fragment shader for rendering quads

Multiple Viewport Transformations

You learned in "Viewport Transformation" back in Chapter 3 about the viewport transformation and how you can specify the rectangle of the window you're rendering into by calling **glViewport()** and **glDepthRange()**. Normally, you would set the viewport dimensions to cover the entire window or screen, depending on whether your application is running on a desktop or is taking over the whole display. However, it's possible to move the viewport around and draw into

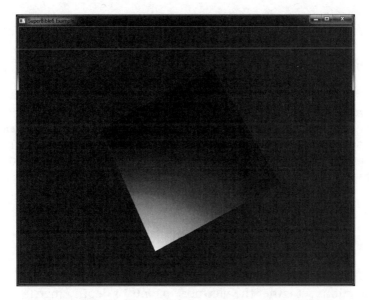

Figure 8.26: Quad rendered using a geometry shader

multiple virtual windows within a single larger framebuffer. Furthermore, OpenGL also allows you to use multiple viewports *at the same time*. This feature is known as viewport arrays.

To use a viewport array, we first need to tell OpenGL what the bounds of the viewports we want to use are. To do this, call **glViewportIndexedf()** or **glViewportIndexedfv()**, whose prototypes are

```
void glViewportIndexedf(GLuint index,
                        GLfloat x,
                        GLfloat y,
                        GLfloat w,
                        GLfloat h);

void glViewportIndexedfv(GLuint index,
                         const GLfloat * v);
```

For both **glViewportIndexedf()** and **glViewportIndexedfv()**, index is the index of the viewport you wish to modify. Also notice that the viewport parameters to the indexed viewport commands are floating-point values rather than the integers used for **glViewport()**. OpenGL supports a minimum[6] of 16 viewports, and so index can range from 0 to 15.

---

6. The actual number of viewports that are supported by OpenGL can be determined by querying the value of GL_MAX_VIEWPORTS.

Likewise, each viewport also has its own depth range, which can be specified by calling **glDepthRangeIndexed()**, whose prototype is

```
void glDepthRangeIndexed(GLuint index,
                         GLdouble n,
                         GLdouble f);
```

Again, index may be between 0 and 15. In fact, **glViewport()** really sets the extent of all of the viewports to the same range, and **glDepthRange()** sets the depth range of all viewports to the same range. If you want to set more than one or two of the viewports at a time, you might consider using **glViewportArrayv()** and **glDepthRangeArrayv()**, whose prototypes are

```
void glViewportArrayv(GLuint first,
                      GLsizei count,
                      const GLfloat * v);

void glDepthRangeArrayv(GLuint first,
                        GLsizei count,
                        const GLdouble * v);
```

These functions set either the viewport extents or depth range for count viewports starting with the viewport indexed by first to the parameters specified in the array v. For **glViewportArrayv()**, the array contains a sequence of x, y, width, height values, in that order. For **glDepthRangeArrayv()**, the array contains a sequence of n, f pairs, in that order.

Once you have specified your viewports, you need to direct geometry into them. This is done by using a geometry shader. Writing to the built-in variable gl_ViewportIndex selects the viewport to render into. Listing 8.36 shows what such a geometry shader might look like.

```
#version 430 core

layout (triangles, invocations = 4) in;
layout (triangle_strip, max_vertices = 3) out;

layout (std140, binding = 0) uniform transform_block
{
    mat4 mvp_matrix[4];
};

in VS_OUT
{
    vec4 color;
} gs_in[];

out GS_OUT
{
    vec4 color;
} gs_out;
```

```
void main(void)
{
    for (int i = 0; i < gl_in.length(); i++)
    {
        gs_out.color = gs_in[i].color;
        gl_Position = mvp_matrix[gl_InvocationID] *
                         gl_in[i].gl_Position;
        gl_ViewportIndex = gl_InvocationID;
        EmitVertex();
    }
    EndPrimitive();
}
```

Listing 8.36: Rendering to multiple viewports in a geometry shader

When the shader of Listing 8.36 executes, it produces four invocations of
the shader. On each invocation, it sets the value of gl_ViewportIndex to
the value of gl_InvocationID, directing the result of each of the geometry
shader instances to a separate viewport. Also, for each invocation, it uses a
separate model-view-projection matrix, which it retrieves from the
uniform block, transform_block. Of course, a more complex shader could
be constructed, but this is sufficient to demonstrate direction of
transformed geometry into a number of different viewports. We have
implemented this code in the multipleviewport sample, and the result of
running this shader on our simple spinning cube is shown in Figure 8.27.

Figure 8.27: Result of rendering to multiple viewports

You can clearly see the four copies of the cube rendered by Listing 8.36 in Figure 8.27. Because each was rendered into its own viewport, it is clipped separately, and so where the cubes extend past the edges of their respective viewports, their corners are cut off by OpenGL's clipping stage.

Summary

In this chapter, you have read about the two tessellation shader stages, the fixed-function tessellation engine, and the way they interact. You have also read about geometry shaders and have seen how both the tessellator and the geometry shader can be used to change the amount of data in the OpenGL pipeline. You have also seen some of the additional functionality in OpenGL that can be accessed using tessellation and geometry shaders. You have seen how, conceptually, tessellation shaders and geometry shaders process vertices in groups — in the case of tessellation shaders, those groups forming *patches*, and in the case of geometry shaders, those groups forming traditional primitives such as lines and triangles. You've seen the special *adjacency* primitive types accessible to geometry shaders. After the geometry shader ends, primitives are eventually sent to the rasterizer and then to per-fragment operations, which will be the subject of the next chapter.

Chapter 9

Fragment Processing and the Framebuffer

WHAT YOU'LL LEARN IN THIS CHAPTER

- How data is passed into fragment shaders, how to control the way it's sent there, and what to do with it once it gets there

- How to create your own framebuffers and control the format of data that they store

- How to produce more than just one output from a single fragment shader

- How to get data out of your framebuffer and into textures, buffers, and your application's memory

This chapter is all about the *back end* — everything that happens after rasterization. We will take an in-depth look at some of the interesting things you can do with a fragment shader, what happens to your data once it leaves the fragment shader, and how to get it back into your application. We're also going to look at ways to improve the quality of the images that your applications produce, from rendering in high dynamic range, to antialiasing techniques (compensating from the pixelating effect of the display) and alternative color spaces that you can render into.

Fragment Shaders

You have already been introduced to the fragment shader stage. It is the stage in the pipeline where your shader code determines the color of each fragment before it is sent for composition into the framebuffer. The fragment shader runs once per fragment, where a fragment is a virtual element of processing that might end up contributing to the final color of a pixel. Its inputs are generated by the fixed-function interpolation phase that executes as part of rasterization. By default, all members of the input blocks to the fragment shader are smoothly interpolated across the primitive being rasterized, with the endpoints of that interpolation being fed by the last stage in the front end (which may be the vertex, tessellation evaluation, or geometry shader stages). However, you have quite a bit of control over how that interpolation is performed and even whether interpolation is performed at all.

Interpolation and Storage Qualifiers

You already read about some of the storage qualifiers supported by GLSL in earlier chapters. There are a few storage qualifiers that can be used to control interpolation that you can use for advanced rendering. They include the `flat` and `noperspective`, and we quickly go over each of these here.

Disabling Interpolation

When you declare an input to your fragment shader, that input is generated, or interpolated, across the primitive being rendered. However, whenever you pass an integer from the front end to the back end, interpolation must be disabled — this is done automatically for you because OpenGL isn't capable of smoothly interpolating integers. It is also possible to explicitly disable interpolation for floating-point fragment shader inputs. Fragment shader inputs for which interpolation has been disabled are known as *flat* inputs (in contrast to *smooth* inputs, referring to the smooth interpolation normally performed by OpenGL). To create a flat input to the fragment shader for which interpolation is not performed, declare it using the `flat` storage[1] qualifier, as in

---

1. It's actually legal to explicitly declare floating-point fragment shader inputs with the `smooth` storage qualifier, although this is normally redundant as this is the default.

```
flat in vec4 foo;
flat in int  bar;
flat in mat3 baz;
```

You can also apply interpolation qualifiers to input blocks, which is where the smooth qualifier comes in handy. Interpolation qualifiers applied to blocks are inherited by its members — that is, they are applied automatically to all members of the block. However, it's possible to apply a different qualifier to individual members of the block. Thus, consider this snippet:

```
flat in INPUT_BLOCK
{
    vec4         foo;
    int          bar;
    smooth mat3 baz;
};
```

Here, foo has interpolation disabled because it inherits flat qualification from the parent block. bar is automatically flat because it is an integer. However, even though baz is a member of a block that has the flat interpolation qualifier, it is smoothly interpolated because it has the smooth interpolation qualifier applied at the member level.

Don't forget that while we are describing this in terms of fragment shader inputs, storage and interpolation qualifiers used on the corresponding outputs in the front end must match those used at the input of the fragment shader. This means that whatever the last stage in your front end, whether it's a vertex, tessellation evaluation, or geometry shader, you should also declare the matching output with the flat qualifier.

When flat inputs to a fragment are in use, their value comes from only one of the vertices in a primitive. When the primitives being rendered are single points, then there is only one choice as to where to get the data. However, when the primitives being rendered are lines or triangles, either the first or last vertex in the primitive is used. The vertex from which the values for flat fragment shader inputs are taken is known as the provoking vertex, and you can decide whether that should be the first or last vertex by calling

```
void glProvokingVertex(GLenum provokeMode);
```

Here, provokeMode indicates which vertex should be used, and valid values are GL_FIRST_VERTEX_CONVENTION and GL_LAST_VERTEX_CONVENTION. The default is GL_LAST_VERTEX_CONVENTION.

Interpolating without Perspective Correction

As you have learned, OpenGL interpolates the values of fragment shader inputs across the face of primitives, such as triangles, and presents a new value to each invocation of the fragment shader. By default, the interpolation is performed smoothly in the space of the primitive being rendered. That means that if you were to look at the triangle flat on, the steps that the shader inputs take across its surface would be equal. However, OpenGL performs interpolation in screen space as it steps from pixel to pixel. Very rarely is a triangle seen directly face on, and so perspective foreshortening means that the step in each varying from pixel to pixel is not constant — that is, they are not linear in screen space. OpenGL corrects for this by using *perspective-correct interpolation*. To implement this, it interpolates values that *are* linear in screen space and uses those to derive the actual values of the shader inputs at each pixel.

Consider a texture coordinate, uv, that is to be interpolated across a triangle. Neither u nor v is linear in screen space. However (due to some math that is beyond the scope of this section), $\frac{u}{w}$ and $\frac{v}{w}$ *are* linear in screen space, as is $\frac{1}{w}$ (the fourth component of the fragment's coordinate). So, what OpenGL actually interpolates is

$$\frac{u}{w}, \frac{v}{w}, \text{ and } \frac{1}{w}$$

At each pixel, it reciprocates $\frac{1}{w}$ to find w and then multiplies $\frac{u}{w}$ and $\frac{v}{w}$ by w to find u and v. This provides perspective-correct values of the interpolants to each instance of the fragment shader.

Normally, this is what you want. However, there may be times when you don't want this. If you actually want interpolation to be carried out in screen space regardless of the orientation of the primitive, you can use the `noperspective` storage qualifier, like this:

```
noperspective out vec2 texcoord;
```

in the vertex shader (or whatever shader is last in the front end of your pipeline), and

```
noperspective in vec2 texcoord;
```

in the fragment shader, for example. The results of using perspective-correct and screen-space linear (`noperspective`) rendering are shown in Figure 9.1.

Figure 9.1: Contrasting perspective-correct and linear interpolation

The top image of Figure 9.1 shows perspective-correct interpolation applied to a pair of triangles as its angle to the viewer changes. Meanwhile, the bottom image of Figure 9.1 shows how the `noperspective` storage qualifier has affected the interpolation of texture coordinates. As the pair of triangles moves to a more and more oblique angle relative to the viewer, the texture becomes more and more skewed.

Per-Fragment Tests

Once the fragment shader has run, OpenGL needs to figure what do to with the fragments that are generated. Geometry has been clipped and transformed into normalized device space, and so all of the fragments that are produced by rasterization are known to be on the screen (or inside the window). However, OpenGL then performs a number of other tests on the fragment to determine if and how it should be written to the framebuffer. These tests (in logical order) are the *scissor test*, the *stencil test*, and the *depth test*. These are covered in pipeline order in the following section.

Scissor Testing

The scissor rectangle is an arbitrary rectangle that you can specify in screen coordinates that allows you to further clip rendering to a particular region.

Unlike the viewport, geometry is not clipped directly against the scissor rectangle, but rather individual fragments are tested against the rectangle as part of post-rasterization[2] processing. As with viewport rectangles, OpenGL supports an array of scissor rectangles. To set them up, you can call **glScissorIndexed()** or **glScissorIndexedv()**, whose prototypes are

```
void glScissorIndexed(GLuint index,
                      GLint left,
                      GLint bottom,
                      GLsizei width,
                      GLsizei height);

void glScissorIndexedv(GLuint index,
                       const GLint * v);
```

For both functions, the index parameter specifies which scissor rectangle you want to change. The left, bottom, width, and height parameters describe a region in window coordinates that defines the scissor rectangle. For **glScissorIndexedv()**, the left, bottom, width, and height parameters are stored (in that order) in an array whose address is passed in v.

To select a scissor rectangle, the gl_ViewportIndex built-in output from the geometry shader is used (yes, the same one that selects the viewport). That means that given an array of viewports and an array of scissor rectangles, the same index is used for both arrays. To enable scissor testing, call

```
glEnable(GL_SCISSOR_TEST);
```

To disable it, call

```
glDisable(GL_SCISSOR_TEST);
```

The scissor test starts off disabled, so unless you need to use it, you don't need to do anything. If we again use the shader of Listing 8.36, which employs an instanced geometry shader to write to gl_ViewportIndex, enable the scissor test, and set some scissor rectangles, we can mask off sections of rendering. Listing 9.1 shows part of the code from the multiscissor, which is to set up our scissor rectangles, and Figure 9.2 shows the result of rendering with this code.

```
// Turn on scissor testing
glEnable(GL_SCISSOR_TEST);

// Each rectangle will be 7/16 of the screen
```

---

2. It may be the case that some OpenGL implementations either apply scissoring at the end of the geometry stage, or in an early part of rasterization. Here, we are describing the logical OpenGL pipeline, though.

```
int scissor_width = (7 * info.windowWidth) / 16;
int scissor_height = (7 * info.windowHeight) / 16;

// Four rectangles - lower left first...
glScissorIndexed(0, 0, 0, scissor_width, scissor_height);

// Lower right...
glScissorIndexed(1,
                 info.windowWidth - scissor_width, 0,
                 info.windowWidth - scissor_width, scissor_height);

// Upper left...
glScissorIndexed(2,
                 0, info.windowHeight - scissor_height,
                 scissor_width, scissor_height);

// Upper right...
glScissorIndexed(3,
                 info.windowWidth - scissor_width,
                 info.windowHeight - scissor_height,
                 scissor_width, scissor_height);
```

Listing 9.1: Setting up scissor rectangle arrays

Figure 9.2: Rendering with four different scissor rectangles

An important point to remember about the scissor test is that when you
clear the framebuffer using **glClear()** or **glClearBufferfv()**, the first
scissor rectangle is applied as well. This means that you can clear an
arbitrary rectangle of the framebuffer using the scissor rectangle, but it can

also lead to errors if you leave the scissor test enabled at the end of a frame and then try to clear the framebuffer ready for the next frame.

Stencil Testing

The next step in the fragment pipeline is the stencil test. Think of the stencil test as cutting out a shape in cardboard and then using that cutout to spray-paint the shape on a mural. The spray paint only hits the wall in places where the cardboard is cut out (just like a real stencil). If pixel format of the framebuffer includes a stencil buffer, you can similarly mask your draws to the framebuffer. You can enable stenciling by calling **glEnable()** and passing GL_STENCIL_TEST in the cap parameter. Most implementations only support stencil buffers that contain 8 bits, but some configurations may support fewer bits (or more, but this is extremely uncommon).

Your drawing commands can have a direct effect on the stencil buffer, and the value of the stencil buffer can have a direct effect on the pixels you draw. To control interactions with the stencil buffer, OpenGL provides two commands: **glStencilFuncSeparate()** and **glStencilOpSeparate()**. OpenGL lets you set both of these separately for front- and back-facing geometry. The prototypes of **glStencilFuncSeparate()** and **glStencilOpSeparate()** are

```
void glStencilFuncSeparate(GLenum face,
                           GLenum func,
                           GLint ref,
                           GLuint mask);

void glStencilOpSeparate(GLenum face,
                         GLenum sfail,
                         GLenum dpfail,
                         GLenum dppass);
```

First let's look at **glStencilFuncSeparate()**, which controls the conditions under which the stencil test passes or fails. The test is applied separately for front-facing and back-facing primitives, each has its own state, and you can pass GL_FRONT, GL_BACK, or GL_FRONT_AND_BACK for face, signifying which geometry will be affected. The value of func can be any of the values in Table 9.1. These specify under what conditions geometry will pass the stencil test.

The ref value is the reference used to compute the pass or fail result, and the mask parameter lets you control which bits of the reference and the buffer are compared. In pseudo-code, the operation of the stencil test is effectively implemented as

```
GLuint current = GetCurrentStencilContent(x, y);
if (compare(current & mask,
            ref & mask,
            front_facing ? front_op : back_op))
{
    passed = true;
}
else
{
    passed = false;
}
```

Table 9.1: Stencil Functions

Function	Pass Condition
GL_NEVER	Never pass test.
GL_ALWAYS	Always pass test.
GL_LESS	Reference value is less than buffer value.
GL_LEQUAL	Reference value is less than or equal to buffer value.
GL_EQUAL	Reference value is equal to buffer value.
GL_GEQUAL	Reference value is greater than or equal to buffer value.
GL_GREATER	Reference value is greater than buffer value.
GL_NOTEQUAL	Reference value is not equal to buffer value.

The next step is to tell OpenGL what to do when the stencil test passes or fails by using **glStencilOpSeparate()**. This function takes four parameters, with the first specifying which faces will be affected. The next three parameters control what happens after the stencil test is performed and can be any of the values in Table 9.2. The second parameter, sfail, is the action taken if the stencil test fails. The dpfail parameter specifies the action taken if the depth buffer test fails, and the final parameter, dppass, specifies what happens if the depth buffer test passes. Note that because stencil testing comes before depth testing (which we'll get to in a moment), should the stencil test fail, the fragment is killed right there and no further processing is performed — which explains why there are only three operations here rather than four.

So how does this actually work out? Let's look at a simple example of typical usage shown in Listing 9.2. The first step is to clear the stencil buffer to 0 by calling **glClearBufferiv()** with buffer set to GL_STENCIL, drawBuffer set to 0, and value pointing to a variable containing zero. Next, a window border is drawn that may contain details such as a player's score and statistics. Set up the stencil test to always pass with the reference value being 1 by calling **glStencilFuncSeparate()**. Next, tell OpenGL to replace the value in the stencil buffer only when the depth test passes by calling **glStencilOpSeparate()** followed by rendering the border geometry. This turns the border area pixels to 1 while the rest of the framebuffer remains at 0. Finally, set up the stencil state so that the stencil test will only pass if the stencil buffer value is 0, and then render the rest of the scene. This causes all pixels that would overwrite the border we just drew to fail the stencil test and not be drawn to the framebuffer. Listing 9.2 shows an example of how stencil can be used.

Table 9.2: Stencil Operations

Function	Result
GL_KEEP	Do not modify the stencil buffer.
GL_ZERO	Set stencil buffer value to 0.
GL_REPLACE	Replace stencil value with reference value.
GL_INCR	Increment stencil with saturation.
GL_DECR	Decrement stencil with saturation.
GL_INVERT	Bitwise invert stencil value.
GL_INCR_WRAP	Increment stencil without saturation.
GL_DECR_WRAP	Decrement stencil without saturation.

```
// Clear stencil buffer to 0
const GLint zero;
glClearBufferiv(GL_STENCIL, 0, &zero);

// Setup stencil state for border rendering
glStencilFuncSeparate(GL_FRONT, GL_ALWAYS, 1, 0xff);
glStencilOpSeparate(GL_FRONT, GL_KEEP, GL_ZERO, GL_REPLACE);

// Render border decorations
. . .

// Now, border decoration pixels have a stencil value of 1
// All other pixels have a stencil value of 0.

// Setup stencil state for regular rendering,
// fail if pixel would overwrite border
glStencilFuncSeparate(GL_FRONT_AND_BACK, GL_LESS, 1, 0xff);
glStencilOpSeparate(GL_FRONT, GL_KEEP, GL_KEEP, GL_KEEP);

// Render the rest of the scene, will not render over stenciled
// border content
. . .
```

Listing 9.2: Example stencil buffer usage, border decorations

There are also two other stencil functions: **glStencilFunc()** and **glStencilOp()**. These behave just as **glStencilFuncSeparate()** and **glStencilOpSeparate()** would if you were to set the face parameter to GL_FRONT_AND_BACK.

Controlling Updates to the Stencil Buffer

By clever manipulation of the stencil operation modes (setting them all to the same value, or judicious use of GL_KEEP, for example), you can perform some pretty flexible operations on the stencil buffer. However, beyond this, it's possible to control updates to individual bits of the stencil buffer. The **glStencilMaskSeparate()** function takes a bitfield of which bits in the stencil buffer should be updated and which should be left alone. Its prototype is

```
void glStencilMaskSeparate(GLenum face, GLuint mask);
```

As with the stencil test function, there are two sets of state — one for front-facing and one for back-facing primitives. Just like **glStencilFuncSeparate()**, the face parameter specifies which types of primitives should be affected. The mask parameter is a bitfield that maps to the bits in the stencil buffer — if the stencil buffer has less than 32 bits (8 is the maximum supported by most current OpenGL implementations), only that many of the least significant bits of mask are used. If a mask bit is set to 1, the corresponding bit in the stencil buffer can be updated. But if the mask bit is 0, the corresponding stencil bit will not be written to. For instance, consider the following code:

```
GLuint mask = 0x000F;
glStencilMaskSeparate(GL_FRONT, mask);
glStencilMaskSeparate(GL_BACK, ~mask);
```

In the preceding example, the first call to **glStencilMaskSeparate()** affects front-facing primitives and enables the lower four bits of the stencil buffer for writing while leaving the rest disabled. The second call to **glStencilMaskSeparate()** sets the opposite mask for back-facing primitives. This essentially allows you to pack two stencil values together into an 8-bit stencil buffer — the lower four bits being used for front-facing primitives, and the upper four bits being used for back-facing primitives.

Depth Testing

After stencil operations are complete and if depth testing is enabled, OpenGL tests the depth value of a fragment against the existing content of the depth buffer. If depth writes are also enabled and the fragment has passed the depth test, the depth buffer is updated with the depth value of the fragment. If the depth test fails, the fragment is discarded and does not pass to the following fragment operations.

The input to primitive assembly is a set of vertex positions that make up primitives. Each has a z coordinate. This coordinate is scaled and biased such that the normal[3] visible range of values lies between zero and one. This is the value that's usually stored in the depth buffer. During depth testing, OpenGL reads the depth value of the fragment from the depth buffer at the current fragment's coordinate and compares it to the generated depth value for the fragment being processed.

You can choose what comparison operator is used to figure out if the fragment "passed" the depth test. To set the depth comparison operator (or *depth function*), call **glDepthFunc()**, whose prototype is

```
void glDepthFunc(GLenum func);
```

Here, func is one of the available depth comparison operators. The legal values for func and what they mean are shown in Table 9.3.

If the depth test is disabled, it is as if the depth test always passes (i.e., the depth function is set to GL_ALWAYS), with one exception: The depth buffer is only updated when the depth test is enabled. If you want your geometry to be written into the depth buffer unconditionally, you must enable the depth test and set the depth function to GL_ALWAYS. By default, the depth test is disabled. To turn it on, call

```
glEnable(GL_DEPTH_TEST);
```

To turn it off again, simply call **glDisable()** with the GL_DEPTH_TEST parameter. It is a very common mistake to disable the depth test and expect it to be updated. Again, the depth buffer is not updated unless the depth test is also enabled.

Controlling Updates of the Depth Buffer

Writes to the depth buffer can be turned on and off, regardless of the result of the depth test. Remember, the depth buffer is only updated if the depth test is turned on (although the test function can be set to GL_ALWAYS if

---

3. It's possible to turn off this visibility check and consider all fragments visible, even if they lie outside the zero-to-one range that is stored in the depth buffer.

you don't actually need depth testing and only wish to update the depth buffer). The `glDepthMask()` function takes a Boolean flag that turns writes to the depth buffer on if it's GL_TRUE and off if GL_FALSE. For example,

```
glDepthMask(GL_FALSE);
```

will turn writes to the depth buffer off, regardless of the result of the depth test. You can use this, for example, to draw geometry that should be tested against the depth buffer, but that shouldn't update it. By default, the depth mask is set to GL_TRUE, which means you won't need to change it if you want depth testing and writing to behave as normal.

Table 9.3: Depth Comparison Functions

Function	Meaning
GL_ALWAYS	The depth test always passes — all fragments are considered to have passed the depth test.
GL_NEVER	The depth test never passes — all fragments are considered to have failed the depth test.
GL_LESS	The depth test passes if the new fragment's depth value is less than the old fragment's depth value.
GL_LEQUAL	The depth test passes if the new fragment's depth value is less than or equal to the old fragment's depth value.
GL_EQUAL	The depth test passes if the new fragment's depth value is equal to the old fragment's depth value.
GL_NOTEQUAL	The depth test passes if the new fragment's depth value is not equal the old fragment's depth value.
GL_GREATER	The depth test passes if the new fragment's depth value is greater than the old fragment's depth value.
GL_GEQUAL	The depth test passes if the new fragment's depth value is greater than or equal to the old fragment's depth value.

Depth Clamping

OpenGL represents the depth of each fragment as a finite number, scaled between zero and one. A fragment with a depth of zero is intersecting the near plane (and would be jabbing you in the eye if it were real), and a fragment with a depth of one is at the farthest representable depth but not infinitely far away. To eliminate the far plane and draw things at any arbitrary distance, we would need to store arbitrarily large numbers in the depth buffer — something that's not really possible. To get around this, OpenGL has the option to turn off clipping against the near and far planes and instead clamp the generated depth values to the range zero to one. This means that any geometry that protrudes behind the near plane or beyond the far plane will essentially be projected onto that plane.

To enable depth clamping (and simultaneously turn off clipping against the near and far planes), call

```
glEnable(GL_DEPTH_CLAMP);
```

and to disable depth clamping, call

```
glDisable(GL_DEPTH_CLAMP);
```

Figure 9.3 illustrates the effect of enabling depth clamping and drawing a primitive that intersects the near plane.

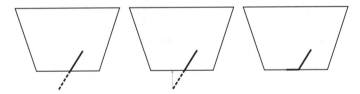

Figure 9.3: Effect of depth clamping at the near plane

It is simpler to demonstrate this in two dimensions, and so on the left of Figure 9.3, the view frustum is displayed as if we were looking straight down on it. The dark line represents the primitive that would have been clipped against the near plane, and the dotted line represents the portion of the primitive that was clipped away. When depth clamping is enabled, rather than clipping the primitive, the depth values that would have been generated outside the range zero to one are clamped into that range, effectively projecting the primitive onto the near plane (or the far plane, if the primitive would have clipped that). The center of Figure 9.3 shows this projection. What actually gets rendered is shown on the right of Figure 9.3. The dark line represents the values that eventually get written into the depth buffer. Figure 9.4 shows how this translates to a real application.

Figure 9.4: A clipped object with and without depth clamping

In the left image of Figure 9.4, the geometry has become so close to the viewer that it is partially clipped against the near plane. As a result, the portions of the polygons that would have been behind the near plane are simply not drawn, and so they leave a large hole in the model. You can see right through to the other side of the object, and the image is quite visibly incorrect. On the right of Figure 9.4, depth clamping has been enabled. As you can see, the geometry that was lost in the left image is back and fills the hole in the object. The values in the depth buffer aren't technically correct, but this hasn't translated to visual anomalies, and the picture produced looks better than that in the left image.

Early Testing

Logically, the depth and stencil tests occur *after* the fragment has been shaded, but most graphics hardware is capable of performing the test before your shader runs and avoiding the cost of executing that shader if the ownership test would fail. However, if a shader has side effects (such as directly writing to a texture) or would otherwise effect the outcome of the test, OpenGL can't perform the tests first, and must always run your shader. Not only that, but it must always wait for the shader to finish executing before it can perform depth testing or update the stencil buffer.

One particular example of something you can do in your shader that would stop OpenGL from performing the depth test before executing it is writing to the built-in `gl_FragDepth` output.

The special built-in variable `gl_FragDepth` is available for writing an updated depth value to. If the fragment shader doesn't write to this variable, the interpolated depth generated by OpenGL is used as the fragment's depth value. Your fragment shader can either calculate an entirely new value for gl_FragDepth, or it can derive one from the value gl_FragCoord.z. This new value is subsequently used by OpenGL both as the reference for the depth test and as the value written to the depth buffer should the depth test pass. You can use this functionality, for example, to slightly perturb the values in the depth buffer and create physically bumpy surfaces. Of course, you'd need to shade such surfaces appropriately to make them appear bumpy, but when new objects were tested against the content of the depth buffer, the result would match the shading.

Because your shader changes the fragment's depth value when you write to gl_FragDepth, there's no way that OpenGL can perform the depth test before the shader runs because it doesn't know what you're going to put there. For this scenario, OpenGL provides some layout qualifiers that let you tell it what you plan to do with the depth value.

Now, remember that the range of values in the depth buffer is between 0.0 and 1.0, and that the depth test comparison operators include functions such as GL_LESS and GL_GREATER. Now, if you set the depth test function to GL_LESS, for example (which would pass for any fragment that is *closer* to the viewer than what is currently in the framebuffer), then if you only ever set gl_FragDepth to a value that is less than it would have been otherwise, then the fragment will pass the depth test regardless of whatever the shader does, and so the original test result remains valid. In this case, OpenGL now knows that it can perform the depth test before running your fragment shader, even though the logical pipeline has it running afterwards.

The layout qualifier you use to tell OpenGL what you're going to do to depth is applied to a *redeclaration* of gl_FragDepth. The redeclaration of gl_FragDepth can take the form of any of the following:

```
layout (depth_any) out float gl_FragDepth;
layout (depth_less) out float gl_FragDepth;
layout (depth_greater) out float gl_FragDepth;
layout (depth_unchanged) out float gl_FragDepth;
```

If you use the depth_any layout qualifier, you're telling OpenGL that you might write *any* value to gl_FragDepth. This is effectively the default — if OpenGL sees that your shader writes to gl_FragDepth, it has no idea what you did to it and assumes that the result could be anything. If you specify depth_less, you're effectively saying that whatever you write to gl_FragDepth will result in the fragment's depth value being *less* than it would have been otherwise. In this case, results from the GL_LESS and GL_LEQUAL comparison functions remain valid. Similarly, using depth_greater indicates that your shader will only make the fragment's depth *greater* than it would have been and, therefore, the result of the GL_GREATER and GL_GEQUAL tests remain valid.

The final qualifier, depth_unchanged, is somewhat unique. This tells OpenGL that whatever you do to gl_FragDepth, it's free to assume you haven't written anything to it that would change the result of the depth test. In the case of depth_any, depth_less, and depth_greater, although OpenGL becomes free to perform depth testing before your shader executes under certain circumstances, there are still times when it must run your shader and wait for it to finish. With depth_unchanged you are telling OpenGL that no matter what you do with the fragment's depth value, the original result of the test remains valid. You might choose to use this if you plan to perturb the fragment's depth slightly, but not in a way that would make it intersect any other geometry in the scene (or if you don't care if it does).

Regardless of the layout qualifier you apply to a redeclaration of gl_FragDepth and what OpenGL decides to do about it, the value you write into gl_FragDepth will be clamped into the range 0.0 to 1.0 and then written into the depth buffer.

Color Output

The color output stage is the last part of the OpenGL pipeline before fragments are written to the framebuffer. It determines what happens to your color data between when it leaves your fragment shader and when it is finally displayed to the user.

Blending

For fragments that pass the per-fragment tests, *blending* is performed. Blending allows you to combine the incoming source color with the color already in the color buffer or with other constants using one of the many supported blend equations. If the buffer you are drawing to is fixed point, the incoming source colors will be clamped to 0.0 to 1.0 before any blending operations occur. Blending is enabled by calling

```
glEnable(GL_BLEND);
```

and disabled by calling

```
glDisable(GL_BLEND);
```

The blending functionality of OpenGL is powerful and highly configurable. It works by multiplying the source color (the value produced by your shader) by the *source factor*, then multiplying the color in the framebuffer by the *destination factor*, and then combining the results of these multiplications using an operation that you can choose called the *blend equation*.

Blend Functions

To choose the source and destination factors by which OpenGL will multiply the result of your shader and the value in the framebuffer, respectively, you can call **glBlendFunc()** or **glBlendFuncSeparate()**. **glBlendFunc()** lets you set the source and destination factors for all four channels of data (red, green, blue, and alpha). **glBlendFuncSeparate()**, on the other hand, allows you to set a source and destination factor for the red, green, and blue channels and another for the alpha channel.

```
glBlendFuncSeparate(GLenum srcRGB, GLenum dstRGB,
                    GLenum srcAlpha, GLenum dstaAlpha);

glBlendFunc(GLenum src, GLenum dst);
```

The possible values for these calls can be found in Table 9.4. There are four sources of data that might be used in a blending function. These are the first source color (R_{s0}, G_{s0}, B_{s0}, and A_{s0}), the second source color (R_{s1}, G_{s1}, B_{s1}, and A_{s1}), the destination color (R_d, G_d, B_d, and A_d), and the constant blending color (R_c, G_c, B_c, and A_c). The last value, the constant blending color, can be set by calling **glBlendColor()**:

```
glBlendColor(GLfloat red, GLfloat green,
             GLfloat blue, GLfloat alpha);
```

In addition to all of these sources, the constant values zero and one can be used as any of the product terms.

As a simple example, consider the code shown in Listing 9.3. This code clears the framebuffer to a mid-orange color, turns on blending, sets the blend color to a mid-blue color, and then draws a small cube with every possible combination of source and destination blending function.

The result of rendering with the code shown in Listing 9.3 is shown in Figure 9.5. This image is also shown in Color Plate 1 and was generated by the `blendmatrix` sample application.

Table 9.4: Blend Functions

Blend Function	RGB	Alpha
`GL_ZERO`	$(0, 0, 0)$	0
`GL_ONE`	$(1, 1, 1)$	1
`GL_SRC_COLOR`	(R_{s0}, G_{s0}, B_{s0})	A_{s0}
`GL_ONE_MINUS_SRC_COLOR`	$(1, 1, 1) - (R_{s0}, G_{s0}, B_{s0})$	$1 - A_{s0}$
`GL_DST_COLOR`	(R_d, G_d, B_d)	A_d
`GL_ONE_MINUS_DST_COLOR`	$(1, 1, 1) - (R_d, G_d, B_d)$	$1 - A_d$
`GL_SRC_ALPHA`	(A_{s0}, A_{s0}, A_{s0})	A_{s0}
`GL_ONE_MINUS_SRC_ALPHA`	$(1, 1, 1) - (A_{s0}, A_{s0}, A_{s0})$	$1 - A_{s0}$
`GL_DST_ALPHA`	(A_d, A_d, A_d)	A_d
`GL_ONE_MINUS_DST_ALPHA`	$(1, 1, 1) - (A_d, A_d, A_d)$	$1 - A_d$
`GL_CONSTANT_COLOR`	(R_c, G_c, B_c)	A_c
`GL_ONE_MINUS_CONSTANT_COLOR`	$(1, 1, 1) - (R_c, G_c, B_c)$	$1 - A_c$
`GL_CONSTANT_ALPHA`	(A_c, A_c, A_c)	A_c
`GL_ONE_MINUS_CONSTANT_ALPHA`	$(1, 1, 1) - (A_c, A_c, A_c)$	$1 - A_c$
`GL_ALPHA_SATURATE`	(f, f, f) $f = \min(A_{s0}, 1 - A_d)$	1
`GL_SRC1_COLOR`	(R_{s1}, G_{s1}, B_{s1})	A_{s1}
`GL_ONE_MINUS_SRC1_COLOR`	$(1, 1, 1) - (R_{s1}, G_{s1}, B_{s1})$	$1 - A_{s1}$
`GL_SRC1_ALPHA`	(A_{s1}, A_{s1}, A_{s1})	A_{s1}
`GL_ONE_MINUS_SRC1_ALPHA`	$(1, 1, 1) - (A_{s1}, A_{s1}, A_{s1})$	$1 - A_{s1}$

```
static const GLfloat orange[] = { 0.6f, 0.4f, 0.1f, 1.0f };
glClearBufferfv(GL_COLOR, 0, orange);

static const GLenum blend_func[] =
{
    GL_ZERO,
    GL_ONE,
    GL_SRC_COLOR,
    GL_ONE_MINUS_SRC_COLOR,
    GL_DST_COLOR,
    GL_ONE_MINUS_DST_COLOR,
    GL_SRC_ALPHA,
    GL_ONE_MINUS_SRC_ALPHA,
    GL_DST_ALPHA,
    GL_ONE_MINUS_DST_ALPHA,
    GL_CONSTANT_COLOR,
    GL_ONE_MINUS_CONSTANT_COLOR,
    GL_CONSTANT_ALPHA,
    GL_ONE_MINUS_CONSTANT_ALPHA,
    GL_SRC_ALPHA_SATURATE,
    GL_SRC1_COLOR,
    GL_ONE_MINUS_SRC1_COLOR,
```

```
        GL_SRC1_ALPHA,
        GL_ONE_MINUS_SRC1_ALPHA
};
static const int num_blend_funcs = sizeof(blend_func) /
                                    sizeof(blend_func[0]);
static const float x_scale = 20.0f / float(num_blend_funcs);
static const float y_scale = 16.0f / float(num_blend_funcs);
const float t = (float)currentTime;

glEnable(GL_BLEND);
glBlendColor(0.2f, 0.5f, 0.7f, 0.5f);
for (j = 0; j < num_blend_funcs; j++)
{
    for (i = 0; i < num_blend_funcs; i++)
    {
        vmath::mat4 mv_matrix =
            vmath::translate(9.5f - x_scale * float(i),
                             7.5f - y_scale * float(j),
                             -50.0f) *
            vmath::rotate(t * -45.0f, 0.0f, 1.0f, 0.0f) *
            vmath::rotate(t * -21.0f, 1.0f, 0.0f, 0.0f);

        glUniformMatrix4fv(mv_location, 1, GL_FALSE, mv_matrix);

        glBlendFunc(blend_func[i], blend_func[j]);

        glDrawElements(GL_TRIANGLES, 36, GL_UNSIGNED_SHORT, 0);
    }
}
```

Listing 9.3: Rendering with all blending functions

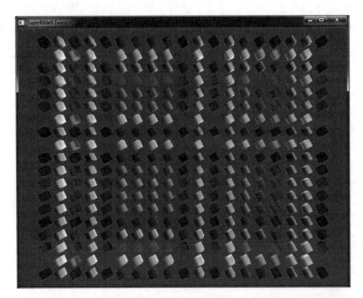

Figure 9.5: All possible combinations of blending functions

Dual-Source Blending

You may have noticed that some of the factors in Table 9.4 use source 0 colors (R_{s0}, G_{s0}, B_{s0}, and A_{s0}), and others use source 1 colors (R_{s1}, G_{s1}, B_{s1}, and A_{s1}). Your shaders can export more than one final color for a given color buffer by setting up the outputs used in your shader by assigning them indices using the index layout qualifier. An example is shown below:

```
layout (location = 0, index = 0) out vec4 color0;
layout (location = 0, index = 1) out vec4 color1;
```

Here, color0_0 will be used for the GL_SRC_COLOR factor, and color0_1 will be used for the GL_SRC1_COLOR. When you use dual source blending functions, the number of separate color buffers that you can use might be limited. You can find out how many dual output buffers are supported by querying the value of GL_MAX_DUAL_SOURCE_DRAW_BUFFERS.

Blend Equation

Once the source and destination factors have been multiplied by the source and destination colors, the two products need to be combined together. This is done using an equation that you can set by calling **glBlendEquation()** or **glBlendEquationSeparate()**. As with the blend functions, you can choose one blend equation for the red, green, and blue channels and another for the alpha channel — use **glBlendEquationSeparate()** to do this. If you want both equations to be the same, you can call **glBlendEquation()**:

```
glBlendEquation(GLenum mode);

glBlendEquationSeparate(GLenum modeRGB,
                        GLenum modeAlpha);
```

For **glBlendEquation()**, the one parameter, mode, selects the same mode for all of the red, green, blue, and alpha channels. For **glBlendEquationSeparate()**, an equation can be chosen for the red, green, and blue channels (specified in modeRGB) and another for the alpha channel (specified in modeAlpha). The values you pass to the two functions are shown in Table 9.5.

In Table 9.5, RGB_s represents the source red, green, and blue values; RGB_d represents the destination red, green, and blue values; A_s and A_d represent the source and destination alpha values; S_{rgb} and D_{rgb} represent the source

Table 9.5: Blend Equations

Equation	RGB	Alpha
GL_FUNC_ADD	$S_{rgb} * RGB_s +$ $D_{rgb} * RGB_d$	$S_a * A_s +$ $D_a * A_d$
GL_FUNC_SUBTRACT	$S_{rgb} * RGB_s -$ $D_{rgb} * RGB_d$	$S_a * A_s -$ $D_a * A_d$
GL_FUNC_REVERSE_ SUBTRACT	$D_{rgb} * RGB_d -$ $S_{rgb} * RGB_s$	$D_a * A_d -$ $S_a * A_s$
GL_MIN	$\min(RGB_s, RGB_d)$	$\min(A_s, A_d)$
GL_MAX	$\max(RGB_s, RGB_d)$	$\min(A_s, A_d)$

and destination blend factors; and S_a and D_a represent the source and destination alpha factors (chosen by **glBlendFunc()** or **glBlendFuncSeparate()**).

Logical Operations

Once the pixel color is in the same format and bit depth as the framebuffer, there are two more steps that can affect the final result. The first allows you to apply a logical operation to the pixel color before it is passed on. When enabled, the effects of blending are ignored. Logic operations do not affect floating-point buffers. You can enable logic ops by calling

```
glEnable(GL_COLOR_LOGIC_OP);
```

and disable it by calling

```
glDisable(GL_COLOR_LOGIC_OP);
```

Logic operations use the values of the incoming pixel and the existing framebuffer to compute a final value. You can pick the operation that computes the final value by calling **glLogicOp()**. The possible options are listed in Table 9.6. The prototype of **glLogicOp()** is

```
glLogicOp(GLenum op);
```

where op is one of the values from Table 9.6.

Table 9.6: Logic Operations

Operation	Result
GL_CLEAR	Set all values to 0
GL_AND	Source & Destination
GL_AND_REVERSE	Source & ~Destination
GL_COPY	Source
GL_AND_INVERTED	~Source & Destination
GL_NOOP	Destination
GL_XOR	Source ^Destination
GL_OR	Source | Destination
GL_NOR	~(Source | Destination)
GL_EQUIV	~(Source ^Destination)
GL_INVERT	~Destination
GL_OR_REVERSE	Source | ~Destination
GL_COPY_INVERTED	~Source
GL_OR_INVERTED	~Source | Destination
GL_NAND	~(Source & Destination)
GL_SET	Set all values to 1

Logic operations are applied separately to each color channel, and operations that combine source and destination are performed bitwise on the color values. Logic ops are not commonly used in today's graphics applications but still remain part of OpenGL because the functionality is still supported on common GPUs.

Color Masking

One of the last modifications that can be made to a fragment before it is written is *masking*. By now you recognize that three different types of data can be written by a fragment shader: color, depth, and stencil data. Just as you can mask off updates to the stencil and depth buffers, you can also apply a mask to the updates of the color buffer.

To mask color writes or prevent color writes from happening, you can use **glColorMask()** and **glColorMaski()**. We briefly introduced **glColorMask()** back in Chapter 5 where we turned on and off writing to the framebuffer. However, you don't have to mask all color channels at once; for instance, you can choose to mask the red and green channels while permitting writes to the blue channel. Each function takes four Boolean parameters that control updates to each of the red, green, blue, and alpha channels of the color buffer. You can pass in GL_TRUE to one of these parameters to allow writes for the corresponding channel to occur, or GL_FALSE to mask these writes off. The first function, **glColorMask()**, allows you to mask all buffers currently enabled for rendering, while the second function, **glColorMaski()**, allows you to set the mask for a specific color buffer (there can be many if you're rendering off screen). The prototypes of these two functions are

```
glColorMask(GLboolean red,
            GLboolean green,
            GLboolean blue,
            GLboolean alpha);

glColorMaski(GLuint index,
             GLboolean red,
             GLboolean green,
             GLboolean blue,
             GLboolean alpha);
```

For both functions, red, green, blue, and alpha can be set to either GL_TRUE or GL_FALSE to determine whether the red, green, blue, or alpha channels should be written to the framebuffer. For **glColorMaski()**, index is the index of the color attachment to which masking should apply. Each color attachment can have its own color mask settings. So, for example, you could write only the red channel to attachment 0, only the green channel to attachment 1, and so on.

Mask Usage

Write masks can be useful for many operations. For instance, if you want to fill a shadow volume with depth information, you can mask off all color writes because only the depth information is important. Or if you want to draw a decal directly to screen space, you can disable depth writes to prevent the depth data from being polluted. The key point about masks is you can set them and immediately call your normal rendering paths, which may set up necessary buffer state and output all color, depth, and stencil data you would normally use without needing any knowledge of the mask state. You don't have to alter your shaders to not write some value, detach some set of buffers, or change the enabled draw buffers. The rest of your rendering paths can be completely oblivious and still generate the right results.

Off-Screen Rendering

Until now, all of the rendering your programs have performed has been directed into a window, or perhaps the computer's main display. The output of your fragment shader goes into the *back buffer*, which is normally owned by the operating system or window system that your application is running on, and is eventually displayed to the user. Its parameters are set when you choose a format for the rendering context. As a platform-specific operation, this means that you have little control over what the underlying storage format really is. Also, in order for the samples in this book to run on many platforms, the book's application framework takes care of setting this up for you, hiding many of the details.

However, OpenGL includes features that allow you to set up your own framebuffer and use it to draw directly into textures. You can then use these textures later for further rendering or processing. You also have a lot of control over the format and layout of the framebuffer. For example, when you use the default framebuffer, it is implicitly sized to the size of the window or display, and rendering outside the display (if the window is obscured or dragged off the side of the screen, for example) is undefined as the corresponding pixels' fragment shaders might not run. However, with user-supplied framebuffers, the maximum size of the textures you render to is only limited by the maximums supported by the implementation of OpenGL you're running on, and rendering to any location in it is always defined.

User-supplied framebuffers are represented by OpenGL as *framebuffer objects*. As with most objects in OpenGL, each framebuffer object has a name that must be reserved before it is created — the actual object is initialized when it is first bound. So, the first thing to do is to reserve a name for a framebuffer object and bind it to the context to initialize it. To generate names for framebuffer objects, call **glGenFramebuffers()**, and to bind a framebuffer to the context, call **glBindFramebuffer()**. The prototypes of these functions are

```
void glGenFramebuffers(GLsizei n,
                       GLuint * ids);

void glBindFramebuffer(GLenum target,
                       GLuint framebuffer);
```

The **glGenFramebuffers()** function takes a count in n and hands you back a list of names in ids that you are able to use as framebuffer objects. The **glBindFramebuffer()** function makes your application-supplied framebuffer object the current framebuffer (instead of the default one). The framebuffer is one of the names that you got from a call to **glGenFramebuffers()**, and target parameter will normally be GL_FRAMEBUFFER. However, it's possible to bind two framebuffers at the same time — one for reading and one for writing.

To bind a framebuffer for reading only, set `target` to GL_READ_FRAMEBUFFER. Likewise, to bind a framebuffer just for rendering to, set `target` to GL_DRAW_FRAMEBUFFER. The framebuffer bound for drawing will be the destination for all of your rendering (including stencil and depth values used during their respective tests and colors read during blending). The framebuffer bound for reading will be the source of data if you want to read back pixel data or copy data from the framebuffer into textures, as we'll explain shortly. Setting `target` to just GL_FRAMEBUFFER actually binds the object to both the read and draw framebuffer targets, and this is normally what you want.

Once you have created a framebuffer object and bound it, you can attach textures to it to serve as the storage for the rendering you're going to do. There are three types of attachment supported by the framebuffer — the depth, stencil, and color attachments, which serve as the depth, stencil, and color buffers. To attach a texture to a framebuffer, we can call **glFramebufferTexture()**, whose prototype is

```
void glFramebufferTexture(GLenum target,
                          GLenum attachment,
                          GLuint texture,
                          GLint level);
```

For **glFramebufferTexture()**, `target` is the binding point where the framebuffer object you want to attach a texture to is bound. This should be GL_READ_FRAMEBUFFER, GL_DRAW_FRAMEBUFFER, or just GL_FRAMEBUFFER. In this case, GL_FRAMEBUFFER is considered to be equivalent to GL_DRAW_FRAMEBUFFER, and so if you use this token, OpenGL will attach the texture to the framebuffer object bound the GL_DRAW_FRAMEBUFFER target.

`attachment` tells OpenGL which attachment you want to attach the texture to. It can be GL_DEPTH_ATTACHMENT to attach the texture to the depth buffer attachment, or GL_STENCIL_ATTACHMENT to attach it to the stencil buffer attachment. Because there are several texture formats that include depth and stencil values packed together, OpenGL also allows you to set `attachment` to GL_DEPTH_STENCIL_ATTACHMENT to indicate that you want to use the same texture for both the depth and stencil buffers.

To attach a texture as the color buffer, set `attachment` to GL_COLOR_ATTACHMENT0. In fact, you can set `attachment` to GL_COLOR_ATTACHMENT1, GL_COLOR_ATTACHMENT2, and so on to attach multiple textures for rendering to. We'll get to that momentarily, but first, we'll look at an example of how to set up a framebuffer object for rendering to. Lastly, `texture` is the name of the texture you want to attach to the framebuffer, and `level` is the mipmap level of the texture you want to render into. Listing 9.4 shows a complete example of setting up a framebuffer object with a depth buffer and a texture to render into.

```
// Create a framebuffer object and bind it
glGenFramebuffers(1, &fbo);
glBindFramebuffer(GL_FRAMEBUFFER, fbo);

// Create a texture for our color buffer
glGenTextures(1, &color_texture);
glBindTexture(GL_TEXTURE_2D, color_texture);
glTexStorage2D(GL_TEXTURE_2D, 1, GL_RGBA8, 512, 512);

// We're going to read from this, but it won't have mipmaps,
// so turn off mipmaps for this texture.
glTexParameteri(GL_TEXTURE_2D, GL_TEXTURE_MIN_FILTER, GL_LINEAR);
glTexParameteri(GL_TEXTURE_2D, GL_TEXTURE_MAG_FILTER, GL_LINEAR);

// Create a texture that will be our FBO's depth buffer
glGenTextures(1, &depth_texture);
glBindTexture(GL_TEXTURE_2D, depth_texture);
glTexStorage2D(GL_TEXTURE_2D, 1, GL_DEPTH_COMPONENT32F, 512, 512);

// Now, attach the color and depth textures to the FBO
glFramebufferTexture(GL_FRAMEBUFFER,
                     GL_COLOR_ATTACHMENT0,
                     color_texture, 0);
glFramebufferTexture(GL_FRAMEBUFFER,
                     GL_DEPTH_ATTACHMENT,
                     depth_texture, 0);

// Tell OpenGL that we want to draw into the framebuffer's color
// attachment
static const GLenum draw_buffers[] = { GL_COLOR_ATTACHMENT0 };
glDrawBuffers(1, draw_buffers);
```

Listing 9.4: Setting up a simple framebuffer object

After this code has executed, all we need to do is call **glBindFramebuffer()** again and pass our newly created framebuffer object, and all rendering will be directed into the depth and color textures. Once we're done rendering into our own framebuffer, we can use the resulting texture as a regular texture and read from it in our shaders. Listing 9.5 shows an example of doing this.

```
// Bind our off-screen FBO
glBindFramebuffer(GL_FRAMEBUFFER, fbo);

// Set the viewport and clear the depth and color buffers
glViewport(0, 0, 512, 512);
glClearBufferfv(GL_COLOR, 0, green);
glClearBufferfv(GL_DEPTH, 0, &one);

// Activate our first, non-textured program
glUseProgram(program1);
```

```
// Set our uniforms and draw the cube.
glUniformMatrix4fv(proj_location, 1, GL_FALSE, proj_matrix);
glUniformMatrix4fv(mv_location, 1, GL_FALSE, mv_matrix);
glDrawArrays(GL_TRIANGLES, 0, 36);

// Now return to the default framebuffer
glBindFramebuffer(GL_FRAMEBUFFER, 0);

// Reset our viewport to the window width and height, clear the
// depth and color buffers.
glViewport(0, 0, info.windowWidth, info.windowHeight);
glClearBufferfv(GL_COLOR, 0, blue);
glClearBufferfv(GL_DEPTH, 0, &one);

// Bind the texture we just rendered to for reading
glBindTexture(GL_TEXTURE_2D, color_texture);

// Activate a program that will read from the texture
glUseProgram(program2);

// Set uniforms and draw
glUniformMatrix4fv(proj_location2, 1, GL_FALSE, proj_matrix);
glUniformMatrix4fv(mv_location2, 1, GL_FALSE, mv_matrix);
glDrawArrays(GL_TRIANGLES, 0, 36);

// Unbind the texture and we're done.
glBindTexture(GL_TEXTURE_2D, 0);
```

Listing 9.5: Rendering to a texture

The code shown in Listing 9.5 is taken from the basicfbo sample and first binds our user-defined framebuffer, sets the viewport to the dimensions of the framebuffer, and clears the color buffer with a dark green color. It then proceeds to draw our simple cube model. This results in the cube being rendered into the texture we previously attached to the GL_COLOR_ATTACHMENT0 attachment point on the framebuffer. Next, we unbind our FBO, returning to the default framebuffer that represents our window. We render the cube again, this time with a shader that uses the texture we just rendered to. The result is that an image of the first cube we rendered is shown on each face of the second cube. Output of the program is shown in Figure 9.6.

Multiple Framebuffer Attachments

In the last section, we introduced the concept of user-defined framebuffers, which are also known as FBOs. An FBO allows you to render into textures that you create in your application. Because the textures are owned and allocated by OpenGL, they are decoupled from the operating or window system and so can be extremely flexible. The upper limit on their size depends only on OpenGL and not on the attached displays, for example. You also have full control over their format.

Figure 9.6: Result of rendering into a texture

Another extremely useful feature of user-defined framebuffers is that they support multiple attachments. That is, you can attach multiple textures to a single framebuffer and render into them simultaneously with a single fragment shader. Recall that to attach your texture to your FBO, you called **glFramebufferTexture()** and passed GL_COLOR_ATTACHMENT0 as the attachment parameter, but we mentioned that you can also pass GL_COLOR_ATTACHMENT1, GL_COLOR_ATTACHMENT2, and so on. In fact, OpenGL supports attaching at least eight textures to a single FBO. Listing 9.6 shows an example of setting up an FBO with three color attachments.

```
static const GLenum draw_buffers[] =
{
    GL_COLOR_ATTACHMENT0,
    GL_COLOR_ATTACHMENT1,
    GL_COLOR_ATTACHMENT2
};

// First, generate and bind our framebuffer object
glGenFramebuffers(1, &fbo);
glBindFramebuffer(GL_FRAMEBUFFER, fbo);

// Generate three texture names
glGenTextures(3, &color_texture[0]);

// For each one...
for (int i = 0; i < 3; i++)
{
    // Bind and allocate storage for it
```

```
glBindTexture(GL_TEXTURE_2D, color_texture[i]);
glTexStorage2D(GL_TEXTURE_2D, 9, GL_RGBA8, 512, 512);

// Set its default filter parameters
glTexParameteri(GL_TEXTURE_2D,
                GL_TEXTURE_MIN_FILTER, GL_LINEAR);
glTexParameteri(GL_TEXTURE_2D,
                GL_TEXTURE_MAG_FILTER, GL_LINEAR);

// Attach it to our framebuffer object as color attachments
glFramebufferTexture(GL_FRAMEBUFFER,
                     draw_buffers[i], color_texture[i], 0);
}

// Now create a depth texture
glGenTextures(1, &depth_texture);
glBindTexture(GL_TEXTURE_2D, depth_texture);
glTexStorage2D(GL_TEXTURE_2D, 9, GL_DEPTH_COMPONENT32F, 512, 512);

// Attach the depth texture to the framebuffer
glFramebufferTexture(GL_FRAMEBUFFER, GL_DEPTH_ATTACHMENT,
                     depth_texture, 0);

// Set the draw buffers for the FBO to point to the color attachments
glDrawBuffers(3, draw_buffers);
```

Listing 9.6: Setting up an FBO with multiple attachments

To render into multiple attachments from a single fragment shader, we must declare multiple outputs in the shader and associate them with the attachment points. To do this, we use a *layout qualifier* to specify each output's location, which is a term used to refer to the index of the attachment to which that output will be sent. Listing 9.7 shows an example of this.

```
layout (location = 0) out vec4 color0;
layout (location = 1) out vec4 color1;
layout (location = 2) out vec4 color2;
```

Listing 9.7: Declaring multiple outputs in a fragment shader

Once you have declared multiple outputs in your fragment shader, you can write different data into each of them and that data will be directed into the framebuffer color attachment indexed by the output's location. Remember, the fragment shader still only executes once for each fragment produced during rasterization, and the data written to each of the shader's outputs will be written at the same position within each of the corresponding framebuffer attachments.

Layered Rendering

In "Array Textures" in Chapter 5, we described a form of texture called the *array texture*, which represents a stack of 2D textures arranged as an array of *layers* that you can index into in a shader. It's also possible to render into array textures by attaching them to a framebuffer object and using a geometry shader to specify which layer you want the resulting primitives to be rendered into. Listing 9.8 is taken from the gslayered sample and illustrates how to set up a framebuffer object that uses a 2D array texture as a color attachment. Such a framebuffer is known as a *layered framebuffer*. In addition to creating an array texture to use as a color attachment, you can create an array texture with a depth or stencil format and attach that to the depth or stencil attachment points of the framebuffer object. That texture will then become your depth or stencil buffer, allowing you to perform depth and stencil testing in a layered framebuffer.

```
// Create a texture for our color attachment, bind it, and allocate
// storage for it. This will be 512 x 512 with 16 layers.
GLuint color_attachment;
glGenTextures(1, &color_attachment);

glBindTexture(GL_TEXTURE_2D_ARRAY, color_attachment);
glTexStorage3D(GL_TEXTURE_2D_ARRAY, 1, GL_RGBA8, 512, 512, 16);

// Do the same thing with a depth buffer attachment.
GLuint depth_attachment;
glGenTextures(1, &depth_attachment);

glBindTexture(GL_TEXTURE_2D_ARRAY, depth_attachment);
glTexStorage3D(GL_TEXTURE_2D_ARRAY, 1, GL_DEPTH_COMPONENT, 512, 512, 16);

// Now create a framebuffer object, and bind our textures to it
GLuint fbo;
glGenFramebuffers(1, &fbo);
glBindFramebuffer(GL_FRAMEBUFFER, fbo);

glFramebufferTexture(GL_FRAMEBUFFER, GL_COLOR_ATTACHMENT0,
                     color_attachment, 0);
glFramebufferTexture(GL_FRAMEBUFFER, GL_DEPTH_ATTACHMENT,
                     depth_attachment, 0);

// Finally, tell OpenGL that we plan to render to the color
// attachment
static const GLuint draw_buffers[] = { GL_COLOR_ATTACHMENT0 };

glDrawBuffers(1, draw_buffers);
```

Listing 9.8: Setting up a layered framebuffer

Once you have created an array texture and attached it to a framebuffer object, you can then render into it as normal. If you don't use a geometry shader, all rendering goes into the first layer of the array — the slice at index zero. However, if you wish to render into a different layer, you will need to write a geometry shader. In the geometry shader, the built-in variable gl_Layer is available as an output. When you write a value into gl_Layer, that value will be used to index into the layered framebuffer to select the layer of the attachments to render into. Listing 9.9 shows a simple geometry shader that renders 16 copies of the incoming geometry, each with a different model-view matrix, into an array texture and passes a per-invocation color along to the fragment shader.

```glsl
#version 430 core

// 16 invocations of the geometry shader, triangles in
// and triangles out
layout (invocations = 16, triangles) in;
layout (triangle_strip, max_vertices = 3) out;

in VS_OUT
{
    vec4 color;
    vec3 normal;
} gs_in[];

out GS_OUT
{
    vec4 color;
    vec3 normal;
} gs_out;

// Declare a uniform block with one projection matrix and
// 16 model-view matrices
layout (binding = 0) uniform BLOCK
{
    mat4 proj_matrix;
    mat4 mv_matrix[16];
};

void main(void)
{
    int i;

    // 16 colors to render our geometry
    const vec4 colors[16] = vec4[16](
        vec4(0.0, 0.0, 1.0, 1.0), vec4(0.0, 1.0, 0.0, 1.0),
        vec4(0.0, 1.0, 1.0, 1.0), vec4(1.0, 0.0, 1.0, 1.0),
        vec4(1.0, 1.0, 0.0, 1.0), vec4(1.0, 1.0, 1.0, 1.0),
        vec4(0.0, 0.0, 0.5, 1.0), vec4(0.0, 0.5, 0.0, 1.0),
        vec4(0.0, 0.5, 0.5, 1.0), vec4(0.5, 0.0, 0.0, 1.0),
        vec4(0.5, 0.0, 0.5, 1.0), vec4(0.5, 0.5, 0.0, 1.0),
        vec4(0.5, 0.5, 0.5, 1.0), vec4(1.0, 0.5, 0.5, 1.0),
        vec4(0.5, 1.0, 0.5, 1.0), vec4(0.5, 0.5, 1.0, 1.0)
    );

    for (i = 0; i < gl_in.length(); i++)
    {
        // Pass through all the geometry
        gs_out.color = colors[gl_InvocationID];
        gs_out.normal = mat3(mv_matrix[gl_InvocationID]) * gs_in[i].normal;
        gl_Position = proj_matrix *
                      mv_matrix[gl_InvocationID] *
                      gl_in[i].gl_Position;
        // Assign gl_InvocationID to gl_Layer to direct rendering
        // to the appropriate layer
        gl_Layer = gl_InvocationID;
        EmitVertex();
    }

    EndPrimitive();
}
```

Listing 9.9: Layered rendering using a geometry shader

The result of running the geometry shader shown in Listing 9.9 is that we have an array texture with a different view of a model in each slice. Obviously, we can't directly display the contents of an array texture, so we must now use our texture as the source of data in another shader. The vertex shader in Listing 9.10, along with the corresponding fragment shader in Listing 9.11, displays the contents of an array texture.

```
#version 430 core

out VS_OUT
{
    vec3 tc;
} vs_out;

void main(void)
{
    int vid = gl_VertexID;
    int iid = gl_InstanceID;
    float inst_x = float(iid % 4) / 2.0;
    float inst_y = float(iid >> 2) / 2.0;

    const vec4 vertices[] = vec4[](vec4(-0.5, -0.5, 0.0, 1.0),
                                   vec4( 0.5, -0.5, 0.0, 1.0),
                                   vec4( 0.5,  0.5, 0.0, 1.0),
                                   vec4(-0.5,  0.5, 0.0, 1.0));

    vec4 offs = vec4(inst_x - 0.75, inst_y - 0.75, 0.0, 0.0);

    gl_Position = vertices[vid] *
                vec4(0.25, 0.25, 1.0, 1.0) + offs;
    vs_out.tc = vec3(vertices[vid].xy + vec2(0.5), float(iid));
}
```

Listing 9.10: Displaying an array texture — vertex shader

```
#version 430 core

layout (binding = 0) uniform sampler2DArray tex_array;

layout (location = 0) out vec4 color;

in VS_OUT
{
    vec3 tc;
} fs_in;

void main(void)
{
    color = texture(tex_array, fs_in.tc);
}
```

Listing 9.11: Displaying an array texture — fragment shader

The vertex shader in Listing 9.10 simply produces a quad based on the vertex index. In addition, it offsets the quad using a function of the instance index such that rendering 16 instances will produce a 4 × 4 grid of quads. Finally, it also produces a texture coordinate using the x and y components of the vertex along with the instance index as the third component. Because we will use this to fetch from an array texture, this third component will select the layer. The fragment shader in Listing 9.11 simply reads from the array texture using the supplied texture coordinates and sends the result to the color buffer.

The result of the program is shown in Figure 9.7. As you can see, 16 copies of the torus have been rendered, each with a different color and orientation. Each of the 16 copies is then drawn into the window by reading from a separate layer of the array texture.

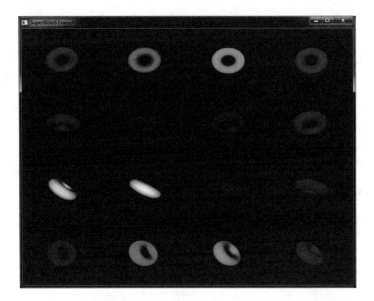

Figure 9.7: Result of the layered rendering example

Rendering into a 3D texture works in almost exactly the same way. You simply attach the whole 3D texture to a framebuffer object as one of its color attachments and then set the gl_Layer output as normal. The value written to gl_Layer becomes the z coordinate of the slice within the 3D texture where data produced by the fragment shader will be written. It's even possible to render into multiple slices of the same texture (array or 3D) at the same. To do this, call **glFramebufferTextureLayer()**, whose prototype is

```
void glFramebufferTextureLayer(GLenum target,
                               GLenum attachment,
                               GLuint texture,
                               GLint level,
                               GLint layer);
```

The **glFramebufferTextureLayer()** function works just like
glFramebufferTexture(), except that it takes one additional parameter,
layer, which specifies the layer of the texture that you wish to attach to
the framebuffer. For instance, the code in Listing 9.12 creates a 2D array
texture with eight layers and attaches each of the layers to the
corresponding color attachment of a framebuffer object.

```
GLuint tex;
glGenTextures(1, &tex);
glBindTexture(GL_TEXTURE_2D_ARRAY, tex);
glTexStorage3D(GL_TEXTURE_2D_ARRAY, 1, GL_RGBA8, 256, 256, 8);

GLuint fbo;
glGenFramebuffers(1, &fbo);
glBindFramebuffer(GL_FRAMEBUFFER, fbo);

int i;
for (i = 0; i < 8; i++)
{
    glFramebufferTextureLayer(GL_FRAMEBUFFER,
                              GL_COLOR_ATTACHMENT0 + i,
                              tex,
                              0,
                              i);
}

static const GLenum draw_buffers[] =
{
    GL_COLOR_ATTACHMENT0, GL_COLOR_ATTACHMENT1,
    GL_COLOR_ATTACHMENT2, GL_COLOR_ATTACHMENT3,
    GL_COLOR_ATTACHMENT4, GL_COLOR_ATTACHMENT5,
    GL_COLOR_ATTACHMENT6, GL_COLOR_ATTACHMENT7
};
glDrawBuffers(8, &draw_buffers[0]);
```

Listing 9.12: Attaching texture layers to a framebuffer

Now, when you render into the framebuffer created in Listing 9.12, your
fragment shader can have up to eight outputs, and each will be written to
a different layer of the texture.

Rendering to Cube Maps

As far as OpenGL is concerned, a cube map is really a special case of an
array texture. A single cube map is just an array of six slices, and a cube
map array texture is an array of an integer multiple of six slices. You attach
a cube map texture to a framebuffer object in exactly the same way as
shown in Listing 9.8, except that rather than creating a 2D array texture,
you create a cube map texture. The cube map has six faces, which are
known as positive and negative x, positive and negative y, and positive
and negative z, and they appear in that order in the array texture. When

you write 0 into gl_Layer in your geometry shader, rendering will go to the positive x face of the cube map. Writing 1 into gl_Layer sends output to the negative x face, writing 2 sends output to the positive y face, and so on, until eventually, writing 5 sends output to the negative z face.

If you create a cube map array texture and attach it to a framebuffer object, writing to the first six layers will render into the first cube, writing the next six layers will write into the second cube, and so on. So, if you set gl_Layer to 6, you will write to the positive x face of the second cube in the array. If you set gl_Layer to 1234, you will render into the positive z face of the 205th face.

Just as with 2D array textures, it's also possible to attach individual faces of a cube map to the various attachment points of a single framebuffer object. In this case, we use the **glFramebufferTexture2D()** function, whose prototype is

```
void glFramebufferTexture2D(GLenum target,
                            GLenum attachment,
                            GLenum textarget,
                            GLuint texture,
                            GLint level);
```

Again, this function works just like **glFramebufferTexture()**, except that it has one additional parameter, textarget. This can be set to specify which face of the cube map you want to attach to the attachment. To attach the cube map's positive x face, set this to GL_CUBE_MAP_POSITIVE_X; for the negative x face, set it to GL_CUBE_MAP_NEGATIVE_X. Similar tokens are available for the y and z faces, too. Using this, you could bind all of the faces of a single cube map[4] to the attachment points on a single framebuffer and render into all of them at the same time.

Framebuffer Completeness

Before we can finish up with framebuffer objects, there is one last important topic. Just because you are happy with the way you set up your FBO doesn't mean your OpenGL implementation is ready to render. The only way to find out if your FBO is set up correctly and in a way that the implementation can use it is to check for *framebuffer completeness*. Framebuffer completeness is similar in concept to texture completeness. If a texture doesn't have all required mipmap levels specified with the right sizes, formats, and so on, that texture is incomplete and can't be used.

---

4. While this is certainly possible, rendering the same thing to all faces of a cube map has limited utility.

There are two categories of completeness: attachment completeness and whole framebuffer completeness.

Attachment Completeness

Each attachment point of an FBO must meet certain criteria to be considered complete. If any attachment point is incomplete, the whole framebuffer will also be incomplete. Some of the cases that cause an attachment to be incomplete are

- No image is associated with the attached object.

- Width or height of zero for attached image.

- A non-color renderable format is attached to a color attachment.

- A non-depth renderable format is attached to a depth attachment.

- A non-stencil renderable format is attached to a stencil attachment.

Whole Framebuffer Completeness

Not only does each attachment point have to be valid and meet certain criteria, but the framebuffer object as a whole must also be complete. The default framebuffer, if one exists, will always be complete. Common cases for the whole framebuffer being incomplete are

- **glDrawBuffers()** has mapped an output to an FBO attachment where no image is attached.

- The combination of internal formats is not supported by the OpenGL driver.

Checking the Framebuffer

When you think you are finished setting up an FBO, you can check to see whether it is complete by calling

```
GLenum fboStatus = glCheckFramebufferStatus(GL_DRAW_FRAMEBUFFER);
```

If **glCheckFramebufferStatus()** returns GL_FRAMEBUFFER_COMPLETE, all is well, and you may use the FBO. The return value of **glCheckFramebufferStatus()** provides clues to what might be wrong if the framebuffer is not complete. Table 9.7 describes all possible return conditions and what they mean.

Many of these return values are helpful when debugging an application but are less useful after an application has shipped. Nonetheless, the first sample application checks to make sure none of these conditions occurred. It pays to do this check in applications that use FBOs, making sure your use case hasn't hit some implementation-dependent limitation. An example of how this might look is shown in Listing 9.13.

Table 9.7: Framebuffer Completeness Return Values

Return Value (GL_FRAMEBUFFER_*)	Description
UNDEFINED	The current FBO binding is 0, but no default framebuffer exists.
COMPLETE	A user-defined FBO is bound and is complete. OK to render.
INCOMPLETE_ATTACHMENT	One of the buffers enabled for rendering is incomplete.
INCOMPLETE_MISSING_ATTACHMENT	No buffers are attached to the FBO and it is not configured for rendering without attachments.
UNSUPPORTED	The combination of internal buffer formats is not supported.
INCOMPLETE_LAYER_TARGETS	Not all color attachments are layered textures or bound to the same target.

```
GLenum fboStatus = glCheckFramebufferStatus(GL_DRAW_FRAMEBUFFER);
if(fboStatus != GL_FRAMEBUFFER_COMPLETE)
{
    switch (fboStatus)
    {
    case GL_FRAMEBUFFER_UNDEFINED:
        // Oops, no window exists?
        break;
    case GL_FRAMEBUFFER_INCOMPLETE_ATTACHMENT:
        // Check the status of each attachment
        break;
    case GL_FRAMEBUFFER_INCOMPLETE_MISSING_ATTACHMENT:
        // Attach at least one buffer to the FBO
        break;
    case GL_FRAMEBUFFER_INCOMPLETE_DRAW_BUFFER:
        // Check that all attachments enabled via
        // glDrawBuffers exist in FBO
    case GL_FRAMEBUFFER_INCOMPLETE_READ_BUFFER:
        // Check that the buffer specified via
        // glReadBuffer exists in FBO
        break;
```

```
    case GL_FRAMEBUFFER_UNSUPPORTED:
        // Reconsider formats used for attached buffers
        break;
    case GL_FRAMEBUFFER_INCOMPLETE_MULTISAMPLE:
        // Make sure the number of samples for each
        // attachment is the same
        break;
    case GL_FRAMEBUFFER_INCOMPLETE_LAYER_TARGETS:
        // Make sure the number of layers for each
        // attachment is the same
        break;
    }
}
```

Listing 9.13: Checking completeness of a framebuffer object

If you attempt to perform any command that reads from or writes to the framebuffer while an incomplete FBO is bound, the command simply returns after throwing the error GL_INVALID_FRAMEBUFFER_OPERATION, retrievable by calling **glGetError()**.

Read Framebuffers Need to Be Complete, Too!

In the previous examples, we test the FBO attached to the draw buffer binding point, GL_DRAW_FRAMEBUFFER. But a framebuffer attached to GL_READ_FRAMEBUFFER also has to be attachment complete and whole framebuffer complete for reads to work. Because only one read buffer can be enabled at a time, making sure an FBO is complete for reading is a little easier.

Rendering in Stereo

Most[5] human beings have two eyes. We use these two eyes to help us judge distance by providing parallax shift — a slight difference between the images our two eyes see. There are many depth queues, including depth from focus, from differences in lighting and the relative movement of objects as we move our point of view. OpenGL is able to produce pairs of images that, depending on the display device used, can be presented separately to your two eyes and increase the sense of depth of the image. There are plenty of display devices available including binocular displays (devices with a separate physical display for each eye), shutter and polarized displays that require glasses to view, and autostereoscopic displays that don't require that you put anything on your face. OpenGL

---

5. Those readers with less than two eyes may wish to skip to the next section.

doesn't really care about how the image is displayed, only that you wish to render two views of the scene — one for the left eye and one for the right.

To display images in stereo requires some cooperation from the windowing or operating system, and therefore the mechanism to create a stereo display is platform specific. The gory details of this are covered for a number of platforms in Chapter 14. For now, we can use the facilities provided by the sb6 application framework to create our stereo window for us. In your application, you can override sb6::application::init, call the base class function, and then set info.flags.stereo to 1 as shown in Listing 9.14. Because some OpenGL implementations may require your application to cover the whole display (which is known as full-screen rendering), you can also set the info.flags.fullscreen flag in your init function to make the application use a full-screen window.

```
void my_application::init()
{
    info.flags.stereo = 1;
    info.flags.fullscreen = 1;   // Set this if your OpenGL
                                 // implementation requires
                                 // fullscreen for stereo rendering.
}
```

Listing 9.14: Creating a stereo window

Remember, not all displays support stereo output, and not all OpenGL implementations will allow you to create a stereo window. However, if you have access to the necessary display and OpenGL implementation, you should have a window that runs in stereo. Now we need to render into it. The simplest way to render in stereo is to simply draw the entire scene twice. Before rendering into the left eye image, call

```
glDrawBuffer(GL_BACK_LEFT);
```

When you want to render into the right eye image, call

```
glDrawBuffer(GL_BACK_RIGHT);
```

In order to produce a pair of images with a compelling depth effect, you need to construct transformation matrices representing the views observed by the left and right eyes. Remember, our model matrix transforms our model into world space, and world space is global, applying the same way regardless of the viewer. However, the view matrix essentially transforms the world into the frame of the viewer. As the viewer is in a different location for each of the eyes, the view matrix must be different for each of the two eyes. Therefore, when we render to the left view, we use the left view matrix, and when we're rendering to the right view, we use the right view matrix.

The simplest form of stereo view matrix pairs simply translates the left and right views away from each other on the horizontal axis. Optionally, you can also rotate the view matrices inwards towards the center of view. Alternatively, you can use the vmath::lookat function to generate your view matrices for you. Simply place your eye at the left eye location (slightly left of the viewer position) and the center of the object of interest to create the left view matrix, and then do the same with the right eye position to create the right view matrix. Listing 9.15 shows how this is done.

```
void my_application::render(double currentTime)
{
    static const vmath::vec3 origin(0.0f);
    static const vmath::vec3 up_vector(0.0f, 1.0f, 0.0f);
    static const vmath::vec3 eye_separation(0.01f, 0.0f, 0.0f);

    vmath::mat4 left_view_matrix =
        vmath::lookat(eye_location - eye_separation,
                      origin,
                      up_vector);

    vmath::mat4 right_view_matrix =
        vmath::lookat(eye_location + eye_separation,
                      origin,
                      up_vector);

    static const GLfloat black[] = { 0.0f, 0.0f ,0.0f, 0.0f };
    static const GLfloat one = 1.0f;

    // Setting the draw buffer to GL_BACK ends up drawing in
    // both the back left and back right buffers. Clear both
    glDrawBuffer(GL_BACK);
    glClearBufferfv(GL_COLOR, 0, black);
    glClearBufferfv(GL_DEPTH, 0, &one);

    // Now, set the draw buffer to back left
    glDrawBuffer(GL_BACK_LEFT);

    // Set our left model-view matrix product
    glUniformMatrix4fv(model_view_loc, 1,
                       left_view_matrix * model_matrix);

    // Draw the scene
    draw_scene();

    // Set the draw buffer to back right
    glDrawBuffer(GL_BACK_RIGHT);

    // Set the right model-view matrix product
    glUniformMatrix4fv(model_view_loc, 1,
                       right_view_matrix * model_matrix);

    // Draw the scene... again.
    draw_scene();
}
```

Listing 9.15: Drawing into a stereo window

Clearly, the code in Listing 9.15 renders the entire scene twice. Depending on the complexity of your scene, that could be very, very expensive — literally doubling the cost of rendering the scene. One possible tactic is to switch between the GL_BACK_LEFT and GL_BACK_RIGHT draw buffers between each and every object in your scene. This can mean that updates to state (such as binding textures or changing the current program) can be performed only once, but changing the draw buffer can be as expensive as any other state-changing function. As we learned earlier in the chapter, though, it's possible to render into more than one buffer at a time by outputting two vectors from your fragment shader. In fact, consider what would happen if you used a fragment shader with two outputs and then call

```
static const GLenum buffers[] = { GL_BACK_LEFT, GL_BACK_RIGHT }
glDrawBuffers(2, buffers);
```

After this, the first output of your fragment shader will be written to the left eye buffer, and the second will be written to the right eye buffer. This is great! Now we can render both eyes at the same time! Well, not so fast. Remember, even though the fragment shader can output to a number of different draw buffers, the location within each of those buffers will be the same. How do we draw a different image into each of the buffers?

What we can do is use a geometry shader to render into a layered framebuffer with two layers, one for the left eye and one for the right eye. We will use geometry shader instancing to run the geometry shader twice, and write the invocation index into the layer to direct the two copies of the data into the two layers of the framebuffer. In each invocation of the geometry shader, we can select one of two model-view matrices and essentially perform all of the work of the vertex shader in the geometry shader. Once we're done rendering the whole scene, the framebuffer's two layers will contain the left and right eye images. All that is needed now is to render a full-screen quad with a fragment shader that reads from the two layers of the array texture and writes the result into its two outputs, which are directed into the left and right eye views.

Listing 9.16 shows the simple geometry shader that we'll use in our application to render both views of our stereo scene in a single pass.

```
#version 430 core

layout (triangles, invocations = 2) in;
layout (triangle_strip, max_vertices = 3) out;

uniform matrices
{
```

```
        mat4 model_matrix;
        mat4 view_matrix[2];
        mat4 projection_matrix;
};

in VS_OUT
{
    vec4 color;
    vec3 normal;
    vec2 texture_coord;
} gs_in[];

out GS_OUT
{
    vec4 color;
    vec3 normal;
    vec2 texture_coord;
} gs_out;

void main(void)
{
    // Calculate a model-view matrix for the current eye
    mat4 model_view_matrix = view_matrix[gl_InvocationID] *
                             model_matrix;

    for (int i = 0; i < gl_in.length(); i++)
    {
        // Output layer is invocation ID
        gl_Layer = gl_InvocationID;
        // Multiply by the model matrix, view matrix for the
        // appropriate eye and then the projection matrix.
        gl_Position = projection_matrix *
                      model_view_matrix *
                      gl_in[i].gl_Position;
        gs_out.color = gs_in[i].color;
        // Don't forget to transform the normals...
        gs_out.normal = mat3(model_view_matrix) * gs_in[i].normal;
        gs_out.texcoord = gs_in[i].texcoord;
        EmitVertex();
    }

    EndPrimitive();
}
```

Listing 9.16: Rendering to two layers with a geometry shader

Now that we've rendered our scene into our layered framebuffer, we can attach the underlying array texture and draw a full-screen quad to copy the result into the left and right back buffers with a single shader. Such a shader is shown in Listing 9.17.

```
#version 430 core

layout (location = 0) out vec4 color_left;
layout (location = 1) out vec4 color_right;

in vec2 tex_coord;

uniform sampler2DArray back_buffer;
```

```
void main(void)
{
    color_left = texture(back_buffer, vec3(tex_coord, 0.0));
    color_right = texture(back_buffer, vec3(tex_coord, 1.0));
}
```

Listing 9.17: Copying from an array texture to a stereo back buffer

A photograph running this application is shown in Figure 9.8. A photograph is necessary here as a screenshot would not show both of the images in the stereo pair. However, the double image produced by stereo rendering is clearly visible in the photograph.

Figure 9.8: Result of stereo rendering to a stereo display

Antialiasing

Aliasing is an artifact of *under-sampling* data. It is a term commonly used in signal processing fields. When aliasing occurs in an audio signal, it can be heard as a high-pitched whining or crunching sound. You may have noticed this in old video games, musical greeting cards, or children's toys that often include low-cost playback devices. Aliasing occurs when the rate at which a signal is sampled (the sampling rate) is too low for the content of that signal. The rate at which a sample must be sampled in order to preserve (most of) its content is known as the Nyquist rate, and is twice the frequency of the highest frequency component present in the signal to be captured. In image terms, aliasing manifests as jagged edges wherever there is sharp contrast. These edges are sometimes referred to as *jaggies*.

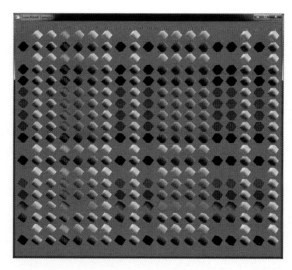

Color Plate 1: All possible combinations of blend functions

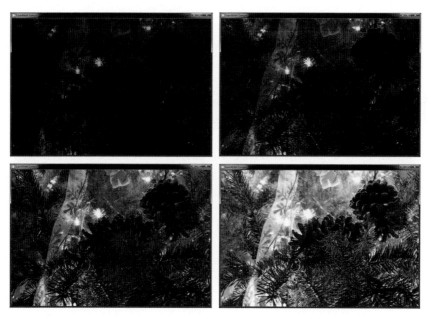

Color Plate 2: Different views of an HDR image

Color Plate 3: Adaptive tone mapping

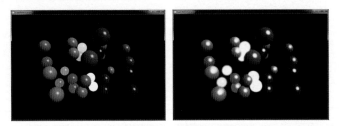

Color Plate 4: Bloom filtering: no bloom (left) and bloom (right)

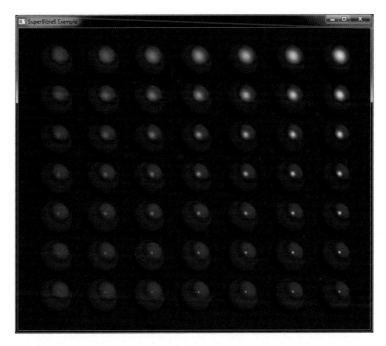

Color Plate 5: Varying specular parameters of a material

Color Plate 6: Result of rim lighting example

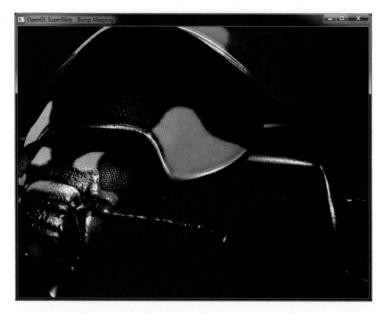

Color Plate 7: Normal mapping in action

Color Plate 8: Depth of field applied to an image

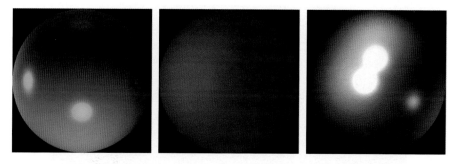

Color Plate 9: A selection of spherical environment maps

Color Plate 10: A golden environment-mapped dragon

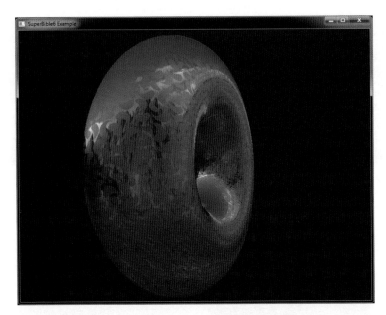

Color Plate 11: Result of per-pixel gloss example

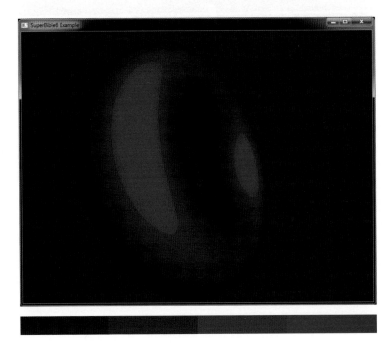

Color Plate 12: Toon shading output with color ramp

Color Plate 13: Real-time rendering of the Julia set

Color Plate 14: Ray tracing with four bounces

Color Plate 15: OpenGL ES rendering on a cell phone

There are two main approaches to deal with aliasing. The first is filtering, which removes high-frequency content from the signal before or during sampling. The second is increasing the sampling rate, which allows the higher frequency content to be recorded. The additional samples captured can then be processed for storage or reproduction. Methods for reducing or eliminating aliasing are known as *antialiasing* techniques. OpenGL includes a number of ways to apply antialiasing to your scene. These include filtering geometry as it is rendered, and various forms of over-sampling.

Antialiasing by Filtering

The first and simplest way to deal with the aliasing problem is to filter primitives as they are drawn. To do this, OpenGL calculates the *amount* of a pixel that is covered by a primitive (point, line, or triangle) and uses it to generate an alpha value for each fragment. This alpha value is multiplied by the alpha value of the fragment produced by your shader and so has an effect on blending when either the source or destination blend factor includes the source alpha term. Now, as fragments are drawn to the screen, they are blended with its existing content using a function of the pixel coverage.

To turn on this form of antialiasing, we need to do two things. First, we need to enable blending and choose an appropriate blending function. Second, we need to enable GL_LINE_SMOOTH to apply antialiasing to lines and GL_POLYGON_SMOOTH to apply antialiasing to triangles. Figure 9.9 shows the result of doing this.

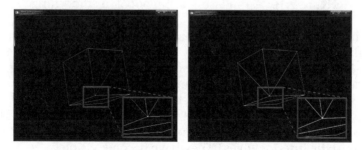

Figure 9.9: Antialiasing using line smoothing

On the left of Figure 9.9, we have drawn our spinning cube in line mode and zoomed in on a section of the image where a number of edges join each other. In the inset, the aliasing artifacts are clearly visible — notice the jagged edges. In the image on the right of Figure 9.9, line smoothing and blending are enabled, but the scene is otherwise unchanged. Notice how the lines appear much smoother and the jagged edges are much reduced. Zooming into the inset, we see that the lines have been blurred slightly. This is the effect of filtering that is produced by calculating the coverage of the lines and using it to blend them with the background color. The code to set up antialiasing and blending in order to render the image is shown in Listing 9.18.

```
glEnable(GL_BLEND);
glBlendFunc(GL_SRC_ALPHA, GL_ONE_MINUS_SRC_ALPHA);
glEnable(GL_LINE_SMOOTH);
```

Listing 9.18: Turning on line smoothing

Listing 9.18 seems pretty simple, doesn't it? Surely, if it's that simple, we should be able to turn this on for any geometry we like and everything will just look better. Well, no, that's not really true. This form of antialiasing only works in limited cases like the one shown in Figure 9.9. Take a look at the images in Figure 9.10.

Figure 9.10: Antialiasing using polygon smoothing

The left image in Figure 9.10 shows our cube rendered in solid white. You can see that the jaggies in the middle where the individual triangles abut aren't visible, but on the edges of the cube, we can see the aliasing effect quite clearly. In the image on the right of Figure 9.10, we have turned on polygon smoothing using code almost identical to that of Listing 9.18, only substituting GL_POLYGON_SMOOTH for GL_LINE_SMOOTH. Now, although the edges of the cube are smoothed and the jaggies are mostly gone, what happened to the interior edges? They have become visible!

Consider what happens when the edge between two adjoining triangles cuts exactly halfway through the middle of a pixel. First, our application clears the framebuffer to black, and then our first white triangle hits that pixel. OpenGL calculates that half the pixel is covered by the triangle, and uses an alpha value of 0.5 in the blending equation. This mixes half and half white and black, producing a mid-gray pixel. Next, our second, adjacent triangle comes along and covers the other half of the pixel. Again, OpenGL figures that half the pixel is covered by the new triangle and mixes the white of the triangle with the existing framebuffer content... except now the framebuffer is 50% gray! Mixing white and 50% gray produces 75% gray, which is the color we see in the lines between the triangles.

Ultimately, whenever a polygon edge cuts part of the way through a pixel and is written to the screen, OpenGL has no way to know *which part* is already covered and which part is not. This leads to artifacts like those seen in Figure 9.10. Another significant issue with this method is that there is only one depth value for each pixel, which means that if a triangle pokes into a not-yet-covered part of a pixel, it may still fail the depth test and not contribute at all if there's already a closer triangle covering a different part of that same pixel.

To circumvent these problems, we need more advanced antialiasing methods, all of which include increasing the sample count.

Multi-sample Antialiasing

To increase the sample rate of the image, OpenGL supports storing multiple samples for every pixel on the screen. This technique is known as *multi-sample antialiasing* or MSAA. Rather than sampling each primitive only once, OpenGL will sample the primitive at multiple locations within the pixel and, if any are hit, run your shader. Whatever color your shader produces is written into all of the hit samples. The actual location of the samples within each pixel might be different on different OpenGL implementations. Figure 9.11 shows an example arrangement of the sample positions for 1, 2, 4, and 8 sample arrangements.

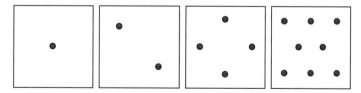

Figure 9.11: Antialiasing sample positions

Turning on MSAA for the default framebuffer is somewhat platform specific. In most cases, you need to specify a multi-sampled format for the default framebuffer when you set up your rendering window. In the sample programs included with this book, the application framework takes care of this for you. To enable multi-sampling with the sb6::application framework, simply override the sb6::application::init() function, call the base class method, and then set the samples member of the info structure to the desired sample count. Listing 9.19 shows an example of this.

```
virtual void init()
{
    sb6::application::init();

    info.samples = 8;
}
```

Listing 9.19: Choosing 8-sample antialiasing

After choosing 8-sample antialiasing and rendering our trusty spinning cube, we are presented with the images shown in Figure 9.12.

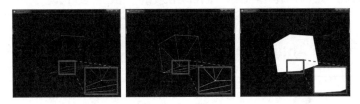

Figure 9.12: No antialiasing (left) and 8-sample antialiasing (center and right)

In the leftmost image of Figure 9.12, no antialiasing is applied and we are given jaggies as normal. In the center image, we can see that antialiasing has been applied to the lines, but the result doesn't look that dissimilar to the image produced by enabling GL_LINE_SMOOTH, as shown in Figure 9.9. However, the real difference is shown in the rightmost image of Figure 9.11. Here, we will have good quality antialiasing along the edges of our polygons, but the inner abutting edges of the triangles no longer show gray artifacts.

If you create a multi-sampled framebuffer, then multi-sampling is enabled by default. However, if you wish to render without multi-sampling even though the current framebuffer has a multi-sampled format, you can turn multi-sampling off by calling

```
glDisable(GL_MULTISAMPLE);
```

and of course, you can turn it back on again by calling

```
glEnable(GL_MULTISAMPLE);
```

When multi-sampling is disabled, OpenGL proceeds as if the framebuffer were a normal single-sample framebuffer and samples each fragment once. The only difference being that the shading results are written to every sample in the pixel.

Multi-sample Textures

You have already learned about how to render into off-screen textures using a framebuffer object, and you have learned about how to perform antialiasing using multi-sampling. However, the multi-sampled color buffer has been owned by the window system. It's possible to combine both of these features and create an off-screen multi-sampled color buffer to render into. To do this, we can create a *multi-sampled texture* and attach it to a framebuffer object for rendering into.

To create a multi-sampled texture, create a texture name as normal and bind it to one of the multi-sampled texture targets such as GL_TEXTURE_2D_MULTISAMPLE or GL_TEXTURE_2D_MULTISAMPLE_ARRAY. Then, allocate storage for it using **glTexStorage2DMultisample()** or **glTexStorage3DMultisample()** (for array textures), whose prototypes are

```
void glTexStorage2DMultisample(GLenum target,
                               GLsizei samples,
                               GLenum internalformat,
                               GLsizei width,
                               GLsizei height,
                               GLboolean fixedsamplelocations);

void glTexStorage3DMultisample(GLenum target,
                               GLsizei samples,
                               GLenum internalformat,
                               GLsizei width,
                               GLsizei height,
                               GLsizei depth,
                               GLboolean fixedsamplelocations);
```

These two functions behave pretty much like **glTexStorage2D()** and **glTexStorage3D()**, but with a couple of extra parameter. The first, samples, tells OpenGL how many samples should be in the texture. The second, fixedsamplelocations, tells OpenGL whether you want it to use standard sample locations for all texels in the texture or whether it is allowed to vary sample locations spatially within the texture. In general, allowing OpenGL to do this can improve image quality, but it may reduce consistency and even cause artifacts if your application relies on the same object being rendered in exactly the same way regardless of where it is in the framebuffer.

Once you have allocated storage for your texture, you can attach it to a framebuffer with **glFramebufferTexture()** as normal. An example of creating a depth and a color multi-sample texture is shown in Listing 9.20.

```
GLuint color_ms_tex;
GLuint depth_ms_tex;

glGenTextures(1, &color_ms_tex);
glBindTexture(GL_TEXTURE_2D_MULTISAMPLE, color_ms_tex);
glTexStorage2DMultisample(GL_TEXTURE_2D_MULTISAMPLE,
                          8, GL_RGBA8, 1024, 1024, GL_TRUE);
glGenTextures(1, &depth_ms_tex);
glBindTexture(GL_TEXTURE_2D_MULTISAMPLE, depth_ms_tex);
glTexStorage2DMultisample(GL_TEXTURE_2D_MULTISAMPLE,
                          8, GL_DEPTH_COMPONENT, 1024, 1024, GL_TRUE);

GLuint fbo;

glGenFramebuffers(1, &fbo);
glBindFramebuffer(GL_FRAMEBUFFER);
glFramebufferTexture(GL_FRAMEBUFFER, GL_COLOR_ATTACHMENT0,
                     color_ms_tex, 0);
glFramebufferTexture(GL_FRAMEBUFFER, GL_DEPTH_ATTACHMENT,
                     depth_ms_tex, 0);
```

Listing 9.20: Setting up a multi-sample framebuffer attachment

Multi-sample textures have several restrictions. First, there are no 1D or 3D multi-sample textures, and second, multi-sample textures cannot have mipmaps. The **glTexStorage3DMultisample()** function is only for allocating storage for 2D multi-sample array textures, and neither it nor **glTexStorage2DMultisample()** accept a levels parameter. As a result, you may only pass 0 as the level parameter to **glFramebufferTexture()**. Furthermore, you can't just use a multi-sample texture like any other texture, and they don't support filtering. Rather, you must explicitly read texels from the multi-sample texture in your shader by declaring a special multi-sampled sampler type. The multi-sample sampler types in GLSL are **sampler2DMS** and **sampler2DMSArray**, which represent 2D multi-sample and multi-sample array textures, respectively. Additionally, there are **isampler2DMS** and **usampler2DMS** types, which represent signed and unsigned integer multi-sample textures, and **isampler2DMSArray** and **usampler2DMSArray**, which represent the array forms.

A typical use for sampling from multi-sample textures in a shader is to perform custom resolve operations. When you render into a window-system-owned multi-sampled back buffer, you don't have a whole lot of control over how OpenGL will combine the color values of the samples contributing to a pixel to produce its final color. However, if you render into a multi-sample texture and then draw a full-screen quad using a fragment shader that samples from that texture and combines its samples with code you supply, then you can implement any algorithm you wish. The example shown in Listing 9.21 demonstrates taking the brightest sample of those contained in each pixel.

```
#version 430 core

uniform sampler2DMS input_image;

out vec4 color;

void main(void)
{
    ivec2 coord = ivec2(gl_FragCoord.xy);
    vec4 result = vec4(0.0);
    int i;

    for (i = 0; i < 8; i++)
    {
        result = max(result, texelFetch(input_image, coord, i));
    }

    color = result;
}
```

Listing 9.21: Simple multi-sample "maximum" resolve

Sample Coverage

Coverage refers to how much of a pixel a fragment "covers." The coverage of a fragment is normally calculated by OpenGL as part of the rasterization process. However, you have some control over this and can actually generate new coverage information in your fragment shader. There are three ways to do this.

First, you can have OpenGL convert the alpha value of a fragment directly to a coverage value to determine how many samples of the framebuffer will be updated by the fragment. To do this, pass the GL_SAMPLE_ALPHA_TO_COVERAGE parameter to **glEnable()**. The coverage value for a fragment is used to determine how many subsamples will be written. For instance, a fragment with an alpha of 0.4 would generate a coverage value of 40%. When you use this method, OpenGL will first calculate the coverage for each of the samples in each pixel, producing a *sample mask*. It then calculates a second mask using the alpha value that your shader produces and then logically ANDs it with the incoming sample mask. For example, if OpenGL determines that 66% the pixel is originally covered by the primitive, and then you produce an alpha value of 40%, then it will produce an output sample mask of 40% × 66%, which is roughly 25%. Thus, for an 8-sample MSAA buffer, two of that pixel's samples would be written to.

Because the alpha value was already used to decide how many subsamples should be written, it wouldn't make sense to then blend those subsamples with the same alpha value. To help prevent these subpixels from also being blended when blending is enabled, you can force the alpha values for those samples to 1 by calling **glEnable()** (GL_SAMPLE_ALPHA_TO_ONE).

Using alpha-to-coverage has several advantages over simple blending. When rendering to a multi-sampled buffer, the alpha blend would normally be applied equally to the entire pixel. With alpha-to-coverage, alpha masked edges are antialiased, producing a much more natural and smooth result. This is particularly useful when drawing bushes, trees, or dense foliage where parts of the brush are alpha transparent.

Next, OpenGL also allows you to set the sample coverage manually by calling **glSampleCoverage()**, whose prototype is

```
void glSampleCoverage(GLfloat value,
                      GLboolean invert);
```

Manually applying a coverage value for a pixel occurs after the mask for alpha-to-coverage is applied. For this step to take effect, sample coverage must be enabled by calling

```
glEnable(GL_SAMPLE_COVERAGE);
glSampleCoverage(value, invert);
```

The coverage value passed into the value parameter can be between 0 and 1. The invert parameter signals to OpenGL if the resulting mask should be inverted. For instance, if you were drawing two overlapping trees, one with a coverage of 60% and the other with 40%, you would want to invert one of the coverage values to make sure the same mask was not used for both draw calls.

```
glSampleCoverage(0.5, GL_FALSE);
// Draw first geometry set
. . .
glSampleCoverage(0.5, GL_TRUE);
// Draw second geometry set
. . .
```

The third way that you can generate coverage information is to explicitly set it right in your fragment shader. To facilitate this, you can use two built-in variables, gl_SampleMaskIn[] and gl_SampleMask[], that are available to fragment shaders. The first is an input and contains the coverage information generated by OpenGL during rasterization. The second variable is an output that you can write to in the shader to update coverage. Each bit of each element of the arrays corresponds to a single sample (starting from the least significant bit). If the OpenGL implementation supports more than 32 samples in a single framebuffer, then the first element of the array contains coverage information for the first 32 samples, the second element contains information about the next 32, and so on.

The bits in gl_SampleMaskIn[] are set if OpenGL considered that particular sample covered. You can copy this array directly into gl_SampleMask[] and pass the information straight through without having any effect on coverage. If, however, you turn samples off during this process, they will effectively be discarded. While you can turn bits on in gl_SampleMask[] that weren't on in gl_SampleMaskIn[], this will have no effect as OpenGL will just turn them off again for you. There's a simple work-around for this. Just disable multi-sampling by calling **glDisable()** and passing GL_MULTISAMPLE as described earlier. Now, when your shader runs, gl_SampleMaskIn[] will indicate that all samples are covered and you can turn bits off at your leisure.

Sample Rate Shading

Multi-sample antialiasing solves a number of issues related to under-sampling geometry. In particular, it captures fine geometric details and correctly handles partially covered pixels, overlapping primitives, and other sources of artifacts at the boundaries of lines and triangles. However, it cannot cope with whatever your shader throws at it elegantly. Remember, under normal circumstances, once OpenGL determines that a triangle hits a pixel, it will run your shader once and broadcast the resulting output to each sample that was covered by the triangle. This cannot accurately capture the result of a shader that itself produces high-frequency output. For example, consider the fragment shader shown in Listing 9.22.

```
#version 430 core

out vec4 color;

in VS_OUT
{
    vec2 tc;
} fs_in;

void main(void)
```

```
{
    float val = abs(fs_in.tc.x + fs_in.tc.y) * 20.0f;
    color = vec4(fract(val) >= 0.5 ? 1.0 : 0.25);
}
```

Listing 9.22: Fragment shader producing high-frequency output

This extremely simple shader produces stripes with hard edges (which produce a high-frequency signal). For any given invocation of the shader, the output will either be bright white or dark gray, depending on the incoming texture coordinates. If you look at the image on the left of Figure 9.13, you will see that the jaggies have returned. The outline of the cube is still nicely smoothed, but *inside* the triangles, the stripes produced by our shader are jagged and badly aliased.

Figure 9.13: Antialiasing of high-frequency shader output

To produce the image on the right of Figure 9.13, we enabled *sample-rate shading*. In this mode, OpenGL will run your shader for each and every sample that a primitive hits. Be careful, though, as for 8-sample buffers, your shader will become 8 times more expensive! To enable sample rate shading, call

```
glEnable(GL_SAMPLE_SHADING);
```

and to disable sample rate shading, call

```
glDisable(GL_SAMPLE_SHADING);
```

Once you have enabled sample shading, you also need to let OpenGL know what portion of the samples it should run your shader for. By default, simply enabling sample shading won't do anything, and OpenGL will still run your shader once for each pixel. To tell OpenGL what fraction of the samples you want to shade independently, call **glMinSampleShading()**, whose prototype is

```
void glMinSampleShading(GLfloat value);
```

For example, if you want OpenGL to run your shader for at least half of the samples in the framebuffer, set the value parameter set to 0.5f. To uniquely shade every sample hit by the geometry, set value to 1.0f. As you can see from the right image of Figure 9.13, the jaggies on the interior of the cube have been eliminated. We set the minimum sampling fraction to 1.0 to create this image.

Centroid Sampling

The centroid storage qualifier controls where in a pixel OpenGL interpolates the inputs to the fragment shader to. It only applies to situations where you're rendering into a multi-sampled framebuffer. You specify the centroid storage qualifier just like any other storage qualifier that is applied to an input or output variable. To create a varying that has the centroid storage qualifier, first, in the vertex, tessellation control, or geometry shader, declare the output with the centroid keyword:

```
centroid out vec2 tex_coord;
```

And then in the fragment shader, declare the same input with the centroid keyword:

```
centroid in vec2 tex_coord;
```

You can also apply the centroid qualifier to an interface block to cause all of the members of the block to be interpolated to the fragment's centroid:

```
centroid out VS_OUT
{
    vec2 tex_coord;
} vs_out;
```

Now tex_coord (or vs_out.tex_coord) is defined to use the centroid storage qualifier. If you have a single-sampled draw buffer, this makes no difference, and the inputs that reach the fragment shader are interpolated to the pixel's center. Where centroid sampling becomes useful is when you are rendering to a multi-sampled draw buffer. According to the OpenGL Specification, when centroid sampling is not specified (the default), fragment shader varyings will be interpolated to "the pixel's center, or anywhere within the pixel, or to one of the pixel's samples" — which basically means anywhere within the pixel. When you're in the middle of a large triangle, this doesn't really matter. Where it becomes important is when you're shading a pixel that lies right on the edge of the triangle — where an edge of the triangle cuts through the pixel. Figure 9.14 shows an example of how OpenGL might sample from a triangle.

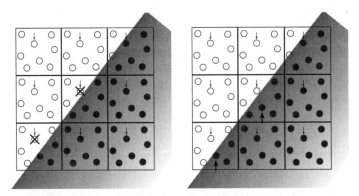

Figure 9.14: Partially covered multi-sampled pixels

Take a look at the left of Figure 9.14. It shows the edge of a triangle passing through several pixels. The solid dots represent samples that are covered by the triangle, and the clear dots represent those that are not. OpenGL has chosen to interpolate the fragment shader inputs to the sample closest to the pixel's center. Those samples are indicated by a small downwards-pointing arrow.

For the pixels in the upper left, this is fine — they are entirely uncovered and the fragment shader will not run for those pixels. Likewise, the pixels in the lower right are fully covered. The fragment shader will run, but it doesn't really matter which sample it runs for. The pixels along the edge of the triangle, however, present a problem. Because OpenGL has chosen the sample closest to the pixel center as its interpolation point, your fragment shader inputs could actually be interpolated to a point that lies *outside* the triangle! Those samples are marked with an X. Imagine what would happen if you used the input, say, to sample from a texture. If the texture was aligned such that its edge was supposed to match the edge of the triangle, the texture coordinates would lie outside the texture. At best, you would get a slightly incorrect image. At worst, it would produce noticeable artifacts.

If we declare our inputs with the `centroid` storage qualifier, the OpenGL Specification says that "the value must be interpolated to a point that lies in both the pixel and in the primitive being rendered, or to one of the pixel's samples that falls within the primitive." That means that OpenGL chooses, for each pixel, a sample that is certainly within the triangle to which to interpolate all varyings. You are safe to use the inputs to the fragment shader for any purpose, and you know that they are valid and have not been interpolated to a point outside the triangle.

Now look at the right side of Figure 9.14. OpenGL has still chosen to interpolate the fragment shader inputs to the samples closest to the pixel centers for fully covered pixels. However, for those pixels that are partially covered, it has instead chosen another sample that lies within the triangle (marked with larger arrows). This means that the inputs presented to the fragment shader are valid and refer to points that are inside the triangle. You can use them for sampling from a texture or use them in a function whose result is only defined within a certain range and know that you will get meaningful results.

You may be wondering whether using the `centroid` storage qualifier guarantees that you're going to get valid results in your fragment shader and not using it may mean that the inputs are interpolated outside the primitive, why not turn on centroid sampling all the time? Well, there are some drawbacks to using centroid sampling.

The most significant is that OpenGL can provide the gradients (or differentials) of inputs to the fragment shader. Implementations may differ, but most use discrete differentials, taking deltas between the values of the same inputs from adjacent pixels. This works well when the inputs are interpolated to the same position within each pixel. In this case, it doesn't matter which sample position is chosen; the samples will always be exactly one pixel apart. However, when centroid sampling is enabled for an input, the values for adjacent pixels may actually be interpolated to different positions within those pixels. That means that the samples are not exactly one pixel apart, and the discrete differentials presented to the fragment shader could be inaccurate. If accurate gradients are required in the fragment shader, it is probably best not to use centroid sampling. Don't forget, the calculations that OpenGL performs during mipmapping depend on gradients of texture coordinates, and so using a `centroid` qualified input as the source of texture coordinates to a mipmapped texture could lead to inaccurate results.

Using Centroid Sampling to Perform Edge Detection

An interesting use case for centroid sampling is hardware-accelerated edge detection. You just learned that using the `centroid` storage qualifier ensures that your inputs are interpolated to a point that definitely lies within the primitive being rendered. To do this, OpenGL chooses a sample that it knows lies inside the triangle at which to evaluate those inputs, and that sample may be different from the one that it would have chosen if the pixel was fully covered or the one that it would choose if the centroid storage qualifier was not used. You can use this knowledge to your advantage.

To extract edge information from this, declare two inputs to your fragment shader, one with and one without the `centroid` storage qualifier, and assign the same value to each of them in the vertex shader. It doesn't matter what the values are, so long as they are different for each vertex. The x and y components of the transformed vertex position are probably a good choice because you know that they will be different for each vertex of any triangle that is actually visible.

```
out vec2 maybe_outside;
```

gives us our non-`centroid` input that may be interpolated to a point outside the triangle, and

```
centroid out vec2 certainly_inside;
```

gives us our `centroid` sampled input that we know is inside the triangle. Inside the fragment shader, we can compare the values of the two varyings. If the pixel is entirely covered by the triangle, OpenGL uses the same value for both input. However, if the pixel is only partially covered by the triangle, OpenGL uses its normal choice of sample for `maybe_outside` and picks a sample that is certain to be inside the triangle for `certainly_inside`. This could be a different sample than was chosen for `maybe_outside`, and that means that the two inputs may have different values. Now you can compare them to determine that you are on the edge of a primitive:

```
bool may_be_on_edge = any(notEqual(maybe_outside,
                                    certainly_inside));
```

This method is not foolproof. Even if a pixel is on the edge of a triangle, it is possible that it covers OpenGL's original sample of choice, and therefore you still get the same values for `maybe_outside` and `certainly_inside`. However, this marks most edge pixels.

To use this information, you can write the value to a texture attached to the framebuffer and subsequently use that texture for further processing later. Another option is to draw only to the stencil buffer. Set your stencil reference to one, disable stencil testing, and set your stencil operation to `GL_REPLACE`. When you encounter an edge, let the fragment shader continue running. When you encounter a pixel that's not on an edge, use the `discard` keyword in your shader to prevent the pixel from being written to the stencil buffer. The result is that your stencil buffer contains ones wherever there was an edge in the scene and zeros wherever there was no edge. Later, you can render a full-screen quad with an expensive fragment shader that only runs for pixels that represent the edges of geometry where a sample would have been chosen that was outside the triangle by enabling the stencil test, setting the stencil function to GL_EQUAL, and leaving the reference value at one. The shader could implement image processing operations at each pixel, for instance. Applying Gaussian blur using a convolution operation can smooth the edges of polygons in the scene, allowing the application to perform its own antialiasing.

Advanced Framebuffer Formats

Until now, you have been using either the window-system-supplied framebuffer (i.e., the default framebuffer), or you have rendered into textures using your own framebuffer. However, the textures you attached to the framebuffer have been of the format GL_RGBA8, which is an 8-bit unsigned normalized format. This means that it can only represent values between 0.0 and 1.0, in 256 steps. However, the output of your fragment shaders has been declared as vec4 — a vector of four floating-point elements. OpenGL can actually render into almost any format you can imagine, and framebuffer attachments can have one, two, three, or four components, can be floating-point or integer formats, can store negative numbers, and can be wider than 8 bits, providing much more definition.

In this section, we explore a few of the more advanced formats that can be used for framebuffer attachments and that allow you to capture more of the information that might be produced by your shaders.

Rendering with No Attachments

Just as you can attach multiple textures to a single framebuffer and render into all of them with a single shader, it's also possible to create a framebuffer and not attach any textures to it at all. This may seem like a strange thing to do. You may ask where your data goes. Well, any outputs declared in the fragment shader have no effect, and data written to them will be discarded. However, fragment shaders can have a number of side effects besides writing to their outputs. For example, they can write into memory using the imageStore function, and they can also increment and decrement atomic counters using the atomicCounterIncrement and atomicCounterDecrement functions.

Normally, when a framebuffer object has one or more attachments, it derives its maximum width and height, layer count, and sample count from those attachments. These properties define the size to which the viewport will be clamped and so on. When a framebuffer object has no attachments, limits imposed by the amount of memory available for textures, for example, are removed. However, the framebuffer must derive this information from another source. Each framebuffer object therefore has a set of parameters that are used in place of those derived from its attachments when no attachments are present. To modify these parameters, call **glFramebufferParameteri()**, whose prototype is

```
void glFramebufferParameteri(GLenum target,
                             GLenum pname,
                             GLint param);
```

target specifies the target where the framebuffer object is bound, and may be GL_DRAW_FRAMEBUFFER, GL_READ_FRAMEBUFFER, or simply GL_FRAMEBUFFER. Again, If you specify GL_FRAMEBUFFER, then it is considered equivalent to GL_DRAW_FRAMEBUFFER, and the framebuffer object bound to the GL_DRAW_FRAMEBUFFER binding point will be modified. pname specifies which parameter you want to modify, and param is the value you want to change it to. pname can be one of the following:

- GL_FRAMEBUFFER_DEFAULT_WIDTH indicates that param contains the width of the framebuffer when it has no attachments.

- GL_FRAMEBUFFER_DEFAULT_HEIGHT indicates that param contains the height of the framebuffer when it has no attachments.

- GL_FRAMEBUFFER_DEFAULT_LAYERS indicates that param contains the layer count of the framebuffer when it has no attachments.

- GL_FRAMEBUFFER_DEFAULT_SAMPLES indicates that param contains the number of samples in the framebuffer when it has no attachments.

- GL_FRAMEBUFFER_DEFAULT_FIXED_SAMPLE_LOCATIONS indicates that param specifies whether the framebuffer uses the fixed default sample locations. If param is non-zero, then OpenGL's default sample pattern will be used; otherwise, OpenGL might choose a more advanced arrangement of samples for you.

The maximum dimensions of a framebuffer without any attachments can be extremely large because no real storage for the attachments is required. Listing 9.23 demonstrates how to initialize a virtual framebuffer that is 10,000 pixels wide and 10,000 pixels high.

```
// Generate a framebuffer name and bind it.
Gluint fbo;

glGenFramebuffers(1, &fbo);
glBindFramebuffer(GL_FRAMEBUFFER, fbo);

// Set the default width and height to 10000
glFramebufferParameteri(GL_FRAMEBUFFER_DEFAULT_WIDTH, 10000);
glFramebufferParameteri(GL_FRAMEBUFFER_DEFAULT_HEIGHT, 10000);
```

Listing 9.23: A 100-megapixel virtual framebuffer

If you render with the framebuffer object created in Listing 9.23 bound, you will be able to use `glViewport()` to set the viewport size to 10,000 pixels wide and high. Although there are no attachments on the framebuffer, OpenGL will rasterize primitives as if the framebuffer were really that size, and your fragment shader will run. The values of the x and y components of `gl_FragCoord` variable will range from 0 to 9,999.

Floating-Point Framebuffers

One of the most useful framebuffer features is the ability to use attachments with floating-point formats. Although internally the OpenGL pipeline usually works with floating-point data, the sources (textures) and targets (framebuffer attachments) have often been fixed point and of significantly less precision. As a result, many portions of the pipeline used to clamp all values between 0 and 1 so they could be stored in a fixed-point format in the end.

The data type passed into your vertex shader is up to you but is typically declared as `vec4`, or a vector of four floats. Similarly, you decide what outputs your vertex shader should write when you declare variables as `out` in a vertex shader. These outputs are then interpolated across your geometry and passed into your fragment shader. You have complete control of the type of data you decide to use for color throughout the whole pipeline, although it's most common to just use floats. You now have complete control over how and in what format your data is in as it travels from vertex arrays all the way to the final output.

Now instead of 256 values, you can color and shade using values from 1.18×10^{-38} all the way to 3.4×10^{38}! You may wonder what happens if you are drawing to a window or monitor that only supports 8 bits per color. Unfortunately, the output is clamped to the range of 0 to 1 and then mapped to a fixed-point value. That's no fun! Until someone invents monitors or displays[6] that can understand and display floating-point data, you are still limited by the final output device.

That doesn't mean floating-point rendering isn't useful though. Quite the contrary! You can still render to textures in full floating-point precision. Not only that, but you have complete control over how floating-point data gets mapped to a fixed output format. This can have a huge impact on the final result and is commonly referred to high dynamic range, or HDR.

Using Floating-Point Formats

Upgrading your applications to use floating-point buffers is easier than you may think. In fact, you don't even have to call any new functions. Instead, there are two new tokens you can use when creating buffers, GL_RGBA16F and GL_RGBA32F. These can be used when creating storage for textures:

```
glTexStorage2D(GL_TEXTURE_2D, 1, GL_RGBA16F, width, height);
glTexStorage2D(GL_TEXTURE_2D, 1, GL_RGBA32F, width, height);
```

In addition to the more traditional RGBA formats, Table 9.8 lists other formats allowed for creating floating-point textures. Having so many floating-point formats available allows applications to use the format that most suits the data that they will produce directly.

Table 9.8: Floating-Point Texture Formats

Format	Content
GL_RGBA32F	Four 32-bit floating-point components
GL_RGBA16F	Four 16-bit floating-point components
GL_RGB32F	Three 32-bit floating-point components
GL_RGB16F	Three 16-bit floating-point components
GL_RG32F	Two 32-bit floating-point components
GL_RG16F	Two 16-bit floating-point components
GL_R32F	One 32-bit floating-point component
GL_R16F	One 16-bit floating-point component
GL_R11F_G11F_B10F	Two 11-bit floating-point components and one 10-bit floating-point component

---

6. Some very high-end monitors are available today that can interpret 10 or even 12 bits of data in each channel. However, they're often prohibitively expensive, and there aren't any displays that accept floating-point data outside of the lab.

As you can see, there are 16- and 32-bit floating-point formats with one, two, three, and four channels. There is also a special format, GL_R11F_G11F_B10F, that contains two 11-bit floating-point components and one 10-bit component, packed together in a single 32-bit word. These are special, unsigned floating-point formats[7] with a 5-bit exponent and a 6-bit mantissa in the 11-bit components, and a 5-bit exponent and mantissa for the 10-bit component.

In addition to the formats shown in Table 9.8, you can also create textures that have the GL_DEPTH_COMPONENT32F or GL_DEPTH_COMPONENT32F_STENCIL8 formats. The first is used to store depth information and such textures can be used as depth attachments on a framebuffer. The second represents both depth and stencil information stored in a single texture. This can be used for both the depth attachment and the stencil attachment of a framebuffer object.

High Dynamic Range

Many modern game applications use floating-point rendering to generate all of the great eye candy we now expect. The level of realism possible when generating lighting effects such as light bloom, lens flare, light reflections, light refractions, crepuscular rays, and the effects of participating media such as dust or clouds are often not possible without floating-point buffers. High dynamic range (HDR) rendering into floating-point buffers can make the bright areas of a scene really bright, keep shadow areas very dark, and still allow you to see detail in both. After all, the human eye has an incredible ability to perceive very high contrast levels well beyond the capabilities of today's displays.

Instead of drawing a complex scene with a lot of geometry and lighting in our sample programs to show how effective HDR can be, we use images already generated in HDR for simplicity. The first sample program, hdr_imaging, loads HDR (floating-point) images from .KTX files that store the original, floating-point data in its raw form. These images are generated by taking a series of aligned images of a scene with different exposures and then combining them together to produce an HDR result.

The low exposures capture detail in the bright areas of the scene while the high exposures capture detail in the dark areas of the scene. Figure 9.15 shows four views of a scene of a tree lit by bright decorative lights (these

---

7. Floating-point data is almost always signed, but it is possible to sacrifice the sign bit if only positive numbers will ever be stored.

images are also shown in Color Plate 2). The top left image is rendered at a very low exposure and shows all of the detail of lights even though they are very bright. The top right image increases the exposure such that you start to see details in the ribbon. On the bottom left, the exposure is increased to the level that you can see details in the pine cones, and finally, on the bottom right, the exposure has increased such that the branches in the foreground become very clear. The four images show the incredible amount of detail and range that are stored in a single image.

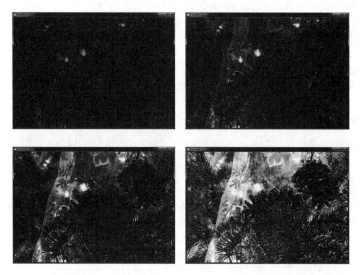

Figure 9.15: Different views of an HDR image

The only way possible to store so much detail in a single image is to use floating-point data. Any scene you render in OpenGL, especially if it has very bright or dark areas, can look more realistic when the true color output can be preserved instead of clamped between 0.0 and 1.0, and then divided into only 256 possible values.

Tone Mapping

Now that you've seen some of the benefits of using floating-point rendering, how do you use that data to generate a dynamic image that still has to be displayed using values from 0 to 255? Tone mapping is the action of mapping color data from one set of colors to another or from one color space to another. Because we can't directly display floating-point data, it has to be tone mapped into a color space that can be displayed.

The first sample program, hdrtonemap, uses three approaches to map the high-definition output to the low-definition screen. The first method, enabled by pressing the 1 key, is a simple and naïve direct texturing of the floating-point image to the screen. The histogram of the HDR image in Figure 9.15 is shown in Figure 9.16. From the graph, it is clear while that most of the image data has values between 0.0 and 1.0, many of the important highlights are well beyond 1.0. In fact, the highest luminance level for this image is almost 5.5!

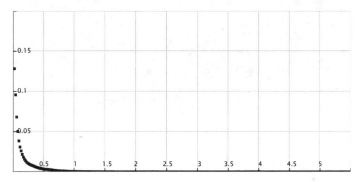

Figure 9.16: Histogram of levels for treelights.ktx

If we send this image directly to our regular 8-bit normalized back buffer, the result is that the image is clamped and all of the bright areas look white. Additionally, because the majority of the data is in the first quarter of the range, or between 0 and 63 when mapped directly to 8 bits, it all blends together to look black. Figure 9.17 shows the result; the bright areas such as the lamps are practically white, and the dark areas such as the pine cones the are nearly black.

The second approach in the sample program is to vary the "exposure" of the image, similar to how a camera can vary exposure to the environment. Each exposure level provides a slightly different window into the texture data. Low exposures show the detail in the very bright sections of the scene; high exposures allow you to see detail in the dark areas but wash out the bright parts. This is similar to the images in Figure 9.15 with the low exposure on the upper left and the high exposure on the lower right. For our tone mapping pass, the hdrtonemap sample program reads from a floating-point texture and writes to the default framebuffer with an 8-bit back buffer. This allows the conversion from HDR to LDR (low dynamic range) to be on a pixel-by-pixel basis, which reduces artifacts that occur when a texel is interpolated between bright and dark areas. Once the LDR image has been generated, it can be displayed to the user. Listing 9.24 shows the simple exposure shader used in the example.

Figure 9.17: Naïve tone mapping by clamping

```
#version 430 core

layout (binding = 0) uniform sampler2D hdr_image;

uniform float exposure = 1.0;

out vec4 color;

void main(void)
{
    vec4 c = texelFetch(hdr_image, ivec2(gl_FragCoord.xy), 0);
    c.rgb = vec3(1.0) - exp(-c.rgb * exposure);
    color = c;
}
```

Listing 9.24: Applying simple exposure coefficient to an HDR image

In the sample application, you can use the plus and minus keys on the numeric keypad to adjust the exposure. The range of exposures for this program goes from 0.01 to 20.0. Notice how the level of detail in different locations in the image changes with the exposure level. In fact, the images shown in Figure 9.15 were generated with this sample program by setting the exposure to different levels.

The last tone mapping shader used in the first sample program performs dynamic adjustments to the exposure level based on the relative brightness of different portions of the scene. First, the shader needs to know the relative luminance of the area near the current texel being tone mapped. The shader does this by sampling 25 texels centered around the current texel. All of the surrounding samples are then converted to luminance values, which are then weighted and added together. The sample program uses a non-linear function to convert the luminance to an exposure. In this example, the default curve is defined by the function

$$y = \sqrt{8.0(x + 0.25)}$$

The shape of the curve is shown in Figure 9.18.

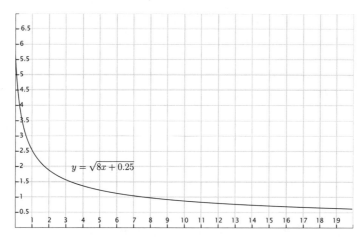

Figure 9.18: Transfer curve for adaptive tone mapping

The exposure is then used to convert the HDR texel to an LDR value using the same expression as in Listing 9.24. Listing 9.25 shows the adaptive HDR shader.

```
#version 430 core
// hdr_adaptive.fs
//
//

in vec2 vTex;

layout (binding = 0) uniform sampler2D hdr_image;

out vec4 oColor;

void main(void)
{
    int i;
    float lum[25];
    vec2 tex_scale = vec2(1.0) / textureSize(hdr_image, 0);
```

```
for (i = 0; i < 25; i++)
{
    vec2 tc = (2.0 * gl_FragCoord.xy +
                3.5 * vec2(i % 5 - 2, i / 5 - 2));
    vec3 col = texture(hdr_image, tc * tex_scale).rgb;
    lum[i] = dot(col, vec3(0.3, 0.59, 0.11));
}

// Calculate weighted color of region
vec3 vColor = texelFetch(hdr_image,
                    2 * ivec2(gl_FragCoord.xy), 0).rgb;

float kernelLuminance = (
    (1.0 * (lum[0] + lum[4] + lum[20] + lum[24])) +
    (4.0 * (lum[1] + lum[3] + lum[5] + lum[9] +
            lum[15] + lum[19] + lum[21] + lum[23])) +
    (7.0 * (lum[2] + lum[10] + lum[14] + lum[22])) +
    (16.0 * (lum[6] + lum[8] + lum[16] + lum[18])) +
    (26.0 * (lum[7] + lum[11] + lum[13] + lum[17])) +
    (41.0 * lum[12])
    ) / 273.0;

// Compute the corresponding exposure
float exposure = sqrt(8.0 / (kernelLuminance + 0.25));

// Apply the exposure to this texel
oColor.rgb = 1.0 - exp2(-vColor * exposure);
oColor.a = 1.0f;
}
```

Listing 9.25: Adaptive HDR to LDR conversion fragment shader

When using one exposure for an image, you can adjust for the best results by taking the range for the whole and using an average. Considerable detail is still lost with this approach in the bright and dim areas. The non-linear transfer function used with the adaptive fragment shader brings out the detail in both the bright and dim areas of the image; take a look at Figure 9.19. The transfer function uses a logarithmic-like scale to map luminance values to exposure levels. You can change this function to increase or decrease the range of exposures used and the resulting amount of detail in different dynamic ranges.

Figure 9.19 is also shown in Color Plate 3. Great, so now you know how to image process an HDR file, but what good is that in a typical OpenGL program? Lots! The HDR image is only a stand-in for any lit OpenGL scene. Many OpenGL games and applications now render HDR scenes and other content to floating-point framebuffer attachments and then display the result by doing a final pass using a technique such as one discussed above. You can use the same methods you just learned to render in HDR, generating much more realistic lighting environments and showing the dynamic range and detail of each frame.

Figure 9.19: Result of adaptive tone mapping program

Making Your Scene Bloom

One of the effects that works very well with high dynamic range images is the bloom effect. Have you ever noticed how the sun or a bright light can sometimes engulf tree branches or other objects between you and the light source? That's called *light bloom*. Figure 9.20 shows how light bloom can affect an indoor scene.

Figure 9.20: The effect of light bloom on an image

Notice how you can see all the detail in the lower exposure of the left side of Figure 9.20. The right side is a much higher exposure, and the grid in the stained glass is covered by the light bloom. Even the wooden post on the bottom right looks smaller as it gets covered by bloom. By adding bloom to a scene you can enhance the sense of brightness in certain areas. We can simulate this bloom effect caused by bright light sources. Although you could also perform this effect using 8-bit precision buffers, it's much more effective when used with floating-point buffers on a high dynamic range scene.

The first step is to draw your scene in with high dynamic range. For the hdrbloom sample program, an framebuffer is set up with two floating-point textures bound as color attachments. The scene is rendered as normal to the first bound texture. But the second bound texture gets only the bright areas of the field. The hdrbloom sample program fills both textures in one pass from one shader (see Listing 9.26). The output color is computed as normal and sent to the color0 output. Then, the luminance (brightness) value of the color is calculated and used to threshold the data. Only the brightest data is used to generate the bloom effect and is written to the second output, color1. The threshold levels used are adjustable via a pair of uniforms, bloom_thresh_min and bloom_thresh_max. To filter for the bright areas, we use the smoothstep function to smoothly force any fragments whose brightness is less than bloom_thresh_min to zero, and any fragments whose brightness is greater than bloom_thresh_max to four times the original color output.

```
#version 430 core

layout (location = 0) out vec4 color0;
layout (location = 1) out vec4 color1;

in VS_OUT
{
    vec3 N;
    vec3 L;
    vec3 V;
    flat int material_index;
} fs_in;

// Material properties
uniform float bloom_thresh_min = 0.8;
uniform float bloom_thresh_max = 1.2;

struct material_t
{
    vec3    diffuse_color;
    vec3    specular_color;
    float   specular_power;
    vec3    ambient_color;
};
```

```
layout (binding = 1, std140) uniform MATERIAL_BLOCK
{
    material_t material[32];
} materials;

void main(void)
{
    // Normalize the incoming N, L, and V vectors
    vec3 N = normalize(fs_in.N);
    vec3 L = normalize(fs_in.L);
    vec3 V = normalize(fs_in.V);

    // Calculate R locally
    vec3 R = reflect(-L, N);

    material_t m = materials.material[fs_in.material_index];

    // Compute the diffuse and specular components for each fragment
    vec3 diffuse = max(dot(N, L), 0.0) * m.diffuse_color;
    vec3 specular = pow(max(dot(R, V), 0.0), m.specular_power)
                        * m.specular_color;
    vec3 ambient = m.ambient_color;

    // Add ambient, diffuse, and specular to find final color
    vec3 color = ambient + diffuse + specular;

    // Write final color to the framebuffer
    color0 = vec4(color, 1.0);

    // Calculate luminance
    float Y = dot(color, vec3(0.299, 0.587, 0.144));

    // Threshold color based on its luminance, and write it to
    // the second output
    color = color * 4.0 * smoothstep(bloom_thresh_min, bloom_thresh_max, Y);
    color1 = vec4(color, 1.0);
}
```

Listing 9.26: Bloom fragment shader; output bright data to a separate buffer

After the first shader has run, we obtain the two images shown in
Figure 9.21. The scene we rendered is just a large collection of spheres
with varying material properties. Some of them are configured to actually
emit light as they have properties that will produce values in the
framebuffer greater than one no matter what the lighting effects are. The
image on the left is the scene rendered with no bloom. You will notice
that it is sharp in all areas, regardless of brightness. The image on the right
is the thresholded version of the image, which will be used as input to the
bloom filters.

Now, after the scene has been rendered, there is still some work to do to
finish the bright pass. The bright data must be blurred for the bloom effect
to work. To implement this, we use a separable Gaussian filter. A separable
filter is a filter that can be separated into two passes — generally one in the
horizontal axis and one in the vertical. In this example, we use 25 taps in

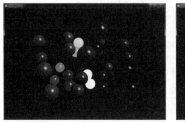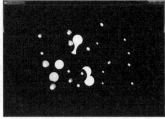

Figure 9.21: Original and thresholded output for bloom example

each dimension, sampling from the 25 samples around the center of the filter and multiplying each texel by a fixed set of weights. To apply a separable filter, we make two passes. In the first pass, we filter in the horizontal dimension. However, you may notice that we use `gl_FragCoord.yx` to determine the center of our filter kernel. This means that we will *transpose* the image during filtering. However, on the second pass, we apply the same filter again. This means that filtering in the horizontal axis is equivalent to filtering in the vertical axis of the original image, and the output image is transposed again, returning it to its original orientation. In effect, we have performed a 2D Gaussian filter with a diameter of 25 samples and a total sample count of 625. The shader that implements this is shown in Listing 9.27.

```glsl
#version 430 core

layout (binding = 0) uniform sampler2D hdr_image;

out vec4 color;

const float weights[] = float[](0.0024499299678342,
                                0.0043538453346397,
                                0.0073599963704157,
                                0.0118349786570722,
                                0.0181026699707781,
                                0.0263392293891488,
                                0.0364543006660986,
                                0.0479932050577658,
                                0.0601029809166942,
                                0.0715974486241365,
                                0.0811305381519717,
                                0.0874493212267511,
                                0.0896631113333857,
                                0.0874493212267511,
                                0.0811305381519717,
                                0.0715974486241365,
                                0.0601029809166942,
                                0.0479932050577658,
                                0.0364543006660986,
                                0.0263392293891488,
                                0.0181026699707781,
                                0.0118349786570722,
                                0.0073599963704157,
```

```
                        0.0043538453346397,
                        0.0024499299678342);

void main(void)
{
    vec4 c = vec4(0.0);
    ivec2 P = ivec2(gl_FragCoord.yx) - ivec2(0, weights.length() >> 1);
    int i;

    for (i = 0; i < weights.length(); i++)
    {
        c += texelFetch(hdr_image, P + ivec2(0, i), 0) * weights[i];
    }

    color = c;
}
```

Listing 9.27: Blur fragment shader

The result of applying blur to the thresholded image shown on the right of
Figure 9.21 is shown in Figure 9.22.

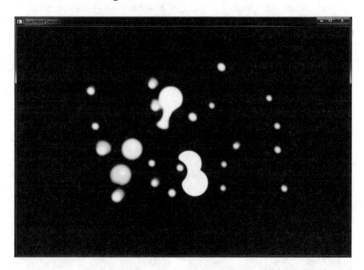

Figure 9.22: Blurred thresholded bloom colors

After the blurring passes are complete, the blur results are combined with
the full color texture of the scene to produce the final results. In
Listing 9.28 you can see how the final shader samples from two textures:
the original full color texture and the blurred version of the bright pass.
The original colors and the blurred results are added together to form the
bloom effect, which is multiplied by a user-controlled uniform. The final
high dynamic range color result is then put through exposure calculations,
which you should be familiar with from the last sample program.

The exposure shader shown in Listing 9.28 is used to draw a screen-sized textured quad to the window. That's it! Dial up and down the bloom effect to your heart's content. Figure 9.23 shows the `hdrbloom` sample program with a high bloom level.

```
#version 430 core

layout (binding = 0) uniform sampler2D hdr_image;
layout (binding = 1) uniform sampler2D bloom_image;

uniform float exposure = 0.9;
uniform float bloom_factor = 1.0;
uniform float scene_factor = 1.0;

out vec4 color;

void main(void)
{
    vec4 c = vec4(0.0);

    c += texelFetch(hdr_image, ivec2(gl_FragCoord.xy), 0) * scene_factor;
    c += texelFetch(bloom_image, ivec2(gl_FragCoord.xy), 0) * bloom_factor;

    c.rgb = vec3(1.0) - exp(-c.rgb * exposure);
    color = c;
}
```

Listing 9.28: Adding bloom effect to scene

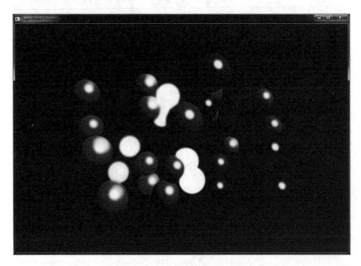

Figure 9.23: Result of the bloom program

A comparison of the output of this program with and without bloom is shown in Color Plate 4.

Integer Framebuffers

By default, the window system will provide your application with a *fixed-point* back buffer. When you declare a floating-point output from your fragment shader (such as a `vec4`), OpenGL will convert the data you write into it into a fixed-point representation suitable for storage in that framebuffer. In the previous section we covered floating-point framebuffer attachments, which provide the capability of storing an arbitrary floating-point value in the framebuffer. It's also possible to create an *integer* framebuffer attachment by creating a texture with an integer internal format and attaching it to a framebuffer object. When you do this, it's possible to use an output with an integer component type such as `ivec4` or `uvec4`. With an integer framebuffer attachment, the bit pattern contained in your output variables will be written verbatim into the texture. You don't need to worry about denormals, negative zero, infinities, or any other special bit patterns that might be a concern with floating-point buffers.

To create an integer framebuffer attachment, simply create a texture with an internal format made up an integer components and attach it to a framebuffer object. Internal formats that are made up of integers generally end in I or UI — for example, `GL_RGBA32UI` represents a format made up of four unsigned 32-bit integers per texel, and `GL_R16I` is a format made up of a single signed 16-bit component per texel. Code to create a framebuffer attachment with an internal format of `GL_RGBA32UI` is shown in Listing 9.29.

```
// Variables for the texture and FBO
GLuint tex;
GLuint fbo;

// Create the texture object
glGenTextures(1, &tex);

// Bind it to the 2D target and allocate storage for it
glBindTexture(GL_TEXTURE_2D, tex);
glTexStorage2D(GL_TEXTURE_2D, 1, GL_RGBA32UI, 1024, 1024);

// Now create an FBO and attach the texure as normal
glGenFrambuffers(1, &fbo);
glBindFramebuffer(GL_FRAMEBUFFER, fbo);

glFramebufferTexture(GL_FRAMEBFUFFER,
                     GL_COLOR_ATTACHMENT0,
                     tex,
                     0);
```

Listing 9.29: Creating integer framebuffer attachments

You can determine the component type of a framebuffer attachment by calling **`glGetFramebufferAttachmentParameteriv()`** with pname set to

GL_FRAMEBUFFER_ATTACHMENT_COMPONENT_TYPE. The value returned in params will be GL_FLOAT, GL_INT, GL_UNSIGNED_INT, GL_SIGNED_NORMALIZED, or GL_UNSIGNED_NORMALIZED depending on the internal format of the color attachments. There is no requirement that the attachments to a framebuffer object all be of the same type. This means that you can have a combination of attachments, some of which are floating point or fixed point and others that are integer formats.

When you render to an integer framebuffer attachment, the output declared in your fragment shader should match that of the attachment in component type. For example, if your framebuffer attachment is an unsigned integer format such as GL_RGBA32UI, then your shader's output variable corresponding to that color attachment should be an unsigned integer format such as `unsigned int`, `uvec2`, `uvec3`, or `uvec4`. Likewise, for signed integer formats, your output should be `int`, `ivec2`, `ivec3`, or `ivec4`. Although the component formats should match, there is no requirement that the number of components match.

If the component width of the framebuffer attachment is less than 32 bits, then the additional most significant bits will be thrown away when you render to it. You can even write floating-point data directly into an integer color buffer by using the GLSL functions `floatBitsToInt` (or `floatBitsToUint`) or the packing functions such as `packUnorm2x16`.

While it may seem that integer framebuffer attachments offer some level of flexibility over traditional fixed- or floating-point framebuffers — especially in light of being able to write floating-point data into them,— there are some trade-offs that must be considered. The first and most glaring is that blending is not available for integer framebuffers. The other is that having an integer internal format means that the resulting texture into which you rendered your image cannot be filtered.

The sRGB Color Space

Eons ago, computer users had large, clunky monitors made from glass vacuum bottles called cathode ray tubes (CRTs). These devices worked by shooting electrons at a fluorescent screen to make it glow. Unfortunately, the amount of light emitted by the screen was not linear in the voltage used to drive it. In fact, the relationship between light output and driving voltage was highly nonlinear. The amount of light output was a power function of the form

$$L_{out} = V_{in}{}^{\gamma}$$

To make matters worse, γ didn't always take the same value. For NTSC systems (the television standard used in North America, much of South America, and parts of Asia), γ was about 2.2. However, with SECAM and PAL systems (the standards used in Europe, Australia, Africa, and other parts of Asia) used a γ value of 2.8. That means that if you put a voltage of half the maximum into a CRT-based display, you'd get a little less than one quarter of the maximum possible light output!

To compensate for this, in computer graphics we apply *gamma correction* (after the γ term in the power function) by raising linear values by a small power, scaling the result, and offsetting it. The resulting color space is known as sRGB, and the pseudo-code to translate from a linear value to an sRGB value is as follows:

```
if (cl >= 1.0)
{
    cs = 1.0;
}
else if (cl <= 0.0)
{
    cs = 0.0;
}
else if (cl < 0.0031308)
{
    cs = 12.92 * cl;
}
else
{
    cs = 1.055 * pow(cl, 0.41666) - 0.055;
}
```

Further, to go from sRGB to linear color space, we apply the transformation illustrated by the following pseudo-code:

```
if (cs >= 1.0)
{
    cl = 1.0;
}
else if (cs <= 0.0)
{
    cl = 0.0;
}
else if (cs <= 0.04045)
{
    cl = cs / 12.92;
}
else
{
    cl = pow((cs + 0.0555) / 1.055), 2.4)
}
```

In both cases, cs is the sRGB color space value, and cl is the linear value. Notice that the transformation has a short linear section and a small bias. In practice, this is so close to raising our linear color values to the powers 2.2 (for sRGB to linear) and 0.454545, which is $\frac{1}{2.2}$ (for linear to sRGB), that some implementations will do this. Figure 9.24 shows the transfer functions of linear to sRGB and sRGB back to linear on the left, and a pair of simple power curves using the powers 2.2 and 0.45454 on the right. You should notice that the shapes of these curves are so close as to be almost indistinguishable.

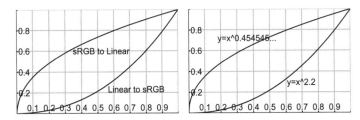

Figure 9.24: Gamma curves for sRGB and simple powers

To use the sRGB color space in OpenGL, we create textures with SRGB internal formats. For example, the GL_SRGB8_ALPHA8 represents the red, green, and blue components with an sRGB gamma ramp (the alpha component) is linear. We can load data into the texture as usual. When you read from an sRGB texture in your shader, the sRGB format is converted to RGB when the texture is sampled but before it is filtered. That is, when bilinear filtering is turned on, the incoming texels are converted from sRGB to linear, and then the linear samples are blended together to form the final value returned to the shader. Also, only the RGB components are converted separately, and the alpha is left as is.

Framebuffers also support storage formats that are sRGB; specifically, the format GL_SRGB8_ALPHA8 must be supported. That means you can attach textures that have an internal sRGB format to a framebuffer object and then render to it. Because we just talked about how sRGB formats are not linear, you probably don't want your writes to sRGB framebuffer attachments to be linear either; that would defeat the whole purpose! The good news is OpenGL can convert the linear color values your shader outputs into sRGB values automatically. However, this isn't performed by default. To turn this feature on, you need to call **glEnable()** with the GL_FRAMEBUFFER_SRGB token. Remember, this only works for color attachments that contain an sRGB surface. You can call **glGetFramebufferAttachmentParameteriv()** with the value GL_FRAMEBUFFER_ATTACHMENT_COLOR_ENCODING to find out if the attached surface is sRGB. sRGB surfaces return GL_SRGB, while other surfaces return GL_LINEAR.

Point Sprites

The term *point sprites* is usually used to refer to textured points. OpenGL represents each point by a single vertex, and so there is no opportunity to specify texture coordinates that can be interpolated as there is with the other primitive types. To get around this, OpenGL will generate an interpolated texture coordinate for you with which you can do anything you like. With point sprites, you can place a 2D textured image anywhere on-screen by drawing a single 3D point.

One of the most common applications of point sprites is for particle systems. A large number of particles moving on-screen can be represented as points to produce a number of visual effects. However, representing these points as small overlapped 2D images can produce dramatic streaming animated filaments. For example, Figure 9.25 shows a well-known screen saver on the Macintosh powered by just such a particle effect.

Figure 9.25: A particle effect in the flurry screen saver

Without point sprites, achieving this type of effect would be a matter of drawing a large number of textured quads (or triangle fans) on-screen. This could be accomplished either by performing a costly rotation to each individual face to make sure that it faced the camera, or by drawing all particles in a 2D orthographic projection. Point sprites allow you to render a perfectly aligned textured 2D square by sending down a single 3D vertex. At one-quarter the bandwidth of sending down four vertices for a quad and no matrix math to keep the 3D quad aligned with the camera, point sprites are a potent and efficient feature of OpenGL.

Texturing Points

Point sprites are easy to use. On the application side, the only thing you have to do is simply bind a 2D texture and read from it in your fragment shader using a built-in variable called gl_PointCoord, which is a two-component vector that interpolates the texture coordinates across the point. Listing 9.30 shows the fragment shader for the PointSprites example program.

```
#version 430 core

out vec4 vFragColor;

in vec4 vStarColor;

layout (binding = 0) uniform sampler2D starImage;

void main(void)
{
    vFragColor = texture(starImage, gl_PointCoord) * vStarColor;
}
```

Listing 9.30: Texturing a point sprite in the fragment shader

Again, for a point sprite, you do not need to send down texture coordinates as an attribute as OpenGL will produce gl_PointCoord automatically. Since a point is a single vertex, you wouldn't have the ability to interpolate across the points surface any other way. Of course, there is nothing preventing you from providing a texture coordinate anyway or deriving your own customized interpolation scheme.

Rendering a Star Field

Let's now take a look at an example program that makes use of the point sprite features discussed so far. The starfield example program creates an animated star field that appears as if you were flying forward through it. This is accomplished by placing random points out in front of your field of view and then passing a time value into the vertex shader as a uniform. This time value is used to move the point positions so that over time they move closer to you and then recycle when they get to the near clipping plane to the back of the frustum. In addition, we scale the size of the stars so that they start off very small but get larger as they get closer to your point of view. The result is a nice realistic effect... all we need is some planetarium or space movie music!

Figure 9.26 shows our star texture map that is applied to the points. It is simply a .KTX file that we load in the same manner we loaded any other

2D texture so far. Points can also be mipmapped, and because they can range from very small to very large, it's probably a good idea to do so.

Figure 9.26: The star texture map

We are not going to cover all of the details of setting up the star field effect, as it's pretty routine and you can check the source yourself if you want to see how we pick random numbers. Of more importance is the actual rendering of code in the RenderScene function:

```
void render(double currentTime)
{
    static const GLfloat black[] = { 0.0f, 0.0f, 0.0f, 0.0f };
    static const GLfloat one[] = { 1.0f };
    float t = (float)currentTime;
    float aspect = (float)info.windowWidth /
                   (float)info.windowHeight;
    vmath::mat4 proj_matrix = vmath::perspective(50.0f,
                                                 aspect,
                                                 0.1f,
                                                 1000.0f);

    t *= 0.1f;
    t -= floor(t);

    glViewport(0, 0, info.windowWidth, info.windowHeight);
    glClearBufferfv(GL_COLOR, 0, black);
    glClearBufferfv(GL_DEPTH, 0, one);

    glEnable(GL_PROGRAM_POINT_SIZE);
    glUseProgram(render_prog);

    glUniform1f(uniforms.time, t);
    glUniformMatrix4fv(uniforms.proj_matrix, 1, GL_FALSE, proj_matrix);

    glEnable(GL_BLEND);
    glBlendFunc(GL_ONE, GL_ONE);

    glBindVertexArray(star_vao);

    glDrawArrays(GL_POINTS, 0, NUM_STARS);
}
```

We are going to use additive blending to blend our stars with the background. Because the dark area of our texture is black (zero in color space), we can get away with just adding the colors together as we draw. Transparency with alpha would require that we depth-sort our stars, and that is an expense we certainly can do without. After turning on point size program mode, we bind our shader and set up the uniforms. Of interest here is that we use the current time, which drives what will end up being the z position of our stars, that recycles so that it just counts smoothly from 0 to 1. Listing 9.31 provides the source code to the vertex shader.

```
#version 430 core

layout (location = 0) in vec4 position;
layout (location = 1) in vec4 color;

uniform float time;
uniform mat4 proj_matrix;

flat out vec4 starColor;

void main(void)
{
    vec4 newVertex = position;

    newVertex.z += time;
    newVertex.z = fract(newVertex.z);

    float size = (20.0 * newVertex.z * newVertex.z);

    starColor = smoothstep(1.0, 7.0, size) * color;

    newVertex.z = (999.9 * newVertex.z) - 1000.0;
    gl_Position = proj_matrix * newVertex;
    gl_PointSize = size;
}
```

Listing 9.31: Vertex shader for the star field effect

The vertex z component is offset by the time uniform. This is what causes the animation where the stars move closer to you. We only use the fractional part of this sum so that their position loops back to the far clipping plane as they get closer to the viewer. At this point in the shader, vertices with a z coordinate of 0.0 are at the far plane and vertices with a z coordinate of 1.0 are at the near plane. We can use the square of the vertex's z coordinate to make the stars grow ever larger as they get nearer and set the final size in the gl_PointSize variable. If the star sizes are too small, you will get flickering sometimes, so we dim the color progressively using the smoothstep function so that any points with a size less than 1.0 will be black, fading to full intensity as they reach 7 pixels in size. This way, they fade into view instead of just popping up near the far clipping plane. The star color is passed to the fragment shader shown in Listing 9.32, which simply fetches from our star texture and multiplies the result by the computed star color.

```
#version 430 core

layout (location = 0) out vec4 color;

uniform sampler2D tex_star;
flat in vec4 starColor;

void main(void)
{
    color = starColor * texture(tex_star, gl_PointCoord);
}
```

Listing 9.32: Fragment shader for the star field effect

The final output of the `starfield` program is shown in Figure 9.27.

Figure 9.27: Flying through space with point sprites

Point Parameters

A couple of features of point sprites (and points in general, actually) can be fine-tuned with the function **glPointParameteri()**. Figure 9.28 shows the two possible locations of the origin (0,0) of the texture applied to a point sprite. On the left, we see the origin on the upper left of the point sprite, and on the right, we see the origin as the lower left.

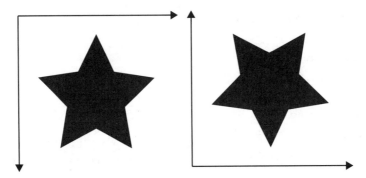

Figure 9.28: Two potential orientations of textures on a point sprite

The default orientation for point sprites is GL_UPPER_LEFT. Setting the GL_POINT_SPRITE_COORD_ORIGIN parameter to GL_LOWER_LEFT places the origin of the texture coordinate system at the lower-left corner of the point:

```
glPointParameteri(GL_POINT_SPRITE_COORD_ORIGIN, GL_LOWER_LEFT);
```

When the point sprite origin is set to its default of GL_UPPER_LEFT, gl_PointCoord will be 0.0, 0.0 at the top left of the point as it is viewed on the screen. However, in OpenGL, window coordinates are considered to start at the lower left of the window (which is the convention that gl_FragCoord adheres to, for example). Therefore, to get our point sprite coordinates to follow the window coordinate conventions and align with gl_FragCoord, we set the point sprite coordinate origin to GL_LOWER_LEFT.

Shaped Points

There is more you can do with point sprites besides apply a texture using gl_PointCoord for texture coordinates. You can use gl_PointCoord to derive a number of things other than just texture coordinates. For example, you can make non-square points by using the **discard** keyword in your fragment shader to throw away fragments that lie outside your desired point shape. The following fragment shader code produces round points:

```
vec2 p = gl_PointCoord * 2.0 - vec2(1.0);
if (dot(p, p) > 1.0)
    discard;
```

Or perhaps an interesting flower shape:

```
vec2 temp = gl_PointCoord * 2.0 - vec2(1.0);
if (dot(temp, temp) > sin(atan(temp.y, temp.x) * 5.0))
    discard;
```

These are simple code snippets that allow arbitrary shaped points to be rendered. Figure 9.29 shows a few more examples of interesting shapes that can be generated this way.

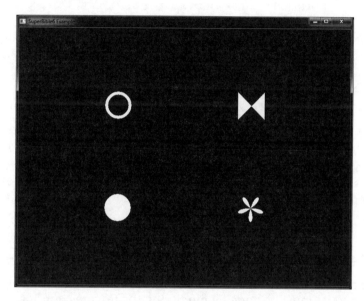

Figure 9.29: Analytically generated point sprite shapes

To create Figure 9.29, we used the fragment shader shown in Listing 9.33.

```
#version 430 core

layout (location = 0) out vec4 color;

flat in int shape;

void main(void)
{
    color = vec4(1.0);
    vec2 p = gl_PointCoord * 2.0 - vec2(1.0);

    if (shape == 0)
    {
        // Simple disc shape
```

```
        if (dot(p, p) > 1.0)
            discard;
    }
    else if (shape == 1)
    {
        // Hollow circle
        if (abs(0.8 - dot(p, p)) > 0.2)
            discard;
    }
    else if (shape == 2)
    {
        // Flower shape
        if (dot(p, p) > sin(atan(p.y, p.x) * 5.0))
            discard;
    }
    else if (shape == 3)
    {
        // Bowtie
        if (abs(p.x) < abs(p.y))
            discard;
    }
}
```

Listing 9.33: Fragment shader for generating shaped points

The advantage of calculating the shape of your points analytically in the fragment shader rather than using a texture is that the shapes are exact and stand up well to scaling and rotation, as you will see in the next section.

Rotating Points

Because points in OpenGL are rendered as axis-aligned squares, rotating the point sprite must be done by modifying the texture coordinates used to read the sprite's texture or to analytically calculate its shape. To do this, you can simply create a 2D rotation matrix in the fragment shader and multiply it by gl_PointCoord to rotate it around the z axis. The angle of rotation could be passed from the vertex or geometry shader to the fragment shader as an interpolated variable. The value of the variable can, in turn, be calculated in the vertex or geometry shader or can be supplied through a vertex attribute. Listing 9.34 shows a slightly more complex point sprite fragment shader that allows the point to be rotated around its center.

This example allows you to generate rotated point sprites. However, the value of angle will not change from one fragment to another within the point sprite. That means that sin_theta and cos_theta will be constant, and the resulting rotation matrix constructed from them will also be the same for every fragment in the point. It is therefore much more efficient

```
#version 430

uniform sampler2D sprite_texture;

in float angle;

out vec4 color;

void main(void)
{
    const float sin_theta = sin(angle);
    const float cos_theta = cos(angle);
    const mat2 rotation_matrix = mat2(cos_theta, sin_theta,
                                      -sin_theta, cos_theta);
    const vec2 pt = gl_PointCoord - vec2(0.5);
    color = texture(sprite_texture, rotation_matrix * pt + vec2(0.5));
}
```

Listing 9.34: Naïve rotated point sprite fragment shader

to calculate `sin_theta` and `cos_theta` in the vertex shader and pass them as a pair of variables into the fragment shader rather than calculating them at every fragment. Here's an updated vertex and fragment shader that allows you to draw rotated point sprites. First, the vertex shader is shown in Listing 9.35.

```
#version 430 core

uniform matrix mvp;

in vec4 position;
in float angle;

flat out float sin_theta;
flat out float cos_theta;

void main(void)
{
    sin_theta = sin(angle);
    cos_theta = cos(angle);

    gl_Position = mvp * position;
}
```

Listing 9.35: Rotated point sprite vertex shader

And second, the fragment shader is shown in Listing 9.36.

```
#version 430 core

uniform sampler2D sprite_texture;

flat in float sin_theta;
```

```
flat in float cos_theta;

out vec4 color;

void main(void)
{
    mat2 m = mat2(cos_theta, sin_theta,
                  -sin_theta, cos_theta);
    const vec2 pt = gl_PointCoord - vec2(0.5);
    color = texture(sprite_texture, rotation_matrix * pt + vec2(0.5));
}
```

Listing 9.36: Rotated point sprite fragment shader

As you can see, the potentially expensive `sin` and `cos` functions have been moved out of the fragment shader and into the vertex shader. If the point size is large, this pair of shaders performs much better than the earlier, brute force approach of calculating the rotation matrix in the fragment shader.

Remember that even though you are rotating the coordinates you derived from `gl_PointCoord`, the point itself is still square. If your texture or analytic shape spills outside the unit-diameter circle inside the point, you will need to make your point sprite larger and scale your texture coordinate down accordingly to get the shape to fit within the point under all angles of rotation. Of course, if your texture is essentially round, you don't need to worry about this at all.

Getting at Your Image

Once everything's rendered, your application will usually show the result to the user. The mechanism to do this is platform specific,[8] and so the book's application framework normally takes care of this for you. However, showing the result to the user might not always be what you want to do. There are many reasons why you might want to gain access to the rendered image directly from your application. For example, perhaps you want to print the image, save a screenshot, or even process it further with an offline process.

---

8. To read the details about how this works on several popular platforms, refer to Chapter 14.

Reading from a Framebuffer

To allow you to read pixel data from the framebuffer, OpenGL includes the **glReadPixels()** function, whose prototype is

```
void glReadPixels(GLint x,
                  GLint y,
                  GLsizei width,
                  GLsizei height,
                  GLenum format,
                  GLenum type,
                  GLvoid * data);
```

The **glReadPixels()** function will read the data from a region of the framebuffer currently bound to the GL_READ_FRAMEBUFFER target, or from the default framebuffer should no user-generated framebuffer object be bound, and write it into your application's memory or into a buffer object. The x and y parameters specify the offset in window coordinates of the lower-left corner of the region, and width and height specify the width and height of the region to be read — remember, the origin of the window (which is at 0,0) is the *lower-left* corner. The format and type parameters tell OpenGL what format you want the data to be read back in. These parameters work similarly to the format and type parameters that you might pass to **glTexSubImage2D()**, for example. For instance, format might be GL_RED or GL_RGBA, and type might be GL_UNSIGNED_BYTE or GL_FLOAT. The resulting pixel data is written into the region specified by data.

If no buffer object is bound to the GL_PIXEL_PACK_BUFFER target, then data is interpreted as a raw pointer into your application's memory. However, if a buffer *is* bound to the GL_PIXEL_PACK_BUFFER target, then data is treated as an offset into that buffer's data store, and the image data is written there. If you want to get at that data, you can then map the buffer for reading by calling **glMapBufferRange()** with the GL_MAP_READ_BIT set and access the data. Otherwise, you could use the buffer for any other purpose.

To specify where the color data comes from, you can call **glReadBuffer()**, passing GL_BACK or GL_COLOR_ATTACHMENT*i*, where *i* indicates which color attachment you want to read from. The prototype of **glReadBuffer()** is

```
void glReadBuffer(GLenum mode);
```

If you are using the default framebuffer rather than your own framebuffer object, then mode should be GL_BACK. This is the default, so if you never use framebuffer objects in your application (or if you only ever read from the default framebuffer), you can get away without calling **glReadBuffer()** at all. However, since user-supplied framebuffer objects can have multiple attachments, you need to specify which attachment you want to read from, and so you must call **glReadBuffer()** if you are using your own framebuffer object.

When you call **glReadPixels()** with the format parameter set to GL_DEPTH_COMPONENT, the data read will come from the depth buffer. Likewise, if format is GL_STENCIL_INDEX, then the data comes from the stencil buffer. The special GL_DEPTH_STENCIL token allows you to read both the depth and stencil buffers at the same time. However, if you take this route, then the type parameter must be either GL_UNSIGNED_INT_24_8 or GL_FLOAT_32_UNSIGNED_INT_24_8_REV, which produces packed data that you would need to interpret to get at the depth and stencil information.

When OpenGL writes the data either into your application's memory or into the buffer object bound to the GL_PIXEL_PACK_BUFFER target (if there is one bound), it writes it from left to right in order of ascending y coordinate, which, remember, has its origin at the bottom of the window and increases in an upward direction. By default, each row of the image starts at an offset from the previous, which is a multiple of four bytes. If the product of the width of the region to be read and the number of bytes per pixel is a multiple of four, then everything works out and the resulting data will be tightly packed. However, if things don't add up, then you could be left with gaps in the output. You can change this by calling **glPixelStorei()**, whose prototype is

```
void glPixelStorei(GLenum pname,
                   GLint param);
```

When you pass GL_PACK_ALIGNMENT in pname, the value you pass in param is used to round the distance in bytes between each row of the image. You can pass 1 in param to set the rounding to a single byte, effectively disabling the rounding. The other values you can pass are 2, 4, and 8.

Taking a Screenshot

Listing 9.37 demonstrates how to take a screenshot of a running application and save it as a .TGA file, which is a relatively simple image file format that is easy to generate.

```
int row_size = ((info.windowWidth * 3 + 3) & ~3);
int data_size = row_size * info.windowHeight;
unsigned char * data = new unsigned char [data_size];
```

```
#pragma pack (push, 1)
struct
{
    unsigned char identsize;      // Size of following ID field
    unsigned char cmaptype;       // Color map type 0 = none
    unsigned char imagetype;      // Image type 2 = rgb
    short cmapstart;              // First entry in palette
    short cmapsize;               // Number of entries in palette
    unsigned char cmapbpp;        // Number of bits per palette entry
    short xorigin;                // X origin
    short yorigin;                // Y origin
    short width;                  // Width in pixels
    short height;                 // Height in pixels
    unsigned char bpp;            // Bits per pixel
    unsigned char descriptor;     // Descriptor bits
} tga_header;
#pragma pack (pop)

glReadPixels(0, 0,                                        // Origin
             info.windowWidth, info.windowHeight,        // Size
             GL_BGR, GL_UNSIGNED_BYTE,                    // Format, type
             data);                                       // Data

memset(&tga_header, 0, sizeof(tga_header));
tga_header.imagetype = 2;
tga_header.width = (short)info.windowWidth;
tga_header.height = (short)info.windowHeight;
tga_header.bpp = 24;

FILE * f_out = fopen("screenshot.tga", "wb");
fwrite(&tga_header, sizeof(tga_header), 1, f_out);
fwrite(data, data_size, 1, f_out);
fclose(f_out);

delete [] data;
```

Listing 9.37: Taking a screenshot with `glReadPixels()`

The .TGA file format simply consists of a header (which is defined by
tga_header) followed by raw pixel data. The example of Listing 9.37 fills
in the header and then immediately writes the raw data into the file
immediately following it.

Copying Data between Framebuffers

Rendering to these off-screen framebuffers is fine and dandy, but
ultimately you have to do something useful with the result. Traditionally,
graphics APIs allowed an application to read pixel or buffer data back to
system memory and also provided ways to draw it back to the screen.
While these methods are functional, they required copying data from the
GPU into CPU memory and then turning right around and copying it
back. Very inefficient! We now have a way to quickly move pixel data
from one spot to another using a blit command. *Blit* is a term that refers

to direct, efficient bit-level data/memory copies. There are many theories of the origin of this term, but the most likely candidates are Bit-Level-Image-Transfer or Block-Transfer. Whatever the etymology of blit may be, the action is the same. Performing these copies is simple; the function looks like this:

```
void glBlitFramebuffer(GLint srcX0, GLint srcY0,
                       GLint srcX1, GLint srcY1,
                       GLint dstX0, GLint dstY0,
                       GLint dstX1, GLint dstY1,
                       GLbitfield mask, GLenum filter);
```

Even though this function has "blit" in the name, it does much more than a simple bitwise copy. In fact, it's more like an automated texturing operation. The source of the copy is the read framebuffer's read buffer specified by calling **glReadBuffer()**, and the area copied is the region defined by the rectangle with corners at (srcX0, srcY0) and (srcX1, srcY1). Likewise, the target of the copy is the current draw framebuffer's draw buffer specified by calling **glDrawBuffer()**, and the area copied to is the region defined by the rectangle with corners at (dstX0, dstY0) and (dstX1, dstY1). Because the rectangles for the source and destination do not have to be of equal size, you can use this function to scale the pixels being copied. If you have set the read and draw buffers to the same FBO and have bound the same FBO to the GL_DRAW_FRAMEBUFFER and GL_READ_FRAMEBUFFER bindings, you can even copy data from one portion of a framebuffer to another (so long as you're careful that the regions don't overlap).

The mask argument can be any or all of GL_DEPTH_BUFFER_BIT, GL_STENCIL_BUFFER_BIT, or GL_COLOR_BUFFER_BIT. The filter can be either GL_LINEAR or GL_NEAREST, but it must be GL_NEAREST if you are copying depth or stencil data or color data with an integer format. These filters behave the same as they would for texturing. For our example, we are only copying non-integer color data and can use a linear filter.

```
GLint width = 800;
GLint height = 600;

GLenum fboBuffs[] = { GL_COLOR_ATTACHMENT0 };

glBindFramebuffer(GL_DRAW_FRAMEBUFFER, readFBO);
glBindFramebuffer(GL_READ_FRAMEBUFFER, drawFBO);

glDrawBuffers(1, fboBuffs);
glReadBuffer(GL_COLOR_ATTACHMENT0);
glBlitFramebuffer(0, 0, width, height,
                  (width *0.8), (height*0.8),
                  width, height,
                  GL_COLOR_BUFFER_BIT, GL_LINEAR );
```

Assume the width and height of the attachments of the FBO bound in the preceding code is 800 and 600. This code creates a copy of the whole of the first color attachment of readFBO, scales it down to 80% of the total size, and places it in the upper-left corner of the first color attachment of drawFBO.

Copying Data into a Texture

As you read in the last section, you can read data from the framebuffer into your application's memory (or into a buffer object) by calling **glReadPixels()**, or from one framebuffer into another using **glBlitFramebuffer()**. If you intend to use this data as a texture, it may be more straightforward to simply copy the data directly from the framebuffer into the texture. The function to do this is **glCopyTexSubImage2D()**, and it is similar to **glTexSubImage2D()**, except that rather than taking source data from application memory or a buffer object, it takes its source data from the framebuffer. Its prototype is

```
void glCopyTexSubImage2D(GLenum target,
                         GLint level,
                         GLint xoffset,
                         GLint yoffset,
                         GLint x,
                         GLint y,
                         GLsizei width,
                         GLsizei height);
```

The target parameter is the texture target to which the destination texture is bound. For regular 2D textures, this will be GL_TEXTURE_2D, but you can also copy from the framebuffer into one of the faces of a cube map by specifying GL_TEXTURE_CUBE_MAP_POSITIVE_X, GL_TEXTURE_CUBE_MAP_NEGATIVE_X, GL_TEXTURE_CUBE_MAP_POSITIVE_Y, GL_TEXTURE_CUBE_MAP_NEGATIVE_Y, GL_TEXTURE_CUBE_MAP_POSITIVE_Z, or GL_TEXTURE_CUBE_MAP_NEGATIVE_Z. width and height represent the size of the region to be copied. x and y are the coordinates of the lower-left corner of the rectangle in the framebuffer, and xoffset and yoffset are the texel coordinates of the rectangle in the destination texture.

If your application renders directly into a texture (by attaching it to a framebuffer object), then this function might not be that useful to you. However if your application renders to the default framebuffer most of the time, you can use this function to move parts of the output into textures. If, on the other hand, you have data in a texture that you want to copy into *another* texture, you can achieve this by calling **glCopyImageSubData()**, which has a monstrous prototype:

```
void glCopyImageSubData(GLuint srcName,
                        GLenum srcTarget,
                        GLint srcLevel,
                        GLint srcX,
                        GLint srcY,
                        GLint srcZ,
                        GLuint dstName,
                        GLenum dstTarget,
                        GLint dstLevel,
                        GLint dstX,
                        GLint dstY,
                        GLint dstZ,
                        GLsizei srcWidth,
                        GLsizei srcHeight,
                        GLsizei srcDepth);
```

Unlike many of the other functions in OpenGL, this function operates *directly* on the texture objects you specify by name, rather than on objects bound to targets. srcName and srcTarget are the name and type of the source texture, and dstName and dstTarget are the name and type of the destination texture. You can pass pretty much any type of texture here, and so you have x, y, and z coordinates for the source and destination regions, and a width, height, and depth for each, too. srcX, srcY, and srcZ are the coordinates of the source region, and dstX, dstY, and dstZ are the coordinates of the destination region. The width, height, and depth of the region to copy is specified in srcWidth, srcHeight, and srcDepth.

If the textures you're copying between don't have a particular dimension (e.g., the z dimension for 2D textures doesn't exist), you should set the corresponding coordinate to zero, and size to one.

If your textures have mipmaps, you can set the source and destination mipmap levels in srcLevel and dstLevel, respectively. Otherwise, set these to zero. Note that there is no destination width, height, or depth — the destination region is the same size as the source region, and no stretching or shrinking is possible. If you want to resize part of a texture and write the result into another texture, you'll need to attach both to framebuffer objects and use **glBlitFramebuffer()**.

Reading Back Texture Data

In addition to being able to read data from the framebuffer, you can also read image data from a texture by binding it to the appropriate texture target and then calling

```
void glGetTexImage(GLenum target,
                   GLint level,
                   GLenum format,
                   GLenum type,
                   GLvoid * img);
```

The `glGetTexImage()` function works similarly to `glReadPixels()`, except that it does not allow a small region of a texture level to be read — instead, it only allows the entire level to be retrieved in one go. The `format` and `type` parameters have the same meanings as in `glReadPixels()`, and the `img` parameter is equivalent to the `data` parameter to `glReadPixels()`, including its dual use as either a client memory pointer or an offset into the buffer bound to the `GL_PIXEL_PACK_BUFFER` target, if there is one. Although only being able to read a whole level of a texture back seems to be a disadvantage, `glGetTexImage()` does possess a couple of pluses. First, you have direct access to all of the mipmap levels of the texture. Second, if you have a texture object from which you need to read data, you don't need to create a framebuffer object and attach the texture to it as you would if you were to use `glReadPixels()`.

In most cases, you would have put the data in the texture using a function such as `glTexSubImage2D()` in the first place. However, there are several ways to get data into a texture without putting it there explicitly or drawing into it with a framebuffer. For example, you can call `glGenerateMipmap()`, which will populate lower resolution mips from the higher resolution mip, or you could write directly to the image from a shader, as explained in "Writing to Textures in Shaders" back in Chapter 5.

Summary

This chapter explained a lot about the back end of OpenGL. First, we covered fragment shaders, interpolation, and a number of the built-in variables that are available to fragment shaders. We also looked into the fixed-function testing operations that are performed using the depth and stencil buffers. Next, we proceeded to color output — color masking, blending, and logical operations, which all effect how the data your fragment shader produces is written into the framebuffer.

Once we were done with the functions that you can apply to the default framebuffer, we proceeded to advanced framebuffer formats. The key advantages of user-specified framebuffers (or framebuffer objects) are that they can have multiple attachments and those attachments can be in advanced formats and color spaces such as floating point, sRGB, and pure integers. We also explored various ways to deal with resolution limits through antialiasing — antialiasing through blending, alpha to coverage, MSAA, and supersampling, and we covered the advantages and disadvantages of each.

Finally, we covered ways to get at the data you have rendered. Putting data into textures falls out naturally from attaching them to framebuffers and rendering directly to them. However, we also showed how you can copy data from a framebuffer into a texture, from framebuffer to framebuffer, from texture to texture, and from the framebuffer to your application's own memory or into buffer objects.

Chapter 10

Compute Shaders

WHAT YOU'LL LEARN IN THIS CHAPTER

- How to create, compile, and dispatch compute shaders

- How to pass data between compute shader invocations

- How to synchronize compute shaders and keep their work in order

Compute shaders are a way to take advantage of the enormous computational power of graphics processors that implement OpenGL. Just like all shaders in OpenGL, they are written in GLSL and run in large parallel groups that simultaneously work on huge amounts of data. In addition to the facilities available to other shaders such as texturing, storage buffers, and atomic memory operations, compute shaders are able to synchronize with each other and share data amongst themselves in order to make general computation easier. They stand apart from the rest of the OpenGL pipeline and are designed to provide as much flexibility to the application developer as possible. In this chapter, we discuss compute shaders, their similarities, and their differences to other shader types in OpenGL and explain some of the unique properties and abilities of compute shaders.

Using Compute Shaders

Modern graphics processors are extremely powerful devices capable of performing a huge amount of numeric calculation. You were briefly introduced to the idea of using compute shaders for non-graphics work back in Chapter 3, but there we only really skimmed the surface. In fact, the compute shader stage is effectively its own pipeline, somewhat disconnected from the rest of OpenGL. It has no fixed inputs or outputs, does not interface with any of the fixed-function pipeline stages, is very flexible, and has capabilities that other stages do not possess.

Having said this, a compute shader is just like any other shader from a programming point of view. It is written in GLSL, represented as a shader object, and linked into a program object. When you create a compute shader, you call **glCreateShader()** and pass the GL_COMPUTE_SHADER parameter as the shader type. You get back a new shader object from this call that you can use to load your shader code with **glShaderSource()**, compile with **glCompileShader()**, and attach to a program object with **glAttachShader()**. Then, you go ahead and link the program object as normal by calling **glLinkProgram()**, just as you would with any graphics program.

You can't mix and match compute shaders with shaders of other types. That means, for example, that you can't attach a compute shader to a program object that also has a vertex or fragment shader attached to it and then link the program object. If you attempt this, the link will fail. Thus, a linked program object can contain only compute shaders or only graphics shaders (vertex, tessellation, geometry, or fragment), but not a combination of the two. We will sometimes refer to a linked program object that contains compute shaders (and so only compute shaders) as a *compute program* (as opposed to a *graphics program*, which contains only graphics shaders).

Example code to compile and link our do-nothing compute shader (first introduced in Listing 3.13) is shown in Listing 10.1.

```
GLuint      compute_shader;
GLuint      compute_program;

static const GLchar * compute_source[] =
{
    "#version 430 core                                      \n"
    "                                                       \n"
    "layout (local_size_x = 32, local_size_y = 32) in;      \n"
    "                                                       \n"
```

```
"void main(void)                                          \n"
"{                                                        \n"
"    // Do nothing                                        \n"
"}                                                        \n"
};

// Create a shader, attach source, and compile.
compute_shader = glCreateShader(GL_COMPUTE_SHADER);
glShaderSource(compute_shader, 1, compute_source, NULL);
glCompileShader(compute_shader);

// Create a program, attach shader, link.
compute_program = glCreateProgram();
glAttachShader(compute_program, compute_shader);
glLinkProgram(compute_program);

// Delete shader as we're done with it.
glDeleteShader(compute_shader);
```

Listing 10.1: Creating and compiling a compute shader

Once you have run the code in Listing 10.1, you will have a ready-to-run compute program in `compute_program`. A compute program can use uniforms, uniform blocks, shader storage blocks, and so on, just as any other program does. You also make it current by calling **glUseProgram()**. Once it is the current program object, functions such as **glUniform4fv()** affect its state as normal.

Executing Compute Shaders

Once you have made a compute program current, and set up any resources that it might need access to, you need to actually execute it. To do this, we have a pair of functions:

```
void glDispatchCompute(GLuint num_groups_x,
                       GLuint num_groups_y,
                       GLuint num_groups_z);
```

and

```
void glDispatchComputeIndirect(GLintptr indirect);
```

The **glDispatchComputeIndirect()** function is to **glDispatchCompute()** as **glDrawArraysIndirect()** is to **glDrawArraysInstancedBaseInstance()**. That is, the indirect parameter is interpreted as an offset into a buffer object that contains a set parameters that could be passed to **glDispatchCompute()**. In code, this structure would look like

```
typedef struct {
    GLuint num_groups_x;
    GLuint num_groups_y;
    GLuint num_groups_z;
} DispatchIndirectCommand;
```

However, we need to understand how these parameters are interpreted in order to use them effectively.

Global and Local Work Groups

Compute shaders execute in what are called *work groups*. A single call to **glDispatchCompute()** or **glDispatchComputeIndirect()** will cause a single *global work group*[1] to be sent to OpenGL for processing. That global work group will then be subdivided into a number of *local work groups* — the amount of local work groups in each of the x, y, and z dimensions is set by the num_groups_x, num_groups_y, and num_groups_z parameters, respectively. A work group is fundamentally a 3D block of *work items*, where each work item is processed by an invocation of a compute shader running your code. The size of each local work group in the x, y, and z dimensions is set using an input layout qualifier in your shader source code. You can see an example of this in our simple compute shader that we introduced earlier, and it looks like this:

```
layout (local_size_x = 4,
        local_size_y = 7,
        local_size_z = 10) in;
```

In this example, the local work group size would be $4 \times 7 \times 10$ work items or invocations for a total of 280 work items per local work group. The maximum size of a work group can be found by querying the values of two parameters, GL_MAX_COMPUTE_WORK_GROUP_SIZE and GL_MAX_COMPUTE_WORK_GROUP_INVOCATIONS. For the first of these, you query it using the **glGetIntegeri_v()** function, passing it as the target parameter and 0, 1, or 2 as the index parameter to specify the x, y, or z dimension, respectively. The maximum size will be at least 1024 items in the x and y dimensions and 64 in the z dimension. The value you get by querying the GL_MAX_COMPUTE_WORK_GROUP_INVOCATIONS constant is the maximum total number of invocations allowed in a single work group, which is the maximum allowed product of the x, y, and z dimensions, or the *volume* of the local work group. That value will be at least 1024 items.

It's possible to launch 1D or 2D work groups by simply setting either the y or z dimensions (or both) to 1. In fact, the default size in all dimensions is 1, and so if you don't include them in your input layout qualifier, you will create a work group size of lower dimension than 3. For example,

---

1. The OpenGL specification doesn't explicitly call the total work dispatched by a single command a *global work group*, but rather uses the unqualified term *work group* to mean *local work group* and never names the global work group.

```
layout (local_size_x = 512) in;
```

will create a 1D local work group of 512 ($\times$ 1 $\times$ 1) items and

```
layout (local_size_x = 64,
        local_size_y = 64) in;
```

will create a 2D local work group of 64 $\times$ 64 ($\times$ 1) items. The local work group size is used when you link the program to determine the size and dimensions of the work groups executed by the program. You can find the local work group size of a program's compute shaders by calling **glGetProgramiv()** with pname set to GL_COMPUTE_WORK_GROUP_SIZE. It will return three integers giving the size of the work groups. For example, you could write:

```
int size[3];

glGetProgramiv(program, GL_COMPUTE_WORKGROUP_SIZE, size);

printf("Work group size is %d x %d % xd items.\n",
       size[0], size[1], size[2]);
```

Once you have defined a local work group size, you can dispatch a 3D block of workgroups to do work for you. The size of this block is specified by the num_groups_x, num_groups_y, and num_groups_z parameters to **glDispatchCompute()** or the equivalent members of the DispatchIndirectCommand structure stored in the buffer object bound to the GL_DISPATCH_INDIRECT_BUFFER target. This block of local work groups is known as the *global work group*, and its dimension doesn't need to be the same as the dimension of the local work group. That is, you could dispatch a 3D global work group of 1D local work groups, or a 2D global work group of 3D local work groups, and so on.

Compute Shader Inputs and Outputs

First and foremost, compute shaders *have no built-in outputs*. Yes, you read correctly — they have no built-in outputs at all, nor can you declare any user-defined outputs as you are able to do in other shader stages. This is because the compute shader forms a kind of single-stage pipeline with nothing before it and nothing after it. However, like some of the graphics shaders, it does have a few built-in input variables that you can use to determine where you are in your local work group and within the greater global work group.

The first variable, gl_LocalInvocationID, is the index of the shader invocation within the local work group. It is implicitly declared as a **uvec3** input to the shader and each element ranges in value from zero to one less than the local work group size in the corresponding dimension (x, y, or z). The local work group size is stored in the gl_WorkGroupSize variable, which is also implicitly declared as a **uvec3** type. Again, even if you only declared your local work group size to be 1D or 2D, the work group will still essentially be 3D, but with the size of the unused dimensions set to one. That is, gl_LocalInvocationID and gl_WorkGroupSize will still be implicitly declared as **uvec3** variables, but the y and z components of gl_LocalInvocationID will be 0, and for gl_WorkGroupSize, they will be 1.

Just as gl_WorkGroupSize and gl_LocalInvocationID store the size of the local work group and the location of the current shader invocation within the work group, gl_NumWorkGroups and gl_WorkGroupID contain the number of work groups and the index of the current work group within the global set, respectively. Again, both are implicitly declared as **uvec3** variables. The value of gl_NumWorkGroups is set by the **glDispatchCompute()** or **glDispatchComputeIndirect()** commands and contains the values of num_groups_x, num_groups_y, and num_groups_z in its three elements. The elements of gl_WorkGroupID range in value from zero to one less than the values of the corresponding elements of gl_NumWorkGroups.

These variables are illustrated in Figure 10.1. The diagram shows a global work group that contains three work groups in the x dimension, four work groups in the y dimension, and eight work groups in the z dimension. Each local work group is a 2D array of work items that contains six items in the x dimension and four items in the y dimension.

Between gl_WorkGroupID and gl_LocalInvocationID, you can tell where in the complete set of work items your current shader invocation is located. Likewise, between gl_NumWorkGroups and gl_WorkGroupSize, you can figure out the total number of invocations in the global set. However, OpenGL provides the global invocation index to you through the gl_GlobalInvocationID built-in variable. This is effectively calculated as

```
gl_GlobalInvocationID = gl_WorkGroupID * gl_WorkGroupSize +
                        gl_LocalInvocationID;
```

Finally, the gl_LocalInvocationIndex built-in variable contains a "flattened" form of gl_LocalInvocationID. That is, the 3D variable is converted to a 1D index using the following code:

```
gl_LocalInvocationIndex =
    gl_LocalInvocationID.z * gl_WorkGroupSize.x * gl_WorkGroupSize.y +
    gl_LocalInvocationID.y * gl_WorkGroupSize.x +
    gl_LocalInvocationID.x;
```

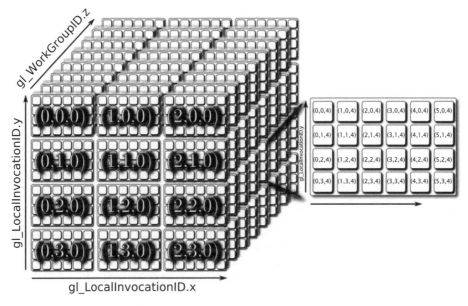

Figure 10.1: Global and local compute work group dimensions

The values stored in these variables allow your shader to know where it is in the local and global work groups and can then be used as indices into arrays of data, texture coordinates, random seeds, or for any other purpose.

Now we come to outputs. We started this section by stating that compute shaders have no outputs. That's true, but it doesn't mean that compute shaders can't output any data — it just means that there are no *fixed* outputs represented by built-in output variables, for example. Compute shaders can still produce data, but it must be stored into memory explicitly by your shader code. For instance, in your compute shader you could write into a shader storage block, use image functions such as `imageStore` or atomics, or increment and decrement the values of atomic counters. These operations have *side effects*, which means that their operation can be detected because they update the contents of memory or otherwise have externally visible consequences.

Consider the shader shown in Listing 10.2, which reads from one image, logically inverts the data, and writes the data back out to another image.

```
#version 430 core

layout (local_size_x = 32,
        local_size_y = 32) in;

layout (binding = 0, rgba32f) uniform image2D img_input;
layout (binding = 1) uniform image2D img_output;

void main(void)
{
    vec4 texel;
    ivec2 p = ivec2(gl_GlobalInvocationID.xy);

    texel = imageLoad(img_input, p);
    texel = vec4(1.0) - texel;
    imageStore(img_output, p, texel);
}
```

Listing 10.2: Compute shader image inversion

In order to execute this shader, we would compile it and link it into a program object and then set up our images by binding a level of a texture object to each of the first two image units. As you can see from Listing 10.2, the local work group size is 32 invocations in x and y, so our images should ideally be integer multiples of 32 texels wide and high. Once the images are bound, we can call **glDispatchCompute()**, setting the num_groups_x and num_groups_y parameters to the width and height of the images divided by 32, respectively, and setting num_groups_z to 1. Code to do this is shown in Listing 10.3.

```
// Bind input image
glBindImageTexture(0, tex_input, 0, GL_FALSE,
                   0, GL_READ_ONLY, GL_RGBA32F);

// Bind output image
glBindImageTexture(1, tex_output, 0, GL_FALSE,
                   0, GL_WRITE_ONLY, GL_RGBA32F);

// Dispatch the compute shader
glDispatchCompute(IMAGE_WIDTH / 32, IMAGE_HEIGHT / 32, 1);
```

Listing 10.3: Dispatching the image copy compute shader

Compute Shader Communication

Compute shaders execute on work items in work groups much as tessellation control shaders execute on control points in patches[2] — both work groups and patches are created from groups of invocations. Within a

---

2. This may also seem similar to the behavior of geometry shaders. However, there is an important difference — compute shaders and tessellation control shaders execute an invocation per work item or per control point, respectively. Geometry shaders, on the other hand, execute an invocation for each primitive, and each of those invocations has access to all of the input data for that primitive.

single patch, tessellation control shaders can write to variables qualified with the `patch` storage qualifier and, if they are synchronized correctly, read the values that other invocations in the same patch wrote to them. As such, this allows a limited form of communication between the tessellation control shader invocations in a single patch. However, this comes with substantial limitations — for example, the amount of storage available for `patch` qualified variables is fairly limited, and the number of control points in a single patch is quite small.

Compute shaders provide a similar mechanism, but offer significantly more flexibility and power. Just as you can declare variables with the `patch` storage qualifier in a tessellation control shader, you can declare variables with the `shared` storage qualifier, which allows them to be *shared* between compute shader invocations running in the *same local work group*. Variables declared with the `shared` storage qualifier are known as *shared variables*. Access to shared variables is generally much faster than access to main memory through images or storage blocks. Thus, if you expect multiple invocations of your compute shader to access the same data, it makes sense to copy the data from main memory into a shared variable (or an array of them), access the data from there, possibly updating it in place, and then write any results back to main memory when you're done.

Keep in mind, though, that you can only use a limited number of shared variables. A modern graphics board might have several gigabytes of main memory, whereas the amount of shared variable storage space might be limited to just a few kilobytes. The amount of shared memory available to a compute shader can be determined by calling `glGetIntegerv()` with pname set to GL_MAX_COMPUTE_SHARED_MEMORY_SIZE. The minimum amount of shared memory required to be supported in OpenGL is only 32KB, so while your implementation may have more than this, you shouldn't count on it being substantially larger.

Synchronizing Compute Shaders

The invocations in a work group most likely run in parallel — this is where the vast computation power of graphics processors comes from. The processor will likely divide each local work group into a number of smaller[3] chunks, executing the invocations in a single chunk in lockstep. These chunks are then *time-sliced* onto the processor's computational resources, and those timeslices may be assigned in any order. It may be

---

3. Chunk sizes of 16, 32, or 64 elements are common.

that a chunk of invocations is completed before any more chunks from the same local work group begin, but more than likely there will be many "live" chunks present on the processor at any given time.

Because these chunks can effectively run out of order but are allowed to communicate, we need a way to ensure that messages received by a recipient are the most recent sent. Imagine if you were told to go to someone's office and perform the duty written on their whiteboard. Each day, they would write a new message on the whiteboard, but you don't know at what time they do it. When you go into the office, how do you know if the message that's there is what you're supposed to do, or if it's left over from the previous day? You'd be in a bit of trouble. Now, if the owner of the office left their door locked until they'd been there and written the message and then you showed up and the door was locked, you'd have to wait outside the office. This is known as a *barrier*. If the door is open, you can go look at the message. If it's locked, you need to wait until the person arrives to open it.

A similar mechanism is available to compute shaders. This is the barrier() function, and it executes a *flow control barrier*. When you call barrier() in your compute shader, it will be blocked until all other shader invocations in the same local work group have reached that point in the shader too. We touched on this back in "Communication between Shader Invocations" in Chapter 8, where we described the behavior of the barrier() function in the context of tessellation control shaders. In a time-slicing architecture, executing the barrier() function means that your shader (along with the chunk it's in) will give up its timeslice so that another invocation can execute until it reaches the barrier. Once all the other invocations in the local work group reach the barrier (or if they'd already gotten there before your invocation did) execution continues as normal.

Flow control barriers are important when shared memory is in use because they allow you to know when other shader invocations in the same local workgroup have reached the same point as the current invocation. If the current invocation has written to some shared memory variable, then you know that all the others must have written to theirs too, and therefore it's safe to go ahead and read the data they wrote. Without a barrier, you would have no idea whether data that was supposed to have been written to shared variables actually has been. At best, you'd leave your application susceptible to *race conditions*, and at worst, the application won't work at all. Consider, for example, the shader in Listing 10.4.

```
#version 430 core

layout (local_size_x = 1024) in;

layout (binding = 0, r32ui) uniform uimageBuffer image_in;
layout (binding = 1) uniform uimageBuffer image_out;

shared uint temp_storage[1024];

void main(void)
{
    // Load from the input image
    uint n = imageLoad(image_in, gl_LocalInvocationID.x).x;

    // Store into shared storage
    temp_storage[gl_LocalInvocationID.x] = n;

    // Uncomment this to avoid the race condition
    // barrier();
    // memoryBarrierShared();

    // Read the data written by the invocation ''to the left''
    n = temp_storage[(gl_LocalInvocationID.x - 1) & 1023];

    // Write new data into the buffer
    imageStore(image_out, gl_LocalInvocationID.x, n);
}
```

Listing 10.4: Compute shader with race conditions

This shader loads data from a buffer image into a shared variable. Each invocation of the shader loads a single item from the buffer and writes it into its own "slot" in the shared variable array. Then, it reads from the slot owned by the invocation to its left and writes the data out to the buffer image. The result *should* be that the data in the buffer is *moved* along by one element. However, Figure 10.2 illustrates what actually happens.

As you can see, multiple shader invocations have been time-sliced onto a single computational resource. At t0, invocation A runs the first couple of lines of the shader and writes its value to temp_storage. At t1, invocation B runs a line, and then at t2, invocation C takes over and runs the same first two lines of the shader. At time t3, A gets its timeslice back again and completes the shader. It's done at this point, but the other invocations haven't finished their work yet. At t4, invocation D finally gets a turn but is quickly interrupted by invocation C, which reads from temp_storage. Now we have a problem — invocation C was expecting to read data from the shared storage that was written by invocation B, but invocation B hasn't reached that point in the shader yet! Execution continues blindly, and invocations D, C, and B all finish the shader, but the data stored by C will be garbage.

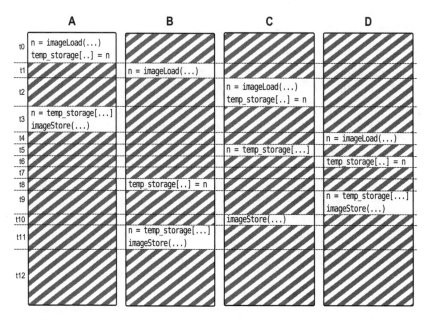

Figure 10.2: Effect of race conditions in a compute shader

This is known as a *race condition*. The shader invocations race each other to the same point in the shader, and some invocations will read from the temp_storage shared variable before others have written their data into it. The result is that they pick up stale data that then gets written into the output buffer image. Uncommenting the call to barrier() in Listing 10.4 produces an execution flow more like that shown in Figure 10.3.

Compare Figures 10.2 and 10.3. Both depict four shader invocations being time-sliced onto the same computational resource, only Figure 10.3 does not exhibit the race condition. In Figure 10.3, we again start with shader invocation A executing the first couple of lines of the shader, but then it calls the barrier() function, which causes it to yield its timeslice. Next, invocation B executes the first couple of lines and then is pre-empted. Then, C executes the shader as far as the barrier() function and so yields. Invocation B executes its barrier but gets no further because D still has not reached the barrier function. Finally, invocation D gets a chance to run, reads from the image buffer, writes its data into the shared storage area, and then calls barrier(). This signals all the other invocations that it is safe to continue running.

Immediately after invocation D executes the barrier, all other invocations are able to run again. Invocation C loads from the shared storage, then D,

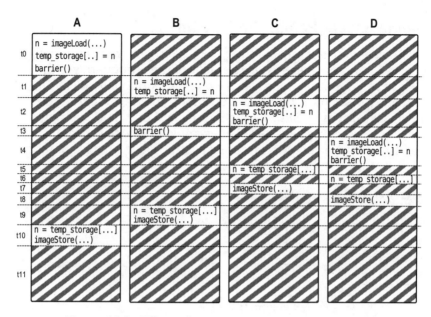

Figure 10.3: Effect of `barrier()` on race conditions

and then C and D both store their results to the image. Finally, invocations A and B read from the shared storage and write their results out to memory. As you can see, no invocation tried to read data that hasn't been written yet. The presence of the `barrier()` functions affected the scheduling of the invocations with respect to one another. Although these diagrams show only four invocations competing for a single resource, in real OpenGL implementations there are likely to be many hundreds of threads competing for perhaps a few tens of resources. As you might guess, the likelihood of data corruption due to race conditions is much higher in these scenarios.

Examples

The following section contains several examples of the use of compute shaders. In our first example, the *parallel prefix sum*, we demonstrate how to implement an algorithm (which at first seems like a very serial process) in an efficient parallel manner. In our second example, an implementation of the classic *flocking* algorithm (also known as *boids*) is shown. In both examples, we make use of local and global work groups, synchronization using the `barrier()` command, and shared local variables — a feature unique to compute shaders.

Compute Shader Parallel Prefix Sum

A *prefix sum operation* is an algorithm that, given an array of input values, computes a new array where each element of the output array is the sum of all of the values of the input array up to (and optionally including) the current array element. A prefix sum operation that includes the current element is known as an *inclusive* prefix sum, and one that does not is known as an *exclusive* prefix sum. For example, the code shown in Listing 10.5 shows a simple C++ implementation of a prefix sum function that can be inclusive or exclusive.

```
void prefix_sum(const float * in_array,
                float * out_array,
                int elements,
                bool inclusive)
{
    float f = 0.0f;
    int i;

    if (inclusive)
    {
        for (i = 0; i < elements; i++)
        {
            f += in_array[i];
            out_array[i] = f;
        }
    }
    else
    {
        for (i = 0; i < elements; i++)
        {
            out_array[i] = f;
            f += in_array[i];
        }
    }
}
```

Listing 10.5: Simple prefix sum implementation in C++

Notice that the only difference between the inclusive and exclusive prefix sum implementations is that the accumulation of the input array is conducted before writing to the output array rather than afterwards. The result of running an inclusive prefix sum on an array of values is illustrated in Figure 10.4.

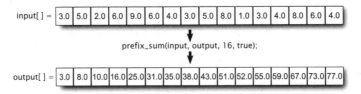

Figure 10.4: Sample input and output of a prefix sum operation

You should appreciate that as the number of elements in the input and output arrays grows, the number of addition operations grows too and can become quite large. Also, as the result written to each element of the output array is the sum of all elements before it (and therefore dependent on all of them), it would seem at first glance that this type of algorithm does not lend itself well to parallelization. However, this is not the case — the prefix sum operation is highly parallelizable. At its core, the prefix sum is nothing more than a huge number of additions of adjacent array elements. Take, for example, a prefix sum of four input elements, I_0 through I_3, producing an output array O_0 through O_3. The result is

$$O_0 = I_0$$
$$O_1 = I_0 + I_1$$
$$O_2 = I_0 + I_1 + I_2$$
$$O_3 = I_0 + I_1 + I_2 + I_3$$

The key to parallelization is to break large tasks into groups of smaller, independent tasks that can be completed independently of one another. Now, you can see that in the computation of O_2 and O_3, we use the sum of I_0 and I_1, which we also need to calculate O_1. So, if we break this operation into multiple steps, we see that we have in the first step

$$O_0 = I_0$$
$$O_1 = I_0 + I_1$$
$$O_2 = I_2$$
$$O_3 = I_2 + I_3$$

Then, in a second step, we can compute

$$O_2 = O_2 + O_1$$
$$O_3 = O_3 + O_1$$

Now, the computations of O_1 and O_3 are independent of one another in the first step and therefore can be computed in parallel as can the updates of the values of O_2 and O_3 in the second step. If you look closely, you will see that the first step simply takes a four-element prefix sum and breaks it into a pair of two-element prefix sums that are trivially computed. In the second step, we use the result of the previous to update the results of the inner sums. In fact, we can break any sized prefix sum into smaller and smaller chunks until we reach a point where we can compute the inner sum directly. This is shown pictorially in Figure 10.5.

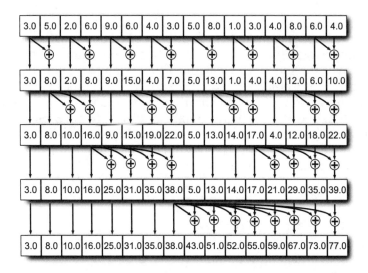

Figure 10.5: Breaking a prefix sum into smaller chunks

The recursive nature of this algorithm is apparent in Figure 10.5. The number of additions required by this method is actually more than the sequential algorithm for prefix sum calculation would require. In this example, we would require 15 additions to compute the prefix sum with a sequential algorithm, whereas here we require 8 additions per step and 4 steps for a total of 32 additions. However, we can execute the 8 additions of each step in parallel, and hence we will be done in 4 steps instead of 15, making the algorithm almost 4 times faster than the sequential one.

As the number of elements in the input array grows, the potential speedup becomes greater. For example, if we expand the input array to 32 elements, we execute 5 steps of 16 additions each rather than 31 sequential additions. Assuming we have enough computational resources to perform 16 additions at a time, we now take 5 steps instead of 31 and go around 6 times faster. Likewise, for an input array size of 64, we'd take 6 steps of 32 additions rather than 63 sequential additions, and go 10 times faster! Of course, we eventually hit a limit in either the number of additions we can perform in parallel, the amount of memory bandwidth we consume reading and writing the input and output arrays, or something else.

To implement this in a compute shader, we can load a chunk of input data into shared variables, compute the inner sums, synchronize with the other invocations, accumulate their results, and so on. An example compute shader that implements this algorithm is shown in Listing 10.6.

```glsl
#version 430 core

layout (local_size_x = 1024) in;

layout (binding = 0) coherent buffer block1
{
    float input_data[gl_WorkGroupSize.x];
};

layout (binding = 1) coherent buffer block2
{
    float output_data[gl_WorkGroupSize.x];
};

shared float shared_data[gl_WorkGroupSize.x * 2];

void main(void)
{
    uint id = gl_LocalInvocationID.x;
    uint rd_id;
    uint wr_id;
    uint mask;

    // The number of steps is the log base 2 of the
    // work group size, which should be a power of 2
    const uint steps = uint(log2(gl_WorkGroupSize.x)) + 1;
    uint step = 0;

    // Each invocation is responsible for the content of
    // two elements of the output array
    shared_data[id * 2] = input_data[id * 2];
    shared_data[id * 2 + 1] = input_data[id * 2 + 1];

    // Synchronize to make sure that everyone has initialized
    // their elements of shared_data[] with data loaded from
    // the input arrays
    barrier();
    memoryBarrierShared();

    // For each step...
    for (step = 0; step < steps; step++)
    {
        // Calculate the read and write index in the
        // shared array
        mask = (1 << step) - 1;
        rd_id = ((id >> step) << (step + 1)) + mask;
        wr_id = rd_id + 1 + (id & mask);

        // Accumulate the read data into our element
        shared_data[wr_id] += shared_data[rd_id];

        // Synchronize again to make sure that everyone
        // has caught up with us
        barrier();
        memoryBarrierShared();
    }

    // Finally write our data back to the output image
    output_data[id * 2] = shared_data[id * 2];
    output_data[id * 2 + 1] = shared_data[id * 2 + 1];
}
```

Listing 10.6: Prefix sum implementation using a compute shader

The shader shown in Listing 10.6 has a local workgroup size of 1024, which means it will process arrays of 2048 elements, as each invocation computes two elements of the output array. The shared variable shared_data is used to store the data that is in flight, and at the start of execution, the shader loads two adjacent elements from the input arrays into the array. Next, it executes the barrier() function. This is to ensure that all of the shader invocations have loaded their data into the shared array before the inner loop begins.

Each iteration of the inner loop performs one step of the algorithm. This loop executes $log_2(N)$ times, where N is the number of elements in the array. For each invocation, the shader calculates the index of the first and second elements to be added together and then computes the sum, writing the result back into the shared array. At the end of the loop, there is another call to barrier(), which ensures that the invocations are fully synchronized before the next iteration of the loop and ultimately when the loop exits. Finally, it writes the result to the output buffer.

Prefix sum algorithms can be applied in a *separable* manner to multi-dimensional data sets such as images and volumes. You have already seen an example of a separable algorithm when we performed Gaussian filtering in our bloom example back in Chapter 9. To produce a prefix sum of an image, we would first apply our prefix sum algorithm across each row of pixels in the image, producing a new image, and then apply another prefix sum on each of the columns of the at result. The output of these two steps is a new 2D grid where each point represents the sum of all of the values contained in the *rectangle* whose corners are at the origin and at the point of interest. Figure 10.6 demonstrates the principle.

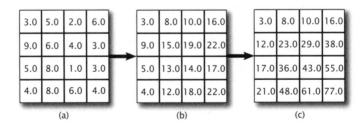

Figure 10.6: A 2D prefix sum

As you can see, given the input in Figure 10.6 (a), the first step simply computes a number of prefix sums over the rows of the image, producing an output image that is comprised of a set of prefix sums shown in Figure 10.6 (b). The second step performs prefix sum operations on the columns of the intermediate image, producing an output containing the 2D prefix sum of the original image, shown in Figure 10.6 (c). Such an image is called a *summed area table,* and is an extremely important data structure with many applications in computer graphics.

We can modify our shader of Listing 10.6 to compute the prefix sums of the rows of an image variable rather than a shader storage buffer. The modified shader is shown in Listing 10.7. As an optimization, the shader reads from the input image's rows but writes to the images *columns.* This means that the output image will be transposed with respect to the input. However, we're going to apply this shader twice, and we know that transposing an image twice returns it to its original orientation, which means that the final result will be correctly oriented with respect to the original input. Also, if we wanted to avoid the transpose operation, the shader to process the rows would need to be different from the shader that processes the columns (or do extra work to figure out how to index the image). With this approach, the shader for both passes is identical.

```
#version 430 core

layout (local_size_x = 1024) in;

shared float shared_data[gl_WorkGroupSize.x * 2];

layout (binding = 0, r32f) readonly uniform image2D input_image;
layout (binding = 1, r32f) writeonly uniform image2D output_image;

void main(void)
{
    uint id = gl_LocalInvocationID.x;
    uint rd_id;
    uint wr_id;
    uint mask;
    ivec2 P = ivec2(id * 2, gl_WorkGroupID.x);

    const uint steps = uint(log2(gl_WorkGroupSize.x)) + 1;
    uint step = 0;

    shared_data[id * 2] = imageLoad(input_image, P).r;
    shared_data[id * 2 + 1] = imageLoad(input_image,
                                        P + ivec2(1, 0)).r;

    barrier();
    memoryBarrierShared();

    for (step = 0; step < steps; step++)
    {
        mask = (1 << step) - 1;
        rd_id = ((id >> step) << (step + 1)) + mask;
        wr_id = rd_id + 1 + (id & mask);

        shared_data[wr_id] += shared_data[rd_id];

        barrier();
```

```
        memoryBarrierShared();
    }

    imageStore(output_image, P.yx, vec4(shared_data[id * 2]));
    imageStore(output_image, P.yx + ivec2(0, 1),
            vec4(shared_data[id * 2 + 1]));
}
```

Listing 10.7: Compute shader to generate a 2D prefix sum

Each local work group of the shader in Listing 10.7 is still one dimensional. However, when we launch the shader for the first pass, we create a one-dimensional global work group containing as many local work groups as there are rows in the image, and then when we launch it for the second pass, we create as many local work groups as there are columns in the image (which are actually rows again at this point due to the transpose operation performed by the shader). Each local work group will therefore process the row or column of the image determined by the global workgroup index.

Given a summed area table for an image, we can actually compute the sum of the elements contained within an arbitrary rectangle of that image. To do this, we simply need four values from the table, each one giving the sum of the elements contained within the rectangle spanning from the origin to its coordinate. Given a rectangle of interest defined by an upper-left and lower-right coordinate, we add the values from the summed area table at the upper-left and lower-right coordinates, and then *subtract* the values at its upper-right and lower-left coordinates. To see why this works, refer to Figure 10.7.

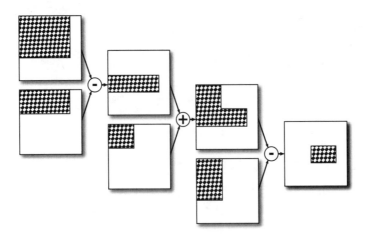

Figure 10.7: Computing the sum of a rectangle in a summed area table

Now, the number of pixels contained in any given rectangle of the summed area table is simply the rectangle's area. Given this, we know that if we take the sum of all the elements contained with the rectangle and divide this through by its area, we will be left with the *average* value of the elements inside the rectangle. Averaging a number of values together is a form of filtering known as a *box filter*, and while it's pretty crude, it can be useful for certain applications. In particular, being able to take the average of an arbitrary number of pixels centered around an arbitrary point in an image allows us to create a variable-sized filter, where the dimensions of the filtered rectangle can be changed per pixel.

As an example, Figure 10.8 shows an image that has a variable-sized filter applied to it. The image is least heavily filtered on the left and more heavily filtered on the right. As you can see, the right side of the image is substantially more blurry than the left side of it.

Figure 10.8: Variable filtering applied to an image

Simple filtering effects like this are great, but we can use this same technique to generate some much more interesting results. One such effect is the *depth of field* effect. Cameras have two properties that are relevant to this effect — *focal distance* and *focal depth*. The focal distance refers to the distance from the camera at which an object must be placed to be perfectly in focus. The focal depth refers to the rate at which an object becomes out of focus as it moves away from this sweet spot.

An example of this is seen in the photograph[4] shown in Figure 10.9. The glass closest to the camera is in sharp focus. However, as the row of glasses progresses from front to back, they become successively less well defined. The basket of oranges in the background is quite out of focus. The true blur of an image due to out of focus lenses is caused by a number of complex optical phenomena, but we can make a pretty good approximation to the visual effect with our rudimentary box filter.

Figure 10.9: Depth of field in a photograph

To simulate our depth of field effect, we'll first render our scene as normal, but save the depth of each fragment (which is approximately equal to its distance from the camera). When this depth value is equal to our simulated camera's focal distance, the image will be sharp and in focus, as it normally is with computer graphics. As the depth of a pixel strays from this perfect depth, the amount of blur we apply to the image should increase too.

We have implemented this in the dof sample. In the program, we convert the rendered image into a summed area table using the compute shader shown in Listing 10.7, modified slightly to operate on **vec3** data rather than a single floating-point value per pixel. Also, as we rendered the image, we stored the per-pixel view-space depth in the fourth *alpha* channel of the image so that our fragment shader, shown in Listing 10.8, would have access to it. The fragment shader then computes the area of confusion (which is a fancy term for the size of the blurred size) for the

___
4. Photograph courtesy of http://www.cookthestory.com.

current pixel and uses it to build a filter width (m), reading data from the summed area table to produce blurry pixels.

```
#version 430 core

layout (binding = 0) uniform sampler2D input_image;

layout (location = 0) out vec4 color;

uniform float focal_distance = 50.0;
uniform float focal_depth = 30.0;

void main(void)
{
    // s will be used to scale our texture coordinates before
    // looking up data in our SAT image.
    vec2 s = 1.0 / textureSize(input_image, 0);
    // C is the center of the filter
    vec2 C = gl_FragCoord.xy;

    // First, retrieve the value of the SAT at the center
    // of the filter. The last channel of this value stores
    // the view-space depth of the pixel.
    vec4 v = texelFetch(input_image, ivec2(gl_FragCoord.xy), 0).rgba;

    // M will be the radius of our filter kernel
    float m;

    // For this application, we clear our depth image to zero
    // before rendering to it, so if it's still zero, we haven't
    // rendered to the image here. Thus, we set our radius to
    // 0.5 (i.e., a diameter of 1.0) and move on.
    if (v.w == 0.0)
    {
        m = 0.5;
    }
    else
    {
        // Calculate a circle of confusion
        m = abs(v.w - focal_distance);

        // Simple smoothstep scale and bias. Minimum radius is
        // 0.5 (diameter 1.0), maximum is 8.0. Box filter kernels
        // greater than about 16 pixels don't look good at all.
        m = 0.5 + smoothstep(0.0, focal_depth, m) * 7.5;
    }

    // Calculate the positions of the four corners of our
    // area to sample from.
    vec2 P0 = vec2(C * 1.0) + vec2(-m, -m);
    vec2 P1 = vec2(C * 1.0) + vec2(-m, m);
    vec2 P2 = vec2(C * 1.0) + vec2(m, -m);
    vec2 P3 = vec2(C * 1.0) + vec2(m, m);

    // Scale our coordinates.
    P0 *= s;
    P1 *= s;
    P2 *= s;
    P3 *= s;

    // Fetch the values of the SAT at the four corners
    vec3 a = textureLod(input_image, P0, 0).rgb;
```

```
vec3 b = textureLod(input_image, P1, 0).rgb;
vec3 c = textureLod(input_image, P2, 0).rgb;
vec3 d = textureLod(input_image, P3, 0).rgb;

// Calculate the sum of all pixels inside the kernel.
vec3 f = a - b - c + d;

// Scale radius -> diameter.
m *= 2;

// Divide through by area
f /= float(m * m);

// Output final color
color = vec4(f, 1.0);
}
```

Listing 10.8: Depth of field using summed area tables

The shader in Listing 10.8 takes as input a texture containing the depth of each pixel and the summed area table of the image computed earlier, along with the parameters of the simulated camera. As the absolute value of the difference between the pixel's depth and the camera's focal distance increases, it uses this value to compute the size of the filtering rectangle (which is known as the area of confusion). It then reads the four values from the summed area table at the corners of the rectangle, computes the average value of its content, and writes this to the framebuffer. The result is that pixels that are "further" from the ideal focal distance are blurred more and pixels that are closer to it are blurred less. The result of this shader is shown in Figure 10.10. This image is also shown in Color Plate 8.

As you can see in Figure 10.10, the depth of field effect has been applied to a row of dragons. In the image, the nearest dragon appears slightly blurred and out of focus, the second dragon is in focus, and the dragons beyond it become successively out of focus again. Figure 10.11 shows several more results from the same program. In the leftmost image of Figure 10.11, the closest dragon is in sharp focus, and the furthest dragon is very blurry. In the middle image of Figure 10.11, the furthest dragon is the one in focus, whereas the closest is the most blurred. To achieve this effect, the depth of field of the simulated camera is quite shallow. By lengthening the camera's depth of field, we can obtain the image on the right of Figure 10.11, where the effect is far more subtle. However, all three images were produced in real time using the same program and varying only two parameters — the focal distance and the depth of field.

In order to simplify this example, we used 32-bit floating-point data for every component of every image. This allows us to not worry about precision issues. Because the precision of floating-point data gets lower as

Figure 10.10: Applying depth of field to an image

Figure 10.11: Effects achievable with depth of field

the magnitude of the data gets higher, summed area tables can suffer from precision loss. As the values of all of the pixels in the image are summed together, the values stored in the summed area tables can become very large. Then, as the output image is reconstructed, the difference between multiple (potentially large valued) floating-point numbers is taken, which can lead to noise.

In order to improve our implementation of the algorithm, we could

- Render our initial image in 16-bit floating point rather than at full 32-bit precision.

- Store the depth of our fragments in a separate texture (or reconstruct them from the depth buffer), eliminating the need to store them in the intermediate image.

- Pre-bias our rendered image by -0.5, which keeps the summed area table values closer to zero even for larger images, thereby improving precision.

Compute Shader Flocking

The following example uses a compute shader to implement a flocking algorithm. Flocking algorithms show emergent behavior within a large group by updating the properties of individual members independently of all others. This kind of behavior is regularly seen in nature, and examples are swarms of bees, flocks of birds, and schools of fish apparently moving in unison even though the members of the group don't communicate globally. That is, the decisions made by an individual are based solely on its perception of the other nearby members of the group. However, no collaboration is made between members over the outcome of any particular decision — as far as we know, schools of fish don't have leaders. Because each member of the group is effectively independent, the new value of each of the properties can be calculated in parallel — ideal for a GPU implementation.

Here, we implement the flocking algorithm in a compute shader. We represent each member of the flock as a single element stored in a shader storage buffer. Each member has a position and a velocity that are updated by a compute shader that reads the current values from one buffer and writes the result into another buffer. That buffer is then bound as a vertex buffer and used as an instanced input to the rendering vertex shader. Each member of the flock is an instance in the rendering draw. The vertex shader is responsible for transforming a mesh (in this case, a simple model of a paper airplane) into the position and orientation calculated in the first vertex shader. The algorithm then iterates, starting again with the compute shader, reusing the positions and velocities calculated in the previous pass. No data leaves the graphics card's memory, and the CPU is not involved in any calculations.

We use a pair of buffers to store the current position of the members of the flock. We also use a set of VAOs to represent the vertex array state for each pass so that we can render the resulting data. These VAOs also hold the vertex data for the model we use to represent them. The flock positions and velocities need to be double-buffered because we don't want to partially update the position or velocity buffer while at the same time using them as a source for drawing commands. Figure 10.12 illustrates the passes that the algorithm makes.

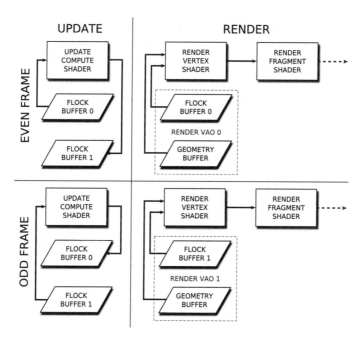

Figure 10.12: Stages in the iterative flocking algorithm

On the top left, we perform the update for an even frame. The first buffer containing position and velocity is bound as a shader storage buffer that can be read by the compute shader, and the second buffer is bound such that it can be written by the compute shader. Next we render, on the top right of Figure 10.12, using the same set of buffers as inputs as in the update pass. We use the same buffers as input in both the update and render passes so that the render pass has no dependency on the update pass. That means that OpenGL may be able to start working on the render pass before the update pass has finished. The buffer containing the position and velocity of the flock members is used to source instanced vertex attributes, and the additional geometry buffer is used to provide vertex position data.

On the bottom left of Figure 10.12, we move to the next frame. The buffers have been exchanged—the second buffer is now the input to the compute shader, and the first is written by it. Finally, on the bottom right of Figure 10.12, we render the odd frames. The second buffer is used as input to the vertex shader. Notice, though, that the flock_geometry buffer is a member of both rendering VAOs because the same data is used in both passes, and so we don't need two copies of it.

The code to set all that up is shown in Listing 10.9. It isn't particularly complex, but there is a fair amount of repetition, making it long. The listing contains the bulk of the initialization.

```
glGenBuffers(2, flock_buffer);
glBindBuffer(GL_SHADER_STORAGE_BUFFER, flock_buffer[0]);
glBufferData(GL_SHADER_STORAGE_BUFFER,
             FLOCK_SIZE * sizeof(flock_member),
             NULL,
             GL_DYNAMIC_COPY);
glBindBuffer(GL_SHADER_STORAGE_BUFFER, flock_buffer[1]);
glBufferData(GL_SHADER_STORAGE_BUFFER,
             FLOCK_SIZE * sizeof(flock_member),
             NULL,
             GL_DYNAMIC_COPY);

glGenBuffers(1, &geometry_buffer);
glBindBuffer(GL_ARRAY_BUFFER, geometry_buffer);
glBufferData(GL_ARRAY_BUFFER, sizeof(geometry), geometry, GL_STATIC_DRAW);

glGenVertexArrays(2, flock_render_vao);

for (i = 0; i < 2; i++)
{
    glBindVertexArray(flock_render_vao[i]);
    glBindBuffer(GL_ARRAY_BUFFER, geometry_buffer);
    glVertexAttribPointer(0, 3, GL_FLOAT, GL_FALSE,
                          0, NULL);
    glVertexAttribPointer(1, 3, GL_FLOAT, GL_FALSE,
                          0, (void *)(8 * sizeof(vmath::vec3)));

    glBindBuffer(GL_ARRAY_BUFFER, flock_buffer[i]);
    glVertexAttribPointer(2, 3, GL_FLOAT, GL_FALSE,
                          sizeof(flock_member), NULL);
    glVertexAttribPointer(3, 3, GL_FLOAT, GL_FALSE,
                          sizeof(flock_member),
                          (void *)sizeof(vmath::vec4));
    glVertexAttribDivisor(2, 1);
    glVertexAttribDivisor(3, 1);

    glEnableVertexAttribArray(0);
    glEnableVertexAttribArray(1);
    glEnableVertexAttribArray(2);
    glEnableVertexAttribArray(3);
}
```

Listing 10.9: Initializing shader storage buffers for flocking

In addition to running the code shown in Listing 10.9, we initialize our flock positions with some random vectors and set all of the velocities to zero.

Now we need a rendering loop to update our flock positions and draw the members of the flock. It's actually pretty simple now that we have our data encapsulated in VAOs. The rendering loop is shown in Listing 10.10. You can clearly see the two passes that the loop makes. First, the update_program is made current and used to update the positions and velocities of the flock members. The position of the goal is updated, the storage buffers are bound to the first and second GL_SHADER_STORAGE_BUFFER binding points for reading and writing, and then the compute shader is dispatched.

Next, the window is cleared, the rendering program is activated, and we update our transform matrices, bind our VAO, and draw. The number of instances is the number of members of our simulated flock, and the number of vertices is simply the amount of geometry we're using to represent our little paper airplane.

```
glUseProgram(flock_update_program);

vmath::vec3 goal = vmath::vec3(sinf(t * 0.34f),
                               cosf(t * 0.29f),
                               sinf(t * 0.12f) * cosf(t * 0.5f));

goal = goal * vmath::vec3(15.0f, 15.0f, 180.0f);

glUniform3fv(uniforms.update.goal, 1, goal);

glBindBufferBase(GL_SHADER_STORAGE_BUFFER, 0, flock_buffer[frame_index]);
glBindBufferBase(GL_SHADER_STORAGE_BUFFER, 1, flock_buffer[frame_index ^ 1]);

glDispatchCompute(NUM_WORKGROUPS, 1, 1);

glViewport(0, 0, info.windowWidth, info.windowHeight);
glClearBufferfv(GL_COLOR, 0, black);
glClearBufferfv(GL_DEPTH, 0, &one);

glUseProgram(flock_render_program);

vmath::mat4 mv_matrix =
    vmath::lookat(vmath::vec3(0.0f, 0.0f, -400.0f),
                  vmath::vec3(0.0f, 0.0f, 0.0f),
                  vmath::vec3(0.0f, 1.0f, 0.0f));
vmath::mat4 proj_matrix =
    vmath::perspective(60.0f,
                       (float)info.windowWidth / (float)info.windowHeight,
                       0.1f,
                       3000.0f);
vmath::mat4 mvp = proj_matrix * mv_matrix;

glUniformMatrix4fv(uniforms.render.mvp, 1, GL_FALSE, mvp);

glBindVertexArray(flock_render_vao[frame_index]);

glDrawArraysInstanced(GL_TRIANGLE_STRIP, 0, 8, FLOCK_SIZE);

frame_index ^= 1;
```

Listing 10.10: The rendering loop for the flocking example

That's pretty much the interesting part of the program side. Let's take a look at the shader side of things. The flocking algorithm works by applying a set of rules for each member of the flock to decide which direction to travel in. Each rule considers the current properties of the flock member and the properties of the other members of the flock as perceived by the individual being updated. Most of the rules require access to the other member's position and velocity data, so `update_program` uses a shader storage buffer containing that information. Listing 10.11 shows the start of the update compute shader. It lists the uniforms we'll use[5] during simulation, the declaration of the flock member, the two buffers used for input and output, and, finally, a `shared` array of members that will be used during the updates.

```
#version 430 core

layout (local_size_x = 256) in;

uniform float closest_allowed_dist2 = 50.0;
uniform float rule1_weight = 0.18;
uniform float rule2_weight = 0.05;
uniform float rule3_weight = 0.17;
uniform float rule4_weight = 0.02;
uniform vec3 goal = vec3(0.0);
uniform float timestep = 0.5;

struct flock_member
{
    vec3 position;
    vec3 velocity;
};

layout (std430, binding = 0) buffer members_in
{
    flock_member member[];
} input_data;

layout (std430, binding = 1) buffer members_out
{
    flock_member member[];
} output_data;

shared flock_member shared_member[gl_WorkGroupSize.x];
```

Listing 10.11: Compute shader for updates in flocking example

Once we have declared all of the inputs to our shader, we have to define our rules that we're going to use to update them. The rules we use in this example are as follows:

- Members try not to hit each other. They need to stay at least a short distance from each other at all times.

- Members try to fly in the same direction as those around them.

---

5. Most of these uniforms are not hooked up to the example program, but their default values can be changed by tweaking the shader.

- Members of the flock try to reach a common goal.

- Members try to keep with the rest of the flock. They will fly toward the center of the flock.

The first two rules are the intra-member rules. That is, the effect of each of the members on each other is considered individually. Listing 10.12 contains the shader code for the first rule. If we're closer to another member than we're supposed to be, we simply move away from that member.

```
vec3 rule1(vec3 my_position,
           vec3 my_velocity,
           vec3 their_position,
           vec3 their_velocity)
{
    vec3 d = my_position - their_position;
    if (dot(d, d) < closest_allowed_dist2)
        return d;
    return vec3(0.0);
}
```

Listing 10.12: The first rule of flocking

The shader for the second rule is shown in Listing 10.13. It returns a change in velocity weighted by the inverse square of the distance from each member to the member. A small amount is added to the squared distance between the members to keep the denominator of the fraction from getting too small (and thus the acceleration too large), which keeps the simulation stable.

```
vec3 rule2(vec3 my_position,
           vec3 my_velocity,
           vec3 their_position,
           vec3 their_velocity)
{
    vec3 d = their_position - my_position;
    vec3 dv = their_velocity - my_velocity;
    return dv / (dot(d, d) + 10.0);
}
```

Listing 10.13: The second rule of flocking

The third rule (that flock members attempt to fly towards a common goal) is applied once per member. The fourth rule (that members attempt to get to the center of the flock) is also applied once per member, but requires the average position of all of the flock members (along with the total number of members in the flock) to calculate.

The main body of the program contains the meat of the algorithm. The flock is broken into groups and each group is represented as a single local workgroup (the size of which we have defined as 256 elements). Because every member of the flock needs to interact in some way with every other member of the flock, this algorithm is considered an $O(N^2)$ algorithm. This means that each of the N flock members will read all of the other N members' positions and velocities, and that each of the N members' positions and velocities will be read N times. Rather than read through the entirety of the input shader storage buffer for every flock member, we copy a local workgroup's worth of data into a shared storage buffer and use the local copy to update each of the members.

For each flock member (which is a single invocation of our compute shader), we loop over the number of work groups and copy a single flock member's data into the shared local copy (the shared_member array declared at the top of the shader in Listing 10.11). Each of the 256 local shader invocations copies one element into the shared array and then executes the barrier() function to ensure that all of the invocations are synchronized and have therefore copied *their* data into the shared array. Then, we loop over all of the data stored in the shared array, apply each of the intra-member rules in turn, sum up the resulting vector, and then execute another call to barrier(). This again synchronizes the threads in the local workgroup and ensures that all of the other invocations have finished using the shared array before we restart the loop and write over it again. Code to do this is given in Listing 10.14.

```
void main(void)
{
    uint i, j;
    int global_id = int(gl_GlobalInvocationID.x);
    int local_id  = int(gl_LocalInvocationID.x);

    flock_member me = input_data.member[global_id];
    flock_member new_me;
    vec3 acceleration = vec3(0.0);
    vec3 flock_center = vec3(0.0);

    for (i = 0; i < gl_NumWorkGroups.x; i++)
    {
        flock_member them =
            input_data.member[i * gl_WorkGroupSize.x +
                              local_id];
        shared_member[local_id] = them;
        memoryBarrierShared();
        barrier();
        for (j = 0; j < gl_WorkGroupSize.x; j++)
        {
            them = shared_member[j];
            flock_center += them.position;
            if (i * gl_WorkGroupSize.x + j != global_id)
            {
                acceleration += rule1(me.position,
                                      me.velocity,
                                      them.position,
                                      them.velocity) * rule1_weight;
```

```
                        acceleration += rule2(me.position,
                                              me.velocity,
                                              them.position,
                                              them.velocity) * rule2_weight;
            }
        }
        barrier();
    }

    flock_center /= float(gl_NumWorkGroups.x * gl_WorkGroupSize.x);
    new_me.position = me.position + me.velocity * timestep;
    acceleration += normalize(goal - me.position) * rule3_weight;
    acceleration += normalize(flock_center - me.position) * rule4_weight;
    new_me.velocity = me.velocity + acceleration * timestep;
    if (length(new_me.velocity) > 10.0)
        new_me.velocity = normalize(new_me.velocity) * 10.0;
    new_me.velocity = mix(me.velocity, new_me.velocity, 0.4);
    output_data.member[global_id] = new_me;
}
```

Listing 10.14: Main body of the flocking update compute shader

In addition to applying the first two rules on a per-member basis and then adjusting acceleration to try to get the members to fly towards the common goal and towards the center of the flock, we also apply a couple more rules to keep the simulation sane. First, if the velocity of the flock member gets too high, we clamp it to a maximum allowed value. Second, rather than output the new velocity verbatim, we perform a weighted average between it and the old velocity. This forms a basic low-pass filter and stops the flock members from accelerating or decelerating too quickly or, more importantly, from changing direction too abruptly.

Putting all this together completes the update phase of the program. Now we need to produce the shaders that are responsible for rendering the flock. This program uses the position and velocity data calculated by the compute shader as instanced vertex arrays and transforms a fixed set of vertices into position based on the position and velocity of the individual member. Listing 10.15 shows the inputs to the shader.

```
#version 430 core

layout (location = 0) in vec3 position;
layout (location = 1) in vec3 normal;

layout (location = 2) in vec3 bird_position;
layout (location = 3) in vec3 bird_velocity;

out VS_OUT
{
    flat vec3 color;
} vs_out;

uniform mat4 mvp;
```

Listing 10.15: Inputs to the flock rendering vertex shader

In this shader, `position` and `normal` are regular inputs from our geometry buffer, which in this example contains a simple model of a paper airplane. The `bird_position` and `bird_velocity` inputs will be the instanced attributes, provided by the compute shader and whose instance divisor is set with the **glVertexAttribDivisor()** function. The body of our shader (given in Listing 10.16) uses the velocity of the flock member to construct a *lookat* matrix that can be used to orient the airplane model such that it's always flying forward.

```
mat4 make_lookat(vec3 forward, vec3 up)
{
    vec3 side = cross(forward, up);
    vec3 u_frame = cross(side, forward);

    return mat4(vec4(side, 0.0),
                vec4(u_frame, 0.0),
                vec4(forward, 0.0),
                vec4(0.0, 0.0, 0.0, 1.0));
}

vec3 choose_color(float f)
{
    float R = sin(f * 6.2831853);
    float G = sin((f + 0.3333) * 6.2831853);
    float B = sin((f + 0.6666) * 6.2831853);

    return vec3(R, G, B) * 0.25 + vec3(0.75);
}

void main(void)
{
    mat4 lookat = make_lookat(normalize(bird_velocity),
                              vec3(0.0, 1.0, 0.0));
    vec4 obj_coord = lookat * vec4(position.xyz, 1.0);
    gl_Position = mvp * (obj_coord + vec4(bird_position, 0.0));

    vec3 N = mat3(lookat) * normal;
    vec3 C = choose_color(fract(float(gl_InstanceID / float(1237.0))));

    vs_out.color = mix(C * 0.2, C, smoothstep(0.0, 0.8, abs(N).z));
}
```

Listing 10.16: Flocking vertex shader body

Construction of the lookat matrix uses a method similar to that described in Chapter 4, "Math for 3D Graphics." Once we have oriented the mesh using this matrix, we add the flock member's position and transform the whole lot by the model-view-projection matrix. We also orient the object's normal by the lookat matrix, which allows us to apply a very simple lighting calculation. We choose a color for the object based on the current instance ID (which is unique per mesh) and use it to compute the final output color, which we write into the vertex shader output. The fragment shader is a simple pass-through shader that writes this incoming color to the framebuffer. The result of rendering the flock is shown in Figure 10.13.

Figure 10.13: Output of compute shader flocking program

A possible enhancement that could be made to this program is to calculate the lookat matrix in the compute shader. Here, we calculate it in the vertex shader and therefore redundantly calculate it for every vertex. It doesn't matter so much in this example because our mesh is small, but if our instanced mesh were larger, generating it in the compute shader and passing it along with the other instanced vertex attributes would likely be faster. We could also apply more physical simulations rather than just ad-hoc rules. For example, we could simulate gravity, making it easier to fly down than up, or we could allow the planes to crash into and bounce off of one another. However, for the purposes of this example, what we have here is sufficient.

Summary

In this chapter, we have taken an in-depth look at compute shaders — the "single-stage pipeline" that allows you to harness the computational power of modern graphics processors for more than just computer graphics. We have covered the execution model of compute shaders where you learned about work groups, synchronization, and intra-workgroup communication. Then, we covered some of the applications of compute shaders. First, we showed you the applications of compute shaders in image processing, which is an obvious fit for computer graphics. Next, we showed you how you might use compute shaders for physical simulation when we implemented the flocking algorithm. This should have allowed you to imagine some of the possibilities for the use of compute shaders in your own applications — from artificial intelligence, pre- and post-processing, or even audio applications!

Chapter 11

Controlling and Monitoring the Pipeline

WHAT YOU'LL LEARN IN THIS CHAPTER

- How to ask OpenGL about the progress of your commands down the graphics pipeline

- How to measure the time taken for your commands to execute

- How to synchronize your application with OpenGL and how to synchronize multiple OpenGL contexts with each other

This chapter is about the OpenGL pipeline and how it executes your commands. As your application makes OpenGL function calls, work is placed in the OpenGL pipeline and makes its way down it one stage at a time. This takes time, and you can measure that. This allows you to tune your application's complexity to match the performance of the graphics system and to measure and control latency, which is important for real-time applications. You'll also learn how to synchronize your application's execution to that of OpenGL commands you've issued and even how to synchronize multiple OpenGL contexts with each other.

Queries

Queries are a mechanism to ask OpenGL what's happening in the graphics pipeline. There's plenty of information that OpenGL can tell you; you just need to know what to ask — and how to ask the question.

Remember way back to your early days in school. The teacher wanted you to raise your hand before asking a question. This was almost like reserving your place in line for asking the question — the teacher didn't know yet what your question was going to be, but she knew that you had something to ask. OpenGL is similar. Before we can ask a question, we have to reserve a spot so that OpenGL knows that the question is coming. Questions in OpenGL are represented by query objects, and much like any other object in OpenGL, query objects must be reserved, or generated. To do this, call **glGenQueries()**, passing it the number of queries you want to reserve and the address of a variable (or array) where you would like the names of the query objects to be placed:

```
void glGenQueries(GLsizei n,
                  GLuint *ids);
```

The function reserves some query objects for you and gives you their names so that you can refer to them later. You can generate as many query objects you need in one go:

```
GLuint one_query;
GLuint ten_queries[10];
glGenQueries(1, &one_query);
glGenQueries(10, ten_queries);
```

In this example, the first call to **glGenQueries()** generates a single query object and returns its name in the variable one_query. The second call to **glGenQueries()** generates 10 query objects and returns 10 names in the array ten_queries. In total, 11 query objects have been created, and OpenGL has reserved 11 unique names to represent them. It is very unlikely, but still possible that OpenGL will not be able to create a query for you, and in this case it returns zero as the name of the query. A well-written application always checks that **glGenQueries()** returns a non-zero value for the name of each requested query object. If there is a failure, OpenGL keeps track of the reason, and you can find that out by calling **glGetError()**.

Each query object reserves a small but measurable amount of resources from OpenGL. These resources must be returned to OpenGL because if they are not, OpenGL may run out of space for queries and fail to generate more for the application later. To return the resources to OpenGL, call **glDeleteQueries()**:

```
void glDeleteQueries(GLsizei n,
                     const GLuint *ids);
```

This works similarly to **glGenQueries()** — it takes the number of query objects to delete and the address of a variable or array holding their names:

```
glDeleteQueries(10, ten_queries);
glDeleteQueries(1, &one_query);
```

After the queries are deleted, they are essentially gone for good. The names of the queries can't be used again unless they are given back to you by another call to **glGenQueries()**.

Occlusion Queries

Once you've reserved your spot using **glGenQueries()**, you can ask a question. OpenGL doesn't automatically keep track of the number of pixels it has drawn. It has to count, and it must be told when to start counting. To do this, use **glBeginQuery()**. The **glBeginQuery()** function takes two parameters: The first is the question you'd like to ask, and the second is the name of the query object that you reserved earlier:

```
glBeginQuery(GL_SAMPLES_PASSED, one_query);
```

GL_SAMPLES_PASSED represents the question you're asking: "How many samples passed the depth test?" Here, OpenGL counts samples because you might be rendering to a multi-sampled display format, and in that case, there could be more than one sample per pixel. In the case of a normal, single-sampled format, there is one sample per pixel and therefore a one-to-one mapping of samples to pixels. Every time a sample makes it past the depth test (meaning that it hadn't previously been discarded by the fragment shader), OpenGL counts one. It adds up all the samples from all the rendering it is doing and stores the answer in part of the space reserved for the query object. A query object that counts samples that might end up visible (because they passed the depth test) is known as an *occlusion query*.

Now OpenGL is counting samples, you can render as normal, and OpenGL keeps track of all the samples generated as a result. Anything that you render is counted toward the total — even samples that have no contribution to the final image due to blending or being covered by later samples, for example. When you want OpenGL to add up everything rendered since you told it to start counting, you tell it to stop by calling **glEndQuery()**:

```
glEndQuery(GL_SAMPLES_PASSED);
```

This tells OpenGL to stop counting samples that have passed the depth test and made it through the fragment shader without being discarded. All the samples generated by all the drawing commands between the call to **glBeginQuery()** and **glEndQuery()** are added up.

Retrieving Query Results

Now that the pixels produced by your drawing commands have been counted, you need to retrieve them from OpenGL. This is accomplished by calling

```
glGetQueryObjectuiv(the_query, GL_QUERY_RESULT, &result);
```

Here, the_query is the name of the query object that's being used to count samples, and result is the variable that you want OpenGL to write the result into (notice that we pass the *address* of the variable). This instructs OpenGL to place the count associated with the query object into your variable. If no pixels were produced as a result of the drawing commands between the last call to **glBeginQuery()** and **glEndQuery()** for the query object, the result will be zero. If anything actually made it to the end of the fragment shader without being discarded, the result will contain the number of samples that got that far. By rendering an object between a call to **glBeginQuery()** and **glEndQuery()** and then checking if the result is zero or not, you can determine whether the object is visible.

Because OpenGL operates as a pipeline, it may have many drawing commands queued up back-to-back waiting to be processed. It could be the case that not all of the drawing commands issued before the last call to **glEndQuery()** have finished producing pixels. In fact, some may not have even started to be executed. In that case, **glGetQueryObjectuiv()** causes OpenGL to wait until everything between **glBeginQuery()** and **glEndQuery()** has been rendered, and it is ready to return an accurate count. If you're planning to use a query object as a performance optimization, this is certainly not what you want. All these short delays could add up and eventually slow down your application! The good news is that it's possible to ask OpenGL if it's finished rendering anything that might affect the result of the query and therefore has a result available for you. To do this, call

```
glGetQueryObjectuiv(the_query, GL_QUERY_RESULT_AVAILABLE, &result);
```

If the result of the query object is not immediately available and trying to retrieve it would cause your application to have to wait for OpenGL to finish what it is working on, the result becomes GL_FALSE. If OpenGL is ready and has your answer, the result becomes GL_TRUE. This tells you that retrieving the result from OpenGL will not cause any delays. Now you can do useful work while you wait for OpenGL to be ready to give you your pixel count, or you can make decisions based on whether the result is available to you. For example, if you would have skipped rendering something had the result been zero, you could choose to just go ahead and render it anyway rather than waiting for the result of the query.

Using the Results of a Query

Now that you have this information, what will you do with it? A very common use for occlusion queries is to optimize an application's performance by avoiding unnecessary work. Consider an object that has a very detailed appearance. The object has many triangles and possibly a complex fragment shader with a lot of texture lookups and intensive math operations. Perhaps there are many vertex attributes and textures, and there's a lot of work for the application to do just to get ready to draw the object. The object is very expensive to render. It's also possible that the object may never end up being visible in the scene. Perhaps it's covered by something else. Perhaps it's off the screen altogether. It would be good to know this up front and just not draw it at all if it's never going to be seen by the user anyway.

Occlusion queries are a good way to do this. Take your complex, expensive object and produce a much lower fidelity version of it. Usually, a simple bounding box will do. Start an occlusion query, render the bounding box, and then end the occlusion query and retrieve the result. If no part of the object's bounding box produces any pixels, then the more detailed version of the object will not be visible, and it doesn't need to be sent to OpenGL.

Of course, you probably don't actually want the bounding box to be visible in the final scene. There are a number of ways you can make sure that OpenGL doesn't actually draw the bounding box. The easiest way is probably to use **glColorMask()** to turn off writes to the color buffer by passing GL_FALSE for all parameters. You could also call **glDrawBuffer()** to set the current draw buffer to GL_NONE. Whichever method you choose, don't forget to turn framebuffer writes back on again afterwards!

Listing 11.1 shows a simple example of how to use **glGetQueryObjectuiv()** to retrieve the result from a query object.

```
glBeginQuery(GL_SAMPLES_PASSED, the_query);
RenderSimplifiedObject(object);
glEndQuery(GL_SAMPLES_PASSED);
glGetQueryObjectuiv(the_query, GL_QUERY_RESULT, &the_result);
if (the_result != 0)
    RenderRealObject(object);
```

Listing 11.1: Getting the result from a query object

RenderSimplifiedObject is a function that renders the low-fidelity version of the object, and RenderRealObject renders the object with all of its detail. Now, RenderRealObject only gets called if at least one pixel is produced by RenderSimplifiedObject. Remember that the call to glGetQueryObjectuiv causes your application to have to wait if the result of the query is not ready yet. This is likely if the rendering done by RenderSimplifiedObject is simple — which is the point of this example. If all you want to know is whether it's safe to skip rendering something, you can find out if the query result is available and render the more complex object if the result is either unavailable (i.e., the object may be visible or hidden), or if the object result is available and nonzero (i.e., the object is certainly visible). Listing 11.2 demonstrates how you might determine whether a query object result is ready before you ask for the actual count, allowing you to make decisions based on both the availability and the value of a query result.

```
GLuint the_result = 0;

glBeginQuery(GL_SAMPLES_PASSED, the_query);
RenderSimplifiedObject(object);
glEndQuery(GL_SAMPLES_PASSED);

glGetQueryObjectuiv(the_query, GL_QUERY_RESULT_AVAILABLE, &the_result);

if (the_result != 0)
    glGetQueryObjectuiv(the_query, GL_QUERY_RESULT, &the_result);
else
    the_result = 1;

if (the_result != 0)
    RenderRealObject(object);
```

Listing 11.2: Figuring out if occlusion query results are ready

In this new example, we determine whether the result is available and if so, retrieve it from OpenGL. If it's not available, we put a count of one into the result so that the complex version of the object will be rendered.

It is possible to have multiple occlusion queries in the graphics pipeline at the same time so long as they don't overlap. Using multiple query objects is another way for the application to avoid having to wait for OpenGL. OpenGL can only count and add up results into one query object at a time, but it can manage several query objects and perform many queries back-to-back. We can expand our example to render multiple objects with multiple occlusion queries. If we had an array of ten objects to render, each with a simplified representation, we might rewrite the example provided as follows in Listing 11.3.

```
int n;

for (n = 0; n < 10; n++)
{
    glBeginQuery(GL_SAMPLES_PASSSED, ten_queries[n]);
    RenderSimplifiedObject(&object[n]);
    glEndQuery(GL_SAMPLES_PASSED);
}

for (n = 0; n < 10; n++)
{
    glGetQueryObjectuiv(ten_queries[n], GL_QUERY_RESULT, &the_result);
    if (the_result != 0)
        RenderRealObject(&object[n]);
}
```

Listing 11.3: Simple, application-side conditional rendering

As discussed earlier, OpenGL is modeled as a pipeline and can have many things going on at the same time. If you draw something simple such as a bounding box, it's likely that won't have reached the end of the pipeline by the time you need the result of your query. This means that when you call **glGetQueryObjectuiv()**, your application may have to wait a while for OpenGL to finish working on your bounding box before it can give you the answer and you can act on it.

In our next example, we render ten bounding boxes before we ask for the result of the first query. This means that OpenGL's pipeline can be filled, and it can have a lot of work to do and is therefore much more likely to have finished working on the first bounding box before we ask for the result of the first query. In short, the more time we give OpenGL to finish working on what we've asked it for, the more likely it is that it'll have the result of your query and the less likely it is that your application will have to wait for results. Some complex applications take this to the extreme and use the results of queries from the previous frame to make decisions about the new frame.

Finally, putting both techniques together into a single example, we have the code shown in Listing 11.4.

```
int n;

for (n = 0; n < 10; n++)
{
    glBeginQuery(GL_SAMPLES_PASSSED, ten_queries[n]);
    RenderSimplifiedObject(&object[n]);
    glEndQuery(GL_SAMPLES_PASSED);
}

for (n = 0; n < 10; n+)
{
    glGetQueryObjectuiv(ten_queries[n],
                        GL_QUERY_RESULT_AVAILABLE,
                        &the_result);
    if (the_result != 0)
        glGetQueryObjectuiv(ten_queries[n],
                            GL_QUERY_RESULT,
                            &the_result);
    else
        the_result = 1;
    if (the_result != 0)
        RenderRealObject(&object[n]);
}
```

Listing 11.4: Rendering when query results aren't available

Because the amount of work sent to OpenGL by RenderRealObject is much greater than by RenderSimplifiedObject, by the time we ask for the result of the second, third, fourth, and additional query objects, more and more work has been sent into the OpenGL pipeline, and it becomes more likely that our query results are ready. Within reason, the more complex our scene, and the more query objects we use, the more likely we are to see positive a performance impact.

Getting OpenGL to Make Decisions for You

The preceding examples show how you can ask OpenGL to count pixels and how to get the result back from OpenGL into your application so that it can make decisions about what to do next. However, in this application, we don't really care about the actual value of the result. We're only using it to decide whether to send more work to OpenGL or to make other changes to the way it might render things. The results have to be sent back from OpenGL to the application, perhaps over a CPU bus or even a network connection when you're using a remote rendering system, just so the application can decide whether to send more commands to OpenGL. This causes latency and can hurt performance, sometimes outweighing any potential benefits to using the queries in the first place.

What would be much better is if we could send all the rendering commands to OpenGL and tell it to obey them only if the result of a query object says it should. This is called predication, and fortunately, it is possible through a technique called *conditional rendering*. Conditional rendering allows you to wrap up a sequence of OpenGL drawing commands and send them to OpenGL along with a query object and a message that says "ignore all of this if the result stored in the query object is zero." To mark the start of this sequence of calls, use

```
glBeginConditionalRender(the_query, GL_QUERY_WAIT);
```

and to mark the end of the sequence, use

```
glEndConditionalRender();
```

Any drawing command, including functions like **glDrawArrays()**, **glClearBufferfv()**, and **glDispatchCompute()** that is called between **glBeginConditionalRender()** and **glEndConditionalRender()** is ignored if the result of the query object (the same value that you could have retrieved using **glGetQueryObjectuiv()**) is zero. This means that the actual result of the query doesn't have to be sent back to your application. The graphics hardware can make the decision as to whether to render for you. Keep in mind, though, that state changes such as binding textures, turning blending on or off, and so on are still executed by OpenGL — only rendering commands are discarded. To modify the previous example to use conditional rendering, we could use the code in Listing 11.5.

```
// Ask OpenGL to count the samples rendered between the start
// and end of the occlusion query
glBeginQuery(GL_SAMPLES_PASSED, the_query);
RenderSimplifiedObject(object);
glEndQuery(GL_SAMPLES_PASSED);

// Only obey the next few commands if the occlusion query says something
// was rendered
glBeginConditionalRender(the_query, GL_QUERY_WAIT);
RenderRealObject(object);
glEndConditionalRender();
```

Listing 11.5: Basic conditional rendering example

The two functions, RenderSimplifiedObject and RenderRealObject, are functions within our hypothetical example application that render simplified (perhaps just the bounding box, for example) and more complex versions of the object, respectively. Notice now that we never call **glGetQueryObjectuiv()**, and we never read any information (such as the result of the query object) back from OpenGL.

The astute reader will have noticed the GL_QUERY_WAIT parameter passed to **glBeginConditionalRender()**. You may be wondering what that's for — after all, the application doesn't have to wait for results to be ready any more. As mentioned earlier, OpenGL operates as a pipeline, which means that it may not have finished dealing with RenderSimplifiedObject before your call to **glBeginConditionalRender()** or before the first drawing function called from RenderRealObject reaches the beginning of the pipeline. In this case, OpenGL can either wait for everything called from RenderSimplifiedObject to reach the end of the pipeline before deciding whether to obey the commands sent by the application, or it can go ahead and start working on RenderRealObject if the results aren't ready in time. To tell OpenGL not to wait and to just go ahead and start rendering if the results aren't available, call

```
glBeginConditionalRender(the_query, GL_QUERY_NO_WAIT);
```

This tells OpenGL, "If the results of the query aren't available yet, don't wait for them; just go ahead and render anyway." This is of greatest use when occlusion queries are being used to improve performance. Waiting for the results of occlusion queries can use up any time gained by using them in the first place. Thus, using the GL_QUERY_NO_WAIT flag essentially allows the occlusion query to be used as an optimization if the results are ready in time and to behave as if they aren't used at all if the results aren't ready. The use of GL_QUERY_NO_WAIT is similar to using GL_QUERY_RESULT_AVAILABLE in the preceding examples. Don't forget, though, if you use GL_QUERY_NO_WAIT, the actual geometry rendered is going to depend on whether the commands contributing to the query object have finished executing. This could depend on the performance of the machine your application is running on and can therefore vary from run to run. You should be sure that the result of your program is not dependent on the second set of geometry being rendered (unless this is what you want). If it is, your program might end up producing different output on a faster system than on a slower system.

Of course, it is also possible to use multiple query objects with conditional rendering, and so a final, combined example using all of the techniques in this section is given in Listing 11.6.

```
// Render simplified versions of 10 objects, each with its own occlusion
// query
int n;

for (n = 0; n < 10; n++)
{
    glBeginQuery(GL_SAMPLES_PASSSED, ten_queries[n]);
    RenderSimplifiedObject(&object[n]);
    glEndQuery(GL_SAMPLES_PASSED);
}
```

```
// Render the more complex versions of the objects, skipping them
// if the occlusion query results are available and zero
for (n = 0; n < 10; n++)
{
    glBeginConditionalRender(ten_queries[n], GL_QUERY_NO_WAIT);
    RenderRealObject(&object[n]);
    glEndConditionalRender();
}
```

Listing 11.6: A more complete conditional rendering example

In this example, simplified versions of ten objects are rendered first, each with its own occlusion query. Once the simplified versions of the objects have been rendered, the more complex versions of the objects are conditionally rendered based on the results of those occlusion queries. If the simplified versions of the objects are not visible, the more complex versions are skipped, potentially improving performance.

Advanced Occlusion Queries

The GL_SAMPLES_PASSED query target counts the exact number of samples that passed the depth test. Even if no significant rendering occurs, OpenGL must still effectively rasterize every primitive to determine the number of pixels it covers and how many of them pass the depth and stencil tests. Even worse, if your fragment shader does something to affect the result (such as using a `discard` statement or modifying the fragment's depth value), then it must run your shader for every pixel as well. Sometimes, this really is what you want. However, very often, you will only care whether *any* sample passed the depth and stencil tests, or even whether any sample *might have* passed the depth and stencil tests.

To provide this kind of functionality, OpenGL provides two additional occlusion query targets. These are the GL_ANY_SAMPLES_PASSED and GL_ANY_SAMPLES_PASSED_CONSERVATIVE targets, and they are known as *Boolean* occlusion queries.

The first of these targets, GL_ANY_SAMPLES_PASSED, will produce a result of zero (or GL_FALSE) if no samples pass the depth and stencil tests, and one (the value of GL_TRUE) if any sample passes the depth test. In some circumstances, performance could be higher if the GL_ANY_SAMPLES_PASSED query target is used because OpenGL can stop counting samples as soon as any sample passes the depth and stencil tests. However, if no samples pass the depth and stencil tests, it is unlikely to provide any benefit.

The second Boolean occlusion query target, GL_ANY_SAMPLES_PASSED_CONSERVATIVE, is even more approximate.

In particular, it will count as soon as a sample *might* pass the depth and stencil tests. Many implementations of OpenGL implement some form of hierarchical depth testing, where the nearest and furthest depth values for a particular region of the screen are stored, and then as primitives are rasterized, the depth values for large blocks of them are tested against this hierarchical information to determine whether to continue to rasterize the interior of the region. A conservative occlusion query may simply count the number of these large regions and not run your shader at all, even if it discards fragments or modifies the final depth value.

Timer Queries

One further query type that you can use to judge how long rendering is taking is the *timer query*. Timer queries are used by passing the GL_TIME_ELAPSED query type as the `target` parameter of **glBeginQuery()** and **glEndQuery()**. When you call **glGetQueryObjectuiv()** to get the result from the query object, the value is the number of nanoseconds that elapsed between when OpenGL executes your calls to **glBeginQuery()** and **glEndQuery()**. This is actually the amount of time it took OpenGL to process all the commands between the **glBeginQuery()** and **glEndQuery()** commands. You can use this, for example, to figure out what the most expensive part of your scene is. Consider the code shown in Listing 11.7.

```
// Declare our variables
GLuint queries[3];      // Three query objects that we'll use
GLuint world_time;      // Time taken to draw the world
GLuint objects_time;    // Time taken to draw objects in the world
GLuint HUD_time;        // Time to draw the HUD and other UI elements

// Create three query objects
glGenQueries(3, queries);

// Start the first query
glBeginQuery(GL_TIME_ELAPSED, queries[0]);

// Render the world
RenderWorld();

// Stop the first query and start the second...
// Note: we're not reading the value from the query yet
glEndQuery(GL_TIME_ELAPSED);
glBeginQuery(GL_TIME_ELAPSED, queries[1]);

// Render the objects in the world
RenderObjects();

// Stop the second query and start the third
glEndQuery(GL_TIME_ELAPSED);
glBeginQuery(GL_TIME_ELAPSED, queries[2]);

// Render the HUD
RenderHUD();
```

```
// Stop the last query
glEndQuery(GL_TIME_ELAPSED);

// Now, we can retrieve the results from the three queries.
glGetQueryObjectuiv(queries[0], GL_QUERY_RESULT, &world_time);
glGetQueryObjectuiv(queries[1], GL_QUERY_RESULT, &objects_time);
glGetQueryObjectuiv(queries[2], GL_QUERY_RESULT, &HUD_time);

// Done. world_time, objects_time, and hud_time contain the values we want.
// Clean up after ourselves.
glDeleteQueries(3, queries);
```

Listing 11.7: Timing operations using timer queries

After this code is executed, `world_time`, `objects_time`, and `HUD_time` will contain the number of nanoseconds it took to render the world, all the objects in the world, and the heads-up display (HUD), respectively. You can use this to determine what fraction of the graphics hardware's time is taken up rendering each of the elements of your scene. This is useful for profiling your code during development — you can figure out what the most expensive parts of your application are, and so know from this where to spend optimization effort. You can also use it during runtime to alter the behavior of your application to try to get the best possible performance out of the graphics subsystem. For example, you could increase or reduce the number of objects in the scene depending on the relative value of `objects_time`. You could also dynamically switch between more or less complex shaders for elements of the scene based on the power of the graphics hardware. If you just want to know how much time passes, according to OpenGL, between two actions that your program takes, you can use **glQueryCounter()**, whose prototype is

```
void glQueryCounter(GLuint id, GLenum target);
```

You need to set id to `GL_TIMESTAMP` and target to the name of a query object that you've created earlier. This function puts the query straight into the OpenGL pipeline, and when that query reaches the end of the pipeline, OpenGL records its view of the current time into the query object. The time zero is not really defined — it just indicates some unspecified time in the past. To use this effectively, your application needs to take deltas between multiple time stamps. To implement the previous example using **glQueryCounter()**, we could write code as shown in Listing 11.8.

```
// Declare our variables
GLuint queries[4];       // Now we need four query objects
GLuint start_time;       // The start time of the application
GLuint world_time;       // Time taken to draw the world
GLuint objects_time;     // Time taken to draw objects in the world
GLuint HUD_time;         // Time to draw the HUD and other UI elements
```

```
// Create four query objects
glGenQueries(4, queries);

// Get the start time
glQueryCounter(GL_TIMESTAMP, queries[0]);

// Render the world
RenderWorld();

// Get the time after RenderWorld is done
glQueryCounter(GL_TIMESTAMP, queries[1]);

// Render the objects in the world
RenderObjects();

// Get the time after RenderObjects is done
glQueryCounter(GL_TIMESTAMP, queries[2]);

// Render the HUD
RenderHUD();

// Get the time after everything is done
glQueryCounter(GL_TIMESTAMP, queries[3]);

// Get the result from the three queries, and subtract them to find deltas
glGetQueryObjectuiv(queries[0], GL_QUERY_RESULT, &start_time);
glGetQueryObjectuiv(queries[1], GL_QUERY_RESULT, &world_time);
glGetQueryObjectuiv(queries[2], GL_QUERY_RESULT, &objects_time);
glGetQueryObjectuiv(queries[3], GL_QUERY_RESULT, &HUD_time);
HUD_time -= objects_time;
objects_time -= world_time;
world_time -= start_time;

// Done. world_time, objects_time, and hud_time contain the values we want.
// Clean up after ourselves.
glDeleteQueries(4, queries);
```

Listing 11.8: Timing operations using `glQueryCounter()`

As you can see, the code in this example is not that much different from
that in Listing 11.7 shown earlier. You need to create four query objects
instead of three, and you need to subtract out the results at the end to find
time deltas. However, you don't need to call `glBeginQuery()` and
`glEndQuery()` in pairs, which means that there are fewer calls to OpenGL,
in total. The results of the two samples aren't quite equivalent. When you
issue a GL_TIMESTAMP query, the time is written when the query reaches the
end of the OpenGL pipeline. However, when you issue a GL_TIME_ELAPSED
query, internally OpenGL will take a timestamp when `glBeginQuery()`
reaches the start of the pipeline and again when `glEndQuery()` reaches the
end of the pipeline, and then subtract the two. Clearly, the results won't
be quite the same. So long as you are consistent in which method you use,
your results should still be meaningful, however.

One important thing to note about the results of timer queries is that, as
they are measured in nanoseconds, their values can get very large in a

small amount of time. A single, unsigned 32-bit value can count to a little over 4 seconds' worth of nanoseconds. If you expect to time operations that take longer than this (hopefully over the course of many frames!), you might want to consider retrieving the full 64-bit results that query objects keep internally. To do this, call

```
void glGetQueryObjectui64v(GLuint id,
                           GLenum pname,
                           GLuint64 * params);
```

Just as with **glGetQueryObjectuiv()**, id is the name of the query object whose value you want to retrieve, and pname can be GL_QUERY_RESULT or GL_QUERY_RESULT_AVAILABLE to retrieve the result of the query or just an indication of whether it's available or not.

Finally, although not technically a query, you can get an instantaneous, synchronous timestamp from OpenGL by calling

```
GLint64 t;
void glGetInteger64v(GL_TIMESTAMP, &t);
```

After this code has executed, t will contain the current time as OpenGL sees it. If you take this timestamp and then immediately launch a timestamp query, you can retrieve the result of the timestamp query and subtract t from it, and the result will be the amount of time that it took the query to reach the end of the pipeline. This is known as the *latency* of the pipeline and is approximately equal to the amount of time that will pass between your application issuing a command and OpenGL fully executing it.

Transform Feedback Queries

If you use transform feedback with a vertex shader but no geometry shader, the output from the vertex shader is recorded, and the number of vertices stored into the transform feedback is the same as the number of vertices sent to OpenGL unless the available space in any of the transform feedback buffers is exhausted. However, if a geometry shader is present, that shader may create or discard vertices, and so the number of vertices written to the transform feedback buffer may be different from the number of vertices sent to OpenGL. Also, if tessellation is active, the amount of geometry produced will depend on the tessellation factors produced by the tessellation control shader. OpenGL can keep track of the number of vertices written to the transform feedback buffers through query objects. Your application can then use this information to draw the resulting data or to know how much to read back from the transform feedback buffer, should it want to keep the data.

Query objects were introduced earlier in this chapter in the context of occlusion queries. It was stated that there are many questions that can be asked of OpenGL. Both the number of primitives generated and the number of primitives actually written to the transform feedback buffers are available as queries.

As before, to generate a query object, call

```
GLuint one_query;
glGenQueries(1, &one_query);
```

or to generate a number of query objects, call

```
GLuint ten_queries[10];
glGenQueries(10, ten_queries);
```

Now that you have created your query objects, you can ask OpenGL to start counting primitives as it produces them by beginning a GL_PRIMITIVES_GENERATED or GL_TRANSFORM_FEEDBACK_PRIMITIVES_WRITTEN query by beginning the query of the appropriate type. To start either query, call

```
glBeginQuery(GL_PRIMITIVES_GENERATED, one_query);
```

or

```
glBeginQuery(GL_TRANSFORM_FEEDBACK_PRIMITIVES_WRITTEN, one_query);
```

After a call to **glBeginQuery()** with either GL_PRIMITIVES_GENERATED or GL_TRANSFORM_FEEDBACK_PRIMTIVES_WRITTEN, OpenGL keeps track of how many primitives were produced by the front end, or how many were actually written into the transform feedback buffers until the query is ended using

```
glEndQuery(GL_PRIMITIVES_GENERATED);
```

or

```
glEndQuery(GL_TRANSFORM_FEEDBACK_PRIMITIVES_WRITTEN);
```

The results of the query can be read by calling **glGetQueryObjectuiv()** with the GL_QUERY_RESULT parameter and the name of the query object. As with other OpenGL queries, the result might not be available immediately because of the pipelined nature of OpenGL. To find out if the results are available, call **glGetQueryObjectuiv()** with the GL_QUERY_RESULT_AVAILABLE parameter. See "Retrieving Query Results" earlier in this chapter for more information about query objects.

There are a couple of subtle differences between the GL_PRIMITIVES_GENERATED and GL_TRANSFORM_FEEDBACK_PRIMITIVES_WRITTEN queries. The first is that the GL_PRIMITIVES_GENERATED query counts the number of primitives emitted by the front end, but the GL_TRANSFORM_FEEDBACK_PRIMITIVES_WRITTEN query only counts primitives that were successfully written into the transform feedback buffers. The primitive count generated by the front end may be more or less than the number of primitives sent to OpenGL, depending on what it does. Normally, the results of these two queries would be the same, but if not enough space is available in the transform feedback buffers, GL_PRIMITIVES_GENERATED will keep counting, but GL_TRANSFORM_FEEDBACK_PRIMITIVES_WRITTEN will stop.

You can check whether all of the primitives produced by your application were captured into the transform feedback buffer by running one of each query simultaneously and comparing the results. If they are equal, then all the primitives were successfully written. If they differ, the buffers you used for transform feedback were probably too small.

The second difference is that GL_TRANSFORM_FEEDBACK_PRIMITIVES_WRITTEN is only meaningful when transform feedback is active. That is why it has TRANSFORM_FEEDBACK in its name but GL_PRIMITIVES_GENERATED does not. If you run a GL_TRANSFORM_FEEDBACK_PRIMITIVES_WRITTEN query when transform feedback is not active, the result will be zero. However, the GL_PRIMITIVES_GENERATED query can be used at any time and will produce a meaningful count of the number of primitives produced by OpenGL. You can use this to find out how many vertices your geometry shader produced or discarded.

Indexed Queries

If you are only using a single stream for storing vertices in transform feedback, then calling **glBeginQuery()** and **glEndQuery()** with the GL_PRIMITIVES_GENERATED or GL_TRANSFORM_FEEDBACK_PRIMITIVES_WRITTEN targets works just fine. However, if you have a geometry shader in your pipeline, then that shader could produce primitives on up to four output streams. In that case, OpenGL provides *indexed* query targets that you can use to count how much data is produced on each stream. The **glBeginQuery()** and **glEndQuery()** functions associate queries with the first stream — the one with index zero. To begin and end a query on a different stream, you

can call **glBeginQueryIndexed()** and **glEndQueryIndexed()**, whose
prototypes are

```
void glBeginQueryIndexed(GLenum target,
                         GLuint index,
                         GLuint id);

void glEndQueryIndexed(GLenum target,
                       GLuint index);
```

These two functions behave just like their non-indexed counterparts,
and the target and id parameters have the same meaning. In fact,
calling **glBeginQuery()** is equivalent to calling **glBeginQueryIndexed()**
with index set to zero. The same is true for **glEndQuery()** and
glEndQueryIndexed(). When target is GL_PRIMITIVES_GENERATED, the
query will count the primitives produced by the geometry shader on the
stream whose index is given in index. Likewise, when target is
GL_TRANSFORM_FEEDBACK_PRIMITIVES_WRITTEN, the query will count the
number of primitives actually written into the buffers associated with the
output stream of the geometry shader whose index is given in index. If no
geometry shader is present, you can still use these functions, but only
stream zero will actually count anything.

You can actually use the indexed query functions with any query target
(such as GL_SAMPLES_PASSED or GL_TIME_ELAPSED), but the only value for
index that is valid for those targets is zero.

Using the Results of a Primitive Query

Now you have the results of the front end stored in a buffer. You also
determined how much data is in that buffer by using a query object. Now
it's time to use those results in further rendering. Remember that the
results of the front end are placed into a buffer using transform feedback.
The only thing making the buffer a transform feedback buffer is that it's
bound to one of the GL_TRANSFORM_FEEDBACK_BUFFER binding points.
However, buffers in OpenGL are generic chunks of data and can be used
for other purposes.

Generally, after running a rendering pass that produces data into a
transform feedback buffer, you bind the buffer object to the
GL_ARRAY_BUFFER binding point so that it can be used as a vertex buffer. If
you are using a geometry shader that might produce an unknown amount
of data, you need to use a GL_TRANSFORM_FEEDBACK_PRIMITIVES_WRITTEN
query to figure out how many vertices to render on the second pass.
Listing 11.9 shows an example of what such code might look like.

```
// We have two buffers, buffer1 and buffer2. First, we'll bind buffer1 as the
// source of data for the draw operation (GL_ARRAY_BUFFER), and buffer2 as
// the destination for transform feedback (GL_TRANSFORM_FEEDBACK_BUFFER).
glBindBuffer(GL_ARRAY_BUFFER, buffer1);
glBindBuffer(GL_TRANSFORM_FEEDBACK_BUFFFER, buffer2);

// Now, we need to start a query to count how many vertices get written to
// the transform feedback buffer
glBeginQuery(GL_TRANSFORM_FEEDBACK_PRIMITIVES_WRITTEN, q);

// Ok, start transform feedback...
glBeginTransformFeedback(GL_POINTS);

// Draw something to get data into the transform feedback buffer
DrawSomePoints();

// Done with transform feedback
glEndTransformFeedback();

// End the query and get the result back
glEndQuery(GL_TRANSFORM_FEEDBACK_PRIMITIVES_WRITTEN);
glGetQueryObjectuiv(q, GL_QUERY_RESULT, &vertices_to_render);

// Now we bind buffer2 (which has just been used as a transform
// feedback buffer) as a vertex buffer and render some more points
// from it.
glBindBuffer(GL_ARRAY_BUFFER, buffer2);
glDrawArrays(GL_POINTS, 0, vertices_to_render);
```

Listing 11.9: Drawing data written to a transform feedback buffer

Whenever you retrieve the results of a query from OpenGL, it has to finish
what it's doing so that it can provide an accurate count. This is true for
transform feedback queries just as it is for any other type of query. When
you execute the code shown in Listing 11.9, as soon as you call
glGetQueryObjectuiv(), the OpenGL pipeline will drain and the graphics
processor will idle. All this just so the vertex count can make a round trip
from the GPU to your application and back again. To get around this,
OpenGL provides two things. First, is the *transform feedback object*, which
represents the state of the transform feedback stage. Up until now, you
have been using the default transform feedback object. However, you can
create your own by calling **glGenTransformFeedbacks()** followed by
glBindTransformFeedback():

```
void glGenTransformFeedbacks(GLsizei n,
                             GLuint * ids);

void glBindTransformFeedback(GLenum target,
                             GLuint id);
```

For **glGenTransformFeedbacks()**, n is the number of object names to
reserve and ids is a pointer to an array into which the new names
will be written. Once you have a new name, you bind it using
glBindTransformFeedback(), whose first parameter, target, must be

GL_TRANSFORM_FEEDBACK and whose second parameter, id, is the name of the transform feedback object to bind. You can delete transform feedback objects using **glDeleteTransformFeedbacks()**, and you can determine whether a given value is the name of a transform feedback object by calling **glIsTransformFeedback()**:

```
void glDeleteTransformFeedbacks(GLsizei n,
                                const GLuint * ids);

GLboolean glIsTransformFeedback(GLuint id);
```

Once a transform feedback object is bound, all state related to transform feedback is kept in that object, and this includes the transform feedback buffer bindings and the counts used to keep track of how much data has been written to each transform feedback stream. This is effectively the same data that would be returned in a transform feedback query, and we can use it to automatically draw the number of vertices captured using transform feedback. This is the second part of functionality that OpenGL provides for this purpose, and it consists of four functions:

```
void glDrawTransformFeedback(GLenum mode,
                             GLuint id);

void glDrawTransformFeedbackInstanced(GLenum mode,
                                      GLuint id,
                                      GLsizei primcount);

void glDrawTransformFeedbackStream(GLenum mode,
                                   GLuint id,
                                   GLuint stream);

void glDrawTransformFeedbackStreamInstanced(GLenum mode,
                                            GLuint id,
                                            GLuint stream,
                                            GLsizei primcount);
```

For all four functions, mode is one of the primitive modes that can be used with other drawing functions such as **glDrawArrays()** and **glDrawElements()**, and id is the name of a transform feedback object that contains the counts.

- Calling **glDrawTransformFeedback()** is equivalent to calling **glDrawArrays()**, except that the number of vertices to process is taken from the first stream of the transform feedback object named in id.

- Calling **glDrawTransformFeedbackInstanced()** is equivalent to **glDrawArraysInstanced()**, with the vertex count again sourced from the first stream of the transform feedback object named in id and with the instance count specified in primcount.

- Calling `glDrawTransformFeedbackStream()` is equivalent to calling `glDrawTransformFeedback()`, except that the stream given in `stream` is used as the source of the count.

- Calling `glDrawTransformFeedbackStreamInstanced()` is equivalent to calling `glDrawTransformFeedbackInstanced()`, except that the stream given in `stream` is used as the source of the count.

When you use one of the functions that take a stream index, data must be recorded into the transform feedback buffers associated with streams other than zero using a geometry shader, as discussed in "Multiple Streams of Storage" back in Chapter 8.

Synchronization in OpenGL

In an advanced application, OpenGL's order of operation and the pipeline nature of the system may be important. Examples of such applications are those with multiple contexts and multiple threads, or those sharing data between OpenGL and other APIs such as OpenCL. In some cases, it may be necessary to determine whether commands sent to OpenGL have finished yet and whether the results of those commands are ready. In this section, we discuss various methods of synchronizing various parts of the OpenGL pipeline.

Draining the Pipeline

OpenGL includes two commands to force it to start working on commands or to finish working on commands that have been issued so far. These are

```
glFlush();
```

and

```
glFinish();
```

There are subtle differences between the two. The first, **glFlush()**, ensures that any commands issued so far are at least placed into the start of the OpenGL pipeline and that they will eventually be executed. The problem is that **glFlush()** doesn't tell you anything about the execution status of the commands issued — only that they will eventually be executed. **glFinish()**, on the other hand actually ensures that all commands issued have been fully executed and that the OpenGL pipeline is empty. While **glFinish()** does ensure that all of your OpenGL commands have been processed, it will empty the OpenGL pipeline, causing a *bubble* and reducing performance, sometimes drastically. In general, it is recommended that you don't call **glFinish()** for any reason.

Synchronization and Fences

Sometimes it may be necessary to know whether OpenGL has finished executing commands up to some point without forcing to empty the pipeline. This is especially useful when you are sharing data between two contexts or between OpenGL and OpenCL, for example. This type of synchronization is managed by what are known as *sync objects*. Like any other OpenGL object, they must be created before they are used and destroyed when they are no longer needed. Sync objects have two possible states: *signaled* and *unsignaled*. They start out in the unsignaled state, and when some particular event occurs, they move to the signaled state. The event that triggers their transition from unsignaled to signaled depends on their type. The type of sync object we are interested in is called a fence sync, and one can be created by calling

```
GLsync glFenceSync(GL_SYNC_GPU_COMMANDS_COMPLETE, 0);
```

The first parameter is a token specifying the event we're going to wait for. In this case, GL_SYNC_GPU_COMMANDS_COMPLETE says that we want the GPU to have processed all commands in the pipeline before setting the state of the sync object to signaled. The second parameter is a flags field and is zero here because no flags are relevant for this type of sync object. The **glFenceSync()** function returns a new GLsync object. As soon as the fence sync is created, it enters (in the unsignaled state) the OpenGL pipeline and is processed along with all the other commands without stalling OpenGL or consuming significant resources. When it reaches the end of the pipeline, it is "executed" like any other command, and this sets its state to signaled. Because of the in-order nature of OpenGL, this tells us that any OpenGL commands issued before the call to **glFenceSync()** have completed, even though commands issued after the **glFenceSync()** may not have reached the end of the pipeline yet.

Once the sync object has been created (and has therefore entered the OpenGL pipeline), we can query its state to find out if it's reached the end of the pipeline yet, and we can ask OpenGL to wait for it to become signaled before returning to the application. To determine whether the sync object has become signaled yet, call

```
glGetSynciv(sync, GL_SYNC_STATUS, sizeof(GLint), NULL, &result);
```

When **glGetSynciv()** returns, result (which is a GLint) will contain
GL_SIGNALED if the sync object was in the signaled state and GL_UNSIGNALED
otherwise. This allows the application to poll the state of the sync object
and use this information to potentially do some useful work while the GPU
is busy with previous commands. For example, consider the code in
Listing 11.10.

```
GLint result = GL_UNSIGNALED;
glGetSynciv(sync, GL_SYNC_STATUS, sizeof(GLint), NULL, &result);
while (result != GL_SIGNALED)
{
    DoSomeUsefulWork();
    glGetSynciv(sync, GL_SYNC_STATUS, sizeof(GLint), NULL, &result);
}
```

Listing 11.10: Working while waiting for a sync object

This code loops, doing a small amount of useful work on each iteration
until the sync object becomes signaled. If the application were to create a
sync object at the start of each frame, the application could wait for the
sync object from two frames ago and do a variable amount of work
depending on how long it takes the GPU to process the commands for
that frame. This allows an application to balance the amount of work
done by the CPU (such as the number of sound effects to mix together or
the number of iterations of a physics simulation to run, for example) with
the speed of the GPU.

To actually cause OpenGL to wait for a sync object to become signaled
(and therefore for the commands in the pipeline before the sync to
complete), there are two functions that you can use:

```
glClientWaitSync(sync, GL_SYNC_FLUSH_COMMANDS_BIT, timeout);
```

or

```
glWaitSync(sync, 0, GL_TIMEOUT_IGNORED);
```

The first parameter to both functions is the name of the sync object that
was returned by **glFenceSync()**. The second and third parameters to the
two functions have the same names but must be set differently.

For **glClientWaitSync()**, the second parameter is a bitfield specifying
additional behavior of the function. The GL_SYNC_FLUSH_COMMANDS_BIT
tells **glClientWaitSync()** to ensure that the sync object has entered the
OpenGL pipeline before beginning to wait for it to become signaled.

Without this bit, there is a possibility that OpenGL could watch for a sync object that hasn't been sent down the pipeline yet, and the application could end up waiting forever and hang. It's a good idea to set this bit unless you have a really good reason not to. The third parameter is a timeout value in nanoseconds to wait. If the sync object doesn't become signaled within this time, **glClientWaitSync()** returns a status code to indicate so. **glClientWaitSync()** won't return until either the sync object becomes signaled or a timeout occurs.

There are four possible status codes that might be returned by **glClientWaitSync()**. They are summarized in Table 11.1.

Table 11.1: Possible Return Values for **glClientWaitSync()**

Returned Status	Meaning
GL_ALREADY_SIGNALED	The sync object was already signaled when **glClientWaitSync()** was called, and so the function returned immediately.
GL_TIMEOUT_EXPIRED	The timeout specified in the timeout parameter expired, meaning that the sync object never became signaled in the allowed time.
GL_CONDITION_SATISFIED	The sync object became signaled within the allowed timeout period (but was not already signaled when **glClientWaitSync()** was called).
GL_WAIT_FAILED	An error occurred (such as sync not being a valid sync object), and the user should check the result of **glGetError()** to get more information.

There are a couple of things to note about the timeout value. First, while the unit of measurement is nanoseconds, there is no accuracy requirement in OpenGL. If you specify that you want to wait for one nanosecond, OpenGL could round this up to the next millisecond or more. Second, if you specify a timeout value of zero, **glClientWaitSync()** will return GL_ALREADY_SIGNALED if the sync object was in a signaled state at the time of the call and GL_TIMEOUT_EXPIRED otherwise. It will never return GL_CONDITION_SATISFIED.

For **glWaitSync()**, the behavior is slightly different. The application won't actually wait for the sync object to become signaled, only the GPU will. Therefore, **glWaitSync()** will return to the application immediately. This makes the second and third parameters somewhat irrelevant. Because the application doesn't wait for the function to return, there is no danger of your application hanging, and so the GL_SYNC_FLUSH_COMMANDS_BIT is not needed and would actually cause an error if specified. Also, the timeout will actually be implementation dependent, and so the special timeout value GL_TIMEOUT_IGNORED is specified to make this clear. If you're interested, you can find out what the timeout value used by your implementation is by calling **glGetInteger64v()** with the GL_MAX_SERVER_WAIT_TIMEOUT parameter.

You might be wondering, "What is the point of asking the GPU to wait for a sync object to reach the end of the pipeline?" After all, the sync object will become signaled when it reaches the end of the pipeline, and so if you wait for it to reach the end of the pipeline, it will of course be signaled. Therefore, won't **glWaitSync()** just do nothing? This would be true if we only considered simple applications that only use a single OpenGL context and that don't use other APIs. However, the power of sync objects is harnessed when using multiple OpenGL contexts. Sync objects can be shared between OpenGL contexts and between compatible APIs such as OpenCL. That is, a sync object created by a call to **glFenceSync()** on one context can be waited for by a call to **glWaitSync()** (or **glClientWaitSync()**) on another context.

Consider this. You can ask one OpenGL context to hold off rendering something until another context has finished doing something. This allows synchronization between two contexts. You can have an application with two threads and two contexts (or more, if you want). If you create a sync object in each context, and then in each context you wait for the sync objects from the other contexts using either **glClientWaitSync()** or **glWaitSync()**, you know that when all of the functions have returned, all of those contexts are synchronized with each other. Together with thread synchronization primitives provided by your OS (such as semaphores), you can keep rendering to multiple windows in sync.

An example of this type of usage is when a buffer is shared between two contexts. The first context is writing to the buffer using transform feedback, while the second context wants to draw the results of the transform feedback. The first context would draw using transform feedback mode. After calling **glEndTransformFeedback()**, it immediately calls **glFenceSync()**. Now, the application makes the second context current and calls **glWaitSync()** to wait for the sync object to become signaled. It can then issue more commands to OpenGL (on the new context), and those are queued up by the drivers, ready to execute. Only when the GPU has finished recording data into the transform feedback buffers with the first context does it start to work on the commands using that data in the second context.

There are also extensions and other functionality in APIs like OpenCL that allow asynchronous writes to buffers. You can use **glWaitSync()** to ask a GPU to wait until the data in a buffer is valid by creating a sync object on the context that generates the data and then waiting for that sync object to become signaled on the context that's going to consume the data.

Sync objects only ever go from the unsignaled to the signaled state. There is no mechanism to put a sync object back into the unsignaled state, even manually. This is because a manual flip of a sync object can cause race conditions and possibly hang the application. Consider the situation where a sync object is created, reaches the end of the pipeline and becomes signaled, and then the application set it back to unsignaled. If another thread tried to wait for that sync object but didn't start waiting until after the application had already set the sync object back to the unsignaled state, it would wait forever. Each sync object therefore represents a one-shot event, and every time a synchronization is required, a new sync object must be created by calling **glFenceSync()**. Although it is always important to clean up after yourself by deleting objects when you're done with them, this is particularly important with sync objects because you might be creating many new ones every frame. To delete a sync object, call

```
glDeleteSync(sync);
```

This deletes the sync object. This may not occur immediately; any thread that is watching for the sync object to become signaled will still wait for its respective timeouts, and the object will actually be deleted once nobody's watching it any more. Thus, it is perfectly legal to call **glWaitSync()** followed by **glDeleteSync()** even though the sync object is still in the OpenGL pipeline.

Summary

This chapter discussed how to monitor the execution of your commands in the pipeline and get some feedback about their progress down it. You saw how to measure the time taken for your commands to complete, and have the tools necessary to measure the latency of the graphics pipeline. This, in turn, allows you to alter your application's complexity to suit the system it's running on and the performance targets you've set for it. We will use these tools for real-world performance tuning exercises in Chapter 13, "Debugging and Performance Optimization." You also saw how it is possible to synchronize the execution of your application to the OpenGL context, and how to synchronize execution of multiple OpenGL contexts.

Part III

In Practice

Chapter 12

Rendering Techniques

WHAT YOU'LL LEARN IN THIS CHAPTER

- How to light the pixels in your scene

- How to delay shading until the last possible moment

- How to render an entire scene without a single triangle

By this point in the book, you should have a good grasp of the fundamentals of OpenGL. You have been introduced to most of its features and should feel comfortable using it to implement graphics rendering algorithms. In this chapter, we take a look at a few of these algorithms — in particular those that might be interesting in a real-time rendering context. First, we will cover a few basic lighting techniques that will allow you to apply interesting shading to the objects in your scene. Then, we will take a look at some approaches to rendering without the goal of photo-realism. Finally, we will discuss some algorithms that are really only applicable outside the traditional forward-rendering geometry pipeline, ultimately culminating with rendering an entire scene without a single vertex or triangle.

Lighting Models

Arguably, the job of any graphics rendering application is the simulation of light. Whether it be the simplest spinning cube, or the most complex movie special effect ever invented, we are trying to convince the user that they are seeing the real world, or an analog of it. To do this, we must model the way that light interacts with surfaces. Extremely advanced models exist that are as physically accurate as far as we understand the properties of light. However, most of these are impractical for real-time implementation, and so we must assume approximations, or *models* that produce plausible results even if they are not physically accurate. The following few sections show how a few of the lighting models that you might use in a real-time application can be implemented.

The Phong Lighting Model

One of the most common lighting models is the Phong lighting model. It works on a simple principle, which is that objects have three material properties, which are the ambient, diffuse, and specular reflectivity. These properties are assigned color values, with brighter colors representing a higher amount of reflectivity. Light sources have these same three properties and are again assigned color values that represent the brightness of the light. The final calculated color value is then the sum of the lighting and material interactions of these three properties.

Ambient Light

Ambient light doesn't come from any particular direction. It has an original source somewhere, but the rays of light have bounced around the room or scene and become directionless. Objects illuminated by ambient light are evenly lit on all surfaces in all directions. You can think of ambient light as a global "brightening" factor applied per light source. This lighting component really approximates scattered light in the environment that originates from the light source.

To calculate the contribution an ambient light source makes to the final color, the ambient material property is scaled by the ambient light values (the two color values are just multiplied), which yields the ambient color contribution. In GLSL shader speak, we would write this like so:

```
uniform vec3 ambient = vec3(0.1, 0.1, 0.1);
```

Diffuse Light

Diffuse light is the directional component of a light source and was the subject of our previous example lighting shader. In the Phong lighting model, the diffuse material and lighting values are multiplied together, as is done with the ambient components. However, this value is then scaled by the dot product of the surface normal and light vector, which is the direction vector from the point being shaded to the light. Again, in shader speak, this might look something like this:

```
uniform vec3 vDiffuseMaterial;
uniform vec3 vDiffuseLight;
float fDotProduct = max(0.0, dot(vNormal, vLightDir));
vec3 vDiffuseColor = vDiffuseMaterial * vDiffuseLight * fDotProduct;
```

Note that we did not simply take the dot product of the two vectors, but also employed the GLSL function max. The dot product can also be a negative number, and we really can't have negative lighting or color values. Anything less than zero needs to just be zero.

Specular Highlight

Like diffuse light, specular light is a highly directional property, but it interacts more sharply with the surface and in a particular direction. A highly specular light (really a material property in the real world) tends to cause a bright spot on the surface it shines on, which is called the *specular highlight*. Because of its highly directional nature, it is even possible that depending on a viewer's position, the specular highlight may not even be visible. A spotlight and the sun are good examples of sources that produce strong specular highlights, but of course they must be shining on an object that is "shiny."

The color contribution to the specular material and lighting colors is scaled by a value that requires a bit more computation than we've done so far. First we must find the vector that is reflected by the surface normal and the inverted light vector. The dot product between these two vectors is then raised to a "shininess" power. The higher the shininess number, the smaller the resulting specular highlight turns out to be. Some shader skeleton code that does this is shown here.

```
uniform vec3 vSpecularMaterial;
uniform vec3 vSpecularLight;
float shininess = 128.0;

vec3 vReflection = reflect(-vLightDir, vEyeNormal);
float EyeReflectionAngle = max(0.0, dot(vEyeNormal, vReflection);
fSpec = pow(EyeReflectionAngle, shininess);
vec3 vSpecularColor = vSpecularLight * vSpecularMaterial * fSpec;
```

The shininess parameter could easily be a uniform just like anything else. Traditionally (from the fixed-function pipeline days), the highest specular power is set to 128. Numbers greater than this tend to have a diminishingly small effect.

Now, we have formed a complete equation for modeling the effect of lighting on a surface. Given material with ambient term k_a, diffuse term k_d, specular term k_s and *shininess factor* α, and a light with ambient term i_a, diffuse term i_d, and diffuse term i_s, the complete lighting formula is

$$I_p = k_a i_a + k_d(\vec{L} \cdot \vec{N})i_d + k_s(\vec{R} \cdot \vec{V})^\alpha i_s$$

This equation is a function of several vectors, $\vec{N}$, $\vec{L}$, $\vec{R}$, and $\vec{V}$, which represent the surface normal, the unit vector from the point being shaded to the light, the reflection of the *negative* of the light vector $\vec{L}$ in the plane defined by $\vec{N}$, and the vector to the viewer $\vec{V}$. To understand why this works, consider the vectors shown in Figure 12.1.

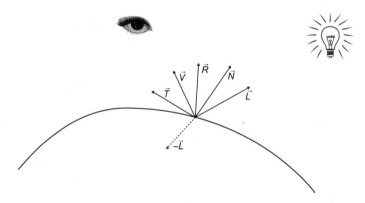

Figure 12.1: Vectors used in Phong lighting

In Figure 12.1, $-\vec{L}$ is shown pointing *away* from the light. If we then reflect that vector about the plane defined by the surface normal $\vec{N}$, it is obvious from the diagram that we end up with $\vec{R}$. This represents the reflection of the light source in the surface. When $\vec{R}$ points away from the viewer, the reflection will not be visible. However, when $\vec{R}$ points directly at the viewer, then the reflection will appear brightest. At this point, the dot product (which, remember, is the cosine of the angle between two normalized vectors) will be greatest. This is the specular highlight, which is view dependent.

The effect of diffuse shading also becomes clearer from Figure 12.1. When the light source shines directly on the surface, the vector $\vec{L}$ will be perpendicular to the surface and therefore be colinear with $\vec{N}$, where the dot product between $\vec{N}$ and $\vec{L}$ is greatest. When the light strikes the surface at a grazing angle, $\vec{L}$ and $\vec{N}$ will be almost perpendicular to one another, and their dot product will be close to zero.

As you can see, the intensity of the light at point p (I_p) is calculated as the sum of a number of terms. The *reflection vector* $\vec{R}$ (called R in the shader) is calculated by reflecting the light vector around the eye-space normal of the point being shaded.

The sample program phonglighting implements just such a shader. The sample implements the *Gouraud* technique known as *Gouraud shading*, where we compute the lighting values per vertex and then simply interpolate the resulting colors between vertices for the shading. This allows us to implement the entire lighting equation in the vertex shader. The complete listing of the vertex shader is given in Listing 12.1.

```
#version 420 core

// Per-vertex inputs
layout (location = 0) in vec4 position;
layout (location = 1) in vec3 normal;

// Matrices we'll need
layout (std140) uniform constants
{
    mat4 mv_matrix;
    mat4 view_matrix;
    mat4 proj_matrix;
};

// Light and material properties
uniform vec3 light_pos = vec3(100.0, 100.0, 100.0);
uniform vec3 diffuse_albedo = vec3(0.5, 0.2, 0.7);
uniform vec3 specular_albedo = vec3(0.7);
uniform float specular_power = 128.0;
uniform vec3 ambient = vec3(0.1, 0.1, 0.1);

// Outputs to the fragment shader
out VS_OUT
{
    vec3 color;
} vs_out;

void main(void)
{
    // Calculate view-space coordinate
    vec4 P = mv_matrix * position;

    // Calculate normal in view space
    vec3 N = mat3(mv_matrix) * normal;
```

```
// Calculate view-space light vector
vec3 L = light_pos - P.xyz;
// Calculate view vector (simply the negative of the
// view-space position)
vec3 V = -P.xyz;

// Normalize all three vectors
N = normalize(N);
L = normalize(L);
V - normalize(V);

// Calculate R by reflecting -L around the plane defined by N
vec3 R = reflect(-L, N);

// Calculate the diffuse and specular contributions
vec3 diffuse = max(dot(N, L), 0.0) * diffuse_albedo;
vec3 specular = pow(max(dot(R, V), 0.0), specular_power) *
                specular_albedo;

// Send the color output to the fragment shader
vs_out.color = ambient + diffuse + specular;

// Calculate the clip-space position of each vertex
gl_Position = proj_matrix * P;
}
```

Listing 12.1: The Gouraud shading vertex shader

The fragment shader for Gouraud shading is very simple. As the final color of each fragment is essentially calculated in the vertex shader and then interpolated before being passed to the fragment shader, all we need to do in our fragment shader is write the incoming color to the framebuffer. The complete source code is shown in Listing 12.2.

```
#version 420 core

// Output
layout (location = 0) out vec4 color;

// Input from vertex shader
in VS_OUT
{
    vec3 color;
} fs_in;

void main(void)
{
    // Write incoming color to the framebuffer
    color = vec4(fs_in.color, 1.0);
}
```

Listing 12.2: The Gouraud shading fragment shader

Unless you use a very high level of tessellation, then for a given triangle, there are only three vertices and usually many more fragments that fill out the triangle. This makes per-vertex lighting and Gouraud shading very efficient, as all the computations are done only once per vertex. Figure 12.2 shows the output of the phonglighting example program.

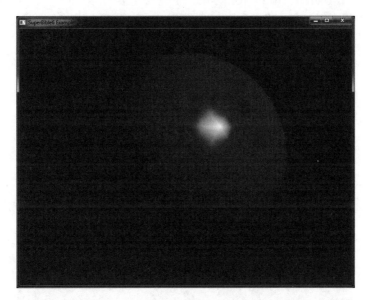

Figure 12.2: Per-vertex lighting (Gouraud shading)

Phong Shading

One of the drawbacks to Gouraud shading is clearly apparent in Figure 12.2. Notice the starburst pattern of the specular highlight. On a still image, this might almost pass as an intentional artistic effect. The running sample program, however, rotates the sphere and shows a characteristic flashing that is a bit distracting and generally undesirable. This is caused by the discontinuity between triangles because the color values are being interpolated linearly through color space. The bright lines are actually the seams between individual triangles. One way to reduce this effect is to use more and more vertices in your geometry.

Another, and higher quality, method is called *Phong shading*. Note that Phong shading and the Phong lighting model are separate things — although they were both invented by the same person at the same time. With Phong shading, instead of interpolating the color values between vertices, we interpolate the surface normals between vertices and then use the resulting normal to perform the entire lighting calculation for each pixel instead of per vertex. The phonglighting example program can be switched between evaluating the lighting equations per vertex (and therefore implementing Gouraud shading) and evaluating them per fragment (implementing Phong shading). Figure 12.3 shows the output from the `phonglighting` sample program performing shading per fragment.

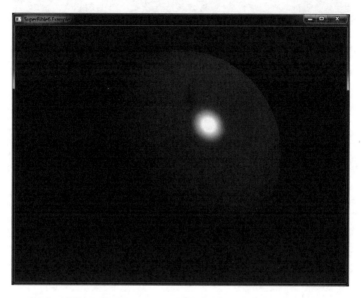

Figure 12.3: Per-fragment lighting (Phong shading)

The trade-off is of course we are now doing significantly more work in the fragment shader, which is going to be executed significantly more times than the vertex shader. The basic code is the same as for the Gouraud shading example, but this time there is some significant rearranging of the shader code. Listing 12.3 shows the new vertex shader.

```
#version 420 core

// Per-vertex inputs
layout (location = 0) in vec4 position;
layout (location = 1) in vec3 normal;

// Matrices we'll need
layout (std140) uniform constants
{
    mat4 mv_matrix;
    mat4 view_matrix;
    mat4 proj_matrix;
};

// Inputs from vertex shader
out VS_OUT
```

```
{
    vec3 N;
    vec3 L;
    vec3 V;
} vs_out;

// Position of light
uniform vec3 light_pos = vec3(100.0, 100.0, 100.0);
void main(void)
{
    // Calculate view-space coordinate
    vec4 P = mv_matrix * position;

    // Calculate normal in view-space
    vs_out.N = mat3(mv_matrix) * normal;

    // Calculate light vector
    vs_out.L = light_pos - P.xyz;

    // Calculate view vector
    vs_out.V = -P.xyz;

    // Calculate the clip-space position of each vertex
    gl_Position = proj_matrix * P;
}
```

Listing 12.3: The Phong shading vertex shader

All the lighting computations depend on the surface normal, light direction, and view vector. Instead of passing a computed color value one from each vertex, we pass these three vectors as the outputs vs_out.N, vs_out.L, and vs_out.V. Now the fragment shader has significantly more work to do than before, and it is shown in Listing 12.4.

```
#version 420 core

// Output
layout (location = 0) out vec4 color;

// Input from vertex shader
in VS_OUT
{
    vec3 N;
    vec3 L;
    vec3 V;
} fs_in;

// Material properties
uniform vec3 diffuse_albedo = vec3(0.5, 0.2, 0.7);
uniform vec3 specular_albedo = vec3(0.7);
uniform float specular_power = 128.0;

void main(void)
{
    // Normalize the incoming N, L, and V vectors
    vec3 N = normalize(fs_in.N);
    vec3 L = normalize(fs_in.L);
    vec3 V = normalize(fs_in.V);
```

```
// Calculate R locally
vec3 R = reflect(-L, N);

// Compute the diffuse and specular components for each
// fragment
vec3 diffuse = max(dot(N, L), 0.0) * diffuse_albedo;
vec3 specular = pow(max(dot(R, V), 0.0), specular_power) *
                specular_albedo;

// Write final color to the framebuffer
color = vec4(diffuse + specular, 1.0);
}
```

Listing 12.4: The Phong shading fragment shader

On today's hardware, higher quality rendering choices such as Phong shading are often practical. The visual quality is dramatic, and performance is often only marginally compromised. Still, on lower powered hardware (such as an embedded device) or in a scene where many other already expensive choices have been made, Gouraud shading may be the best choice. A general shader performance optimization rule is to move as much processing out of the fragment shaders and into the vertex shader as possible. With this example, you can see why.

The main parameters that are passed to the Phong lighting equations (whether they be evaluated per vertex or per fragment) are the diffuse and specular *albedo* and the specular power. The first two are the colors of the diffuse and specular lighting effect produced by the material being modeled. Normally, they are either the same color or the diffuse albedo is the color of the material and the specular albedo is white. However, it's also possible to make the specular albedo a completely different color to the diffuse albedo. The specular power controls the sharpness of the specular highlight. Figure 12.4 shows the effect of varying the specular parameters of a material (this image is also shown in Color Plate 5). A single white point light is in the scene. From left to right, the specular albedo varies from almost black to pure white (essentially increasing the specular contribution), and from top to bottom, the specular power increases exponentially from 4.0 to 256.0, doubling in each row. As you can see, the sphere on the top left looks dull and evenly lit, whereas the sphere on the bottom right appears highly glossy.

Although the image in Figure 12.4 shows only the effect of a white light on the scene, colored lights are simulated by simply multiplying the color

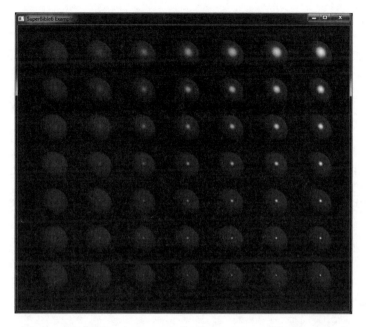

Figure 12.4: Varying specular parameters of a material

of the light by the diffuse and specular components of each fragment's color.

Blinn-Phong Lighting

The Blinn-Phong lighting model could be considered an extension to or possibly an optimization of the Phong lighting model. Notice that in the Phong lighting model, we calculate $\vec{R} \cdot \vec{N}$ at each shaded point (either per vertex or per fragment). However, as an approximation, we can replace $\vec{R} \cdot \vec{N}$ with $\vec{N} \cdot \vec{H}$, where $\vec{H}$ is the halfway vector between the light vector $\vec{L}$ and the eye vector $\vec{E}$. This vector is can be calculated as

$$\vec{H} = \frac{\vec{L} + \vec{E}}{\left| \vec{L} + \vec{E} \right|}$$

Technically, this calculation should also be applied wherever the Phong equations would have been applied, requiring a normalization at each step (the division by the vectors' magnitude in the above equation). However, this comes in exchange for no longer needing to calculate the vector $\vec{R}$, avoiding the call to the `reflect` function. Modern graphics processors are generally powerful enough that the difference in cost between the vector normalization required to calculate $\vec{H}$ and the call to `reflect` is negligible. However, if the curvature of the underlying surface represented by a triangle is relatively small and if the triangle is small relative to the distance from the surface to the light and viewer, the value of $\vec{H}$ won't change much, so it's even possible to calculate $\vec{H}$ in the vertex (or geometry or tessellation) shader and pass it to the fragment shader as a `flat` input. Even when the result of this is inaccurate, this can often be remedied by increasing the shininess (or specular) factor α. Listing 12.5 provides a fragment shader that implements Blinn-Phong lighting per fragment. This shader is included in the `blinnphong` example program.

```
#version 420 core

// Output
layout (location = 0) out vec4 color;

// Input from vertex shader
in VS_OUT
{
    vec3 N;
    vec3 L;
    vec3 V;
} fs_in;

// Material properties
uniform vec3 diffuse_albedo = vec3(0.5, 0.2, 0.7);
uniform vec3 specular_albedo = vec3(0.7);
uniform float specular_power = 128.0;

void main(void)
{
    // Normalize the incoming N, L, and V vectors
    vec3 N = normalize(fs_in.N);
    vec3 L = normalize(fs_in.L);
    vec3 V = normalize(fs_in.V);

    // Calculate the half vector, H
    vec3 H = normalize(L + V);

    // Compute the diffuse and specular components for each fragment
    vec3 diffuse = max(dot(N, L), 0.0) * diffuse_albedo;

    // Replace the R.V calculation (as in Phong) with N.H
    vec3 specular = pow(max(dot(N, H), 0.0), specular_power) * specular_albedo;

    // Write final color to the framebuffer
    color = vec4(diffuse + specular, 1.0);
}
```

Listing 12.5: Blinn-Phong fragment shader

Figure 12.5 shows the result of using plain Phong shading (left) next to the result of using Blinn-Phong shading. In Figure 12.5, the specular exponent used for the Phong rendering is 128, whereas the specular exponent used for the Blinn-Phong rendering is 200. As you can see, after adjustment of the specular powers, the results are very similar.

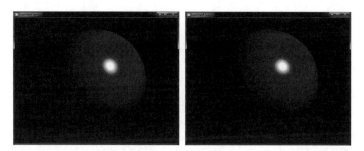

Figure 12.5: Phong lighting (left) vs. Blinn-Phong lighting (right)

Rim Lighting

Rim lighting, which is also known as back-lighting, is an effect that simulates the bleeding of light "around" an object from sources that are behind it or otherwise have no effect on the shaded surfaces of the model. Rim lighting is so called because it produces a bright rim of light around the outline of the object being lit. In photography, this is attained by physically placing a light source behind the subject such that the object of interest sits between the camera and the light source. In computer graphics, we can simulate the effect by determining how closely the view direction comes to glancing the surface.

To implement this, all we need is the surface normal and the view direction — two quantities we have at hand from any of the lighting models we have already described. When the view direction is face on to the surface, the view vector will be colinear to the surface normal and so the effect of rim lighting will be least. When the view direction glances the surface, the surface normal and view vector will be almost perpendicular to one another and the rim light effect will be greatest.

You can see this in Figure 12.6. Near the edge of the object, the vectors $\vec{N_1}$ and $\vec{V_1}$ are almost perpendicular, and this is where the most light from the lamp behind the object will leak around it. However, in the center of the object, $\vec{N_2}$ and $\vec{V_2}$ point in pretty much the same direction. The lamp will be completely obscured by the object, and the amount of light leaking through will minimal.

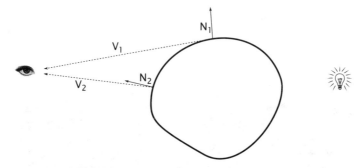

Figure 12.6: Rim lighting vectors

A quantity that is easy to calculate and is proportional to the angle between two vectors is the dot product. When two vectors are colinear, the dot product between them will be one. As the two vectors become closer to orthogonal, the dot product becomes closer to zero. Therefore, we can produce a rim light effect by taking the dot product between the view direction and the surface normal and making the intensity of the rim light inversely proportional to it. To provide further control over the rim light, we include a scalar brightness and an exponential sharpness factor. Thus, our rim lighting equation is

$$L_{rim} = C_{rim} \left(1.0 - \vec{N} \cdot \vec{V}\right)^{P_{rim}}$$

Here, $\vec{N}$ and $\vec{V}$ are our usual normal and view vectors, C_{rim} and P_{rim} are the color and power of the rim light, respectively, and L_{rim} is the resulting contribution of the rim light. The fragment shader to implement this is quite simple, and is shown in Listing 12.6.

```
// Uniforms controlling the rim light effect
uniform vec3 rim_color;
uniform float rim_power;

vec3 calculate_rim(vec3 N, vec3 V)
{
    // Calculate the rim factor
    float f = 1.0 - dot(N, V);

    // Constrain it to the range 0 to 1 using a smooth step function
    f = smoothstep(0.0, 1.0, f);

    // Raise it to the rim exponent
    f = pow(f, rim_power);

    // Finally, multiply it by the rim color
    return f * rim_color;
}
```

Listing 12.6: Rim lighting shader function

Figure 12.7 shows a model illuminated with a Phong lighting model as described earlier in this chapter, but with a rim light effect applied. The code to produce this image is included in the rimlight example program. The top-left image has the rim light disabled for reference. The top-right image applies a medium strength rim light with a moderate fall-off exponent. The bottom-left image increases both the exponent and the strength of the light. As a result, the rim is sharp and focused. The image on the bottom right of Figure 12.7 has the light intensity turned down but also has the rim exponent turned down. This causes the light to bleed further around the model producing more of an ambient effect.

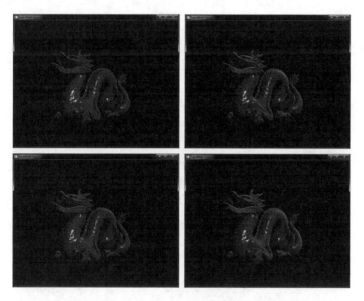

Figure 12.7: Result of rim lighting example

Two of the images included in Figure 12.7 are also shown in Color Plate 6. For a given scene, the color of the rim light would normally be fixed or perhaps vary as a function of world space (otherwise it would seem as though the different objects were lit by different lights, which might look odd). However, the power of the rim light is essentially an approximation of bleeding, which may vary by material. For example, soft materials such as hair, fur or translucent materials such as marble might bleed quite a bit, whereas harder materials such as wood or rock might not bleed as much light.

Normal Mapping

In the examples shown so far, we have calculated the lighting contributions either at each vertex in the case of Gouraud shading, or at each pixel, but with vectors derived from per-vertex attributes that are then smoothly interpolated across each triangle in the case of Phong shading. To really see surface features, that level of detail must be present in the original model. In most cases, this leads to an unreasonable amount of geometry that must be passed to OpenGL and to triangles that are so small that each one only covers a small number of pixels.

One method for increasing the perceived level of detail without actually adding more vertices to a model is *normal mapping*, which is sometimes also called *bump mapping*. To implement normal mapping, we need a texture that stores a surface normal in each texel. This is then applied to our model and used in the fragment shader to calculate a local surface normal for each fragment. Our lighting model of choice is then applied in each invocation to calculate per-fragment lighting. An example of such a texture is shown in Figure 12.8.

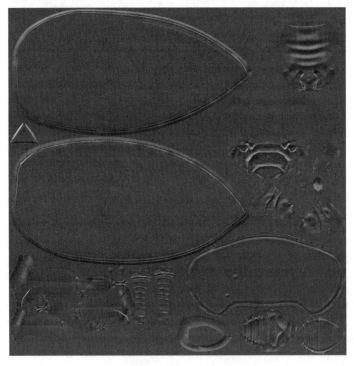

Figure 12.8: Example normal map

The most common coordinate space used for normal maps is tangent space, which is a local coordinate system where the positive z axis is aligned with the surface normal. The other two vectors in this coordinate space are known as the *tangent* and *bitangent* vectors, and for best results, these vectors should line up with the direction of the u and v coordinates used in the texture. The tangent vector is usually encoded as part of the geometry data and passed as an input to the vertex shader. As an orthonormal basis, given two vectors in the frame, the third can be calculated using a simple cross product. This means that given the normal and tangent vectors, we can calculate the bitangent vector using the cross product.

The normal, tangent, and bitangent vectors can be used to construct a rotation matrix that will transform a vector in the standard Cartesian frame into the frame represented by these three vectors. We simply insert the three vectors as the rows of this matrix. This gives us the following:

$$\vec{N} = \text{normal}$$
$$\vec{T} = \text{tangent}$$
$$\vec{B} = \vec{N} \times \vec{T}$$
$$TBN = \begin{bmatrix} \vec{T}.x & \vec{T}.y & \vec{T}.z \\ \vec{B}.x & \vec{B}.y & \vec{B}.z \\ \vec{N}.x & \vec{N}.y & \vec{N}.z \end{bmatrix}$$

The matrix produced here is often referred to as the TBN matrix, which stands for Tangent, Bitangent, Normal. Given the TBN matrix for a vertex, we can transform any vector expressed in Cartesian coordinates into the local frame at the vertex. This is important because the dot product operations we use in our lighting calculations are relative to pairs of vectors. As long as these two vectors are in the same frame, then the results will be correct. By transforming our view and light vectors into the local frame at each vertex and then interpolating them across each polygon as we would with normal Phong shading, we are presented with view and light vectors at each fragment that are in the same frame as the normals in our normal map. We can then simply read the local normal at each fragment and perform our lighting calculations in the usual manner.

A vertex shader that calculates the TBN matrix for a vertex, determines the light and view vectors, and then multiplies them by the TBN matrix before passing them to the fragment shader is shown in Listing 12.7. This shader, along with the rest of the code for this example is included in the bumpmapping sample application.

```
#version 420 core

layout (location = 0) in vec4 position;
layout (location = 1) in vec3 normal;
layout (location = 2) in vec3 tangent;
layout (location = 4) in vec2 texcoord;

out VS_OUT
{
    vec2 texcoord;
    vec3 eyeDir;
    vec3 lightDir;
} vs_out;

uniform mat4 mv_matrix;
uniform mat4 proj_matrix;
uniform vec3 light_pos = vec3(0.0, 0.0, 100.0);

void main(void)
{
    // Calculate vertex position in view space.
    vec4 P = mv_matrix * position;

    // Calculate normal (N) and tangent (T) vectors in view space from
    // incoming object space vectors.
    vec3 N = normalize(mat3(mv_matrix) * normal);
    vec3 T = normalize(mat3(mv_matrix) * tangent);
    // Calculate the bitangent vector (B) from the normal and tangent
    // vectors.
    vec3 B = cross(N, T);

    // The light vector (L) is the vector from the point of interest to
    // the light. Calculate that and multiply it by the TBN matrix.
    vec3 L = light_pos - P.xyz;
    vs_out.lightDir = normalize(vec3(dot(V, T), dot(V, B), dot(V, N)));

    // The view vector is the vector from the point of interest to the
    // viewer, which in view space is simply the negative of the position.
    // Calculate that and multiply it by the TBN matrix.
    vec3 V = -P.xyz;
    vs_out.eyeDir = normalize(vec3(dot(V, T), dot(V, B), dot(V, N)));

    // Pass the texture coordinate through unmodified so that the fragment
    // shader can fetch from the normal and color maps.
    vs_out.texcoord = texcoord;

    // Calculate clip coordinates by multiplying our view position by
    // the projection matrix.
    gl_Position = proj_matrix * P;
}
```

Listing 12.7: Vertex shader for normal mapping

The shader in Listing 12.7 calculates the view and light vectors expressed in the local frame of each vertex and passes them along with the vertex's texture coordinates to the fragment shader. In our fragment shader, which

is shown in Listing 12.8, we simply fetch a per-fragment normal map and
use it in our shading calculations.

```
#version 420 core

out vec4 color;

// Color and normal maps
layout (binding = 0) uniform sampler2D tex_color;
layout (binding = 1) uniform sampler2D tex_normal;

in VS_OUT
{
    vec2 texcoord;
    vec3 eyeDir;
    vec3 lightDir;
} fs_in;

void main(void)
{
    // Normalize our incoming view and light direction vectors.
    vec3 V = normalize(fs_in.eyeDir);
    vec3 L = normalize(fs_in.lightDir);
    // Read the normal from the normal map and normalize it.
    vec3 N = normalize(texture(tex_normal, fs_in.texcoord).rgb * 2.0
    - vec3(1.0));
    // Calculate R ready for use in Phong lighting.
    vec3 R = reflect(-L, N);

    // Fetch the diffuse albedo from the texture.
    vec3 diffuse_albedo = texture(tex_color, fs_in.texcoord).rgb;
    // Calculate diffuse color with simple N dot L.
    vec3 diffuse = max(dot(N, L), 0.0) * diffuse_albedo;
    // Uncomment this to turn off diffuse shading
    // diffuse = vec3(0.0);

    // Assume that specular albedo is white - it could also come from a
    texture
    vec3 specular_albedo = vec3(1.0);
    // Calculate Phong specular highlight
    vec3 specular = max(pow(dot(R, V), 5.0), 0.0) * specular_albedo;
    // Uncomment this to turn off specular highlights
    // specular = vec3(0.0);

    // Final color is diffuse + specular
    color = vec4(diffuse + specular, 1.0);
}
```

Listing 12.8: Fragment shader for normal mapping

Rendering a model with this shader clearly shows specular highlights on
details that are present only in the normal map and do not have geometric
representation in the model data. In Figure 12.9, the top-left image shows
the diffuse shading result, the top-right image shows the specular shading
results, and the bottom left shows the image produced by adding these
two results together. For reference, the bottom-right image of Figure 12.9
shows the result of applying per-pixel Phong shading using only the

normals that are interpolated by OpenGL and does not use the normal map. It should be clear from contrasting the bottom-left and bottom-right images that normal mapping can add substantial detail to an image. The bottom-left image from Figure 12.9 is also shown in Color Plate 7.

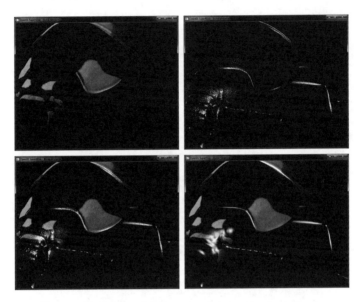

Figure 12.9: Result of normal mapping example

Environment Mapping

In the previous few subsections, you have learned how to compute the effect of lighting on the surface of objects. Lighting shaders can become extremely complex, but eventually they become so intensive that they start to affect performance. Also, it's virtually impossible to create an equation that can represent an arbitrary environment. This is where *environment maps* come in. There are a few types of environment maps that are commonly used in real-time graphics applications — the spherical environment map, the equirectangular map, and the cube map. The spherical environment map is represented as the image of a sphere illuminated by the simulated surroundings. As a sphere map can only represent a single hemisphere of the environment, an equirectangular map is a mapping of spherical coordinates onto a rectangle that allows a full 360° view of the environment to be represented. A cube map, on the other hand, is a special texture made up of six faces that essentially represent a box made of glass through which, if you were standing in its center, you would see your surroundings. We'll dig into these three methods of simulating an environment in the next couple of subsections.

Spherical Environment Maps

As noted, a spherical environment map is a texture map that represents the lighting produced by the simulated surroundings on a sphere made from the material being simulated. This works by taking the view direction and surface normal at the point being shaded and using these two vectors to compute a set of texture coordinates that can be used to look up into the texture to retrieve the lighting coefficients. In the simplest case, this is simply the color of the surface under these lighting conditions, although any number of parameters could be stored in such a texture map. A few examples[1] of environment maps are shown in Figure 12.10. These environment maps are also shown in Color Plate 9.

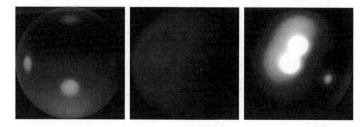

Figure 12.10: A selection of spherical environment maps

The first step in implementing spherical environment mapping is to transform the incoming normal into view-space and to calculate the eye-space view direction. These will be used in our fragment shader to compute the texture coordinates to look up into the environment map. Such a vertex shader is shown in Listing 12.9.

```
#version 420 core

uniform mat4 mv_matrix;
uniform mat4 proj_matrix;

layout (location = 0) in vec4 position;
layout (location = 1) in vec3 normal;

out VS_OUT
{
    vec3 normal;
```

1. The images shown in Figure 12.10 were produced by simply ray tracing a sphere using the popular POVRay ray tracer using different materials and lighting conditions.

```
    vec3 view;
} vs_out;

void main(void)
{
    vec4 pos_vs = mv_matrix * position;

    vs_out.normal = mat3(mv_matrix) * normal;
    vs_out.view = pos_vs.xyz;

    gl_Position = proj_matrix * pos_vs;
}
```

Listing 12.9: Spherical environment mapping vertex shader

Now, given the per-fragment normal and view direction, we can calculate
the texture coordinates to look up into our environment map. First, we
reflect the incoming view direction about the plane defined by the
incoming normal. Then, by simply scaling and biasing the x and y
components of this reflected vector, we can use them to fetch from the
environment and shade our fragment. The corresponding fragment shader
is given in Listing 12.10.

```
#version 420 core

layout (binding = 0) uniform sampler2D tex_envmap;

in VS_OUT
{
    vec3 normal;
    vec3 view;
} fs_in;

out vec4 color;

void main(void)
{
    // u will be our normalized view vector
    vec3 u = normalize(fs_in.view);

    // Reflect u about the plane defined by the normal at the fragment
    vec3 r = reflect(u, normalize(fs_in.normal));

    // Compute scale factor
    r.z += 1.0;
    float m = 0.5 * inversesqrt(dot(r, r));

    // Sample from scaled and biased texture coordinate
    color = texture(tex_envmap, r.xy * m + vec2(0.5));
}
```

Listing 12.10: Spherical environment mapping fragment shader

The result of rendering a model with the shader given in Listing 12.10 is
shown in Figure 12.11. This image was produced by the envmapsphere

example program, using the environment map in the rightmost image of Figure 12.10.

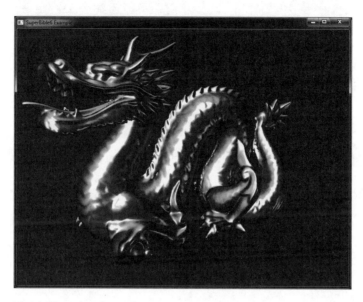

Figure 12.11: Result of rendering with spherical environment mapping

Equirectangular Environment Maps

The equirectangular environment map is similar to the spherical environment map except that it is less susceptible to the pinching effect sometimes seen when the poles of the sphere are sampled from. An example equirectangular environment texture is shown in Figure 12.12. Again, we use the view-space normal and view direction vectors, calculated in the vertex shader, interpolated and passed to the fragment shader, and again the fragment shader reflects the incoming view direction about the plane defined by the local normal. Now, instead of directly using the scaled and biased x and y components of this reflected vector, we extract the y component and then project the vector onto the xz plane by setting the y component to zero and normalizing it again. From this normalized vector, we extract the x component, producing our second texture coordinate. These extracted x and y components effectively form the altitude and azimuth angles for looking up into our equirectangular texture.

A fragment shader implementing equirectangular environment mapping is included in the equirectangular example application and is shown in

Figure 12.12: Example equirectangular environment map

Listing 12.11. The result of rendering an object with this shader is shown in Figure 12.13.

```
#version 420 core

layout (binding = 0) uniform sampler2D tex_envmap;

in VS_OUT
{
    vec3 normal;
    vec3 view;
} fs_in;

out vec4 color;

void main(void)
{
    // u will be our normalized view vector
    vec3 u = normalize(fs_in.view);

    // Reflect u about the plane defined by the normal at the fragment
    vec3 r = reflect(u, normalize(fs_in.normal));

    // Compute texture coordinate from reflection vector
    vec2 tc;

    tc.y = r.y; r.y = 0.0;
    tc.x = normalize(r).x * 0.5;

    // Scale and bias texture coordinate based on direction
    // of reflection vector
    float s = sign(r.z) * 0.5;

    tc.s = 0.75 - s * (0.5 - tc.s);
    tc.t = 0.5 + 0.5 * tc.t;

    // Sample from scaled and biased texture coordinate
    color = texture(tex_envmap, tc);
}
```

Listing 12.11: Equirectangular environment mapping fragment shader

Figure 12.13: Rendering result of equirectangular environment map

Cube Maps

A cube map is treated as a single texture object, but it is made up of six square (yes, they must be square!) 2D images that make up the six sides of a cube. Applications of cube maps range from 3D light maps to reflections and highly accurate environment maps. Figure 12.14 shows the layout of six square images composing a cube map that we use for the Cubemap sample program.[2] The images are arranged in a cross shape with their matching edges abutting. If you wanted to, you could cut and fold the image into a cube and the edges would align.

To load a cube map texture, we create a texture object by binding a new name to the GL_TEXTURE_CUBE_MAP target, call **glTexStorage2D()** to specify the storage dimensions of the texture, and then load the cube map data into the texture object by calling **glTexSubImage2D()** once for each face of the cube map. The faces of the cube map each have a special target named GL_TEXTURE_CUBE_MAP_POSITIVE_X, GL_TEXTURE_CUBE_MAP_NEGATIVE_X, GL_TEXTURE_CUBE_MAP_POSITIVE_Y, GL_TEXTURE_CUBE_MAP_NEGATIVE_Y, GL_TEXTURE_CUBE_MAP_POSITIVE_Z, and GL_TEXTURE_CUBE_MAP_NEGATIVE_Z. They are assigned numerical values in

---

2. The six images used for the Cubemap sample program were provided courtesy of The Game Creators, Ltd. (www.thegamecreators.com).

Figure 12.14: The layout of six cube faces in the Cubemap sample program

this order, and so we can simply create a loop and update each face in turn. Example code to do this is shown in Listing 12.12.

```
GLuint texture;

glGenTextures(1, &texture);
glBindTexture(GL_TEXTURE_CUBE_MAP, texture);

glTexStorage2D(GL_TEXTURE_CUBE_MAP,
               levels, internalFormat,
               width, height);
for (face = 0; face < 6; face++)
{
    glTexSubImage2D(GL_TEXURE_CUBE_MAP_POSITIVE_X + face,
                    0,
```

```
                    0, 0,
                    width, height,
                    format, type,
                    data + face * face_size_in_bytes);
    }
```

Listing 12.12: Loading a cube map texture

Cube maps also support mipmaps, and so if your cube map has mipmap data, the code in Listing 12.12 would need to be modified to load the additional mipmap levels. The Khronos Texture File format has native support for cube map textures, and so the book's .KTX file loader is able to do this for you.

Texture coordinates for cube maps have three dimensions, even though it they are collections of 2D images. This seem a little odd at first glance. Unlike a true 3D texture, the S, T, and R texture coordinates represent a signed vector from the center of the texture map pointing outwards. This vector will intersect one of the six sides of the cube map. The texels around this intersection point are then sampled to create the filtered color value from the texture.

A very common use of cube maps is to create an object that reflects its surroundings. The cube map is applied to a sphere, creating the appearance of a mirrored surface. The same cube map is also applied to the sky box, which creates the background being reflected.

A sky box is nothing more than a big box with a picture of the sky on it. Another way of looking at it is as a picture of the sky on a big box! Simple enough. An effective sky box contains six images that contain views from the center of your scene along the six directional axes. If this sounds just like a cube map, congratulations, you're paying attention!

To render a cube map, we could simply draw a large cube around the viewer and apply the cube map texture to it. However, there's an even easier way to do it! Any part of the virtual cube that is outside the viewport will be clipped away, but what we need is for the entire viewport to be covered. We can do this by rendering a full-screen quad. All we need to do then is to compute the texture coordinates at each of the four corners of the viewport, and we'll be able to use them to render our cube map.

Now, if the cube map texture were mapped directly to our virtual cube, the cube's vertex positions would be our texture coordinates. We would take the cube's vertex positions, multiply their x, y, and z components by the rotational part of our view matrix (which is the upper-left 3×3

submatrix) to orient them in the right direction, and render the cube in world space. In world space, the only face we'd see is the one we are looking directly at. Therefore, we can render a full-screen quad, and transform its corners by the view matrix in order to orient it correctly. All this occurs in the vertex shader, which is shown in Listing 12.13.

```glsl
#version 420 core

out VS_OUT
{
    vec3    tc;
} vs_out;

uniform mat4 view_matrix;

void main(void)
{
    vec3[4] vertices = vec3[4](vec3(-1.0, -1.0, 1.0),
                               vec3( 1.0, -1.0, 1.0),
                               vec3(-1.0,  1.0, 1.0),
                               vec3( 1.0,  1.0, 1.0));

    vs_out.tc = mat3(view_matrix) * vertices[gl_VertexID];

    gl_Position = vec4(vertices[gl_VertexID], 1.0);
}
```

Listing 12.13: Vertex shader for sky box rendering

Notice that because the vertex coordinates *and* the resulting texture coordinates are hard-coded into the vertex shader, we don't need any vertex attributes, and therefore don't need any buffers to store them. If we wished, we could scale the field of view by scaling the z component of the vertex data — the larger the z component becomes, the smaller the x and y become after normalization, and so the smaller the field of view. The fragment shader for rendering the cube map is also equally simple and is shown in its entirety in Listing 12.14.

```glsl
#version 420 core

layout (binding = 0) uniform samplerCube tex_cubemap;

in VS_OUT
{
    vec3    tc;
} fs_in;

layout (location = 0) out vec4 color;

void main(void)
{
    color = texture(tex_cubemap, fs_in.tc);
}
```

Listing 12.14: Fragment shader for sky box rendering

Once we've rendered our sky box, we need to render something into the scene that reflects the sky box. The texture coordinates used to fetch from a cube map texture are interpreted as a vector pointing from the origin outwards towards the cube. OpenGL will determine which face this vector eventually hits, and the coordinate within the face that it hits and then retrieve data from this location. What we need to do is for each fragment, calculate this vector. Again, we need the incoming view direction and the normal at each fragment.

These are produced in the vertex shader as before and passed to the fragment shader and normalized. Again, we reflect the incoming view direction about the plane defined by the surface normal at the fragment to compute an outgoing reflection vector. Under the assumption that the scenery shown in the sky box is sufficiently far away, this reflection vector can be considered to emanate from the origin and so can be used as the texture coordinate for our sky box. The vertex and fragment shaders are shown in Listings 12.15 and 12.16.

```
#version 420 core

uniform mat4 mv_matrix;
uniform mat4 proj_matrix;

layout (location = 0) in vec4 position;
layout (location = 1) in vec3 normal;

out VS_OUT
{
    vec3 normal;
    vec3 view;
} vs_out;

void main(void)
{
    vec4 pos_vs = mv_matrix * position;

    vs_out.normal = mat3(mv_matrix) * normal;
    vs_out.view = pos_vs.xyz;

    gl_Position = proj_matrix * pos_vs;
}
```

Listing 12.15: Vertex shader for cube map environment rendering

```
#version 420 core

layout (binding = 0) uniform samplerCube tex_cubemap;

in VS_OUT
{
    vec3 normal;
    vec3 view;
} fs_in;
```

```
out vec4 color;

void main(void)
{
    // Reflect view vector about the plane defined by the normal
    // at the fragment
    vec3 r = reflect(fs_in.view, normalize(fs_in.normal));

    // Sample from scaled using reflection vector
    color = texture(tex_cubemap, r);
}
```

Listing 12.16: Fragment shader for cube map environment rendering

The result of rendering an object surrounded by a sky box using the shaders shown in Listings 12.13 through 12.16 is shown in Figure 12.15. This image was produced by the cubemapenv example program.

Figure 12.15: Cube map environment rendering with a sky box

Of course, there is no reason that the final color of the fragment must be taken directly from the environment map. For example, you could multiply it by the base color of the object you're rendering to tint the environment it reflects. Color Plate 10 shows a golden version the dragon being rendered.

Material Properties

In the examples presented so far in this chapter, we have used a single material for the entire model. This means that our dragons are uniformly shiny, and our ladybug looks somewhat plastic. However, there is no reason that every part of our models must be made from the same material. In fact, we can assign material properties per surface, per triangle, or even per pixel by storing information about the surface in a texture. For example, the specular exponent can be stored in a texture and applied to a model when rendering. This allows some parts of the model to be more reflective than others.

Another technique that allows a sense of roughness to be applied to a model is to pre-blur an environment map and then use a gloss factor (also stored in a texture) to gradually fade between a sharp and blurred version of the map. In this example, we will again use a simple spherical environment map. Figure 12.16 shows two environment maps and a shininess map used to blend between them. The left image shows a fully sharp environment map, whereas the image in the center contains a pre-blurred version of the same environment. The rightmost image is our gloss map and will be used to filter between the sharp and blurry versions of the environment map. Where the gloss map is brightest, the sharper environment map will be used. Where it is darkest, we will use the blurrier environment map.

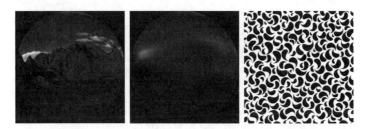

Figure 12.16: Pre-filtered environment maps and gloss map

We can combine the two environment textures together into a single, 3D texture that is only two texels deep. Then, we can sample from our gloss texture and use the fetched texel value as the third component of the texture coordinate used to fetch from the environment map (with the first two being calculated as normal). With the sharp image as the first layer of the 3D environment texture and the blurry image as the second layer of the 3D environment, OpenGL will smoothly interpolate between the sharp and the blurry environment maps for you.

Listing 12.17 shows the fragment shader that reads the material property texture to determine per-pixel gloss and then reads the environment map texture using the result.

```
#version 420 core

layout (binding = 0) uniform sampler3D tex_envmap;
layout (binding = 1) uniform sampler2D tex_glossmap;

in VS_OUT
{
    vec3 normal;
    vec3 view;
    vec2 tc;
} fs_in;

out vec4 color;

void main(void)
{
    // u will be our normalized view vector
    vec3 u = normalize(fs_in.view);

    // Reflect u about the plane defined by the normal at the fragment
    vec3 r = reflect(u, normalize(fs_in.normal));

    // Compute scale factor
    r.z += 1.0;
    float m = 0.5 * inversesqrt(dot(r, r));

    // Sample gloss factor from glossmap texture
    float gloss = texture(tex_glossmap, fs_in.tc * vec2(3.0, 1.0) * 2.0).r;

    // Sample from scaled and biased texture coordinate
    vec3 env_coord = vec3(r.xy * m + vec2(0.5), gloss);

    // Sample from two-level environment map
    color = texture(tex_envmap, env_coord);
}
```

Listing 12.17: Fragment shader for per-fragment shininess

Figure 12.17 was produced by the perpixelgloss example and shows the result of rendering a torus with the map applied.

Casting Shadows

The shading algorithms presented so far have all assumed that each light will contribute to the final color of each fragment. However, in a complex scene with lots of objects, this is not the case. Objects will cast shadows on each other and upon themselves. If these shadows are omitted from the rendered scene, a great deal of realism can be lost. This section outlines some techniques for simulating the effects of shadowing on objects.

Shadow Mapping

The most basic operation of any shadow calculation must be to determine whether the point being considered has any light hitting it. In effect, we

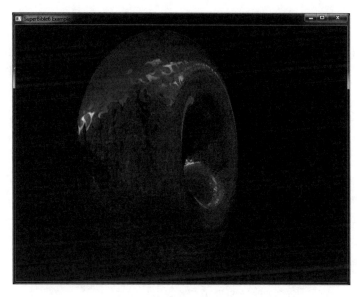

Figure 12.17: Result of per-pixel gloss example

must determine whether there is line of sight from the point being shaded to a light and, therefore, from the light to the point being shaded. This turns out to be a visibility calculation, and as luck might have it, we have extremely fast hardware to determine whether a piece of geometry is visible from a given vantage point — the depth buffer.

Shadow mapping is a technique that produces visibility information for a scene by rendering it from the point of view of a light source. Only the depth information is needed, and so to do this, we can use a framebuffer object with only a depth attachment. After rendering the scene into a depth buffer from the light's perspective, we will be left with a per-pixel distance of the nearest point to the light in the scene. When we render our geometry in a forward pass, we can calculate, for each point, what the distance to the light is and compare that to the distance stored in the depth buffer. To do this, we project our point from view space (where it is being rendered) into the coordinate system of the light.

Once we have this coordinate, we simply read from the depth texture we rendered earlier, compare our calculated depth value against the one stored in the texture, and if we are not the closest point to the light for that particular texture, we know we are in shadow. In fact, this is such a common operation in graphics that OpenGL even has a special sampler type that does the comparison for us, the *shadow sampler*. In GLSL, this is declared as a variable with a `sampler2DShadow` type for 2D textures, which we'll be using in this example. You can also create show samplers for 1D textures (`sampler1DShadow`), cube maps (`samplerCubeShadow`), and rectangle textures (`samplerRectShadow`), and for arrays of these types (except, of course, rectangle textures).

Listing 12.18 shows how to set up a framebuffer object with only a depth attachment ready for rendering the shadow map into.

```
GLuint shadow_buffer; GLuint shadow_tex;

glGenFramebuffers(1, &shadow_buffer);
glBindFramebuffer(GL_FRAMEBUFFER, shadow_buffer);

glGenTextures(1, &shadow_tex);
glBindTexture(GL_TEXTURE_2D, shadow_tex);
glTexStorage2D(GL_TEXTURE_2D, 1, GL_DEPTH_COMPONENT32,
               DEPTH_TEX_WIDTH, DEPTH_TEX_HEIGHT);
glTexParameteri(GL_TEXTURE_2D, GL_TEXTURE_MIN_FILTER, GL_LINEAR);
glTexParameteri(GL_TEXTURE_2D, GL_TEXTURE_MAG_FILTER, GL_LINEAR);
glTexParameteri(GL_TEXTURE_2D, GL_TEXTURE_COMPARE_MODE,
                GL_COMPARE_REF_TO_TEXTURE);
glTexParameteri(GL_TEXTURE_2D, GL_TEXTURE_COMPARE_FUNC, GL_LEQUAL);

glFramebufferTexture(GL_FRAMEBUFFER, GL_DEPTH_ATTACHMENT,
                     shadow_tex, 0);

glBindFramebuffer(GL_FRAMEBUFFER, 0);
```

Listing 12.18: Getting ready for shadow mapping

You will notice in Listing 12.18 two calls to **glTexParameteri()** with the parameters GL_TEXTURE_COMPARE_MODE and GL_TEXTURE_COMPARE_FUNC. The first of these turns on texture comparison, and the second sets the function that should be used. Once we have created our FBO for rendering depth, we can render the scene from the point of view of the light. Given a light position, `light_pos`, which is pointing at the origin, we can construct a matrix that represents the model-view-projection matrix for the light. This is shown in Listing 12.19.

```
vmath::mat4 model_matrix = vmath::rotate(currentTime, 0.0f, 1.0f, 0.0f);
vmath::mat4 light_view_matrix =
    vmath::lookat(light_pos,
                  vmath::vec3(0.0f),
                  vmath::vec3(0.0f, 1.0f, 0.0f));
vmath::mat4 light_proj_matrix =
    vmath::frustum(-1.0f, 1.0f, -1.0f, 1.0f,
                   1.0f, 1000.0f);
vmath::mat4 light_mvp_matrix = light_projection_matrix *
                               light_view_matrix *
                               model_matrix;
```

Listing 12.19: Setting up matrices for shadow mapping

Rendering the scene from the light's position results in a depth buffer that contains the distance from the light to each pixel in the framebuffer. This can be visualized as a grayscale image with black being the closest possible depth value (zero) and white being the furthest possible depth value (white). Figure 12.18 shows the depth buffer of a simple scene rendered with the above shader.

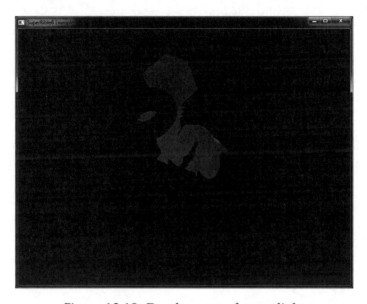

Figure 12.18: Depth as seen from a light

To make use of this stored depth information to generate shadows, we need to make a few modifications to our rendering shader. First, of course, we need to declare our shadow sampler and read from it. The interesting part is how we determine the coordinates at which to read from the depth texture. In fact, it turns out to be pretty simple. In our vertex shader, we normally calculate the output position in clip coordinates, which is a projection of the vertex's world-space coordinate into the view space of our virtual camera and then into the camera's frustum. At the same time, we need to perform the same operations using the light's view and frustum matrices. As the resulting coordinate is interpolated and passed to the fragment shader, that shader then has the coordinate of each fragment in the light's clip space.

In addition to the coordinate space transforms, we must scale and bias the resulting clip coordinates. Remember, OpenGL's normal clip coordinate frame ranges from -1.0 to 1.0 in the x and y axis and 0.0 to 1.0 in the z

axis. The matrix that transforms vertices from object space into the light's clip space is known as the *shadow matrix,* and the code to calculate it is shown in Listing 12.20.

```
const vmath::mat4 scale_bias_matrix =
    vmath::mat4(vmath::vec4(0.5f, 0.0f, 0.0f, 0.0f),
                vmath::vec4(0.0f, 0.5f, 0.0f, 0.0f),
                vmath::vec4(0.0f, 0.0f, 0.5f, 0.0f),
                vmath::vec4(0.5f, 0.5f, 0.5f, 1.0f));

vmath::mat4 shadow_matrix = scale_bias_matrix *
                           light_proj_matrix *
                           light_view_matrix *
                           model_matrix;
```

Listing 12.20: Setting up a shadow matrix

The shadow matrix can be passed as a single uniform to the original vertex shader. A simplified version of the shader is shown in Listing 12.21.

```
#version 420 core

uniform mat4 mv_matrix;
uniform mat4 proj_matrix;
uniform mat4 shadow_matrix;

layout (location = 0) in vec4 position;

out VS_OUT
{
    vec4 shadow_coord;
} vs_out;

void main(void)
{
    gl_Position = proj_matrix * mv_matrix * position;
    vs_out.shadow_coord = shadow_matrix * position;
}
```

Listing 12.21: Simplified vertex shader for shadow mapping

The shadow_coord output is sent from the vertex shader, interpolated, and passed into the fragment shader. This coordinate must be *projected* into normalized device coordinates in order to use them to look up into the shadow map we made earlier. This would normally mean dividing the whole vector through by its own w component. However, as projecting a coordinate in this way is such a common operation, there is a version of the overloaded texture function that will do this for us called textureProj. When we use textureProj with a shadow sampler, it first divides the x, y, and z components of the texture coordinate by its own w

component and then uses the resulting x and y components to fetch a value from the texture. It then compares the returned value against the computed z component using the chosen comparison function, producing a value 1.0 or 0.0 depending on whether the test passed or failed, respectively.

If the selected texture filtering mode for the texture is GL_LINEAR or would otherwise require multiple samples, then OpenGL applies the test to each of the samples individually before averaging them together. The result of the textureProj function is therefore a value between 0.0 and 1.0 based on which and how many of the samples passed the comparison. All we need to do, then, is to call textureProj with our shadow sampler containing our depth buffer using the interpolated shadow texture coordinate, and the result will be a value that we can use to determine whether the point is in shadow or not. A highly simplified shadow mapping fragment shader is shown in Listing 12.22.

```
#version 420 core

layout (location = 0) out vec4 color;

layout (binding = 0) uniform sampler2DShadow shadow_tex;

in VS_OUT
{
    vec4 shadow_coord;
} fs_in;

void main(void)
{
    color = textureProj(shadow_tex, fs_in.shadow_coord) * vec4(1.0);
}
```

Listing 12.22: Simplified fragment shader for shadow mapping

Of course, the result of rendering a scene with the shader shown in Listing 12.22 is that no real lighting is applied and everything is drawn in black and white. However, as you can see in the shader code, we have simply multiplied the value vec4(1.0) by the result of the shadow map sample. In a more complex shader, we would apply our normal shading and texturing and multiply the result of *those* calculations by the result of the shadow map sample. Figure 12.19 shows a simple scene rendered as just shadow information on the left and with full lighting calculations on the right. This image was produced by the shadowmapping example.

Shadow maps have their advantages and disadvantages. They can be very memory intensive as each light requires its own shadow map. Each light

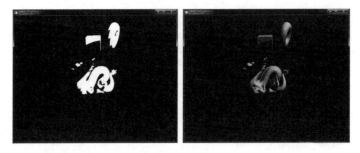

Figure 12.19: Results of rendering with shadow maps

also requires a pass over the scene, which costs performance. This can quickly add up and slow your application down. The shadow maps must be of a very high resolution as what might have mapped to a single texel in the shadow map may cover several pixels in screen space, which is effectively where the lighting calculations are performed. Finally, effects of self-occlusion may be visible in the output as stripes or a "sparkling" image in shadowed regions. It is possible to mitigate this to some degree using *polygon offset*. This is a small offset that can be applied automatically by OpenGL to all polygons (triangles) in order to push them towards or away from the viewer. To set the polygon offset, call

```
void glPolygonOffset(GLfloat factor,
                     GLfloat units);
```

The first parameter, `factor`, is a scale factor that is multiplied by the change in depth of the polygon relative to its screen area, and the second parameter, `units`, is an implementation-defined scaling value that is internally multiplied by the smallest change guaranteed to produce a different value in the depth buffer. If this sounds a bit handwavy — it can be. You need to play with these two values until the depth fighting effects go away. Once you've set up your polygon offset scaling factors, you can enable the effect by calling **glEnable()** with the GL_POLYGON_OFFSET_FILL parameter, and disable it again by passing the same parameter to **glDisable()**.

Atmospheric Effects

In general, rendering in computer graphics is the modeling of light as it interacts with the world around us. Most of the rendering we've done so far has not taken into consideration the medium in which the light travels. Usually, this is air. The air around us isn't perfectly transparent, and it contains particles, vapor, and gases that absorb and scatter light as it travels. We use this scattering and absorption to gauge depth and infer distance as we look out into the world. Modeling it, even approximately, can add quite a bit of realism to our scenes.

Fog

We are all familiar with fog. On a foggy day, it might be impossible to see more than a few feet in front of us, and dense fog can present danger. However, even when fog is not heavy, it's still there — you may just need to look further to see it. Fog is caused by water vapor hanging in the air or by other gases or particles such as smoke or pollution. As light travels through the air, two things happen — some of the light is absorbed by the particles, and some bounces off the particles (or is possibly re-emitted by those particles). As light is absorbed by fog, this is known as *extinction* as eventually all of the light will have been absorbed and none will be left. However, light will generally find a way to get out of the fog as it will bounce around and be absorbed and re-emitted by the fog particles. We call this *inscattering*. We can build a simple model of both extinction and inscattering to produce a simple yet effective simulation of fog.

For this example, we will return to the tessellated landscape example of Chapter 8, "Primitive Processing." If you refer back to Figure 8.12, you will notice that we left the sky black and used only a simple texture with shading information baked into it to render the landscape. It is quite difficult to infer depth from the rendered result, and so we will adapt the sample to apply fog.

To add fog effects to the sample, we modify our tessellation evaluation shader to send both the world- and eye-space coordinates of each point to the fragment shader. The modified tessellation evaluation shader is shown in Listing 12.23.

```
#version 420 core

layout (quads, fractional_odd_spacing) in;

uniform sampler2D tex_displacement;

uniform mat4 mv_matrix;
uniform mat4 proj_matrix;
uniform float dmap_depth;

out vec2 tc;

in TCS_OUT
{
    vec2 tc;
```

```
    } tes_in[];

out TES_OUT
{
    vec2 tc;
    vec3 world_coord;
    vec3 eye_coord;
} tes_out;

void main(void)
{
    vec2 tc1 = mix(tes_in[0].tc, tes_in[1].tc, gl_TessCoord.x);
    vec2 tc2 = mix(tes_in[2].tc, tes_in[3].tc, gl_TessCoord.x);
    vec2 tc = mix(tc2, tc1, gl_TessCoord.y);

    vec4 p1 = mix(gl_in[0].gl_Position,
                  gl_in[1].gl_Position, gl_TessCoord.x);
    vec4 p2 = mix(gl_in[2].gl_Position,
                  gl_in[3].gl_Position, gl_TessCoord.x);
    vec4 p = mix(p2, p1, gl_TessCoord.y);
    p.y += texture(tex_displacement, tc).r * dmap_depth;

    vec4 P_eye = mv_matrix * p;

    tes_out.tc = tc;
    tes_out.world_coord = p.xyz;
    tes_out.eye_coord = P_eye.xyz;

    gl_Position = proj_matrix * P_eye;
}
```

Listing 12.23: Displacement map tessellation evaluation shader

In the fragment shader, we fetch from our landscape texture as normal,
but then we apply our simple fog model to the resulting color. We use the
length of the eye-space coordinate to determine the distance from the
viewer to the point being rendered. This tells us how far through the
atmosphere light from the point of interest must travel to reach our eyes,
which is the input term to the fog equations. We will apply exponential
fog to our scene. The extinction and inscattering terms will be

$$f_e = e^{-zd_e}$$

$$f_i = e^{-zd_i}$$

Here, f_e is the extinction factor, and f_i is the inscattering factor. Likewise,
d_e and d_i are the extinction and inscattering coefficients, which we can
use to control our fog effect. z is the distance from the eye to the point
being shaded. As z approaches zero, the exponential term then tends
towards one. As z increases (i.e., the point being shaded gets further
from the viewer), the exponential term gets smaller and smaller,
tending towards zero. These curves are illustrated by the graph in
Figure 12.20.

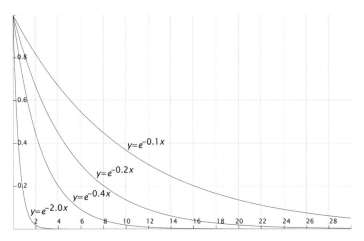

$y=e^{-0.1x}$

$y=e^{-0.2x}$

$y=e^{-0.4x}$

$y=e^{-2.0x}$

Figure 12.20: Graphs of exponential decay

The modified fragment shader that applies fog is shown in Listing 12.24.

```
#version 420 core

out vec4 color;

layout (binding = 1) uniform sampler2D tex_color;

uniform bool enable_fog = true;
uniform vec4 fog_color = vec4(0.7, 0.8, 0.9, 0.0);

in TES_OUT
{
    vec2 tc;
    vec3 world_coord;
    vec3 eye_coord;
} fs_in;

vec4 fog(vec4 c)
{
    float z = length(fs_in.eye_coord);

    float de = 0.025 * smoothstep(0.0, 6.0,
                                  10.0 - fs_in.world_coord.y);
    float di = 0.045 * smoothstep(0.0, 40.0,
                                  20.0 - fs_in.world_coord.y);

    float extinction   = exp(-z * de);
    float inscattering = exp(-z * di);

    return c * extinction + fog_color * (1.0 - inscattering);
}

void main(void)
{
    vec4 landscape = texture(tex_color, fs_in.tc);

    if (enable_fog)
    {
```

```
        color = fog(landscape);
    }
    else
    {
        color = landscape;
    }
}
```

Listing 12.24: Application of fog in a fragment shader

In our fragment shader, the `fog` function applies fog to the incoming
fragment color. It first calculates the fog factor for the extinction and
inscattering components of the fog. It then multiplies the original
fragment color by the extinction term. As the extinction term approaches
zero, so this term approaches black. It then multiplies the fog color by one
minus the inscattering term. As the distance from the viewer increases, so
the inscattering term approaches zero (just like the extinction term).
Taking one minus this causes it to approach one as the distance to the
viewer increases, meaning that as the scene gets further from the viewer,
its color approaches the color of the fog. The results of rendering the
tessellated landscape scene with this shader is shown in Figure 12.21. The
left image shows the original scene without fog, and the right image
shows the scene with fog applied. You should be able to see that the sense
of depth is greatly improved in the image on the right.

Figure 12.21: Applying fog to tessellated landscape

Non-Photo-Realistic Rendering

Normally, the goal of rendering and computer graphics is to produce an
image that appears as realistic as possible. However, for some applications
or artistic reasons, it may be desirable to render an image that isn't realistic
at all. For example, perhaps we want to render using a pencil-sketch effect
or in a completely abstract manner. This is known as non-photo-realistic
rendering, or NPR.

Cell Shading — Texels as Light

Many of our examples of texture mapping in the last few chapters have used 2D textures. Two-dimensional textures are typically the simplest and easiest to understand. Most people can quickly get the intuitive feel for putting a 2D picture on the side of a piece of 2D or 3D geometry. Let's take a look now at a one-dimensional texture mapping example that is commonly used in computer games to render geometry that appears on-screen like a cartoon. Toon shading, which is often referred to as cell shading, uses a one-dimensional texture map as a lookup table to fill geometry with a solid color (using GL_NEAREST) from the texture map.

The basic idea is to use the diffuse lighting intensity (the dot product between the eye space surface normal and light directional vector) as the texture coordinate into a one-dimensional texture that contains a gradually brightening color table. Figure 12.22 shows one such texture, with four increasingly bright red texels (defined as RGB unsigned byte color components).

Figure 12.22: A one-dimensional color lookup table

Recall that the diffuse lighting dot product varies from 0.0 at no intensity to 1.0 at full intensity. Conveniently, this maps nicely to a one-dimensional texture coordinate range. Loading this one-dimensional texture is pretty straightforward as shown here:

```
static const GLubyte toon_tex_data[] =
{
    0x44, 0x00, 0x00, 0x00,
    0x88, 0x00, 0x00, 0x00,
    0xCC, 0x00, 0x00, 0x00,
    0xFF, 0x00, 0x00, 0x00
};

glGenTextures(1, &tex_toon);
glBindTexture(GL_TEXTURE_1D, tex_toon);
glTexStorage1D(GL_TEXTURE_1D, 1, GL_RGB8, sizeof(toon_tex_data) / 4);
glTexSubImage1D(GL_TEXTURE_1D, 0,
                0, sizeof(toon_tex_data) / 4,
                GL_RGBA, GL_UNSIGNED_BYTE,
                toon_tex_data);
glTexParameteri(GL_TEXTURE_1D, GL_TEXTURE_MAG_FILTER, GL_NEAREST);
glTexParameteri(GL_TEXTURE_1D, GL_TEXTURE_MIN_FILTER, GL_NEAREST);
glTexParameteri(GL_TEXTURE_1D, GL_TEXTURE_WRAP_S, GL_CLAMP_TO_EDGE);
```

This code is from the example program toonshading, which renders a spinning torus with the toon shading effect applied. Although the torus model file, which we use to create the torus, supplies a set of two-dimensional texture coordinates, we ignore them in our vertex shader, which is shown in Listing 12.25, and only use the incoming position and normal.

```
#version 420 core

uniform mat4 mv_matrix;
uniform mat4 proj_matrix;

layout (location = 0) in vec4 position;
layout (location = 1) in vec3 normal;

out VS_OUT
{
    vec3 normal;
    vec3 view;
} vs_out;

void main(void)
{
    vec4 pos_vs = mv_matrix * position;

    // Calculate eye-space normal and position
    vs_out.normal = mat3(mv_matrix) * normal;
    vs_out.view = pos_vs.xyz;

    // Send clip-space position to primitive assembly
    gl_Position = proj_matrix * pos_vs;
}
```

Listing 12.25: The toon vertex shader

Other than the transformed geometry position, the outputs of this shader are an interpolated eye-space normal and position that are passed to the fragment shader, which is shown in Listing 12.26. The computation of the diffuse lighting component is virtually identical to the earlier diffuse lighting examples.

```
#version 420 core

layout (binding = 0) uniform sampler1D tex_toon;

uniform vec3 light_pos = vec3(30.0, 30.0, 100.0);

in VS_OUT
{
    vec3 normal;
    vec3 view;
} fs_in;

out vec4 color;

void main(void)
{
    // Calculate per-pixel normal and light vector
    vec3 N = normalize(fs_in.normal);
    vec3 L = normalize(light_pos - fs_in.view);
```

```
// Simple N dot L diffuse lighting
float tc = pow(max(0.0, dot(N, L)), 5.0);

// Sample from cell shading texture
color = texture(tex_toon, tc) * (tc * 0.8 + 0.2);
}
```

Listing 12.26: The toon fragment shader

The fragment shader for our toon shader calculates the diffuse lighting coefficient as normal, but rather than using it directly, it uses it to look up into a texture containing our four cell colors. In a traditional toon shader, the diffuse coefficient would be used unmodified as a texture coordinate, and the resulting color would be sent directly to the output of the fragment shader. However, here we raise the diffuse coefficient to a small power and then scale that color returned from the ramp texture by the diffuse lighting coefficient before outputting the result. This makes the toon highlights slightly sharper and also leaves the image with some depth rather than the plain flat shading that would be achieved with the content of the toon ramp texture only.

The resulting output is shown in Figure 12.23, where the banding and highlighting due to the toon shader are clearly visible. Both the red color ramp texture and the toon-shaded torus are also shown together in Color Plate 12.

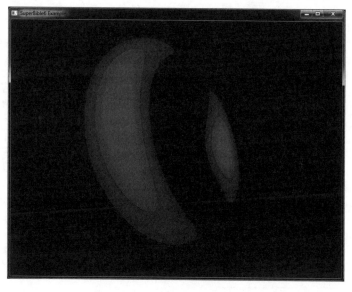

Figure 12.23: A toon-shaded torus

Alternative Rendering Methods

Traditional forward rendering executes the complete graphics pipeline, starting with a vertex shader and following through with any number of subsequent stages, most likely terminating with a fragment shader. That fragment shader is responsible for calculating the final color of the fragment[3] and after each drawing command, the content of the framebuffer becomes more and more complete. However, it doesn't have to be this way. As you will see in this section, it's quite possible to partially calculate some of the shading information and finish the scene after all of the objects have been rendered, or even to forego traditional vertex-based geometry representations and do all of your geometry processing in the *fragment shader*.

Deferred Shading

In almost all of the examples you've seen so far, the fragment shader is used to calculate the final color of the fragment that it's rendering. Now, consider what happens when you render an object that ends up covering something that's already been drawn to the screen. This is known as *overdraw*. In this case, the result of the previous calculation is replaced with the new rendering, essentially throwing away all of the work that the first fragment shader did. If the fragment shader is expensive, or if there is a lot of overdraw, this can add up to a large drain on performance. To get around this, we can use a technique called *deferred shading*, which is a method to delay the heavy processing that might be performed by a fragment shader until the last moment.

To do this, we first render the scene using a very simple fragment shader that outputs into the framebuffer any parameters of each fragment that we might need for shading it later. In most cases, multiple framebuffer attachments will be required. If you refer to the earlier sections on lighting, you will see that the types of information you might need for lighting the scene would be the diffuse color of the fragment, its surface normal, and its position in world space. The latter can usually be reconstructed from screen space and the depth buffer, but it can be convenient to simply store the world-space coordinate of each fragment in a framebuffer attachment. The framebuffer used for storing this intermediate information is often referred to as a *G-buffer*. Here, G stands

---

3. Post processing notwithstanding.

for geometry as it stores information about the geometry at that point rather than image properties.

Once the G-buffer has been generated, it is possible to shade each and every point on the screen using a single full-screen quad. This final pass will use the full complexity of the final lighting algorithms, but rather than being applied to each pixel of each triangle, it is applied to each pixel in the framebuffer exactly once. This can substantially reduce the cost of shading fragments, especially if many lights or a complex shading algorithm are in use.

Generating the G-Buffer

The first stage of a deferred renderer is to create the G-buffer, which is implemented using a framebuffer object with several attachments. OpenGL can support framebuffers with up to eight attachments, and each attachment can have up to four 32-bit channels (using the GL_RGBA32F internal format, for example). However, each channel of each attachment consumes some *memory bandwidth*, and if we don't pay attention to the amount of data we write to the framebuffer, we can start to outweigh the savings of deferring shading with the added cost of the memory bandwidth required to save all of this information.

In general, 16-bit floating-point values are more than enough to store colors[4] and normals. 32-bit floating-point values are normally preferred to store the world-space coordinates in order to preserve accuracy. Additional components that might be stored for the purposes of shading might be derived from the material. For example, we may store the specular exponent (or shininess factor) at each pixel. Given all of the data, the varying precision requirements, and the consideration of efficiency of memory bandwidth, it's a good idea to attempt to pack the data together into otherwise unrelated components of wider framebuffer formats.

In our example, we'll use three 16-bit components to store the normal at each fragment, three 16-bit components to store the fragment's albedo (flat color), three 32-bit floating-point components to store[5] the

---

4. Even when rendering in HDR, the color content of a G-buffer can be stored as 8-bit values so long as the final passes operate at higher precision.

5. Several methods exist to reconstruct the world-space coordinates of a fragment from its screen-space coordinates, but for this example, we'll store them directly in the framebuffer.

world-space coordinate of the fragment, and a 32-bit integer component to store a per-pixel object or material index, and a 32-bit component to store the per-pixel specular power factor.

The sum total of these bits is six 16-bit components and five 32-bit components. How on earth will we represent this with a single framebuffer? Actually, it's fairly simple. For the six 16-bit components, we can pack them into the first three 32-bit components of a GL_RGBA32UI format framebuffer. This leaves a fourth component that we can use to store our 32-bit object identifier. Now, we have four more 32-bit components to store — the three components of our world-space coordinate and the specular power. These can simply be packed into a GL_RGBA32F format framebuffer attachment. The code to create our G-buffer framebuffer is shown in Listing 12.27.

```
GLuint gbuffer;
GLuint gbuffer_tex[3];

glGenFramebuffers(1, &gbuffer);
glBindFramebuffer(GL_FRAMEBUFFER, gbuffer);

glGenTextures(3, gbuffer_tex);
glBindTexture(GL_TEXTURE_2D, gbuffer_tex[0]);
glTexStorage2D(GL_TEXTURE_2D, 1, GL_RGBA32UI,
               MAX_DISPLAY_WIDTH, MAX_DISPLAY_HEIGHT);
glTexParameteri(GL_TEXTURE_2D, GL_TEXTURE_MIN_FILTER, GL_NEAREST);
glTexParameteri(GL_TEXTURE_2D, GL_TEXTURE_MAG_FILTER, GL_NEAREST);

glBindTexture(GL_TEXTURE_2D, gbuffer_tex[1]);
glTexStorage2D(GL_TEXTURE_2D, 1, GL_RGBA32F,
               MAX_DISPLAY_WIDTH, MAX_DISPLAY_HEIGHT);
glTexParameteri(GL_TEXTURE_2D, GL_TEXTURE_MIN_FILTER, GL_NEAREST);
glTexParameteri(GL_TEXTURE_2D, GL_TEXTURE_MAG_FILTER, GL_NEAREST);

glBindTexture(GL_TEXTURE_2D, gbuffer_tex[2]);
glTexStorage2D(GL_TEXTURE_2D, 1, GL_DEPTH_COMPONENT32F,
               MAX_DISPLAY_WIDTH, MAX_DISPLAY_HEIGHT);

glFramebufferTexture(GL_FRAMEBUFFER, GL_COLOR_ATTACHMENT0,
                     gbuffer_tex[0], 0);
glFramebufferTexture(GL_FRAMEBUFFER, GL_COLOR_ATTACHMENT1,
                     gbuffer_tex[1], 0);
glFramebufferTexture(GL_FRAMEBUFFER, GL_DEPTH_ATTACHMENT,
                     gbuffer_tex[2], 0);

glBindFramebuffer(GL_FRAMEBUFFER, 0);
```

Listing 12.27: Initializing a G-buffer

Now that we have a framebuffer to represent our G-buffer, it's time to start rendering into it. We mentioned packing multiple 16-bit components into half as many 32-bit components. This can be achieved using the GLSL function packHalf2x16. Assuming our fragment shader has all of the necessary input information, it can export all of the data it needs into two color outputs as seen in Listing 12.28.

```glsl
#version 420 core

layout (location = 0) out uvec4 color0;
layout (location = 1) out vec4 color1;

in VS_OUT
{
    vec3    ws_coords;
    vec3    normal;
    vec3    tangent;
    vec2    texcoord0;
    flat uint    material_id;
} fs_in;

layout (binding = 0) uniform sampler2D tex_diffuse;

void main(void)
{
    uvec4 outvec0 = uvec4(0);
    vec4 outvec1 = vec4(0);

    vec3 color = texture(tex_diffuse, fs_in.texcoord0).rgb;

    outvec0.x = packHalf2x16(color.xy);
    outvec0.y = packHalf2x16(vec2(color.z, fs_in.normal.x));
    outvec0.z = packHalf2x16(fs_in.normal.yz);
    outvec0.w = fs_in.material_id;

    outvec1.xyz = fs_in.ws_coords;
    outvec1.w = 60.0;

    color0 = outvec0;
    color1 = outvec1;
}
```

Listing 12.28: Writing to a G-buffer

As you can see from Listing 12.28, we have made extensive use of the packHalf2x16 function. Although this seems like quite a bit of code, it is generally "free" relative to the memory bandwidth cost of storing all of this data. Once you have rendered your scene to the G-buffer, it's time to calculate the final color of all of the pixels in the framebuffer.

Consuming the G-Buffer

Given a G-buffer with diffuse colors, normals, specular powers, world-space coordinates, and other information, we need to read from it and reconstruct the original data that we packed in Listing 12.28. Essentially, we employ the inverse operations to our packing code and make use of the unpackHalf2x16 and uintBitsToFloat functions to

convert the integer data stored in our textures into the floating-point data
we need. The unpacking code is shown in Listing 12.29.

```
layout (binding = 0) uniform usampler2D gbuf0;
Layout (binding = 1) uniform sampler2D gbuf1;

struct fragment_info_t
{
    vec3 color;
    vec3 normal;
    float specular_power;
    vec3 ws_coord;
    uint material_id;
};

void unpackGBuffer(ivec2 coord,
                   out fragment_info_t fragment)
{
    uvec4 data0 = texelFetch(gbuf_tex0, ivec2(coord), 0);
    vec4 data1 = texelFetch(gbuf_tex1, ivec2(coord), 0);
    vec2 temp;

    temp = unpackHalf2x16(data0.y);
    fragment.color = vec3(unpackHalf2x16(data0.x), temp.x);
    fragment.normal = normalize(vec3(temp.y, unpackHalf2x16(data0.z)));
    fragment.material_id = data0.w;

    fragment.ws_coord = data1.xyz;
    fragment.specular_power = data1.w;
}
```

Listing 12.29: Unpacking data from a G-buffer

We can visualize the contents of our G-buffer using a simple fragment
shader that reads from the resulting textures that are attached to it,
unpacks the data into its original form, and then outputs the desired
parts to the normal color framebuffer. Rendering a simple scene into
the G-buffer and visualizing it gives the result shown in Figure 12.24.

The upper-left quadrant of Figure 12.24 shows the diffuse albedo, the
upper right shows the surface normals, the lower left shows the
world-space coordinates, and the lower right of Figure 12.24 shows the
material ID at each pixel, represented as different levels of gray.

Once we have unpacked the content of the G-buffer into our shader, we
have everything we need to calculate the final color of the fragment. We
can use any of the techniques covered in the earlier part of this chapter. In
this example, we use standard Phong shading. Taking the fragment_info_t
structure unpacked in Listing 12.29, we can pass this directly to a lighting
function that will calculate the final color of the fragment from the lighting
information. Such a function is shown in Listing 12.30.

Figure 12.24: Visualizing components of a G-buffer

```
vec4 light_fragment(fragment_info_t fragment)
{
    int i;
    vec4 result = vec4(0.0, 0.0, 0.0, 1.0);

    if (fragment.material_id != 0)
    {
        for (i = 0; i < num_lights; i++)
        {
            vec3 L = fragment.ws_coord - light[i].position;
            float dist = length(L);
            L = normalize(L);
            vec3 N = normalize(fragment.normal);
            vec3 R = reflect(-L, N);
            float NdotR = max(0.0, dot(N, R));
            float NdotL = max(0.0, dot(N, L));
            float attenuation = 50.0 / (pow(dist, 2.0) + 1.0);

            vec3 diffuse_color = light[i].color * fragment.color *
                             NdotL * attenuation;
            vec3 specular_color = light[i].color *
                              pow(NdotR, fragment.specular_power)
                              * attenuation;

            result += vec4(diffuse_color + specular_color, 0.0);
        }
    }

    return result;
}
```

Listing 12.30: Lighting a fragment using data from a G-buffer

The final result of lighting a scene using deferred shading is shown in Figure 12.25. In the scene, over 200 copies of an object are rendered using instancing. Each pixel in the frame has some overdraw. The final pass over the scene calculates the contribution of 64 lights. Increasing and decreasing the number of lights in the scene has little effect on performance. In fact, the most expensive part of rendering the scene is generating the G-buffer in the first place and then reading and unpacking it in the lighting shader, which is performed once in this example, regardless of the number of lights in the scene. In this example, we have used a relatively inefficient G-buffer representation for the sake of clarity. This consumes quite a bit of memory bandwidth, and the performance of the program could probably be increased somewhat by reducing the storage requirements of the buffer.

Figure 12.25: Final rendering using deferred shading

Normal Mapping and Deferred Shading

Earlier in this chapter, you read about normal mapping, which is a technique to store local surface normals in a texture and then use them to add detail to rendered models. To achieve this, most normal mapping algorithms (including the one described earlier in this chapter) use *tangent space normals* and perform all lighting calculations in that coordinate space. This involves calculating the light and view vectors, $\vec{L}$ and $\vec{V}$, in the vertex shader, transforming them into tangent space using the TBN matrix, and passing them to the fragment shader where lighting calculations are performed. However, in deferred renderers, the normals that you store in the G-buffer are generally in world or view space.

In order to generate view-space normals[6] that can be stored into a G-buffer for deferred shading, we need to take the tangent-space normals read from the normal map and transform them into view-space during G-buffer generation. This requires minor modifications to the normal mapping algorithm.

First, we do not calculate $\vec{V}$ or $\vec{L}$ in the vertex shader, nor do we construct the TBN matrix there. Instead, we calculate the view-space normal and tangent vectors $\vec{N}$ and $\vec{T}$ and pass them to the fragment shader. In the fragment shader, we re-normalize $\vec{N}$ and $\vec{T}$ and take their cross product to produce the bitangent vector $\vec{B}$. This is used in the fragment shader to construct the TBN matrix local to the fragment being shaded. We read the tangent-space normal from the normal map as usual, but transform it through the inverse of the TBN matrix (which is simply its transpose, assuming it encodes only rotation). This moves the normal vector from tangent-space into view-space. The normal is then stored in the G-buffer. The remainder of the shading algorithm that performs lighting calculations is unchanged from that described earlier.

The vertex shader used to generate the G-buffer with normal mapping applied is almost unmodified from the version that does not apply normal mapping. However, the updated fragment shader is shown in Listing 12.31.

```
#version 420 core

layout (location = 0) out uvec4 color0;
layout (location = 1) out vec4 color1;

in VS_OUT
{
    vec3        ws_coords;
    vec3        normal;
    vec3        tangent;
    vec2        texcoord0;
    flat uint   material_id;
} fs_in;
```

---

6. View space is generally preferred for lighting calculations over world space as it has consistent accuracy independent of the viewer's position. When the viewer is placed at a large distance from the origin, world space precision breaks down near the viewer, and that can affect the accuracy of lighting calculations.

```
layout (binding = 0) uniform sampler2D tex_diffuse;
layout (binding = 1) uniform sampler2D tex_normal_map;

void main(void)
{
    vec3 N = normalize(fs_in.normal);
    vec3 T = normalize(fs_in.tangent);
    vec3 B = cross(N, T);
    mat3 TBN = mat3(T, B, N);

    vec3 nm = texture(tex_normal_map, fs_in.texcoord0).xyz * 2.0 - vec3(1.0);
    nm = TBN * normalize(nm);

    uvec4 outvec0 = uvec4(0);
    vec4 outvec1 = vec4(0);

    vec3 color = texture(tex_diffuse, fs_in.texcoord0).rgb;

    outvec0.x = packHalf2x16(color.xy);
    outvec0.y = packHalf2x16(vec2(color.z, nm.x));
    outvec0.z = packHalf2x16(nm.yz);
    outvec0.w = fs_in.material_id;

    outvec1.xyz = floatBitsToUint(fs_in.ws_coords);
    outvec1.w = 60.0;

    color0 = outvec0;
    color1 = outvec1;
}
```

Listing 12.31: Deferred shading with normal mapping (fragment shader)

Finally, Figure 12.26 shows the difference between applying normal maps
to the scene (left) and using the interpolated per-vertex normal (right). As
you can see, substantially more detail is visible in the left image that has
normal maps applied. All of this code is contained in the
deferredshading example, which generated these images.

Figure 12.26: Deferred shading with and without normal maps

Deferred Shading — Downsides

While deferred shading can reduce the impact of complex lighting or
shading calculations on the performance of your application, it won't

solve all of your problems. Besides being very bandwidth heavy and requiring a lot of memory for all of the textures you attach to your G-buffer, there are a number of other downsides to deferred shading. With a bit of effort, you might be able to work around some of them, but before you launch into writing a shiny new deferred renderer, you should consider the following.

First, the bandwidth considerations of a deferred shading implementation should be considered carefully. In our example, we used 256 bits of information for each pixel in the G-buffer, and we didn't make particularly efficient use of them either. We packed our world-space coordinates directly in the G-buffer, consuming 96 bits of space (remember, we used three 32-bit floating-point entries for this). However, we have the screen-space coordinates of each pixel when we render our final pass, which we can retrieve from the x and y components of gl_FragCoord and from the content of the depth buffer. To obtain world-space coordinates, we need to undo the viewport transform (which is simply a scale and bias) and then move the resulting coordinates from clip space into world space by applying the inverse of the projection and view matrices (which normally transforms coordinates from world space to view space). As the view matrix usually only encodes translation and rotation, it is generally easy to invert. However, the projection matrix and subsequent homogenous division is more difficult to reverse.

We also used 48 bits to encode our surface normals in the G-buffer by using three 16-bit floating-point numbers per normal. We could instead store only the x and y components of the normal and reconstruct the z coordinate using the knowledge that the normal should a unit-length vector and, therefore, $z = \sqrt{x^2 + y^2}$. We must also deduce the sign of z. However, if we make the assumption that no surface with a negative z component in view space will ever be rendered, we'd usually be right. Finally, the specular power and material ID components were stored using full 32-bit quantities. It is likely that you won't have more than 60,000 unique materials in your scene and can therefore use 16 bits for a material ID. Also, it is reasonable to store specular powers as logarithms and raise 2 to the power of the shininess factor in your lighting shader. This will require substantially fewer bits to store the specular power factor in the G-buffer.

Another downside of deferred shading algorithms is that they generally don't play well with antialiasing. Normally, when OpenGL *resolves* a multi-sample buffer, it will take a (possibly weighted) average of the samples in the pixel. Averaging depth values, normals, and in particular meta-data such as material IDs just doesn't work. So, if you want to implement antialiasing, you'll need to use multi-sampled textures for all of the off-screen buffers attached to your G-buffer. What's worse, because the final pass consists of a single large polygon (or possibly two) that covers the entire scene, none of the interior pixels will be considered edge pixels, breaking traditional multi-sample antialiasing. For the resolve pass, you will either need to write a special custom resolve shader or run the whole thing at sample rate, which will substantially increase the cost of lighting your scene.

Finally, most deferred shading algorithms can't deal with transparency. This is because at each pixel in the G-buffer, we store only the information for a single fragment. In order to properly implement transparency, we would need to know all of the information for every fragment starting closest to the viewer until an opaque fragment is hit. There are algorithms that do this, and they are often used to implement order-independent transparency, for example. Another approach is simply to render all non-transparent surfaces using deferred shading and then to render transparent materials in a second pass through the scene. This requires your renderer to either keep a list of transparent surfaces that it skipped as it traversed the scene, or to traverse your scene twice. Either option can be pretty expensive.

In summary, deferred shading can bring substantial performance improvements to your application if you keep in mind the limitations of the techniques and restrict yourself to algorithms that it handles well.

Screen-Space Techniques

Most of the rendering techniques described in this book so far have been implemented per primitive. However, in the previous section, we discussed deferred shading, which suggested that at least some of the rendering procedures can be implemented in screen space. In this subsection, we discuss a few more algorithms that push shading into screen space. In some cases, this is the only way to implement certain techniques, and in other cases, we can achieve a pretty significant performance advantage by delaying processing until all geometry has already been rendered.

Ambient Occlusion

Ambient occlusion is a technique for simulating one component of *global illumination*. Global illumination is the observed effect of light bouncing from object to object in a scene such that surfaces are lit indirectly by the light reflected from nearby surfaces. Ambient light is an approximation to this scattered light and is a small, fixed amount added to lighting calculations. However, in deep creases or gaps between objects, less light will light them due to the nearby surfaces *occluding* the light sources — hence the term *ambient occlusion*. Real-time global illumination is a topic of current research, and while some fairly impressive work has been presented, this is an unsolved problem. However, we can produce some reasonably good results with ad-hoc methods and gross approximations. One such approximation is *screen space ambient occlusion* (or SSAO), which we will discuss here.

To explain the technique, we will start in two dimensions. Ambient light could be considered to be the amount of light that would hit a point on a surface if it were surrounded by an arbitrarily large number of small point lights. On a perfectly flat surface, any point is visible to all of the lights above that surface. However, on a bumpy surface, not all of the lights will be visible from all points on that surface — the bumpier the surface, the fewer the number of lights that will be visible from any given point. This is illustrated in Figure 12.27.

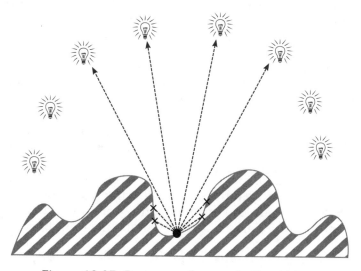

Figure 12.27: Bumpy surface occluding points

In the diagram, you can see that we have eight point lights distributed roughly equally around a surface. For the point under consideration, we draw a line from that point to each of the eight lights. You can see that a point at the bottom of a valley in the surface can only see a small number of the lights. However, it should be clear that a point at the top of a peak should be able to see most, if not all of the lights. The bumps in the surface occlude the lights from points at the bottom of valleys, and therefore, they will receive ambient light. In a full global illumination simulation, we would literally trace lines (or rays) from each point being shaded in hundreds, perhaps thousands, of directions and determine what was hit. However, that's far too expensive for a real-time solution, and so we use a method that allows us to calculate the occlusion of a point directly in screen space.

To implement this technique, we are going to march rays from each position in screen space along a random direction and determine the amount of occlusion at each point along that ray. First, we render our scene into depth and color buffers attached to an FBO. Along with this, we also render the normal at each fragment and its linear depth[7] in view space into a second color attachment on the same FBO. In a second pass, we will use this information to compute the level of occlusion at each pixel. In this pass, we render a full-screen quad with our ambient occlusion shader. The shader reads the depth value that we render in our first pass, selects a random direction to walk in, and takes several steps along that direction. At each point along the walk, it tests whether the value in the depth buffer is less than the depth value computed along the ray. If it is, then we consider the point occluded.

To select a random direction, we pre-initialize a uniform buffer with a large number of random vectors in a unit radius sphere. Although our random vectors may point in any direction, we only really want to consider vectors that point *away* from the surface. That is, we only consider vectors lying in the hemisphere oriented around the surface normal at the point. To produce a random direction oriented in this hemisphere, we take the dot product of the surface normal (which we rendered into our color buffer earlier) and the selected random direction. If the result is negative, then the selected direction vector points into the surface, and so we negate it in order to point it back into the correctly oriented hemisphere. Figure 12.28 demonstrates the technique.

In Figure 12.28, you can see that vectors V_0, V_1, and V_4 already lie in the hemisphere that is aligned with the normal vector, N. This means that the dot product between any of these three vectors and N will be positive.

---

7. We could reconstruct a linear view-space depth from the content of the depth buffer produced in the first pass by inverting the mapping of eye-space z into the 0.0 to 1.0 range stored in the depth buffer. However, for simplicity, we're going to use the extra channel on our framebuffer attachment.

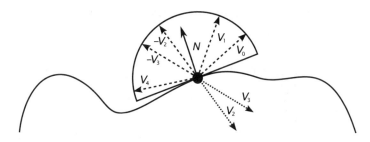

Figure 12.28: Selection of random vector in an oriented hemisphere

However, V_2 and V_3 lie outside the desired hemisphere, and it should be clear that the dot product between either of these two vectors and N will be negative. In this case, we simply negate V_2 and V_3, reorienting them into the correct hemisphere.

Once we have our random set of vectors, it's time to walk along them. To do this, we start at the point on the surface and step a small distance along our chosen distance vector. This produces a new point, complete with x, y, and z coordinates. We use the x and y components to read from the linear depth buffer that we rendered earlier and look up the value stored there. We compare this depth to that of the interpolated position vector, and if it is closer (i.e., lower) than the interpolated value, then our interpolated point is obscured from view in the image, and thus we consider the original point to be occluded for the purposes of the algorithm. While this is clearly far from accurate, *statistically* it works out. The number of random directions to choose, the number of steps along each direction, and how far that step is are all parameters that we can choose to control the output image quality. The more directions we choose, the farther we step, and the more steps we take in each direction, the better the output image quality will be. Figure 12.29 shows the effect of adding more sample directions on the result of the ambient occlusion algorithm.

In Figure 12.29, directions are added from left to right, top to bottom, starting with a single direction on the top left, with 4 on the top right, 16 on the bottom left, and 64 on the bottom right. As you can see, it is not until we have 64 directions that the image becomes smooth. With fewer directions, severe banding is seen in the image. There are many approaches to reduce this, but one of the most effective is to *randomize* the distance along each of the occlusion rays we take for each sample. This introduces noise into the image, but also smoothes the result, improving overall quality. Figure 12.30 shows the result of introducing this randomness into the image.

Figure 12.29: Effect of increasing direction count on ambient occlusion

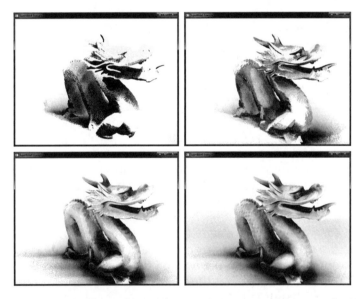

Figure 12.30: Effect of introducing noise in ambient occlusion

As you can see in Figure 12.30, the introduction of randomness in the step rate along the occlusion rays has improved image quality substantially. Again, from left to right, top to bottom, we have taken 1, 4, 16, and 64 directions, respectively. With random ray step rates, the image produced by considering only a single ray direction has gone from looking quite corrupted to looking noisy, but correct. Even the 4-direction result (shown on the top right of Figure 12.30) has acceptable quality, whereas the equivalent image in Figure 12.29 still exhibits considerable banding. The 16-sample image on the bottom left of Figure 12.30 is almost as good as the 64-sample image of Figure 12.29, and the 64-sample image of Figure 12.30 does not show much improvement over it. It is even possible to compensate for the noise introduced by this method, but that is beyond the scope of this example.

Once we have our ambient occlusion term, we need to apply it to our rendered image. Ambient occlusion is simply the amount by which ambient light is occluded. Therefore, all we need to do is multiply our ambient lighting term in our shading equation by our occlusion term, which causes the creases of our model to have less ambient lighting applied to them. Figure 12.31 shows the effect of applying the screen space ambient occlusion algorithm to a rendered scene.

Figure 12.31: Ambient occlusion applied to a rendered scene

In Figure 12.31, the image on the left is the diffuse and specular terms of the lighting model only. The dragon is suspended just over a plane although depth is very hard to judge in the image. The image on the right has screen space ambient occlusion applied. As you can see, not only is the definition of some of the dragon's details more apparent, but the dragon also casts a soft shadow on the ground below it, increasing the sense of depth.

In our first pass, we simply render the diffuse and specular terms into one color attachment as usual, and then we render the surface normal and linear eye-space depth into a second color attachment. The shader to do this is relatively straightforward and is similar to many of the shaders presented thus far in the book. The second pass of the algorithm is the interesting part — this is where we apply the ambient occlusion effect. It is shown in its entirety in Listing 12.32, which is part of the `ssao` sample application.

```glsl
#version 430 core

// Samplers for pre-rendered color, normal, and depth
layout (binding = 0) uniform sampler2D sColor;
layout (binding = 1) uniform sampler2D sNormalDepth;

// Final output
layout (location = 0) out vec4 color;

// Various uniforms controlling SSAO effect
uniform float ssao_level = 1.0;
uniform float object_level = 1.0;
uniform float ssao_radius = 5.0;
uniform bool weight_by_angle = true;
uniform uint point_count = 8;
uniform bool randomize_points = true;

// Uniform block containing up to 256 random directions (x,y,z,0)
// and 256 more completely random vectors
layout (binding = 0, std140) uniform SAMPLE_POINTS
{
    vec4 pos[256];
    vec4 random_vectors[256];
} points;

void main(void)
{
    // Get texture position from gl_FragCoord
    vec2 P = gl_FragCoord.xy / textureSize(sNormalDepth, 0);
    // ND = normal and depth
    vec4 ND = textureLod(sNormalDepth, P, 0);
    // Extract normal and depth
    vec3 N = ND.xyz;
    float my_depth = ND.w;

    // Local temporary variables
    int i;
    int j;
    int n;

    float occ = 0.0;
    float total = 0.0;

    // n is a pseudo-random number generated from fragment coordinate
    // and depth
    n = (int(gl_FragCoord.x * 7123.2315 + 125.232) *
         int(gl_FragCoord.y * 3137.1519 + 234.8)) ^
         int(my_depth);
    // Pull one of the random vectors
    vec4 v = points.random_vectors[n & 255];

    // r is our "radius randomizer"
    float r = (v.r + 3.0) * 0.1;
    if (!randomize_points)
        r = 0.5;
```

```
// For each random point (or direction)...
for (i = 0; i < point_count; i++)
{
    // Get direction
    vec3 dir = points.pos[i].xyz;

    // Put it into the correct hemisphere
    if (dot(N, dir) < 0.0)
        dir = -dir;

    // f is the distance we've stepped in this direction
    // z is the interpolated depth
    float f = 0.0;
    float z = my_depth;

    // We're going to take 4 steps - we could make this
    // configurable
    total += 4.0;

    for (j = 0; j < 4; j++)
    {
        // Step in the right direction
        f += r;
        // Step _towards_ viewer reduces z
        z -= dir.z * f;

        // Read depth from current fragment
        float their_depth =
            textureLod(sNormalDepth,
                       (P + dir.xy * f * ssao_radius), 0).w;

        // Calculate a weighting (d) for this fragment's
        // contribution to occlusion
        float d = abs(their_depth - my_depth);
        d *= d;

        // If we're obscured, accumulate occlusion
        if ((z - their_depth) > 0.0)
        {
            occ += 4.0 / (1.0 + d);
        }
    }
}

// Calculate occlusion amount
float ao_amount = vec4(1.0 - occ / total);

// Get object color from color texture
vec4 object_color =  textureLod(sColor, P, 0);

// Mix in ambient color scaled by SSAO level
color = object_level * object_color +
        mix(vec4(0.2), vec4(ao_amount), ssao_level);
}
```

Listing 12.32: Ambient occlusion fragment shader

Rendering without Triangles

In the previous section, we covered techniques that can be applied in
screen space, all of which are implemented by drawing a full-screen quad

over geometry that's already been rendered. In this section, we take it one step further and demonstrate how it's possible to render entire scenes entirely with a single full-screen quad.

Rendering Julia Fractals

In this next example, we render a *Julia set*, creating image data from nothing but the texture coordinates. Julia sets are related to the *Mandelbrot set* — the iconic bulblike fractal. The Mandelbrot image is generated by iterating the formula

$$Z_n = Z_{n-1}{}^2 + C$$

until the magnitude of Z exceeds a threshold and calculating the number of iterations. If the magnitude of Z never exceeds the threshold within the allowed number of iterations, that point is determined to be inside the Mandelbrot set and is colored with some default color. If the magnitude of Z exceeds the threshold within the allowed number of iterations, then the point is outside the set. A common visualization of the Mandelbrot set colors the point using a function of the iteration count at the time the point was determined to be outside the set. The primary difference between the Mandelbrot set and the Julia set is the initial conditions for Z and C.

When rendering the Mandelbrot set, Z is set to $(0 + 0i)$, and C is set to the coordinate of the point at which the iterations are to be performed. When rendering the Julia set, on the other hand, Z is set to the coordinate of the point at which iterations are performed, and C is set to an application-specified constant. Thus, while there is only one Mandelbrot set, there are infinitely many Julia sets — one for every possible value of C. Because of this, the Julia set can be controlled parametrically and even animated. Just as in some of the previous examples, we invoke this shader at every fragment by drawing a full-screen quad. However, rather than consuming and post-processing data that might already be in the framebuffer, we generate the final image directly.

Let's set up the fragment shader with an input block containing just the texture coordinates. We also need a uniform to hold the value of C. To apply interesting colors to the resulting Julia image, we use a one-dimensional texture with a color gradient in it. When we've iterated a point that escapes from the set, we color the output fragment by indexing into this texture using the iteration count. Finally, we also define a uniform containing the maximum number of iterations we want to perform. This allows the application to balance performance against the level of detail in the resulting image. Listing 12.33 shows the setup for our Julia renderer's fragment shader.

```
#version 430 core

in Fragment
{
    vec2 tex_coord;
} fragment;

// Here's our value of c
uniform vec2 c;

// This is the color gradient texture
uniform sampler1D tex_gradient;

// This is the maximum iterations we'll perform before we consider
// the point to be outside the set
uniform int max_iterations;

// The output color for this fragment
out vec4 output_color;
```

Listing 12.33: Setting up the Julia set renderer

Now that we have the inputs to our shader, we are ready to start rendering the Julia set. The value of C is taken from the uniform supplied by the application. The initial value of Z is taken from the incoming texture coordinates supplied by the vertex shader. Our iteration loop is shown in Listing 12.34.

```
int iterations = 0;
vec2 z = fragment.tex_coords;
const float threshold_squared = 4.0;

// While there are iterations left and we haven't escaped from
// the set yet...
while (iterations < max_iterations &&
       dot(z, z) < threshold_squared)
{
    // Iterate the value of Z as Z^2 + C
    vec2 z_squared;
    z_squared.x = z.x * z.x - z.y * z.y;
    z_squared.y = 2.0 * z.x * z.y;
    z = z_squared + c;
    iterations++;
}
```

Listing 12.34: Inner loop of the Julia renderer

The loop terminates under one of two conditions — either we reach the maximum number of iterations allowed (iterations == max_iterations) or the magnitude of Z passes our threshold. Note that in this shader, we compare the squared magnitude of Z (found using the dot function) to the square of the threshold (the threshold_squared uniform). The two operations are equivalent, but this way avoids a square root in the shader, improving performance. If, at the end of the loop, `iterations` is equal to `max_iterations`, we know that we ran out of iterations and the point is inside the set — we color it black. Otherwise, our point left the set *before* we ran out of iterations, and we can color the point accordingly. To do this, we can just figure out what fraction of the total allowed iterations we used up and use that to look up into the gradient texture. Listing 12.35 shows what the code looks like.

```
if (iterations == max_iterations)
{
    output_color = vec4(0.0, 0.0, 0.0, 0.0);
}
else
{
    output_color = texture(tex_gradient,
                           float(iterations) / float(max_iterations));
}
```

Listing 12.35: Using a gradient texture to color the Julia set

Now all that's left is to supply the gradient texture and set an appropriate value of c. For our application, we update c on each frame as a function of the `currentTime` parameter passed to our `render` function. By doing this, we can animate the fractal. Figure 12.32 shows a few frames of the Julia animation produced by the `julia` example program. (See Color Plate 13 in the color insert for another example.)

Figure 12.32: A few frames from the Julia set animation

Ray Tracing in a Fragment Shader

OpenGL usually works by using rasterization to generate fragments for primitives such as lines, triangles, and points. This should be obvious to you by now. We send geometry into the OpenGL pipeline, and for each triangle, OpenGL figures out which pixels it covers, and then runs your shader to figure out what color it should be. Ray tracing effectively inverts the problem. We throw a bunch of pixels into the pipeline (actually represented by rays), and then for each one, we figure out which pieces of geometry cover that pixel (which means our per-pixel ray hits the geometry). The biggest disadvantage of this when compared to traditional rasterization is that OpenGL doesn't include direct support for it, which means we have to do all of the work in our own shaders. However, this provides us with a number of advantages — in particular, we aren't limited[8] to just points, lines, and triangles, *and* we can figure out what happens to a ray after it hits an object. Using the same techniques as we use for figuring out what's visible from the camera, we can render reflections, shadows, and even refraction with little additional code.

In this subsection, we discuss the construction of a simple recursive ray tracer using a fragment shader. The ray tracer we produce here will be capable of rendering images consisting of simple spheres and infinite planes — enough to produce the classic "glossy spheres in a box" image. Certainly, substantially more advanced implementations exist, but this should be sufficient to convey the basic techniques. Figure 12.33 shows a simplified, 2D illustration of the basics of a simple ray tracer.

In Figure 12.33, we see the eye position, which forms the origin of a ray O shot towards the image plane (which is our display) and intersecting it at point P. This ray is known as the primary ray and is denoted here by $R_{primary}$. The ray intersects a first sphere at the intersection point I_0. At this point, we create two additional rays. The first is directed towards the light source and is denoted by R_{shadow}. If this ray intersects anything along its way to the light source, then point I_0 is in shadow; otherwise, it is lit by the point. In addition to the shadow ray, we shoot a second ray $R_{reflected}$ by reflecting the incoming ray $R_{primary}$ around the surface normal at I_0, N.

Shading for ray tracing isn't all that different from the types of shading and lighting algorithms we've looked at already in this book. We can still calculate diffuse and specular terms, apply normal maps and other

---

8. In fact, points, lines, and triangles are amongst the more complex shapes to render in a ray tracer.

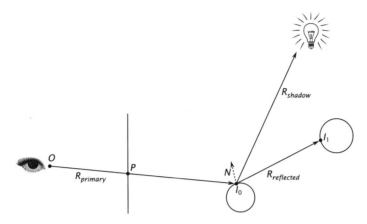

Figure 12.33: Simplified 2D illustration of ray tracing

textures, and so on. However, we also consider the contribution of the rays that we shoot in other directions. So, for I_0, we'll shade it using $R_{primary}$ as our view vector, N as our normal, R_{shadow} as our light vector, and so on. Next, we'll shoot a ray off towards I_1 ($R_{reflected}$), shade the surface *there*, and then add that contribution (scaled by the reflectivity of the surface at I_0) back to the color accumulated at P. The result is crisp, clean reflections.

Now, given the origin (O), which is usually at the origin in view space, and point P, we calculate the direction of ray $R_{primary}$ and begin the ray tracing process. This involves calculating the intersection of a line (our ray) and an object in the scene (each sphere). The intersection of a ray with a sphere works as follows.

Given a ray R with origin O and direction $\vec{D}$, then at time t, a point on that ray is $O + t\vec{D}$. Also, given a sphere at center C with radius r, any point on its surface is at distance r from C, and moreover, the squared distance between C and any point on the sphere's surface is r^2. This is convenient as the dot product of a vector with itself is its squared distance. Thus, we can say that for a point P at $O + t\vec{D}$

$$(P - C) \cdot (P - C) = r^2$$

Substituting for P, we have

$$(O + t\vec{D} - C) \cdot (O + t\vec{D} - C) = r^2$$

Expanding this gives us a quadratic equation in t:

$$(\vec{D} \cdot \vec{D})t^2 + 2(O - C) \cdot \vec{D}t + (O - C) \cdot (O - C) - r^2 = 0$$

To write this in the more familiar form of $At^2 + Bt + C = 0$

$$A = \vec{D} \cdot \vec{D}$$
$$B = 2(O - C) \cdot \vec{D}$$
$$C = (O - C) \cdot (O - C) - r^2$$

As a simple quadratic equation, we can solve for t, knowing that there are either zero, one, or two solutions:

$$t = \frac{-B \pm \sqrt{B^2 - 4AC}}{2A}$$

Given that we know that our direction vector $\vec{D}$ is normalized, then its length is one, and therefore, A is one also. This simplifies things a little, and we can simply say that our solution for t is

$$t = \frac{-B \pm \sqrt{B^2 - 4C}}{2}$$

If $4C$ is greater than B^2, then the term under the square root is negative, and there is no solution for t, which means that there is no intersection between the ray and the sphere. If B^2 is equal to $4C$, then there is only one solution, meaning that the ray just grazes the sphere. If that solution is positive, then this occurs in front of the viewer and we have found our intersection point. If the single solution for t is negative, then the intersection point is behind the viewer. Finally, if there are two solutions to the equation, we take the smallest non-negative solution for t as our intersection point. We simply plug this value back into $P = O + t\vec{D}$ and retrieve the coordinates of the intersection point in 3D space.

Shader code to perform this intersection test is shown in Listing 12.36.

```
struct ray
{
    vec3 origin;
    vec3 direction;
};

struct sphere
{
    vec3 center;
    float radius;
};
```

```
float intersect_ray_sphere(ray R,
                           sphere S,
                           out vec3 hitpos,
                           out vec3 normal)
{
    vec3 v = R.origin - S.center;
    float B = 2.0 * dot(R.direction, v);
    float C = dot(v, v) - S.radius * S.radius;
    float B2 = B * B;

    float f = B2 - 4.0 * C;

    if (f < 0.0)
        return 0.0;

    float t0 = -B + sqrt(f);
    float t1 = -B - sqrt(f);
    float t = min(max(t0, 0.0), max(t1, 0.0)) * 0.5;

    if (t == 0.0)
        return 0.0;

    hitpos = R.origin + t * R.direction;
    normal = normalize(hitpos - S.center);

    return t;
}
```

Listing 12.36: Ray-sphere intersection test

Given the structures ray and sphere, the function intersect_ray_sphere
in Listing 12.36 returns 0.0 if the ray does not hit the sphere and the
value of t if it does. If an intersection is found, the position of that
intersection is returned in the output parameter hitpos, and the normal
of the surface at the intersection point is returned in the output parameter
normal. We use the returned value of t to determine the closest
intersection point along each ray by initializing a temporary variable to
the longest allowed ray length, and taking the minimum between it and
the distance returned by intersect_ray_sphere for each sphere in the
scene. The code to do this is shown in Listing 12.37.

```
// Declare a uniform block with our spheres in it.
layout (std140, binding = 1) uniform SPHERES
{
    sphere       S[128];
};

// Textures with the ray origin and direction in them
layout (binding = 0) uniform sampler2D tex_origin;
layout (binding = 1) uniform sampler2D tex_direction;

// Construct a ray using the two textures
ray R;

R.origin = texelFetch(tex_origin, ivec2(gl_FragCoord.xy), 0).xyz;
R.direction = normalize(texelFetch(tex_direction,
                ivec2(gl_FragCoord.xy), 0).xyz);
```

```
float min_t = 1000000.0f;
float t;

// For each sphere...
for (i = 0; i < num_spheres; i++)
{
    // Find the intersection point
    t = intersect_ray_sphere(R, S[i], hitpos, normal);

    // If there is an intersection
    if (t != 0.0)
    {
        // And that intersection is less than our current best
        if (t < min_t)
        {
            // Record it.
            min_t = t;
            hit_position = hitpos;
            hit_normal = normal;
            sphere_index = i;
        }
    }
}
```

Listing 12.37: Determining closest intersection point

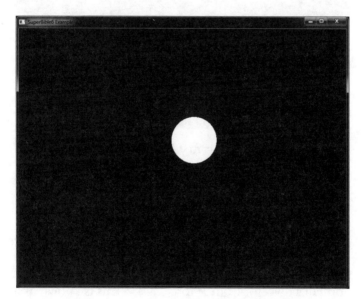

Figure 12.34: Our first ray-traced sphere

If all we do at each point is write white wherever we hit something, and then trace rays into a scene containing a single sphere, we produce the image shown in Figure 12.35.

However, this isn't particularly interesting — we'll need to light the point. The surface normal is important for lighting calculations (as you have read already in this chapter), and this is returned by our intersection function. We perform lighting calculations as normal in the ray tracer — taking the surface normal, the view-space coordinate (calculated during the intersection test), and material parameters and shade the point. By applying the lighting equations you've already learned about, we can retrieve the image shown in Figure 12.35.

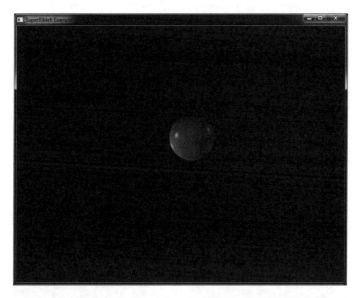

Figure 12.35: Our first lit ray-traced sphere

Although the normal is used in lighting calculations, it is also very important for the next few steps in the ray tracer. For each light in the scene, we calculate its contribution to the surface's shading and accumulate this to produce the final color. This is where the first real advantage of ray tracing comes in. Given a surface point P and a light coordinate L, we form a new ray, setting its origin O to P and its direction $\vec{D}$ to the normalized vector from P to L, $\frac{L-P}{|L-P|}$. This is known as a *shadow ray* (pictured as R_{shadow} in Figure 12.33). We can then test the objects in the scene to see if the light is visible from that point — if the ray doesn't hit anything, then there is line of sight from the point being shaded to the light; otherwise, it is occluded and therefore in shadow. As you can imagine, shadows are something that ray tracers do very well.

However, it doesn't end there. Just as we constructed a new ray starting from our intersection and pointing in the direction of our light source, we can construct a ray pointing in any direction. For example, given that we know the surface normal at the ray's intersection with the sphere, we can use GLSL's reflect to reflect the incoming ray direction around the plane defined by this normal and shoot a new ray away from the plane in this direction. This ray is simply sent as input to our ray tracing algorithm, the intersection point it generates is shaded, and the resulting color is simply added into the scene.

You may have noticed in Listing 12.37 that at each pixel, we read an origin and a direction from a texture. Ray tracing is a recursive algorithm — you trace a ray, shade the point, create a new ray, trace it, and continue. GLSL doesn't allow recursion, so instead, we implement it using a stack maintained in an array of textures.

To maintain all the data that we'll need for our ray tracer, we create an array of framebuffer objects, and to each we attach four textures as color attachments. These hold, for each pixel in the framebuffer, the final composite color, the origin of a ray, the current direction of the ray, and the accumulated reflected color of the ray. In our application, we allow each ray to take up to five bounces, and we need five framebuffer objects, each with four textures attached to it. The first (the composite color) is common to all framebuffer objects, but the other three are unique to each framebuffer. During each pass, we read from one set of textures and write into the next set via the framebuffer object. This is illustrated in Figure 12.36.

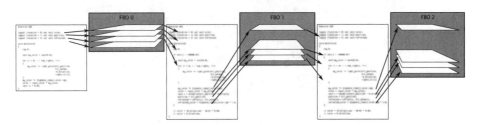

Figure 12.36: Implementing a stack using framebuffer objects

To initialize our ray tracer, we run a shader that writes the starting origin and ray direction into the first origin and direction textures. We also initialize our accumulation texture to zeros, and our reflection color texture to all ones. Next, we run our actual ray tracing shader by drawing a full-screen quad once for each bounce of the rays we want to trace. On each pass, we bind the origin, direction, and reflected color textures from the previous pass. We also bind a framebuffer that has the outgoing origin, direction, and reflection textures attached to it as color attachments — these textures will be used in the next pass. Then, for each pixel, the shader forms a ray using the origin and direction stored in the first two textures, traces it into the scene, lights the intersection point, multiplies the result by the value stored in the reflected color texture, and sends it to its first output.

To enable composition into the final output texture, we attach it to the first color attachment of each framebuffer object and enable blending for that attachment with the blending function set to GL_ONE for both the source and destination factors. This causes the output to be simply added to the existing content of that attachment. To the other outputs, we write the intersection position, the reflected ray direction, and the reflectivity coefficient of the material that we use for shading the ray's intersection point.

If we add a few more spheres to the scene, we can have them reflect each other by applying this technique. Figure 12.37 shows the scene with a few more spheres thrown in with an increasing number of bounces of each ray.

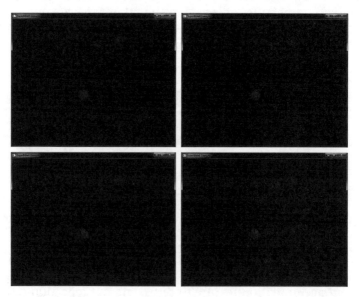

Figure 12.37: Ray-traced spheres with increasing ray bounces

As you can see in Figure 12.37, the top-left image (which includes no secondary rays) is pretty dull. As soon as we introduce the first bounce in the top-right image, we begin to see reflections of the spheres. Adding a second bounce in the bottom left, we can see reflections of spheres in the reflections of the spheres... in the third bounce on the lower right, the effect is more subtle, but if you look very closely, there are reflections of spheres in spheres in spheres.

Now, a scene made entirely of spheres really isn't very exciting. What we need to do is add more object types. Although in theory, any object could be ray traced, another form that is relatively easy to perform intersection tests with is the plane. One representation of a plane is a normal (which is constant for a plane) and a distance from the origin of the point on the plane that lies along that normal. The normal is a three-dimensional vector, and the distance is a scalar value. As such, we can describe a plane with a single four-component vector. We pack the normal into the x, y, and z components of the vector and the distance from the origin into the w component. In fact, given a plane normal N and distance from origin d, the implicit equation of a plane can be represented as

$$P \cdot N + d = 0$$

where P is a point in the plane. Given that we have P, a point on our ray defined as

$$P = O + t\vec{D}$$

we can simply substitute this value of P into the implicit equation to retrieve

$$(O + t\vec{D}) \cdot N + d = 0$$

Solving for t, we arrive at

$$O \cdot N + t\vec{D} \cdot N + d = 0$$
$$t\vec{D} \cdot N = -(O \cdot N + d)$$
$$t = \frac{-(O \cdot N + d)}{\vec{D} \cdot N}$$

As you can see from the equation, if $\vec{D} \cdot N$ is zero, then the denominator of the fraction is zero and there is no solution for t. This occurs when the ray direction is parallel to the plane (thus, it is perpendicular to the plane's normal and their dot product is zero), and so never intersects it.

Otherwise, we can find a real value for t. Again, once we know the value of t, we can substitute it back into our ray equation, $P = O + t\vec{D}$, to retrieve our intersection point. If t is less than zero, then we know that the ray intersects the plane *behind* the viewer, which we consider here to be a miss. Code to perform this intersection test is shown in Listing 12.38.

```
float intersect_ray_plane(ray R,
                          vec4 P,
                          out vec3 hitpos,
                          out vec3 normal)
{
    vec3 O = R.origin;
    vec3 D = R.direction;
    vec3 N = P.xyz;
    float d = P.w;

    float denom = dot(N, D);

    if (denom == 0.0)
        return 0.0;

    float t = -(d + dot(O, N)) / denom;

    if (t < 0.0)
        return 0.0;

    hitpos = O + t * D;
    normal = N;

    return t;
}
```

Listing 12.38: Ray-plane intersection test

Adding a plane to our scene behind our spheres produces the image shown on the left of Figure 12.38. Although this adds some depth to our scene, it doesn't show the full effect of the ray tracer. By adding a couple of bounces, we can clearly see the reflections of the spheres in the plane, and of the plane in the spheres.

Figure 12.38: Adding a ray-traced plane

Now, if we add a few more planes, we can enclose our scene in a box. The resulting image is shown on the top left of Figure 12.39. However, now, when we bounce the rays further, the effect of reflection becomes more and more apparent. You can see the result of adding more bounces as we progress from left to right, top to bottom in Figure 12.39 with no bounces, one, two, and three bounces, respectively. A higher resolution image using four bounces is shown in Color Plate 14.

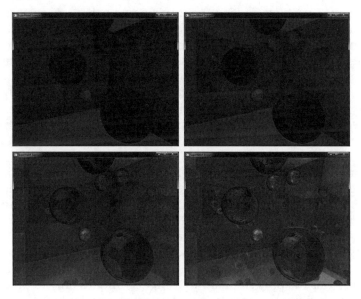

Figure 12.39: Ray-traced spheres in a box

The ray tracing implementation presented here and in the raytracer example application is a *brute force* approach that simply intersects every ray against every object. As your objects get more complex and the amount of them in the scene becomes greater, you may wish to implement *acceleration structures*. An acceleration structure is a data structure constructed in memory that allows you to quickly determine which objects *might* be hit by a ray given an origin and a direction. As you have seen from this example, ray tracing is actually pretty easy so long as you know an intersection algorithm for your primitive of choice. Shadows, reflections, and even refraction just come for free with ray tracing. However, ray tracing is certainly not cheap, and without dedicated hardware support, it leaves a lot of work for you to do in your shaders. Using an acceleration structure is vital if you really want to use ray trace scenes containing more than a handful of spheres and bunch of planes in real time. Current research in ray tracing is almost entirely focused on efficient acceleration structures and how to generate them, store them, and traverse them.

Summary

In this chapter, we have applied the fundamentals that you have learned throughout the book to a number of rendering techniques. At first, we focused heavily on lighting models and how to shade the objects that you're drawing. This included a discussion of the Phong lighting model, the Blinn-Phong model, and rim lighting. We also looked at how to produce higher frequency lighting effects than are representable by your geometry by using normal maps, environment maps, and other textures. We showed how you can cast shadows and simulate basic atmospheric effects. We also discussed some techniques that have no basis in reality.

In the final section, we stepped away from shading at the same time as rendering our geometry and looked at some techniques that can be applied in screen space. Deferred shading allows expensive shading calculations to be decoupled from the initial pass that renders our geometry. By storing positions, normals, colors, and other surface attributes in framebuffer attachments, we are able to implement arbitrarily complex shading algorithms without worrying about wasting work. At first, we use this to apply standard lighting techniques only to pixels we know will be visible. However, with screen space ambient occlusion, we demonstrated a technique that relies on having data from neighboring pixels available in order to function at all. Ultimately, we introduced the topic of ray tracing, and in our implementation, we render an entire scene without a single triangle.

Chapter 13

Debugging and Performance Optimization

WHAT YOU'LL LEARN IN THIS CHAPTER

- How to figure out what's wrong when your application isn't doing what you want it to

- How to achieve the highest possible performance

- How to make sure you're making the best use of OpenGL that you can

By now, you've learned a lot about OpenGL. You'll probably have started writing some pretty complex programs of your own, and chances are they won't work first time — and even when you get them working, they won't go as fast as you'd like them to. In this chapter, we take a look at two important skill sets: debugging and performance tuning. The first helps you to just get your application running *correctly*. The second helps you to get it to run *fast*. Both are important for production-quality applications that must run on the widest range of hardware possible.

Debugging Your Applications

It is an all-too-common scenario that you'll invent a nifty new algorithm for rendering something; set up all your textures, vertices, framebuffers, and other data that you'll need; start calling drawing commands; and either see nothing, or see something other than what you wanted. In this section we'll cover two very powerful assets that are available to you to assist in the debugging of your application. The first is the *debug context*, which is a mode of OpenGL that provides thorough error checking and feedback about your use of the OpenGL API. The second is the tools that are freely available to help you debug your application. Running your application inside one of these tools can provide you with great insight about its behavior and the use of OpenGL, and some tools can even give you advice about how you might change your application to make it run faster.

Debug Contexts

When you create an OpenGL context, you have the option of creating it in one of several modes. One of these modes is the *debug context*. When you create a debug context, OpenGL installs additional layers between your application and the normal paths it will take into the drivers and ultimately to the GPU. These additional layers perform strict error checking, analysis of your parameters, recording of errors, and a number of other things that would normally be too expensive to penalize a production-ready, debugged application with. The method with which you create a debug context is platform specific and will be covered in Chapter 14. For now, we can use the sb6 application class to create a debug context for us. To explicitly create a debug context, override the sb6::application::init() function, and set the debug flag in the application info structure as shown in Listing 13.1.

```
void my_application::init()
{
    sb6::application::init();

    info.flags.debug = 1;
}
```

Listing 13.1: Creating a debug context with the sb6 framework

In debug builds, the sb6 base class automatically sets this bit, and if debug contexts are available, it will create one. In this case, you don't need to do anything. If you want to create a debug context in release builds of your application (or if you want to force a non-debug context in a debug build), you'll need to override the init() function as shown in Listing 13.1.

Once you have created a debug context, you need to give it a way to notify your application when something goes wrong. To do this, OpenGL uses a *callback function* that is specified using a function pointer. The definition of the callback function pointer type is

```
typedef void (APIENTRY * GLDEBUGPROC)(GLenum source,
                                      GLenum type,
                                      GLuint id,
                                      GLenum severity,
                                      GLsizei length,
                                      const GLchar* message,
                                      void* userParam);
```

The function is defined to have the same calling conventions as OpenGL API functions — this is the purpose of the APIENTRY macro, which is defined by the OpenGL header files to the correct thing for the platform for which the code is being compiled. To implement the debug callback, create a function with the appropriate signature, and then call **glDebugMessageCallback()**, whose prototype is

```
void glDebugMessageCallback(GLDEBUGPROC callback,
                            void * userParam);
```

Here, callback is a pointer to your debug output callback function, and the userParam parameter is simply stored by OpenGL and passed back to your callback function in its userParam parameter. An example of this is shown in Listing 13.2.

```
static void APIENTRY simple_print_callback(GLenum source,
                                           GLenum type,
                                           GLuint id,
                                           GLenum severity,
                                           GLsizei length,
                                           const GLchar* message,
                                           void* userParam)
{
    printf("Debug message with source 0x%04X, type 0x%04X, "
           "id %u, severity 0x%0X, '%s'\n",
           source, type, id, severity, message);
}

void initialize_debug_output()
{
    glDebugMessageCallback(&simple_print_callback, NULL);
}
```

Listing 13.2: Setting the debug callback function

Once you have set up a debug callback function, OpenGL will call it whenever it needs to report information to your application. You should be careful not to call any OpenGL functions from inside the callback function. This is not legal and, should your OpenGL code cause an error (which might end up calling your callback function again), could easily cause an infinite loop and crash your program. In the simple example of Listing 13.2, we just print the message along with the raw values of several of the parameters using the C function `printf`. Again, in debug builds, the `sb6` application framework installs a default debug callback function that simply prints the received message. However, if you want more advanced control over the formatting of your messages, or if you're not using the `sb6` application framework, you can use the parameters of the callback function to your advantage.

In the callback function, the `source` parameter indicates which part of OpenGL the message originated from. It may be one of the following values:

- `GL_DEBUG_SOURCE_API` indicates that the message was generated by the use of the OpenGL API — perhaps you passed an incorrect value for a parameter for example. The message will tell you which parameter, why the value was incorrect, and what the range of acceptable values is.

- `GL_DEBUG_SOURCE_SHADER_COMPILER` is normally used by OpenGL to send compilation errors and warning messages to your application. Very often, this will be the same information that is stored in the shader and program information logs.

- `GL_DEBUG_SOURCE_WINDOW_SYSTEM` indicates that the issue was raised by some interaction with the window system or perhaps the operating system.

- `GL_DEBUG_SOURCE_THIRD_PARTY` suggests that the message came from a tool, utility library, or other source outside the OpenGL driver.

- `GL_DEBUG_SOURCE_APPLICATION` says that the message came from *your application*. That's right — you can insert messages into the log, which we will get to in a moment.

- `GL_DEBUG_SOURCE_OTHER` is a catch-all category for anything that doesn't fit anywhere else.

The `type` parameter gives you further information about what the message is for. It can take one of the following values:

- `GL_DEBUG_TYPE_ERROR` means that an error has occurred. For example, if the source is the OpenGL API, **glGetError()** will probably return an error code. If the source is the shader compiler, then it probably means that one of your shaders failed to compile.

- GL_DEBUG_TYPE_DEPRECATED_BEHAVIOR means that you've attempted to use features that are marked for deprecation (which means that they will removed from future versions of OpenGL).

- GL_DEBUG_TYPE_UNDEFINED_BEHAVIOR indicates that something your application is trying to do will produce undefined behavior, and that even if it might work on *this particular* OpenGL implementation, this is not standard and might break if you run it on another computer.

- GL_DEBUG_TYPE_PERFORMANCE messages are generated by OpenGL when it is trying to warn you that something you're doing isn't likely to perform well. The message may even include information about what you could consider doing instead.

- GL_DEBUG_TYPE_PORTABILITY suggests that you are using OpenGL in a way that is well defined, but possibly only on your implementation of OpenGL. This means that your code might not be portable.

- GL_DEBUG_TYPE_MARKER is used to insert events into the OpenGL command stream that can be picked up by tools and other debugging aids.

- GL_DEBUG_TYPE_PUSH_GROUP and GL_DEBUG_TYPE_POP_GROUP messages are generated when you use the **glPushDebugGroup()** and **glPopDebugGroup()** functions that are explained later in this section.

- GL_DEBUG_TYPE_OTHER is used for any messages that don't cleanly fit into any of the preceding categories.

The severity argument may be one of GL_DEBUG_SEVERITY_LOW, GL_DEBUG_SEVERITY_MEDIUM, or GL_DEBUG_SEVERITY_HIGH to indicate that the message is of low, medium, or high severity, respectively. It could also be GL_DEBUG_SEVERITY_NOTIFICATION if the message is for informational purposes and has no negative connotations.

In addition to the source, type, and severity properties, each message is assigned a unique identifier, which is passed to your callback function in the id parameter. Its actual value is implementation defined, but it can be used to refer to a specific message. The other parameters to the debug callback function are the length of the message string (in length), a pointer to the string itself (in message), and the userParam parameter that you passed to **glDebugMessageCallback()**. You can use this for whatever you want. For example, you could put a pointer to an instance of a class in it, a file handle, or any other type of object that can be represented as a pointer.

You can tell OpenGL which types of messages you want to receive by calling the **glDebugMessageControl()** function. Its prototype is

```
void glDebugMessageControl(GLenum source,
                           GLenum type,
                           GLenum severity,
                           GLsizei count,
                           const GLuint * ids,
                           GLboolean enabled);
```

The source, type, and severity parameters together form a filter that is used to select the group of debugging messages that the function will affect. Each of the parameters can have one of the values that are passed in the similarly named parameters to the debug message callback function described earlier. Additionally, any combination of these parameters can be set to GL_DONT_CARE. If one of the parameters is GL_DONT_CARE, then it is effectively ignored for the purposes of filtering; otherwise, any message whose source, type, or severity matches the value passed will be included in the filter. Furthermore, if ids is not NULL, then it is considered to be a pointer to an array of count message identifiers. Any message whose identifier is in this list will be considered part of the filter.

Once the filter has been formed, the reporting of the resulting group of messages is enabled if enabled is GL_TRUE and is disabled if it is GL_FALSE. Using **glDebugMessageControl()**, you can effectively turn on or off reporting of particular classes of messages. For example, to turn on all high severity messages, but turn off any message produced by the shader compiler, you could call

```
// Enable all messages with high severity
glDebugMessageControl(GL_DONT_CARE,                   // Source
                      GL_DONT_CARE,                   // Type
                      GL_DEBUG_SEVERITY_HIGH,         // Severity
                      0, NULL,                        // Count, ids
                      GL_TRUE);                       // Enable

// Disable messages from the shader compiler
glDebugMessageControl(GL_DEBUG_SOURCE_SHADER_COMPILER,
                      GL_DONT_CARE,
                      GL_DONT_CARE,
                      0, NULL,
                      GL_FALSE);
```

In addition to debug messages that might be produced by the OpenGL implementation, you can insert your own messages into the debug output stream. When you do this, your debug callback function will be called, and so you can record these messages using the same logging mechanisms you might implement for regular debugging messages. To inject your own message into the debug output log, call

```
void glDebugMessageInsert(GLenum source,
                          GLenum type,
                          GLuint id,
                          GLenum severity,
                          GLsizei length,
                          const char * message);
```

Again, the source, type, id, and severity parameters have the same meanings as they do in the debug callback function. In fact, you can even pass sources such as GL_DEBUG_SOURCE_SHADER_COMPILER in these parameters, but really the GL_DEBUG_SOURCE_APPLICATION token is reserved for application use and the GL_DEBUG_SOURCE_THIRD_PARTY is designed for tools and utility libraries. OpenGL will not generate messages with these sources. As most of the debug messages are intended to warn you of bad behavior, the GL_DEBUG_TYPE_MARKER is reserved for informational messages. Tools may intercept this message stream and treat it specially. The length parameter contains the length of the string pointed to by message. If length is 0, then message is considered to be a null-terminated string.

You can group messages together into hierarchical sets called *debug groups*. Tools that capture debug output may, for instance, indent groups of messages or color them differently in a log viewer. When OpenGL starts up, it will use the default group. Further groups can be created by pushing them onto the debug group stack. To do this, call

```
void glPushDebugGroup(GLenum source,
                      GLuint id,
                      GLsizei length,
                      const char * message);
```

When you do this, a copy of the current debug state will made and copied to the top location of the debug stack. At the same time, a debug message will be generated and sent to your callback function. It will have its type set to GL_DEBUG_TYPE_PUSH_GROUP and its severity set to GL_DEBUG_SEVERITY_NOTIFICATION. It will have the source and identifier specified in the source and id parameters, respectively. As with **glDebugMessageInsert()**, message and length specify the address of the message string and its length, respectively, and if length is 0, then message is considered to point to a null-terminated string.

When you want to leave a debug group, call

```
void glPopDebugGroup(void);
```

Again, **glPopDebugGroup()** will produce another debug message, this time with the type parameter set to GL_DEBUG_TYPE_POP_GROUP but with all the other parameters set to the same thing as the corresponding message from when the group was pushed.

When OpenGL produces debug messages, it will usually refer to objects such as textures, buffers, framebuffers, and so on by their number (the name you pass to OpenGL functions). This might be a bit confusing if you need to trawl through hundreds of lines of log looking for usage of a specific texture. To make this a little easier, you can assign human-readable names to objects by calling **glObjectLabel()** or **glObjectPtrLabel()**, whose prototypes are

```
void glObjectLabel(GLenum identifier,
                   GLuint name,
                   GLsizei length,
                   const char * label);

void glObjectPtrLabel(void * ptr,
                      GLsizei length,
                      const char * label);
```

When you call **glObjectLabel()**, you should pass in identifier the type of object referred to by name, which is the name of the object. identifier may be one of the following:

- GL_BUFFER if name is the name of a buffer object.

- GL_FRAMEBUFFER if name is the name of a framebuffer object.

- GL_PROGRAM_PIPELINE if name is the name of a program pipeline object.

- GL_PROGRAM if name is the name of a program object.

- GL_QUERY if name is the name of a query object.

- GL_RENDERBUFFER if name is the name of a renderbuffer object.

- GL_SAMPLER if name is the name of a sampler object.

- GL_SHADER if name is the name of a shader object.

- GL_TEXTURE if name is the name of a texture object.

- GL_TRANSFORM_FEEDBACK if name is the name of a transform feedback object.

- GL_VERTEX_ARRAY if name is the name of a vertex array object.

For **glObjectPtrLabel()**, the object is identified by a pointer type. This function is used for objects that have pointer types in OpenGL, which is currently only sync objects.

For both functions, the label and length parameters specify the name of the object and the length of the name, respectively. Again, if length is 0, then label is considered to point to a null-terminated string. Once you've given an object a name, OpenGL will use the text name rather than the raw number in debug messages. For example, you could set the debug object label of texture objects to the name of the file from which they were loaded.

Performance Optimization

Once your application is running correctly, you might want to undertake some level of performance optimization and tuning. Improving the performance of your application does two things:

- It lowers the minimum specification of the computer needed to run the application, increasing the potential user base.

- It increases the amount of time you might have in any given frame to apply additional special effects, render more geometry, or run more complex shaders.

In this section, we will cover the use of performance analysis tools to measure where your application might be spending its time and possibly highlight some areas where you might be able to improve its usage of the computing resources at your disposal. Next, we'll take a look at some things that you can do in your application to make sure that it's efficient.

Performance Analysis Tools

In this section, we'll cover some of the performance analysis tools that are freely available and don't rely on any non-free tools. That is, you can go download and install them right now! The first of these tools is *GPUView*, which is part of the *Windows Performance Toolkit* by Microsoft. The second is AMD's *GPU PerfStudio 2*. Both of these tools are available for download from their respective vendors' Web sites.

Windows Performance Toolkit and GPUView

Microsoft's Windows Performance Toolkit (WPT) is a suite of tools for measuring the performance of various parts of the Windows operating system. It can measure CPU usage and events, memory and disk accesses, network activity, and a multitude of other things. What we are most interested in here is GPU activity.

Modern graphics processors operate by processing *command buffers*, which are sequences of commands encoded in some form of byte code and sent from the application (or in this case, the OpenGL driver) to the graphics card. Sending a command buffer to the graphics card is sometimes known as submission. The GPU picks up the command buffers, interprets their contents, and acts on the instructions they contain. Command buffers are stored in one or more queues. When the driver first submits a command buffer for execution, the operating system (or some component of it) manages that queue and holds the command buffer in a ring waiting to send it to the hardware — this queue is referred to as the *software queue* or *CPU queue*. Once the hardware is ready to execute a new command buffer, a low level component of the graphics driver signals the GPU to pick up the command buffer at the front of the queue and execute it. The GPU can usually get one or more command buffers lined up and ready to execute while it is still working on previously enqueued buffers. The command buffers that have been sent to the hardware but are still waiting to execute are held in a *hardware queue*.

GPUView is a tool that is included in the WPT that is designed to allow you to visualize command buffer submission and the activity in the hardware and software queues. It can track all of the submissions that the application makes (through the OpenGL driver) into the operating system queues, tell you what type of submissions are being made, and show how they get batched up, sent to the hardware, and executed. You can see how long each command buffer spent waiting in the software queues before being sent to the hardware, how long each spent in the hardware queue, and how long it spent being executed. An annotated screenshot of GPUView running is shown in Figure 13.1.

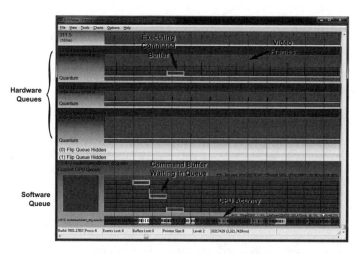

Figure 13.1: GPUView in action

The application under analysis is Figure 13.1 is the asteroid field example
from Chapter 7, a screenshot of which is shown in Figure 7.9. This
particular application uses almost all of the available GPU time. The
system used to capture this trace contained an AMD Phenom X6 1050T
processor with six CPU cores and an NVIDIA GeForce GTX 560 SE graphics
card with two displays attached to it. The application was running in full
screen on one of the displays while the other display was used for
development tools. The top hardware queue is clearly executing the
application under test. The small submissions on the second queue are
Windows' Desktop Window Manager (DWM) performing composition on
the second display. The vertical lines running through the trace are the
vertical refresh events that are associated with the display. In this
application, synchronization to vertical refresh (also known as vsync) is
off. Now take a look at Figure 13.2.

In Figure 13.2, we start running the application in full-screen mode with
vsync turned off (which is the default). Then, during the run, we turn
on vsync. This point is clearly visible in the GPUView image. When vsync
is turned on, the software and hardware queues drain, and the operating
system takes over presentation of the rendered frames. When vsync is off,
OpenGL tells the graphics hardware to get done with what it's rendering
and show the result to the user as soon as possible. When it's on, the
operating system holds back the graphics hardware and tells it to wait for
a vertical refresh event before showing the frame to the user. This causes
the GPU to idle for short periods of time between each frame, which

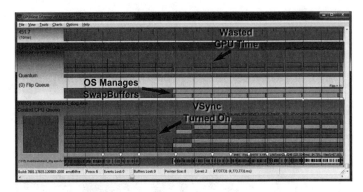

Figure 13.2: VSync seen in GPUView

shows up as gaps in the hardware queue. This is effectively wasted time.
Here, we have wasted time on purpose in order to not allow the
application to get too far ahead of the display (and to show what this
looks like in the tool). However, anything that causes the GPU to have to
wait will waste GPU time.

When you install the WPT, its program directory will contain a gpuview
folder, which is where the GPUView tool is located. In that same directory
is the file log.cmd, which is a script for starting and stopping recording of
logging events into ETL files — Event Trace Logs. This is the raw data that
is interpreted by the GPUView tool. ETL files can be extremely large. To
start recording data, run log.cmd from a command prompt with
administrative privileges, and then to stop it, run log.cmd again. Even
running a simple application for a minute or so can generate gigabytes of
data, so it's best to keep recording times short and sweet. Other
suggestions include minimizing the number of other applications running
(especially those with graphical output) and disabling the Aero user
interface (which turns off DWM composition). Also, you can implement a
pause feature in your application such that it can be made to stop
rendering. Then, pause the application, start logging, allow the
application to render for a few seconds, pause it again, and then stop
logging. When logging is active, a number of ETL files are written into the
directory from which logging is started. One file is created for each of
several of the major Windows subsystems, and then when logging is
terminated, they are all merged together into a single file called
Merged.etl, which is what is loaded into GPUView.

In addition to regular command buffer submissions (referred to by
GPUView as *standard queue packets* in the CPU queue and *standard*

DMA packets once they reach the hardware), the tool can show you a number of other events that might be inserted into the graphics pipeline. For example, *present packets* are events that instruct the operating system to display the results of rendering (triggered by the **SwapBuffers()** command) and are displayed with a crosshatch pattern by GPUView. Clicking on a packet brings up a dialog similar to the one shown in Figure 13.3.

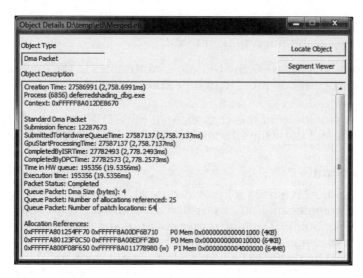

Figure 13.3: A packet dialog in GPUVIew

You can see a number of useful pieces of information in the dialog shown in Figure 13.3. First, we see several timestamps. The first is the packet creation time, which is the time that the command buffer was allocated (which is when the OpenGL would start filling it in). Next, we see the `SubmittedToHardwareQueueTime`, which is when the packet was sent to the hardware for processing. It is then picked up by the hardware at the time noted by `GpuStartProcessingTime`. When the GPU is done processing the packet, it triggers an interrupt, which is handled by an Interrupt Service Routine (ISR) — the time at which this interrupt is serviced by the ISR is shown in `CompletedByISRTime`. Next, the graphics subsystem processes the packet using a Deferred Procedure Call (DPC), and the time at which this completes is shown as `CompletedByDPCTime`. The total time between when the command buffer is submitted to the hardware (`SubmittedToHardwareQueueTime`) until the command buffer is completed and signals the ISR (`CompletedByISRTime`) is given by `Time in HW Queue`. This is effectively the amount of time it took the GPU to execute the command buffer, and the sum of these packets for a given frame places the upper limit on the frame rate of your application.

GPUView can show you quite a bit more information than this about your application's use of the graphics processor. As your applications become more and more complex, they will start to exhibit behavior that only a tool such as GPUView can show you. The goal of performance tuning is twofold:

• Ensure that the GPU does as much work as it is able to by feeding it efficiently and not causing it to stall.

• Ensure that the work the GPU does contributes to the final scene and that it doesn't do more than it needs to.

During the remainder of this chapter, we'll use GPUView to analyze our applications and show the effects of the tuning advice we'll give.

GPU PerfStudio 2

GPU PerfStudio 2 is a free tool provided by AMD that's designed for the analysis of graphics applications written using OpenGL and other graphics APIs. GPU PerfStudio 2 supports three major modes of operation — an API trace tool, a frame debugger, and a frame profiler. The frame profiler requires AMD hardware to be present, but the API trace and the frame debugger, work well on hardware from any vendor. Figure 13.4 shows a screenshot of GPU PerfStudio's API trace window running the displacement example from Chapter 8.

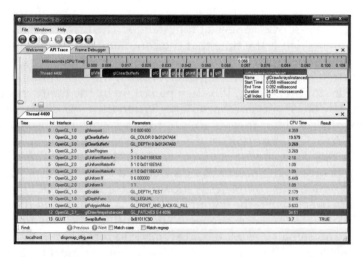

Figure 13.4: GPU PerfStudio 2 running the displacement mapping example

As you can see, the GPU PerfStudio has captured all of the OpenGL calls made by the application and has produced a timeline of the application making those calls. Along with each OpenGL command, the amount of CPU time taken to execute the call is shown in both the timeline and the function call list. The function call list also logs the parameters sent to each command. The frame debugger window of GPU PerfStudio 2 is shown in Figure 13.5 below.

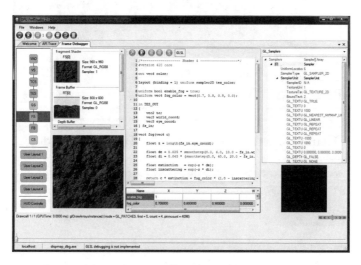

Figure 13.5: GPU PerfStudio 2 frame debugger

In the GPU PerfStudio 2 frame debugger, you can see the OpenGL pipeline with the vertex array object (VAO), vertex shader (VS), tessellation control and evaluation shaders (TCS and TES), fragment shader (FS), and framebuffer (FB) active in Figure 13.5. We also see that this particular drawing command is not using the geometry or compute shader stages (GS and CS). The fragment shader stage is selected, and in the main window, we see the source code of the current fragment shader along with the texture that's bound for rendering.

Finally, in addition to being able to display information about the timing of drawing commands, the resources bound, and the code used for shaders, GPU PerfStudio is able to overlay data *in your application*. By clicking on the HUD Controls button in the frame debugger, we receive the window shown in Figure 13.6.

By using the HUD control window shown in Figure 13.6, we can select certain textures for viewing inside the application whenever the application is paused. A screenshot of the landscape example from

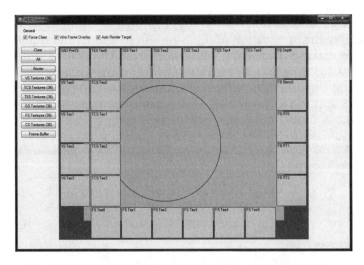

Figure 13.6: GPU PerfStudio 2 HUD control window

Figure 13.7: GPU PerfStudio 2 overlaying information

Chapter 8 with the in-use textures is shown in Figure 13.7. You can see in the figure that at the top left, the height map used by the tessellation evaluation shader is visible. On the top right of the screenshot is the depth buffer (pure white because it's been cleared to 1.0) and the content of the framebuffer. At the bottom left is the texture used by the fragment shader for shading the terrain.

If you happen to have access to AMD hardware, GPU PerfStudio 2 can read a number of hardware *performance counters* from OpenGL to measure the impact of the drawing commands that your application makes. This includes measurements of things like primitives processed, the amount of texture data read, the amount of information written to the framebuffer, and so on. This feature is called the Frame Profiler, and a screenshot of GPU PerfStudio in this mode is shown in Figure 13.8.

Figure 13.8: GPU PerfStudio 2 showing AMD performance counters

Because this mode isn't universally available, we will leave it as an exercise for AMD users to explore this feature on their own. GPU PerfStudio 2 comes with some excellent help documentation and more is available online.

Tuning Your Application for Speed

In this section, we discuss a number of things that you can do to make sure that your application runs more efficiently, minimize the amount of work that the OpenGL driver needs to do, and maximizes the amount of work you can get from a GPU.

Reading State or Data from OpenGL

In general, reading state or data back from OpenGL into your application is not a great idea. If we can offer one piece of advice, it's to not do anything that might stall the OpenGL pipeline. This includes reading the framebuffer using **glReadPixels()**; reading the results[1] of occlusion queries, transform feedback queries, or other objects whose results depend on rendering; or performing a wait on a fence that is unlikely to have completed. In particular, it should never be necessary to call **glFinish()**.

Furthermore, cases that might be less obvious can be avoided. For example, functions such as **glGetError()**, **glGetIntegerv()**, **glGetUniformLocation()**, and so on may not stall the GPU, but could well stall a multi-threaded driver and damage application performance. It's best to stay away from functions that have the words "Get" or "Is" in their names. Also, while it should be common sense to not allocate and destroy objects frequently during the normal operation of your application, try to avoid generating names through the various "Gen" functions.

In cases where reading data from OpenGL back into client memory, there are ways to achieve this without stalling — most of which involve allowing the GPU to lag far enough behind your application that it's almost certainly done gathering the information you need before you read it.

The first case we cover here is reading data from the framebuffer using **glReadPixels()**. If the intent is to use the resulting data for some other purpose in OpenGL, simply bind a buffer to the GL_PIXEL_PACK_BUFFER target, read pixel data into it, then bind the buffer to whichever target you want to use it with, and continue rendering. There is no reason for the pixel data to ever leave the graphics card's memory or for the CPU to ever see it. If, however, you really must have the data in application memory, you can get at it in a number of ways.

First, and simplest, is simply to call **glReadPixels()** and pass the address of a region of your application's memory into which OpenGL should place the data. In almost all cases, this will cause a bubble to form in the OpenGL pipeline. You can see the effect of this in Figure 13.9.

In Figure 13.9, the application starts by not calling **glReadPixels()** at all, and as you can see on the left of the capture, the GPU is nicely utilized, is not stalling, and always has at least one frame queued up ready to render. As soon as the application starts calling **glReadPixels()**, the CPU and GPU synchronize, and we can clearly see that the GPU is starving for work to do, with big gaps in its execution queue. Of course, we can bind a buffer

---

1. As noted in "Getting OpenGL to Make Decisions for You" back in Chapter 11, you can use conditional rendering to avoid reading the result of occlusion queries.

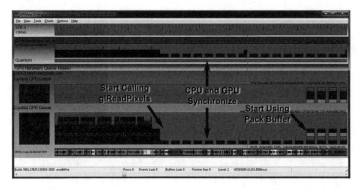

Figure 13.9: GPUView showing the effect of **glReadPixels()** into system memory

to the GL_PIXEL_PACK_BUFFER target before calling **glReadPixels()** to retrieve data into a pixel pack buffer, which is what we're doing towards the end of the trace in Figure 13.9. However, although there seems to be a significant change in activity, there are still gaps in the queue, which is not what we want at all.

What's happening here is that we're still calling **glReadPixels()**, but with a buffer bound to the GL_PIXEL_PACK_BUFFER target. This allows the GPU to complete rendering and then copy the resulting data into the buffer object without interruption. However, we then *read the data back* into the application by calling **glMapBufferRange()**. This means that our application has to wait for OpenGL to copy the data from the framebuffer into the buffer object before it can continue. This is even worse! Not only do we stall the GPU, but it actually does *more* work between each stall. Now take a look at Figure 13.10.

In this new trace, we see something interesting going on. Again, at first, we continue to call **glReadPixels()** to get the data into the buffer object and then immediately map it in order to get the data into our application. This is causing stalls and inefficient use of the GPU. However, part way through Figure 13.10 we change our strategy to one where we still call **glReadPixels()** to transfer data from the framebuffer into a buffer object, but then map the buffer from the *previous frame*. We create multiple buffer objects, and because we only map buffers that haven't been written to in at least one frame time, this gives the GPU more time to keep up with us. Although you can still see quite a bit of work going on, the GPU remains fully utilized, and the performance of our application is not significantly impacted.

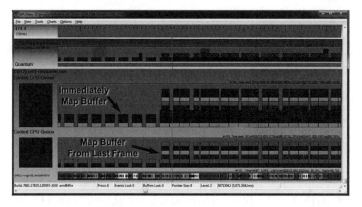

Figure 13.10: GPUView showing the effect of **glReadPixels()** into a buffer

Effective Buffer Mapping

Once you have a buffer object whose data store has been allocated using a call to **glBufferData()**, you can map the entire buffer into the application's memory by calling **glMapBuffer()**. However, there are several caveats to the use of this function. First, if you only want to overwrite some part of the buffer, the rest of the buffer remains intact, meaning that OpenGL has to keep that data alive. Another is that the buffer itself could be quite large, and OpenGL could fail to find enough available address space to provide you with a single pointer to one contiguous region of memory representing the buffer. Finally, if you want to write into the buffer, OpenGL either has to wait until the GPU is done reading from it before giving you the pointer, or it must keep multiple copies of the data around, giving you a pointer to one of the copies that is not in use by the GPU.

To address these issues, we can use the **glMapBufferRange()** function, which allows you to only map *part* of the buffer into your application, and also provides several more flags that can be used to control how the data is mapped and how synchronization is performed with the rest of the OpenGL pipeline. The prototype of **glMapBufferRange()** is

```
void *glMapBufferRange(GLenum target,
                       GLintptr offset,
                       GLsizeiptr length,
                       GLbitfield access);
```

The target parameter is the buffer target to which the buffer you wish to map is bound, just as in the other buffer functions such as **glMapBuffer()** and **glBindBuffer()**. The offset and length parameters specify the range of the buffer that you want to map. Their units are bytes, with offset zero being the first byte in the buffer and length being the size of the mapped range, in bytes. Besides being able to map a small part of the buffer, the additional power of **glMapBufferRange()** comes from the last parameter, access, which is used to specify a number of flags that control how the mapping is performed. Table 13.1 shows the possible bitfield values that can be passed in access.

Table 13.1: Map Buffer Access Types

Access Flags (GL_MAP_*)	Usage
READ_BIT	Returned pointer may be used for reading the buffer.
WRITE_BIT	Returned pointer may be used for modifying the buffer.
INVALIDATE_RANGE_BIT	Signals that OpenGL can throw away the previous contents of the mapped range. Data in the range is undefined unless updated by the application.
INVALIDATE_BUFFER_BIT	Signals that OpenGL can throw away the previous contents of the entire buffer. Data in the buffer is undefined unless updated by the application.
FLUSH_EXPLICIT_BIT	Using this bit with GL_MAP_WRITE_BIT requires an application to explicitly flush each range updated by calling **glFlushMappedBufferRange()**. If this bit is not specified, the entire mapped range will be flushed when **glUnmapBuffer()** is called.
UNSYNCHRONIZED_BIT	Tells OpenGL to avoid trying to synchronize any pending GPU writes to this buffer before mapping.

As you can see, **glMapBufferRange()** gives you quite a bit of control over how OpenGL performs the requested mapping operation. The GL_MAP_READ_BIT and GL_MAP_WRITE_BIT flags are pretty self-explanatory. Setting the read bit indicates that you wish to read from the buffer, and setting the write bit indicates that you want to write to it. They're a bit more strictly enforced with **glMapBufferRange()** than the equivalent GL_READ_ONLY and GL_WRITE_ONLY parameters to **glMapBuffer()**, though. Incorrect use can cause your application to crash, so get them right!

Of course, you can specify both the GL_MAP_READ_BIT and GL_MAP_WRITE_BIT flags at the same time by simply ORing them together.

The GL_MAP_INVALIDATE_RANGE_BIT and GL_MAP_INVALIDATE_BUFFER_BIT tell OpenGL that you don't care about the data in the buffer anymore and that it's free to throw it out if it wishes. If you don't need the old contents of the buffer after the mapping operation, it's important to set one of these bits;[2] otherwise, OpenGL has to make sure that whatever you don't write in the buffer has valid data after you unmap it. Setting the GL_MAP_INVALIDATE_RANGE_BIT tells OpenGL to discard the data in the range being mapped, whereas setting GL_MAP_INVALIDATE_BUFFER_BIT tells it to discard everything in the buffer, even parts outside the mapped range. If you map the whole range of the buffer by setting offset to zero and length to the size of the buffer object, then these two bits become equivalent.

You use the GL_MAP_FLUSH_EXPLICIT_BIT flag if you want to overwrite only part of the buffer, but you don't know which parts, when you call **glMapBufferRange()**. This tells OpenGL that you might overwrite the whole range, or just a single byte of it, and that when you know what got overwritten, you will tell it. To do that, call **glFlushMappedBufferRange()**, whose prototype is

```
GLvoid glFlushMappedBufferRange(GLenum target,
                                GLintptr offset,
                                GLsizeiptr length);
```

You can also use **glFlushMappedBufferRange()** if you want to update multiple independent regions of the buffer but don't want to make multiple calls to **glMapBufferRange()**. A second possible benefit of calling **glFlushMappedBufferRange()** is that if you map a very large buffer and then update different ranges of it over time, you can use **glFlushMappedBufferRange()** to tell OpenGL that you're done with updating parts of it as you go. This might allow OpenGL to overlap work such as moving data to the GPU's memory with any additional work that your application might be doing, such as reading data from a file. You should be careful with GL_MAP_FLUSH_EXPLICIT_BIT as setting it and then not calling **glFlushMappedBufferRange()** correctly will likely result in your new data not being used.

---

2. You could set both, but GL_MAP_INVALIDATE_BUFFER_BIT is clearly a superset of GL_MAP_INVALIDATE_RANGE_BIT.

Finally, GL_MAP_UNSYNCHRONIZED_BIT tells OpenGL not to wait until it's done using the data in a buffer before giving you a pointer to the buffer's memory. If you don't set this flag and OpenGL is planning to give you a pointer to the same memory that's about to be used by a previously issued command, it will wait for that command to finish executing before returning, which can slow your application down. However, if you know that you won't overwrite any data that hasn't already been used, you can set this bit to turn off that synchronization. If you do this, though, you're on your own. There are a number of mechanisms to provide your own synchronization, from calling **glFinish()** (which is a bit like a sledgehammer — don't call this), to fences, which we covered in "Synchronization and Fences" back in Chapter 11.

Finally, it should be clear that calling **glMapBufferRange()** with offset set to zero and length set to the size of the buffer object being mapped, and with the GL_MAP_READ_BIT and GL_MAP_WRITE_BIT flags set appropriately, is essentially equivalent to calling **glMapBuffer()**. However, **glMapBufferRange()** gives you so much additional flexibility that it's recommended that you always prefer **glMapBufferRange()** over **glMapBuffer()**, making sure to set the read, write, invalidation, and synchronization flags appropriately.

Use the Features OpenGL Gives You

OpenGL is a large and feature-packed programming interfaces. Some parts of it are more advanced than others, while other things aren't quite optimal. One advantage of this is that this makes it relatively easy to just get something simple working quickly. The disadvantage, of course, is that you need to know an awful lot in order to make a OpenGL program that truly makes use of all of the advanced features of the API.

One of the things that OpenGL has quite a few of is *container objects*. These are objects that represent blocks of state, and examples are vertex array objects, framebuffer objects, and transform feedback objects. In general, you should prefer to use a container object rather than modifying lots of state. For example, a vertex array object contains the state for all of the vertex arrays associated with the front end of OpenGL. This includes the bound buffer stores; the vertex attribute formats, strides, and offsets within those stores; and which attributes are enabled and disabled. You can very quickly switch between complete sets of information using a single call to **glBindVertexArray()**. The sb6::object object wrapper internally uses a vertex array object to represent all of its vertex array state. When you call `sb6::object::render`, it simply binds the vertex array object and calls the appropriate drawing command, giving it extremely low software overhead.

Likewise, for framebuffer state, framebuffer objects wrap up all of the parameters describing the color, depth, and stencil attachments of the current framebuffer. It is far more efficient to create a framebuffer once at initialization time and then bind it before rendering than it is to explicitly reconfigure the current attachments on a single framebuffer object right before rendering.

Finally, transform feedback objects wrap up all of the state required to represent the transform feedback stage of OpenGL. Not only is it required to use a transform feedback object if you want to make use of `glDrawTransformFeedback()` or any of its variants, but it is substantially more efficient to make a single call to `glBindTransformFeedback()` than it is to reconfigure all of the transform-feedback-related state directly before use.

Use Only the Data You Need

Just because the inputs to your vertex shader are floating point, or the return value from the GLSL `texture` function are floating point, doesn't mean that you need to store the data in memory as floating-point data. In many cases, smaller data formats are sufficient to represent the data you'll actually be using. Using more data than you need can have two effects:

- Your application will use more memory than is really necessary, meaning that OpenGL may not be able to fit all your data in the most optimal areas of memory — or worse, it may just fail to allocate data for your objects at all.

- The more data OpenGL must read from your buffers, the more pressure will be put on resources such as caches, memory controllers, and so on. This can reduce absolute performance. Also, the buses that connect GPUs to memories are big power consumers, and so producing more memory accesses can increase power consumption of a device and drain batteries faster.

For example, for position data (which is normally stored in object space), there is almost no requirement for full floating-point precision. In a preprocessing step, try normalizing your object-space data such that it lies in the region −1.0 to 1.0. This will allow you to store coordinates using signed normalized data — for example by passing GL_SHORT to `glVertexAttribPointer()` and setting the `normalized` parameter to GL_TRUE. You can then include a scale factor in any model matrices to return the object to its original scale, for free. This allows you to use only 16 bits per component rather than the 32 that would be needed for full-precision floating-point data, and at the same time provides for more precision than would be afforded by 16-bit half-precision floating-point data.

Furthermore, for object-space coordinate data, the w component is virtually always 1.0. Therefore, there's really no reason to store it — you may as well store only three components and assume that the fourth is 1.0. Similar tactics can be used for object normals and tangents. In object files, normals (and tangents) are usually stored in object space. When you want to perform normal mapping, bump mapping or any other technique that might rely on tangents and normals (see "Normal Mapping" back in Chapter 12), we use those the tangent and normal to construct the binormal by taking their cross product, and then use the tangent, binormal, and normal to construct our TBN matrix. The precision required for the normal and tangent vectors is generally not that high. In fact, 10 bits is generally enough, and so you could consider using packed data for them. To do this, pass GL_INT_2_10_10_10_REV as the `type` parameter to `glVertexAttribPointer()`. Again, this uses signed normalized data (the `normalized` parameter being set to GL_TRUE) and provides a similar level of precision as 16-bit half-precision floating-point data in the range -1.0 to 1.0.

When it comes to storing normals in textures, you can take this one step further by making the assumption that because normals are in tangent space and that they all point *away* from the surface, their z components are always positive. Now, also considering that the normals stored in your normal map are always unit length (that is, they are normalized), we know that

$$x^2 + y^2 + z^2 = 1.0$$
$$z^2 = 1.0 - x^2 - y^2$$
$$z = \sqrt{1.0 - x^2 - y^2}$$

Given this, we can store only the x and y components of our tangent space normals in our normal maps and then reconstruct the z component in our fragment shader. This is known as trading texture performance for ALU (Arithmetic and Logic Unit) performance. Graphics processors generally have substantially more performance available for performing general math operations than memory transactions. It can often turn out to be a net win to do more math in your shader if it can avoid consumption of memory bandwidth. A reasonable format for normal maps is a two-component, 8-bit signed normalized format. Here, x and y are stored with 7 bits of precision (plus the sign bit), and the z component is reconstructed from the x and y components on use.

Applying texture compression to normal maps usually doesn't turn out well. There are some texture compression formats that are designed to be able to cope with normal data, but all too often discontinuities in normals are seen. However, for other data such as diffuse and specular albedos, compressed textures can work well. You should always consider whether a compressed texture can adequately represent your data.

The preceding advice focuses on data that might be read by OpenGL, but it also holds for data *written* by OpenGL. For example, if you are rendering to an off-screen texture using an FBO and want to use HDR, it might be tempting to make all of your framebuffer attachments use the GL_RGBA32F internal format and be done with it. However, this consumes very large amounts of memory both for storage and in bandwidth terms. If you don't need the rendered textures to hold an alpha channel, don't allocate one! Rather, use GL_RGB32F. Better yet, if you don't need a full 32-bits of precision, consider using GL_RGBA16F.

Similar advice holds true for operations such as writing into images from shader or using transform feedback, although you should be aware that the number of formats that are writable with these methods may not be as great as those that are writable through framebuffer operations, or are readable by the front end. Even so, in many of these cases, it's quite possible to use GLSL's packing functions to construct the data in your shader and then write it into integer images or buffers.

Shader Compilation Performance

Not only does OpenGL do graphics well, but it also includes a complete compiler environment! Of course, you've been using this all throughout this book, and by now you should have realized that GLSL is pretty complex, and so GLSL compilers have to do quite a bit of work to make sure that your shaders are compiled correctly and efficiently to run on the underlying graphics hardware. While you might not think that shader compilation performance can affect the running time of your application (after all, you don't compile shaders in the middle of rendering... do you?), it actually does impact the user's experience when they run your application.

First, and most obviously, the startup time of your application is going to be affected by how quickly you can get all the shaders ready for running. Some OpenGL implementations may use additional CPU threads to compile your shaders and may even be able to compile multiple shaders in parallel. However, just as you should consider the OpenGL pipeline as something that shouldn't be stalled, you can consider OpenGL drivers and implementations as pipelines — even before the GPU gets involved. So, if you compile a shader using `glCompileShader()` and then immediately call `glGetShaderiv()` to get the compilation status or the shader's info log, you will stall such an implementation because it must complete compilation of your shader in order to give you your answer. Rather than simply running through all the shaders your application needs, compiling them one at a time and then querying their compilation results, you can do the following:

- Run through the list of shaders that you'll need to compile, create their shader objects, and call `glCompileShader()` on each one, but don't query the compilation result.

- In *debug* or *development* builds of your application, either query the compilation results and the information log after all of the shaders have been compiled, or simply rely on debug output to send the log to you. Make sure you have a way to turn this off, though. Presumably, once your shaders are debugged and your application is ready to ship, you won't need the compilation status as you can assume that it's always successful.

- Likewise, for your program objects, run through a list of all of the program objects your application needs, attach shaders to them, and call `glLinkProgram()`, but don't query the link result — again, this can be deferred or only included in debug builds of your application.

In large applications, you will undoubtedly have a very large number of shaders, and possibly a huge number of combinations of shaders, that need to be linked into program objects. A naïve way to manage this is to simply create a set of shader objects for each combination, re-compile each shader as it's referenced, and attach it to the resulting program objects in a one-to-one relationship. However, seeing as you can attach a shader to multiple program objects, it's reasonable to load all of the shaders you might need, compile them each once, then attach the compiled shaders as needed to program objects, and link them. This allows the OpenGL implementation to cache compiled shader data inside the shader objects and not have to regenerate it multiple times.

There may be some GPU-side performance advantages to using large, monolithic program objects, but more often than not, well-written shaders don't see much gain from this. Therefore, if you have a large number of shaders, you might want to consider compiling and linking them into *separable program objects*. You might want to have a program object for each combination of front-end shaders that you're likely to use, and a program object with just a fragment shader in it just for the back end. This might allow the OpenGL implementation to, for example, optimize tessellation control and evaluation shaders together, or vertex and geometry shaders, whilst leaving the interface from the front end and back end as separable.

When you do use separate shader objects and link your program in separable mode, you attach them to another container object, the *program pipeline object*. This object can store validated information about the stages in the current pipeline, and it will be more efficient to switch between multiple program pipeline objects than to reconfigure a single program pipeline object when you want to switch shaders. While creating a program pipeline object for each combination of shaders your application is going to use might land you with the same combinatorial explosion of pipeline objects, it may be worthwhile maintaining a list of 100 or so objects and then using them as a cache. If the pipeline object you need is still in the cache, pull it out and use it. If not, either add a new object to the cache, or pull an object from the cache and reconfigure it for your use. This allows you to rapidly switch between combinations of program stages without necessarily maintaining a pipeline object for each combination of states.

Once you have done your best to keep your application's shader management in good shape, it might be worthwhile taking a look at the complexity of your shaders themselves. Shader compilation consists of many parts. First, the preprocessor is run, which expands macros, removes comments, and so on. Next, the shader is tokenized, checked for syntax, and finally compiled into an internal format, at which place optimization and code generation takes place. Often, code optimizers will operate by making a pass over a section of code, performing local optimizations as it can, and then saving the result. It will then make subsequent passes, repeating the process until no more optimizations can be made, or until some maximum number of passes is performed. When the optimizer stops running, one of two things will have happened:

- If the optimizer stops because it cannot find any more transformations to make on your code, the resulting executable is probably as efficient as its going to get, but the optimizer may have taken many passes over the shader to reach this point, increasing optimization time.

- If the optimizer stops because it has run out of available passes, it's quite possible that the code is not as optimal as it could be. Plus, the optimizer has burned all of the time that it has allotted to it.

To cope with this, it is in your best interest as a developer to help the shader compiler to do the best job that it can. First, and most obviously, try to write efficient shader code. However, you can also do a number of other things to improve the run-time performance of OpenGL shader compilers. First, you can run your compiler through a preprocessor offline, ahead of shipping your application. This allows you to use macros, preprocessor definitions, and other features of the preprocessor, but doesn't place a burden on the shader compiler to produce the final shader for you.

If you want take things further, you can *pre-optimize* your shaders. This effectively involves running them through an off-line shader compiler that preprocesses, parses, and compiles your shader code into an intermediate representation and then performs many common optimizations on it (such as dead code elimination, constant folding and propagation, common sub-expression elimination, and so forth) and then spits the optimized code back out *as GLSL*. When the run-time GLSL compiler takes this shader and tries to optimize it, it should find that there's not much to do and finish quickly.

Finally, we covered *program binaries* back in Chapter 6. Program binaries offer you a way to compile your shaders and link them into program objects once, and then save off the results into files. When you need the program again, rather than compiling it from source code, you can simply load up the program binary and hand it to OpenGL to use. OpenGL can almost certainly skip most, if not all, of the compilation procedures by caching information in the binaries it gives you. With program binaries, you may be able to completely eliminate shader compilation or at least greatly reduce the time it takes.

Making Use of Multiple GPUs

Some users choose to install multiple graphics cards in a single machine and produce what is known as a *multi-gpu* system. AMD calls this *CrossFire*, whilst NVIDIA calls it *SLI*. Whatever the name, the technique used to improve performance by using multiple graphics cards is usually to render in what is known as *alternate frame rendering* (or AFR) mode, where one GPU renders a frame, the next GPU renders the next frame, and so on for as many GPUs as there are in the system. Most such systems have only two GPUs in them, but some may have three, four, or even more present. Also, AFR isn't the only way to achieve scaling using multiple GPUs, but it certainly the most common.

There is one single piece of advice that is commonly given when optimizing for AFR systems: Avoid producing data on one GPU and then using it on another. There are two reasons for this. First, it means that the two GPUs must be synchronized — as one relies on the output of the other, the GPUs can't run in parallel, and the performance advantages of having two or more GPUs in a single system are lost. Second, the cost of actually moving the data from one GPU to another is high as it must generally cross a bus (such as PCI-express), which has much lower throughput than the memory on the graphics card.

While this advice might seem obvious, it's not obvious at first what types of operations might trigger OpenGL to have to transfer data from one GPU to another. Here is list of behaviors that might trigger a copy operation from one GPU to another.

- Rendering into a texture and then using it in the next frame. This is perhaps the most obvious reason to need to transfer a texture between GPUs. For example, if you write an application that produces a dynamic environment map and try to optimize it by only updating the environment every other frame, you might find that it does indeed go faster on single GPU systems. However, on a multi-GPU system that environment must cross the bus after being rendered into, and this will cause a GPU synchronization. It may be better to generate a new environment map every frame in this case, and avoid the copy. If you must reuse resources, try to always reuse the resource from *two* frames ago if there is a chance you're running on a dual GPU system.

- Rendering into a texture without clearing it first. This was a common trick used in the late 1990s to avoid the memory bandwidth costs of clearing the framebuffer when the application developer knows that they will overwrite the whole thing by the end of the frame anyway. This is almost universally a bad idea on modern graphics hardware. First, any hardware designed in the last decade likely implements some form of compression for framebuffers, allowing it to *very* quickly clear the framebuffer. Not clearing the framebuffer will likely turn off compression and make your application run slower, even on single-GPU systems. On multi-GPU systems, the issue is more severe. If you don't clear the framebuffer, then OpenGL doesn't know that when you start drawing into it again that you're going to overwrite everything, which means that before it can execute the first drawing command, it must wait for the previous frame to complete (on the other GPU), and then transfer the result to the new GPU so that any part of it that's not overwritten has valid data in it.

- Writing into buffer objects in one frame and then using the result in another frame can cause synchronization and transfers. For example, if you implement one of the physics simulation algorithms described earlier in the book, you may find that the application doesn't scale because each step of the algorithm relies on data produced in the previous frame. If your application has some awareness that it's running on two GPUs, you may want to effectively run two copies of the physics simulation in parallel, the second a half step ahead of the other and occasionally synchronize them.

- Using conditional rendering with the result of an occlusion query generated by one GPU used to determine execution of commands on the other will cause GPUs to synchronize. While the amount of data transferred to convey the result of the occlusion query probably isn't large, the synchronization may have a devastating effect on performance. If you can, either issue the occlusion queries very early in the frame and then use their results very late in the frame, or use two sets of occlusion queries in order to use the result of queries issued two frames earlier. Don't forget, you'll need to make this delay longer if there are more GPUs present.

Unfortunately, there is no standard way of determining whether your application is running on a multi-GPU system, or how many GPUs are present. Although some extensions exist for this purpose, there are also extensions that allow you to create contexts that render explicitly to one of the GPUs in a multi-GPU set. If these are available, and you're willing to go that far, you might want to see if you can scale the performance of your application by rendering different parts of your scene on different GPUs and explicitly merging the results.

Using Multiple Threads

OpenGL is fully multi-threaded and has a well-defined threading model. Each thread owns a "current context," and changing contexts for a thread is performed by calling `wglMakeCurrent()`, `glXMakeCurrent()`, or the equivalent for your platform from that thread. Once contexts are current for a thread, the thread can create objects, compile shaders, load textures, and even render into windows at the same time. This is in addition to any multi-threading that OpenGL drivers may implement internally on your behalf. In fact, if you look at your application running inside a debugger or other profiling tool, you may well see multiple threads that have their starting procedure inside the OpenGL driver for your graphics card.

Although OpenGL does have a well-supported multi-threading system, and a well-defined object sharing model that allows multiple contexts that are current in different threads to use the same set of objects, this may not be what you want. For example, it's very tempting to simply decide that you'll create two contexts, make one current in each of two threads, and then use one for loading textures and compiling shaders while the other does the rendering. If you do this, though, you might find that you don't get the performance scaling that you want. Ultimately, there is one GPU and one command buffer, and OpenGL guarantees that everything is rendered in a well-defined order. That means that most access to OpenGL will be serialized, and the overhead of synchronizing and coordinating access to OpenGL from multiple threads may well outweigh any benefits of having multiple CPUs work on your application for you.

To avoid the serialization issues, it's also tempting to create two or more contexts and just switch between them using `wglMakeCurrent()` (or your platform's equivalent) in a single thread. While this does help you isolate state changes from one context to another, switching contexts can be an expensive operation. In particular, most window system bindings specify that switching contexts comes with an implicit flush.

Having said that, there are many ways to use multiple threads in an OpenGL application. First, most complex applications will have non-graphics tasks (such as artificial intelligence, sound effects, object management, input and network handling, physics simulation, and so on) going on that can be offloaded to other threads. Now, create a single OpenGL context, and make it current in your main "rendering" thread. This thread will be the only one that actually talks to OpenGL — it will be the arbiter of all things graphics.

Next, suppose you want to upload some texture data from a file into a texture object. Here, your main OpenGL thread will create a buffer object, bind it to the GL_PIXEL_UNPACK_BUFFER target, and then map it for writing into. It will then signal a worker thread that the buffer is ready for writing and send it a pointer to write to. The worker thread will then go read the texture data from the file and into the buffer object via the pointer it received from the main thread, signaling back to the main thread when it has finished loading the texture. At this point, the main thread can call `glTexSubImage2D()` to copy the now loaded data from the buffer into the target texture object.

This same technique can be applied to any data that's stored in buffer objects, including vertex and index data, shader constants stored in uniform blocks, image data for textures and images, and even parameters to drawing commands via the `GL_DRAW_INDIRECT_BUFFER` target. You can use this to your advantage and essentially make your rendering engine *data driven*. In your rendering thread, create two sets of all the buffers that might be dynamically updated by your application. Before rendering a frame, map all of the buffers for *the next frame*. You can of course bind new buffers for rendering while the buffers for the next frame are mapped. Now, in one or more worker threads, prepare all of the data for the next frame — perform CPU culling, implement dynamic vertex generation, update constants, and set up drawing parameters. Each batch of drawing should have its constants placed at a new offset within any uniform buffers. You can allocate space in these buffers in a thread-safe manner using atomic additions on the CPU.

While your worker threads are busy getting ready for the next frame, the OpenGL thread is rendering the current frame. This thread walks a list of draws generated by the worker threads, binding objects needed by each draw — for example, textures, buffers (or ranges of them), and so on, and then issuing drawing commands. If you can merge textures together into texture arrays and store the offsets within the arrays in uniform blocks, even that data preparation can be offloaded to other threads. The upshot is that while scene traversal, culling, data preparation, and so on is fully offloaded to worker threads and should scale nicely across multiple CPU cores (keeping in mind, of course, that some CPU time should be preserved for sound, AI, physics, communication, etc.), only the main OpenGL thread actually calls any OpenGL commands. However, the workload of the main thread is really light, as it performs only buffer maps and un-maps, basic state changes and draws, and does not do any work in between. Between this and efficient multi-threading implemented in most OpenGL drivers, good scaling across multiple CPU cores should be achievable in most scenarios.

Throw Out What You Don't Need

Graphics applications can use a tremendous amount of memory. Textures, framebuffer attachments, and the buffers you use for vertices and other data can all consume a lot of resources. In the previous subsections, we recommended that you always clear a framebuffer before you start rendering to it. This is partly so that optimizations such as framebuffer compression can be effective. It's also a signal to OpenGL that you're done with the contents of the framebuffer and that it should be free to reuse that memory for something else. After all, it's pretty easy for OpenGL to recreate the cleared framebuffer attachments if it needs to.

This is fine, but it's not ideal to rely on hints and suggestions for optimization. In fact, OpenGL allows you to tell it much more explicitly which resources it should keep around and which ones it's free to throw out. First, for textures, we have two functions — **glInvalidateTexImage()** and **glInvalidateTexSubImage()**. Their prototypes are

```
void glInvalidateTexImage(GLuint texture,
                          GLint level);

void glInvalidateTexSubImage(GLuint texture,
                             GLint level,
                             GLint xoffset,
                             GLint yoffset,
                             GLint zoffset,
                             GLsizei width,
                             GLsizei height,
                             GLsizei depth);
```

The first function, **glInvalidateTexImage()**, tells OpenGL that you're done with an entire mipmap level of a texture. The name of the texture object should be given in texture, and the mipmap level given in level. When you call this function, OpenGL knows that it's free to throw out the data in the image (although the texture itself remains allocated). At this point, the contents of the texture's mipmap level become undefined. In a multi-GPU setup, for example, OpenGL would then know that it doesn't need to copy data from one GPU to another to keep the texture in sync across the system. The second function, **glInvalidateTexSubImage()**, is slightly more gentle in that it only invalidates the region you specify in the xoffset, yoffset, zoffset, width, height, and depth parameters. The first three are the origin of the region, and the last three are its size — these parameters have the same meanings as they do in **glTexSubImage3D()**.

Next, we have similar functions for buffer objects: **glInvalidateBufferData()** and **glInvalidateBufferSubData()**, whose prototypes are

```
void glInvalidateBufferData(GLuint buffer);

void glInvalidateBufferSubData(GLuint buffer,
                               GLintptr offset,
                               GLsizeiptr length);
```

As with **glInvalidateTexImage()**, **glInvalidateBufferData()** throws out any data contained in the buffer object whose name you pass in buffer. After you call this function, the entire contents of the buffer become undefined, but are still allocated and owned by OpenGL. You might call this function, for example, if you store data into an intermediate buffer using transform feedback and then immediately draw from the buffer by calling **glDrawTransformFeedback()**. After calling **glDrawTransformFeedback()**, you can call **glInvalidateBufferData()** to tell OpenGL that you're done with the data and that it's free to re-use the buffer for another pass if it needs to. The second function, **glInvalidateBufferSubData()**, is the finer version and only throws out the contents of the buffer defined by the offset and length parameters.

The final two functions essentially perform the same operations on framebuffer attachments. They are **glInvalidateFramebuffer()** and **glInvalidateSubFramebuffer()**. Their prototypes are

```
void glInvalidateFramebuffer(GLenum target,
                             GLsizei numAttachments,
                             const GLenum * attachments);

void glInvalidateSubFramebuffer(GLenum target,
                                GLsizei numAttachments,
                                const GLenum * attachments,
                                GLint x,
                                GLint y,
                                GLint width,
                                GLint height);
```

For both functions, target is the target of the operation and can be GL_FRAMEBUFFER, GL_DRAW_FRAMEBUFFER, or GL_READ_FRAMEBUFFER (where GL_FRAMEBFUFER is treated as equivalent to GL_DRAW_FRAMEBUFFER). The numAttachments parameter is the number of elements in the array pointed to by attachments, which is a list of attachments to invalidate. The elements of the array should be values such as GL_COLOR_ATTACHMENT0, GL_DEPTH_ATTACHMENT, or GL_STENCIL_ATTACHMENT.

The **glInvalidateFramebuffer()** throws out the contents of the whole of each of the attachments in the attachments array. However, again, the **glInvalidateSubFramebuffer()** function is a little gentler and allows you to throw away only a region of the framebuffer attachments. This region is specified by the x, y, width, and height parameters.

Invalidating resources allows OpenGL to do a number of things that otherwise might have adverse effects. For example,

- It may be able to reclaim memory for buffers or textures that have been invalidated and are no longer in use.

- It can avoid copying data from resource to resource, especially in multi-GPU systems.

- It can return framebuffer attachments to a compressed state without necessarily making their contents valid.

In general, you should call one of the invalidation functions when you're done with the contents of a resource but may reuse it for something else later. At worst, OpenGL will ignore you and do nothing. At best, you can avoid expensive copies, clears, paging operations, or memory starvation that may otherwise occur.

Summary

This chapter introduced you to a number of debugging techniques, including the use of debug contexts in your application and some of the tools available to help you solve problems. We have discussed several methods to analyze the performance of your application and to figure out how to make it go faster and to use the graphics processing resources as efficiently as possible. By ensuring that your program doesn't generate any errors, doesn't produce any warnings when running on a debug context, and performs as well as it possibly can, you increase the range of hardware that can run it and end up with a larger potential user base.

Chapter 14

Platform Specifics

WHAT YOU'LL LEARN IN THIS CHAPTER

- How OpenGL interacts with major operating systems and window systems

- How to create an application without using the book's framework

- How OpenGL translates onto mobile devices such as tablets and smart phones

Throughout the book, we've been using a simple application framework to allow our example programs to easily port from one operating system to another. This framework in turn relies on a couple of other libraries to help it interact with the window system and with OpenGL. In this chapter, we tear away the layers and show you the bare metal — the inner workings of your favorite operating system. We'll cover Windows, Linux, and Mac OS X, and we'll also take a look at *extensions* — an important feature of OpenGL that allows you to get bleeding-edge access to new hardware features as they become available. Finally, we'll touch on OpenGL on mobile platforms and the OpenGL ES API.

Using Extensions in OpenGL

All of the examples shown in this book so far have relied on the core functionality of OpenGL. However, one of OpenGL's greatest strengths is that it can be extended and enhanced by hardware manufacturers, operating system vendors, and even publishers of tools and debuggers. Extensions can have many different effects on OpenGL functionality.

An extension is any addition to a core version of OpenGL. Extensions are listed in the OpenGL extension registry[1] on the OpenGL Web site. These extensions are written as a list of differences to a particular version of the OpenGL specification, and note what that version of OpenGL is. That means the text of the extensions describes how the core OpenGL specification must be changed if the extension is supported. However, popular and generally useful extensions are normally "promoted" into the core versions of OpenGL, which means that if you are running on the latest and greatest version of OpenGL, there might not actually be that many extensions that are interesting but are not part of the core profile. A complete list of the extensions that were promoted to each version of OpenGL and a brief synopsis of what they do is included at the back of the OpenGL specification.

There are three major classifications of extensions: vendor, EXT, and ARB. Vendor extensions are written and implemented on one vendor's hardware. Initials representing the specific vendor are usually part of the extension name — "AMD" for Advanced Micro Devices or "NV" for NVIDIA, for example. It is possible that more than one vendor might support a specific vendor extension, especially if it becomes widely accepted. EXT extensions are written together by two or more vendors. They often start their lives as a vendor-specific extensions, but if another vendor is interested in implementing the extension, perhaps with minor changes, they may collaborate with the original authors to produce an EXT version. ARB extensions are an official part of OpenGL because they are approved by the OpenGL governing body, the Architecture Review Board (ARB). These extensions are often supported by most or all major hardware vendors and may also have started out as vendor or EXT extensions.

This extension process may sound confusing at first. Hundreds of extensions currently are available! But new versions of OpenGL are often

---

1. Find the OpenGL extension registry at `http://www.opengl.org/registry/`.

constructed from extensions programmers have found useful. In this way each extension gets its time in the sun. The ones that shine can be promoted to core; the ones that are less useful are not considered. This "natural selection" process helps to ensure only the most useful and important new features make it into a core version of OpenGL.

A useful tool to determine which extensions are supported in your computer's OpenGL implementation is Realtech VR's OpenGL Extensions Viewer. It is freely available from the Realtech VR Web site (see Figure 14.1).

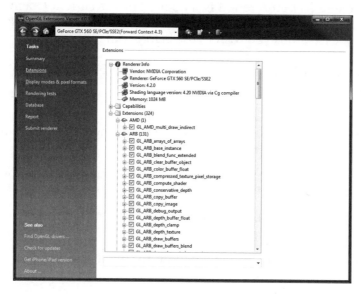

Figure 14.1: Realtech VR's OpenGL Extensions Viewer

Enhancing OpenGL with Extensions

Before using any extensions, you *must* make sure that they're supported by the OpenGL implementation that your application is running on. To find out which extensions OpenGL supports, there are two functions that you can use. First, to determine the *number* of supported extensions, you can call **glGetIntegerv()** with the GL_NUM_EXTENSIONS parameter. Next, you can find out the name of each of the supported extensions by calling

```
const GLubyte* glGetStringi(GLenum name,
                            GLuint index);
```

You should pass GL_EXTENSIONS as the name parameter, and a value between zero and one less than the number of supported extensions in index. The function returns the name of the extension as a string. To see if a specific extension is supported, you can simply query the number of extensions, and then loop through each supported extension and compare its name to the one you're looking for. The book's source code comes with a simple function that does this for you. **sb6IsExtensionSupported()** has the prototype

```
int sb6IsExtensionSupported(const char * extname);
```

This function is declared in the <sb6ext.h> header, takes the name of an extension, returns non-zero if it is supported by the current OpenGL context, and zero if it is not. Your application should always check for support for extensions you wish to use before using them.

Extensions generally add to OpenGL in some combination of four different ways:

- They can make things legal that weren't before, by simply removing restrictions from the OpenGL specification.

- They can add tokens or extend the range of values that can be passed as parameters to existing functions.

- They can extend GLSL to add functionality, built-in functions, variables, or data types.

- They can add entirely new functions to OpenGL itself.

In the first case, where things that once were considered errors no longer are, your application doesn't need to do anything besides start using the newly allowed behavior (once, of course, you have determined that the extension is supported). Likewise, for the second case, you can just start using the new token values in the relevant functions, presuming that you have their values. The values of the tokens are in the extension specifications, so you can look them up there if they are not included in your system's header files.

To enable use of extensions in GLSL, you must first include a line at the beginning of shaders that use them to tell the compiler that you're going to need their features. For example, to enable the hypothetical

`GL_ABC_foobar_feature` extension in GLSL, include the following in the beginning of your shader:

```
#extension GL_ABC_foobar_feature : enable
```

This tells the compiler that you intend to use the extension in your shader. If the compiler knows about the extension, it will let you compile the shader, even if the underlying hardware doesn't support the feature. If this is the case, the compiler should issue a warning if it sees that the extension is actually being used. Typically, extensions to GLSL will add preprocessor tokens to indicate their presence. For example, `GL_ABC_foobar_feature` will implicitly include

```
#define GL_ABC_foobar_feature 1
```

This means that you could write code such as

```
#if GL_ABC_foobar_feature
    // Use functions from the foobar extension
#else
    // Emulate or otherwise work around the missing functionality
#endif
```

This allows you to conditionally compile or execute functionality that is part of an extension that may or may not be supported by the underlying OpenGL implementation. If your shader absolutely requires support for an extension and will not work at all without it, you can instead include the more assertive

```
#extension GL_ABC_foobar_feature : require
```

If the OpenGL implementation does not support the `GL_ABC_foobar_feature` extension, then it will fail to compile the shader and report an error on the line including the `#extension` directive. In effect, GLSL extensions are opt-in, and applications must[2] tell compilers up front which extensions they intend to use.

Next, we come to extensions that introduce new functions to OpenGL. On most platforms, you do not have direct access to the OpenGL driver, and extension functions don't just magically appear as available to your applications to call. Rather, you must ask the OpenGL driver for a

---

2. In practice, many implementations enable functionality included in some extensions by default and don't require that your shaders include these directives. However, if you rely on this behavior, your application is likely to not work on other OpenGL drivers, and so you should always explicitly enable the extensions that you plan to use.

function pointer that represents the function you want to call. Function pointers are generally declared in two parts: The first is the definition of the function pointer type, and the second is the function pointer variable itself. Consider this code as an example:

```
typedef void
(APIENTRYP PFNGLDRAWTRANSFORMFEEDBACKPROC) (GLenum mode,
                                            GLuint id);
PFNGLDRAWTRANSFORMFEEDBACKPROC glDrawTransformFeedback = NULL;
```

This declares the `PFNGLDRAWTRANSFORMFEEDBACKPROC` type as a pointer to a function taking a `GLenum` and a `GLuint` parameter. Next, it declares the `glDrawTransformFeedback` variable as an instance of this type. In fact, on many platforms, the declaration of the **glDrawTransformFeedback()** function is actually just like this. This seems pretty complicated, but fortunately, the following header files include declarations of all of the function prototypes, function pointer types, and token values introduced by all registered OpenGL extensions:

```
#include <glext.h>
#include <glxext.h>
#include <wglext.h>
```

These files can be found at the OpenGL extension registry Web site. The `glext.h` header contains both standard OpenGL extensions and many vendor-specific OpenGL extensions, the `wglext.h` header contains a number of extensions that are Windows specific, and the `glxext.h` header contains definitions that are X specific (X is the windowing system used on Linux and many other Unix derivatives and implementations).

The method for querying the address of extension functions is actually platform specific. The book's application framework wraps up these intricacies into a handy function that is declared in the `<sb6ext.h>` header file. The function **sb6GetProcAddress()** has the prototype

```
void * sb6GetProcAddress(const char * funcname);
```

Here, `funcname` is the name of the extension function that you wish to use. The return value is the address of the function, if it's supported, and `NULL` otherwise. Even if OpenGL returns a valid function pointer for a function that's part of the extension you want to use, that doesn't mean the extension is present. Sometimes the same function is part of more than one extension, and sometimes vendors ship drivers with partial implementations of extensions present. Always check for support for extensions using the official mechanisms or the **sb6IsExtensionSupported()** function.

OpenGL on Windows

OpenGL is a powerful API. Its low-level nature leaves all of the control in the hands of application developers. Additionally, the core OpenGL code is portable across many different platforms and operating systems. Because every operating system has a different means of window management, each operating system has a different layer to help applications interface with OpenGL. This helps the driver implementation understand what types of buffers, color formats, and other characteristics should be used for any specific instance.

On Microsoft Windows desktop operating systems (netbooks, laptops, desktops, servers, and so on), a set of functions specifically tied to the Windows API is used, called WGL (Windows-GL). WGL functions have the prefix wgl at the front of function names and WGL_ at the front of token names, symbolizing that these functions are for interfaces between Windows and OpenGL. They are also sometimes referred to as *wiggle* functions because of their prefix. From here on in, we use real WGL functions to directly interface with Windows and the OpenGL drivers instead of using the application framework. The framework is great for getting simple apps up and running but comes at the cost of reduced control and flexibility.

In this section, you'll learn how to use WGL to probe a system's capabilities, create and manage windows, as well as handle applicable system messages. The concepts of this chapter are introduced gradually, as we build a model OpenGL program that provides a framework for Windows-specific OpenGL support. Up until now, this book has not required prior knowledge or experience with 3D graphics or OpenGL. But for this chapter, we assume you have at least an entry-level knowledge of Windows programming. Otherwise, we would have wound up writing a book twice the size of this one. We would have spent more time on the details of writing programs for Windows and less on OpenGL programming. Many good books and resources exist that explain the details of writing Windows applications.

OpenGL Implementations on Windows

OpenGL first became natively available for the Win32 platform with the release of Windows NT version 3.5. Later, it was released as an add-on for Windows 95 and then began shipping as part of the Windows 95 operating system with the OSR2 release. OpenGL is now a native API on any full Windows platform (Windows XP, Vista, Win 7, Server 2003, Server 2008, and so on), with its functions exported through the opengl32.dll library and supporting components in user32.dll. Many different levels of OpenGL hardware are available for Windows platforms, from chipsets with part of OpenGL implemented by software, to entry level video cards, to screaming fast workstation class cards. You should be aware that your application may be running on any one of these platforms.

Microsoft's OpenGL

Microsoft currently ships a generic implementation of OpenGL as the default version with its operating systems. If no 3D hardware exists on a system or if the appropriate hardware drivers have not been installed, the Microsoft version of the OpenGL implementation is the one you will get. Microsoft has not contributed to OpenGL in many years, although the company used to contribute to the OpenGL specification and was a member of the ARB. The version of OpenGL supported on most Microsoft operating systems is 1.1. This is simply not sufficient for any modern 3D application. In addition, a software implementation is often not fast enough to support any meaningful graphics. For this reason, many OpenGL applications will check the supported version of OpenGL and decide to not run if a newer version of the OpenGL specification is not supported. In particular, early versions of OpenGL such as Microsoft's default installation do not support core profile contexts, which all of this book's samples rely on.

Modern Graphics Drivers

The Installable Client Driver (ICD) was the original hardware driver interface provided for Windows NT. The ICD must implement the entire OpenGL pipeline using a combination of software and the specific hardware for which it was written. Creating an ICD from scratch is a considerable amount of work for a vendor to undertake.

Vendor-supplied ICDs drop in and work with Microsoft's OpenGL implementation much like a plug-in for a Web browser, for example. When an application linked to opengl32.dll attempts to create a context, the library will check whether a vendor-supplied driver is available, and if so, it will load that driver and pass any OpenGL calls through to it. Because a common interface exists, drivers and applications do not have to be recompiled to take advantage of OpenGL hardware on a system, even if it changes.

The ICD is actually a part of the display driver and does not affect the existing opengl32.dll system DLL. The name of the driver is completely up to the hardware vendor, and other vendors will use their own naming conventions. For example, AMD's OpenGL driver for Windows is packaged in atioglxx.dll, and NVIDIA's OpenGL driver is packaged in nvoglv32.dll. The name of the ICD for a particular display adapter is stored in Windows' system registry, and opengl32.dll uses this to find and load the appropriate OpenGL driver for a given graphics device. The ICD exposes a common interface that opengl32.dll understands. The interfaces exposed by the AMD and NVIDIA OpenGL drivers are shown in Figure 14.2. As you can see, both ICDs expose a common set of functions.

Figure 14.2: AMD and NVIDIA OpenGL drivers

This driver model provides the vendor with the most opportunities to optimize its driver and hardware combination. All major hardware vendors currently use the ICD model. If a given piece of hardware does not support[3] some part of OpenGL natively, the ICD must implement the missing functionality through some type of emulation. In this way, all ICD drivers should support the entire feature set for the version(s) of OpenGL exported by that driver.

Because the opengl32.dll portion of the OpenGL call stack belongs to the operating system, applications and drivers have to use the library that ships with a given operating system. Because the Microsoft software implementation only supports OpenGL 1.1, the functions exposed by opengl32.dll also only support the same version of OpenGL. This has created a dilemma as OpenGL has grown, evolved, and added new functionality. We have come a long way in the years since OpenGL 1.1 was released.

---

3. In practice, all current hardware from all vendors supports every part of the core OpenGL specification, and this isn't something you need to worry about.

Because a display driver cannot modify the opengl32.dll to add new features for the current version, OpenGL needed a way to allow applications to access parts that were not exposed by the opengl32.dll. This is done through the extension mechanism and an interface that allows applications to get the address of the functions for any supported interfaces. Not only does this work for the newer versions of OpenGL, but this mechanism can be used by hardware vendors to extend the feature set of OpenGL as we will see later in this chapter.

OpenGL on Windows Vista and Beyond

OpenGL on Windows Vista and beyond works in much the same way as on earlier versions of the operating system. The operating system still has a version of the opengl32.dll, and applications call OpenGL functions much the same way. But on these newer operating systems, desktop compositing is used to create the final image a user sees. On previous operating systems, each window rendered into the desktop pixels it owned. But on Windows Vista and onwards, each window renders into a region of memory that is handed off a new component of the operating system called the Desktop Window Manager, or DWM. This is the part of Windows that is responsible for presenting the Aero user interface, where the borders of windows become translucent, and low resolution previews of windows are available in the task switcher, for example.

Each window is known as a *surface* and is "presented" to the DWM, which directly interfaces with the graphics kernel driver, known as DXGI. DWM takes all of the windows from each running 2D and 3D application and uses the GPU to combine them together with desktop components to create a final image that the user sees. This new mechanism separates the rendering surfaces for each window and allows the operating system to take advantage of advanced GPU capabilities to provide cool blending and 3D effects.

The version of opengl32.dll on Windows Vista and later still only supports OpenGL 1.4. However, Microsoft has implemented an OpenGL to D3D emulator that supports OpenGL version 1.4 and so provides some level of hardware acceleration for legacy applications. This implementation looks like an ICD, but only shows up if a real ICD is not installed. Windows Vista, like XP, does not ship with ICD drivers on the distribution media. Once a user downloads a new display driver from a vendor's Web site, however, she will get a true ICD-based driver and full OpenGL support in both windowed and full-screen games.

Basic Window Setup

Now it's time to get back to setting up your application using WGL. The book's application framework provides only one window, and OpenGL function calls always produced output in that window. (Where else would they go?) Your own real-world Windows applications, however, will often have more than one window. In fact, dialog boxes, controls, and even menus are actually all windows at a fundamental level; having a useful program that contains only one window is nearly impossible (well, okay, maybe games are an important exception!). Also, the book's application framework owns the application's main loop and requires that you put all of your drawing code in the render function. This works fine for simple applications but doesn't work with libraries or any time your code doesn't control the main event loop. Let's look at more flexible ways of managing windows and contexts.

GDI Device Contexts

There are many methods for drawing into a window on a Microsoft operating system. The oldest and most widely supported is the Windows GDI (Graphics Device Interface). GDI has since been updated with the release of GDI+. GDI is strictly a 2D drawing interface and was widely hardware accelerated before Windows Vista. Although GDI is still available on Windows Vista and beyond, it is no longer hardware accelerated in the same way. The preferred high-level drawing technology is based on the .NET framework and is called the Windows Presentation Foundation (WPF). WPF is also available via a download for Windows XP. Over the years some minor 2D API variations have come and gone, as well as many incarnations of Direct3D. On Windows Vista, the new low-level rendering interface is called Windows Graphics Foundation (WGF) and is essentially just Direct3D 10.

The one native rendering API common to all versions of Windows (even Windows Mobile) is GDI. This is fortunate because GDI is how we initialize OpenGL and interact with OpenGL on all versions of Windows (except Windows Mobile, where OpenGL is not natively supported by Microsoft). On Windows Vista and onwards, GDI is no longer hardware accelerated, but this is irrelevant because we will never (at least when using OpenGL) actually use GDI for any drawing operations anyway.

When using GDI, each window has a *device context* (or DC) that actually receives the graphics output, and each GDI function takes a device context as an argument to indicate which context you want the function to affect. You can have multiple device contexts, but only one for each window.

Before you jump to the conclusion that OpenGL should work in a similar way, remember that GDI is Windows specific. OpenGL was designed to be completely portable across environments and hardware platforms (and it didn't start on Windows anyway!). Adding a device context parameter to OpenGL functions would render your OpenGL code useless in any environment other than Windows.

OpenGL does have a context identifier, however, and it is called the *rendering context* (or RC). The OpenGL rendering context has many similarities to the GDI device context because it is the rendering context that remembers current bindings, state settings, and so on, much like the device context holds onto the current brush or pen color for Windows.

Creating a Window

Before you can render anything, you need an OpenGL context, and before you can create an OpenGL context, you need a GDI context, and before you can get a GDI context, you need a window — the operating system is called Windows after all. To create a window, we use the `CreateWindowEx` function and tell it what kind of window you want to use. Before you can create a window, you need a *class* for the window that, amongst other things, tells Windows which function will be used to handle messages for the window. To set up our window class, we'll call `RegisterClass`, whose prototype is

```
ATOM WINAPI RegisterClass(const WNDCLASS *lpWndClass);
```

The `RegisterClass` function takes a pointer to a `WNDCLASS` structure, which defines our class. We're not going to use all of the fields in the class, but a few of them are important. Listing 14.1 registers our new window class.

```
WNDCLASS cls;

::ZeroMemory(&cls, sizeof(cls));

cls.style = CS_HREDRAW | CS_VREDRAW | CS_OWNDC;
cls.lpfnWndProc = &WindowProc;
cls.hInstance = ::GetModuleHandle(NULL);
cls.lpszClassName = TEXT("OPENGL");

::RegisterClass(&cls);
```

Listing 14.1: Registering a window class

In Listing 14.1, we first initialize the contents of the structure to zero using ZeroMemory (this is similar to memset, but does not depend on the C runtime). This means that any fields of the structure we don't otherwise fill in will be zeros — which is what we want for most of them. We set the structure's style member to CS_HREDRAW | CS_VREDRAW | CS_OWNDC, which tells Windows to redraw the window if either its width or height changes, and to give each window of this class its own device context (DC). WindowProc is our message handling function that we will write, the hInstance field stores the instance of the application, and the lpszClassName field is the address of a string with which we can refer to our new class. We'll set this to "OPENGL".

Next, we can create our window by calling CreateWindowEx. The prototype for CreateWindowEx is

```
HWND WINAPI CreateWindowEx(DWORD dwExStyle,
                           LPCTSTR lpClassName,
                           LPCTSTR lpWindowName,
                           DWORD dwStyle,
                           int x,
                           int y,
                           int nWidth,
                           int nHeight,
                           HWND hWndParent,
                           HMENU hMenu,
                           HINSTANCE hInstance,
                           LPVOID lpParam);
```

The dwExStyle and dwStyle are the style of the window. The lpClassName parameter is the name of the class of the window, which we just registered and so we can set this to "OPENGL". The x, y, nWidth, and nHeight parameters specify the position and size of the window. hWndParent is the handle of the parent window. We would use this if we were nesting this window inside another, but in this case, we are going to create a top-level window and so will set this parameter to NULL. Likewise, our window will have no menu, and so we set hMenu to NULL, too. hInstance is the instance of our application. The lpParam is a pointer value that we can use for anything we want. When the window is created, Windows will call its window function, and we will be able to get at this parameter. In this example, we're not using lpParam, and so we'll set that to NULL. In a more complex application, you could use this as a pointer to a class instance or for any other purpose. The code to create our window and get its device context is shown in Listing 14.2.

```
HWND hWnd = ::CreateWindowEx(WS_EX_APPWINDOW | WS_EX_WINDOWEDGE,
                             TEXT("OPENGL"),
                             TEXT("OpenGL Window"),
                             WS_CLIPSIBLINGS | WS_CLIPCHILDREN |
                             WS_OVERLAPPEDWINDOW | WS_VISIBLE,
```

```
                                    0, 0,
                                    800, 600,
                                    NULL,
                                    NULL,
                                    hInstance,
                                    NULL);

        HDC dc = ::GetDC(hWnd);
```

Listing 14.2: Creating a simple window

In Listing 14.2, once we've created our window, we get its device context using the GetDC function. Now we're ready to set up the DC for rendering with OpenGL.

Pixel Formats

The Windows concept of the GDI device context is limited for 3D graphics because it was designed for 2D graphics applications. In Windows, you request a device context identifier for a given window. The nature of the device context depends on the nature of the device. If your desktop is set to 16-bit color, the device context Windows gives you knows about and understands 16-bit color only. You cannot tell Windows, for example, that one window is to be a 16-bit color window and another is to be a 32-bit color window. You, the programmer, have no control over the intrinsic characteristics of a windows device context.

Any window or device that will be rendering 3D graphics has far more characteristics to it than simply color depth. Up until now, the application framework has taken care of these details for you. When you initialized the application framework, you told it what version of OpenGL you wanted, whether you wanted to be full screen or not, and that's about it. The rest was hidden from you.

Before OpenGL can render into a window, you must first configure that window according to your rendering needs. Will the rendering be single or double buffered? Do you need a depth buffer? How about stencil or destination alpha? After you set these parameters for a window, you cannot change them later. To switch from a window with only a depth and color buffer to a window with only a stencil and color buffer, you have to destroy the first window and re-create a new window with the characteristics you need.

OpenGL on Windows uses *pixel formats* to encapsulate all of this information into grouped capabilities. You need to find a pixel format that has the characteristics and capabilities that match the needs of your application. This pixel format is then used to create an OpenGL rendering context. There are two ways to go about looking for a pixel format. The first method is the more preferred and capable mechanism exposed by OpenGL directly. The second method uses the original Windows interfaces, which have been around for as long as OpenGL has been supported on Windows.

Choosing a Pixel Format

Windows exposes several functions that can be used for finding an OpenGL pixel format. However, many newer OpenGL features such as multi-sample buffers are not accessible through the old pixel format selection methods — we'll get to ways to access these formats shortly.

The 3D characteristics of the window are set one time, usually just after window creation. The collective name for these settings is the pixel format. Windows provides a structure named PIXELFORMATDESCRIPTOR that describes the pixel format. This structure is defined in Listing 14.3.

```
typedef struct tagPIXELFORMATDESCRIPTOR
{
    WORD  nSize;            // Size of this structure
    WORD  nVersion;         // Version of structure (should be 1)
    DWORD dwFlags;          // Pixel buffer properties
    BYTE  iPixelType;       // Type of pixel data (RGBA or Color Index)
    BYTE  cColorBits;       // Number of color bit planes in color buffer
    BYTE  cRedBits;         // How many bits for red
    BYTE  cRedShift;        // Shift count for red bits
    BYTE  cGreenBits;       // How many bits for green
    BYTE  cGreenShift;      // Shift count for green bits
    BYTE  cBlueBits;        // How many bits for blue
    BYTE  cBlueShift;       // Shift count for blue
    BYTE  cAlphaBits;       // How many bits for destination alpha
    BYTE  cAlphaShift;      // Shift count for destination alpha
    BYTE  cAccumBits;       // How many bits for accumulation buffer
    BYTE  cAccumRedBits;    // How many red bits for accumulation buffer
    BYTE  cAccumGreenBits;  // How many green bits for accumulation buffer
    BYTE  cAccumBlueBits;   // How many blue bits for accumulation buffer
    BYTE  cAccumAlphaBits;  // How many alpha bits for accumulation buffer
    BYTE  cDepthBits;       // How many bits for depth buffer
    BYTE  cStencilBits;     // How many bits for stencil buffer
    BYTE  cAuxBuffers;      // How many auxiliary buffers
    BYTE  iLayerType;       // Obsolete - ignored
    BYTE  bReserved;        // Number of overlay and underlay planes
    DWORD dwLayerMask;      // Obsolete - ignored
    DWORD dwVisibleMask;    // Transparent color of underlay plane
    DWORD dwDamageMask;     // Obsolete - ignored
} PIXELFORMATDESCRIPTOR;
```

Listing 14.3: Declaration of PIXELFORMATDESCRIPTOR

For a given OpenGL device (hardware or software), the values of these members are not arbitrary. Only a limited number of pixel formats is available for a specific window. Pixel formats are said to be exported by the OpenGL driver. To find a format that suits your needs, you should create an instance of this structure, fill in as many fields as you need (setting the rest to zero), and call the ChoosePixelFormat function, whose prototype is

```
int ChoosePixelFormat(IIDC hdc,
                      const PIXELFORMATDESCRIPTOR *ppfd);
```

The ChoosePixelFormat function returns the index of the closest matching format from those supported by the installed OpenGL driver. You can then call **SetPixelFormat()** using this index to set the pixel format of the device context into which your OpenGL application will render. Code to do this is shown in Listing 14.4.

```
PIXELFORMATDESCRIPTOR pfd;

::ZeroMemory(&pfd, sizeof(pfd));

pfd.nSize            = sizeof(pfd);
pfd.nVersion         = 1;
pfd.dwFlags          = PFD_DRAW_TO_WINDOW |
                       PFD_SUPPORT_OPENGL |
                       PFD_GENERIC_ACCELERATED |
                       PFD_DOUBLEBUFFER;
pfd.iPixelType       = PFD_TYPE_RGBA;
pfd.cColorBits       = 24;
pfd.cRedBits         = 8;
pfd.cGreenBits       = 8;
pfd.cBlueBits        = 8;
pfd.cDepthBits       = 32;

int iPixelFormat = ::ChoosePixelFormat(dc, &pfd);
::SetPixelFormat(dc, iPixelFormat, &pfd);
```

Listing 14.4: Choosing and setting a pixel format

The original contents of the PIXELFORMATDESCRIPTOR structure do not affect the functioning of the **SetPixelFormat()** function. Pass in the window device context handle in the hDC parameter and your chosen pixel format in the nPixelFormat parameter. **SetPixelFormat()** can only be called once for a given DC. To change the pixel format, your window will have to be destroyed and re-created.

The OpenGL Rendering Context

A typical Windows application can consist of many windows. You can even set a pixel format for each one (using that windows device context) if you want! When you call an OpenGL command, how does the driver know which window to send its output to? In the previous chapters, we used the book's application framework, which provided a single window to display OpenGL output. Recall that with normal Windows GDI-based drawing, each window has its own device context.

To accomplish the portability of the core OpenGL functions, each environment must implement some means of specifying a current rendering window before executing any OpenGL commands. Just as the Windows GDI functions use the window's device contexts, the OpenGL environment is embodied in what is known as the *rendering context*. The rendering context remembers OpenGL settings and state.

The data type of an OpenGL rendering on Windows context is HGLRC, and you can create one by calling **wglCreateContext()**. If everything succeeds, the new context handle is returned, and you can make the context current by calling **wglMakeCurrent()**. The code to do this is as follows:

```
HGLRC rc = wglCreateContext(dc);
wglMakeCurrent(dc, rc);
```

Once you have a current context, you're ready to enter the application's *main loop*. On Windows, the paradigm is based around a message pump, where each window is the target of a queue of messages. Your application should contain a loop that checks whether there are any messages in the queue for your window and, if so, deals with it. The message loop for our simple Windows application is shown in Listing 14.5.

```
for (;;)
{
    if (::PeekMessage(&msg, hWnd, 0, 0, PM_REMOVE))
    {
        if (msg.message == WM_QUIT)
        {
            break;
        }
        ::TranslateMessage(&msg);
        ::DispatchMessage(&msg);
    }
    DrawScene();
    ::SwapBuffers(dc);
}
```

Listing 14.5: Windows main message loop

Normally, the application handles messages by calling the TranslateMessage and DispatchMessage functions as we have done in

Listing 14.5. These in turn call the function associated with the window's class (the `lpfnWndProc` member of the window class structure that we set to `WindowProc` earlier).

Double Buffering

The example program in the previous section requests a double buffered pixel format by specifying `PFD_DOUBLEBUFFER` the in the `PIXELFORMATDESCRIPTOR` when searching for a pixel format using **`ChoosePixelFormat()`**. By this time, you have seen many sample programs that are double buffered — in fact, the book's application framework creates double buffered contexts by default. But let's revisit briefly given that this is relevant to how we allocate the pixel format and how the program is controlled. When a double buffered pixel format is used, two surfaces the size of the window are allocated. One acts as the front buffer and the other as the back buffer. You can draw to them by calling **`glDrawBuffers()`** with `GL_FRONT` or `GL_BACK`. However, in practice, modern windowing systems with composited desktops (such as Windows' DWM) don't really support rendering to the front buffer, and so all contexts are double buffered under the covers.

Double buffering allows OpenGL to draw your entire scene to the back buffer without any intermediate results showing up on the screen. This can provide a smoother and more visually pleasing experience for your users.

But how do users see anything if you are always rendering to a buffer that is not visible? Easy — just tell OpenGL when you are done drawing and the buffers need to be swapped. This is done simply by calling **`SwapBuffers()`** with the device handle of the window. Once this call is made, the back buffer will be displayed, and our program will have a new back buffer to work with.

```
// Do the buffer swap
SwapBuffers(dc);
```

You might have noticed the call to **`SwapBuffers()`** in Listing 14.5. That just about does it for basic rendering with OpenGL on Windows. However, there's actually more to it. Before we can go further, we'll need to look at how the WGL interface is extended.

Extending WGL

As previously discussed, the main mechanism through which OpenGL is enhanced is via extensions. Some of the available extensions add functions to OpenGL, and this is true for WGL too. The Windows OpenGL implementation has a function named **wglGetProcAddress()** that allows you to retrieve a pointer to an OpenGL function supported by the driver, and its prototype is

```
PROC wglGetProcAddress(LPSTR lpszProc);
```

This function takes the name of an OpenGL function and returns a function pointer that you can use to call it directly. You will notice that this is very similar to the **sb6GetProcAddress()** function and that is because the Windows implementation of **sb6GetProcAddress()** is simply a wrapper around **wglGetProcAddress()**.

WGL also supports extensions, but before we can start using them, we need to determine which extensions are supported by the installed OpenGL drivers. To do this, we actually use a function from an extension. This seems circular, but a special exception is made in this case to allow us to break the dependency. The function in question is **wglGetExtensionsStringARB()**, which returns a string containing the name of all of the WGL extensions supported by the OpenGL driver. If **wglGetProcAddress()** returns a valid pointer for the **wglGetExtensionsStringARB()** function, then the WGL_ARB_extensions_string extension is present and supported. Its use is as follows:

```
PFNWGLGETEXTENSIONSSTRINGARBPROC wglGetExtensionsStringARB;

wglGetExtensionsStringARB = (PFNWGLGETEXTENSIONSSTRINGARBPROC)
                        wglGetProcAddress("wglGetExtensionsStringARB");

const char * extension_string = wglGetExtensionsStringARB();
```

After executing this code, the extension_string variable is a pointer to a string containing a space-separated list of all the extensions supported by the OpenGL drivers. If this string contains WGL_ARB_create_context, then we're ready to go! It means that advanced context creation functions exist, and we can use the extension to create a more advanced context version than the default provided by **wglCreateContext()**. Likewise, the WGL_ARB_pixel_format allows us to choose more advanced pixel formats. You may have noticed that the PIXELFORMATDESCRIPTOR omitted fields for things like multi-sampling. WGL_ARB_pixel_format fixes that.

This extension defines a long list of attributes that can be associated with a context, listed in Table 14.1.

Table 14.1: Pixel Format Attributes

Constant (WGL_*)	Description
NUMBER_PIXEL_FORMATS_ARB	The number of pixel formats for this device.
DRAW_TO_WINDOW_ARB	Non-zero if the pixel format can be used with a window.
DRAW_TO_BITMAP_ARB	Non-zero if the pixel format can be used with a memory Device Independent Bitmap (DIB).
DEPTH_BITS_ARB	The number of bits in the depth buffer.
STENCIL_BITS_ARB	The number of bits in the stencil buffer.
ACCELERATION_ARB	Should be set to WGL_FULL_ACCELERATION_ARB to specify that hardware acceleration is required.
NEED_PALETTE_ARB	Non-zero if a palette is required.
NEED_SYSTEM_PALETTE_ARB	Non-zero if the hardware supports one palette only in 256-color mode.
SWAP_LAYER_BUFFERS_ARB	Non-zero if the hardware supports swapping layer planes.
SWAP_METHOD_ARB	The method by which the buffer swap is accomplished for double-buffered pixel formats. It is one of the values listed in Table 14.2.
NUMBER_OVERLAYS_ARB	The number of overlay planes.
NUMBER_UNDERLAYS_ARB	The number of underlay planes.
SAMPLES_ARB	The number of multi-sample samples per pixel. Default is 1.
TRANSPARENT_ARB	Non-zero if transparency is supported.
TRANSPARENT_RED_VALUE_ARB	Transparent red color.
TRANSPARENT_GREEN_VALUE_ARB	Transparent green color.
TRANSPARENT_BLUE_VALUE_ARB	Transparent blue color.
TRANSPARENT_ALPHA_VALUE_ARB	Transparent alpha color.
SHARE_DEPTH_ARB	Non-zero if layer planes share a depth buffer with the main plane.

continued

Constant (`WGL_*`)	Description
`SHARE_STENCIL_ARB`	Non-zero if layer planes share a stencil buffer with the main plane.
`SHARE_ACCUM_ARB`	Non-zero if layer planes share an accumulation buffer with the main plane.
`SUPPORT_GDI_ARB`	Non-zero if GDI rendering is supported (front buffer only).
`SUPPORT_OPENGL_ARB`	Non-zero if OpenGL is supported.
`DOUBLE_BUFFER_ARB`	Non-zero if double buffered.
`STEREO_ARB`	Non-zero if left and right buffers are supported.
`PIXEL_TYPE_ARB`	`TYPE_RGBA_ARB` for RGBA color modes; `TYPE_COLORINDEX_ARB` for color index mode.
`COLOR_BITS_ARB`	Number of bit planes in the color buffer.
`RED_BITS_ARB`	Number of red bit planes in the color buffer.
`RED_SHIFT_ARB`	Shift count for red bit planes.
`GREEN_BITS_ARB`	Number of green bit planes in the color buffer.
`GREEN_SHIFT_ARB`	Shift count for green bit planes.
`BLUE_BITS_ARB`	Number of blue bit planes in the color buffer.
`BLUE_SHIFT_ARB`	Shift count for blue bit planes.
`ALPHA_BITS_ARB`	Number of alpha bit planes in the color buffer.
`ALPHA_SHIFT_ARB`	Shift count for alpha bit planes.

Table 14.2: Buffer Swap Values for `WGL_SWAP_METHOD_ARB`

Constant (`WGL_*`)	Description
`SWAP_EXCHANGE_ARB`	Swapping exchanges the front and back buffers.
`SWAP_COPY_ARB`	The back buffer is copied to the front buffer.
`SWAP_UNDEFINED_ARB`	The back buffer is copied to the front buffer, but the back buffer contents remain undefined after the buffer swap.

The function **wglChoosePixelFormatARB()** is a more advanced version of **ChoosePixelFormat()** that can used to find pixel formats that match requirements using the attributes in Table 14.1. Its prototype is

```
BOOL wglChoosePixelFormatARB(HDC hdc,
                             const int *piAttribIList,
                             const float *pfAttribFList,
                             UINT nMaxFormats,
                             const int *piFormats,
                             UINT *nNumFormats);
```

It's important to notice the "ARB" suffix on this function. **wglChoosePixelFormatARB()** is not the same as **ChoosePixelFormat()**. For most applications you should always prefer **wglChoosePixelFormatARB()**. Also note that an OpenGL context must be created before you can set up this extension and call **wglChoosePixelFormatARB()**. To do this, you can create a dummy context that gets deleted as soon as you find the pixel format you need.

There are a lot of arguments to handle here. The first, hdc, is the device context of the window that the pixel format will be used for. The second and third arguments are used to specify the attributes you are searching for. Both arguments are lists of attribute and value pairs. piAttribIList is a list of integer values, and pfAttribIList is a list of float values. Some attributes are better defined as floats than integers. To use these attributes, create an array of one type and then set the first index to the value of the first attribute you'd like to specify. Set the second index to the minimum value you require. Repeat for the second attribute in the third index and so on. Once you have added all attributes, add a zero to the end of the array. Some attributes such as WGL_DRAW_TO_WINDOW_ARB and WGL_SWAP_METHOD require an exact match, while others such as WGL_COLOR_BITS_ARB and WGL_ALPHA_BITS_ARB only specify a minimum acceptable value.

You have to allocate a second array to hold the results of the search. Then pass the size of the results array into nMaxFormats, and pass a pointer to the integer array into piFormats. The actual number of formats that were written into the results array is passed back in the nNumFormats argument. Normally this is also the number of formats found, but if your array is too small and nNumFormats is the same as nMaxFormats, the driver found more matching formats than fit into your results array. If you don't specify an attribute in piAttribIList or pfAttribIList, the function ignores it when looking for matches; no default is used. If you pass in NULL for piAttribIList and pfAttribIList, you get all supported formats back.

The results returned by **wglChoosePixelFormatARB()** in the piFormats attribute are sorted with the "best" matching formats at the start of the list. The "best" match is defined by the implementation and is device dependent. It is usually advantageous to pick formats that the implementation thinks are the best match as long as they meet the requirements of your application.

Some attributes are required on most queries for the resulting pixel formats to be useful. Most programs should request the WGL_SUPPORT_OPENGL_ARB, WGL_DRAW_TO_WINDOW_ARB, and WGL_ACCELERATION_ARB attributes. These attributes are described in more detail in the next section. All this information may seem confusing, but finding a pixel format is easier than it may seem. Listing 14.6 gives an example of how to choose a pixel format.

```
int nPixCount = 0;

// Specify the important attributes we care about
int pixAttribs[] = {
            WGL_SUPPORT_OPENGL_ARB, 1,  // Must support OGL rendering
            WGL_DRAW_TO_WINDOW_ARB, 1,  // pf that can run a window
            WGL_RED_BITS_ARB,       8,  // At least 8 bits of red
            WGL_GREEN_BITS_ARB,     8,  // At least 8 bits of green
            WGL_BLUE_BITS_ARB,      8,  // At least 8 bits of blue
            WGL_DEPTH_BITS_ARB,    16,  // At least 16 bits of depth
            WGL_ACCELERATION_ARB,
            WGL_FULL_ACCELERATION_ARB, // Must be HW accelerated
            WGL_PIXEL_TYPE_ARB,
            WGL_TYPE_RGBA_ARB,          // pf should be RGBA type
            0} ;                        // Zero termination

// Ask \GL to find the most relevant format matching our attribs
// Only get one format back.
wglChoosePixelFormatARB(dc,
                        &pixAttribs[0],
                        NULL,
                        1,
                        &nPixelFormat,
                        (UINT*)&nPixCount);

if (nPixelFormat == -1)
{
    // Couldn't find a format, perhaps no 3D HW or drivers are installed
    g_hDC = 0;
    g_hDC = 0;
    bRetVal = false;
    printf("!!! An error occurred trying to find a pixel format with "
            "the requested attributes.\ n");
}
```

Listing 14.6: Finding a pixel format with **wglChoosePixelFormatARB()**

Enumerating Pixel Formats

Although the **wglChoosePixelFormatARB()** can choose a pixel format that matches your requirements, sometimes it is necessary to ask the OpenGL driver for a list of all of the formats that it supports and query their properties. The **wglGetPixelFormatAttribivARB()** and **wglGetPixelFormatAttribfvARB()** functions can be used for this purpose and their prototypes are

```
BOOL wglGetPixelFormatAttribivARB(HDC hdc, int iPixelFormat,
                       int iLayerPlane, UINT nAttributes,
                       const int *piAttributes, int *piValues);

BOOL wglGetPixelFormatAttribfvARB(HDC hdc, int iPixelFormat,
                       int iLayerPlane, UINT nAttributes,
                       const int *piAttributes, float *pfValues);
```

These two variations of the same function allow you to query the properties of a particular pixel format index and retrieve an array containing the attribute data for that pixel format. The first argument, hdc, is the device context of the window that the pixel format will be used for, followed by the pixel format index in iPixelFormat. The iLayerPlane argument specifies which layer plane to query (0 on Windows Vista and later, and other implementations that do not support layer planes). Next, nAttributes specifies how many attributes you are querying for this pixel format, and the array piAttributes contains the list of attribute names to be queried. The attributes that can be specified are listed in Table 14.1. The final argument, pfValues, is an array that will be filled with the corresponding pixel format attributes.

You many have noticed in Table 14.1 that one of the possible values that can be queried by **wglGetPixelFormatAttribivARB()** and **wglGetPixelFormatAttribfvARB()** is WGL_NUMBER_PIXEL_FORMATS_ARB. You can make an initial call to **wglGetPixelFormatAttribivARB()** to get the total number of formats and then use that information to step through the entire list and query the information you care about for each pixel format available. Listing 14.7 shows code to do this.

```
GLint pfAttribCount[]= { WGL_NUMBER_PIXEL_FORMATS_ARB };
GLint pfAttribList[] = { WGL_DRAW_TO_WINDOW_ARB,
                         WGL_ACCELERATION_ARB,
                         WGL_SUPPORT_OPENGL_ARB,
                         WGL_DOUBLE_BUFFER_ARB,
                         WGL_DEPTH_BITS_ARB,
                         WGL_STENCIL_BITS_ARB,
                         WGL_RED_BITS_ARB,
                         WGL_GREEN_BITS_ARB,
```

```
                      WGL_BLUE_BITS_ARB,
                      WGL_ALPHA_BITS_ARB };

int nPixelFormatCount = 0;
wglGetPixelFormatAttribivARB(g_hDC, 1, 0, 1, pfAttribCount,
                             &nPixelFormatCount);
for (int i=0; i<nPixelFormatCount; i++)
{
    GLint results[10];
    printf("Pixel format %d details:\n", i);
    wglGetPixelFormatAttribivARB(g_hDC, i, 0, 10, pfAttribList, results);
    printf("    Draw to Window   = %d:\n", results[0]);
    printf("    HW Accelerated   = %d:\n", results[1]);
    printf("    Supports \GL     = %d:\n", results[2]);
    printf("    Double Buffered  = %d:\n", results[3]);
    printf("    Depth Bits       = %d:\n", results[4]);
    printf("    Stencil Bits     = %d:\n", results[5]);
    printf("    Red Bits         = %d:\n", results[6]);
    printf("    Green Bits       = %d:\n", results[7]);
    printf("    Blue Bits        = %d:\n", results[8]);
    printf("    Alpha Bits       = %d:\n", results[9]);
}
```

Listing 14.7: Enumerating pixel formats on Windows

This code prints a list of pixel formats, but you could use the same method to choose your own pixel format if you didn't want to use the more automated method provided by **wglChoosePixelFormatARB()**.

Advanced Context Creation

Many different versions of OpenGL have been released in the last 20 years. Some are not backward compatible with others. For this reason, you can pick the specific version of OpenGL your application will use. If OpenGL did not allow you to do this, your application could stop working when a new version of OpenGL was released that was not compatible with the one you designed your application for. If you create a context with the **wglCreateContext()** function, you will get back a context which is backwards compatible with OpenGL 1.0. However, if you want to get a context that breaks that backwards compatibility (perhaps adding new features along the way), this won't work for you. Instead, you need to create an OpenGL rendering context by calling the **wglCreateContextAttribsARB()** function, which is part of another WGL extension called WGL_ARB_create_context. Its prototype is

```
HGLRC wglCreateContextAttribsARB(HDC hDC,
                                 HGLRC hShareContext,
                                 const int *attribList);
```

The attribList parameter is a value-pair list of attributes you can request in a new context. First, specify the attribute name in the array followed by

the value for the attribute. The attributes
WGL_CONTEXT_MAJOR_VERSION_ARB and WGL_CONTEXT_MINOR_VERSION_ARB
are used to explicitly ask for a specific context version of OpenGL. If your
application was written for OpenGL 3.3, for example, you would pass in 3
as the major version and 3 as the minor version.

Similarly, if your application needed an OpenGL 4.0 context, you could
ask for that. However, OpenGL drivers are allowed to return any version
that is 100% backward compatible with the version you requested. If you
do not specify a version of OpenGL or if you ask for version 1.0, the driver
will probably create an OpenGL 3.1 context or a more recent compatibility
profile context. The exact behavior differs between vendors. The best idea
is to ask for a specific OpenGL version that is the minimum required by
your application. For new applications you create, it's pretty safe to rely
on OpenGL 3.3 or later being available.

There are several other types of attributes you can request through the
attrib_list. The attribute WGL_CONTEXT_PROFILE_MASK_ARB is followed
by a bitfield containing either WGL_CONTEXT_CORE_PROFILE_BIT_ARB or
WGL_CONTEXT_COMPATIBILITY_PROFILE_BIT_ARB. Only one bit can be used
at a time. Setting the WGL_CONTEXT_CORE_PROFILE_BIT_ARB bit causes the
driver to return a context containing only core functionality, no
deprecated OpenGL functionality. Using this bit is a good way to
prepare an application for the next revision of OpenGL where
deprecated functionality may be removed. Setting the
WGL_CONTEXT_COMPATIBILITY_PROFILE_BIT_ARB bit asks the driver
to create a context that is backward compatible with all older versions of
OpenGL. In other words, no deprecated functionality will be removed. A
context created with this bit may run slower than a core profile context
because of the additional state and functionality that needs to be
tracked.

The WGL_CONTEXT_FLAGS_ARB attribute can be used to set other flags for
context creation. The only supported flag is WGL_CONTEXT_DEBUG_BIT.
Specifying this bit creates a context with additional debugging
information available for applications under development. What
information and how it can be accessed is vendor specific.

If any of the attributes you have specified are not supported by
the OpenGL driver on your system, **wglCreateContextAttribsARB()**
returns NULL, and an error is generated. The error
WGL_ERROR_INVALID_VERSION_ARB is thrown if the combination of minor
and major version attributes with the forward-compatible context bit is

not a valid OpenGL version. If any of the bits specified for
`WGL_CONTEXT_PROFILE_MASK_ARB` are not supported, the error
`WGL_ERROR_INVALID_PROFILE_ARB` is thrown.

OpenGL can share objects (textures, buffers, sync objects, and so on)
between contexts. If you want to share objects between two or more
contexts, create the first context, and then pass its handle in the
hShareContext parameter to **wglCreateContextAttribsARB()**. If you pass
NULL to the new context, no other existing contexts will share data with
the new context. A simple example of how to create two OpenGL 4.2 core
profile contexts that share objects using **wglCreateContextAttribsARB()** is
shown in Listing 14.8.

```
GLint attribs[] =
{
    WGL_CONTEXT_MAJOR_VERSION_ARB, 4,
    WGL_CONTEXT_MINOR_VERSION_ARB, 2,
    WGL_CONTEXT_PROFILE_MASK_ARB, WGL_CONTEXT_CORE_PROFILE_BIT_ARB,
    0
};
HGLRC  oglRC1 = wglCreateContextAttribsARB(g_hDC, 0, attribs);
HGLRC  oglRC2 = wglCreateContextAttribsARB(g_hDC, oglRC1, attribs);
```

Listing 14.8: Creating shared contexts on Windows

Advanced Pixel Formats

The pixel format for a window is identified by a one-based integer index
number. An implementation exports a number of pixel formats from
which to choose. The Windows interfaces for OpenGL have not grown
along with OpenGL. As a result, features were added to OpenGL that could
not be accessed using traditional Windows functions. Thankfully, OpenGL
added a way to get at these new features. The new mechanisms also
provide advanced search capabilities to save you time in finding the right
pixel format for your application.

Now it's time to use our first and maybe the most important WGL
extension. The `WGL_ARB_pixel_format` extension provides a mechanism
that allows you to check for and select pixel format features that go
beyond what Windows provides access to. For example, you can use this
extension to find a pixel format that supports multi-sampled rendering.

Pixel Format Attributes

Once your application has chosen a pixel format, or while walking
through the entire list yourself, you can get information on any particular

attribute of a pixel format by using the `wglGetPixelFormatAttribivARB()` function.

There is, however, a catch-22 to these and all other OpenGL extensions. You must have a valid OpenGL rendering context before you can call either `glGetString()` or `wglGetProcAddress()` of most OpenGL functions. This means that you must first create a temporary window, set a pixel format (we can actually cheat and just specify pixel format 1, which will be the first hardware accelerated format), and then obtain a pointer to one of the `wglGetPixelFormatAttribARB()` functions. A convenient place to do this might be the splash screen or perhaps an initial options dialog box that is presented to the user. You should not, however, try to use the Windows desktop because your application does not own it!

The following simple example queries for a single attribute — the number of pixel formats supported — so that you know how many you may need to look at:

```
int attrib[] = { WGL_NUMBER_PIXEL_FORMATS_ARB } ;
int nResults[1] = { 0} ;
int pixFmt = 1;
wglGetPixelFormatAttribivARB (hDC, pixFmt, 0, 1, attrib, nResults);
// nResults[0] now contains the number of exported pixelformats
```

It's also important to understand that all entrypoints you get for OpenGL are only valid for the current OpenGL context. If you delete a context and create another, you should fill in the entrypoints again. It is possible that the entrypoints are different between contexts, especially if you create contexts that support different versions of OpenGL or might be on different monitors driven by multiple graphics cards.

Full-Screen Rendering

Windowed OpenGL apps are great, but it's hard to create an immersive game if your application isn't in full screen! One of the most common developer questions is "How do I do full-screen rendering with OpenGL?" The truth is, if you've read this chapter, you already know how to do full-screen rendering with OpenGL — it's just like rendering into any other window! The real question is "How do I create a window that takes up the entire screen and has no borders?" Once you do this, the OpenGL driver will see what you are trying to do and give your application full control of the whole screen. Rendering into this window looks no different to your application than rendering into any other window in any other sample in this book, but OpenGL will do what it needs to do to make your application run in full-screen mode.

Even though this issue isn't strictly related to OpenGL, it is of enough interest to a wide number of our readers that we give this topic some coverage here. Creating a full-screen window is almost as simple as creating a regular window the size of the screen and starting at (0,0). We also use a different window style because we have no need for a title bar or border because none of that is visible. The code in Listing 14.9 does just that.

```
if(bUseFS)
{
    // Prepare for a mode set to the requested resolution
    DEVMODE dm;
    memset(&dm,0,sizeof(dm));
    dm.dmSize=sizeof(dm);
    dm.dmPelsWidth       = nWidth;
    dm.dmPelsHeight      = nHeight;
    dm.dmBitsPerPel      = 32;
    dm.dmFields=DM_BITSPERPEL|DM_PELSWIDTH|DM_PELSHEIGHT;

    long error = ChangeDisplaySettings(&dm, CDS_FULLSCREEN);

    if (error != DISP_CHANGE_SUCCESSFUL)
    {
        // Oops, something went wrong, let the user know.
        if (MessageBox(NULL, "Could not set full-screen mode.\ n"
            "Your video card may not support the requested mode.\ n"
            "Use windowed mode instead?", g_szAppName,
            MB_YESNO|MB_ICONEXCLAMATION)==IDYES)
        {
            g_InFullScreen = false;
            dwExtStyle  = WS_EX_APPWINDOW | WS_EX_WINDOWEDGE;
            dwWindStyle = WS_OVERLAPPEDWINDOW;
        }
        else
        {
            MessageBox(NULL, "Program will exit.",
                    "ERROR", MB_OK|MB_ICONSTOP);
            return false;
        }
    }
    else
    {
        // Mode set passed, set up the styles for full screen
        g_InFullScreen = true;
        dwExtStyle  = WS_EX_APPWINDOW;
        dwWindStyle = WS_POPUP;
        ShowCursor(FALSE);
    }
}

AdjustWindowRectEx(&g_windowRect, dwWindStyle, FALSE, dwExtStyle);

// Create the window again
    . . .
```

Listing 14.9: Setting up a full-screen window

Eliminating Visual Tearing

If your application is able to draw quickly and call SwapBuffers at a faster rate than the refresh rate of the monitor, an ugly effect called tearing can occur. If your application calls SwapBuffers before the previous frame is finished being scanned out, someone using your application will see part of one frame and part of the next.

The widely supported extension WGL_EXT_swap_control comes to the rescue! You can tell OpenGL how many video frames, or V-Syncs, are allowed to happen at minimum between swap calls. Just use the following function to set the interval:

```
BOOL wglSwapIntervalEXT(GLint interval);
```

If you pass in 0 for interval, the calls to SwapBuffers are unrestricted just as they are without this extension. But if you pass 1 for interval, only one SwapBuffers call is allowed to return for every vertical refresh of the monitor (every video frame). This is exactly what you want to eliminate tearing! All of the additional CPU time can be used for other things while your app waits for the swap to complete.

You can also pass larger intervals to **wglSwapIntervalEXT()** to wait more frames between swaps, but this can cause considerable stutter in your applications.

Cleaning Up

When you're all done with your application (or at least with OpenGL), you'll want to clean up after yourself. Recall that we have registered a class with RegisterClass, created a window with CreateWindowEx, got its device context (DC) using GetDC, created an OpenGL context with **wglCreateContextAttribsARB()**, and made it current. To tear down OpenGL, we need to first destroy any OpenGL objects that you may have created (such as textures, buffers, and so on), and then delete all of the window-system objects.

First, we delete the OpenGL context using **wglDeleteContext()**:

```
BOOL wglDeleteContext(HGLRC hglrc);
```

Next, we release the DC using ReleaseDC:

```
int ReleaseDC(HWND hWnd, HDC hDC);
```

Then, we delete the window using `DestroyWindow`:

```
BOOL DestroyWindow(HWND hWnd);
```

Finally, we can unregister the window class using `UnregisterClass`:

```
BOOL UnregisterClass(LPCTSTR lpClassName, HINSTANCE hInstance);
```

By calling each of these functions in the reverse order to which their corresponding setup functions were called, we return resources to the operating system and effectively clean up after ourselves.

OpenGL on Mac OS X

OpenGL is the native and preferred 3D rendering API on the Mac OS X platform. In fact, OpenGL is used at the lowest levels of the operating system for the desktop, GUI, and Mac OS X's own 2D graphics APIs and compositing engine (Quartz). The importance of OpenGL on the Mac platform cannot be overstated. With its favored status in the eyes of Apple (somewhat analogous to Direct3D's status with Microsoft), it enjoys significant support and investment by Apple in continual tuning and extension to the API. Despite this, there is no denying that they have been slow to adopt and keep pace with OpenGL's rapid evolution when it comes to keeping their implementation up to date with the latest specifications. While new GPU features are exposed on OS X as extensions, an official OpenGL 3+ implementation was not included in OS X until OS X 10.7, and this was OpenGL version 3.2, at a time when OpenGL 4.x was already becoming widespread on Windows. As of this writing, OS X 10.8 (Mountain Lion) still only supports OpenGL 3.2 Core Profile.

There are reasons for this, and Apple has always done things their own way for their own reasons. Mac OS X is not Windows, or Linux, and Apple places the customer experience above other considerations, and they prize uniformity in an app's ability to run on all currently shipping hardware. If you want to ship an OpenGL application that will run on every customer's Mac without worry (well, MOSTLY without worry) about driver revisions, worries about graphics cards, and so on, then the Mac platform is for you. If you want to really push the envelope with OpenGL in your application, using the latest features and the latest available graphics hardware, then the Mac is simply not for you. In what might be considered a bold move by Apple, OpenGL 3.2 is only available via a core context. The OpenGL compatibility context supports OpenGL 2.1 only, with some extensions that do penetrate into later hardware capabilities. However, if you want true OpenGL 3.2, with shader enhancements to boot, then you must create and use a core profile rendering context.

Since this book has left the compatibility context behind, we focus exclusively on using OpenGL 3.2 with Apple technologies. Many, but not all, of the examples elsewhere in the book can be made to run on OS X with some modification. OpenGL is a C API, and Apple technologies are sometimes C based as well, but more typically use Objective-C. Fortunately, Objective-C is a superset of C, so using OpenGL with Objective-C is as trivial as using OpenGL with C++.

The Faces of OpenGL on the Mac

There are four non-deprecated (notably, the well-known AGL interface popular with Carbon programmers has not been brought forward to the 64-bit world) OpenGL programming technologies available on the Mac, each with its own personality, history, and uses. Which one you use will vary greatly depending on how you prefer to create applications on the Mac and your specific rendering needs. You encounter all four of these technologies as you traverse the OS X OpenGL programming landscape, and actually all of these technologies can be used simultaneously and are complementary. They are enumerated in Table 14.3.

Table 14.3: OpenGL Technologies in OS X

Name	Description
GLUT	Provides a complete and portable framework for simple rendering-based applications. This interface is layered on top of NSOpenGL on OS X. GLUT has been around for many years and is available on multiple platforms.
NSOpenGL	Provides the OpenGL interface for developers using the Cocoa object-oriented framework for their applications.
CGL	The lowest-level OpenGL interface, available to all applications technologies.
GLKit	An OpenGL "helper" library available on iOS, with some functionality also available on OS X.

We use these interfaces to do the setup for OpenGL in a window or on a display device. After that is out of the way, OpenGL is just OpenGL! GLUT is really a legacy framework (it was used for all sample programs for previous editions of this and many other OpenGL books), and we will talk about it only briefly last in this chapter. Our primary focus, then, for this chapter will be Cocoa-based OpenGL programming because this is by and large the primary means by which you will structure your application framework and OpenGL initialization. CGL will be discussed within the context of a Cocoa-based program, using it for our full-screen example. GLKit is a library on iOS that was intended to make developing OpenGL ES 2.0 apps easier, especially for programmers used to the old fixed-function pipeline available in OpenGL ES 1.x. Some of GLKit, however, has migrated to the desktop, and of particular use are the 3D math routines and utilities. For this chapter, we'll be using the GLKit math routines to demonstrate their use rather than the vmath math class library used in the rest of the book.

So, What'cha Got Under the Hood There?

Before we get to the programming part, it is really useful to know ahead of time what version of OpenGL you have on your Mac, and what OpenGL extensions are available. The easiest way to get an X-ray view of your current OpenGL implementation is to download the Mac version of the OpenGL Extensions Viewer mentioned earlier (and shown in Figure 14.3), which is available on the app store for free. It's instructive to run this program every time you upgrade your OS X installation, or change graphics cards (Mac Pro users only).

OpenGL with Cocoa

Many programming languages are available to developers on Mac OS X. One very popular language on the Mac (but not as popular elsewhere) is Objective-C. To the uninitiated, Objective-C may appear a strange blend of C and C++ with some completely new syntax thrown in. But Objective-C is also the foundation of a very pervasive application development technology in the Apple world called Cocoa.

Cocoa is best described as both a collection of application framework classes and a visual programming paradigm. Developers do quite a bit of work in Interface Builder (now rolled in as part of XCode), designing user interfaces, assigning properties, and even making connections between

Figure 14.3: The OpenGL Extensions Viewer is free on the Mac App Store.

events. Objective-C classes are sub-classed from controls or are created from scratch to add application functionality. Fortunately, OpenGL is a first-class citizen in this development environment.

Creating a Cocoa Program

A Cocoa-based program can be created using the New Project Assistant in XCode. Figure 14.4 shows the newly created CocoaGL project after we have added the OpenGL and GLKit frameworks.

Adding an OpenGL View

Cocoa applications store resources and GUI layouts in a XIB file (a compiled version of the old NIB, which for historic reasons stands for NEXTSTEP Interface Builder). Select the MainMenu.xib file under the Resources folder. This starts the integrated Interface Builder portion of the XCode environment, and opens this XIB for editing. You may need to expand the utilities view on the right, after which your screen should look very similar to that shown in Figure 14.5.

You may also need to select the Window icon on the vertical toolbar to show the main window of our newly created application contained by this

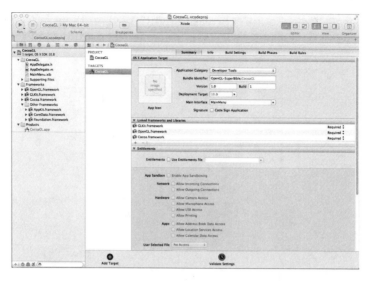

Figure 14.4: The initial `CocoaGL` project

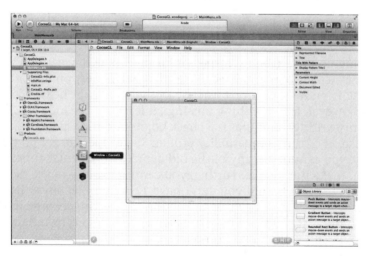

Figure 14.5: Interface Builder is ready to build your OpenGL app.

.xib file. In the object library, scroll down until you see the OpenGL View object. Click and drag this view over to the main window, and resize it to fill the main window. You can also resize the main window to taste. As shown in Figure 14.6, we now have an OpenGL-enabled window nearly ready to go. This view now needs to be connected to a Cocoa class derived from `NSOpenGLView`. Couldn't be easier right? Well, in the words of the late Amelia Pond, "Okay Kid, THIS, is where it gets complicated."

Figure 14.6: The OpenGL window ready to go... or is it?

Core Profile Support in Cocoa

If you bring up the attributes inspector for the OpenGL view, you will find all sorts of nice settings and checkboxes that will allow you to configure the OpenGL rendering context used by this view to your heart's content. There is however, just one thing missing (at least as of XCode 4.5.2 at the time of this writing), and that is a check box to use the OpenGL Core Profile instead of the Compatibility profile. Since OpenGL 3.2 on OS X is core only, you cannot use any of the old deprecated OpenGL functionality when you make this choice. Further, you cannot use any of the new OpenGL 3+ features then if you don't have a core profile. Since the interface builder does not give us the option of selecting a core profile context in the first place, we have to take things into our own hands. Of course no, it isn't really THAT complicated!

Overriding `NSOpenGL`

We begin by creating our own Objective-C view class derived from NSView, shown in Figure 14.7. This creates two files and adds them to the project: GLCoreProfile.h and GLCoreProfile.m. We now have a choice to make. We could actually add the features to an NSView class such that it would support OpenGL rendering (in which case we actually could have just a regular view in Interface Builder), or we could change the class we created to be derived from NSOpenGLView. The latter choice requires that less functionality of the base class be reimplemented, and in the likely event that Apple adds core profile functionality in the future, this choice will require less refactoring should we need to modernize the code later.

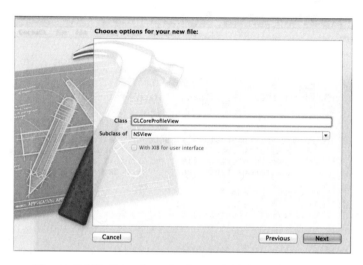

Figure 14.7: Creating the basic NSView view class

Listing 14.10 shows the definition of our view class. XCode created the file for us, we've modified it to be derived from NSOpenGLView instead of NSView, and we have specified the four main methods that we are going to need to implement and override to get a skeleton core context supporting view up and going.

```
@interface GLCoreProfileView : NSOpenGLView
{

}
- (id)    initWithCoder:(NSCoder *)aDecoder;
- (void) drawRect:(NSRect) bounds;
- (void) prepareOpenGL;
- (void) reshape;

@end
```

Listing 14.10: Definition of the Objective-C GLCoreProfileView class

Naturally, for a full-fledged application we are going to want to flesh out our view class considerably more than this. We are showing here the minimal skeleton for a well-behaved OpenGL view. Now let's look at our overridden methods, the most important of which is initWithCoder, the method that initializes our view and OpenGL context, shown in Listing 14.11.

```
-(id)initWithCoder:(NSCoder *)aDecoder
{
 NSOpenGLPixelFormatAttribute pixelFormatAttributes[] =
     {
     NSOpenGLPFAColorSize,         32,
     NSOpenGLPFADepthSize,         24,
     NSOpenGLPFAStencilSize,        8,
     NSOpenGLPFAAccelerated,
     NSOpenGLPFAOpenGLProfile, NSOpenGLProfileVersion3_2Core,
     0
     };

 NSOpenGLPixelFormat *pixelFormat = [[[NSOpenGLPixelFormat alloc]
             initWithAttributes:pixelFormatAttributes] autorelease];
 NSOpenGLContext* openGLContext = [[[NSOpenGLContext alloc]
             initWithFormat:pixelFormat shareContext:nil] autorelease];

 [super initWithCoder:aDecoder];
 [self setOpenGLContext:openGLContext];
 [openGLContext makeCurrentContext];

 return self;
}
```

Listing 14.11: Initialization of our core context OpenGL view

Before OpenGL can be initialized for a window, you must first select an appropriate pixel format. A pixel format describes the hardware buffer configuration for 3D rendering — things like the depth of the color buffer, the size of the stencil buffer, and whether the buffer is on-screen (the default) or off-screen. The pixel format is described by the Cocoa data type NSOpenGLPixelformat.

To select an appropriate pixel format for your needs, you first construct an array of integer attributes of type NSOpenGLPixelFormatAttribute. For example, the following array from our initialization code requests a 32-bit color buffer (usually 8 bits of red, green, blue, and alpha), a 24-bit depth buffer, 8-bit stencil, and an accelerated pixel format, not the software OpenGL renderer provided for Apple as a fallback. The final two entries specifically request an OpenGL 3.2 Core Context profile. You may get other attributes as well, but you are essentially saying these are all you really care about:

```
NSOpenGLPixelFormatAttribute pixelFormatAttributes[] =
    {
    NSOpenGLPFAColorSize,         32,
    NSOpenGLPFADepthSize,         24,
```

```
NSOpenGLPFAStencilSize,     8,
NSOpenGLPFAAccelerated,
NSOpenGLPFAOpenGLProfile, NSOpenGLProfileVersion3_2Core,
0
};
```

Note that you must terminate the array with 0 or nil. Next, you allocate the pixel format using this array of attributes. If the pixel format cannot be created, the allocation routine returns nil, and you should do something appropriate because as far as your OpenGL rendering is concerned, it's game over.

```
NSOpenGLPixelFormat *pixelFormat = [[[NSOpenGLPixelFormat alloc]
                    initWithAttributes:pixelFormatAttributes] autorelease];
```

Most attributes are either a Boolean flag or contain an integer value. The Boolean flags set the attribute by simply being present, for example, NSOpenGLPFAAccelerated in the preceding example. An integer flag on the other hand, such as NSOpenGLPFADepthSize, is expected to be followed by an integer value that specifies the number of bits desired for the depth buffer. The available attributes and their meanings are listed in Table 14.4.

Table 14.4: Cocoa Pixel Format Attributes

Attribute (NSOpenGLPFA*)	Description
AllRenderers	A Boolean attribute that indicates all available renderers should be considered.
OpenGLProfile	Set to either NSOpenGLProfileVersion3_2Core or NSOpenGLProfileVersionLegacy (the default).
DoubleBuffer	A Boolean attribute that indicates a double buffered pixel format is required.
Stereo	A Boolean attribute that indicates only stereo (left/right) pixel formats are to be considered.
ColorSize	A numeric attribute specifying the desired depth of the color buffer. In this attribute's absence, the color buffer will always match the screen's color depth.
AlphaSize	A numeric attribute specifying the desired depth of the alpha color channel.
DepthSize	A numeric attribute specifying the desired depth of the depth buffer.

continued

OpenGL on Mac OS X   **655**

Table 14.4: *Continued*

Attribute (NSOpenGLPFA*)	Description
StencilSize	A numeric attribute specifying the desired depth of the stencil buffer.
MinimumPolicy	A Boolean attribute that indicates the pixel format choosing policy should select color, depth, and stencil buffers equal or greater than the sizes specified by the previous attributes.
MaximumPolicy	A Boolean attribute that indicates for the color, depth, and stencil buffer values, if non-zero is requested, the pixel format choosing policy should select the maximum value available.
OffScreen	A Boolean attribute that indicates only renderers capable of rendering to an off-screen buffer should be considered.
FullScreen	A Boolean attribute that indicates only renderers capable of full-screen rendering should be considered.
SampleBuffers	A numeric attribute indicating the number of multi-sample buffers desired.
Samples	A numeric attribute indicating the number of samples per multi-sample buffer.
ColorFloat	A Boolean attribute that indicates only formats that use floating-point color buffers should be considered. Note: The value of NSOpenGLPFAColorSize should be 64 for half-float pixel components, or 128 for full 32-bit floating-point components. Not all hardware supports these formats; be sure and check for a null pixel format return value.
Multisample	A Boolean attribute that when used with NSOpenGLPFASampleBuffers and NSOpenGLPFASamples hints to OpenGL to prefer multi-sampling over super-sampling.
Supersample	A Boolean attribute that when used with NSOpenGLPFASampleBuffers and NSOpenGLPFASamples hints to OpenGL to prefer super-sampling.

continued

Attribute (NSOpenGLPFA*)	Description
SampleAlpha	A Boolean attribute that when used with NSOpenGLPFASampleBuffers and NSOpenGLPFASamples hints to OpenGL that alpha values should be included in multi-sampling operations.
RendererID	A numeric attribute that specifies a specific OpenGL renderer ID. A notable example is kCGLRendererGenericID, which selects the Apple software renderer.
SingleRenderer	A Boolean attribute that specifies only single renderer can be used. This disables OpenGL's ability to render on different screens when driven by different graphics accelerator cards.
NoRecovery	A Boolean attribute that prevents OpenGL from switching to an alternate renderer should the accelerated renderer fail due to lack of resources.
Accelerated	A Boolean attribute that indicates only hardware-accelerated renderers are to be considered.
ClosestPolicy	A Boolean attribute that indicates a color buffer closest to the one requested should be selected regardless of the actual color buffer depth supported by the device.
Robust	A Boolean attribute that indicates only renderers that do not have failure modes (for lack of resources) are to be considered.
BackingStore	A Boolean attribute that indicates only renderers that have a back store the same size as the front color buffer.
MPSafe	A Boolean attribute that specifies only renderers that are multi-processor safe are to be considered.
Window	A Boolean attribute that indicates only renderers that can render to a window are to be considered.
MultiScreen	A Boolean attribute that indicates only renderers that can drive multiple screens are to be considered.

continued

Table 14.4: *Continued*

Attribute (NSOpenGLPFA*)	Description
Compliant	A Boolean attribute that requires only OpenGL-compliant renderers be considered. This is implied unless the NSOpenGLPFAAllRenderers attribute has been specified.
ScreenMask	A numeric attribute that is a bit mask of supported physical screens.
AllowOfflineRenderers	A Boolean attribute that indicates offline renderers may be considered.
AcceleratedCompute	A Boolean attribute that indicates only renderers that support OpenCL should be used.
VirtualScreenCount	A numeric attribute that indicates the number of virtual screens in this format.

The actual creation of an OpenGL context by selecting a renderer matching our desired pixel format is shown here:

```
NSOpenGLContext* openGLContext = [[[NSOpenGLContext alloc]
    initWithFormat:pixelFormat shareContext:nil] autorelease];
```

It would be best practice to check this as well for nil, but for the purposes of an abbreviated code sample, we will dispense and move on to actually setting the context for our view and making it current:

```
[self setOpenGLContext:openGLContext];
[openGLContext makeCurrentContext];
```

On most platforms, you may have more than one OpenGL rendering context, but only one can be "current" at a time for a given thread. The current rendering context receives all OpenGL commands on that thread. You can have multiple contexts and multiple threads of course, but having multiple threads rendering to a single context is not recommended if not outright prohibited. The additional overhead of thread synchronization is not worth any other benefits. On the other hand, multiple threads rendering to multiple rendering contexts is readily done, and if the two contexts refer to different graphics cards, for example, on a multi-display system, then there are clear advantages to this approach. In addition, multiple contexts can "share" resources such that you could have a background thread loading textures and other data into a shared OpenGL context, which can then be used by another thread controlling a foreground context.

A Couple More Wires

Before any of our code in our custom derived class will be called, we have to actually connect out class to this view in Interface Builder. Do this in the identity inspector with the OpenGL window selected. The class name will be NSOpenGLView, but we will change it to our GLCoreProfileView. Finally, we also have to change the parent window so that it does not use One Shot memory. This flag is on by default, and it tells the parent window that it is okay to delete the sub-window objects when it is minimized to the dock or hidden. With an OpenGL window, this would have the unfortunate side effect of breaking the link between the view and the OpenGL context, which would prevent further rendering operations from being displayed. Figure 14.8 shows the One Shot box unchecked in the Attributes tab. Click the caption of the main window to get to it.

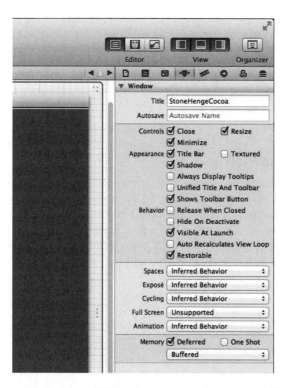

Figure 14.8: Turn off the One Shot memory attribute.

Do Me First!

Typical OpenGL rendering tasks usually require some one-time setup. Perhaps to preload all the textures, shaders, geometry, and so on that will be used during repeated rendering operations. The NSOpenGLView class has a method that is called before any other rendering operations occur called prepareOpenGL. Listing 14.12 shows the body from our example that merely prints to the console information about the selected rendering context, and sets the color buffer clear color to a very dark gray.

```
- (void)prepareOpenGL
    {
    glClearColor(0.1f, 0.1f, 0.1f, 1.0f);

    printf("Version: %s\r\n", glGetString(GL_VERSION));
    printf("Renderer: %s\r\n", glGetString(GL_RENDERER));
    printf("Vendor: %s\r\n", glGetString(GL_VENDOR));
    printf("GLSL Version: %s\r\n",
                        glGetString(GL_SHADING_LANGUAGE_VERSION));
    }
```

Listing 14.12: Outputting information about the OpenGL context

The output, verifying an OpenGL Core Context on the author's MacBook Pro, is shown below:

```
Version: 3.2 NVIDIA-8.0.61
Renderer: NVIDIA GeForce 9400M OpenGL Engine
Vendor: NVIDIA Corporation
GLSL Version: 1.50
```

Managing Your Viewport

Whenever an NSOpenGLView-derived view is created or resized, the reshape method is called. Shown in Listing 14.13, this is a good place to reset the viewport dimensions. In addition, most projection matrices also need to take into account the size of the window, so this is also a great place to put any code that creates this matrix for you. Even if you are rendering full screen (discussed later), this method will be called at least one time before rendering begins.

```
- (void) reshape
    {
    NSRect bounds = [self bounds];
    glViewport(0, 0, NSWidth(bounds), NSHeight(bounds));
    }
```

Listing 14.13: Code called whenever the view changes size

Draw Your Stuff!

Finally, we get to where all the action takes place. The typical NSView (or derived class such as NSOpenGLView) calls the drawRect method to fill the view. This is where we can put our OpenGL rendering code. Listing 14.14 shows our short example rendering code, which does nothing more than clear the color buffer.

```
- (void)drawRect:(NSRect)bounds
    {
    glClear(GL_COLOR_BUFFER_BIT);
    glFlush();
    }
```

Listing 14.14: Code called whenever the view changes size

Double or Single Buffered?

At this point, the astute reader may be imagining the sound of screeching tires on pavement. Was that a **glFlush()** you saw in Listing 14.14 instead of some sort of buffer swap call? Indeed it was, and this brings us to an interesting subtlety of OpenGL on Mac OS X.

On Mac OS X, the entire desktop is actually OpenGL accelerated. Anytime you are rendering with OpenGL, you are always rendering to an off-screen buffer. A buffer swap does nothing but signal the OS that your rendering is ready to be composited with the rest of the desktop. You can think of the desktop compositing engine as your front buffer. Thus, in windowed OpenGL applications (this applies to both Cocoa and the now deprecated Carbon), all OpenGL windows are really single buffered. Depending on how you look at it, it would also be okay to say that all OpenGL windows are really double buffered, with the desktop composite being the front buffer. Pick whichever one helps you sleep best at night! In fact, if you were to execute a **glDrawBuffer()** with the GL_FRONT parameter, the drivers on the Mac actually would fall into a triple-buffered mode! In reality, all OpenGL windows on the Mac should be treated as single buffered. The buffer swap calls are really just doing a **glFlush()**, unless you are working with a full-screen context. For this reason (and many others — the least of which is that you are bypassing the driver's own good sense as to when to flush), you should avoid glFlush in Cocoa views until you have completed all of your OpenGL rendering. You don't need to worry about what will happen if the OpenGL command buffer gets full and is flushed automatically either. The desktop compositing engine knows not to display the contents of the "back" buffer until a **glFlush()** has been called. We will show you how to create genuine double-buffered contexts with real buffer swaps when we get to the full-screen section a little later.

Introducing GLKit

GLKit is a helper framework intended to ease the transition from the OpenGL ES 1.x fixed-function pipeline to the new OpenGL ES 2.0 shader-based pipeline. Originally available on iOS 5.0, GLKit migrated to the desktop with OS X 10.8 and is now available for desktop applications as well. There are four main areas GLKit covers: texture loading, math libraries, effects, and view/controllers. Of these four, the view and view controller classes are only available on iOS and so are not going to be covered in this chapter. In addition, the effects classes, intended to wrap up portions of the fixed-function pipeline in a shader compatible way, will also not be covered as this violates the spirit of intent for this book... modern OpenGL with shaders. This leaves us with some texture loading utilities and a collection of math routines optimized and intended for use directly with OpenGL.

All 3D programmers need a collection of 3D math routines for manipulation of vectors, matrices, and such. Elsewhere in the book, we used the vmath library, which is a convenient C++ class library that mimics the behavior of the OpenGL Shading Language. In this chapter, we will use GLKit exclusively for our example program, a 3D walkthrough of Stonehenge. For a complete and thorough breakdown of GLKit, you should see the "Introduction to GLKit" document on the Apple Developer Relations Web site.

The data types in GLKit are very OpenGL-esque in their naming conventions. GLKMatrix3 is a 3×3 matrix, and GLKMatrix4 is a 4×4 matrix, for example. In addition there is GLKVector2, GLKVector3, and GLKVector4 representing 2, 3, and 4 component vectors, respectively. Numerous functions provide all the typically necessary operations, dot and cross products, matrix multiplication, transposes, vector transformations, and even a GLKMatrix4MakeLookAt method for creating a camera transform. There is also a GLKMatrixStack that may be very useful for keeping track of hierarchical transformations.

Two classes in GLKit handle the responsibility of loading and managing textures. The GLKTextureLoader class handles the task of loading textures, returning objects of the type GLKTextureInfo. These classes can be used to load 2D textures and cube maps, and the GLKTextureLoader class can work asynchronously loading textures in the background using a shared OpenGL context on another thread.

The GLKTextureInfo class contains all the useful information to know about a loaded texture, its size, OpenGL target type, and so on. These read-only properties are listed and described in Table 14.5 below.

Table 14.5: Read-Only Properties of the GLKTextureInfo Class

Method	Description
alphaState	Describes how alpha information is stored in the image's pixel data. A property of type GLKTextureInfoAlphaState equal to GLKTextureInfoAlphaStateNone, GLKTextureInfoAlphaStateNonPremultiplied, or GLKTextureInfoAlphaStatePremultiplied.
containsMipmaps	A Boolean value indicating the presence of mipmaps.
height	The height in pixels of the loaded texture.
name	The GLuint "name" of the texture used with **glBindTexture()** to bind a texture to a context.
target	The target of the texture. Only GL_TEXTURE_2D and GL_TEXTURE_CUBEMAP are currently supported.
textureOrigin	The location of the origin of the source image, either GLKTextureInfoOriginUnknown, GLKTextureInfoOriginTopLeft, or GLKTextureInfoOriginBottomLeft. This is set by the GLKTextureLoader class call and indicates if the texture was flipped on load.
width	The width in pixels of the loaded texture.

We will show the most important GLKit classes and methods in action within the context of our main example program for this chapter, a 3D walkthrough of Stonehenge.

Stonehenge

When OpenGL first came to the Windows platform on Windows NT, there was an example program that rendered a 3D view of Stonehenge. Software rendered, with no texture or special effects to speak of, it was a clunky and plain demo by today's standards. In the spirit of this original demonstration of OpenGL on a non-SGI platform, the rendering example program for this chapter is a recreation of the original Stonehenge. Largely an artist's conception, the model does attempt to hold to what the original structure was thought at least by some to be. Having a real example program then gives us some more reasonable context for demonstrating Mac-specific OpenGL nuances. The geometry for this model was created by Ed Womack some years ago on commission from the author for other projects.

We will build the Stonehenge example using a single C++ class that manages the model creation, texture and shader loading, and navigation within the model. We will use GLKit for all 3D math needs and texture loading, and then include this C++ rendering engine in our Objective-C Cocoa-view-based example, then go full screen, and finally drop it into a GLUT-based framework for completeness' sake. A sample of the completed Stonehenge demo is shown in Figure 14.9.

Figure 14.9: This chapter's demo rendering in a Cocoa view

The GLStonehenge class can easily be wired into any application framework using the following five public interfaces.

Load models, shaders, textures, and so on, and set up the world for rendering:

```
void GLStonehenge::initModels(void);
```

Call this anytime the window changes size for the correct viewport and projection matrix settings:

```
void GLStonehenge::resized(int w, int h);
```

Call this to update the scene from the current camera position to move forward:

```
void GLStonehenge::render(void);
```

Move the camera position forward within the environment:

```
void GLStonehenge::moveForward(float distance);
```

Rotate the camera left/right (in radians):

```
void GLStonehenge::rotateLocalY(float angle);
```

You can only walk around in a single plane in "Stonehenge World."

The majority of this book is about how to write shaders, load them, create and use buffer objects, and so on. We will not belabor the fundamentals of OpenGL here by killing space with a blow by blow of how the entire scene is put together in OpenGL. Instead, let's take a look at how GLKit is used to manage our textures, and take care of our 3D math chores.

Although the Stonehenge engine is written in C++, the GLKit classes are Objective-C classes and make use of other Objective-C frameworks. To show how easy it is to mix these two programming languages, the GLStonehenge class will be implemented in GLStonehenge.mm. The .mm file extension denotes Objective-C++, which is simply a C++ compatible version of Objective-C. In fact, to use C++ in our projects, we will also make all of our Objective-C modules C++ compatible by naming them with the .mm file extension.

Loading Textures with GLKit

Our 3D environment contains only five textures, all stored as .png files. Each texture will be kept track of with an instance of GLKTextureInfo. The declarations for our five textures in the GLStonehenge.h header are listed here:

```
GLKTextureInfo          *textureStones;
GLKTextureInfo          *textureNormalMap;
GLKTextureInfo          *textureSky;
GLKTextureInfo          *textureGround;
GLKTextureInfo          *textureGroundDetail;
```

For a larger or more involved environment, you might well consider making an array of GLKTextureInfo pointers, but for the purposes of demonstration code, this makes the code easier to follow.

In the GLStonehenge.mm file, the member function initModels is called to load all the model information for the environment. Typically on the Mac, we store application resources in the app bundle in the /Resources folder. We will need the path to the .PNG file as a Cocoa NSString type, and the following code returns the file path to the resource we need to load our first texture:

```
NSString *path = [[NSBundle mainBundle] pathForResource:@"rock" ofType:@"png"];
```

Next, we ask the GLKTextureLoader class, using a static function, to load the requested texture as shown here:

```
NSError *error = nil;
textureStones = [GLKTextureLoader textureWithContentsOfFile:path options:nil
error:&error];
[textureStones retain];

if(!textureStones)
    NSLog(@"Texture load failure: %@", error);
```

The textureWithContentsOfFile method loads the file using the default settings for texture loading. If the return value is nil, then an error has occurred, and the NSError object can be used to get details on what went wrong.

The GLKTextureLoader can load textures of any data type supported by the Mac's native Quartz graphics engine, with or without alpha channels. When textures are loaded in this way, they have a filter mode of GL_LINEAR and an edge wrap mode of GL_CLAMP_TO_EDGE. For our purposes, we want to generate mipmaps from a single resolution .PNG file, and we need the texture coordinates to repeat. All of our textures will follow this convention, and the following code then sets up our texture in the manner we need:

```
glBindTexture(GL_TEXTURE_2D, textureStones.name);
glTexParameteri(GL_TEXTURE_2D, GL_TEXTURE_WRAP_S, GL_REPEAT);
glTexParameteri(GL_TEXTURE_2D, GL_TEXTURE_WRAP_T, GL_REPEAT);
glTexParameteri(GL_TEXTURE_2D, GL_TEXTURE_MIN_FILTER,
                              GL_LINEAR_MIPMAP_NEAREST);
glTexParameteri(GL_TEXTURE_2D, GL_TEXTURE_MAG_FILTER, GL_LINEAR);
glGenerateMipmap(GL_TEXTURE_2D);
```

Whenever we need to reactivate this texture during rendering, we'll again use the texture object name supplied by the GLKTextureInfo object:

```
glBindTexture(GL_TEXTURE_2D, textureStones.name);
```

3D Math with GLKit

Our 3D math needs for the Stonehenge demo are relatively simple. For our shaders, we need a perspective projection matrix, a camera transform, and a normal matrix for lighting purposes, and we'll need to transform our lighting vector into eye space.

A 4 × 4 projection matrix is defined in the header like so:

```
GLKMatrix4  mProjection;
```

When the view is created, and if subsequently resized, the resized member function needs to be called. Here, we use the width and height of our window to set the viewport, and create an appropriate perspective matrix using the GLKit utility function GLKMatrix4MakePerspective:

```
void GLStoneHenge::resized(int w, int h)
    {
    glViewport(0, 0, w, h);

    mProjection = GLKMatrix4MakePerspective(GLKMathDegreesToRadians(60.0f),
                                            float(w)/float(h), 0.1f,
                                            1000.0f);
    }
```

For this example, the model-view matrix is simply nothing more than the camera transform. A single GLKMatrix4 instance named mCamera will contain this matrix. We'll use a simple frame of reference technique to represent our camera's position and orientation in space, and so the header also contains this structure definition

```
struct CAMERA_FRAME {
    GLKVector3  vWhere;        // Location of camera
    GLKVector3  vUp;           // Up Vector of camera
    GLKVector3  vForward;      // Forward vector of camera
    };
```

and an instance thereof named cameraFrame. The camera's position and orientation data are then used to build a camera transformation matrix using the GLKMatrix4MakeLookAt function:

```
// Set up camera transform
GLKVector3 vLooking = GLKVector3Add(cameraFrame.vWhere, cameraFrame.vForward);
```

```
mCamera = GLKMatrix4MakeLookAt(
cameraFrame.vWhere.x, cameraFrame.vWhere.y, cameraFrame.vWhere.z,
vLooking.x, vLooking.y, vLooking.z,
cameraFrame.vUp.x, cameraFrame.vUp.y, cameraFrame.vUp.z);
```

Note that the GLKMatrix4MakeLookAt wants a point where the camera is looking, not the vector. We calculate this vector ourselves by simply adding the location to the direction in which we are looking (assuming a vector length of 1.0) using the GLKVector3Add function.

Whenever the mvp (model-view-projection) matrix is required for a shader uniform, it can be found simply enough now by multiplying these two matrices together using the GLKMatrix4Multiply function:

```
GLKMatrix4 matrixMVP = GLKMatrix4Multiply(mProjection, mCamera);
```

Our final matrix magic trick is to get the 3×3 normal matrix from the camera matrix. The normal matrix contains just the rotation component of the model-view transform and is used to rotate lighting vectors for proper lighting calculations in a shader. Extraction of the upper 3×3 portion of a 4×4 matrix is done with a single function call to GLKMatrix4GetMatrix3:

```
GLKMatrix3 mNormal = GLKMatrix4GetMatrix3(mCamera);
```

Camera motion in the Stonehenge example is handled by two functions: one to move the camera forward or backward, and one to allow the camera to rotate left or right. Forward motion with a vector-based camera is trivial. The forward vector is multiplied by the distance to move (use a negative distance to move backward!), and then added to the camera location. The short moveForward function is shown here in its entirety:

```
/////////////////////////////////////////////////////////////
// Moving forward is just an addition along the forward vector
void GLStoneHenge::moveForward(float distance)
    {
    // Scale forward vector by distance
    GLKVector3 vForward =
        GLKVector3MultiplyScalar(cameraFrame.vForward, distance);

    // Add result to location
    cameraFrame.vWhere = GLKVector3Add(cameraFrame.vWhere, vForward);
    }
```

Our example program uses a very simplified camera system, and in addition to moving forward or backward along your line of sight (we will tie these to the arrow keys, by the way), you can also turn left or right. This rotation is about the y axis in camera space, and is simply accomplished by rotating the forward vector appropriately. We can create an appropriate rotation matrix with GLKMatrix4MakeRotation, and then transform our vector with it using GLKMatrix4MultiplyVector3. The complete source for this short function is shown here, also in its entirety:

```
///////////////////////////////////////////////////////////////
// The Camera can turn left or right only
void GLStoneHenge::rotateLocalY(float angle)
    {
    // Create a rotation matrix around the camera's up vector
    GLKMatrix4 rot = GLKMatrix4MakeRotation(angle,
            cameraFrame.vUp.x, cameraFrame.vUp.y, cameraFrame.vUp.z);

    // Rotate the camera's z axis around this vector... that's all
    GLKVector3 vNewForward =
            GLKMatrix4MultiplyVector3(rot, cameraFrame.vForward);

    cameraFrame.vForward = GLKVector3Normalize(vNewForward);
    }
```

Passing GLKit vectors and matrices into shaders as uniforms is trivial. The GLKVectorX data types have a .v member that returns a pointer to an array containing the vector elements, and the GLKMatrixX data types have a .m member that yields an appropriate array of floating-point values as well.

Putting It Together in Cocoa

Now that we've seen how the Stonehenge model is manipulated with GLKit, let's return to our earlier Cocoa example program, but this time we'll expand it considerably by incorporating our Stonehenge rendering class and some other window dressing. We'll start by creating a new project and proceeding much like we did with the CocoaGL example program. We'll call this example StonehengeCocoa and create the same NSOpenGLView-derived view class as before. We add the Stonehenge class files and the resources needed for the project, a few model files, textures, and shaders. We have also modified some OpenGL text output code from the Apple OpenGL examples to work with the new core profile. We'll use this to display a frames per second indicator. The completed project file with all the added files is shown in Figure 14.10.

Wiring in the Stonehenge code and adding smooth motion to the GLOpenGLCoreProfileView class is pretty simple. In the header, we simply add an instance of the GLStonehenge class:

```
GLStonehenge    stonehenge;
```

In the main body, we need a little extra Cocoa plumbing, but that's all. In the previously discussed prepareOpenGL method, we call the initializer on the Stonehenge engine and set up a timer so that the screen is continually

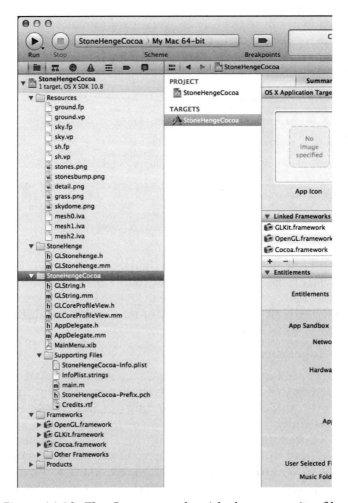

Figure 14.10: The Cocoa sample with the supporting files

updated. In this case, we set the update interval to 0.0 seconds to get the highest frame rate possible. Setting this to 1.0/60.0 would attempt to render at 60 fps. We'll see later another way to limit the frame rate, and why you might want to, but we want to see the frame rate change as we monkey with this project, so we'll leave it as fast as possible for the moment. The timer calls the idle function, which simply calls our method to refresh the screen:

```
- (void)prepareOpenGL
    {
    stonehenge.initModels();
```

```
NSTimer *pTimer =
        [NSTimer timerWithTimeInterval: 0.0f target:self
        selector:@selector(idle:) userInfo:nil repeats:YES];

[[NSRunLoop currentRunLoop]addTimer:pTimer forMode:NSDefaultRunLoopMode];
}


- (void)idle:(NSTimer*)pTimer
    {
    [self drawRect:[self bounds]];
    }
```

Next, the reshape function tells the engine that the screen has changed size:

```
- (void) reshape
    {
    NSRect bounds = [self bounds];
    stonehenge.resized(NSWidth(bounds), NSHeight(bounds));
    }
```

Using the Arrow Keys

Movement is a bit more involved. We will use the keyboard's arrow keys to move the camera forward and backward, and allow rotation left and right. We could move the camera a small amount every time a key is pressed, and use the keyboard repeat rate of the computer to determine how quickly the camera is updated. This tends to give less than ideal results. Even if the frame rate is very high, the keyboard repeat rate is typically much lower, and it will make the frame rate and resulting animation to appear choppy.

A better approach is to set up an array of flags for the movement keys, and turn the flags on when the key is pressed, and turn the flag off when the key is released. The initial key press is still dependent on the keyboard response time, but fast subsequent frames will see the key as down, and motion will be smooth. At the top of GLCoreProfileView.mm, we have created a bit field called moveFlags, and a set of bit definitions to indicate the various degrees of freedom to move about in the environment:

```
#define MOVE_NONE_BIT       0X00
#define MOVE_FORWARD_BIT    0x01
#define MOVE_BACKWARD_BIT   0x02
#define MOVE_LEFT_BIT       0x04
#define MOVE_RIGHT_BIT      0x08
GLuint   moveFlags = 0x0;
```

Child windows in Cocoa do not by default receive keyboard notifications. In order to receive them, the view must respond to acceptsFirstResponder and return TRUE. It must also register itself as the new first responder. The first responder is simply the first view in a hierarchy that is given the opportunity to respond to window events, such as keystrokes:

```
- (BOOL)acceptsFirstResponder
    {
    [[self window] makeFirstResponder:self];
    return YES;
    }
```

Next, we need to respond to the keyUp and keyDown messages, and toggle the appropriate flags based on the key pressed or released. Then, in our drawRect routine, we will move the camera appropriately based on which key flags have been set. This complete dance is listed in Listing 14.15.

```
/////////////////////////////////////////////////////////
// When the key is up, turn the bit off
- (void)keyUp:(NSEvent *)event
    {
    int key = (int)[[event characters] characterAtIndex:0];

    switch(key)
        {
        case NSUpArrowFunctionKey:
            moveFlags &= ~MOVE_FORWARD_BIT;
            break;
        case NSDownArrowFunctionKey:
            moveFlags &= ~MOVE_BACKWARD_BIT;
            break;
        case NSLeftArrowFunctionKey:
            moveFlags &= ~MOVE_LEFT_BIT;
            break;
        case NSRightArrowFunctionKey:
            moveFlags &= ~MOVE_RIGHT_BIT;
            break;
        }
    }

/////////////////////////////////////////////////////////
// When the key goes down, turn the bit on
- (void)keyDown:(NSEvent*)event
    {
    int key = (int)[[event characters] characterAtIndex:0];

    switch(key)
        {
        case NSUpArrowFunctionKey:
            moveFlags |= MOVE_FORWARD_BIT;
            break;
        case NSDownArrowFunctionKey:
            moveFlags |= MOVE_BACKWARD_BIT;
            break;
        case NSLeftArrowFunctionKey:
            moveFlags |= MOVE_LEFT_BIT;
            break;
        case NSRightArrowFunctionKey:
```

```
                moveFlags |= MOVE_RIGHT_BIT;
                break;
        }
    }

- (void)drawRect:(NSRect)bounds
    {
    static float fDistance = 0.025f;
    static CStopWatch cameraTimer;
    float deltaT = cameraTimer.GetElapsedSeconds();
    cameraTimer.Reset();

    if(moveFlags & MOVE_FORWARD_BIT)
        stonehenge.moveForward(fDistance * deltaT);

    if(moveFlags & MOVE_BACKWARD_BIT)
        stonehenge.moveForward(fDistance * -deltaT);

    if(moveFlags & MOVE_LEFT_BIT)
        stonehenge.rotateLocalY(fDistance * 30.0f * deltaT);

    if(moveFlags & MOVE_RIGHT_BIT)
        stonehenge.rotateLocalY(fDistance * -30.0f * deltaT);

    stonehenge.render();
    glFlush();
    }
```

Listing 14.15: Controlling movement smoothly with keyboard bit flags and a timer

In the drawRect method, note the use of a timer class, CStopWatch (the code for this timer is also included in this project). This class simply returns the time passed in seconds as a floating-point value. We want the movement to be smooth, but we also want time-based motion, both forward and backwards, as well as rotations. After updating the camera position appropriately, the Stonehenge engine is told to render, and we call glFlush() to finish the frame.

Retina Displays

In 2012, Apple released laptops with "Retina" displays. These are exceptionally high-resolution displays, so called "Retina" because the pixels are so small and close together that the human eye cannot distinguish any further resolution increase at a normal viewing distance. This concept was first introduced on Apple's popular iOS devices.

The approach Apple took for this technology is interesting. If the displays were simply twice the resolution, then applications, GUI elements, fonts, and text would all appear half their physical size on the screen. Instead device independent coordinates are actually half the values they would be if the coordinate system were based on pixels. Fonts and GUI elements are then rendered at full resolution and everything looks "normal"...yet crisper because of the additional pixel density.

An OpenGL application rendering at full-pixel resolution would then have considerably more pixels to fill, taking quite a fill hit performance-wise. We've seen in a previous section that we can easily reduce the back buffer size by half, which results in a quarter the number of pixels that need to be written to. As it turns out something akin to this is the default behavior on Retina-equipped computers. This default behavior keeps existing applications from suffering a 4x fill performance penalty, yet the rendered results are still equivalent to a non-Retina system.

If you wish to take advantage of the extra high resolution (as an alternative to multi-sampling, for example), you must "opt-in" to the high-resolution surface with the following function call when setting up your NSOpenGLView:

```
[self setWantsBestResolutionOpenGLSurface:YES];
```

This affects only the view on which it is called, and the rendering context must be currently bound when this is called. The StonehengeCGL example program is coded to run at full resolution on Retina-equipped hardware. Some OpenGL functions work in pixels, notably **glViewport()**. The normal Cocoa functions for screen rectangles return point units and not pixels. Usually these are the same, but not so with Retina displays. We will need to get the actual pixel dimensions of our view before we call the GLStonehenge method resized. We can do this with the convertRectToBacking method of NSOpenGLView. This is shown in the new Retina-aware reshape function below:

```
- (void) reshape
{
// Get the dimensions of the screen
NSRect bounds = [self bounds];

// Retina display ready... and we want ALL the pixels
NSRect backRect = [self convertRectToBacking:bounds];
stonehenge.resized(NSWidth(backRect), NSHeight(backRect));
}
```

Core OpenGL

CGL (Core OpenGL) is the lowest level, and the most direct access to OpenGL available on OS X. It works seamlessly with all other OpenGL technologies and APIs as well, and we can use it for our Stonehenge example rendering as well. We cover here just a few quick and easy but useful recipes for using CGL in our Cocoa-based application. There may be Cocoa equivalents to some of these, but the CGL version will also work with your GLUT-based or any other higher-level third-party applications frameworks you might choose to use. You can also use CGL exclusively without NSOpenGLView to create a full-screen context and render to it as needed, but this is no longer necessary on modern OS X.

All CGL functions we are interested in require the current CGL context as one of the parameters. In any OpenGL application, you can retrieve the current CGL context by calling CGLGetCurrentContext:

```
CGLContextObj;
CGLGetCurrentContext(void);
```

Full-Screen Rendering

Many OpenGL applications need to render to the entire screen, rather than live within the confines of a window. This would include many games, media players, kiosk-hosted applications, and other specialized types of applications. One way to accomplish this is to simply make a large window that is the size of the entire display. Prior to OS X 10.6 (Snow Leopard), this was not the most optimal approach, and it was necessary to use the CGL functions to "capture" the display for full-screen rendering to get the best results.

With Snow Leopard and forward, these APIs are still supported but are no longer necessary, and in fact the screen capturing technique is discouraged by Apple. When rendering to a full-screen window, you get a special context flag, and OS X automatically tries to optimize the rendering output in a manner that the old screen capturing technique did. However, by not capturing the display, critical UI messages or other windows are also allowed to pop up over the full-screen window. Capturing the display by modern standards is a bit heavy handed. There is even a simple way now to render into a smaller back buffer to improve fill performance without having to change the display resolution. Let's start by creating a full-screen version of our stonehengeCocoa example.

We can begin StonehengeCGL with the same code and setup as for StonehengeCocoa, with only a couple of exceptions. We will not be making any changes to the MainMenu.xib file at all. The

`GLCoreProfileView` class is still used and is identical except for two changes. First, we can remove the `initWithCoder` method completely from the class, as we will be setting the pixel format from the outside this time. Next, in the `drawRect` method, we are going to replace the **`glFlush()`** call with a bona-fide buffer swap:

```
[[self openGLContext] flushBuffer];
```

Our OpenGL view is now created "manually," if you will, outside the plumbing of the Interface Builder `.xibs`. We place our view creation code in the `AppDelegate.mm` file, within the `applicationDidFinishLaunching` method. Listing 14.16 shows this method in its entirety, which creates a full-screen window with a double-buffered rendering context.

```
- (void)applicationDidFinishLaunching:(NSNotification *)aNotification
{
    // Insert code here to initialize your application
    NSRect mainDisplayRect = [[NSScreen mainScreen] frame];

    NSWindow *fullScreenWindow = [[NSWindow alloc]
                    initWithContentRect:mainDisplayRect
                    styleMask:NSBorderlessWindowMask
                    backing:NSBackingStoreBuffered defer:YES];

    [fullScreenWindow setLevel:NSMainMenuWindowLevel+1];
    [fullScreenWindow setOpaque:YES];
    [fullScreenWindow setHidesOnDeactivate:YES];

    NSOpenGLPixelFormatAttribute pixelFormatAttributes[] =
    {
        NSOpenGLPFAColorSize,      32,
        NSOpenGLPFADepthSize,      24,
        NSOpenGLPFAStencilSize,    8,
        NSOpenGLPFAAccelerated,
        NSOpenGLPFADoubleBuffer,
        NSOpenGLPFAOpenGLProfile, NSOpenGLProfileVersion3_2Core,
        0
    };

    NSOpenGLPixelFormat* pixelFormat =
            [[NSOpenGLPixelFormat alloc]
            initWithAttributes:pixelFormatAttributes];

    NSRect viewRect = NSMakeRect(0.0, 0.0,
                            mainDisplayRect.size.width,
                            mainDisplayRect.size.height);

    GLCoreProfileView *fullScreenView = [[GLCoreProfileView alloc]
initWithFrame:viewRect
            pixelFormat: pixelFormat];
    [fullScreenWindow setContentView: fullScreenView];
```

```
[fullScreenWindow makeKeyAndOrderFront:self];

makeFirstResponder:fullScreenView];
}
```

Listing 14.16: Creating and initializing the full-screen window

Listing 14.16 is taken almost verbatim from the official Apple OpenGL Programming guide. OS X automatically detects the full-screen window and will optimize the rendering and buffer swaps for best performance of a full screen application or game. The advantage to no longer using the CGL methods of locking the screen is that critical system messages and windows can still be displayed... like for a laptop user... say, "You are now running on reserve power".... That might be useful to know.

Sync Frame Rate

In our previous example programs, our event loop ran and rendered at full speed as many frames per second as possible. This is useful when doing performance testing of your rendering or processing code, as the frames per second is a simple metric of just how fast your code can execute. In a shipping application, there are two drawbacks to this however. First, in addition to excessive use of the GPU, you are also taking up all the cycles on one of your CPU cores (at least!). If you consider that your display refreshes typically 60 times per second, there is no real need or purpose to displaying more than 60 frames per second. That excess GPU power could be used to generate more sophisticated rendering effects, or the CPU power could be used to improve other application processing performance or perhaps add more detail or features to the application or game.

Second, because the display only refreshes so many times per second, rendering more frames per second than the display can show causes tearing. Tearing occurs when the buffer swap occurs at any point other than the vertical retrace of the screen. Essentially, you get two different frames displayed on-screen at the same time. The old frame occupies the area of the display above the current display refresh position, and the bottom of the screen is then filled with the new buffer contents. This is especially jarring when the view is moving horizontally in the scene. Figure 14.11 shows a typical tearing example, where the display briefly shows two different frames.

In a double-buffered application, such as our previous full-screen example, the swap interval sets the number of vertical retraces that should occur before the buffer swap occurs. Setting this value to one forces no more

Figure 14.11: Tearing caused by an unsynced buffer swap

than one frame per vertical retrace, while setting it to two allows two vertical retraces between buffer swaps. For example, if the swap interval was set to one, and the display refresh rate was 60 (about typical), you would get no more than 60 fps. For a swap interval of two, you'd get a maximum of 30 fps, and so on. You set the swap interval with the CGL function CGLSetParameter:

```
GLint sync = 1;
CGLSetParameter(CGLGetCurrentContext(), kCGLCPSwapInterval, &sync);
```

Note that this does not "fix" the frame rate to equal the refresh rate of the monitor. If your rendering, or CPU code for that matter, takes an excessive amount of time, you may get less than the full refresh rate of your monitor. What you gain, however is that the buffer swaps only occur between refreshes, thus eliminating the tearing issue. You might also consider when using this approach that your primary rendering thread is blocked while waiting, and background threads may wake up to do other important processing tasks. You may set this parameter at any time, and it takes effect immediately.

Increasing Fill Performance

Fill performance refers to the performance overhead in rendering that specifically relates to the time spent writing data to pixels in the frame buffer. One easy way to improve fill performance is to simply render to a smaller window, or in the case of a full-screen application such as a game, to change the screen resolution to a smaller value. Before Snow Leopard, it was not uncommon for a full-screen OpenGL game, for example, to change the screen resolution before running, capture the display, and so on. Now that we no longer need a display capturing solution, we can make use of CGL's ability to change the size of the back buffer instead of changing the screen resolution. Changing the back buffer to be smaller than the front buffer has the added fill performance benefit, without the need for a display mode change. The contents of the back buffer are then automatically stretched to fill the entire display when the buffer swap occurs.

To set the back surface size, we set the CGL parameter kCGLCPSurfaceBackingSize to the integer dimensions that we want. In addition, we must enable the kCGLCESurfaceBackingSize feature with CGLEnable. The following code shows how you would do this for a desired new size of newWidth × newHeight:

```
GLint dim[2] = { newWidth, newHeight };
CGLSetParameter(CGLGetCurrentContext(), kCGLCPSurfaceBackingSize, dim);
CGLEnable(CGLGetCurrentContext(), kCGLCESurfaceBackingSize);
```

When using a smaller back buffer in this manner, remember to also adjust the size of the rectangle in your call to **glViewport()**. For example, in the StonehengeCGL example, we might reduce the back buffer store by half with the following code:

```
- (void) reshape
  {
  // Get the dimensions of the screen
  NSRect bounds = [self bounds];

  // Reduces the back buffer by half
  GLint dim[2] = { int(NSWidth(bounds)) / 2,
                   int(NSHeight(bounds)) / 2  };

  CGLSetParameter(CGLGetCurrentContext(),
                  kCGLCPSurfaceBackingSize, dim);

  CGLEnable(CGLGetCurrentContext(), kCGLCESurfaceBackingSize);

  stonehenge.resized(NSWidth(bounds)/2, NSHeight(bounds)/2);
  }
```

Multi-threaded OpenGL

The OpenGL driver does a significant amount of processing of your rendering data before it eventually shows up on the hardware for rendering. On OS X 10.5 or later, you can enable a multi-threaded

OpenGL core that offloads some of these tasks to another thread. On a multi-core system, this can have a positive performance impact. You can enable this feature by calling CGLEnable on the kCGLCEMPEngine flag:

```
CGLEnable(CGLGetCurrentContext(), kCGLCEMPEngine);
```

This does not always improve performance, and in fact, sometimes, it can reduce performance! If your OpenGL code is not hampered by CPU processing, this may have little to no effect on your rendering performance, for example. For another, if your rendering code calls a lot of functions that produce pipeline stalls (**glGetFloatv()**, **glGetIntegerv()**, **glReadPixels()**, etc.), these too can interfere with this potential optimization.

GLUT

GLUT is the short name of the OpenGL Utility Toolkit, a window-system-independent toolkit for writing OpenGL programs. GLUT has a long history, dating back to its first release in late 1994. Written by Mark J. Kilgard when he was working for Silicon Graphics, GLUT was intended as a simple demonstration or learning framework. In some niches over the years, GLUT took on a life of its own, being extended even to support rudimentary game programming features. As a teaching framework, GLUT has been featured in numerous OpenGL books, including the first five editions of this book.

GLUT, however, has been, if not completely abandoned, left somewhat to age gracefully and has not been seriously maintained for years. There are still a good many programs and programmers who use it regularly through, and it bears mentioning that Apple's implementation has been extended somewhat for OS X.

When OS X 10.7 shipped with OpenGL core profile 3.2 support, the GLUT framework was not updated. It was thus not possible to use GLUT as is, and create example or useful simple OpenGL programs that made use of the latest OpenGL features. In OS X 10.8 (Mountain Lion), however, Apple added a new token to their GLUT implementation, GLUT_32_CORE_PROFILE. This token, when added to the init line would create an OpenGL 3.2 core context profile.

To create a GLUT-based program with XCode, start with a fresh Cocoa-based app (GLUT is actually built on top of the Cocoa framework).

Remove the `AppDelegate.m/.h` and `main.m` files, and then add the OpenGL and GLUT frameworks (you should know how to do this by now).

Add your GLUT C and/or C++ files, and you are ready to go. Let's go over a quick example. The body of `main` in a typical GLUT program is shown in Listing 14.17.

```
//////////////////////////////////////////////////////////////////////////////
// Main entry point for GLUT-based programs
int main(int argc, char* argv[])
    {
    glutInit(&argc, argv);
    glutInitDisplayMode(GLUT_DOUBLE | GLUT_RGBA | GLUT_DEPTH |
                                 GLUT_STENCIL | GLUT_3_2_CORE_PROFILE);
    glutInitWindowSize(800, 600);
    glutCreateWindow("GLUT Core Profile Demo");

    glutReshapeFunc(ChangeSize);
    glutKeyboardFunc(KeyPressFunc);
    glutDisplayFunc(RenderScene);

    SetupRC();

        printf("Version: %s\r\n", glGetString(GL_VERSION));
        printf("Renderer: %s\r\n", glGetString(GL_RENDERER));
        printf("Vendor: %s\r\n", glGetString(GL_VENDOR));
        printf("GLSL Version: %s\r\n", glGetString(GL_SHADING_LANGUAGE_VERSION));

        glutMainLoop();
        return 0;
        }
```

Listing 14.17: GLUT `main` function to set up OpenGL

Ignoring rendering operations temporarily, the output of the program in the console (or output pane in XCode) is as follows:

```
Version: 3.2 NVIDIA-8.0.61
Renderer: NVIDIA GeForce 9400M OpenGL Engine
Vendor: NVIDIA Corporation
GLSL Version: 1.50
```

On the author's laptop, you can see the specific OpenGL renderer, the version of OpenGL, and of the GLSL supported.

Admittedly a legacy framework, GLUT may yet have some life left on the OS X platform as an easy-to-use OpenGL rendering framework. We won't go into the details of GLUT programming here, but we do provide a complete `StonehengGLUT` example program in the examples directory for this chapter.

OpenGL on Linux

One great thing about OpenGL is that it's supported on so many different platforms. We looked at how to use OpenGL on Windows and on Macs. Now let's dig into 3D rendering on one of the most popular open source platforms — Linux.

This section looks at how Linux supports OpenGL, how to pick a specific version of OpenGL, what interfaces are available for developers, and how to set up an application. We also touch on GLUT, context management, and how to allocate, render to, and deal with windows on X Windows.

The Basics

OpenGL has been the go-to API for 3D rendering on various versions of Linux, UNIX, and similar platforms for nearly as long as 3D rendering has been possible. Linux offers several ways to access OpenGL. Most major graphics hardware provides some form of acceleration. Mesa3D, a software implementation that does not depend on hardware, can also be installed on most X server configurations.

Brief History

In the late 1980s, Silicon Graphics (SGI) introduced a proprietary API for 2D and 3D graphics on its workstations called IRIS GL (Integrated Raster Imaging System Graphics Library). In 1992, SGI revised the specification and published it as an open industry standard called OpenGL. In 1993, Brian Paul started a project to create a software-only implementation of OpenGL called Mesa3D, opening the door to wider support of 3D rendering not tied to a specific hardware vendor. Recent versions of Mesa use the Gallium3D architecture to allow hardware acceleration to be implemented, and hardware accelerated implementations of OpenGL based on Mesa are widely available.

Most computer systems available today contain some sort of 3D acceleration. Modern 3D hardware vendors provide support for the latest versions of OpenGL either through contributions to Mesa or other Open Source projects, or through the release or proprietary graphics drivers. In general, the proprietary graphics drivers tend to be more up-to-date. For example, currently both AMD and NVIDIA provide Linux OpenGL drivers that support OpenGL 4.3. The most recent version of Mesa at the time of publication (9.0.x) supports OpenGL 3.1.

What Is X?

The X Window System is a graphical user interface that provides a more intuitive environment for users than a command prompt, similar to Microsoft Windows and Mac OS. X Window sessions are not restricted to use on local systems. For instance, you can start an X server session from your computer that accesses a supercomputer halfway across the country. This allows you to use the remote computer as if you were sitting right in front of it. In X Window terminology, the computer providing the user display services is called the X Window server, and the computer running the actual application is referred to as the client. This may be counter to the common roles known as server and client. In our supercomputer example, you would open a shell to the supercomputer and run your application there. It would connect (as the client) back to your computer at your desk (acting as the server) and tell it what to render. All of the OpenGL rendering would occur on your machine, while the supercomputer did all the heavy number crunching.

We run our Linux OpenGL applications inside X Windows. Most Linux distributions use either the XFree86 implementation of the X Window System, or the X.Org Server, which is a derivative of it. Many different desktop managers are available, such as KDE and Gnome, which run atop the basic X Windows software and provide user interaction for moving and resizing windows, launching programs, and other basic operations. More recently, Wayland has emerged as a higher-performance alternative to compositing desktop managers for X and is likely to gain traction with Linux desktop distributors.

Getting Started

You need several components set up for your OpenGL applications to compile and run. First and most obviously, you need a Linux system. Different Linux distributions such as OpenSUSE, Fedora, and Ubuntu are available for free download. Next, it is highly recommended you have a modern graphics card or system with a graphics chip that supports current versions of OpenGL. It is also important that recent drivers be available and installed. Although it is possible to run a software implementation of OpenGL, these software implementations may not support all features of

OpenGL and are considerably slower. You also need the header files and libraries for OpenGL and GLX. These are necessary for compiling your own applications.

Checking for OpenGL

Let's quickly look at how you can make sure OpenGL is supported on your system. Without that, the rest of this chapter is pretty meaningless. Try running the glxinfo command, as shown here:

```
glxinfo | grep rendering
```

You should get one of two responses:

```
direct rendering: Yes
```

or

```
direct rendering: No
```

If the answer is yes, good news! You have hardware support for 3D rendering. If no, then you may not have hardware that supports OpenGL, or you may not have drivers installed for OpenGL. If hardware support is not available, try running the following:

```
glxinfo | grep "OpenGL vendor"
glxinfo | grep "OpenGL version"
```

This prints out the currently installed OpenGL driver information. Remember to be careful about capitalization! If you do not have hardware drivers but do have Mesa installed, the information for the Mesa driver will be displayed. You will also get the current version of OpenGL your Mesa implementation supports.

If the glxinfo command fails or no vendor/version information is available, your Linux distribution is not set up for rendering with OpenGL. You have several options. First, you can install Mesa. Or you could install a video card that supports 3D rendering and has driver support for Linux. Most Linux distributions use one of several package managers (based on RPM or deb files) to manage installed software. If your Linux system does not have OpenGL itself, OpenGL hardware drivers, or the OpenGL development headers/libraries installed, you may need to utilize your package manager to obtain and install them. Additional components like Mesa3D, GLUT, and GLEW may also be available as packages in your distribution, permitting easy installation. However, package-distributed versions of these tools may be outdated compared to those available by direct download from the project's Web site.

Setting Up Mesa

The latest version of Mesa can be downloaded from the Mesa3D Web site; a link is provided in Appendix A, "Further Reading." There you will find the download link for the Mesa project on SourceForge. Once downloaded, unpack the files (example shown for Mesa 7.7):

```
gunzip MesaLib-7.7.tar.gz
tar xf MesaLib-7.7.tar
```

Next, you need to compile the source that you just unpacked. Go to the directory that was just created from the tar package, and run the following:

```
make linux-x86
```

It takes a while to build the Mesa software for your system. After the build has finished, a number of libraries will have been created. Now you need to install the libraries and headers to allow the operating system and build environment to find them when necessary. To do the install, run the following command:

```
make install
```

The library and include locations are usually located in the following directories:

```
Libraries: /usr/X11R6/lib
Includes: /usr/include/
```

You have now finished the Mesa install. If you have more questions about the Mesa setup or install, visit the Mesa3D Web site.

Setting Up Hardware Drivers

If you have modern graphics hardware, you want to make sure you have drivers installed and that they are up to date. Driver support for Linux differs by hardware vendor. Both AMD and NVIDIA provide a proprietary driver package that can be downloaded from their Web sites. The install process is usually simple, just a matter of running the downloaded package and following the prompts. Specific installation instructions can be found on manufacturer Web sites.

Some hardware vendors may also provide an open source version of their display drivers. Although it is often nice to have the source for the driver build, these drivers are often slower, updated less frequently, and have fewer features or more limitations than their proprietary counterparts. It's worth noting that some distros may have drivers prepackaged. These can be outdated, and it is often easiest to simply not install the packaged versions and install the newest vendor drivers instead.

Setting Up GLFW and GL3W

This book's application framework uses GLFW to interact with the operating system and its windowing system. X is fairly complex, and while it is certainly possible to write OpenGL applications that run directly on top of X, it's more convenient to install a thin layer such as GLFW that will abstract much of the gory details away for you.

GLFW is available for download and install on Linux as well as other operating systems. This helps to make any applications that use GLFW very portable given that the code can be compiled on Windows, Mac, and Linux. It is also a good way to get applications up and running quickly because no window management is required. GLFW does not allow for direct interface with the X server. This means some things that can be done directly communicating with the OS or the X server are more difficult or impossible when using GLFW.

The GL3W library is also used by the book's application framework to load and initialize OpenGL function pointers. GL3W is actually a single source file that is generated directly from the official OpenGL header files using a Python script. Like GLFW, GL3W is available for many different operating systems and platforms. By using GL3W, applications can focus on 3D rendering and worry less about making applications work across different platforms.

Installing GLFW

GLFW may not be already installed on your system. If that's the case, it can be easily downloaded. Then, go to the GLFW directory and perform the following commands:

```
sh ./compile.sh
make x11
make x11-install
```

The first command creates the make files you use to compile the code. The make files are custom made for each system because different resources may be located in different places on each system. The second command actually compiles the code, and the third installs the result.

To use GLFW in your applications, you need to add the GLFW library to your link command:

```
-lglfw
```

Installing GL3W

GL3W is pretty straightforward and is contained in a single source file that is generated by a Python script. A pregenerated file, gl3w.c is included in the source distribution for the book. You should feel free to simply include this source file in your project. Then, call gl3wInit() when your application starts up before any OpenGL calls are made. All the function pointers for core features up to the most recently supported version of OpenGL will be set up automatically. If the gl3wInit function fails, it returns an error, and the extension pointers may not be initialized.

Building OpenGL Apps

Now that we've gone through all that setup and our system is prepped for running and compiling OpenGL programs, let's take a look at how to build these programs. If you have spent time working with Linux, you are probably already familiar with creating makefiles. If so, skip ahead.

Makefiles are used on Linux systems to compile and link source code, creating an executable file. Makefiles hold instructions for the compiler and linker, telling them where to find files and what to do with them. A sample makefile follows. It can be modified and expanded to accommodate your own projects.

```
LIBDIRS = -L/usr/X11R6/lib -L/usr/X11R6/lib64 -L/usr/local/lib
INCDIRS = -I/usr/include -L/usr/local/include

CC = gcc
CFLAGS = $(COMPILERFLAGS) -g $(INCDIRS)
LIBS = -lX11 -lXi -lXmu -lglfw -lGL -lm

example : example.o
    $(CC) $(CFLAGS) -o example $(LIBDIRS) example.c $(LIBS)
clean:
    rm -f *.o
```

The first line creates a variable that contains the link parameters for libraries to be included. The one used here looks in both the standard lib directory for X11 as well as the version for 64-bit specific libraries. The second line lists the include paths the compiler should use when trying to find header files. `CC = gcc` selects the compiler to use. The next line specifies the compile flags to use with this instance. Then `LIBS =` selects all the libraries that need to be linked into our program.

Finally, we compile and link the single source file specified for this example, called `example.c`. The last line cleans up intermediate objects that were created during the process. This example can be used while substituting your file in the script. Other files can also be compiled together as well. Many resources and tutorials are on the Web; two good makefile primers are listed in Appendix A, "Further Reading," to help you get started.

GLX-Interfacing with X Windows

Although we have used higher level abstraction libraries such as GLFW for many of the samples in this book, it is possible to write directly to the X interfaces. On X Windows, a common interface called GLX exists for allowing applications that use OpenGL to communicate with X Windows. This interface is similar to WGL on Windows and AGL on Mac. There are many different versions of GLX; version 1.4 is the most recent. GLX 1.4 is similar to GLX version 1.3 but includes a few minor changes. GLX 1.2 is much older and is missing much of the functionality of the newer versions. For this reason, GLX 1.4 is used for our applications.

To find out more information about your installation of GLX, you can use the `glxinfo` command again. Try the following:

```
glxinfo | grep "glx vendor"
glxinfo | grep "glx version"
```

This displays the GLX information for both server and client components of X Windows. The effective version you can use is the older of the server and client versions. So if your client reports 1.4 and your server reports 1.3, then you can only use version GLX 1.3. If your client or server driver does not support GLX 1.4, you can try updating your display driver as described earlier.

From inside a program, you can also call **glXQueryVersion()** to get the GLX version:

```
Bool glXQueryVersion(Display * dpy, int *major, int *minor);
```

This call would look like

```
int majorVer, minorVer;
glXQueryVersion(dpy, majorVer, minorVer);
```

Displays and X Windows

Before we get too far into using GLX, there are a few prerequisites for understanding how GLX works on Linux (or many of the other UNIX derivatives for that matter). An OpenGL application runs inside a window on the X server. We mentioned earlier that X Windows supports client and server components running on separate systems, essentially allowing you to run your desktop from somewhere else. Additionally, an X server can have multiple displays active or even multiple graphics cards.

Before we can create a window, we need to find out what display the OpenGL application will be executing on. The display helps the X server understand where we are rendering. Use the **XOpenDisplay()** function to get the current display.

```
Display *dpy = XOpenDisplay(getenv("DISPLAY"));
```

This gives us a pointer to the display object for the default display. We can use this later to tell the X server where we are. After our application is done, it also needs to close the display using the **XCloseDisplay()** function. This tells the X server that we are finished, and it can close the connection:

```
XCloseDisplay(Display * display);
```

Config Management and Visuals

Before we can create a window or an OpenGL rendering context, we need to know what sort of traits are required. Configs on Linux are similar to configs on EGL or pixel formats on Windows. A config is an enumerated set of attributes supported by X Windows or the OpenGL/GLX driver. An implementation often supports many combinations of window and rendering attributes, and therefore a large number of configs. Because there are so many factors all tied into configs, they can be tricky to handle.

For starters, you can use the **glXGetFBConfigs()** interface to get information on all of the configs supported:

```
GLXFBConfig *glXGetFBConfigs(Display * dpy,
                             int screen,
                             int *nelements);
```

Use the display handle that you got from calling **XOpenDisplay()**. For our purposes, we can use the default screen for the screen parameter. When the call returns, nelements tells you how many configs were returned.

There's more to each config than its index. Each config has a unique set of attributes that represent the functionality of that config. These attributes and their descriptions are listed in Table 14.6.

Table 14.6: GLX Config Attribute List

Attribute (GLX_*)	Description
BUFFER SIZE	Total number of bits of the color buffer.
RED_SIZE	Number of bits in red channel of color buffer.
GREEN_SIZE	Number of bits in green channel of color buffer.
BLUE_SIZE	Number of bits in blue channel of color buffer.
ALPHA_SIZE	Number of bits in alpha channel of color buffer.
DEPTH_SIZE	Number of bits in depth buffer.
STENCIL_SIZE	Number of bits in stencil buffer.
CONFIG_CAVEAT	Set to one of the following caveats: NONE, SLOW_CONFIG, or NON_CONFORMANT_CONFIG. These can warn of potential issues for this config. A slow config may be software emulated because it exceeds HW limits. A nonconformant config will not pass the conformance test.
X_RENDERABLE	Is set to TRUE if the X server can render to this surface.
VISUAL_ID	The XID of the related visual.
X_VISUAL_TYPE	Type of an X visual if config supports window rendering (associated visual exists).
DRAWABLE_TYPE	Valid surface targets supported. May be any or all of WINDOW_BIT, PIXMAP_BIT, or PBUFFER_BIT.
RENDER_TYPE	Bitfield indicating the types of contexts that can be bound. May be RGBA_BIT or COLOR_INDEX_BIT.

continued

Attribute (GLX_*)	Description
FBCONFIG_ID	The XID for the GLXFBConfig.
LEVEL	The frame buffer level.
DOUBLEBUFFER	Is TRUE if color buffers are double buffered.
STEREO	Is TRUE if color buffers support stereo rendering.
SAMPLE_BUFFERS	Number of multi-sample buffers. Must be 0 or 1.
SAMPLES	Number of samples per pixel for multi-sample buffers. Will be 0 if SAMPLE_BUFFERS is 0.
TRANSPARENT_TYPE	Indicates support of transparency. Value may be NONE, TRANSPARENT_RGB, or TRANSPARENT_INDEX. If transparency is supported, a transparent pixel is drawn when the pixel's components are all equal to the respective transparent RGB values.
TRANSPARENT_RED_VALUE	Red value a framebuffer pixel must have to be transparent.
TRANSPARENT_GREEN_VALUE	Green value a framebuffer pixel must have to be transparent.
TRANSPARENT_BLUE_VALUE	Blue value a framebuffer pixel must have to be transparent.
TRANSPARENT_ALPHA_VALUE	Alpha value a framebuffer pixel must have to be transparent.
TRANSPARENT_INDEX_VALUE	Index value a framebuffer pixel must have to be transparent. For color index configs only.
AUX_BUFFERS	The number of supported auxiliary buffers.
ACCUM_RED_SIZE	Number of bits in red channel of the auxiliary buffer.
ACCUM_GREEN_SIZE	Number of bits in green channel of the auxiliary buffer.
ACCUM_BLUE_SIZE	Number of bits in blue channel of the auxiliary buffer.
ACCUM_ALPHA_SIZE	Number of bits in alpha channel of the auxiliary buffer.

You can query any configs to find the value of each of these attributes by using the **glXGetFBConfigAttrib()** command:

```
int glXGetFBConfigAttrib(Display * dpy, GLXFBConfig config,
                         int attribute, int *value);
```

Set the config parameter to the config number you are interested in querying and the attribute parameter to the attribute you would like to query. The result is returned in the value parameter. If the **glXGetFBConfigAttrib()** call fails, it may return the error GLX_BAD_ATTRIBUTE if the attribute you are requesting doesn't exist.

GLX also provides a method for getting a subset of configs that meet a set of criteria. This can help narrow down the total set to just those that you care about, making it much easier to find a config that works for your application. For instance, if you have an application for rendering into a window, the config you select needs to support rendering to a window.

```
GLXFBConfig *glXChooseFBConfig(Display * dpy,
                               int screen,
                               const int *attrib_list,
                               int *nelements);
```

Pass in the screen that you are interested in as the screen parameter and specify the elements that are required for a config match. This is done with a NULL-terminated list of parameter and value pairs. These attributes are the same config attributes listed in Table 14.6.

```
static const int attrib_list[] =
{
    attribute1, attribute_value1,
    attribute2, attribute_value2,
    attribute3, attribute_value3,
    0
};
```

Similar to **glXGetFBConfigs()**, the number of configs that match the attribute list is returned in nelements. A pointer to a list of matching configs is returned by the function. Remember to use **XFree()** to clean up the memory that was returned by the **glXChooseFBConfig()** call. All configs returned will match the minimum criteria you set in the attrib list.

You may want to pay attention to a few key attributes when creating a config. For instance, GLX_X_RENDERABLE should be GLX_TRUE so that you can use OpenGL to perform rendering, GLX_DRAWABLE_TYPE needs to include GLX_WINDOW_BIT if you are rendering to a window, GLX_RENDER_TYPE should be GLX_RGBA_BIT, and GLX_CONFIG_CAVEAT should be set to GLX_NONE or at the very least not have the GLX_SLOW_CONFIG bit set. After that you may also want to make sure the color, depth, and stencil channels meet minimum requirements. The pBuffer, accumulation, and transparency values are less commonly used.

For attributes you don't specify, the **glXChooseFBConfig()** command uses default values implicitly. These are listed in the GLX specification. The sort mechanism automatically sorts the list of returned configs using an attribute priority. The order for the highest priority attributes is GLX_CONFIG_CAVEAT, the color buffer bit depths, GLX_BUFFER_SIZE, and then GLX_DOUBLEBUFFER.

If a config has the GLX_WINDOW_BIT set for the GLX_DRAWABLE_TYPE attribute, the config will have an associated X visual. The visual can be queried using the following command:

```
XVisualInfo *glXGetVisualFromFBConfig(Display * dpy,
                                      GLXFBConfig config);
```

NULL is returned if there isn't an associated X visual. Don't forget to free the returned memory with **XFree()**.

Windows and Render Surfaces

Now that we're through the messy stuff, let's create a window. We can do this by calling the X server function **XCreateWindow()**. The result is a handle for the new X Window. The function needs a parent window, but you can also use the main X Window for this, and you should already be familiar with the Display parameter here. You also need to tell X how big of a window you would like and where to put it using the x, y position and the width and height parameters.

Also tell the X server what kind of a window you want with the window class. This can be one of three values: InputOnly, InputOutput, or CopyFromParent. An InputOnly window cannot be used as a source or destination for graphics requests, and the CopyFromParent value inherits the value that the parent window was created with, so InputOutput is most useful. The attributes and valuemask fields let you tell X what types of characteristics the window should have. The attributes field holds the values, and the valuemask tells X which values it should pay attention to. To get more information on attributes, refer to the X server documentation. The full function declaration looks like this:

```
Window XCreateWindow(Display * dpy,
                     Window parent,
                     int x, int y,
                     unsigned int width,
                     unsigned int height,
```

```
unsigned int border_width,
int depth,
unsigned int class,
Visual *visual,
unsigned_long valuemask,
XSetWindowAttributes *attributes);
```

After choosing good values for creating your window and calling **XCreateWindow()**, the handle to the new window is returned. This window handle can then be used to create a corresponding GLX window. When creating the GLX window, the configs you use must be compatible with the visual you created the X Window with. Use the **glXCreateWindow()** command to create a new on-screen OpenGL rendering area associated with your newly created X Window:

```
GLXWindow glXCreateWindow(Display * dpy,
                          GLXFBConfig config,
                          Window win,
                          const int *attrib_list);
```

By now, you are already familiar with the Display parameter. You can use the config you selected in the section using **glXGetFBConfigs()** or **glXChooseFBConfig()**. The Window handle is the same handle returned from **XCreateWindow()**. The attrib_list currently does not support any parameters and is for future expansion, so you should pass in NULL.

glXCreateWindow() throws an error and fails if the config is not compatible with the window visual, if the config doesn't support window rendering, if the window parameter is invalid, if a GLXFBConfig has already been associated with the window, if the GLXFBConfig is invalid, or if there was a general failure creating the GLX window. Also remember that **glXCreateWindow()** is only supported in GLX 1.3 or later. It does not work on older versions. Remember we checked the GLX versions earlier by running glxinfo | grep "glx version" in a terminal.

Once you are done rendering, you also have to clean up the windows you created. To destroy the GLX window, call **glXDestroyWindow()** with the GLX window handle returned when you called **glXCreateWindow()**:

```
glXDestroyWindow(Display * dpy,
                 GLXWindow window);
```

Finally, destroy the X Window you originally created. You can use the similarly named **XDestroyWindow()** command and pass back the X Window handle:

```
XDestroyWindow(Display * dpy, Window win);
```

GLX Strings

You can query various GLX strings to get more information on what your system can do. One of the most important strings is the extension string. This is a list of all the extensions the current implementation of GLX supports. To get the extension string, use

```
const char *glXQueryExtensionsString(Display *dpy, int screen);
```

The returned string, or character array, is a list of extension names separated by spaces. The array is terminated by the value 0.

You can also call **glXGetClientString()** or **glXQueryServerString()** to find out information about the client library or the server, respectively. Pass one of the following enums for the name argument: GLX_VENDOR, GLX_VERSION, or GLX_EXTENSIONS.

```
const char *glXGetClientString(Display *dpy,  int name);
const char *glXQueryServerString(Display *dpy, int screen, int name);
```

Extending OpenGL and GLX

Before going any further, let's look at how GLX can be extended without creating a whole new version of GLX. Vendors can write new extensions for GLX and OpenGL to add new functionality for applications to use. This allows applications to use features that are either vendor specific or are available before they can become part of the core specification. You just learned how to get the list of GLX extensions by calling **glXQueryExtensionsString()**. Earlier in this chapter, you also learned how to get a list of all OpenGL extensions. The descriptions of new extensions can be found in the OpenGL extension repository on the Web. Once you know what extensions are available and what they do, you may have to get new entrypoints to use them. GLX provides the **glXGetProcAddress()** to look up function addresses for extensions:

```
void (*glXGetProcAddress(const ubyte *procname))();
```

Context Management

A context is a set of OpenGL state that is associated with a handle. A context must be bound to a drawable (such as a window) for state to be set or for rendering to occur. Multiple contexts can be created, but only one can be bound to a drawable at a time. At least one context must be created for your app to be able to render.

Creating Contexts

One way you can create a new context is with the **glXCreateNewContext()** command:

```
GLXContext glXCreateNewContext(Display * dpy,
                               GLXFBConfig config,
                               int render_type,
                               GLXContext share_list,
                               bool direct);
```

When successful, this function returns a context handle that you can use when telling GLX which context you want to use when rendering. The config that you use to create this context needs to be compatible with the render surface you intend to draw on. For common cases, it is easiest to use the same config that was used to create the GLX window.

The render_type parameter accepts GLX_RGBA_TYPE or GLX_COLOR_INDEX_TYPE. GLX_RGBA_TYPE should be used because we are not using color index mode. Most implementations no longer support color index mode. Normally, you should also pass NULL in the share_list parameter. However, if you have multiple contexts for an app and want to share OpenGL objects such as textures, buffers, and so on, you can pass the first context handle in when creating the second. This causes both contexts to use the same namespace. Specifying TRUE for the direct parameter requests a direct hardware context for a local X server connection; FALSE may create a context that renders through the X server.

If creation fails, the function returns NULL; otherwise, it initializes the context to default OpenGL state. The function throws an error if you pass an invalid handle as the share_list parameter, if the config is invalid, or if the system is out of resources.

The OpenGL version of the context created will be up to OpenGL 3.1 if your implementation supports that version or any newer context version if it is 100% backward compatible with OpenGL 3.1. Because you can't be sure what version of the OpenGL context you are going to get when calling **glXCreateNewContext()**, this is not the preferred method. Instead, use the newer version: **glXCreateContextAttribsARB()**.

Before using **glXCreateContextAttribsARB()**, you should check that the extension string GLX_ARB_create_context_profile is in the list of GLX extensions. Then, you need to get the function pointer for this extension. After that, you are all set to use the preferred way of creating context:

```
GLint attribs[] = {
    GLX_CONTEXT_MAJOR_VERSION_ARB, 3,
    GLX_CONTEXT_MINOR_VERSION_ARB, 3,
    0 };
rcx->ctx = glXCreateContextAttribsARB(rcx->dpy, fbConfigs[0], 0,
                                      True, attribs);
glXMakeCurrent(rcx->dpy, rcx->win, rcx->ctx);
```

The new method, **glXCreateContextAttribsARB()**, takes an additional
parameter and allows you to select exactly the context you want:

```
GLXContext glXCreateContextAttribsARB(Display * dpy,
                                      GLXFBConfig config,
                                      int render_type,
                                      GLXContext share_list,
                                      bool direct,
                                      const int *attrib_list);
```

The attrib_list parameter is a value-pair list of attributes you can
request in a new context. First, specify the attribute name in the array
followed by the value for the attribute. The attributes
GLX_CONTEXT_MAJOR_VERSION_ARB and GLX_CONTEXT_MINOR_VERSION_ARB
are used to explicitly ask for a specific context version of OpenGL. If your
application was written for OpenGL 3.3, you would pass in 3 as the major
version and 3 as the minor version. Similarly, if your application was older
and you needed an OpenGL 3.0 context, you could ask for that. However,
OpenGL drivers are allowed to return any version that is 100% backward
compatible with the version you requested. If you do not specify a version
of OpenGL or if you ask for version 1.0, the driver will probably create an
OpenGL 3.1 context. The exact behavior differs between vendors. The
best idea is to ask for a specific OpenGL version.

You can only create a context up to the version supported by your
OpenGL driver. You can find out what the newest supported version is by
calling glGetString with the GL_VERSION enum:

```
ubyte *verString = glGetString(GL_VERSION);
```

Or the version can also be queried through the **glGetIntegerv()**
command, which returns the version as integer components:

```
int majorVer, minorVer;
glGetIntegerv(GL_MAJOR_VERSION, &majorVer);
glGetIntegerv(GL_MINOR_VERSION, &minorVer);
```

There are several other types of attributes you can request through the
attrib_list. The attribute GLX_CONTEXT_PROFILE_MASK_ARB is followed
by a bitfield containing either GLX_CONTEXT_CORE_PROFILE_BIT_ARB or
GLX_CONTEXT_COMPATIBILITY_PROFILE_BIT_ARB. Only one can be used at a

time. Setting the `GLX_CONTEXT_CORE_PROFILE_BIT_ARB` bit causes the driver to return a context containing only core functionality, no deprecated OpenGL functionality. Using this bit is a good way to prepare an application for the next revision of OpenGL where deprecated functionality may be removed. Setting the `GLX_CONTEXT_COMPATIBILITY_PROFILE_BIT_ARB` bit asks the driver to create a context that is backward compatible with all older versions of OpenGL. In other words, no deprecated functionality is removed. A context created with this bit may run slower than a core profile context because of the additional state and functionality that needs to be tracked.

The `GLX_CONTEXT_FLAGS_ARB` attribute can be used to set other flags for context creation. The only supported flag is `GLX_CONTEXT_DEBUG_BIT`. Specifying this bit creates a context with additional debugging information available for applications under development. What information and how it can be accessed is vendor specific.

If any of the attributes you have specified are not supported by the OpenGL driver on your system, errors will be generated. The error `GLXBadMatch` is thrown if the combination of minor and major version attributes with the forward-compatible context bit is not a valid OpenGL version. If any of the bits specified for `GLX_CONTEXT_PROFILE_MASK_ARB` are not supported, the error `GLXBadProfileARB` is thrown.

When finished with a context, it is important to destroy the context so the implementation can free all related resources. Use the **glXDestroyContext()** command to destroy contexts:

```
glXDestroyContext(Display * dpy, GLXContext ctx);
```

If the context is currently bound to any thread, the context will not be destroyed until it is no longer current. The function throws an error if you pass an invalid context handle.

One other handy feature provided by GLX is the ability to copy data from one context to another with **glXCopyContext()**. Pass in the source and destination context handles as well as a mask to specify the pieces of OpenGL state that you would like to copy. To copy everything, you can pass `GL_ALL_ATTRIB_BITS`. Client-side state will not be copied.

```
glXCopyContext(Display * dpy, GLXContext source,
               GLXContext dest, unsigned long mask);
```

In GLX, a direct context is one that supports direct rendering to a local X server. To find out if an existing context is a direct context, you can call **glXIsDirect()**. This returns true if the context is a direct rendering context.

```
glXIsDirect(Display * dpy, GLXContext ctx);
```

Using Contexts

To use a context you have created, call **glXMakeContextCurrent()**:

```
glXMakeContextCurrent(Display * dpy, GLXDrawable draw,
                      GLXDrawable read, GLXContext ctx);
```

For most cases, you should specify the same drawable for read and draw for a context. This means that the same context will be used for both read and draw operations. If a different context was bound before you made this call, it will be flushed and marked as no longer current. If the context you pass is not valid or either drawable is not valid, the function throws an error. It also throws an error if the context's config is not compatible with the config used to create the drawables. Contexts can be released from a thread by passing None in the read and draw drawable parameters and NULL as the context. Without passing None for the drawables, GLX throws an error.

Synchronization

GLX has several synchronization commands that are similar to those on other OSs:

```
void glXWaitGL(void);
```

Making a call to **glXWaitGL()** guarantees that all GL rendering will finish for a window before other native rendering occurring after the call to **glXWaitGL()** is allowed to proceed. This allows an app to ensure that all rendering happens in the correct order and that rendering is not incorrectly overlapped or overwritten.

On some implementations, a call to **glXWaitGL()** may return immediately with no rendering visible. An implementation may wait for other rendering to be initiated before completing earlier rendering:

```
void glXWaitX(void);
```

Likewise, a call to **glXWaitX()** ensures that all native rendering made before the call to **glXWaitX()** completes before any OpenGL rendering after the call is allowed to happen:

```
void glXSwapBuffers(Display *dpy, GLXDrawable draw);
```

When using a double buffered config, a call to **glXSwapBuffers()** presents the contents of the back buffer to the window. The call also performs an implicit glFlush before the swap occurs. In addition, the contents of the new back buffer are undefined. You should not assume after a call to **glXSwapBuffers()** the new back buffer will have the same contents as the old back buffer, the old contents of the front buffer, or any other defined content to maintain portability between vendors. GLX throws an error if the drawable or display are invalid, or if the window is no longer valid.

GLX Queries

GLX allows you to query certain attributes of a context as well. Use the **glXQueryContext()** command to query GLX_FBCONFIG_ID, GLX_RENDER_TYPE, or GLX_SCREEN attributes associated with the context:

```
int glXQueryContext(Display * dpy, GLXContext ctx,
                    int attribute, int *value);
```

There are a few other context-related commands in GLX; these are mostly self-descriptive. **glXGetCurrentReadDrawable()** returns the current read drawable handle:

```
GLXDrawable glXGetCurrentReadDrawable(void);
```

In addition, the current context, drawable, and display can be queried with the following functions:

```
GLXContext glXGetCurrentContext(void);
GLXDrawable glXGetCurrentDrawable(void);
GLXDrawable glXGetCurrentReadDrawable(void);
Display glXGetCurrentDisplay(void);
```

There are a few less-common components of GLX we haven't covered yet. For completeness, let's take a quick look at them. You can query certain state from the current drawable with the function **glXQueryDrawable()**. Pass the drawable that you are interested in as well as the attribute you are interested in: GLX_WIDTH, GLX_HEIGHT, GLX_PRESERVED_CONTENTS, GLX_LARGEST_PBUFFER, or GLX_FBCONFIG_ID. The result is returned in the value field:

```
void glXQueryDrawable(Display *dpy, GLXDrawable draw,
                      int attribute, unsigned int *value);
```

There also is a set of functions for creating, dealing with, and deleting
pixmaps and pBuffers. These are not covered here because we are not
using and do not recommend you use pixmaps or pBuffers.

Putting It All Together

Now, for the fun part! Let's put all this GLX stuff together and create
applications that use GLX for window creation and maintenance instead
of GLFW. GLFW is great for creating quick, simple apps but does not allow
for very granular control over the GLX environment. The GLXBasics
sample is an application written from scratch that uses GLX and also
demonstrates handling of GLX callbacks, including how to interpret the
mouse position. The first step is to open a connection to the X server:

```
rcx->dpy = XOpenDisplay(NULL);
```

Then, let's check the supported GLX version to make sure that the
functionality we use later is supported:

```
glXQueryVersion(rcx->dpy, &nMajorVer, &nMinorVer);
printf("Supported GLX version - %d.%d\ n", nMajorVer, nMinorVer);

if (nMajorVer == 1 && nMinorVer < 3)
{
    printf("ERROR: GLX 1.3 or greater is necessary\ n");
    XCloseDisplay(rcx->dpy);
    exit(0);
}
```

Now that we know we are good to go, look for a config that meets our
requirements. We aren't picky here, considering this app doesn't have any
complex interactions with the framebuffer:

```
GLXFBConfig *fbConfigs;
int numConfigs = 0;
static const int fbAttribs[] =
{
    GLX_RENDER_TYPE,   GLX_RGBA_BIT,
    GLX_X_RENDERABLE,  True,
    GLX_DRAWABLE_TYPE, GLX_WINDOW_BIT,
    GLX_DOUBLEBUFFER,  True,
    GLX_RED_SIZE,      8,
    GLX_BLUE_SIZE,     8,
    GLX_GREEN_SIZE,    8,
    0
};
// Get a new fb config that meets our attrib requirements
fbConfigs = glXChooseFBConfig(rcx->dpy, DefaultScreen(rcx->dpy),
                              fbAttribs, &numConfigs);
```

We also need a visual to create the X Window. Once we have a config, we can get the corresponding visual from it:

```
XVisualInfo *visualInfo;
visualInfo = glXGetVisualFromFBConfig(rcx->dpy, fbConfigs[0]);
```

After we have a visual, we can use it to create a new X Window. Before calling into **XCreateWindow()**, we have to figure out what things we want the window to do. Pick the events that are of interest, and add them to the event mask. Do the same with the window mask. Set the border size and gravity we want. We also have to create a color map for the window to use. While we are at it, map the window to the display:

```
winAttribs.event_mask = ExposureMask | VisibilityChangeMask |
                        KeyPressMask | PointerMotionMask     |
                        StructureNotifyMask ;

winAttribs.border_pixel = 0;
winAttribs.bit_gravity = StaticGravity;
winAttribs.colormap = XCreateColormap(rcx->dpy,
                        RootWindow(rcx->dpy, visualInfo->screen),
                        visualInfo->visual, AllocNone);
winmask = CWBorderPixel | CWBitGravity | CWEventMask| CWColormap;

rcx->win = XCreateWindow(rcx->dpy, DefaultRootWindow(rcx->dpy), 20, 20,
                        rcx->nWinWidth, rcx->nWinHeight, 0,
                        visualInfo->depth, InputOutput,
                        visualInfo->visual, winmask, &winAttribs);

XMapWindow(rcx->dpy, rcx->win);
```

Great! We have a window! A few steps still need to be completed before we can render. First, let's create a context and make it the current context. Remember, to create the context we need the config that corresponds with the visual used to create the window:

```
// Also create a new GL context for rendering
GLint attribs[] =
{
    GLX_CONTEXT_MAJOR_VERSION_ARB, 3,
    GLX_CONTEXT_MINOR_VERSION_ARB, 3,
    0
} ;
rcx->ctx = glXCreateContextAttribsARB(rcx->dpy, fbConfigs[0], 0,
                                    True, attribs);
glXMakeCurrent(rcx->dpy, rcx->win, rcx->ctx);
```

Once a context is bound, we can make GL calls. First, set the viewport:

```
glViewport(0, 0, rcx->nWinWidth, rcx->nWinHeight);
```

Next, clear the color buffer and prepare to render:

```
glClearColor(0.0f, 1.0f, 1.0f, 1.0f);
glClear(GL_COLOR_BUFFER_BIT);
```

This little demo application shown in Figure 14.12 just draws two eyeballs that do their best to follow your mouse pointer around the window. Some math is done to figure out where to put the eyeballs, where the mouse pointer is, and where the eyeballs should be looking. You can take a look at the rest of the GLXBasics sample program to see how all this works together. Only the important GLX snippets are listed here because this chapter is not introducing new OpenGL functionality.

Figure 14.12: Here's looking at you!

Now OpenGL setup is complete, and we can concentrate on rendering something. When the window changes or user input such as the pointer position moves are received, the contents of the window are redrawn. Afterward, **glXSwapBuffers()** is called:

```
// Flush drawing commands
glXSwapBuffers(rcx->dpy, rcx->win);
```

Before the app closes, some cleanup needs to be done. Remember when we started the application, a connection to the X server was opened, an X Window was created, and a context was created and bound. Now, before we quit, all of the resources we allocated have to be cleaned up. Note that the context should be unbound before it is destroyed.

```
glXMakeCurrent(rcx->dpy, None, NULL);

glXDestroyContext(rcx->dpy, rcx->ctx);
rcx->ctx = NULL;
```

```
XDestroyWindow(rcx->dpy, rcx->win);
rcx->win = (Window)NULL;

XCloseDisplay(rcx->dpy);
rcx->dpy = 0;
```

Going Full Screen on X

Just as with the other platforms, X-based systems such as most Linux
desktops also support applications taking control of an entire screen.
Modern Linux distributions ship with some form of intelligent window
manager, and so it's best to cooperate with it in order to achieve stable and
predictable results. In order to go full screen on X, we're going to send the
window manager an *event* to request control of the display.

First, we create *atoms* to represent two strings that we want to
communicate to the X server; "_NET_WM_STATE" and
"_NET_WM_STATE_FULLSCREEN". Then, we construct an XEvent structure
using the atoms and send it as a client event to the X server via the
window we've created. The X server responds by resizing our window to
cover the entire screen. The code to do this is pretty simple and is shown
here:

```
Atom wm_state = XInternAtom(rcx->dpy,
                            "_NET_WM_STATE",
                            False);
Atom fullscreen = XInternAtom(rcx->dpy,
                              "_NET_WM_STATE_FULLSCREEN",
                              False);

XEvent xev;
memset(&xev, 0, sizeof(xev));
xev.type = ClientMessage;
xev.xclient.window = rcx->win;
xev.xclient.message_type = wm_state;
xev.xclient.format = 32;
xev.xclient.data.l[0] = 1;
xev.xclient.data.l[1] = fullscreen;
xev.xclient.data.l[2] = 0;

XSendEvent(rcx->dpy, DefaultRootWindow(rcx->dpy), False,
           SubstructureRedirectMask | SubstructureNotifyMask, &xev);
```

After receiving this event, the X server will resize your window to cover
the entire display, remove its window borders, and allow your application
to run in full-screen mode. Once you close the window (at the end of you
application, for example), the X server will return the user's desktop to
normal.

OpenGL on Mobile Platforms

This section peeks into the world of OpenGL ES rendering. This set of APIs is intended for use in embedded environments where traditionally resources have been much more limited. OpenGL ES dares to go where other rendering APIs can only dream of.

There is a lot of ground to cover, and so we will focus on the basics for getting started. There are several versions of OpenGL ES in existence, but we will focus on the newest and most relevant, OpenGL ES 3.0. We also cover the windowing interfaces designed for use with OpenGL ES and touch on some issues specific to dealing with embedded environments. We will demonstrate using OpenGL ES on Android as well as iOS. This chapter is not an attempt to cover OpenGL ES in its entirety, but instead to be a primer for OpenGL ES development as well as point out major differences between full OpenGL and OpenGL ES.

OpenGL on a Diet

You will find that OpenGL ES is similar to regular OpenGL. This isn't accidental; the OpenGL ES specifications were developed from different versions of OpenGL. As you have seen up until now, OpenGL provides a great interface for 3D rendering. It is very flexible and can be used in many applications, from gaming to full-blown CAD workstations to medical imaging.

What's the "ES" For?

Over time, the OpenGL API has been expanded to support new features. This has caused older versions of the OpenGL application programming interface to grow very large, providing many different methods of doing the same thing. Take, for instance, drawing a single point. In older versions of OpenGL this could be accomplished through immediate mode, or through display lists that captured and replayed immediate mode commands. You could also use `glDrawArrays()` with points specified in arrays or through vertex buffer objects.

The simple action of drawing a point can be done four different ways, each having different advantages. Although it is nice to have many choices when implementing your own application, all of this flexibility has produced a very large API. This in turn requires a large and complex driver to support it. In addition, special hardware is often required to make each path efficient and fast. The OpenGL APIs streamline the feature set, only including a subset of the most common and useful portions of related OpenGL APIs. Recent versions of OpenGL have drastically reduced the functionality overlap, but these revisions include features and functionality that most OpenGL ES hardware can only dream about! OpenGL ES 3.0 provides a good balance between flexibility and usability for embedded and mobile environments.

A Brief History

As hardware costs have come down and more functionality fits into smaller areas on semiconductors, user interfaces have become more and more complex for embedded devices. A common example is the automobile. In the 1980s the first visual feedback from car computers was provided in the form of single- and multi-line text. These interfaces provided warnings about seatbelt usage, current gas mileage, and so on. After that, two-dimensional displays became prevalent. These often used bitmap-like rendering to present 2D graphics. Most recently, 3D-capable systems have been integrated to help support GPS navigation, environment control, entertainment, and other graphics-intensive features. In fact, the instrument cluster on many newer models is now rendered using OpenGL ES 2.0. A similar technological history exists for aeronautical instrumentation and cell phones.

Early embedded 3D interfaces were often proprietary and tied closely to the specific hardware features. This was often the case because the supported feature set was small and varied greatly from device to device. But as each vendor's 3D engine increased in complexity, it became time-consuming and challenging to port applications between devices and vendors. The only solution was a standard interface. With this in mind, a consortium was formed to help define an interface that would be flexible and portable, yet tailored to embedded environments and conscious of their limitations. This standards body would be called the Khronos Group.

Khronos

The Khronos Group was originally founded in 2000 by members of the OpenGL ARB, the OpenGL governing body. Many capable graphics APIs existed for the PC space, but the goal of Khronos was to help define interfaces that were more applicable to devices beyond the personal computer. The first embedded API it developed was OpenGL ES.

Khronos consists of many industry leaders in both hardware and software. Some of the current members are AMD, Apple, ARM, Intel, Google, NVIDIA, and Qualcomm. The complete list is long and distinguished. You can visit the Khronos Web site for more information (http://www.khronos.org).

Version Development

The first version of OpenGL ES released, cleverly called OpenGL ES 1.0, was an attempt to drastically reduce the API footprint of a full-featured PC API. This release used the OpenGL 1.3 specification as a basis. Although very capable, OpenGL ES 1.0 removed many of the less frequently used or very complex portions of the full OpenGL specification. Just like its big brother, OpenGL ES 1.0 defines a fixed-functionality pipe for vertex transform and fragment processing. OpenGL ES SC 1.0 is a separate specification based on OpenGL ES 1.0 and was designed for execution environments with extreme reliability requirements. These applications are considered "Safety Critical," hence the *SC* designator. Typical applications are in avionics, automobiles, and military environments. In these areas, 3D applications are often used for instrumentation, mapping, and representing terrain.

ES 1.1 was completed soon after the first specification was released. Although similar to OpenGL ES 1.0, the 1.1 specification is based on the OpenGL 1.5 specification. In addition, a more advanced texture path, buffer objects, and a draw texture interface were added. All in all, the ES 1.1 release was similar to ES 1.0 but added a few new interesting features.

ES 2.0 was a complete break from the pack. It is not backward compatible with the ES 1.x versions. The biggest difference is that the fixed-functionality portions of the pipeline have been removed. Instead, programmable shaders are used to perform the vertex and fragment processing steps. The ES 2.0 specification is based on the OpenGL 2.0 specification.

To fully support programmable shaders, ES 2.0 employs the OpenGL ES Shading Language. This is a high-level shading language that is similar to the OpenGL Shading Language that is paired with OpenGL 2.0+. The reason ES 2.0 is such a large improvement is that all the fixed functionality no longer encumbers the API. This means applications can implement and use only the methods they need in their own shaders.

The latest version of OpenGL ES is 3.0. It is based on and is backwards compatible with OpenGL ES 2.0. This version adds a laundry list of features and formats lifted from various versions of the full OpenGL spec to bring the mobile version a much-needed facelift. In addition, a new version of ES SL was defined to expand the capabilities of the shading language as well. OpenGL ES 3.0 supports ES SL 3.0 as well as earlier versions.

So, to recap, the OpenGL ES versions currently defined and the OpenGL version they were based on are listed in Table 14.7.

Table 14.7: Base OpenGL Versions for OpenGL ES

OpenGL ES Version	OpenGL Version
OpenGL ES 1.0	OpenGL 1.3
OpenGL ES SC 1.0	OpenGL 1.3
OpenGL ES 1.1	OpenGL 1.5
OpenGL ES 2.0	OpenGL 2.0
OpenGL ES 3.0	OpenGL 4.0+

Which Version Is Right for You?

Often hardware is created with a specific API in mind. These platforms may support only a single accelerated version of ES. It is sometimes helpful to think of the different versions of ES as profiles that represent the functionality of the underlying hardware.

For traditional OpenGL, typically new hardware is designed to support the latest version available. OpenGL ES is a little different. The type of features targeted for new hardware are chosen based on several factors; targeted production cost, typical uses, and system support are a few. That said, semiconductor technology has come a long way in the last five years; it's now feasible to make very small, cost-effective, and efficient chips. Almost all smartphones such as Google Android Phones and the Apple iPhone use OpenGL ES. Rather than introduce you to the older versions of ES, this chapter focuses on OpenGL ES 3.0. To get the most out of this chapter, you should be comfortable with most of the OpenGL feature set. This chapter is more about showing you what the major differences are between regular OpenGL and OpenGL ES and less about describing each feature again in detail.

OpenGL ES 3.0

OpenGL ES 3.0 and OpenGL 4.3 are surprisingly similar at the API level. Both have slimmed-down interfaces that have removed old cruft. However, OpenGL 4.3 has added many new features not yet available on embedded hardware. Geometry shaders, tessellation, compute shaders, float buffers, and many other newer additions to OpenGL are simply too complex to implement on most existing mobile or embedded hardware. But as time goes on, the lines have become increasingly blurred between what is embedded hardware and fully featured desktop graphics. Is a tablet computer a mobile device or more similar to a laptop? What about a handheld gaming device or an automobile? As time progresses, expect to see embedded hardware become more and more capable, reaching into the functional areas of the full OpenGL feature set.

Vertex Processing and Coloring

One of the first steps in rendering is defining the vertices of your geometry. Vertex buffer objects, or the client-side vertex arrays, must be used for vertex specification. Vertex buffer objects can be mapped just as OpenGL 4.3 allows. Specify vertex attributes by using **glVertexAttribPointer()**:

```
void glVertexAttribPointer(GLuint index,
                           GLuint size,
                           GLenum type,
                           GLboolean normalized,
                           sizei stride,
                           const void *ptr);
```

To draw geometry, you can use **glDrawArrays()**, **glDrawArraysInstanced()**, **glDrawElements()**, **glDrawElementsInstanced()**, and **glDrawRangeElements()**. However, the more specialized commands in OpenGL 4.3, such as **glMultiDrawArrays()**, **glMultiDrawElements()**, and so on, are not available in OpenGL ES 3.0. Additionally, OpenGL ES 3.0 supports vertex array objects. These objects are used to define the buffer objects consumed by the vertex processing stage and are operated on by calling **glGenVertexArrays()**, **glDeleteVertexArrays()**, and **glBindVertexArray()**. Vertex array objects operate as described earlier in this book.

Shaders

OpenGL ES 2.0 and 3.0 use programmable shaders in much the same way as OpenGL 4.3. However, the only two supported shader stages are vertex and fragment processing. OpenGL ES 2.0 and 3.0 use a shading language similar to the GLSL language specification, called the OpenGL ES Shading Language. This version has changes that are specific to embedded environments and the hardware they contain.

Several years ago, when OpenGL ES 2.0 was gaining popularity, it was common for mobile platforms to not include a built-in compiler. These platforms relied on programs to compile shaders at the time applications were developed and then ship a binary for every platform that program might run on. Most mobile platforms now include a built-in compiler. Some embedded environments may still not support run-time compilation.

Either way, using shaders in OpenGL ES is very similar to full OpenGL. The same semantics of program and shader management are still in play. The first step in using the programmable pipeline is to create the necessary shader and program objects. This is done with the following commands:

```
GLuint glCreateShader(GLenum type);
GLuint glCreateProgram(void);
```

After that, shader objects can be attached to program objects:

```
glAttachShader(GLuint program, GLuint shader);
```

Then, pass your shader strings in directly and compile them at runtime using the familiar functions we already saw with OpenGL 4.3:

```
void glShaderSource(GLuint shader,
                    GLsizei count,
                    const char **string,
                    const GLint *length);
void glCompileShader(GLuint shader);
```

If you are running on a platform that only supports binary shaders, this is the point where you load your precompiled binary instead of shader source. One way you can check for binary support at runtime is to query GL_NUM_SHADER_BINARY_FORMATS. Refer to your device's SDK for more information on what these formats might be. A single binary can be loaded for a fragment-vertex pair if they were compiled together offline.

```
void glShaderBinary(GLsizei count,
                    const GLuint *shaders,
                    GLenum binaryformat,
                    const void *binary,
                    GLsizei length);
```

All platforms supporting OpenGL ES must accept either source or binary shaders. OpenGL ES 3.0 requires a runtime compiler be present, while binary shader support is optional. Check your device documentation to see which option works best for your platform. If you are targeting Android or iOS platforms, you'll be fine using source shaders. Once your shaders are loaded and compiled, bind the attribute channels to the attribute names used in your shaders:

```
glBindAttribLocation(GLuint program,
                     GLuint index,
                     const char *name);
```

The program can then be linked. If the shader binary interface is supported, the shader binaries for the compiled shaders need to be loaded before the link method is called:

```
glLinkProgram(GLuint program);
```

After the program has been successfully linked, you can set it as the currently executing program by calling **glUseProgram()**. Also, at this point uniforms can be set as needed. Most of the normal OpenGL 4.3 attribute and uniform interfaces are supported. However, the transpose bit for setting uniform matrices must be GL_FALSE. This feature is not essential to the functioning of the programmable pipeline. Trying to draw without a valid program bound generates undefined results. You can directly set individual uniforms using the following interfaces:

```
void glUseProgram(GLuint program);
void glUniform{1234}{if}(GLint location, T values);
void glUniform{1234}{if}v(GLint location, GLsizei count, T value);
void glUniformMatrix{234}fv(GLint location, GLsizei count,
                           GLboolean transpose, T value);
```

Also, uniform blocks are now part of OpenGL ES 3.0. To interact with uniform blocks you can use:

```
glGetUniformBlockIndex(GLuint program, const char *uniformBlockName);
glGetActiveUniformBlockName(GLuint program, GLuint uniformBlockIndex,
                           GLsizei bufSize, GLsizei *length,
                           char *uniformBlockName);
```

The shader language paired with OpenGL ES 3.0 is pretty similar to GLSL 3.3. In fact, you can often get started with your ES shaders by developing them on a PC or Mac and then transferring them over to ES once things work as you expect.

While OpenGL ES 3.0 does not natively support Geometry or Tessellation shaders, it does support transform feedback mode. This rendering mode allows you to capture the output of the vertex shader directly into a buffer object. This might allow you to run only the vertex shader on a set of vertex data or to capture the output of complex vertex shaders for replaying later. We already covered transform feedback in Chapter 7. To use transform feedback mode on OpenGL ES 3.0, you can use the commands

```
void glGenTransformFeedback(GLsizei n, GLuint *ids);
void glDeleteTransformFeedback(GLsizei n, const uint *ids);
void glBindTransformFeedback(GLenum target, GLunit id);
void glBeginTransformFeedback(GLenum primitiveMode);
void glEndTransformFeedback();
void glPauseTransformFeedback();
void glResumeTransformFeedback();
```

Rasterization

Antialiased lines are not supported. OpenGL ES 3.0 does not have polygon smooth, polygon antialiasing, or multiple polygon modes.

Texturing

With OpenGL ES 3.0, 2D textures, 2D texture arrays, 3D textures, and cube maps are supported. OpenGL ES 3.0 has also added support for sampler objects. Sampler objects split the data backing a texture object from the state used to sample the texture data. We covered sampler objects back in Chapter 5. OpenGL ES also introduces a new way of specifying an entire texture mip chain at once. This can greatly decrease the validation a driver has to do when loading a new texture, making for faster texture loading. You can use this new method by calling

```
void glTextureStorage2D(GLenum target,
                        GLsizei levels,
                        GLenum internalformat,
                        GLsizei width,
                        GLsizei height);
```

The number of texture formats supported by OpenGL ES 3.0 is significantly larger than the number supported by OpenGL ES 2.0, but still considerably smaller than what is supported in OpenGL 4.3. Before using a texture format, check to make sure it's supported in the OpenGL APIs you plan to use.

Framebuffers

Similar to OpenGL 4.3, OpenGL ES 3.0 also supports framebuffer and renderbuffer objects. Applications can create and bind their own framebuffer objects, attaching render buffers or textures to do off-screen rendering. An improvement over OpenGL ES 2.0, now OpenGL ES 3.0 will allow multi-sampled renderbuffers and depth textures to be used with framebuffer objects. You can also attach any mip level from a texture to a framebuffer object.

Fragment Operations

There are also a few differences to the per-fragment operations allowed in OpenGL ES 3.0. It is required that there be at least one config available that supports both a depth buffer and a stencil buffer. This guarantees that an application depending on the use of depth information and stencil compares will function on any implementation that supports OpenGL ES 3.0.

A few things have also been removed relative to the OpenGL 4.3 spec. First, the alpha test stage has been removed given that an application can implement this stage in a fragment shader. The `glLogicOp()` interface is no longer supported. Only the new Boolean occlusion query mechanism is part of OpenGL ES. Boolean occlusion queries work similarly to those in OpenGL 4.3, but instead of returning a count of the number of primitives that were passed through the pipeline, OpenGL ES just tells you if any or none passed.

Blending works as it does in OpenGL 4.3, but the scope is more limited. Blending cannot be set differently for each render target, and dual source blending is not supported.

State

OpenGL ES 3.0 state can be queried in the same way as OpenGL 4.3 state. You can use `glGetBooleanv()`, `glGetIntegerv()`, and `glGetFloatv()` to query most state. OpenGL ES 3.0 also adds support for `glGetInteger64v()`. OpenGL ES 3.0 has added a significant number of query mechanisms to read back the current state. Many of these did not exist in OpenGL ES 2.0. Most queries available in OpenGL 4.3 are also available in OpenGL ES 3.0.

The OpenGL ES Environment

Now that we have seen what the major spec differences are from the full OpenGL, we are almost ready to take a peek at an example. Figure 14.13

shows an example of OpenGL ES running in a game on a cell phone. This figure is also shown in Color Plate 15. But before that, there are a few issues unique to embedded systems that you should keep in mind while working with OpenGL ES and targeting embedded environments.

Figure 14.13: OpenGL ES rendering on a cell phone

Application Design Considerations

For first-timers to the embedded world, things are a bit different here than when working on a PC. The OpenGL ES world spans a wide variety of hardware profiles. The most capable of these might be multi-core systems with extensive dedicated graphics resources, such as the Sony PlayStation 3. Alternatively, and probably more often, you may be developing for or porting to an entry-level smartphone with a 1-2GHz processor and 1GB of memory.

On limited systems, special attention must be paid to instruction count because every cycle counts if you are looking to maintain reasonable performance. Certain operations can be very slow. An example might be finding the sine of an angle. Instead of calling sin() in a math library, it would be much faster to do a lookup in a precalculated table if a close approximation would do the job. In general, the types of calculations and algorithms that might be part of a PC application should be updated for use in an embedded system. One example might be physics calculations, which are often very expensive. These can usually be simplified and approximated for use on embedded systems like cell phones.

ARM CPUs dominate most of the embedded environment and are part of nearly every mobile phone or tablet. This can ease the burden when porting between mobile platforms, but is also a challenge as the instruction set and performance profile are different from desktop systems. ARM processors and mobile systems are typically regarded as being more power efficient than traditional computers and they need to be able to survive a day or more on one charge. But this means that the power your application uses is also an important factor to pay attention to. Generally, performance and power are direct trade-offs. But you must also be careful to not be wasteful when executing in a mobile environment. Using features like occlusion query to help determine when to process unseen geometry is one tool that can be used to optimize your power usage. There are many others, but power optimization is beyond the scope of this chapter and this book.

Dealing with a Limited Environment

Not only can the environment be limiting when working on embedded systems, but the graphics processing power itself is unlikely to be on par with the bleeding edge of PC graphics. These restrictions force you to pay special attention to resources when you're looking to optimize the performance of your app, or just to get it to load and run at all!

It may be helpful to create a budget for storage space. In this way, you can break up into pieces the maximum graphics and system memory available for each memory-intensive category. This helps to provide a perspective on how much data each unique piece of your app can use and when you are starting to run low. One of the most obvious areas is texturing. Large, detailed textures can help make for rich and detailed environments on PC-targeted applications. This is great for user experience, but textures can be a huge resource hog in most embedded systems. These situations can cause large performance drops when many fragments are textured or multi-textured, especially if each piece of overlapping geometry is textured and drawn in the wrong order.

In addition to core hardware texturing performance, texture sizes can also be a major limitation. Both 3D and cube map textures can quickly add up to a large memory footprint, which is why 3D textures are optional for OpenGL ES 2.0. Usually when the amount of graphics and system memory is limited, the screen size is also small. This means that a much smaller texture can be used with similar visual results. Also, it may be worth avoiding multi-texture because it requires multiple texture passes as well as more texture memory.

Vertex storage can also impact memory, similar to textures. In addition to setting a cap for the total memory used for vertices, it may also be helpful to decide which parts of a scene are important and divide up the vertex allotment along those lines.

One trick to keeping rendering smooth while many objects are on the screen is to change the vertex counts for objects relative to their distance from the viewer. This is a level-of-detail approach to geometry management. For instance, if you want to generate a forest scene, three different models of trees could be used. One level would have a very small vertex count and would be used to render the farthest of the trees. A medium vertex count could be used for trees of intermediate distance, and a larger count would be used on the closest. This would allow many trees to be rendered much quicker than if they were all at a high detail level. Because the least detailed trees are the farthest away, and may also be partially occluded or cover only a few pixels, it is unlikely the lower detail would be noticed. But there may be significant savings in vertex processing as a result.

Fixed-Point Math

You may ask yourself, "What is fixed-point math, and why should I care?" The truth is that you may not care if your hardware supports floating-point numbers, and the version of OpenGL ES you are using does as well. OpenGL ES 3.0 does support full floating point. Some older platforms do not natively support floating point. Floating-point calculations in CPU emulation are very slow and should be avoided. In those instances, a representation of a floating-point number can be used to communicate non-whole numbers. Even if your processor and GPU hardware understand full floating point, leveraging fixed point can provide for significantly smaller data storage, faster data loading, and many other benefits.

We are definitely not going to turn this into a math class! But instead a few basic things about fixed-point math are covered to give you an idea of what's involved. If you need to know more, many great resources are available that go to great lengths in discussing fixed-point math.

First, let's review how floating-point numbers work. There are basically two components to a floating-point number: The mantissa describes the fractional value, and the exponent is the scale or power. In this way, large numbers are represented with the same number of significant digits as small numbers. They are related by $m \times 2^e$, where m is the mantissa and e is the exponent.

Fixed-point representation is different. It looks more like a normal integer. The bits are divided into two parts, with one part being the integer portion and the other part being the fractional. The position between the integer and fractional components is the "imaginary point." There also may be a sign bit. Putting these pieces together, a fixed-point format of s15.16 means that there is 1 sign bit, 15 bits represent the integer, and 16 bits represent the fraction. This is the format used natively by OpenGL ES to represent fixed-point numbers.

Addition of two fixed-point numbers is simple. Because a fixed-point number is basically an integer with an arbitrary "point," the two numbers can be added together with a common scalar addition operation. The same is true for subtraction. There is one requirement for performing these operations. The fixed-point numbers must be in the same format. If they are not, one must be converted to the format of the other first. So to add or subtract a number with format s23.8 and one with s15.16, one format must be chosen and both numbers converted to that format.

Multiplication and division are a bit more complex. When two fixed-point numbers are multiplied together, the imaginary point of the result is the sum of that in the two operands. For instance, if you were multiplying two numbers with formats of s23.8 together, the result would be in the format of s15.16. So it is often helpful to first convert the operands into a format that allows for a reasonably accurate result format. You probably don't want to multiply two s15.16 formats together if they are greater than 1.0 — the result format would have no integer portion! Division is similar, except the size of the fractional component of the second number is subtracted from the first.

When using fixed-point numbers, you have to be especially careful about overflow issues. With normal floating point, when the fractional component would overflow, the exponent portion is modified to preserve accuracy and prevent the overflow. This is not the case for fixed point. To avoid overflowing fixed-point numbers when performing operations that might cause problems, the format can be altered. The numbers can be converted to a format that has a larger integer component and then converted back before calling into OpenGL ES. With multiplication, similar issues result in precision loss of the fractional component when the result is converted back to one of the operand formats. There are also math packages available to help you convert to and from fixed-point formats, as well as perform math functions. This is probably the easiest way to handle fixed-point math if you need to use it for an entire application.

That's it! Now you have an idea how to do basic math operations using fixed-point formats. This will help get you started if you find yourself stuck having to use fixed-point values when working with embedded systems. There are many great references for learning more about fixed-point math. One is *Essential Mathematics for Games and Interactive Applications* by James Van Verth and Lars Bishop (Elsevier, Inc., 2004).

EGL: A New Windowing Environment

You have already heard about GLX, AGL, and WGL. These are the OpenGL-related system interfaces for operating systems like Linux, Apple's Mac OS, and Microsoft Windows. These interfaces are necessary to do the setup and management for system-side resources that OpenGL uses. The EGL implementation often is also provided by the graphics hardware vendor. Unlike the other windowing interfaces, EGL is not OS specific. It's an interface that's designed to run under Windows, Linux, or embedded OSs such as Android and iOS. A block diagram of how EGL and OpenGL ES fit into an embedded system is shown in Figure 14.14.

EGL has its own native types just like OpenGL does. `EGLBoolean` has two values that are named similarly to their OpenGL counterparts: `EGL_TRUE` and `EGL_FALSE`. EGL also defines the type `EGLint`. This is an integer that is sized the same as the native platform integer type. The most current version of EGL as of this writing is EGL 1.4.

EGL Displays

Most EGL entrypoints take a parameter called EGLDisplay. This is a reference to the rendering target where drawing can take place. It might be easiest to think of this as corresponding to a physical monitor. The first step in setting up EGL is to get the default display. This can be done through the following function:

```
EGLDisplay eglGetDisplay(NativeDisplayType display_id);
```

The native display ID that is taken as a parameter is dependent on the system. For instance, if you were working with an EGL implementation on

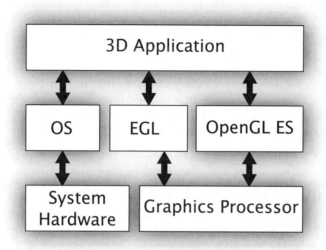

Figure 14.14: A typical embedded system diagram

Windows, the display_id parameter you pass would be the device context. You can also pass EGL_DEFAULT_DISPLAY if you don't have the display ID and just want to render on the default device. If EGL_NO_DISPLAY is returned, an error occurred. Now that you have a display handle, you can use it to initialize EGL. If you try to use other EGL interfaces without initializing EGL first, you get an EGL_NOT_INITIALIZED error.

```
EGLBoolean eglInitialize(EGLDisplay dpy, EGLint *major, EGLint *minor);
```

The other two parameters returned are the major and minor EGL version numbers. By calling the initialize command, you tell EGL you are getting ready to do rendering, which allows it to allocate and set up any necessary resources. EGL also exposes an interface called **eglBindAPI()**. This allows an application to select from different rendering APIs, such as OpenGL, OpenGL ES, and OpenVG. Only one context can be current for each API per thread. Use this interface to tell EGL which interface it should use for subsequent calls to **eglMakeCurrent()** in a thread. Pass in one of EGL_OPENGL_API, EGL_OPENGL_ES_API, or EGL_OPENVG_API to signify the correct API. The call fails if an invalid enum is passed in. OpenVG is a different open API supporting vector graphics found on a few older embedded systems:

```
EGLBoolean eglBindAPI(EGLenum api);
```

EGL also provides a method to query the current API, **eglQueryAPI()**. This interface returns one of the three EGLenum values previously listed: EGL_OPENGL_API, EGL_OPENGL_ES_API, or EGL_OPENVG_API:

```
EGLenum eglQueryAPI(void);
```

On exit of your application, or after you are done rendering, a call must be made to EGL again to clean up all allocated resources. After this call is made, further references to EGL resources with the current display will be invalid until **eglInitialize()** is called on it again:

```
EGLBoolean eglTerminate(EGLDisplay dpy);
```

Also on exit and when finished rendering from a thread, call **eglReleaseThread()**. This allows EGL to release any resources it has allocated in that thread. If a context is still bound, **eglReleaseThread()** releases it as well. It is still valid to make EGL calls after calling **eglReleaseThread()**, but that causes EGL to reallocate any state it just released.

```
EGLBoolean \eglReleaseThread(EGLDisplay dpy);
```

Creating a Window

As on most platforms, creating a window to render in can be a complex task. Windows are created in the native operating system. Later we look at how to tell EGL about native windows. Thankfully the process is similar enough to that for Windows and Linux.

Display Configs

An EGL config is analogous to a pixel format on Windows or a visual on Linux. Each config represents a group of attributes or properties for a set of render surfaces. In this case, the render surface is a window on a display. It is typical for an implementation to support multiple configs. Each config is identified by a unique number. Different constants are defined that correlate to attributes of a config. They are defined in Table 14.8.

It is necessary to choose a config before creating a render surface. But with all the possible combinations of attributes, the process may seem difficult. EGL provides several tools to help you decide which config best supports your needs. If you have an idea of the kind of options you need for a window, you can use the **eglChooseConfig()** interface to let EGL choose the best config for your requirements:

```
EGLBoolean eglChooseConfig(EGLDisplay dpy, const EGLint *attrib_list,
                           EGLConfig *configs,EGLint config_size,
                           EGLint *num_configs);
```

Table 14.8: EGL Config Attribute List

Attribute (EGL_*)	Description
BUFFER_SIZE	Total depth in bits of color buffer.
RED_SIZE	Number of bits in red channel of color buffer.
GREEN_SIZE	Number of bits in green channel of color buffer.
BLUE_SIZE	Number of bits in blue channel of color buffer.
ALPHA_SIZE	Number of bits in alpha channel of color buffer.
DEPTH_SIZE	Number of bits in depth buffer.
LUMINANCE_SIZE	Number of bits of luminance in the color buffer.
STENCIL_SIZE	Number of bits in stencil buffer.
BIND_TO_TEXTURE_RGB	True if config is bindable to RGB textures.
BIND_TO_TEXTURE_RGBA	True if config is bindable to RGBA textures.
CONFIG_CAVEAT	Set to one of the following caveats: EGL_NONE, EGL_SLOW_CONFIG, or EGL_NON_CONFORMANT_CONFIG. These can warn of potential issues for this config. A slow config may be software emulated because it exceeds hardware limits. A nonconformant config will not pass the conformance test.
CONFIG_ID	Unique identifier for this config.
LEVEL	Framebuffer level.
NATIVE_RENDERABLE	Is set to EGL_TRUE if native APIs can render to this surface.
NATIVE_VISUAL_ID	May represent the ID of the native visual if the config supports a window; otherwise, is 0.
NATIVE_VISUAL_TYPE	Type of a native visual if config supports window rendering.

continued

Attribute (EGL_*)	Description
RENDERABLE_TYPE	Native type of visual. May be EGL_OPENGL_ES_BIT or EGL_OPENVG_BIT.
SURFACE_TYPE	Valid surface targets supported. May be any or all of EGL_WINDOW_BIT, EGL_PIXMAP_BIT, or EGL_PBUFFER_BIT.
COLOR_BUFFER_TYPE	Type of color buffer. May be EGL_RGB_BUFFER or EGL_LUMINANCE_BUFFER.
MIN_SWAP_INTERVAL	Smallest value that can be accepted by **eglSwapInterval()**. Smaller values will be clamped to this minimum.
MAX_SWAP_INTERVAL	Largest value that can be accepted by **eglSwapInterval()**. Larger values will be clamped to this maximum.
SAMPLE_BUFFERS	Number of multi-sample buffers supported. Must be 0 or 1.
SAMPLES	Number of samples per pixel for multi-sample buffers. Will be 0 if EGL_SAMPLE_BUFFERS is 0.
ALPHA_MASK_SIZE	Number of bits of alpha mask.
TRANSPARENT_TYPE	Indicates support of transparency. Value may be EGL_NONE or EGL_TRANSPARENT_RGB. If transparency is supported, a transparent pixel is drawn when the pixel's components are all equal to the respective transparent RGB values.
TRANSPARENT_RED_VALUE	Red value a framebuffer pixel must have to be transparent.
TRANSPARENT_GREEN_VALUE	Green value a framebuffer pixel must have to be transparent.
TRANSPARENT_BLUE_VALUE	Blue value a framebuffer pixel must have to be transparent.

First, decide how many matches you are willing to look through. Then, allocate memory to hold the returned config handles. The matching config handles will be returned through the `configs` pointer. The number of configs will be returned through the `num_configs` pointer. Next comes the tricky part. You have to decide which parameters are important to you in a functional config. Then, you create a list of each attribute followed by the corresponding value. For simple applications, some important attributes might be the bit depths of the color and depth buffers, and the surface type. The list must be terminated with `EGL_NONE`. An example of an attribute list is shown here:

```
EGLint attributes[] = { EGL_BUFFER_SIZE,   24,
                        EGL_RED_SIZE,      6,
                        EGL_GREEN_SIZE,    6,
                        EGL_BLUE_SIZE,     6,
                        EGL_DEPTH_SIZE,    12,
                        EGL_SURFACE_TYPE,  EGL_WINDOW_BIT,
                        EGL_NONE} ;
```

For attributes that are not specified in the array, the default values are used. During the search for a matching config, some of the attributes you list are required to make an exact match, whereas others are not. Table 14.9 lists the default values and the compare method for each attribute.

Table 14.9: EGL Config Attribute List

Attribute (EGL_*)	Comparison Operator	Default
BUFFER SIZE	Minimum	0
RED_SIZE	Minimum	0
GREEN_SIZE	Minimum	0
BLUE_SIZE	Minimum	0
ALPHA_SIZE	Minimum	0
DEPTH_SIZE	Minimum	0
LUMINANCE_SIZE	Minimum	0
STENCIL_SIZE	Minimum	0
BIND_TO_TEXTURE_RGB	Equal	EGL_DONT_CARE
BIND_TO_TEXTURE_RGBA	Equal	EGL_DONT_CARE
CONFIG_CAVEAT	Equal	EGL_DONT_CARE
CONFIG_ID	Equal	EGL_DONT_CARE
LEVEL	Equal	0
NATIVE_RENDERABLE	Equal	EGL_DONT_CARE

continued

Attribute (EGL_*)	Comparison Operator	Default
NATIVE_VISUAL_TYPE	Equal	EGL_DONT_CARE
RENDERABLE_TYPE	Mask	EGL_OPENGL_ES_BIT
SURFACE_TYPE	Equal	EGL_WINDOW_BIT
COLOR_BUFFER_TYPE	Equal	EGL_RGB_BUFFER
MIN_SWAP_INTERVAL	Equal	EGL_DONT_CARE
MAX_SWAP_INTERVAL	Equal	EGL_DONT_CARE
SAMPLE_BUFFERS	Minimum	0
SAMPLES	Minimum	0
ALPHA_MASK_SIZE	Minimum	0
TRANSPARENT_TYPE	Equal	EGL_NONE
TRANSPARENT_RED_VALUE	Equal	EGL_DONT_CARE
TRANSPARENT_GREEN_VALUE	Equal	EGL_DONT_CARE
TRANSPARENT_BLUE_VALUE	Equal	EGL_DONT_CARE

EGL uses a set of rules to sort the matching results before they are returned to you. Basically, the caveat field is matched first, followed by the color buffer channel depths, then the total buffer size, and next the sample buffer information. So the config that is the best match should be first. After you receive the matching configs, you can peruse the results to find the best option for you. The first one will often be sufficient.

To analyze the attributes for each config, you can use **eglGetConfigAttrib()**. This allows you to query the attributes for a config, one at a time:

```
EGLBoolean eglGetConfigAttrib(EGLDisplay dpy, EGLConfig config,
                        EGLint attribute, EGLint *value);
```

If you prefer a more "hands-on" approach to choosing a config, a more direct method for accessing supported configs is also provided. You can use **eglGetConfigs()** to get all the configs supported by EGL:

```
EGLBoolean eglGetConfigs(EGLDisplay dpy, EGLConfig *configs,
                        EGLint config_size, EGLint *num_configs);
```

This function is similar to **eglChooseConfig()** except that it returns a list that is not dependent on some search criteria. The number of configs returned is either the maximum available or the number passed in by config_size, whichever is smaller. Here also, a buffer needs to be preallocated based on the expected number of formats. After you have the list, it is up to you to pick the best option, examining each with **eglGetConfigAttrib()**. It is unlikely that multiple different platforms will have the same configs or list configs in the same order. So it is important to properly select a config instead of blindly using the config handle.

Creating Rendering Surfaces

Now that we know how to pick a config that will support our needs, it's time to look at creating an actual render surface. The focus will be window surfaces, although it is also possible to create nondisplayable surfaces such as pBuffers and pixmaps. The first step is to create a native window that has the same attributes as those in the config you chose. Then you can use the window handle to create a window surface. The window handle type is related to the platform or OS you are using. In this way, the same interface supports many different OSs without having to define a new method for each:

```
EGLSurface eglCreateWindowSurface(EGLDisplay dpy,
                                  EGLConfig config,
                                  NativeWindowType win,
                                  EGLint *attrib_list);
```

The handle for the on-screen surface is returned if the call succeeds. The `attrib_list` parameter is intended to specify window attributes, but currently none is defined. After you are done rendering, you have to destroy your surface using the **eglDestroySurface()** function:

```
EGLBoolean eglDestroySurface(EGLDisplay dpy, EGLSurface surface);
```

After a window render surface has been created and the hardware resources have been configured, you are almost ready to go!

Context Management

The last step is to create a render context to use. The rendering context is a set of state used for rendering. Creation of at least one context must be supported on all hardware:

```
EGLContext eglCreateContext(EGLDisplay dpy,
                            EGLConfig config,
                            EGLContext share_context,
                            const EGLint *attrib_list);
```

To create a context, call the **eglCreateContext()** function with the display handle you have been using all along. Also pass in the config used to create the render surface. The config used to create the context must be compatible with the config used to create the window. The share_context parameter is used to share objects like textures and shaders between contexts. Pass in the context you want to share with. Normally you pass EGL_NO_CONTEXT here given that sharing is not necessary. The context handle is passed back if the context was successfully created; otherwise, EGL_NO_CONTEXT is returned.

Now that you have a rendering surface and a context, you're ready to go! The last thing to do is to tell EGL which context you want to use first since it can use multiple contexts for rendering. Use **eglMakeCurrent()** to set a context as current. You can use the surface you just created as both the read and the draw surfaces:

```
EGLBoolean eglMakeCurrent(EGLDisplay dpy, EGLSurface draw,
                          EGLSurface read, EGLContext ctx);
```

You get an error if the draw or read surfaces are invalid or if they are not compatible with the context. To release a bound context, you can call **eglMakeCurrent()** with EGL_NO_CONTEXT as the context. You must use EGL_NO_SURFACE as the read and write surfaces when releasing a context. To delete a context you are finished with, call **eglDestroyContext()**:

```
EGLBoolean eglDestroyContext(EGLDisplay dpy, EGLContext ctx);
```

Presenting Buffers and Rendering Synchronization

For rendering, there are certain EGL functions you may need to help keep things running smoothly. The first is **eglSwapBuffers()**. This interface allows you to present a color buffer to a window. Just pass in the window surface you would like to post to:

```
EGLBoolean eglSwapBuffers(EGLDisplay dpy, EGLSurface surface);
```

Just because **eglSwapBuffers()** is called doesn't mean it's the best time to actually post the buffer to the monitor. It's possible that the display is in the middle of displaying a frame when **eglSwapBuffers()** is called. This case causes an artifact called tearing that looks like the frame is slightly skewed on a horizontal line. EGL provides a way to decide if it should wait until the current display update is complete before posting the swapped buffer to the display:

```
EGLBoolean eglSwapInterval(EGLDisplay dpy, EGLint interval);
```

By setting the swap interval to 0, you are telling EGL to not synchronize swaps and that an **eglSwapBuffers()** call should be posted immediately. The default value is 1, which means each swap is synchronized with the next post to the display. The interval is clamped to the values of EGL_MIN_SWAP_INTERVAL and EGL_MAX_SWAP_INTERVAL.

If you plan to render to your window using other APIs besides OpenGL ES
and EGL, there are some things you can do to ensure that rendering is
posted in the right order:

```
EGLBoolean eglWaitGL(void);
EGLBoolean eglWaitNative(EGLint engine);
```

Use **eglWaitGL()** to prevent other API rendering from operating on a
window surface before OpenGL ES rendering completes. Use
eglWaitNative() to prevent OpenGL ES from executing before native API
rendering completes. The engine parameter can be defined in EGL
extensions specific to an implementation, but EGL_CORE_NATIVE_ENGINE
can also be used and will refer to the most common native rendering
engine besides OpenGL ES. This is implementation and system specific.

More EGL

We covered the most important and commonly used EGL interfaces.
There are a few more EGL functions left to talk about that are more
peripheral to the common execution path.

EGL Errors

EGL provides a method for getting EGL-specific errors that may be thrown
during EGL execution. Most functions return EGL_TRUE or EGL_FALSE to
indicate whether they were successful, but in the event of a failure, a
Boolean provides very little information on what went wrong. In this case,
eglGetError() may be called to get more information:

```
EGLint eglGetError();
```

The last error encountered is returned. This will be one of the following
self-explanatory errors: EGL_SUCCESS, EGL_NOT_INITIALIZED,
EGL_BAD_ACCESS, EGL_BAD_ALLOC, EGL_BAD_ATTRIBUTE, EGL_BAD_CONTEXT,
EGL_BAD_CONFIG, EGL_BAD_CURRENT_SURFACE, EGL_BAD_DISPLAY,
EGL_BAD_SURFACE, EGL_BAD_MATCH, EGL_BAD_PARAMETER,
EGL_BAD_NATIVE_PIXMAP, EGL_BAD_NATIVE_WINDOW, or EGL_CONTEXT_LOST.

Getting EGL Strings

A few EGL state strings may be of interest. These include the EGL version
string and extension string. To get these, use the **eglQueryString()**
interface with the EGL_VERSION and EGL_EXTENSIONS enums:

```
const char *eglQueryString(EGLDisplay dpy, EGLint name);
```

Extending EGL

Like OpenGL, EGL provides support for various extensions. These are often extensions specific to the current platform and can provide for extended functionality beyond that of the core specification. To find out what extensions are available on your system, you can use the `eglQueryString()` function discussed earlier. To get more information on specific extensions, you can visit the Khronos Web site listed in the reference section. Some of these extensions may require additional entrypoints. To get the entrypoint address for these extensions, pass the name of the new entrypoint into the following function:

```
void (*eglGetProcAddress(const char *procname))();
```

Use of this entrypoint is similar to `wglGetProcAddress()`. A NULL return means the entrypoint does not exist. But just because a non-NULL address is returned does not mean the function is actually supported. The related extensions must exist in the EGL extension string or the OpenGL ES extension string. It is important to ensure that you have a valid function pointer (non-NULL) after calling `eglGetProcAddress()`.

Negotiating Embedded Environments

After examining how OpenGL ES and EGL work on an embedded system, it's time to look closer at the environment of an embedded system and how it affects an OpenGL ES application. The environment plays an important role in how you approach creating ES applications.

Popular Operating Systems

Because OpenGL ES is not limited to certain platforms as many 3D APIs are, a wide variety of OSs can be used. The two most common mobile platforms today are Google's Android and Apple's iOS. If you are dealing with a strictly embedded platform, this decision is often already made for you because most embedded systems are designed for use with certain OSs and certain OSs are intended for use on specific hardware.

Vendor-Specific Extensions

Each OpenGL ES vendor often has a set of extensions that are specific to its hardware and implementation. These often extend the number and types of formats available. Because these extensions are useful only for limited sets of hardware, they are not discussed here.

For the Home Gamer

For those of us not lucky enough to be working on a hardware emulator or hardware itself, there are other options if you still want to try your hand at OpenGL ES. Several OpenGL ES implementations are available that execute on desktop operating systems. These are also great for doing initial development. NVIDIA and AMD allow you to create ES profiles when creating OpenGL contexts on discrete graphics cards. You can use these profiles to get started writing OpenGL ES 2.0 or 3.0 applications right on your desktop computer. Additionally, Google and Apple make it easy for you to get started developing for their platforms.

Android Handheld Platforms

Android currently dominates the smartphone market with more than 50% share. When you create an app for the Android Play market, your app gains exposure to tens of millions of phones and tablets. Because Android ships on devices from many manufacturers, you do have to make sure you plan for different levels of hardware capability and performance. Android supports OpenGL ES 1.1 and ES 2.0 on Android versions 2.2 and newer. Android is also adding support for ES 3.0. To develop OpenGL applications on Android, you should have a newer phone or tablet, one supporting at least Android 2.2. If you do not have one, Google sells Android devices that can be used for development on the Google Play store. Visit `http://play.google.com`, and browse the Devices category to learn more about Nexus mobile devices Google sells directly.

Google has done an excellent job providing developer support for the Android platform. There is a wealth of knowledge and instructions on how to get started. The basics of setting up for and developing for Android are beyond the scope of this book. To learn more about Android development, visit `http://developer.android.com/index.html`. It's free to develop Android applications and run them on your local devices, but there's a small fee to publish your apps in the Android Market.

Android Development Environments

Google provides many sample apps that help get you started using various features of the Android OS. At a high level, there are two development kits you can use to develop for Android, the Native Development Kit (NDK) and the Software Development Kit (SDK).

The NDK allows developers to use native-code languages like C and C++. This is particularly useful if you are porting an existing source base to Android already written in C or C++. This can be an ideal method for larger game engines, especially if they use existing non-Java libraries. There may also be some performance advantages to going this route. You also have more control over the windowing system and setting up EGL to match the needs of your application. On the other hand, using the NDK can add to code complexity and affect the portability of your application.

The SDK provides easy access to API libraries that make app development and debugging easier. The SDK is also the ideal place for new Android developers to start. It also includes tools and components to let you develop in the Eclipse IDE. The SDK helps take care of most of the details of managing EGL and GL setup, instead allowing you to access OpenGL ES calls directly through the Java bindings. Most Android applications go the SDK route. For our sample app, we will also use the SDK.

I'll assume you have Eclipse set up on your computer, and the Android SDK installed and set up, as well as having an Android device to be able to try the examples here.

Setting Up an Android Project

Once you have Eclipse installed and the Android SDK installed, add the StonehengeES project to your workspace by selecting File → Import → General → Existing Projects into Workspace. At this point if you are missing any of the required packages, you may see errors appear in some of the code. To add missing packages, go to Window → Android SDK Manager and update any missing packages. API 17 was used for this project; you will need it.

To run your program on your Android device, you will need the USB debug drivers installed. These are different for every platform. You can find more info here: `http://developer.android.com/tools/device.html`. Next, enable USB debugging on your device. For most devices you can bring up the settings dialog, select Developer Options, and then select USB Debugging. On some devices there might be a few tricks[4] to exposing the debug menu if you don't already see it. Each device's might be a bit different as many manufacturers customize the Android settings app. You can refer to your device's documentation for more information on how to enable debugging.

---

4. `http://www.androidcentral.com/how-enable-developer-settings-android-42` shows a few of those tricks.

Once your hardware is set up, you are ready to run the app. Make sure your device is plugged into your computer via USB. Select Run in Eclipse and select your device from the list. That's it! You should now be seeing the StonehengeES app render using OpenGL ES on your device as shown in Figure 14.15.

Figure 14.15: StonehengeES rendered on an Android phone

Setting Up and Rendering

Android uses Activities to manage the actions in the lifecycle of an app. onCreate is where we set up after the app has been launched. onPause is used when the app loses focus, possibly because another app has started. onResume is called when the user returns to using this app. The details of how Activities work is beyond the scope of this example, but more information is available at `http://developer.android.com/`. This application uses `GLSurfaceView` to manage much of the system state. `GLSurfaceView` can manage setting up the EGL display and all EGL state for you. Or if you prefer, you can modify chose your config by using the `setEGLConfigChooser` method. `GLSurfaceView` allows you to control other state as well.

Listing 14.18 runs through the basics of how we set up `GLSurfaceView` in `GLview.java`. In the constructor, the context is created first. Then, the `GLSurfaceView` Renderer is created, and `setRenderer` is called. At this point, a rendering thread is created, and rendering is kicked off.

Further down in Listing 14.18, we handle touch events in the onTouchEvent class. This class gets the touch position on move events. It calculates where a user is touching the screen and then either tilts the view or moves the viewer forward. If the user is swiping, detected by comparing the time the user first touched the screen, the view is rotated in the direction of the swipe.

```java
public class GLView extends GLSurfaceView {

    protected Context context = null;
    protected GLStoneHenge renderer = null;
    protected StopWatch stopwatch = new StopWatch();

    protected long controlLastTouchTime = 0;
    protected float controlLastX = 0.0f;
    protected float controlSensitivity = 150.0f;

    public GLView(Context context) {
        super(context);
        this.context = context;
        setEGLContextClientVersion(2);
        renderer = new GLStoneHenge(context);
        setRenderer(renderer);
        setRenderMode(GLSurfaceView.RENDERMODE_CONTINUOUSLY);
    }

    @Override
    public boolean onTouchEvent(MotionEvent touch) {
        float x = touch.getX();
        float y = touch.getY();
        long holdTime = touch.getEventTime() - touch.getDownTime();

        if (y < getHeight() / 3) {
                renderer.addTilt(-0.5f);
        } else if (y > getHeight() - (getHeight() / 3)) {
                renderer.addTilt(0.5f);
        } else {
                renderer.moveForward(0.5f);
        }

        float scaledX = x / getWidth();
        if (touch.getDownTime() != controlLastTouchTime) {
                controlLastTouchTime = touch.getDownTime();
        } else {
                float deltaX = scaledX - controlLastX;
                renderer.rotateLocalY(controlSensitivity * deltaX);
        }
        controlLastX = scaledX;
        return true;
    }
}
```

Listing 14.18: Extending `GLSurfaceView`

Listing 14.19 covers some of the interesting parts of the initialization for our main class, GLStoneHenge. Note that parts of the function have been removed to allow room for the members we are talking about without having the listing run on for pages. The constructor allocates the models that hold the stone textures. initModels loads the textures, sets up the vertex arrays, loads the shaders, and sets up all necessary OpenGL state. onSurfaceChanged handles resizes by calling resized, which makes sure the viewport and model-view matrix are set up correctly. onSurfaceCreated is what kicks off the OpenGL initialization by calling initModels.

```
class GLStoneHenge implements GLSurfaceView.Renderer {
...
    public GLStoneHenge(Context context) {
        this.context = context;
        for (int i = 0; i < OBJECT_LAST; i++) {
            models[i] = new GLModel();
        }
    }

    public void initModels() throws IOException {
        // Load models.
...
        modelsInitialized = true;
    }

    public void resized(int w, int h) {
        GLES20.glViewport(0, 0, w, h);
        fScreenWidth = (float)w;
        fScreenHeight = (float)h;
        mProjection.perspective(
            45.0f,                          // Field of view.
            fScreenWidth / fScreenHeight,   // Aspect ratio.
            1.0f,                           // Near clipping plane.
            15000.0f                        // Far clipping plane.
            );
    }

    public void onSurfaceChanged(GL10 arg0, int arg1, int arg2) {
        this.resized(arg1, arg2);
    }

    public void onSurfaceCreated(GL10 arg0, EGLConfig arg1) {
        try {
            Log.d("DebugTag", "initModels()");
            this.initModels();
        catch (IOException e) {
            e.printStackTrace();
        }
    }
}
```

Listing 14.19: Setting up and rendering

That's the condensed version of the key components of running StonehengeES on Android. Please take a look through the actual source to get a feel for the pieces we haven't had space to cover here. Developing OpenGL ES applications for Android is surprisingly easy, and Android devices are readily available. Enjoy bringing your OpenGL ES projects to a mobile device near you!

iOpenGL

Apple has three mainstream devices that are powered by OpenGL ES. The iPhone, the iPod Touch, and the iPad. All three devices are available in varying screen resolutions and support both OpenGL ES 2.0 and, via emulation, the older OpenGL ES 1.1. Although not yet supporting the new OpenGL ES 3.0 specification, many of the 3.0 features are available via extensions on the Apple devices. We are of course not going to concern ourselves with OpenGL ES 1.1 at all any longer.

To make things simple in this chapter, we are not going to bother saying iPhone/iPod Touch/iPad all over the place. We'll just say iOS, and you should know this includes all the iOS devices, as they are essentially the same as far as OpenGL ES programming is concerned. By the time this book reaches the press, this may well include iTV, iWatch, and iMicrowaves for all we know!

Apple's iOS SDK includes OpenGL ES 2.0 and GLKit, a framework to ease the creation of OpenGL projects on iOS devices. You were introduced to GLKit in the section on Mac development, as some elements of GLKit are also available on the desktop version of OS X. Here, we will go through the exercise of getting our Stonehenge example program up and running on an iOS device.

Setting Up an iOS Project

The very first thing you need to do is acquire the iOS SDK from Apple's Developer Relations Web site, http://developer.apple.com. Launching Xcode (the Apple development IDE) presents the familiar welcome screen shown in Figure 14.16.

If you have been working on other projects recently, you'll see them listed to the right under Recents. Click the Create a New Xcode Project button to open the project wizard screen. On the New Project screen, shown in Figure 14.17, select Application under the iOS group (see, no devices listed, they are all the same thing). You will see various application

Figure 14.16: The Xcode welcome screen

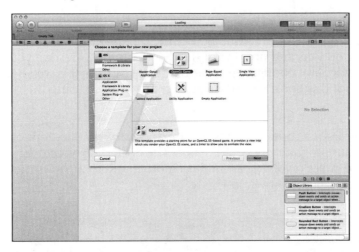

Figure 14.17: Selecting an OpenGL-ES-based game (application) template

templates in the upper pane, one of which is OpenGL Game. Even though we aren't necessarily going to build a game, select this by clicking on it, select Next to specify a project folder where the new project will be created, and click the Create button.

Once the project is created, you will see a screen similar to the one shown in Figure 14.18. We have expanded the groups so you can see all the files and frameworks that make up your project. Also, make sure you've

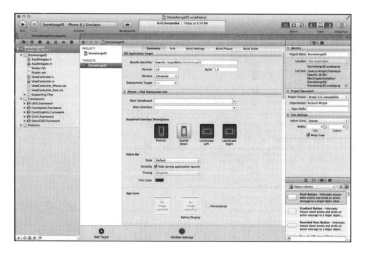

Figure 14.18: The starter OpenGL ES application

selected or changed the combo box in the upper left to be one of the
Simulator options and not one of the device options. Getting your app
on the device and configuring your hardware certificate is well beyond
the scope of this book, so we will restrict ourselves to using the
simulator.

As is typical for Xcode, just press Command-R to compile, link, and
launch your program in the simulator. The default OpenGL ES application
is just two cubes revolving around each other and rotating as they go. The
simulator output is shown in Figure 14.19.

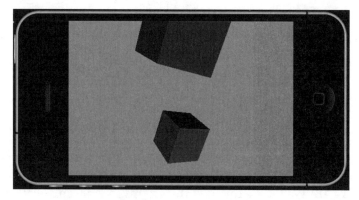

Figure 14.19: The "dancing cubes" default OpenGL ES code

Using C++ on iOS

The native iOS programming environment uses the Objective-C programming language. There is a good bit of passion and sometimes vitriol about this, as the majority of non-Mac programmers in the world would much rather use C or C++. In fact, a good number of Mac programmers would rather use C++ as it turns out. Other than making use of Apple's frameworks, however, there is no reason why anyone cannot use C++ for other portions of their code, and in fact, we are going to make use of Objective-C only as necessary as we move our Stonehenge C++ class over to iOS. Since we are already using this class with the Objective-C Cocoa framework in the Mac chapter, and are already making use of GLKit, this is going to be relatively painless.

Objective-C is essentially C with objects. These objects, however, do not act like C++ objects, and incorporating C++ into Objective-C does not work as well as incorporating C into Objective-C. There is a simple and almost trivial solution to this: Rename all the Objective-C files from *.m to *.mm. Now, you are essentially using Objective-C++, and you can incorporate C++ code with ease in the project, create and use C++ classes in Objective-C++ code, and call C++ methods from Objective-C++ modules.

GLKit

GLKit is a helper framework that was initially intended to help ease the transition from OpenGL ES 1.1's fixed-function pipeline to the new shader-based ES 2.0. Introduced in iOS 5.0, parts of GLKit have migrated to the desktop version of OS X as well, and it continues to be enhanced and supported with subsequent OS releases. A full and complete breakdown of GLKit can be had in the "Introduction to GLKit" document on the Apple Developer Relations Web site. We also went over some details of GLKit in the Mac OS chapter, particularly the 3D Math routines and texture loading code, none of which changes for iOS.

What has changed for iOS is that our main view class is no longer derived from the Cocoa NSOpenGLView, but instead the view is based on GLKView, and using the pervasive model-view-controller paradigm on iOS, we use a view controller based on GLKViewController. The Xcode project wizard has done all of this for us, and you'll see in ViewController.h, that our view controller is indeed derived directly from GLKViewController:

```
@interface ViewController : GLKViewController
```

Listing 14.20 shows the construction of the GLKView object, which contains the actual OpenGL ES context that we are rendering with. This object is created when the nib is loaded initially, and by default contains only a color buffer and a 24-bit depth buffer.

```
- (void)viewDidLoad
  {
  [super viewDidLoad];

  self.context = [[[EAGLContext alloc]
                    initWithAPI:kEAGLRenderingAPIOpenGLES2]
                                  autorelease];

  if (!self.context) {
     NSLog(@"Failed to create ES context");
     }

  GLKView *view = (GLKView *)self.view;
  view.context = self.context;
  view.drawableDepthFormat = GLKViewDrawableDepthFormat24;

  [self setupGL];
  }
```

Listing 14.20: Construction and initialization of the GLKView

Buffer configuration for the GLKView is much simpler than on the desktop, as there are fewer options (and pitfalls) available on the limited number of iOS device configurations. The drawableDepthFormat member may be GLKViewDrawableDepthFormatNone for no depth buffer, or either of GLKViewDrawableDepthFormat16 or GLKViewDrawableDepthFormat24 for a 16-bit or 24-bit formatted depth buffer, respectively. The complete list of buffer members and the valid flags for each is listed in Table 14.10 below.

Table 14.10: Configuration Members and Flags for GLKView

Member	Available Flags
drawableColorFormat	GLKViewDrawableColorFormatRGBA888, GLKViewDrawableColorFormatRGB565
drawableDepthFormat	GLKViewDrawableDepthFormatNone, GLKViewDrawableDepthFormat16, GLKViewDrawableDepthFormat24
drawableStencilFormat	GLKViewDrawableStencilFormatNone, GLKViewDrawableStencilFormat8
drawableMultisample	GLKViewDrawableMultisampleNone, GLKViewDrawableMultisample4X

Core to ES

Moving our core profile Stonehenge example from the desktop to an iOS device is very straightforward. We'll begin with the client code, then talk about the shader differences. We begin by adding the needed resources and source code to the project, using nearly the same code as we did in the Mac chapter. Our Xcode project post this process is shown in Figure 14.20.

Figure 14.20: The Xcode project with the Stonehenge model code added

We've had to update some of the core profile function calls to ES equivalents, and make some changes to the GLSL shader code. Some of the core profile functions we used actually aren't a part of OpenGL ES 2.0, but are extensions supported by iOS, and have since been brought into OpenGL ES 3.0. These extensions are defined by the OpenGL ES Working Group, and have the extension identifier "OES." For example, OpenGL ES 2.0 does not provide for vertex arrays, but an extension is available that allows you to use them much like you would in a desktop environment. They are named familiarly enough, just with an OES suffix on the end:

```
glGenVertexArraysOES(...
glBindVertexArrayOES(...
glDeleteVertexArraysOES(...
```

When loading geometry from disk, we also made use of buffer mapping using the **glMapBuffer()** call. This is also an OES extension, with the further requirement that only GL_WRITE_ONLY access is permitted when

mapping a buffer. We of course have to use the `GL_WRITE_ONLY_OES`
extension enumerate as well.

```
float *pData = (float *)glMapBufferOES(GL_ARRAY_BUFFER, GL_WRITE_ONLY_OES);
...
glUnmapBufferOES(GL_ARRAY_BUFFER);
```

GLSL on iOS

Shaders on OpenGL ES 2.0 have a few quirks from the desktop OpenGL
Core profile equivalents. Although OpenGL ES 3.0 GLSL code requires a

```
#version 300 ES
```

as the first non-commented line of executable code, OpenGL ES 2.0 on
iOS will not recognize this preprocessor directive. Instead, GLSL for ES 2.0
on iOS is based on an older desktop version of GLSL from OpenGL 2.0. See
Appendix A for some good and thorough references on OpenGL ES and
the ES-specific GLSL. A good quick-start however can be had by comparing
the shaders from the desktop version of the Stonehenge demo and the
mobile versions.

First, `in` and `out` are not used to pass data between shader stages. The ES
2.0 GLSL is based on simpler times when there were only two shader
stages. Anything coming `in` therefore the vertex program is an attribute,
and is therefore declared like so:

```
attribute vec4 vVertexPos;
```

Data passed from the vertex shader to the fragment shader "varies," and so
is called a *varying*, both in the vertex shader and the fragment shader.

```
varying vec2 vTexCoordVary;
```

There is no fine-tuning of interpolation between varyings either, so don't
try using the `smooth` or `centroid` keywords here either.

In the fragment shader, things get more fun. For starters, just like we have
a built-in `gl_Position` for the output of the vertex program, we also have
a built-in `gl_FragColor` to represent the output of a fragment color. We
also do not have the overloaded version of `texture()` to sample a texture,
but have to explicitly sample the type of texture. For example, to sample
from a 2D texture as the fragment color, you would see something like
this:

```
gl_FragColor = texture2D(colorMap, vTexCoordVary.st);
```

Finally, we need to set the default precision for floating-point variables in the fragment program. Desktop GLSL also now has precision qualifiers, but this feature first débuted on OpenGL ES 2.0, and fragment programs for handheld devices require a default precision to be specified for floats. Typically, this is just a single line of code you'll see at the top of the shader:

```
precision mediump float;
```

Typically, medium precision is sufficient for floats, especially where color computations are concerned, and thus making high precision the default for fragment programs might be a poor performance choice. While precision qualifiers are only a "hint" to the implementation about the intended use of a variable, these qualifiers are taken advantage of by the PowerVR hardware most iOS devices are based on, and careful application of them can yield substantial performance gains.

Wiring It In

Similar to our demonstration in the OS X section, we will create an instance of the GLStonehenge class, but this time it will belong to GLKViewController, and we'll place it in the ViewController.h header file:

```
#import <UIKit/UIKit.h>
#import <GLKit/GLKit.h>
#import "GLStonehenge.h"

@interface ViewController : GLKViewController
    {
    GLStonehenge     stoneHenge;
    }
@end
```

The GLKViewController class has four key methods where you will wire in your OpenGL rendering maintenance and rendering code: setupGL, teardownGL, update, and finally drawInRect.

First is the setupGL method, where the OpenGL context is set current for the first time. It's a good place to preload textures, geometry, shaders, and so on. In our example code, we'll remove the default setup code and make a call to our Stonehenge class's GLStonehenge::initModels(void) method:

```
- (void)setupGL
    {
    [EAGLContext setCurrentContext:self.context];

    stoneHenge.initModels();
    }
```

The reverse of this allows you to free up any dynamically allocated memory or resources associated with the OpenGL context:

```
- (void)tearDownGL
    {
    [EAGLContext setCurrentContext:self.context];

    stoneHenge.cleanupModels();
    }
```

Note the context is made current before any operations that free OpenGL resources will be valid.

From frame to frame, you are given a chance to update your model. In the update method, we will simply set the current projection by calling GLStonehenge::resized(). When the device changes orientation, this method is called with new width and height values appropriate to the device's new position.

```
- (void)update
    {
    stoneHenge.resized(self.view.bounds.size.width,
        self.view.bounds.size.height);
    }
```

Finally, and perhaps most importantly, we need to execute the OpenGL code to render our scene. The drawInRect method is actually a delegate method of the GLView class, and here we simply call GLStonehenge::render():

```
- (void)glkView:(GLKView *)view drawInRect:(CGRect)rect
    {
    stoneHenge.render();
    }
```

There is one more thing we really have to do before our ported desktop code will work on the iOS device. We need to change the current default working directory so that file open calls to locate the shaders will find them. The following "hack" to main.mm works on both desktop OS X applications and iOS applications:

```
int main(int argc, char *argv[])
    {
    static char szParentDirectory[255];

    ///////////////////////////////////////////////////////////
    // Get the directory where the .exe resides
    char *c;
    strncpy( szParentDirectory, argv[0], sizeof(szParentDirectory) );
    szParentDirectory[254] = '\0'; // Make sure we are NULL terminated
```

```
c = (char*) szParentDirectory;

while (*c != '\0')       // go to end
  c++;

while (*c != '/')        // back up to parent
  c--;

*c++ = '\0';             // cut off last part (binary name)

////////////////////////////////////////////////////////////
// Change to directory. Any data files added to the project
// will be placed here.
chdir(szParentDirectory);


@autoreleasepool {
    return UIApplicationMain(argc, argv, nil,
                            NSStringFromClass([AppDelegate class]));
}
}
```

Listing 14.21: Redirecting the current folder to point our resources

The primary advantage to the code in Listing 14.21 is that the main body of the Stonehenge object is far more portable between the mobile iOS world and the desktop worlds of Windows, Mac OS X, and Linux. One of the great advantages of OpenGL over other 3D APIs is portability after all. We did remove a great deal of sample code however from the supplied template OpenGL ES program. This sample code does show how to load a shader file from local resources in the "iOS way" if portability is not a concern. The final output of our Stonehenge example model is shown in Figure 14.21.

Figure 14.21: The completed Stonehenge model on an iOS device

We'll leave it to you to explore the project in its entirety to see how the touch events are used to move the camera and navigate the model.

Summary

This chapter covered how to build native applications that use OpenGL on Windows with nothing but calls to the Win32 API, on Mac OS X with Interface Builder and Cocoa, and with direct calls to X on Linux. On Windows, we have shown how to work around the lack of updates in the OpenGL window system binding. On Mac, while the legacy GLUT framework still has its uses, here we covered how to create an OpenGL-capable Mac application using the native application frameworks in Objective-C. We also showed how new technologies introduced in OS X 10.6 and GLKit, introduced in OS X 10.8, make high-performance and full-screen applications easier to build than ever, and we saw how to take advantage, or not, of the new Retina displays. Finally, we also looked at some simple tricks we can pull with Mac's lowest-level OpenGL interface, CGL.

OpenGL is a core foundational technology for the Macintosh. A basic understanding of OpenGL and how applications can natively interact with it is an essential skill for any Mac OS X developer. This chapter only scratched the surface of a potentially deep and complex topic. We purposely stayed in the shallow end of the pool as it were, so that you can get going quickly and experiment as much as possible with OpenGL on this wonderful platform. In Appendix A, "Further Reading," you will find some additional great coverage of this exciting topic.

Furthermore, OpenGL is an important part of Linux because it is the only commonly supported hardware 3D API available. Although we have seen how GLUT can be used with Linux, direct use of GLX is necessary for defining buffer resources, window management, and other Linux-specific interfaces with OpenGL. Just as with Mac, GLUT can be used to handle window management on Linux, but GLX 1.4 and related extensions allow greater control for an application to choose a specific version of OpenGL when creating new contexts. GLX provides methods to synchronize rendering with the OS, similar to the native Windows and Mac interfaces.

On all platforms, you've learned how to search for configs that meet your rendering needs. You also learned how to create a context supporting a specific version of OpenGL. Finally, you saw how to clean up window system state after your application is finished.

Finally, we touched on OpenGL's leaner cousin, OpenGL ES, which is the dominant graphics API on mobile platforms. An example of porting an application from Mac to iOS (which is used on Apple's mobile platforms), and then to Android was presented.

Appendix A

Further Reading

Real-time 3D graphics and OpenGL are popular topics. More information is available and more techniques are in practice than can ever be published in a single book. You might find the following resources helpful as you further your knowledge and experience.

Other Good OpenGL Books

McReynolds, T., and Blythe, D. (2005). *Advanced Graphics Programming Using OpenGL*. Morgan Kaufmann.

Angel, E., and Shreiner, D. (2011). *Interactive Computer Graphics: A Top-Down Approach with Shader-Based OpenGL (6th Edition)*. Addison-Wesley.

Astle, D. (ed.) (2006). *More OpenGL Game Programming*. Thomson Course Technology.

Munshi, A., Ginsburg, D., and Shreiner, D. (2008). *OpenGL ES 2.0 Programming Guide*. Addison-Wesley.

Shreiner, D., Sellers, G., Kessenich, J., and Licea-Kane, B. (2013). *OpenGL Programming Guide, 8th Edition: The Official Guide to Learning OpenGL, Version 4.3*. Addison-Wesley.

Cozzi, P., and Riccio, C. (eds.) (2012). *OpenGL Insights*. CRC Press.

Wolff, D. (ed.) (2011). *OpenGL 4.0 Shading Language Cookbook*. Packt Publishing.

3D Graphics Books

Watt, A. (1999). *3D Computer Graphics, 3rd Edition*. Addison-Wesley.

Dunn, F., and Parberry, I. (2011). *3D Math Primer for Graphics and Game Development, 2nd Edition*. A.K. Peters / CRC Press.

Van Verth, J., and Bishop, L. (2008). *Essential Mathematics for Games and Interactive Applications, 2nd Edition*. Morgan Kaufmann.

Foley, J. D., et al. (1993). *Introduction to Computer Graphics*. Addison-Wesley.

Lengyel, E. (2011). *Mathematics for 3D Game Programming & Computer Graphics, 3rd Edition*. Course Technology PTR.

Akenine-Moller, T., Haines, E., and Hoffman, N. (2008). *Real-Time Rendering, 3rd Edition*. A.K. Peters.

Engel, W. (ed.) (2006). *Shader X 4: Advanced Rendering Techniques*. Charles River Media.

Web Sites

- The *OpenGL® SuperBible, Sixth Edition,* Web site:
  http://www.openglsuperbible.com/
- The official OpenGL Web site: http://www.opengl.org/
- The OpenGL SDK (lots of tutorials and tools):
  http://www.opengl.org/sdk/

The preceding three Web sites are the gateways to OpenGL information on the Web and, of course, the official source of information for all things OpenGL and SuperBible related. The following sites also pertain to information covered in this book and offer vendor-specific OpenGL support, tutorials, demos, and news.

- The Khronos Group OpenGL ES home page: `http://www.khronos.org/opengles/`.

- The OpenGL Extension Registry: `http://www.opengl.org/registry/`

- AMD's developer home page: `http://www.amd.com/developer/`

- NVIDIA's developer home page: `http://developer.nvidia.com/`

- The Mesa 3D OpenGL "work-alike": `http://www.mesa3d.org`

- GLView OpenGL Extension Viewer: `http://www.realtech-vr.com/glview`

Appendix B

The SBM File Format

The SBM model file format is a simple geometry data file format devised
specifically for this book. The format is chunk based and extensible, with
several chunk types defined for use in the book's examples. This appendix
documents the file format. SBM files begin with a file header, followed by
a number of chunks, each started with a header, followed by raw data that
may be referenced by chunks. Multi-byte fields in structures are defined to
follow little-endian byte ordering. All structures are tightly packed.

File Header

All SBM files start with a header of the following form:

```
typedef struct SB6M_HEADER_t
{
    union
    {
        unsigned int    magic;
        char            magic_name[4];
    };
    unsigned int        size;
    unsigned int        num_chunks;
    unsigned int        flags;
} SB6M_HEADER;
```

The magic and magic_name fields are contained in a union and therefore
occupy the same 4 bytes of the file header. SBM files start with the magic
number 0x4d364253, which when encoded as a little-endian 32-bit word
causes the magic_name field to contain the characters
{'S', 'B', '6', 'M'} (SuperBible 6 Model).

751

The following field, `size`, encodes the size of the file header, in bytes. This represents the offset in bytes from the start of the file header to the start of the first chunk header, described in the next section. The size of the `SB6_HEADER` structure as defined is 16 bytes, and so `size` will normally be `0x10`. However, it is legal to store data between the header and the first chunk, and as such, loaders should add the value of `size` to the location of the file header to find the first chunk.

The `num_chunks` field stores the number of chunks contained in the SBM file. It is legal for loaders to skip chunks that are not recognized. The `num_chunks` field is therefore necessary to know when the chunk list is fully parsed and that the chunk ID is not just garbage following the last valid chunk.

The final field, `flags`, is a bitfield that encodes a series of flags further defining the SB6M file. At this time, no flags are defined, and this field should be set to zero.

Chunk Headers

Following the file header is a list of chunks. Each chunk starts with a chunk header with the following form:

```
typedef struct SB6M_CHUNK_HEADER_t
{
    union
    {
        unsigned int    chunk_type;
        char            chunk_name[4];
    };
    unsigned int        size;
} SB6M_CHUNK_HEADER;
```

Again, the `chunk_type` and `chunk_name` fields are members of a union and therefore share storage space in memory. The `chunk_type` field encodes the type of the chunk and is unique per chunk type and is documented in the following section and its subsections. The `size` field stores the number of bytes contained in the chunk, *including the header*. The next chunk in the file begins `size` bytes beyond the start of the current chunk's header. Loaders may skip unrecognized chunks by simply adding `size` bytes to the current file pointer, although this may result in loading or rendering errors.

Defined Chunks

This section documents the chunks that have been defined at this time.

Index Data Chunk

The index data chunk encodes a reference to index data stored in the file's data chunk (which follows the last chunk in the file). Its structure is as follows:

```
typedef struct SB6M_CHUNK_INDEX_DATA_t
{
    SB6M_CHUNK_HEADER    header;
    unsigned int         index_type;
    unsigned int         index_count;
    unsigned int         index_data_offset;
} SB6M_CHUNK_INDEX_DATA;
```

The first member of the chunk (as with all chunks) is the chunk header. The chunk_type field of the index data chunk's header is 0x58444e49, and its chunk_name field will contain {'I', 'N', 'D', 'X'}. The normal size of the index data chunk is 20 bytes, and so the header's size field is expected to be 0x14 although, again, it is legal to store arbitrary data between the chunks.

The following fields describe the index data. The index_type field encodes the value of an OpenGL token that determines the types. Legal values for the index type are 0x1401 (GL_UNSIGNED_BYTE), 0x1403 (GL_UNSIGNED_SHORT), and 0x1405 (GL_UNSIGNED_INT). Whilst other values could be encoded in this field, these values would be considered unsupported and proprietary. Loaders will generally fail to load the SBM file, or pass the value unaltered to OpenGL, resulting in failure to render correctly on unextended implementations.

The index_count field stores the number of indices that are contained in the file. To determine the total size of the index data, the element size of an index must be determined from the index_type field and multiplied by the index_count field. The index_data_offset field stores the offset, in bytes, from the start of the first data chunk where the index data starts.

Vertex Data Chunk

Raw vertex data is stored in SBM files and is then referenced by vertex data chunks, whose structure is as follows:

```
typedef struct SB6M_CHUNK_VERTEX_DATA_t
{
    SB6M_CHUNK_HEADER    header;
    unsigned int         data_size;
    unsigned int         data_offset;
    unsigned int         total_vertices;
} SB6M_CHUNK_VERTEX_DATA;
```

The header of a vertex data chunk has the chunk_type 0x58545256, which corresponds to a chunk_name of {'V', 'R', 'T', 'X'}. The size of a vertex data chunk is expected to be 20 (0x14) bytes. The data_size member contains the raw size in bytes of the vertex data and the data_offset field contains the offset in bytes from the start of the first data chunk of the vertex data. The total number of vertices encoded in the vertex data chunk is stored in total_vertices.

Vertex Attribute Chunk

The vertex attribute chunk stores the definitions of vertex attributes. It is made up of a header followed by a *variable sized* array of vertex attribute declarations. Its structure is as follows:

```
typedef struct SB6M_VERTEX_ATTRIB_CHUNK_t
{
    SB6M_CHUNK_HEADER           header;
    unsigned int                attrib_count;
    SB6M_VERTEX_ATTRIB_DECL     attrib_data[1];
} SB6M_VERTEX_ATTRIB_CHUNK;
```

The chunk_type field for vertex attributes is 0x42525441, corresponding to a chunk_name of {'A', 'T', 'R', 'B'}. The size of the vertex attribute chunk is variable and will depend on the number of vertex attributes contained in the chunk, which is stored in its attrib_count field. The attrib_data field is declared here as an array of size 1, but is in fact a variable length array with attrib_count element. At least one vertex attribute is assumed to be contained in the file, hence the minimal size declaration.

The attrib_data field is an array of SB6M_VERTEX_ATTRIB_DECL structures, whose definition is

```
typedef struct SB6M_VERTEX_ATTRIB_DECL_t
{
    char                name[64];
    unsigned int        size;
    unsigned int        type;
    unsigned int        stride;
    unsigned int        flags;
    unsigned int        data_offset;
} SB6M_VERTEX_ATTRIB_DECL;
```

Each attribute is given a name that may be up to 64 characters long, including the terminating NULL character and is stored in the name field. The size field encodes the number of elements per vertex encoded by the attribute, and the type contains the value of an OpenGL token that defines the data type of the attribute. Examples are 0x1406 (GL_FLOAT), 0x1400 (GL_BYTE), and 0x140B (GL_HALF_FLOAT) although any legal OpenGL type token may be used here. It is expected that loaders will cast this field to a GLenum token and pass it to OpenGL unmodified. The stride field encodes the number of bytes between the start of each element. As with OpenGL, a stride value of zero indicates that the data is tightly packed. Again, this value can be directly passed to OpenGL unmodified.

The flags field is a bitfield encoding information about the vertex attribute. Currently, the defined flags are

```
#define SB6M_VERTEX_ATTRIB_FLAG_NORMALIZED    0x00000001
#define SB6M_VERTEX_ATTRIB_FLAG_INTEGER       0x00000002
```

If flags contains SB6M_VERTEX_ATTRIB_FLAG_NORMALIZED, then the attribute is assumed to be normalized integer data, and this information will be conveyed to OpenGL, for example, by setting the normalized parameter to GL_TRUE in a call to **glVertexAttribPointer()**. If flags contains SB6M_VERTEX_ATTRIB_FLAG_INTEGER, then the vertex attribute is assumed to be an integer attribute. In this case, loaders could use a function such as **glVertexAttribIPointer()** to initialize vertex attributes in preference to **glVertexAttribPointer()**, for example.

Finally, the data_offset field encodes the offset, in bytes, of the start of the vertex attribute data from the start of the first data chunk in the file.

Comment Chunk

The comment chunk is provided to allow arbitrary data to be stored inside the SBM file. There is no requirement to parse the comment chunk, although it is guaranteed to never be used for any purpose that will affect rendering of a model.

```
typedef struct SB6M_CHUNK_COMMENT_t
{
    SB6M_CHUNK_HEADER          header;
    char                       comment[1];
} SB6M_CHUNK_COMMENT;
```

The header field of the comment chunk has a chunk_type field of 0x544E4D43, which corresponds to a chunk_name of { 'C', 'M', 'N', 'T' }. Parsers are expected to skip comment chunks, although it is possible to embed text, meta-data, or even rendering information in a proprietary chunk.

Object List Chunk

Object list chunks represent sub-objects within a single SBM file. Each SBM file may contain many sub-objects. Sub-objects share a single vertex declaration, and their vertex and index data is contained within the same buffers.

```
typedef struct SB6M_CHUNK_SUB_OBJECT_LIST_t
{
    SB6M_CHUNK_HEADER           header;
    unsigned int                count;
    SB6M_SUB_OBJECT_DECL        sub_object[1];
} SB6M_CHUNK_SUB_OBJECT_LIST;
```

The header field of the sub-object list chunk has chunk_type field of 0x54534C4F, which corresponds to a chunk_name of { 'O','L','S','T'}. The count field specifies how many sub-objects are contained in the SBM file. Following the count field is an array of one or more SB6M_SUB_OBJECT_DECL structures, whose definition is

```
typedef struct SB6M_SUB_OBJECT_DECL_t
{
    unsigned int                first;
    unsigned int                count;
} SB6M_SUB_OBJECT_DECL;
```

Each sub-object consists of a first vertex and a count of the number of vertices in the object, stored in the first and count fields, respectively. If the object data is indexed, then the first and count fields specify the first index and the number of indices, respectively, in the sub-object. If the object has no index data, then first and count specify the first vertex and number of vertices in the sub-object.

Example

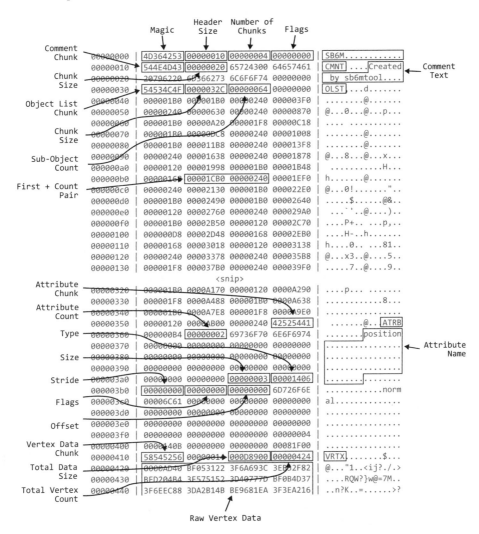

Figure B.1: Dump of example SBM file

Example   **757**

Appendix C

The SuperBible Tools

This book's source code not only includes most of the examples from the book in compilable form for many platforms, but it also includes a number of tools that were used to create the .SBM and .KTX files used by those examples. You can use these tools to create and manipulate .SBM and .KTX files to use in your own applications.

The ktxtool Utility

The ktxtool program is a utility for processing .KTX files. Its usage is as follows:

```
ktxtool -i <inputfile> [-i <inputfile>*] [-o output file] {options}
```

Input files are sent to ktxtool by specifying them with the -i option. More than one input file can be specified by simply including multiple -i options.

The --info option prints information about the input files as they are read. For example, taking a look at the aliens.ktx texture file that contains the array texture full of little monsters used in the "Alien Rain" sample back in Chapter 5, we see the following:

```
$ ktxtool.exe -i aliens.ktx --info
endianness           = 0x04030201
gltype               = 0x00001401 (GL_UNSIGNED_BYTE)
gltypesize           = 0x00000001
glformat             = 0x000080E1 (GL_BGRA)
glinternalformat     = 0x00008058 (GL_RGBA8)
glbaseinternalformat = 0x000080E1 (GL_BGRA)
pixelwidth           = 0x00000100
```

```
pixelheight      = 0x00000100
pixeldepth       = 0x00000000
arrayelements    = 0x00000040
faces            = 0x00000000
miplevels        = 0x00000001
keypairbytes     = 0x00000000
```

As we can see from the output of ktxtool, the aliens.ktx file is an array texture containing GL_BGRA data stored in unsigned bytes. It is 0x100 × 0x100 (256 × 256) texels in size, and there are 0x40 (64) slices in the array. The texture does not include mipmaps and has no additional data stored in key-pairs.

The --fromraw option allows you to create a .KTX file from raw data by specifying all of the parameters that are to be included in the file header, which is prepended to the raw data you specify. First, the raw data in all of the input files is loaded and appended together to make one large blob. Next, the following arguments are used to assign properties to the output file:

--width specifies the width of the output texture, in texels.

--height specifies the height of the output texture, in texels.

--depth specifies the depth of the output texture, in texels.

--slices specifies the number of slices in an output array texture.

--glformat specifies the OpenGL format and is placed in the glformat field of the header.

--gltype specifies the OpenGL type and is placed in the gltype field of the header.

--glinternalformat specifies the OpenGL format and is placed in the glinternalformat field of the header.

As an example, the following converts the raw file data.raw into a 256 × 256 2D array texure with 32 slices and the data format GL_R32F, and then saves it into the array.ktx output file:

```
$ ktxtool.exe -i data.raw --fromraw -o array.ktx --width 256 --height 256 \
--slices 32 --glformat GL_RED --gltype GL_FLOAT --glinternalformat GL_R32F
```

ktxtool will automatically figure out the base internal format and the required size of the data. Note that ktxtool doesn't do any data processing or validation of your arguments — it simply puts into the header whatever you tell it to. This can result in invalid .KTX files.

The `--toraw` option will take data the other way — simply stripping the .KTX header from the file and writing the raw data into the output.

Next, we come to the `--makearray`, `--make3d`, and `--makecube` options, which allow you to construct array textures, 3D textures, and cube maps from separate .KTX files. To use these options, the input textures must be compatible with one another and with the resulting outputs.

First, `--makearray` will take a sequence of 1D or 1D array textures and create a new 1D array texture from it, or take a sequence of 2D or 2D array textures and create a new 2D array texture from it. For 1D textures, the widths of all of the textures must be the same, and for 2D textures, the widths and heights of all of the textures must be the same. All of the input textures must have the same data format. The texture data from the inputs is concatenated in the order that the inputs were specified, and if array textures are encountered in the inputs, then their slices are simply concatenated to the end of the resulting array texture. For example, the following will take the `slice1.ktx`, `slice2.ktx`, and `slice3.ktx` files and create a three-slice array texture from them in `array.ktx`:

```
$ ktxtool.exe -i slice1.ktx -i slice2.ktx -i slice3.ktx -o array.ktx --makearray
```

Again, `ktxtool` does no format conversion. If the files' data formats don't match, `ktxtool` will simply refuse to create the output file. The `--make3d` option works similarly to the `--makearray` option, except that it creates a 3D texture rather than an array texture. Only 2D or 3D input textures are accepted, and each must have the same width, height, and data format. All of the slices of the input textures are stacked in the order that the inputs are encountered.

The `dds2ktx` Utility

The `dds2ktx` utility is a tool for converting .DDS format files to .KTX files. .DDS is a file format used in many content creation tools for storing textures for use in DirectX applications. DDS stands for DirectDraw Surface, and although DirectDraw, the API, is long deprecated, the format lives on and is capable of representing almost any texture format that can be consumed by Direct3D. Virtually every Direct3D texture type and format is also supported by OpenGL and can be represented as a .KTX file.

dds2ktx takes two parameters — the input file name and the output file name. It attempts to do a blind conversion of the .DDS file into a .KTX file.

It decodes the .DDS file header, translates the parameters to a .KTX file header, and then dumps the data from the .DDS file into the .KTX file. It does very little error checking or sanity checking. However, it does allow common content creation tools, including several texture compressors, to produce .DDS files that can then be converted to .KTX files for use with this book's .KTX loader.

The sb6mtool Utility

The sb6mtool utility is a general purpose tool for dealing with the .SBM model files used in this book. The command line parameters and syntax are similar to the ktxtool utility. One or more input files are specified with the --input or -i parameters, each followed by a filename.

The --info parameter instructs sb6mtool to dump information about the object. For example, to dump the information about the asteroids.sbm object file that was used for the asteroid field example back in Chapter 7, we can issue the following command:

```
$ sb6mtool --input asteroids.sbm --info
FILE: asteroids.sbm
Raw data size: 888100 bytes
No indices
Vertex count = 44352, data offset = 0x00000424
Attribute count: 2
    Attribute 0:
        name        = position
        size        = 3
        format      = 0x1406 (GL_FLOAT)
        stride      = 0
        flags       = 0x00000000
        data_offset = 0x00000000
    Attribute 1:
        name        = normal
        size        = 4
        format      = 0x140B (GL_HALF_FLOAT)
        stride      = 0
        flags       = 0x00000000
        data_offset = 0x00081F00
Number of sub-objects: 100
    Sub-object 0: first 0, count 432
    Sub-object 1: first 432, count 576
    Sub-object 2: first 1008, count 576
    Sub-object 3: first 1584, count 576
    Sub-object 4: first 2160, count 432
    Sub-object 5: first 2592, count 504
    Sub-object 6: first 3096, count 432
    Sub-object 7: first 3528, count 576
    Sub-object 8: first 4104, count 432
    Sub-object 9: first 4536, count 576
<...>
    Sub-object 89: first 39528, count 504
    Sub-object 90: first 40032, count 576
    Sub-object 91: first 40608, count 288
```

```
Sub-object 92: first 40896, count 432
Sub-object 93: first 41328, count 288
Sub-object 94: first 41616, count 504
Sub-object 95: first 42120, count 432
Sub-object 96: first 42552, count 432
Sub-object 97: first 42984, count 504
Sub-object 98: first 43488, count 288
Sub-object 99: first 43776, count 576
```

As we can see, the `asteroids.sbm` file contains roughly 850K of raw data. There are two vertex attributes named `position` and `normal`, the data does not have indices, and the file contains 100 sub-objects. The start vertex and vertex count for each of the sub-objects are listed. Each of the sub-objects in this particular file is one of the unique asteroids from the sample application.

To do more than just print the information from the input file(s), we need to specify an output file. To do this, we use the `--output` command line option, followed by a file. It is possible to convert the format of one or more of the model's attributes by using the `--convertattrib` command line option. This option takes the attribute name followed by one of the OpenGL format enumerants. For example, to convert the `position` attribute to `GL_RGB16F` (three components of half-precision 16-bit floating-point data) and write the output to an output file called `asteroids2.sbm`, we can issue

```
$ sb6mtool --input asteroids.sbm --output asteroids2.sbm \
          --convertattrib position GL_RGB16F
```

If you just want to nuke an attribute altogether, you can instead use the `--deleteattrib` command line option. This simply takes the name of the attribute to delete. To delete the `normal` attribute, for instance, we can issue

```
$ sb6mtool --input asteroids.sbm --output asteroids2.sbm \
          --deleteattrib normal
```

The `sb6mtool` utility can also stitch objects together into sub-objects of the same file. To do this, all of the input files must have the same number, layout, and type of attributes. Simply specify all of the input files on the command line, each with its own `--input` argument, set the output file, and then use the `--makesubobj` command. For example, to stitch a bunch of rock models together to make an asteroid field, issue the following command:

```
$ sb6mtool --input rock1.sbm \
          --input rock2.sbm \
          --input rock3.sbm \
          --input rock4.sbm \
```

```
--input rock5.sbm \
--input rock6.sbm \
--input rock7.sbm \
--output asteroids.sbm --makesubobj
```

The tool will take all of the sub-objects in each of the files, in the order that they're specified, and stuff them all into one big output file. You can even keep reading and outputting to the same file to append more and more data onto the end of it. This is exactly how we made the asteroids.sbm file that accompanies the asteroid field example.

Glossary

Aliasing Technically, the loss of signal information in an image reproduced at some finite resolution. It is most often characterized by the appearance of sharp jagged edges along points, lines, or polygons due to the nature of having a limited number of fixed-sized pixels.

Alpha A fourth color value added to provide a degree of transparency to the color of an object. An alpha value of 0.0 means complete transparency; 1.0 denotes no transparency (opaque).

Ambient light Light in a scene that doesn't come from any specific point source or direction. Ambient light illuminates all surfaces evenly and on all sides.

Antialiasing A rendering method used to smooth lines and curves and polygon edges. This technique averages the color of pixels adjacent to the line. It has the visual effect of softening the transition from the pixels on the line and those adjacent to the line, thus providing a smoother appearance.

ARB The Architecture Review Board. The committee body consisting of 3D graphics hardware vendors, previously charged with maintaining the OpenGL Specification. This function has since been assumed by the Khronos Group.

Aspect ratio The ratio of the width of a window to the height of the window. Specifically, the width of the window in pixels divided by the height of the window in pixels.

Associativity An sequence of operations is said to be associative if changing the order of the operations (but not the order of the arguments) does not affect the result. For example, addition is associative because $a + (b + c) = (a + b) + c$.

Atomic operation A sequence of operations that must be indivisible for correct operation. Usually refers to a read-modify-write sequence on a single memory location.

Barrier A barrier is a point in a computer program that serves as a marker across which operations may not be reordered. Between barriers, certain operations may be exchanged if their movement does not logically change the operation of the program.

Bézier curve A curve whose shape is defined by control points near the curve rather than by the precise set of points that define the curve itself.

Bitplane An array of bits mapped directly to screen pixels.

Branch prediction An optimization strategy used in processor design whereby the processor tries to guess (or predict) the outcome of some conditional code and start executing the more likely branch before it is certain that it is required. If it's right, it gets ahead by a few instructions. If it's wrong, it needs to throw away the work and start again with the other branch.

Buffer An area of memory used to store image information. This can be color, depth, or blending information. The red, green, blue, and alpha buffers are often collectively referred to as the color buffers.

Cartesian A coordinate system based on three directional axes placed at a 90° orientation to one another. These coordinates are labeled x, y, and z.

Clip coordinates The 2D geometric coordinates that result from the model-view and projection transformation.

Clipping The elimination of a portion of a single primitive or group of primitives. The points that would be rendered outside the clipping region or volume are not drawn. The clipping volume is generally specified by the projection matrix. Clipped primitives are reconstructed such that the edges of the primitive do not lie outside the clipping region.

Commutative An operation is said to be commutative if changing the order of its operands does not change its result. For example, addition is commutative whereas subtraction is not.

Compute shader A shader that executes a work item per invocation as part of a local work group, a number of which may be grouped together into a global work group.

Concave A reference to the shape of a polygon. A polygon is said to be concave if there is a straight line through it that will enter and subsequently exit the polygon more than once.

Contention A term used to describe the condition where two or more threads of execution attempt to use a single shared resource.

Convex A reference to the shape of a polygon. A convex polygon has no indentations, and no straight line can be drawn through the polygon that intersects it more than twice (once entering, once leaving).

Culling The elimination of graphics primitives that would not be seen if rendered. Backface culling eliminates the front or back face of a primitive so that the face isn't drawn. Frustum culling eliminates whole objects that would fall outside the viewing frustum.

Destination color The stored color at a particular location in the color buffer. This terminology is usually used when describing blending operations to distinguish between the color already present in the color buffer and the color coming into the color buffer (source color).

Dispatch A term used to describe a command that begins the execution of compute shaders.

Dithering A method used to simulate a wider range of color depth by placing different-colored pixels together in patterns that give the illusion of shading between the two colors.

Double buffered A drawing technique used by OpenGL. The image to be displayed is assembled in memory and then placed on the screen in a single update operation, rather than built primitive by primitive on the screen. Double buffering is a much faster and smoother update operation and can produce animations.

Extruded The process of taking a 2D image or shape and adding a third dimension uniformly across the surface. This process can transform 2D fonts into 3D lettering.

Eye coordinates The coordinate system based on the position of the viewer. The viewer's position is placed along the positive z axis, looking down the negative z axis.

FMA Fused multiply-add. An operation commonly implemented in a single piece of hardware that multiplies two numbers together and adds a third with the intermediate result generally computed at higher precision than a stand-alone multiplication or addition operation.

Fragment A single piece of data that may eventually contribute to the color of a pixel in an image.

Fragment shader A shader that executes once per fragment and generally computes the final color of that fragment.

Frustum A pyramid-shaped viewing volume that creates a perspective view. (Near objects are large; far objects are small.)

Garbage A term used to refer to uninitialized data that is read and consumed by a computer program, often resulting in corruption, crashes, or other undesired behavior.

Geometry shader A shader that executes once per primitive, having access to all vertices making up that primitive.

Gimbal lock A state where a sequence of rotations can essentially become stuck on a single axis. This occurs when one of the rotations early in the sequence rotates one Cartesian axis onto another. After this, rotation around either of the axes results in the same rotation, making it impossible to escape from the locked position.

GLSL Acronym for the OpenGL Shading Language, a high-level C-like shading language.

GPU An acronym standing for graphics processing unit — a specialized processor that does most of the heavyweight lifting for OpenGL.

Hazard In reference to memory operations, a hazard is a situation in which undefined order of transactions on memory may lead to undefined or undesired results. Typical examples include read-after-write (RAW) hazards, write-after-write (WAW) hazards, and write-after-read (WAR) hazards.

Implementation A software- or hardware-based device that performs OpenGL rendering operations.

Invocation A single execution of a shader. Most commonly used to describe compute shaders, but applicable to any shader stage.

Khronos Group The industry consortium that manages the maintenance and promotion of the OpenGL specification.

Literal A value, not a variable name. A specific string or numeric constant embedded directly in source code.

Matrix A 2D array of numbers. Matrices can be operated on mathematically and are used to perform coordinate transformations.

Mipmapping A technique that uses multiple levels of detail for a texture. This technique selects from among the different sizes of an image available, or possibly combines the two nearest sized matches to produce the final fragments used for texturing.

Model-view matrix The OpenGL matrix that transforms position vectors from model (or object) space to view (or eye) space.

Normal A directional vector that points perpendicularly to a plane or surface. When used, normals must be specified for each vertex in a primitive.

Normalize The reduction of a normal to a unit normal. A unit normal is a vector that has a length of exactly 1.0.

Occlusion query An occlusion query is a graphics operation whereby hidden (or, more accurately, visible) pixels are counted and the count returned to the application.

Orthographic A drawing mode in which no perspective or foreshortening takes place. Also called parallel projection. The lengths and dimensions of all primitives are undistorted regardless of orientation or distance from the viewer.

Out-of-order execution The ability of a processor to determine inter-instruction dependencies and start executing those instructions whose inputs are ready *before* other instructions that may have preceded them in program order.

Overloading In computer languages, overloading is the practice of creating two or more functions that share the same name but differ in their function signatures.

Perspective A drawing mode in which objects farther from the viewer appear smaller than nearby objects.

Pixel Condensed from the words "picture element." This is the smallest visual division available on the computer screen. Pixels are arranged in rows and columns and are individually set to the appropriate color to render any given image.

Pixmap A two-dimensional array of color values that comprise a color image. Pixmaps are so called because each picture element corresponds to a pixel on the screen.

Polygon A 2D shape drawn with any number of sides (must be at least three sides).

Primitive A group of one or more vertices formed into a geometric shape by OpenGL such as a line, point, or triangle. All objects and scenes are composed of various combinations of primitives.

Projection The transformation of lines, points, and polygons from eye coordinates to clipping coordinates on the screen.

Quadrilateral A polygon with exactly four sides.

Race condition A state encountered when multiple parallel processes such as threads in a program or invocations of a shader attempt to communicate or otherwise depend on each other in some way, but where no insurance of ordering is performed.

Rasterization The process of converting projected primitives and bitmaps into pixel fragments in the framebuffer.

Render The conversion of primitives in object coordinates to an image in the framebuffer. The rendering pipeline is the process by which OpenGL commands and statements become pixels on the screen.

Scintillation A sparkling or flashing effect produced on objects when a non-mipmapped texture map is applied to a polygon that is significantly smaller than the size of the texture being applied.

Scissor A fragment ownership test that rejects fragments that lie outside a window-aligned rectangle.

Shader A small program that is executed by the graphics hardware, often in parallel, to operate on individual vertices or pixels.

Source color The color of the incoming fragment, as opposed to the color already present in the color buffer (destination color). This terminology is usually used when describing how the source and destination colors are combined during a blending operation.

Specification The design document that specifies OpenGL operation and fully describes how an implementation must work.

Spline A general term used to describe any curve created by placing control points near the curve, which have a pulling effect on the curve's shape. This is similar to the reaction of a piece of flexible material when pressure is applied at various points along its length.

Stipple A binary bit pattern used to mask out pixel generation in the framebuffer. This is similar to a monochrome bitmap, but one-dimensional patterns are used for lines and two-dimensional patterns are used for polygons.

Super scalar A term used to describe a processor architecture that is capable of executing two or more independent instructions at the same time on multiple processor pipelines, which may or may not have the same capabilities.

Tessellation The process of breaking down a complex polygon or analytic surface into a mesh of convex polygons. This process can also be applied to separate a complex curve into a series of less complex lines.

Tessellation control shader A shader that runs before fixed-function tessellation occurs. Executes once per control-point in a patch primitive and produces tessellation factors and a new set of control points as an output primitive.

Tessellation evaluation shader A shader that runs after fixed-function tessellation occurs. Executes once per vertex generated by the tessellator.

Tessellation shader A term used to describe either a tessellation control shader or a tessellation evaluation shader.

Texel Similar to pixel (picture element), a texel is a texture element. A texel represents a color from a texture that is applied to a pixel fragment in the framebuffer.

Texture An image pattern of colors applied to the surface of a primitive.

Texture mapping The process of applying a texture image to a surface. The surface does not have to be planar (flat). Texture mapping is often used to wrap an image around a curved object or to produce patterned surfaces such as wood or marble.

Token A constant value used by OpenGL to represent parameters. Examples are GL_RGBA and GL_COMPILE_STATUS.

Transformation The manipulation of a coordinate system. This can include rotation, translation, scaling (both uniform and non-uniform), and perspective division.

Translucence A degree of transparency of an object. In OpenGL, this is represented by an alpha value ranging from 1.0 (opaque) to 0.0 (transparent).

Vector A directional quantity usually represented by x, y, and z components.

Vertex A single point in space. Except when used for point and line primitives, it also defines the point at which two edges of a polygon meet.

Vertex shader A shader that executes once per incoming vertex.

Viewing volume The area in 3D space that can be viewed in the window. Objects and points outside the viewing volume are clipped (cannot be seen).

Viewport The area within a window that is used to display an OpenGL image. Usually, this encompasses the entire client area. Stretched viewports can produce enlarged or shrunken output within the physical window.

Wireframe The representation of a solid object by a mesh of lines rather than solid shaded polygons. Wireframe models are usually rendered faster and can be used to view both the front and back of an object at the same time.

Index

a 100 megapixel virtual framebuffer listing
(9.23), 401
1D textures, 244
2D
array textures, loading, 163–165
Gaussian filters, 411
pixel formats, 630
prefix sums, 452
3D
Linux, 682
math with GLKit, 667–669

abstraction layers, 4, 5
acceleration
calculating, 269
structures, 579
access
map buffer types, 601
synchronization
atomic counters, 137
images, 176–177
memory, 129–133
textures, arrays, 163–165
adaptive HDR to LDR conversion fragment
shader listing (9.25), 407–408
adding
basevertex, 234–235
bloom effect to scene listing (9.28), 414
device context parameters, 628
fog effects, 541–544
views, 650–652
addresses, querying extension functions, 622
adjacency primitive types, 340
advanced framebuffer formats, 399–418
advanced occlusion queries, 483–484

Aero user interfaces, 592
AFR (alternate frame rendering), 610
algorithms
flocking, 462–471
prefix sum, 452
aliasing, 140
allocating memory using buffers, 92–95
alpha-to-coverage, 392
alternate frame rendering. See AFR
alternative rendering methods, 548–580
ALU (Arithmetic and Logic Unit) performance,
605
ambient light, 504
ambient occlusion, 558–565
fragment shader listing (12.32), 564–565
AMD drivers, 625, 682
a more complete conditional rendering
example listing (11.6), 482–483
analysis
graphics processors, 594
performance analysis tools, 589–597
AND operator, 47
Android
development environments, 729–734
handheld platforms, 729
angles, Euler, 72
animating color over time listing (2.2), 16
antialiasing, 384–399
by filtering, 385–387
multi-sample, 387–389
AoSs (array-of-structures), 102
APIENTRY macro, 583
APIs (Application Programming Interfaces), 3,
7. See also interfaces
trace tools, 594
Windows, 623

application of fog in a fragment shader listing
(12.24), 543–544
Application Programming Interfaces. *See* APIs
applications
  barriers, 131–132
  cleaning up, 646–647
  Cocoa, 650
  debugging, 582–589
  design (OpenGL ES 3.0), 714
  frameworks, 14–16
  geometry shaders, 313–317
  Linux, 687–693
  loading textures from files, 144
  performance optimization, 589–616
  shaders, 5
  starting, 21
  tuning for speed, 597–616
applying
  arrow keys, 671–673
  contexts, 699–701
  extensions, 618–622
  simple exposure coefficient to an HDR image
    listing (9.24), 406
ARB (Architectural Review Board), 7, 8, 618
areas, signed, 40
Arithmetic and Logic Unit performance. *See*
    ALU performance
array-of-structures (AoSs), 102
arrays, 15, 192–194
  accessing, 163–165
  allocating, 638
  indexes, 245
  instanced, 288
  multi-dimensional, 194
  sizes of input, 315
  textures, 160–165
  VAOs (vertex array objects), 272
arrow keys, 671–673
assigning binding points, 117
associative, 62
asteroids
  configuring, 254
  field vertex shader listing (7.14), 255–257
  rendering, 257
  vertex shader inputs for, 254
atmospheric effects, 540–544
atomic counters, 133–137
atomic operations, 126, 128–129, 171–176
attachments
  completeness, 377
  multiple framebuffer, 368–370
  rendering with no, 399–401
  texture layers to a framebuffer
    listing (9.12), 375
  textures, 367
attenuation, distance-based point size, 230
attributes, 51
  Cocoa pixel format, 655–658

configs, 690
instancing, 245
pixel format, 636–637
vertices, 28–29, 97, 224
averaging values, 457
axes, coordinates, 68

back buffers, 365
back end processes, 11, 341
back-facing, 39
back-lighting, 515–517
bandwidth, memory, 178, 549
barriers, 446
  applications, 131–132
  shaders, 132–133
barycentric coordinates, 35, 284–285, 288
baseinstance parameter, 239
basevertex parameter, 234–235, 239, 240
basic conditional rendering example listing
    (11.5), 481
basic setup of Windows operating systems,
    627–632
Bézier curves, 85, 86, 87
big-picture views, 11
binaries, programs, 216–218, 609
binding, 92
  buffers, 261
  framebuffers, 366
  points, 117, 262
Bishop, Lara, 718
Bit-Level-Image-Transfer, 432
bittangent vectors, 519
blending, 357–363
  blend equations, 358, 361–362
  color, 406
  dual-source, 361
  factor, 406
  functions, 358–360
Blinn-Phong fragment shader listing (12.5), 514
Blinn-Phong lighting model, 513–515
blit, 431
Block Partitioned Texture Compression (BPTC),
    179
blocks
  interfaces, 31–32
  shaders, storage, 126–133
  uniforms, 108–121
Block Transfer, 432
bloom, light, 409–414
bloom fragment shader listing (9.26), 410–411
blur fragment shader listing (9.27), 412–413
boids, 449
Boolean flags, 655
Boolean occlusion queries, 483
Boolean vectors, 196
border color, texture, 159
BPTC (Block Partitioned Texture Compression),
    179

brute force, 579
bubble, 494
buffers, 10, 92–95
  asteroids, 254
  back, 365
  binding, 261
  command, 590
  data
    allocating memory using, 92–95
    feeding vertex shaders from, 97–103
    filling and copying in, 95–97
  depth, 46
  double buffering, 634, 661
  element array, 279
  EGL, 726–727
  G-buffers, 548, 549–551
  mapping, 600–603
  object storage, 251
  point indexes, 228
  swap values, 637
  TBO (texture buffer object), 266, 269
  textures, 140
  UBO (Uniform Buffer Object), 108
building. *See also* configuration
  Linux applications, 687–693
  model-view matrices listing (5.21), 122
built-in functions, 194–201
built-in outputs, 441
built-in variables, 24
  gl_InstanceID, 288
  gl_FrontFacing, 223
  gl_Position, 277
  gl_VertexID, 92
  gl_int, 146
  fragment, 43
  tessellation, 35
bump mapping, 518

C++, 737
calculations. *See also* math
  acceleration, 269
  antialiasing, 385
  colors, fragments, 152
  contributions to ambient light, 504
  damping force, 270
  dot products, 54–55
  formulas, indexes, 250
  G-buffers, 552
  lighting models. *See* lighting models
  orientation, 257
  per-fragment lighting, 518
  per-instance rotations, 163
  reflection and refraction, 57–58
  shadow maps, 539
  toon shaders, 547
callback functions, 583, 584. *See also* functions
camera space, 64, 65
Cartesian frames, 519

casting shadows, 534–540
Cathode Ray Tubes (CRTs), 416
cell shading, 545–547
centroid sampling, 395–399
CGL (Core OpenGL), 648, 674–675
  specifications, 625n3
checking completeness of a framebuffer object
    listing (9.13), 378–379
child windows (in Cocoa), 671
choosing. *See also* selecting
  8 sample antialiasing listing (9.19), 388
  and setting a pixel format listing (14.4), 632
chunks, SBM model file format, 752–756
clamping
  depth, 354–355
  tone mapping, 406
classes, 628
  GLKit, 662
  GLKTextureInfo, 663
  GLKViewController, 741
  textures, 183
cleaning up applications, 646–647
clipping, 38–39, 276–282
  an object against a plane and a sphere listing
    (7.20), 281
  lines, 276
clip spaces, 17, 38, 64, 66
Cocoa
  GLKit, 669–671
  Mac OS X, 649–662
  pixel format attributes, 655–658
code
  called when the view changes size listing
    (14.14), 661
  errors, 584
colors
  calculating, 257
  grass, 244
  inputs, vertex shaders, 225
  masking, 363–364
  OpenGL ES 3.0, 709
  output, 357–364
  sRGB color spaces, 416–418
  tone mapping, 404
columns
  column major, 60
  column primary, 60
  images, 454
  layouts, 60
combining geometry and primitive restart,
    235–237
commands
  buffers, 590
  drawing, 231–259, 595
    clipping, 276–282
    indexed, 231–237
    indirect draws, 250–259
    instancing, 237–250

commands (*continued*)
    stencil buffers, 348
    storing transformed vertices, 259–275
    glxinfo, 684
    SwapBuffers(), 593
    synchronization, 699
comments, chunks, 755
communication
    compute shaders, 444–449
    between shader invocations, 299
commutativity, 110
comparison operators, 352
compatibility profiles, 9
compiling
    makefiles, 687
    programs, 201–219
    shaders, 218, 606–609
    simple shaders listing (2.5), 18–19
completeness
    attachments, 377
    framebuffers, 377
    whole framebuffer, 377
complex number, 75
complex shader, 339
compressing textures, 177–181, 606
compute shaders, 47–48, 437–472
    applying, 438–439
    communication, 444–449
    examples, 450–471
    executing, 439–444
    flocking, 462–471
    to generate a 2D prefix sum listing (10.7), 455–456
    image inversion listing (10.2), 444
    parallel prefix sum, 450–462
    with race conditions listing (10.4), 447
    synchronizing, 445–449
    for updates in flocking example listing (10.11), 466
concatenation
    model-view transformations, 76–79
    transformations, 73–75
concave polygons, 10
conditions
    conditionally emitting geometry in a geometry shader listing (8.22), 319
    conditional rendering, 481, 598
    race, 446, 447
configs
    EGL, 720–725
    management and visuals, 689–693
configuration
    Android projects, 730–731
    asteroids, 270–271
    comparison operators, 352
    cubes, geometry, 233
    the custom culling geometry shader listing (8.20), 318

GL3W, 686
GLFW, 686
iOS projects, 734–736
Mesa, 685
scalars, 105–106
separable program pipelines listing (6.3), 208
uniforms
    arrays, 106–107
    matrices, 107–108
Windows operating systems, 627–632
connecting vertices, 267
construction
    and initialization of the GLKView listing (14.20), 738
    matrices, 60–63
consuming G-buffers, 551–554
container objects, 603
contention, 129
contexts
    advanced creation, 641–643
    applying, 699–701
    current, 611
    debug, 582–589
    devices, 627, 629
    managing, 695–699, 725–726
controlling
    movement smoothly with keyboard bit flags and a timer listing (14.15), 672–673
    winding order, 296
control points, 83, 284, 324
control shaders, tessellation, 33–34
coordinates
    barycentric, 35, 284–285, 288
    eye-space, 542
    floating point, 152
    homogeneous, 39
    normalized device, 39
    objects, 64–65
    spaces, 62
    textures, 141, 146–148, 529
    transformations, 63–66, 66–73
    view, 65–66
    window, 40
    world, 65
copying
    from an array texture to a stereo back buffer listing (9.17), 383–384
    data between framebuffers, 431–433
    data in buffers, 95–97
    data into a texture, 433–434
Core OpenGL. *See* CGL
core profiles, 9, 652. *See also* profiles
counters
    atomic, 133–137
    performance, 597
counting are using atomic counters listing (5.31), 135
coverage, sample, 391–393

CPU (central processing unit) queues, 590
creating. *See also* configuration; formatting
  and compiling a compute shader listing
    (10.1), 438–439
  a debug context with the sb6 framework
    listing (13.1), 582
  and initializing the full-screen window
    listing (14.16), 676–677
  integer framebuffer attachments listing
    (9.29), 415
  program member variables listing (2.6), 21
  shared contexts on Windows listing (14.8),
    643
  a simple window listing (14.2), 629–630
  a stereo window listing (9.14), 380
cross products, 56–57
CRTs (Cathode Ray Tubes), 416
csplines, 90
cube maps, 527–532
cubes
  geometry
    configuring, 233
    drawing indexed, 234
  maps, rendering to, 375–376
  spinning, 121
cubic Bézier curves, 85, 86
cubic Bézier patches
  fragment shader listing (8.15), 309
  tessellation control shader listing (8.13),
    307
  tessellation evaluation shader listing (8.14),
    308
  tessellation example, 304–310
  vertex shader listing (8.12), 306
cubic Bézier splines, 88
cubic Hermite splines, 89
culling, 40–41, 175
  geometry, 320
current context, 611
curves, 82, 83–87
  Bézier, 85
  gamma, 418
  Hermite, 198
  quintic Bézier, 87
  transfer, 407

damping force, calculating, 270
data, 91
  atomic counters, 133–137
  buffers, 92–95
    allocating memory using, 92–95
    feeding vertex shaders from, 97–103
    filling and copying in, 95–97
  driven rendering engines, 613
  manipulation, built-in functions, 199–201
  shader storage blocks, 126–133
  stores, 92
  textures, 137–185

types, 188–194
uniforms, 103–126
dds2ktx utility, 761–762
debugging applications, 581, 582–589
decay, exponential, 543
declaration
  arrays, 192–193
  atomic counters, 133
  multiple outputs in a fragment shader listing
    (9.7), 370
  of multiple vertex attributes listing (7.1),
    225
  of PIXELFORMATDESCRIPTOR listing (14.3),
    631
  shader storage blocks, 126
  two inputs to vertex shaders listing (5.6),
    100
  uniform blocks listing (5.10), 110
  of vertex attributes listing (3.1), 28
  vertices, 227
default block uniforms, 104–105
default framebuffer, 365
Deferred Procedure Call. *See* DPC
deferred shading, 548–558
  downsides to, 556–558
  normal mapping, 554–556
  with normal mapping listing (12.31), 556
definitions
  of gl_in[] listing (8.19), 314
  of the Objective-C GLCorePorfileViewClass
    listing (14.10), 653
degenerate primitives, 24
denormals, 189
depth
  buffers, 46
  clamping, 354–355
  of field effect, 457
  of field using summed area tables listing
    (10.8), 459–460
  functions, 352
  as seen from light, 537
  tests, 46, 351–355
deriving a fragment's color from its position
    listing (3.10), (3.12), 43, 44
design, 4–5, 714
destinations
  factors, 358
  subsystems, 132
detection of edges, 397–399
determining closest intersection point listing
    (12.37), 572–573
development
  Android environments, 729–734
  builds, 607
  OpenGL ES, 707–708
devices, context, 627, 629
diffuse light, 504, 505
disabling interpolation, 342–343

discarding
    geometry in geometry shaders, 317–320
    rasterizers, 273
dispatching the image copy compute shader
    listing (10.3), 444
dispatch, indirect, 439–441
displacement mapping, 300
    GPU PerfStudio 2, 594
    tessellation evaluation shader listing (12.23),
        542
displaying. *See also* viewing
    an array texture–fragment shader listing
        (9.11), 373
    an array texture–vertex shader listing (9.10),
        373
    EGL, 718–720
    objects and X Window System, 689
distance-based point size attenuation, 230
distributions
    grass, 242, 243
    Linux. *See* Linux
DMA packets, 593
domains, 306
    parameterization, 334
dot products, 54–55
double buffering, 634, 661
    sync frame rates, 677
double precision, 53, 60, 107
downsides to deferred shading, 556–558
DPC (Deferred Procedure Call), 593
drain, queues, 591
drawing
    asteroids listing (7.15), 257–258
    commands, 231–259, 595
        clipping, 276–282
        indexed, 231–237
        indirect draws, 250–259
        instancing, 237–250
        stencil buffers, 348
        storing transformed vertices, 259–275
    data written to a transform feedback buffer
        listing (11.9), 491
    a face normal in the geometry shader listing
        (8.33), 327–328
    indexed cube geometry listing (7.3), 234
    the same geometry many times listing (7.4),
        238
    into a stereo window listing (9.15), 381
    Stonehenge, 663–665
    triangles, 24–25
drivers
    Linux, 685–686
    Windows graphics, 624–626
dual-source blending, 361

EAC (Ericsson Alpha Compression), 179
early testing, 355–357

edges
    detection of, 397–399
    jaggies, 384
effects, atmospheric, 540–544
EGL, 718–728
    configs, 720–725
    displays, 718–720
    eglBindAPI(), 767
    eglChooseConfig(), 720, 724
    eglCreateContext(), 725
    eglDestroyContext(), 726
    eglDestroySurface(), 725
    eglGetConfigAttrib(), 724, 725
    eglGetConfigs(), 724
    eglGetError(), 727
    eglGetProcAddress(), 728
    eglInitialize(), 720
    eglMakeCurrent(), 726
    eglQueryAPI(), 720
    eglQueryString(), 727
    eglReleaseThread(), 720
    eglSwapBuffers(), 726
    eglSwapInterval(), 722
    eglWaitGL(), 727
    eglWaitNative(), 727
    errors, 727
    extensions, 728
    strings, 727
    windows, 720
elements, types, 193
eliminating visual tearing, 646
embedded environments, negotiating, 728–729
emitting a single triangle from a geometry
    shader listing (8.28), 324
EmitVertex() function, 36
endianness, 145
engines
    data driven rendering, 613
    Quartz, 647
    tessellation, 34, 285
enumerating pixel formats, 640–641
environment mapping, 522–532
    cube maps, 527–532
    equirectangular, 525–527
    spherical environment maps, 523–525
environments
    Android development, 729–734
    EGL, 718–728
    negotiating embedded, 728–729
    OpenGL ES, 713–718
equal spacing mode, 295
equations
    blend, 358, 361–362
    quadratic, 85
equirectangular environment mapping,
    525–527
    fragment shader listing (12.11), 526

Ericsson Alpha Compression (EAC), 179
Ericsson Texture Compression (ETC2), 179
errors
    code, 584
    compiling, 201
    EGL, 727
    linker, 204
    shaders, 203
*Essential Mathematics for Games and Interactive
        Applications*, 718
ETC2 (Ericsson Texture Compression), 179
Euler angles, 72
evaluation, TES (tessellation evaluation shader),
        284
Event Trace Logs, 592
examples
    compute shaders, 450–471
    shader storage block declaration listing
        (5.27), 127
    stencil buffer usage listing (9.1), 350
    subroutine uniform declaration listing (6.5),
        213
    uniform blocks
        declaration listing (5.9), 109
        with offsets listing (5.11), 111
    use of indirect draw commands listing
        (7.10), 253
executing compute shaders, 439–444
exponential decay, 543
exponents
    bits, 189
    shared, 181
extending GLSurfaceView listing (14.18), 732
extensions, 8, 617
    applying, 618–622
    EGL, 728
    GLX, 695
    vendor-specific, 728
    WGL (Windows-GL), 634–639
EXT extensions, 618
extinction, 541, 542
eye space, 64, 65, 542

fades, 533
failures, programs, 204
FBOs (user-defined framebuffers), 368, 606
    attachment completeness, 377
    tests, 379
feedback, transforms
    applying, 260–265
    starting, pausing, and stopping, 264–266
feeding vertex shaders from buffers, 97–103
fetching vertices, 28
figuring out if occlusion query results are ready
        listing (11.2), 478
files
    loading

objects, 102–103
    from textures, 144–148
    SBM model file format, 751–757
filling
    data in buffers, 95–97
    a linked-list in a fragment shader listing
        (5.45), 174
fill performance, increasing, 678–679
filtering
    2D Gaussian filters, 411
    antialiasing by, 385–387
    mipmapping, 155–157
    modes, 148
    textures, 151–153
    trilinear, 156
    variables, 457
finding. *See also* searching
    a face normal in a geometry shader listing
        (8.21), 318
    a pixel format with
        wglChoosePixelFormatARB() listing
        (14.6), 639
first fragment shaders listing (2.4), 18
first geometry shader listing (3.9), 37
first OpenGL application listing (2.1), 14
first rule of flocking listing (10.12), 467
first tessellation control shader listing (3.7), 34
first vertex shaders listing (2.3), 18
fixed-function stages, 5
fixed outputs, 443
fixed-point
    data, 227
    math, 716–718
flags, 671
    Boolean, 655
flat inputs, 342
floating-point
    coordinates, 152
    data, 604
    fragment shaders, 342n1
    framebuffers, 401–414
    numbers, 189
    texture formats, 402–403
flocking
    compute shaders, 462–471
    vertex shader body listing (10.16), 470
flow control barriers, 446
FMA (fused multiply-add), 198, 199
focal depth, 457
focal distance, 457
fog, 541–544
format layout qualifiers, 169
formatting
    advanced framebuffers, 399–418
    applications, 14–16
    contexts, 696–699
    enumerating pixels, 640–641

formatting (*continued*)
  pixels, 630–632
  SBM model file format, 751–757
  textures, 138–139, 182–185
  windows, 628–630
formulas, calculating indexes, 250
fractals, rendering Julia, 566–568
fractional even spacing, 295
fractional segments, 295
fragments, 341–435
  antialiasing, 384–399
  color output, 357–364
  depth testing, 351–355
  early testing, 355–357
  off-screen rendering, 364–384
  opacity, 15
  OpenGL ES 3.0, 713
  pre-fragment tests, 345–357
  rasterization, 41
  redeclaration of, 356
  stencil testing, 348–351
fragment shaders, 42–45, 342–345, 595
  for the Alien Rain sample listing (5.42), 163
  with an input listing (3.4), 31
  for cube map environment rendering listing
    (12.16), 531–532
  with external function declaration listing
    (6.2), 206
  for generating shaped points listing (9.33),
    425–426
  with input interface blocks listing (3.6), 32
  for normal mapping listing (12.8), 521
  performing image loads and stores listing
    (5.44), 171
  for per-fragment shininess listing (12.17),
    534
  producing high-frequency output listing
    (9.22), 393–394
  ray tracing in, 568–580
  for rendering quads listing (8.35), 336
  with single texture coordinate listing (5.39),
    147
  for sky box rendering listing (12.14), 530
  for the star field effect listing (9.32), 423
  for terrain rendering listing (8.11), 304
framebuffers, 341–435
  advanced framebuffer formats, 399–418
  antialiasing, 384–399
  binding, 366
  completeness, 377
  copying data between, 431–433
  default, 365
  floating-point, 401–414
  integers, 415–416
  layered, 371, 382, 383
  logical operations, 363–364
  multiple attachments, 368–370

objects, 366
off-screen rendering, 364–384
OpenGL ES 3.0, 713
operations, 45–47, 135
reading from a, 429–431
stacks, 575
frames
  AFR (alternate frame rendering), 610
  Cartesian, 519
  sync frame rates, 677–679
frameworks, applications, 14–16
front end processes, 10
front-facing, 39
frustrum matrix, 81
full-screen
  rendering, 644–645, 675–677
  views (X Window System), 704
functionality, 621
functions. *See also* gl functions
  blending, 358–360
  built-in, 194–201
  callback, 583, 584
  depth, 352
  EmitVertex(), 36
  EndPrimitive(), 36
  init(), 582
  main(), 311
  multi versions of, 252
  normalization, 200
  overloading, 143, 166, 194
  pointers, 622
  portability of, 633
  RegisterClass, 628
  shaders, 19–20
  stencils, 349
  vmath::perspective, 82
  vmath::rotate, 72
fused multiply-add. *See* FMA

gamers, 729
gamma curves, 418
G-buffers, 548
  consuming, 551–554
  generating, 549–551
  unpacking, 552
  visualizing, 552
GDI (Graphics Device Interface), 627–628
  ChoosePixelFormat(), 634, 638
  SetPixelFormat(), 632
  SwapBuffers(), 593, 634
generating
  binding, and initializing buffers listing (5.1),
    94
  binding, and initializing textures listing
    (5.33), 138
  G-buffers, 549–551

geometry in geometry shaders, 322–325
new vertices in a geometry shader listing
    (8.27), 323–324
geometry, 10
  cubes
    configuring, 233
    drawing indexed, 234
  drawing commands, 249. *See also* drawing
    commands
  primitive restart, combining, 235–237
  transformations, 63
  uniforms, 121–126
geometry shaders, 36–38, 310–340
  changing the primitive type in, 35–328
  discarding geometry in, 317–320
  generating geometry in, 322–325
  layered rendering, 371
  layout qualifiers listing (8.17), 311
  modifying geometry in, 320–322
  multiple streams of storage, 328–329
  multiple viewport transformations, 336–340
  new primitive types introduced by, 329–336
  pass-through, 311–313
  quads (quadrilaterals), rendering using,
    332–336
  for rendering quads listing (8.34), 335–336
  using in an application, 313–317
getting ready for instanced rendering listing
    (7.9), 248
getting ready for shadow mapping listing
    (12.18), 536
getting the result from a query object listing
    (11.1), 478
gimbal locks, 72, 76
GL3W
  configuring, 686
  installing, 687
gl functions
  glActiveTexture(), 146, 150
  glAttachShader(), 19, 20, 47, 313, 438
  glBeginConditionalRender(), 481, 482
  glBeginQuery(), 484, 486, 488, 489, 490
  glBeginQueryIndexed(), 490
  glBeginTransformFeedback(), 265, 266
  glBindBuffer(), 93, 263, 600
  glBindBufferBase(), 262, 263
  glBindBufferRange(), 262, 263
  glBindFramebuffer(), 365, 367
  glBindImageTexture(), 167
  glBindProgramPipeline(), 209, 216
  glBindSampler(), 149
  glBindTexture(), 138, 663
  glBindTransformFeedback(), 491, 604
  glBindVertexArray(), 20, 21, 258, 603, 709
  glBindVertexBuffer(), 224, 229
  glBlendColor(), 358
  glBlendEquation(), 361

glBlendEquationSeparate(), 361
glBlendFunc(), 358, 362
glBlendFuncSeparate(), 358, 362
glBlitFramebuffer(), 433, 434
glBufferData(), 92–95, 109, 113, 127, 262,
    600
glBufferSubData(), 94, 95, 113, 134
glCheckFramebufferStatus(), 377
glClear(), 347
glClearBufferfv(), 15, 18, 347, 481
glClearBufferiv(), 349
glClearBufferSubData(), 95, 96, 134
glClientWaitSync(), 495–497
glColorMask(), 363, 364, 477
glColorMaski(), 363, 364
glCompileShader(), 19, 20, 47, 201, 204,
    313, 438, 607
glCompressedTexSubImage2D(), 180
glCompressedTexSubImage3D(), 181
glCopyBufferSubData(), 96, 262
glCopyImageSubData(), 433
glCopyTexSubImage2D(), 433
glCreateProgram(), 19, 439
glCreateShader(), 19, 20, 313, 438
glCreateShaderProgramv(), 209
glCullFace(), 41
glDebugMessageCallback(), 583, 585
glDebugMessageControl(),586
glDebugMessageInsert(), 587
glDeleteProgram(), 21, 205
glDeleteQueries(), 475
glDeleteShader(), 20, 21, 202
glDeleteSync(), 498
glDeleteTextures(), 146
glDeleteTransformFeedbacks(), 492
glDeleteVertexArrays(), 709
glDepthFunc(), 353
glDepthMask(), 353
glDepthRange(), 88
glDepthRangeArrayv(), 338
glDepthRangeIndexed(), 338
glDisable(), 280, 352, 393, 540
glDisableVertexAttribArray(), 100
glDispatchCompute(), 439–442, 444, 481
glDispatchComputeIndirect(), 439, 440, 442
glDrawArrays(), 21–22, 24–26, 122, 164,
    231, 234–236, 238–240, 265, 273, 313,
    321, 481, 492, 705, 709
glDrawArraysIndirect(), 250–252, 449
glDrawArraysInstanced(), 239–240, 245,
    492, 709
glDrawArraysInstancedBaseInstance(), 232,
    239, 250, 258, 439
glDrawBuffer(), 432, 477, 661
glDrawBuffers(), 377, 634
glDrawElements(), 231, 234–240, 251–252,
    275, 321, 492, 709

gl functions (*continued*)

glDrawElementsBaseVertex(), 234, 235, 239
glDrawElementsIndirect(), 250, 251, 252
glDrawElementsInstanced(), 239, 240, 245, 709
glDrawElementsInstancedBaseVertex(), 239
glDrawRangeElements(), 709
glDrawTransformFeedback(), 492, 493, 604, 615, 622
glDrawTransformFeedbackInstanced(), 492, 493
glDrawTransformFeedbackStream(), 493
glEnable(), 41, 348, 391, 392, 540
glEnableVertexAttribArray(), 98, 99
glEndConditionalRender(), 481, 483
glEndQuery(), 476, 484, 486, 489, 490
glEndQueryIndexed(), 490
glEndTransformFeedback(), 491, 497, 712
glFenceSync(), 494, 495, 497, 498
glFinish(), 493, 494, 598, 603
glFlush(), 493, 661, 673, 676
glFlushMappedBufferRange(), 601, 602
glFramebufferParameteri(), 400
glFramebufferTexture(), 366, 375, 376, 390
glFramebufferTexture2D(), 376
glFramebufferTextureLayer(), 374
glFrontFace(), 41
glGenBuffers(), 93
glGenerateMipmap(), 157, 435
glGenFramebuffers(), 365
glGenProgramPipelines(), 207
glGenQueries(), 474, 475
glGenTextures(), 137, 138, 145, 167, 182
glGenTransformFeedbacks(), 491
glGenVertexArrays(), 20, 21, 709
glGetActiveSubroutineName(), 215
glGetActiveUniformsiv(), 114, 115
glGetAttribLocation(), 100, 240
glGetBooleanv(), 713
glGetBufferSubData(), 259
glGetCompressedTexImage(), 180
glGetError(), 379, 474, 496, 584, 598, 727
glGetFloatv(), 680, 713
glGetInteger64v(), 497, 713
glGetIntegeri_v(), 440
glGetIntegerv(), 116, 117, 120, 150, 230, 263, 280, 316, 446, 598, 619, 680, 697, 713
glGetInternalFormativ(), 180
glGetProgramBinary(), 217, 219
glGetProgramInfoLog(), 205, 206
glGetProgramInterfaceiv(), 210
glGetProgramiv(), 205, 217, 441
glGetProgramResourceIndex(), 214
glGetProgramResourceiv(), 210, 211, 212
glGetProgramResourceName(), 211
glGetProgramStageiv(), 215
glGetQueryObjectuiv(), 476, 477, 479, 481, 484, 487, 488, 491

glGetShaderInfoLog(), 202, 206
glGetShaderiv(), 201, 202, 204, 205, 607
glGetString(), 644
glGetSynciv(), 495
glGetTexImage(), 435
glGetTexLevelParameteriv(), 180
glGetTexParameteriv(), 180
glGetUniformBlockIndex(), 117
glGetUniformLocation(), 104, 105, 151, 598
glInvalidateBufferData(), 614, 615
glInvalidateBufferSubData(), 614, 615
glInvalidateFramebuffer(), 615
glInvalidateSubFramebuffer(), 615
glInvalidateTexImage(), 614, 615
glInvalidateTexSubImage(), 614
glIsTransformFeedback(), 492
glLinkProgram(), 20, 47, 204, 206, 217, 264, 313, 438, 608
glLogicOp(), 362, 713
glMapBuffer(), 95, 109, 113, 127, 259, 600, 601, 603, 739
glMapBufferRange(), 134, 429, 599, 600, 601, 602, 603
glMemoryBarrier(), 131, 132, 137, 177
glMinSampleShading(), 394
glMultiDrawArrays(), 709
glMultiDrawArraysIndirect(), 232, 257, 258
glMultiDrawElements(), 709
glMultiDrawElementsIndirect(), 232
glObjectLabel(), 588
glObjectPtrLabel(), 588, 589
glPatchParameterfv(), 298
glPatchParameteri(), 33, 298
glPixelStorei(), 430
glPointParameteri(), 423
glPointSize(), 22, 26, 37, 230
glPolygonMode(), 36, 296
glPopDebugGroup(), 585, 588
glProgramBinary(), 219
glProgramParameteri(), 207, 217
glPushDebugGroup(), 585
glQueryCounter(), 485, 486
glReadBuffer(), 429, 430
glReadPixels(), 429, 430, 431, 433, 435, 598, 599, 600, 680
glSampleCoverage(), 392
glSamplerParameterf(), 149, 150
glSamplerParameterfv(), 159
glSamplerParameteri(), 149, 150, 158
glScissorIndexed(), 346
glScissorIndexedv(), 346
glShaderSource(), 19, 20, 47, 203, 209, 313, 438
glStencilFunc(), 351
glStencilFuncSeparate(), 348, 350, 351
glStencilMaskSeparate(), 351
glStencilOp(), 351
glStencilOpSeparate(), 348, 349, 350, 351

glTexBuffer(), 273
glTexParameteri(), 536
glTexStorage2D(), 138, 144, 154, 156, 167, 180, 389, 527
glTexStorage2DMultisample(), 389, 390
glTexStorage3D(), 161, 180, 389
glTexStorage3DMultisample(), 389, 390
glTexSubImage2D(), 138, 139, 144, 154, 185, 429, 433, 435, 527, 613
glTexSubImage3D(), 161, 614
glTextureView(), 182
glTransformFeedbackVaryings(), 260, 261, 263, 264
glUniform*(), 105, 106, 108
glUniform1i(), 151
glUniform4fv(), 439
glUniformBlockBinding(), 118, 119
glUniformSubroutinesuiv(), 215
glUnmapBuffer(), 601
glUseProgram(), 21, 120, 215, 216, 439, 711
glUseProgramStages(), 207, 215
glVertexAttrib*(), 29, 30, 99, 100, 165
glVertexAttrib4fv(), 29
glVertexAttribBinding(), 224, 228
glVertexAttribDivisor(), 470
glVertexAttribFormat(), 224, 225, 227, 228
glVertexAttribI*(), 165
glVertexAttribIFormat(), 227
glVertexAttribIPointer(), 755
glVertexAttribPointer(), 98, 99, 101, 102, 224, 245 , 263, 605, 709
glViewport(), 40, 122, 336, 337, 338, 401, 674, 679
glViewportArrayv(), 338
glViewportIndexedf(), 337
glViewportIndexedfv(), 337
glWaitSync(), 497–498
GLFW
    configuring, 686
    installing, 686–687
GLKit, 648, 662–673
    3D math with, 667–669
    Cocoa, 669–671
    iOS, 737–738
GLKTextureInfo class, 663
GLKViewController class, 741
global illumination, 558
global work groups, 440–441, 456
gloss maps, 533
GLSL (OpenGL Shading Language), 17, 740–741
GL_TRIANGLES_ADJACENCY primitive mode, 330, 331
GLUT (OpenGL Utility Toolkit), 648, 680–681
    main function to set up OpenGL listing (14.17), 681
GLX
    glXChooseFBConfig(), 692, 693, 694
    glXCopyContext(), 698
    glXCreateContextAttribsARB(), 696, 697

glXCreateNewContext(), 696
glXCreateWindow(), 694
glXDestroyContext(), 698
glXDestroyWindow(), 694
glXGetClientString(), 695
glXGetCurrentReadDrawable(), 700
glXGetFBConfigAttrib(), 692
glXGetFBConfigs(), 689, 692, 694
glXGetProcAddress(), 695
glXIsDirect(), 699
glXMakeContextCurrent(), 699
glXMakeCurrent(), 611
glXQueryContext(), 700
glXQueryDrawable(), 700
glXQueryExtensionsString(), 695
glXQueryServerString(), 695
glXQueryVersion(), 688
glXSwapBuffers(), 700, 703
glXWaitGL(), 699
glXWaitX(), 700
queries, 700–701
strings (Linux), 695
synchronization, 699
windows, 701–704
GLX-interfacing with X Window System, 688–689
Google, 707
Gouraud shading, 507
    fragment shader listing (12.2), 508
    vertex shader listing (12.1), 507–508
GPU PerfStudio 2, 594–597
GPUs (Graphics Processing Units), 5, 609–611
GPUView, 590–594
graphics, 3
    math, 49. See also math
    output, 627
    pipelines, 4–6, 27–48. See also pipelines
    processors, 218, 594
    programs, 438
Graphics Device Interface. See GDI
graphics drivers (Windows), 624–626
Graphics Processing Units. See GPUs
graphics processors, compute shaders, 437–472
graphs, exponential decay, 543
grass
    colors, 244
    distribution, 242, 243
    length of, 245
    positioning, 241
gravity, 270
groups
    messages, 587
    outputs, 296
    work, 440–441
guard bands, 278

hardware, 4, 9
  Linux, 685–686
  queues, 590
  rasterizers, 10
  support, 625
hazards, 129, 137
HDR (High Dynamic Range), 403–404, 606
header of a .KTX file listing (5.36), 144–145
heads-up display (HUD), 485
Hermite curve, 198
High Dynamic Range. *See* HDR
higher order surfaces, 324
highlights, specular, 505–509
hints, 209, 614
histograms, 405
history, 3, 6–10
  of Linux, 682–683
  of OpenGL ES, 706
homogenous coordinates, 39
homogenous vectors, 53
Hooke's law, 269, 270, 271
HUD (heads-up display), 485, 595

ICD (Installable Client Driver), 624, 626
identity matrix, 67–68
IEEE-754, 188
illumination, global, 558
images
  access synchronization, 176–177
  atomic operations on, 171–176
  columns, 454
  stereo, viewing in, 380
  transposing, 412
  units, 167
  variables, 165
increasing fill performance, 678–679
indexes
  arrays, 245
  data chunks (SBM model file format), 753
  drawing commands, 231–237
  formulas, calculating, 250
  global work groups, 456
  queries, 489–490
  uniforms, 112
indirect draws, 250–259
infinity, 200
in flight (executing hardware commands), 4
init() function, 582
initializing
  array textures listing (5.40), 161–162
  core context views listing (14.11), 654
  a G-buffer listing (12.27), 550
  shader storage buffers for flocking listing
    (10.9), 464
  textures, 138–139
inner loop of the julia renderer listing (12.34),
    567

inner products, 54–55
inputs
  compute shaders, 441–444
  flat, 342
  to the flock rendering vertex shader listing
    (10.15), 469
  primitive types, 315
  smooth, 342
  vertex shaders, 224–229
inscattering, 541
inserting geometry shaders, 37
Installable Client Driver. *See* ICD
installing
  GL3W, 687
  GLFW, 686–687
instancing
  arrays, 288
  drawing commands, 237–250
  rendering, 245–250, 249
integers, 189
  framebuffers, 415–416
Integrated Raster Imaging System Graphics
    Library. *See* IRIS GL
Interface Builder, 651, 659
interfaces
  Aero user, 592
  APIs (Application Programming Interfaces),
    3
  blocks, 31–32
  GDI (Graphics Device Interface), 627–628
  GLX-interfacing with X Window System,
    688–689
  Mac OS X, 648–649
  matching, 209–213
  overriding, 652–659
interleaved attributes, 101
internal formats, 138
interpolation, 44, 82
  curves, 85
  disabling, 342
  Hermite, 198
  linear, 83
  perspective-correct, 344, 345
  splines, 88
  and storage qualifiers, 342–345
Interrupt Service Routine. *See* ISR
invocations, 188
iOpenGL, 734–744
iOS
  C++, 737
  configuring, 734–736
  GLKit, 737–738
  GLSL (OpenGL Shading Language), 740–741
IRIS GL (Integrated Raster Imaging System
    Graphics Library), 682
isoline spirals tessellation evaluation shader
    listing (8.7), 292

ISR (Interrupt Service Routine), 593
items, work, 47
iterating over elements of gl_in[] listing (8.18), 312

jaggies, 384
Julia set, 566–568

Khrones Group, 706–707
Khronos Texture File format, 529
Kilgard, Mark J., 680
knots, 87n4
.KTX (Khronos TeXture) format, 144, 145
ktxtool utility, 759–761

languages, overview of, 188–201
layers, 162
    abstraction, 4, 5
    rendering, 370–376
    rendering using a geometry shader listing
        (9.9), 372
layouts
    columns, 60
    qualifiers, 29, 104, 370
        binding, 118
        control points, 33
        depth, 356, 357
        format, 169
        geometry shader, 311
        location, 370
    shared, 110
    standard, 110, 116
length
    of grass, 245
    of vectors, 57
levels, 138
    generating mipmapping, 157
libraries, math, 54, 59, 61
light bloom, 409–414
lighting a fragment using data from a G-buffer
    listing (12.30), 553
lighting models, 504–544
    Blinn-Phong lighting model, 513–515
    environment mapping, 522–532
    normal mapping, 518–522
    Phong lighting model, 504–513
    rim lighting, 515–517
light spaces, occluding, 559
linear interpolation, 83
linear texturing, 245
lines, 82
    clipping, 276–282
    parallel, 80
    smoothing, 385
links
    makefiles, 687
    programs, 204–206

Linux, 682–704
    applications, building, 687–693
    applying contexts, 699–701
    config management and visuals, 689–693
    GLX
        creating windows, 701–704
        strings, 695
    history of, 682–683
    managing contexts, 695–699
    rendering, 693–694
    starting, 683–687
    windows, 693–694
    X Window System, 683
loading
    2D array textures, 163–165
    a cube map texture listing (12.12), 528–529
    a .KTX file listing (5.37), 145
    objects from files, 102–103
    textures, 144–148, 665–667
local work groups, 47, 440–441, 444
locations, 104
    uniforms, 114
    of vertex attributes to zero, 29
locks, gimbal, 72, 76
logical operations, 363–364
logs, Event Trace Logs, 592
lookout matrix, 77–79
loops
    main, 633
    rendering, 273

Mac OS X, 647–681
    CGL (Core OpenGL), 674–675
    Cocoa, 649–662
    full-screen rendering, 675–677
    GLUT (OpenGL Utility Toolkit),
        680–681
    interfaces, 648–649
    multi-threaded OpenGL, 679–680
    OpenGL on, 647–681
    rendering in, 660
    retina displays, 673–674
    sync frame rates, 677–679
macros, APIENTRY, 583
magnification filters, 152
main body of the flocking update compute
    shader listing (10.14), 468–469
main() function, 311
main loops, 633
makefiles, 687
managing
    config management and visuals,
        689–693
    context, 695–699, 725–726
    viewports, 660
Mandelbrot sets, 566
mantissa bits, 189

mapping
    buffers, 600–603
    a buffer's data store listing (5.3), 95
    bump, 518
    displacement, 300
    environment, 522–532
        cube maps, 527–532
        equirectangular, 525–527
        spherical environment maps,
           523–525
    gloss maps, 533
    GPU PerfStudio 2, 594
    normal, 518–522, 554–556, 605
    rendering to cubes, 375–376
    shadows, 534–540
    tone, 404–409
    vertex shader inputs, 228
marching rays, 560
masking colors, 363–364
matching interfaces, 209–213
material properties, 532–534
math, 49
    3D math with GLKit, 667–669
    built-in functions, 197–199
    curves, 83–87
    fixed-point, 716–718
    library, 54, 59, 61
    matrices, construction and operators,
        60–63
    operators, 54–58
    quaternions, 75–76
    splines, 87–90
    transformations, 63–82
        concatenation, 73–75
        model-view transforms, 76–79
        projection, 79–81
    vectors, 51–54
matrices, 53, 58–60, 190–192
    built-in functions, 195–197
    construction, 60–63
    drawing commands, 232
    frustrum, 82
    identity, 67–68
    lookout, 77–79
    operators, 60–63
    perspective, 81
    rotation, 70–72
    scaling, 72–73
    shadows, 538
    transformations, 62, 66
    translation, 68–70
    uniforms, 107–108
member variables, 21
memory
    access synchronization, 129–133
    allocation using buffers, 92–95
    atomic operations, 128–129

    bandwidth, 178, 549
    hazards. *See* hazards
    optimization, 613–616
Mesa, 682, 685
messages
    debug, 586, 587
    loops, 633
methods, 14, 194
minification filters, 152
mipmapping, 138, 153–155
    cube map support, 529
    example program, 158
    filtering, 155–157
    levels, 157–158
mobile platforms, 705–744
    Android development environments,
        729–734
    EGL, 718–728
    gamers, 729
    iOpenGL, 734–744
    negotiating embedded environments,
        728–729
    OpenGL ES, 705–709
    OpenGL ES 3.0, 709–713
models
    lighting, 504–544
        Blinn-Phong lighting model, 513–515
        environment mapping, 522–532
        normal mapping, 518–522
        Phong lighting model, 504–513
        Rim lighting model, 515–517
    SBM model file format, 751–757
    transformations, 63, 67
model space, 64
model-view transforms, 76–79, 667
modes
    filtering, 148
    parameters, 265
    separable, 207
    wrapping, 148
modifying
    geometry in geometry shaders, 320–322
    the primitive type in geometry shaders,
        325–328
monolithic program objects, 206
movement keys, 671
MSAA (multi-sample antialiasing), 387–389
multi-dimensional arrays, 194
multiple framebuffer attachments, 368–370
multiple GPUs, 609–611
multiple interleaved vertex attributes listing
    (5.8), 102
multiple separate vertex attributes listing (5.7),
    101
multiple streams of storage, 328–329
multiple textures, 150–151
multiple threads, 611–613

multiple vertices, 24
  attributes, 225
  shader inputs, 100–102
multiple viewport transformations, 336–340
multiplication, 62
  coordinate spaces, 63–66
  matrices, 62
  model-view transformations, 76–79
  quaternions, 75–76
multi-sampling, 46n3
  aliasing, 140
  antialiasing, 387–389
  textures, 389–393
multi-threaded OpenGL, 679–680
multi versions of functions, 252

naïve rotated point sprite fragment shader
    listing (9.34), 427
names, 92, 138
NaN (Not a Number), 189, 200
NDC (Normalized Device Coordinate) Space,
    64, 66
negative reflections, 506
negotiating embedded environments,
    728–729
new primitive types introduced by geometry
    shaders, 329–336
Newton's laws, 269, 270, 271
noninstanced rendering, 245–250
non-photo-realistic rendering, 544–547
normalization, 52
  buffers, 98
  functions, 200
  positive values, 226
Normalized Device Coordinate Space. *See* NDC
    Space
normalized device spaces, 39
normal mapping, 518–522, 605
  deferred shading, 554–556
normals, finding, 328
Not a Number (NaN), 189, 200
NSOpenGL, 648, 652–659
NULL pointers, 94
NVIDIA drivers, 625, 682
Nyquist rate, 384

objects
  buffers, storage, 251
  container, 603
  coordinates, 64–65
  display objects and X Window System, 689
  files, loading, 102–103
  framebuffers, 366
  instancing, 237–250
  list chunks, 756
  monolithic program, 206
  program pipeline, 207, 608

programs, 17
queries, 474
rotation, 70–72
samplers, 148
separable program, 608
shaders, 17
space, 64
stacks, 575
sync, 494
TBO (texture buffer object), 266, 269
texture, 148
UBO (Uniform Buffer Object), 108
VAOs (vertex array objects), 272
object-space coordinate data, 605
occlusion
  ambient, 558–565
  queries, 475–484
off-screen rendering, 364–384
offsets, 250
  polygons, 540
opacity fragments, 15
OpenGL
  Mac OS X on, 647–681. *See also* Mac OS X
  multi-threaded, 679–680
  in Windows, 623–647. *See also* Windows
OpenGL ES, 705–709, 713–718
OpenGL ES 3.0, 709–713
OpenGL Shading Language. *See* GLSL
operating systems. *See* platforms
operators
  AND, 47
  comparison, 352
  matrices, 60–63
  OR, 47
  standard, 192
  vectors, 54–58
optimization
  compute shaders, 437–472
  with extensions, 619–622
  memory, 613–616
  performance. *See* performance optimization
orientation, calculating, 257
origin of OpenGL, 6–10
OR operator, 47
orthographic projections, 80, 81, 83
orthonormal, 519
outputs
  colors, 357–364
  compute shaders, 441–444
  graphics, 627
  groups, 296
  vertex shaders, 229–230
outputting information about the OpenGL
    context listing (14.12), 660
overdraw, 548
overloading functions, 15, 143, 166, 194
overriding NSOpenGL, 652–659

packed data formats, 227
packed vertex attributes, 247
packets
    DMA, 593
    present, 593
    standard queue, 592
parallax, 379
parallelism, 4, 42
parallel lines, 80
parallel prefix sum (compute shader example),
    450–462
parallization, 450–462
parameters
    domains, 334
    mode, 265
    points, 423–424
passing data between tessellation shaders,
    296–299
pass-through
    geometry shaders, 311–313
    vertex shader listing (8.25), 323
    vertex shader that includes normals listing
        (8.30), 326
patches, 284, 340
    cubic Bézier patches (tessellation example),
        304–310
    domains, 306
    processes, 284
Paul, Brian, 682
pausing transform feedback, 264–266
performance
    counters, 597
    increasing fill, 678–679
    optimization, 581, 589–616, 597–616
performance analysis tools, 589–597
    GPU PerfStudio 2, 594–597
    GPUView, 590–594
    WPT (Windows Performance Toolkit),
        590–594
per-fragment lighting, calculating, 518
per-indirect draw attribute setup listing (7.13),
    255
per-instance rotations, calculating, 163
per-patch inner/outer tessellation factors, 284
perspective
    coordinates, 66
    division, 39
    matrices, 81
    perspective-correct interpolation, 344–345
    projections, 80, 81, 82
perturbations, random, 242
per-vertex lighting (Gouraus shading), 509
Phong lighting model, 504–513
Phong shading, 509–513, 519, 521
    fragment shader listing (12.4), 511–512
    vertex shader listing (12.3), 510–511
physical simulation example, 266–275

pipelines, 10–11, 17, 27–48
    clipping, 38–39
    compute shaders, 47–48
    fragment shaders, 42–45
    framebuffer operations, 45–47
    geometry shaders, 36–38
    graphics, 4–6
    interface blocks, 31–32
    tessellation, 32–36
    vertices
        passing data from stage to stage,
            29–32
        passing data to shaders, 28–29
pixels, 10–11, 17
    advanced formats, 643
    calculating, 385
    centroid sampling, 396, 397
    counting, 480
    enumerating formats, 640–641
    format attributes, 643–644
    formatting, 630–632
    Phong shading, 521
platforms, 617
    extensions, 618–622
    Linux, 682–704
    Mac OS X on, 647–681. *See also*
        Mac OS X
    mobile, 705–744
    Windows, 623–647. *See also* Windows
pointers, 15
    functions, 622
    NULL, 94
point mode, tessellation, 292–294
points
    binding, 117, 262
    clipping, 276
    control, 83, 284, 304
    parameters, 423–424
    rotation, 426–428
    shaped, 424–426
    sizing, 22
    sprites, 419–428
    textures, 420
    variables, 230
polygons
    concave, 10
    offsets, 540
    smoothing, 386
portability of functions, 633
positioning
    antialiasing sample, 387
    calculating, 257
    control points, 284
    grass, 241
    math, 51
positive value normalization, 226
predication, 481

prefix sum, 450–462
    implementation using a compute shader
        listing (10.6), 453
pre-fragment tests, 345–357
pre-optimizing shaders, 609
present packets, 593
primitive mode tessellation, 285–294
primitiveMode values, 265
primitive processing, 283–340
    communication between shader
        invocations, 299
    cubic Bézier patches (tessellation example),
        304–310
    geometry shaders, 310–340
    terrain rendering (tessellation example),
        300–304
    tessellation, 284–310
primitives, 10–11
    assembly, 10, 36, 175
    degenerate, 24
    restart, combining geometry, 235–237
    types, adjacency, 340
printing interface information listing (6.4), 212
processes
    back end, 11, 341
    fragments, 341–435
    front end, 10
    primitive, 283–340. See also primitive
        processing
    vertices, 224–230
processors
    GPUs (Graphics Processing Units), 5
    graphics, 218, 594
producing
    lines from normals in the geometry shader
        listing (8.32), 327
    multiple vertices in a vertex shaders listing
        (2.8), 24
products
    cross, 56–57
    dot, 54–55
    inner, 54–55
    vectors, 55
profiles, 9. See also core profiles
programmable stages, 28
programs, 13, 187. See also applications
    binaries, 216–219, 609
    compiling, 201–219
    compute, 438. See also compute shaders
    linking, 204–206
    monolithic objects, 206
    objects, 17
    pipeline objects, 207, 608
    separaable, 206–213
    shaders, 5
projection
    matrices, 123

orthographic, 419
perspective, 76, 80, 667
transformations, 79–81
properties, material, 532–534
pseudo-code
    for glDrawArraysInstanced() listing (7.5),
        240
    for glDrawElementsInstanced() listing (7.6),
        240
publication dates, 7
pulling vertices, 28
pushing a face out along its normal listing
    (8.24), 321

quadratic Bézier curves, 85, 86
quadratic equations, 86
quads (quadrilaterals)
    geometry shaders, rendering using, 332–336
    tessellation using, 285–288
qualifiers
    binding layout, 119
    centroid, 395
    format layout, 169
    layout, 29, 104, 370
    storage, interpolation and, 342–345
Quartz, 647
quaternions, 72, 75–76
queries, 474–493
    extension functions, 622
    GLX, 700–701
    indexed, 489–490
    objects, 522
        result availability, 475
        retrieving, 476
        timer, 484
        transform feedback, 487–489
    occlusion, 475–484
    results, 476–480, 490–493
    timer, 484–487
    transform feedback, 487–493
queues
    CPU, 590
    drain, 591
    hardware, 590
    software, 590
    standard queue packets, 592

race conditions, 446, 447
radians, 199
random perturbations, 242
rasterization, 41–42
    back end processes, 341
    OpenGL ES 3.0, 712
rasterizers, 10
    discard, 273
    guards bands, 278

rates, sync frame, 677–679
RAW (Read-After-Write), 129
ray-plane intersection test listing (12.38), 578
rays, 560, 568–580
ray-sphere intersection test listing (12.36), 572
RC (rendering context), 628, 632–634
Read-After-Write (RAW), 129
reading
    back texture data, 434–435
    from a framebuffer, 429–431
    state or data from OpenGL, 597–600
    textures, 148–165
    from textures in GLSL listing (5.35), 141
Realtech VR OpenGL Extensions Viewer, 619
rectangles
    prefix sums, 460
    textures, 140n4
redeclaration of fragments, 356
Red-Green Texture Compression (RGTC), 179
redirecting the current folder to point our
        resources listing (14.21), 742–743
reflection, 57–58, 507
reflectivity, 504
refraction, 57–58
RegisterClass function, 628
registering a window class listing (14.1), 628
rendering, 503
    3D graphics, 630
    AFR (alternate frame rendering), 610
    with all blending functions listing (9.3),
        359–360
    alternative rendering methods, 548–580
    Android projects, 731–734
    asteroids, 257
    atmospheric effects, 540–544
    casting shadows, 534–540
    conditional, 481, 598
    context. See RC
    cube maps, 375–376, 529
    data driven engines, 613
    deferred shading, 548–558
    environment mapping, 522–532
    full-screen, 644–645, 675–677
    HDR (High Dynamic Range), 403–404
    instancing, 238, 245–250, 249
    Julia fractals, 566–568
    layers, 370–376
    lighting models, 504–544
    Linux, 693–694
    loops, 273
        for the Alien Rain sample listing (5.43), 164
        for the flocking example listing (10.10), 465
        listing (5.23), (5.26), 123, 125–126
    in Mac OS X, 660
    material properties, 532–534
    to multiple viewports in a geometry shader
        listing (8.36), 338–339
    with no attachments, 399–401
    noninstanced, 245–250
    non-photo-realistic, 544–547
    off-screen, 364–384
    pipelines. See pipelines
    quads (quadrilaterals) using geometry
        shaders, 332–336
    scissor tests, 347
    screen-space techniques, 558–565
    single points listing (2.7), 22
    single triangles listing (2.9), 25
    sky boxes, 531
    starfields, 420–423
    in stereo, 379–384
    Stonehenge, 663–665
    surfaces, 725
    synchronization, 726–727
    terrain, 300–304
    a texture listing (9.5), 367–368
    textures, 610
    to two layers with a geometry shader listing
        (9.16), 382–383
    when query results aren't available listing
        (11.4), 480
    without a TCS (tessellation control shader),
        298–299
    without triangles, 565–580
render() method, 14
resolution, retina displays (Mac OS X),
        673–674
resources
    3D graphics books, 748
    OpenGL books, 747–748
    web sites, 748–749
restarting geometry and primitives, 235–237
results
    primitive queries, 490–493
    queries, 476–480
retina displays (Mac OS X), 673–674
retrieving
    compiler logs from a shader listing (6.1),
        202–203
    indices of uniform block members listing
        (5.12), (5.15), 112, 115
    information about uniform block members
        listing (5.13), 113
    a program binary listing (6.7), 217–218
return values, framebuffer completeness, 378
RGTC (Red-Green Texture Compression), 179
rim lighting, 515–517
    shader function listing (12.6), 516
rotated point sprites
    fragment shader listing (9.36), 427
    vertex shader listing (9.35), 427–428
rotation
    matrices, 70–72
    points, 426–428

roughness, 533
rules, uniform blocks, 111

samples
    centroid sampling, 395–399
    coverage, 391–393
    multi-sample
        antialiasing, 387–389
        textures, 389–393
    objects, 148
    parameters, 149
    rate shading, 393–395
    types, 142
    variables, 141
sampling rates, 384
SB6
    sb6GetProcAddress(), 622, 635
    sb6IsExtensionSupported(), 620, 622
sb6mtool utility, 762–764
SBM model file format, 751–757
    chunk headers, 752
    defined chunks, 752–756
    examples, 757
    file headers, 751–752
scalability, 4, 67
scalars, 105–106, 188–189
scaling matrix, 72–73
scissor tests, 46, 345–348
screen-space techniques, 558–565
searching bind sections of buffers, 262
segments, fractional, 295
selecting
    OpenGL ES versions, 708–709
    pixel formats, 631–662, 654
selectors, 150
separable mode, 207
separable program objects, 608
separate attributes, 100
separate programs, 206–213
serialization, 129
servers (X Window System), 693
sets
    julia, 566–568
    Mandelbrot, 566
setting. *See also* configuration
    the debug callback function listing (13.2), 583
    single floats in uniform blocks listing
        (5.14), 114
    up a full-screen window listing (14.9), 645
    up a layered framebuffer listing (9.8), 371
    up a multisample framebuffer attachment
        listing (9.20), 390
    up and rendering Android listing (14.19), 733
    up an FBO with multiple attachments listing
        (9.6), 369–370
    up a shadow matrix listing (12.20), 538
    up a simple framebuffer object listing (9.4), 367

up atomic counter buffers listing (5.29),
    (5.30), 134
up cube geometry listing (5.20), 121–122
up indexed cube geometry listing (7.2), 233
up indirect draw buffers for Asteroids listing
    (7.11), 254
up matrices for shadow mapping listing
    (12.19), 536
up matrices in uniform blocks listing (5.17),
    116
up scissor rectangle arrays listing (9.1),
    346–347
up the "Explode" geometry shader listing
    (8.23), 321
up the julia set renderer listing (12.33), 567
up the "Normal Visualizer" geometry shader
    listing (8.31), 326–327
up the "Tesellator" geometry shader listing
    (8.26), 323
up vertex attributes listing (5.4), 99
values of subroutine uniforms listing (6.6),
    216
SGI (Silicon Graphics, Inc.), 6, 682
shaders, 5, 187
    applying, 16–23
    barriers, 132–133
    blocks, storage, 126–133
    communication between invocations, 299
    compiling, 218, 606–609
    compute, 47–48, 437–472
        applying, 438–439
        communication, 444–449
        examples, 450–471
        executing, 439–444
        flocking, 462–471
        synchronizing, 445–449
    cores, 5
    fragments, 42–45, 342–345
    geometry, 36–38, 310–340
        changing the primitive type in, 325–328
        discarding geometry in, 317–320
        generating geometry in, 322–325
        layered rendering, 371
        modifying geometry in, 320–322
        multiple streams of storage, 328–329
        multiple viewport transformations,
            336–340
        new primitive types introduced by,
            329–336
        pass-through, 311–313
        storage blocks, 126, 129
        tessellation. *See* tessellation
        using in an application, 313–317
        vertex. *See* vertex shaders
    objects, 17
    OpenGL ES 3.0, 710–712
    pre-optimizing, 609

shaders (*continued*)
subroutines, 213–216
TCS (tessellation control shader), 284
TES (tessellation evaluation shader), 284
tessellation
control, 33–34
evaluation, 34–36
passing data, 296–299
textures
reading from in, 141–144
writing to in, 165–176
vertices, 24
feeding from buffers, 97–103
inputs, 224–229
multiple inputs, 100–102
outputs, 229–230
passing to data to, 28–29
shading
cell, 545–547
deferred, 548–558
downsides to, 556–558
normal mapping, 554–556
Gouraud, 507
Phong, 509–513, 519
sample rate, 393–395
shadows
casting, 534–540
mapping, 534–540
matrix, 538
sampler, 535
shaped points, 424–426
shared memory, 445
sharing
exponents, 181
layouts, 110
variables, 444
shininess factor, 506
shutting down applications, 21
side effects, 443
signaled states, 494
signed areas, 40
signed integers, 189
Silicon Graphics, Inc. (SGI), 6, 680
simple
application side conditional rendering
listing (11.3), 479
do-nothing compute shader listing (3.13), 47
instanced vertex shader listing (7.8), 247
isoline tessellation control shader example
listing (8.5), 291
isoline tessellation control shader example
listing (8.6), 291
multisample maximum resolve listing
(9.21), 391
prefix sum implementation in C++ listing
(10.5), 450
quad tessellation control shader example
listing (8.1), 287

quad tessellation evaluation shader example
listing (8.2), 287–288
simplified fragment shader for shadow
mapping listing (12.22), 539
simplified vertex shader for shadow
mapping listing (12.21), 538
triangle tessellation control shader example
listing (8.3), (8.4), 289, 290
vertex shader with pre-vertex color listing
(7.7), 246
single buffering, 661
sizing
input arrays, 315
points, 22
variables, points, 230
sky boxes, 529, 531
smoothing
inputs, 342
lines, 385
polygons, 386
SoAs (structure-of-arrays), 101
software queues, 590
source code for a simple geometry shader listing
(8.16), 311
source factors, 358
spaces, color, 416–418
specifications, CGL (Core OpenGL), 625n3
specifying
bindings for uniform blocks listing
(5.18), 119
data for arrays in uniform blocks listing
(5.16), 115
varyings, 260
specular albedo, 512
specular highlights, 505–509
speed, tuning applications for, 597–616
spherical environment mapping, 523–525
fragment shader listing (12.10), 524
vertex shader listing (12.9), 523–524
spinning cube
fragment shader listing (5.25), 124
vertex shader listing (5.24), 123
splines, 82, 87–90
spring mass system
example, 266
iteration loop listing (7.18), 273
rendering loop listing (7.19), 273
vertex setup listing (7.16), 269
vertex shader listing (7.17), 271–272
sprites, points, 419–428
sRGB color spaces, 416–418
SSAO (screen space ambient occlusion), 559
stacks, implementing, 575
stages, 5
fixed-function, 5
shaders, 17
standard layouts, 110, 116
standard operators, 192

standard queue packets, 592
starfields, rendering, 420–423
starting
    applications, 21
    Linux, 683–687
    transform feedback, 264–266
state, OpenGL ES 3.0, 713
stencil tests, 46, 348–351
stereo, rendering in, 379–384
Stonehenge, 663–665
stopping transform feedback, 264–266
storage
    buffer objects, 251
    multiple streams of, 328–329
    qualifiers
        interpolation and, 342–345
        patch, 445
        shared, 445
    shaders, blocks, 126–133
    transforms, vertices, 259–275
strings
    EGL, 727
    GLX, 695
structure-of-arrays (SoAs), 101
structures, 192–194
    acceleration, 579
    VERTEX, 225
subdivision modes, tessellation, 294–296
subroutines, shaders, 213–216
subsystems, destination, 132
summed area tables, 456, 460
sums, prefixes, 450–462
support
    core profiles, 652
    hardware, 625
    ICD (Installable Client Driver), 624, 626
    on Linux, 684
surfaces, render, 626, 693–694, 725
SwapBuffers() command, 593
swap values, buffers, 637
swizzling, 191
sync frame rates, 677–679
sync objects, 494
synchronization, 493–498
    access
        to atomic counters, 137
        to images, 176–177
        to memory, 129–133
    compute shaders, 445–449
    and fences, 494–498
    GLX, 699
    rendering, 726–727

tables, summed area, 456, 460
taking a screenshot with glReadPixels() listing
    (9.37), 430–431
tangents
    space normals, 554

vectors, 519
targets, 92, 137, 139–140
TBN (Tangent, Bitangent, Normal) matrix, 519,
    555
TBO (texture buffer object), 266, 269
TCS (tessellation control shader), 284, 298–299,
    595
    for terrain rendering listing (8.9), 302–303
terrain, rendering, 300–304
TES (tessellation evaluation shader), 34–36,
    284, 595
    for terrain rendering listing (8.10), 303
tessellation, 32–36, 284–310
    control shaders, 33–34
    engines, 34
    evaluation shaders, 34–36
    examples
        cubic Bézier patches, 304–310
        terrain rendering, 300–304
    isolines, 290–292
    point mode, 292–294
    primitive modes, 285–294
    quads (quadrilaterals), 285–288
    shaders, passing data, 296–299
    subdivision modes, 294–296
    triangles, 288–290
tessellation control shader. See TCS
tessellation evaluation shader. See TES
tests
    depth, 46, 351–355
    early testing, 355–357
    FBOs (user-defined framebuffers), 379
    pre-fragment, 345–357
    scissor, 46, 345–348
    stencil, 46, 348–351
texels as light, 545–547
texture buffer object. See TBO
textures, 19, 137–185
    1D, 244
    arrays, 160–165, 163–165, 370
    attaching, 367
    base level, 154
    border color, 159
    compression, 177–181, 606
    coordinates, 146–148, 529
    copying data into a, 433–434
    files, loading from, 144–148
    filtering, 151–153
    floating-point, 402–403
    formatting, 138–139
    initializing, 138–139
    linear, 245
    loading, 665–667
    max level, 154
    multiple, 150–151
    multi-sample, 389–393
    objects, 160
    OpenGL ES 3.0, 712

textures (*continued*)
points, 420
a point sprite in the fragment shader listing
(9.30), 420
reading, 148–165, 434–435
rendering, 610
shaders
reading from in, 141–144
writing to in, 165–176
stars, 420
targets, 139–140
TBO (texture buffer object), 266, 269
views, 181–185
wrap mode, 158–160
threads, multiple, 611–613
three-component vertices, 53
tightly packed arrays, 101
timer queries, 484–487
timeslicing, 446
timing operations
using glQueryCounter() listing (11.8),
485–486
using timer queries listing (11.7), 484–485
tokens, 96, 226
tone mapping, 404–409
tools, 759–764
dds2ktx utility, 761–762
GLUT (OpenGL Utility Toolkit), 680–681
ktxtool utility, 759–761
performance analysis, 589–597
Realtech VR OpenGL Extensions Viewer, 619
sb6mtool utility, 762–764
toon fragment shader listing (12.26), 546–547
toon vertex shader listing (12.25), 546
transfer curves, tone mapping, 407
transformations
concatenation, 73–75
coordinates, 66–73
coordinate spaces, 63–66
geometry, 63
matrices, 62, 66
rotation, 70–72
scaling, 72–73
perspective, 68–70
models, 63
model-view, 76–79, 667
multiple viewport transformations, 336–340
order of, 105
overview of, 63–82
projection, 79–81
uniforms, geometry, 121–126
vertices, storage, 259–275
view, 76
viewports, 76
transform feedback
applying, 260–265
ending the pipeline with, 266

physical simulation example, 266–275
queries, 487–493
starting, pausing, and stopping, 264–266
translation, 68–70
transparency, 558
transposing images, 412
traversing a linked-list in a fragment shader
listing (5.46), 175–176
triangles, 10
clipping, 277, 278
drawing, 24–25
GL_TRIANGLES_ADJACENCY primitive mode,
330, 331
guard bands, 278–279
rendering without, 565–580
tessellation using, 288–290
troubleshooting, 581
tuning applications for speed, 597–616
turning on line smoothing listing (9.18), 386
types
buffers, assigning to, 92
data, 188–194
elements, 193
matrices, 190–192
of projection transformations, 79–81
samplers, 132
scalars, 188–189
textures, 139–140
tokens, 96
vectors, 190–192
vertex attributes, 226

UBO (Uniform Buffer Object), 108
unary negation, 76
under sampling data, 384
uniform blocks binding layout qualifiers listing
(5.19), 119
Uniform Buffer Object. *See* UBO
uniforms, 103–126
arrays, 106
blocks, 108–121
buffers, 92, 109
default block, 104–105
geometry, 121–126
matrices, 107
subroutines, 213, 215
units
images, 167
textures, 137
vectors, 52
unpacking data from a G-buffer listing (12.29),
552
unsignaled states, 494
unsigned integers, 189
updating
the content of buffers listing (5.2), 94
depth buffers, 352–353

projection matrices listing (5.22), 123
stencil buffers, 351
texture data listing (5.34), 138–139
uniforms, 108
vertex attributes listing (3.2), 29
user-defined clipping, 279–282
user-defined framebuffers. *See* FBOs
using. *See also* applying
    attributes in vertex shaders listing (5.5), 99
    a function to produce faces in a geometry
        shader listing (8.29), 324
    a gradient texture to color a julia set listing
        (12.35), 568
    results of atomic counters in uniform blocks
        listing (5.32), 136
    shader storage blocks in place of vertex
        attributes listing (5.28), 127–128
    shader storage blocks listing (5.28), 127–128
utilities. *See* tools

values, 15
    averaging, 456
    coverage, 392
    interpolation, 44
    normalization, 226
    primitiveMode, 265
    return, framebuffer completeness, 378
Van Verth, James, 718
VAOs (vertex array objects), 20, 97, 272, 595
variables
    built-in, 24
    filtering, 457
    images, 165
    members, 21
    point sizes, 230
    sampler, 141
    sharing, 444
varyings, 260, 261
    centroid sampling, 395
    per-patch user-defined, 284
vectors, 15, 51–54, 190–192
    bittangent, 519
    Boolean, 196
    built-in functions, 195–197
    homogenous, 53
    length of, 57
    operators, 54–58
    Phong lighting, 506
    products, 55
    reflection, 507
    rim lighting, 516
    tangent, 519
    uniforms, 105–106
    unit, 52
vendor extensions, 618, 728
versions, 7
    development (OpenGL ES), 707–708

vertex array objects. *See* VAOs
vertex shaders, 22, 24, 595. *See also* shaders
    for the Alien Rain sample (5.41), 162–163
    with an output listing (3.3), (3.11), 30, 44
    for cube map environment rendering
        listing (12.15), 531
    feeding from buffers, 97–103
    inputs, 224–229
    inputs for Asteroids listing (7.12), 255
    multiple inputs, 100–102
    for normal mapping listing (12.7), 520
    with output interface blocks listing (3.5), 31
    outputs, 229–230
    with single texture coordinate listing
        (5.38), 147
    for sky box rendering listing (12.13), 530
    for the star field effect listing (9.31), 422
    for terrain rendering listing (8.8), 301
VERTEX structure, 225
vertices
    attributes, 28–29, 97
    basevertex, adding, 234–235
    buffers, 92
    clipping, 38–39
    connections, 267
    data chunks (SBM model file format),
        753–755
    fetching, 28
    multiple, 24
    OpenGL ES 3.0, 709
    per-patch, 284n1
    pipelines
        passing data from stage to stage, 29–32
        passing data to shaders, 28–29
    processing, 224–230
    shaders. *See* vertex shaders
    transforms, storage, 259–275
viewing
    images in stereo, 380
    normals, 328
    Realtech VR OpenGL Extensions Viewer, 619
    retina displays (Mac OS X), 673–674
    X Window System, 704
viewports
    managing, 660
    multiple, 336–340
    transformation, 39–40
views
    adding, 650–652
    coordinates, 65–66
    model-view transforms, 667
    space, 64, 555n6
    textures, 181–185
    transformations, 76–79
visuals
    config management and, 689–693
    tearing, 646, 678

vmath::perspective function, 82
vmath::rotate function, 72
volume, 140
    clipping, 276
    local work groups, 441
vsync, 591

WAR (Write-After-Read), 131
warnings, shaders, 203
WAW (Write-After-Write), 131
web sites, 748–749
WGF (Windows Graphics Foundation), 627
WGL (Windows-GL), 623, 634–639
    wglChoosePixelFormatARB(), 638–641
    wglCreateContext(), 633, 635, 641
    wglCreateContextAttribsARB(), 641, 642,
        643, 646
    wglDeleteContext(), 646
    wglGetExtensionsStringARB(), 635
    wglGetPixelFormatAttribARB(), 644
    wglGetPixelFormatAttribfvARB(), 640
    wglGetPixelFormatAttribivARB(), 640, 644
    wglGetProcAddress(), 636, 646, 725
    wglMakeCurrent(), 611, 612, 633
    wglSwapIntervalEXT(), 646
whole framebuffer completeness, 377
Win32, 623
winding order, 41, 296
windows
    child windows (in Cocoa), 671
    coordinates, 40
    EGL, 720
    formatting, 628–630
    GLX, 701–704
    Linux, 693–694
    space, 64
    surfaces, 626
Windows-GL. See WGL
Windows Graphics Foundation. See WGF
Windows main message loop listing (14.5), 633

Windows operating systems, 623–647
    basic setup, 627–632
    graphics drivers, 624–626
    Windows 95, 623
    Windows NT version 3.5, 623
    Windows Vista, 626
Windows Performance Toolkit. See WPT
Windows Presentation Foundation. See WPF
workgroups, 47
    maximum size of, 440–441
working while waiting for a sync object listing
    (11.10), 495
work items, 493
world coordinates, 65
world space, 64
WPF (Windows Presentation Foundation), 627
WPT (Windows Performance Toolkit), 590–594
wrapping
    modes, 148
    textures, 147, 148, 158–160
Write-After-Read (WAR), 131
Write-After-Write (WAW), 131
writing to a G-buffer listing (12.28), 551

XCloseDisplay(), 689
Xcode, 649, 739–740
XCreateWindow(), 693, 694, 702
XDestroyWindow(), 694
XFree(), 692, 693
XOpenDisplay(), 689, 690
XOR operator, 47
X Window System, 683
    display objects and, 689
    full-screen views, 704
    GLX-interfacing with, 688–689

y-axis, 243

z-axis, 76
zeroes, 24

FREE
Online Edition

Safari
Books Online

Your purchase of **OpenGL® SuperBible, Sixth Edition,** includes access to a free online edition for 45 days through the **Safari Books Online** subscription service. Nearly every Addison-Wesley Professional book is available online through **Safari Books Online**, along with thousands of books and videos from publishers such as Cisco Press, Exam Cram, IBM Press, O'Reilly Media, Prentice Hall, Que, Sams, and VMware Press.

Safari Books Online is a digital library providing searchable, on-demand access to thousands of technology, digital media, and professional development books and videos from leading publishers. With one monthly or yearly subscription price, you get unlimited access to learning tools and information on topics including mobile app and software development, tips and tricks on using your favorite gadgets, networking, project management, graphic design, and much more.

Activate your FREE Online Edition at
informit.com/safarifree

STEP 1:   Enter the coupon code: PEXGFAA.

STEP 2:   New Safari users, complete the brief registration form.
Safari subscribers, just log in.

If you have difficulty registering on Safari or accessing the online edition,
please e-mail customer-service@safaribooksonline.com